The Philokalia

VOLUME IV

THE PHILOKALIA

THE COMPLETE TEXT
compiled by
ST NIKODIMOS OF THE HOLY MOUNTAIN
and
ST MAKARIOS OF CORINTH

translated from the Greek
and edited by
G. E. H. PALMER
PHILIP SHERRARD
KALLISTOS WARE

with the assistance of
THE HOLY TRANSFIGURATION MONASTERY
(BROOKLINE)
CONSTANTINE CAVARNOS
DANA MILLER
BASIL OSBORNE
NORMAN RUSSELL

VOLUME IV

faber and faber

First published in 1995
by Faber and Faber Limited
3 Queen Square London WC1N 3AU
This paperback edition first published in 1998

Photoset by Wilmaset Ltd, Wirral
Printed and bound in Great Britain by
Mackays of Chatham plc, Chatham, Kent

A CIP record for this book
is available from the British Library
ISBN 0-571-19382-X

2 4 6 8 10 9 7 5 3

CONTENTS

INTRODUCTORY NOTE   page 7

NOTE ON BIBLICAL QUOTATIONS AND REFERENCES   9

ST SYMEON THE NEW THEOLOGIAN
  Introductory Note   11
  On Faith   16
  One Hundred and Fifty-Three Practical and Theological
    Texts   25
  Attributed to St Symeon the New Theologian:
    The Three Methods of Prayer   64

NIKITAS STITHATOS
  Introductory Note   76
  On the Practice of the Virtues:
    One Hundred Texts   79
  On the Inner Nature of Things and on the Purification
    of the Intellect: One Hundred Texts   107
  On Spiritual Knowledge, Love and the Perfection of Living:
    One Hundred Texts   139

THEOLIPTOS, METROPOLITAN OF PHILADELPHIA
  Introductory Note   175
  On Inner Work in Christ and the Monastic Profession   177
  Texts   188

NIKIPHOROS THE MONK
  Introductory Note   192
  On Watchfulness and the Guarding of the Heart   194

ST GREGORY OF SINAI

Introductory Note   page   207
On Commandments and Doctrines, Warnings and Promises;
    on Thoughts, Passions and Virtues, and also on
    Stillness and Prayer:
        One Hundred and Thirty-Seven Texts   212
Further Texts   253
On the Signs of Grace and Delusion, Written for the
    Confessor Longinos: Ten Texts   257
On Stillness: Fifteen Texts   263
On Prayer: Seven Texts   275

ST GREGORY PALAMAS

Introductory Note   287
To the Most Reverend Nun Xenia   293
A New Testament Decalogue   323
In Defence of Those who Devoutly Practise a Life
    of Stillness   331
Three Texts on Prayer and Purity of Heart   343
Topics of Natural and Theological Science and on the
    Moral and Ascetic Life:
        One Hundred and Fifty Texts   346
The Declaration of the Holy Mountain in Defence of
    Those who Devoutly Practise a Life of Stillness   418

GLOSSARY   427

INDEX
Authors and Sources   439
Subjects   441

INTRODUCTORY NOTE

The editorial revision of this fourth volume has been undertaken entirely by the two editors whose names appear below. We felt keenly the absence of G. E. H. Palmer, who died on 7 February 1984. As in the earlier volumes, the introductory notes before each text or series of texts by a single author, and also the footnotes, are the work of the editors. We are likewise responsible for the Glossary, which reproduces that in volumes ii and iii.

We wish to express our gratitude to Dr Hans-Veit Beyer, of the Kommission für Byzantinistik (Österreichische Akademie der Wissenschaften, Vienna), who generously supplied us with material from his forthcoming critical edition of St Gregory of Sinai; and to the late Dr Panagiotis K. Christou, formerly Professor of the History of Ecclesiastical Literature in the University of Thessalonica, who kindly sent us, prior to its publication, material from volume v of the collected works of St Gregory Palamas. We would also like to thank the Abbess and nuns of the Monastery of St Nicolas, Galataki, for their generous hospitality during the final editing of the texts of this volume, and Selga Sherrard and Jenny Gerrard for their invaluable work.

Philip Sherrard
Bishop Kallistos of Diokleia

Dr Philip Sherrard died on 30 May 1995, shortly before the publication of this volume. Eternal Memory!

NOTE ON BIBLICAL QUOTATIONS
AND REFERENCES

All Biblical passages have been translated directly from the Greek as given in the original *Philokalia*. This means that quotations from the Old Testament are normally based on the Greek Septuagint text. Where this differs significantly from the Hebrew, we have indicated the fact by adding the Roman numeral LXX after the reference.

Even though we follow the Septuagint text, in giving references we use the numbering and titles of the Hebrew, as reproduced in the Authorized Version (King James Bible), since this is more widely familiar in the Western world. In particular the following differences between the Hebrew and the Septuagint should be noted:

NUMBERING OF PSALMS

Hebrew (Authorized Version)	Greek (Septuagint)
1–8	1–8
9 and 10	9
11–113	Subtract one from the number of each Psalm in the Hebrew
114 and 115	113
116:1–9	114
116:10–16	115
117–146	Subtract one from the number of each Psalm in the Hebrew
147:1–11	146
147:12–20	147
148–150	148–150

TITLES OF BOOKS

Hebrew (Authorized Version)	*Greek (Septuagint)*
1 Samuel	1 Kingdoms
2 Samuel	2 Kingdoms
1 Kings	3 Kingdoms
2 Kings	4 Kingdoms

Where authors in the *Philokalia* merely refer to a passage or paraphrase it, but do not quote it exactly, 'cf.' is added before the reference.

ABREVIATIONS

P.G.   J. P. Migne, *Patrologia Graeca*
E. T.   English translation

ST SYMEON THE NEW THEOLOGIAN

Introductory Note

Among the Greek Fathers there are few if any who are better known to us than St Symeon the New Theologian (949–1022). We are fortunate to have not only the biography composed by his disciple Nikitas Stithatos but also frequent personal references, of the utmost vividness, in the writings of St Symeon himself.[1] His life-story illustrates the central significance of spiritual fatherhood within the Orthodox mystical tradition. Born in Asia Minor, from parents belonging to the lesser provincial nobility, St Symeon was sent as a child of eleven to an uncle in Constantinople, probably with the expectation that he would eventually follow a career in the imperial service. But when he was fourteen there occurred an encounter that proved decisive for his future life – his meeting with a monk at Constantinople, also named Symeon and usually styled 'the Pious' or 'the Devout' (ὁ Εὐλαβής), who belonged to the celebrated monastery of Studios. St Symeon the Studite (c. 917–986/7), who soon became spiritual father to the young Symeon, was a lay monk, never ordained priest; for in the Christian East the ministry of spiritual direction has often been exercised by monks not in holy orders, and also, although less frequently, by nuns and even by non-monastics. St Symeon the New Theologian himself wrote a treatise specifically defending the right of monks who are not priests to 'bind' and 'loose', that is, to receive confessions and to confer absolution.[2]

[1] The fullest treatment of St Symeon's life and teaching is by Archbishop Basil (Krivocheine), *In the Light of Christ: Saint Symeon the New Theologian* (Crestwood, 1986). For further bibliography, see H.J.M. Turner, *St Symeon the New Theologian and Spiritual Fatherhood* (Leiden, 1990), pp. ix–xii; and the article by T. Špidlík in *Dictionnaire de Spiritualité* xiv (1990), cols 1387–1401. The *Life* by Nikitas Stithatos has been edited (with a French translation) by I. Hausherr and G. Horn, *Vie de Syméon le Nouveau Théologien (949–1022) par Nicétas Stéthatos* (*Orientalia Christiana* xii [45]: Rome, 1928). In our introductory note we follow the generally accepted dating of St Symeon's life; but it is possible that in fact he was born in 957 and died in 1035, in which case the dating of the other events in his life must also be adjusted.

[2] See K. Holl, *Enthusiasmus und Bussgewalt beim griechischen Mönchtum* (Leipzig, 1898), pp. 110–27.

Under the Studite's guidance, the young Symeon's life of prayer developed rapidly. When he was aged about twenty – and still fully involved in a secular career – he received a vision of the divine and uncreated light, the first in a series of such visions that marked his later years. After an unhappy relapse to a worldly manner of life, in 977 he entered the monastery of Studios as a novice. But a group of monks in the community, resenting his close relationship with his spiritual father Symeon the Studite, forced him to leave within less than a year. His spiritual father placed him in the nearby Constantinopolitan monastery of St Mamas, and here in quick succession he was professed as a monk, and then (c. 980) ordained to the priesthood and elected abbot, an office that he held for the next twenty-five years. The monastery, at that time in a state of decline, underwent a striking revival under his leadership. St Symeon became well known in the capital as a spiritual father, with many prominent lay people coming to him for counsel and confession.

There is every reason to believe that St Symeon was a loving and compassionate shepherd to his monks. But he was also, in his own words, an 'enthusiastic zealot' who set high standards. He expected, for example, that each monk would receive communion frequently and, following the teaching of St Symeon the Studite, he urged that no one should ever do so without shedding tears. His demanding expectations led in 996–8 to a revolt among the monks, but St Symeon eventually succeeded in reconciling the dissidents. More seriously, a few years later he was denounced to the church authorities by persons outside the monastery, among other reasons because, after the death of his spiritual father Symeon the Studite, he had at once begun to honour him publicly as a saint. Doubtless the New Theologian's teaching on lay confession also brought him under suspicion. These continuing attacks led him to resign his position as abbot in 1005. Four years later, in 1009, he was tried before the patriarch and the holy synod and condemned to exile at Paloukiton, on the Asiatic coast of the Bosphorus. Although the sentence was soon revoked and he was even offered a bishopric, he chose to continue living at his place of exile, in the company of a few disciples. Here he died on 12 March 1022.

The high respect felt for St Symeon by his followers is evident in the title that they ascribed to him, 'the New Theologian'. The term 'theologian' is to be understood in this context, not in its modern academic sense, but to signify a person of prayer, who speaks about the vision of God on the basis of his own immediate experience. Before St Symeon's time, the title 'theologian' had been reserved in the Orthodox Church chiefly for two writers: for St John the Evangelist, author of the most 'mystical' of the four Gospels, and for St Gregory of Nazianzos, writer of contemplative poetry, honoured in the Christian East as one of the Three Great Hierarchs. If St Symeon is called 'the New Theologian', this means that he is to be ranked with the other two as a faithful witness to the continuing tradition of inner prayer. As well as being in this experiential sense a 'theologian', St Symeon may also be regarded as a 'missionary' of the mystical life. Convinced that contemplative union with God is possible for all alike, he believed that it was his duty to share with others his experiences of divine grace. When he spoke in this way about his visions, it was not from pride but from a radical humility. 'If God has shown such mercy to me a sinner,' he was saying in effect, 'then certainly He can and will do as much and more for you. The best is for all – if only you will accept it.'

From the voluminous writings of St Symeon, the editors St Makarios and St Nikodimos have selected two for inclusion in the *Philokalia*. The first work, *On Faith*, is one of the catecheses or homilies which St Symeon delivered to his monks while abbot of St Mamas.[1] Here he speaks in the third person about the inner life of a young man named George. It is generally agreed that this is none other than Symeon himself; possibly George was the baptismal name that he used before entering the monastic life. The narrative makes abundantly plain how crucial was the role played in his development by his spiritual father Symeon the Studite, the 'holy monk' as he is termed in the text. It is significant that, in the work by Mark the Ascetic that the young Symeon was given to read, he was struck particularly by the injunction, 'Listen to your conscience', and by the reference to 'the energies of the Holy Spirit': an insistence on the need for direct personal experience is one of the *leitmotifs* in the New Theologian's teaching. When describing his initial vision of divine light, accompanied by tears of joy, he emphasizes that this happened to him

[1] In the *Philokalia*, the work *On Faith* (= *Cathechesis* 22) is given in a modern Greek paraphrase. We have based our translation on the critical text of the original Greek in the edition of the *Catecheses* by Archbishop Basil (Krivocheine), *Sources chrétiennes* 104 (Paris, 1964), pp. 364–93. E.T. of the *Catecheses*: C.J. deCatanzaro, *Symeon the New Theologian: The Discourses* (*The Classics of Western Spirituality*: New York, 1980).

while still a layman, heavily burdened by worldly distractions: this shows that the heights of contemplation are accessible to anyone with genuine faith in God, whatever their outward circumstances.

The second piece, *One Hundred and Fifty-Three Practical and Theological Texts*, is a composite work. The opening section, §§ 1–118, comes from a longer series of 226 texts by St Symeon the New Theologian.[1] The section that follows, §§ 119–52, is by the New Theologian's teacher, St Symeon the Studite, while the first part of § 153 is from the *Life* of St Symeon the New Theologian by Nikitas Stithatos, § 31.

The section by the New Theologian alludes to many of his favourite themes: to the vision of divine light (§§ 68, 105–6) and the gift of tears (§§ 67, 69); to the need for conscious experience of the Holy Spirit (§ 85); to the ministry of the spiritual father (§§ 16–19, 38–9, 41) – but note that the disciple's obedience is not wholly unqualified (§ 33). St Symeon's rigour as an 'enthusiastic zealot' is evident in his demand for a definitive break on the monk's part with all past links, especially with his family (§§ 3–8). At the same time the New Theologian is generous in his recognition of the variety of individual vocations: we cannot speak in the abstract of any one form of life as higher than another – of the hermit life, for example, as superior to the cenobitic – for the best and highest form of life is, for each one, the particular way to which he or she is personally called (§§ 88–92). The fullness of contemplation is accessible to married people living in cities as well as to the desert-dweller.

In the texts that follow, from the pen of St Symeon the Studite, the situation envisaged is that of a large, highly organized community such as the Studios monastery itself. The author insists upon strict poverty, the cutting-off of self-will, simplicity in personal relationships, the avoidance of all unnecessary complications. He speaks about compunction (*katanyxis*) as an experience that is not so much penitential as joyful (§ 140), about the vision of divine light (§ 150), and about the importance of obedience to the spiritual father (§§ 129, 141) – themes which his disciple the New Theologian was later to develop. In a

---

[1] There is a critical text of the full series by J. Darrouzès, *Syméon le Nouveau Théologien: Chapitres Théologiques Gnostiques et Pratiques* (*Sources chrétiennes* 51: 2nd ed., Paris, 1980); E.T., P. McGuckin (*Cistercian Studies Series* 41: Kalamazoo, 1982). For §§ 1–118 our translation follows the critical text of Darrouzès; for §§ 119–53 we have used the text in the Greek *Philokalia*. On the significance of the number 153, see *The Philokalia*, vol. i (London & Boston, 1979), p. 56.

memorable phrase – 'Love is greater than prayer' (§ 143)[1] – the Studite affirms the primacy of love. St Symeon the New Theologian would not have disagreed (see § 61).

[1] A quotation from St John Klimakos, *The Ladder of Divine Ascent*, Step 26 (*P.G.* lxxxviii, 1028B); E.T., C. Luibheid and N. Russell (*The Classics of Western Spirituality*: New York, 1982), p. 239.

On Faith

Brethren and fathers, it is good that we make God's mercy known to all and speak to those close to us of the compassion and inexpressible bounty He has shown us. For as you know I neither fasted, nor kept vigils, nor slept on bare ground, but – to borrow the Psalmist's words – 'I humbled myself' and, in short, 'the Lord saved me'.

Or, to put it even more briefly, I did no more than believe and the Lord accepted me (cf. Ps. 116 : 6, 10; 27 : 10. LXX). Many things stand in the way of our acquiring humility, but there is nothing that prevents us from having faith. For if we want it with all our heart, it will immediately become active in us, since it is God's gift to us and a pre-eminent characteristic of our nature, even though it is also subject to our individual power of free will. That is why even Scythians and other outlandish peoples have faith in each other's words. Yet to demonstrate through actual facts the effect of our deeply rooted faith and to confirm what I have just said, I will tell you a story related to me by someone who was entirely trustworthy.

A man by the name of George, young in age – he was about twenty – was living in Constantinople during our own times. He was good-looking, and so studied in dress, manners and gait, that some of those who take note only of outer appearances and harshly judge the behaviour of others began to harbour malicious suspicions about him. This young man, then, made the acquaintance of a holy monk who lived in one of the monasteries in the city; and to him he opened his soul and from him he received a short rule which he had to keep in mind. He also asked him for a book giving an account of the ways of monks and their ascetic practices; so the elder gave him the work of Mark the Monk, *On the Spiritual Law*. This the young man accepted as though it had been sent by God Himself, and in the expectation that he would reap richly from it he read it from end to end with eagerness and attention. And though he benefited from the whole work, there were three passages only which he fixed in his heart.

The first of these three passages read as follows: 'If you desire spiritual health, listen to your conscience, do all it tells you, and you will benefit.' The second passage read: 'He who seeks the energies of the Holy Spirit before he has actively observed the commandments is like someone who sells himself into slavery and who, as soon as he is bought, asks to be given his freedom while still keeping his purchase-money.' And the third passage said the following: 'Blind is the man crying out and saying: "Son of David, have mercy upon me" (Luke 18 : 38). He prays with his body alone, and not yet with spiritual knowledge. But when the man once blind received his sight and saw the Lord, he acknowledged Him no longer as the Son of David but as the Son of God, and worshipped Him' (cf. John 9 : 38).[1]

On reading these three passages the young man was struck with awe and fully believed that if he examined his conscience he would benefit, that if he practised the commandments he would experience the energy of the Holy Spirit, and that through the grace of the Holy Spirit he would recover his spiritual vision and would see the Lord. Wounded thus with love and desire for the Lord, he expectantly sought His primal beauty, however hidden it might be. And, he assured me, he did nothing else except carry out every evening, before he went to bed, the short rule given to him by the holy elder. When his conscience told him, 'Make more prostrations, recite additional psalms, and repeat "Lord, have mercy" more often, for you can do so', he readily and unhesitatingly obeyed, and did everything as though asked to do it by God Himself. And from that time on he never went to bed with his conscience reproaching him and saying, 'Why have you not done this?' Thus, as he followed it scrupulously, and as daily it increased its demands, in a few days he had greatly added to his evening office.

During the day he was in charge of a patrician's household and each day he went to the palace, engaging in the tasks demanded by such a life, so that no one was aware of his other pursuits. Every evening tears flowed from his eyes, he multiplied the prostrations he made with his face to the ground, his feet together and rooted to the spot on which

---

[1] St Mark the Ascetic, *On the Spiritual Law* 69; *On Those who Think that They are Made Righteous by Works* 64; *On the Spiritual Law* 13–14; E.T., *The Philokalia*, vol. i, pp. 115, 130, 111.

he stood. He prayed assiduously to the Mother of God with sighs and tears, and as though the Lord was physically present he fell at His most pure feet, while like the blind man he besought mercy and asked that the eyes of his soul should be opened. As his prayers lasted longer every evening, he continued in this way until midnight, never growing slack or indolent during this period, his whole body under control, not moving his eyes or looking up. He stood still as a statue or a bodiless spirit.

One day, as he stood repeating more in his intellect than with his mouth the words, 'God, have mercy upon me, a sinner' (Luke 18 : 13), suddenly a profuse flood of divine light appeared above him and filled the whole room. As this happened the young man lost his bearings, forgetting whether he was in a house or under a roof; for he saw nothing but light around him and did not even know that he stood upon the earth. He had no fear of falling, or awareness of the world, nor did any of those things that beset men and bodily beings enter his mind. Instead he was wholly united to non-material light, so much so that it seemed to him that he himself had been transformed into light. Oblivious of all else, he was filled with tears and with inexpressible joy and gladness. Then his intellect ascended to heaven and beheld another light, more lucid than the first. Miraculously there appeared to him, standing close to that light, the holy, angelic elder of whom we have spoken and who had given him the short rule and the book.

When I heard this story, I thought how greatly the intercession of this saint had helped the young man, and how God had chosen to show him to what heights of virtue the holy man had attained.

When this vision was over and the young man, as he told me, had come back to himself, he was struck with joy and amazement. He wept with all his heart, and sweetness mingled with his tears. Finally he fell on his bed, and at that moment the cock crowed, announcing the middle of the night. Shortly after the church bells rang for matins and he got up as usual to chant the office, not having had a thought of sleep during the whole night.

As God knows – for He brings things about according to decisions of which He alone is aware – all this happened without the young man having done anything more than you have heard. But what he did he did with true faith and unhesitating expectation. And let it not be said that he did these things by way of an experiment, for he had never spoken or thought of acting in such a spirit. Indeed, to make experiments and to try things out is evidence of a lack of faith. On the contrary, after rejecting every passion-charged and self-indulgent thought this young man, as he himself assured me, paid such attention to what his conscience said that he regarded all material things of life with indifference, and did not even find pleasure in food and drink, or want to partake of them frequently.

You have heard, my brethren, what great things faith in God can bring about when it is confirmed by actions. You will have realized that youth is not to be despised and that without understanding and fear of God old age is useless. You have learnt that the heart of a city cannot prevent us from practising God's commandments so long as we are diligent and watchful, nor can stillness or withdrawal from the world be of any benefit if we are lazy and negligent. We have certainly all heard of David, and we admire him and say that he is unique and there cannot be another like him. Yet here, lo and behold, is something more than David. For David was specially chosen by God: he was anointed to be prophet and king; he was inspired by the Holy Spirit; and he was granted many revelations concerning God. Thus when he sinned and was deprived of the grace of the Spirit and of his gift of prophecy, and was estranged from his usual communion with God, is there anything astonishing in the fact that he should recall the state of grace from which he had fallen and should ask to enjoy those privileges once more (cf. Ps. 51 : 11–12)? But our young man had never even conceived of any of these things. He was devoted only to what is transient and worldly, and he could imagine nothing superior to such things. Yet – how unpredictable are Thy ways, Lord – he had only to hear of these divine realities and he believed in them immediately; indeed, he believed so surely that he implemented his faith in corresponding action. It was thanks to this action that his mind took wing and rose to heaven, drawing to it the compassion of Christ's Mother. Through her intercession God was appeased and bestowed on him the grace of the Spirit. This gave him the strength to rise to heaven and to behold the light that everyone longs for but very few attain.

This young man had not observed long fasts or slept on the ground, worn a hair shirt or shaved his head, nor had he shunned the world physically, though he had in spirit, by keeping a few vigils; yet he appeared to be superior to Lot, so renowned in Sodom (cf. Gen. 19). Or, rather, although in a body, he was an angel, constrained yet unconstrained, visible but transcending physicality, human in appearance but immaterial when perceived spiritually, outwardly all things to all men (cf. 1 Cor. 9 : 22) but inwardly solely present to God alone, the knower of all things. Thus when the visible sun set, he found that its place was taken by the tender light of spiritual luminosity, which is the pledge and foretaste of the unceasing light that is to succeed it. And this was as it should be; for the love of that for which he was searching took him out of the world, beyond nature and all material things, filling him wholly with the Spirit and transforming him into light. And all this happened to him while he was living in the middle of the city, and was steward of a house, having in his charge slaves and free men and carrying out all the tasks incumbent on such a life.

Enough has been said in praise of this young man and to stimulate you to a similar longing, in imitation of him. Or would you still like me to speak of other things, greater than these – things which perhaps you might not be able to take in? Yet what can be greater or more perfect than the fear of God? Indeed, nothing is greater than this. It is as St Gregory of Nazianzos has written: ' "Fear of the Lord is the beginning of wisdom" (Prov. 1 : 7). For where there is fear, there the commandments are kept, and where the commandments are kept the flesh is purified, together with the cloud that envelops the soul and prevents it from clearly seeing the divine radiance. Where there is this purification there is illumination, and illumination is the fulfilment of the longing of those who desire the greatest of all supernal things or even that which is above all greatness.'[1] With these words he showed that illumination by the Spirit is the endless end of every virtue, and that whoever attains it has finished with everything sensory and has begun to experience the knowledge of spiritual realities.

Such, my brethren, are the wonders of God. And God reveals His hidden saints so that some may emulate them and others have no excuse for not doing so. Provided they live a worthy life, both those who choose to dwell in the midst of noise and hubbub and those who dwell in monasteries, mountains and caves can achieve salvation. Solely because of their faith in Him God bestows great blessings on them. Hence those who because of their laziness have failed to attain salvation will have no excuse to offer on the day of judgment. For He who promised to grant us salvation simply on account of our faith in Him is not a liar. So show mercy to yourselves and to us who love you

[1] St Gregory of Nazianzos, *Oration* 39,8 (*P.G.* xxxvi, 344A).

and often grieve and shed tears for you – for this is what the merciful and compassionate God has asked us to do. Trust in the Lord with all your soul. Leave the world and everything that passes away, and draw close to God and cleave to Him; for in a little while 'heaven and earth will pass away' (Matt. 24 : 35), and apart from Him there will be no firm ground on which to stand, no limit, nothing to check the fall of sinners. God is infinite and cannot be grasped. Tell me, then, if you can, what place there will be for those who fall away from His kingdom?

I grieve, I exhaust my heart, I pine for you when I bring to mind that we have a Lord so bountiful and compassionate that simply if we have faith in Him He grants us gifts beyond our imagination – gifts we have never heard or thought of and that 'man's heart has not grasped' (1 Cor. 2 : 9). Yet we, like beasts, prefer the earth and the things of the earth that through His great mercy it yields in order to supply our bodily needs; and if we use these things modestly, then our soul may ascend unhampered towards divine realities, nourished spiritually by the Holy Spirit according to the degree of our purification and to the level to which we have ascended.

This is our purpose, for this we were created and brought forth: that after having received lesser blessings in this world we may through our gratitude to God and our love for Him enjoy great and eternal blessings in the life to come. But, alas, far from having any concern for the blessings in store, we are even ungrateful for those at hand, and we are like the demons, or – if truth be told – even worse. Thus we deserve greater punishment than they, for we have been given greater blessings. For we know that God became for our sakes like us in everything except sin, so that He might deliver us from delusion and free us from sin. But what is the use of saying this? The truth is that we believe in all these things only as words, while we deny them where our acts are concerned. Is not Christ's name uttered everywhere, in towns and villages, in monasteries and on mountains? Search diligently, if you will, and find out whether anyone keeps His commandments. Among thousands and myriads you will scarcely find one who is a Christian both in word and in act. Did not our Lord and God say in the Gospel, 'He that believes in Me will also do what I do – indeed, he will do greater things' (John 14 : 12)? But which of us dares to say, 'I do Christ's work and I truly believe in Christ?' Do you not see, brethren, that on the day of judgment we risk being classed among the unbelievers and will be chastised more severely even than those ignorant of Christ? Inevitably either we must be chastised as unbelievers or Christ is a liar – and that, my brethren, is impossible.

I have written this not to dissuade you from withdrawing from the world or to encourage you to live in the midst of it. Rather I have written it so that all who happen to read it may be assured that whoever wants to act rightly will receive from God the power so to do, wherever he may be. In fact, the tale I have told actually encourages withdrawal. For if the young man in question, who lived in the world and never had a thought of renouncing it, or of shedding his possessions, or of submitting to the rule of obedience, received such mercy from God simply because he trusted in Him and called on Him with his whole soul, how much greater blessings should those hope to attain who have abandoned all worldly things and all worldly relationships and who as God commanded have for His sake surrendered their very souls to death (cf. Luke 14 : 26)? Moreover, if, unhesitating in your faith and wholehearted in your determination, you do begin to act rightly and to experience the blessing that comes from so doing, you will of your own accord realize that worldly cares and living in the world are a great obstacle to those who wish to live in conformity with God. What we have related about this young man is amazing and unexpected, and we have never heard of anything like it happening to anyone else. Even though it may have happened to others or may happen in the future, they should realize that they will lose the blessing they have received unless they do promptly abandon the world. This is exactly what I learnt from that young man.

I subsequently met him after he had become a monk, in the third or fourth year of his monastic life. He was then thirty-two. I knew him very well: we had been friends from childhood and had been brought up together. On account of this he also told me the following: 'A few days after that incredible change in my life and the more than human help I received, I was continually attacked by the temptations of my worldly life – temptations that thwarted my secret activities and that little by little deprived me of the blessings I had been given. As a result I longed to get completely away from the world and in solitude to seek out Him who had appeared to me. For, brother, I was convinced that He had appeared to me solely in order to draw me, unworthy as I was, to Himself and to separate me entirely from the world. Yet lacking the strength to respond straight away I gradually forgot everything I have told you about and fell into utter darkness, to such an extent that I no longer remembered or even thought of anything, major or minor, connected with those experiences. Rather, I plunged into evil ways more deeply than ever before and ended up in such a state that it was as if I had never understood or heard Christ's holy words. Even the saint who had once shown me such mercy and who had given me that short rule and had sent me that book became for me merely someone I had happened to meet, and I gave no thought to the things I had seen because of him. I am telling you this,' he continued, 'so you can see quite clearly the pit of perdition into which I fell, contemptible as I was, because of my sloth and negligence, and so you will be filled with amazement at the inexpressible blessings that God subsequently bestowed on me.

'For – though I do not know how to explain it – unknown to myself love and trust toward that saintly elder had remained in my unhappy heart; and it was I think for this reason that, as a result of his prayers, after many years God in His compassion had mercy on me. Through him God again dragged me out of my chronic state of delusion and rescued me from the pit of evil. In spite of my unworthiness I had not completely broken with the elder, but when I was in the city I often visited him in his cell and confessed to him what had happened to me, although, without conscience as I was, I did not carry out any of his instructions. But now, as you see, the merciful God has forgiven my many sins, and through that same saintly elder has granted me the grace to become a monk and – in spite of my being truly unworthy of it – has permitted me to be constantly with him. After great labours and many tears, combined with strict solitude, total obedience, the complete elimination of my own will and many other rigorous practices and actions, I have been going forward resolutely and unremittingly along my path, and have again been granted a vision, faint as it is, of a small ray of that most gentle divine light, although up to now I have not been privileged to see it as I saw it on that original occasion.'

This and many other things he told me with tears. And I, hapless that I am, as I listened to his holy words realized that he was entirely filled with divine grace and was truly wise, despite his lack of worldly wisdom. Moreover, since he had acquired his unerring knowledge of spiritual realities through actual experience, I asked him to tell me how faith could bring about such miracles and to instruct me by setting it down in writing. He began to speak to me about these matters and was quite ready to write down his observations. Not to lengthen this present text, I have set forth what he said elsewhere for the delight of those who seek with faith to learn from such writings.

Thus I beg you, brethren in Christ, let us also diligently follow the path of Christ's commandments, so that our faces are not covered in shame (cf. Ps. 34 : 5). To everyone who knocks resolutely He opens the gates of His kingdom, and on him who asks He at once bestows the Holy Spirit (cf. Luke 11 : 13). Nor is it possible for the person who seeks with all his soul not to find (cf. Matt. 7 : 7–8) and not to be enriched with the richness of His gifts. Thus you, too, will be nourished by the inexpressible blessings that He has prepared for those who love Him (cf. 1 Cor. 2 : 9). Here, in this present life, you will enjoy them in part, in accordance with His supernal wisdom; while in the life to come you will enjoy them fully, in company with the saints of all time, in Christ Jesus our Lord, to whom be glory throughout the ages. Amen.

One Hundred and Fifty-Three Practical and Theological Texts

1. To have faith is to die for Christ and for His commandments; to believe that this death brings life; to regard poverty as wealth, and lowliness and humiliation as true glory and honour; to believe that by not possessing anything one possesses everything (cf. 2 Cor. 6 : 9–10) or, rather, that not possessing anything is to possess the 'unsearchable riches' of the knowledge of Christ (Eph. 3 : 8); and to look upon all visible things as dross and smoke.

2. To have faith in Christ means not only to stand aloof from the delights of this life, but also to endure patiently every temptation and test that brings upon us distress, affliction and misfortune, for as long as God wishes and until He comes to us. 'I waited patiently for the Lord and He heard me' (Ps. 40 : 1).

3. Those who in any way esteem their parents above the commandments of God do not possess faith in Christ (cf. Matt. 10 : 37). Their own conscience will certainly accuse them – if their conscience is still alive to their lack of faith. People who possess faith never transgress at any point the commandment of our great God and Saviour Jesus Christ.

4. Faith in God engenders desire for spiritual blessings and fear of punishment. Desire for spiritual blessings and fear of punishment induce a strict keeping of the commandments. The strict keeping of the commandments teaches us our own weakness. Awareness of our true weakness generates mindfulness of death. The person who is mindful of death will insistently strive to discover what awaits him after his exit from this present life. But he who seeks to know what is to come should first of all detach himself from the things of this world; for whoever is constrained by an attachment, however small, to these

things cannot acquire full knowledge of his post-mortal state. Even should God in His mercy give him some taste of this knowledge, it will be taken away from him unless he speedily severs his worldly attachments and dedicates himself wholly to it, not willingly giving thought to anything extraneous to it.

5. The renunciation of and total separation from this world – which includes self-alienation from all material things, from the modes, attitudes and forms of this present life, as well as the denial of one's own body and will – swiftly brings great rewards whenever it is zealously accomplished.

6. If you are intent on renouncing the world, do not permit yourself the solace of dwelling in it for the time being, even if all your relatives and friends try to compel you to do so. It is the demons who provoke them in this way in order to extinguish the ardour of your heart; for even if they cannot thwart your purpose completely, they will try to slacken and enfeeble it.

7. When you are courageously impervious to all the pleasures of this life, then the demons will promote in your relatives a spurious compassion for you, making them weep and lament over you before your eyes. You will realize that it is spurious when you stick firmly to your purpose, for you will then see them becoming suddenly infuriated with you: they will no longer want to set eyes on you and will reject you as if you were an enemy.

8. When you see the pain which your parents, relatives and friends experience because of you, mock the demon who in his subtlety has provoked these feelings against you. Withdraw with fear and determination, and entreat God insistently to bring you swiftly into His haven, where He will give rest to your tired and over-burdened soul. The sea of life nourishes many forms of danger and even of utter destruction.

9. He who would hate the world must love God from the depths of his soul and always have Him in mind; nothing else leads us to abandon the world more joyfully and to turn away from it as though it were so much trash.

10. Once called, do not seek to remain in the world for any reason at all, good or bad; obey the call straight away. God rejoices at nothing so much as our promptitude; and swift obedience involving a life of frugality is better than procrastination amidst great wealth.

11. If the world and everything in it passes away, while God alone is

eternal and immortal, then rejoice, since for His sake you have renounced what is corruptible. Not merely wealth and possessions, but every sensual pleasure and sinful enjoyment are corruptive. Only the commandments of God are light and life, and everyone acknowledges them as such.

12. If, brother, consumed by spiritual ardour you have entered a monastery or placed yourself under a spiritual father, do not indulge in baths, food or other bodily consolations, even if urged to do so by your spiritual father himself or by your monastic brethren. On the contrary, always be ready to fast, to endure hardship, to exercise the utmost self-control. If, however, your spiritual father insists that you should enjoy some comfort, you will obey him, not even in such a case acting according to your own will. But if he does not insist, then gladly endure what you have freely chosen to do, and your soul will benefit. By keeping to this rule, you will find that always, in every situation, you are abstinent and self-controlled, prompt to renounce your own will in all things. Moreover, you will keep alight in your heart that flame which constrains you to stand aloof from everything.

13. When the demons have done all they can to shake our resolve to live a spiritual life and to hinder us from carrying it out, and have failed in their efforts, they enter pious hypocrites and through them try to obstruct us. First, as if moved by love and compassion, they exhort us to give our bodies some relaxation, on the grounds that otherwise we will become physically exhausted and listless. Then they invite us to join in useless discussions, making us waste whole days in them. If we pay attention to these hypocrites and model ourselves on them, the demons change tactics, mocking us for falling in this way; but if we take no notice of their suggestions, and hold ourselves aloof from all, recollected and reserved, they are consumed with jealousy and do everything they can until they have driven us from the monastery. Arrogance cannot bear to see itself scorned and humility held in honour.

14. A man full of self-esteem suffers torture when he sees a humble person weeping and being doubly compensated: by God, who is moved to pity because of his tears, and by men, who are moved to give him praise that he never sought.

15. Once you have entrusted yourself wholly to your spiritual father, you will find yourself alienated from all things human, worldly or material, that might lead you astray. Without his consent you will

not have any desire to concern yourself with such things; nor will you ask him to allow you anything, great or small, unless he himself on his own initiative either tells you to take it or gives it to you with his own hands.

16. Without the permission of your spiritual father, do not give alms from the money you brought with you, and do not even allow an agent acting on your behalf to distribute any of your wealth. It is better for others to regard you as poor and destitute than to distribute your wealth to those in need while you are still a novice. A person of pure faith will entrust everything to the decision of his spiritual father as if putting it into the hands of God.

17. Even if you are burning with thirst, do not ask for a drink of water until on his own initiative your spiritual father urges you to drink. Constrain yourself, force yourself in all things, prevail over yourself, saying to yourself: 'If God wills. . . .' And if you deserve a drink, God will certainly reveal this to your spiritual father and he will say to you, 'Drink.' Thus you will drink with a pure conscience, even if it is not the correct moment to do so.

18. Someone with experience of spiritual grace and possessing an unadulterated faith once said, invoking God as witness of its truth: 'I resolved never to ask for anything to eat or drink from my spiritual father, or to take anything at all without his consent, but to wait until God prompted him to give me an order. Acting in this way, I never deviated from my aim.'

19. Whoever possesses unclouded faith in his spiritual father will, on seeing him, think that he is seeing Christ Himself; when with him or following him, he will firmly believe that he is with and following Christ. Such a person will never want to associate with anyone else, nor will he value anything in the world more than his thought of him and his love for him. For what is finer or more profitable in this world or in the next than to be with Christ? What is more gracious or beautiful than the sight of Him? If someone is privileged to enjoy His companionship, he draws from this eternal life.

20. If you truly love and pray for those who slander and maltreat you, who hate and defraud you, you will make rapid progress, for when your heart is fully aware that this is happening, your thoughts and, indeed, your whole soul with all its three powers are drawn down into the depths of humility and washed with tears. This in its turn raises your intellect to the heaven of dispassion, conferring on it the

gift of contemplation. Because you have tasted such blessing, you come to regard all the things in this life as mere dross, so that you do not even take food or drink with pleasure or any frequency.

21. The spiritual contestant must not only abstain from evil actions, but must also strive to be free from hostile thoughts and notions. He should always concentrate on ideas of a soul-nourishing and spiritual nature, thus remaining detached from worldly cares.

22. A person who strips his whole body bare, but keeps his eyes covered with a cloth, cannot see the light despite his nakedness. Similarly a person detached from all things, including possessions, and even delivered from the passions themselves, will never see the spiritual light – our Lord and God, Jesus Christ – until he frees his soul's eye from worldly concerns and evil thoughts.

23. Worldly thoughts and material concerns blind the mind, or eye of the soul, like a cloth that covers the physical eyes: so long as we are not free of them, we cannot see. But once they are removed by mindfulness of death, then we clearly see the true light, that which illumines everyone who attains the spiritual world.

24. The person blind from birth will not recognize or believe the significance of what I have just written; but the person privileged with sight will bear witness that what I have said is true.

25. The person who sees with physical eyes knows when it is night and when it is day; the blind man is unaware of both. The person who has come to see with the eyes of the spirit, and who has beheld the true and quenchless light, is consciously aware when he is deprived of it should he return, out of laziness, to his former blindness; and he will not be ignorant of why this has happened. But the person blind from birth, and remaining so, knows nothing of these things from personal experience of their operation. He knows about them only from hearsay, but has never actually seen them; and if he tells others what he has heard, neither he nor his audience will know what he is talking about.

26. We cannot both sate ourselves with food and spiritually enjoy divine and noumenal blessings; the more we pander to the stomach the less can we experience such enjoyment. But to the degree that we discipline the body we are filled with spiritual nourishment and grace.

27. We should abandon all that is earthly. We should not only renounce riches and gold and other material things, but should also expel desire for such things completely from our soul. We should hate

not only the body's sensual pleasure, but also its mindless impulses; and we should strive to mortify it through suffering. For it is through the body that our desires are roused and stirred into action; and so long as it is alive, our soul will inevitably be dead, slow to respond and even impervious to every divine command.

28. Just as a flame always rises no matter in what direction one turns the wood on which it burns, so the heart of an arrogant person cannot humble itself; the more one says to help him, the greater his self-inflation. Corrected or admonished, he reacts violently; and when praised or encouraged, his exultation knows no bounds.

29. A person in the habit of contradicting others becomes a two-edged sword to himself. Unwittingly he destroys his own soul and alienates it from eternal life.

30. A contentious person is like someone who deliberately gives himself over to the enemies of his king. Contentiousness is a trap whose bait is self-justification; deceived by it we swallow the hook of sin. Then our unhappy soul is caught, tongue and throat, by the demons. Sometimes they exalt it to the heights of pride and sometimes cast it down into the depths of sin, to be judged with those who have fallen from heaven.

31. A person who suffers bitterly when slighted or insulted should recognize from this that he still harbours the ancient serpent in his breast. If he quietly endures the insult or responds with great humility, he weakens the serpent and lessens its hold. But if he replies acrimoniously or brazenly, he gives it strength to pour its venom into his heart and to feed mercilessly on his guts. In this way the serpent becomes increasingly powerful; it destroys his soul's strength and his attempts to set himself right, compelling him to live for sin and to be completely dead to righteousness.

32. If you want to renounce the world and to be instructed in life according to the Gospels, do not place yourself in the hands of an inexperienced master or one subject to the passions; for then you will be taught, not the ways of the Gospels, but those of the devil. Good masters impart good teaching, but the evil teach evil. Bad seed produces rotten fruit.

33. Implore God with prayers and tears to send you a guide who is dispassionate and holy. But you yourself should also study the divine writings – especially the works of the fathers that deal with the practice of the virtues – so that you can compare the teachings of your

master with them; for thus you will see and observe them as in a mirror. Take to heart and keep in mind those of his teachings that agree with the divine writings, but separate out and reject those that are false and incongruent. Otherwise you will be led astray. For in these days there are all too many deceivers and false prophets.

34. A blind person who undertakes to guide others is a deceiver plunging into the pit of destruction those who follow him. As the Lord said: 'If the blind lead the blind, both will fall into the pit' (Matt. 15 : 14).

35. The person blind to the One is utterly blind to everything; but he who sees in the One contemplates all things. He abstains from the contemplation of all things and at the same time enters into the contemplation of all things while remaining outside what he contemplates. Being in the One he sees all things; and being in all things he sees nothing. The person who sees in the One perceives through the One both himself and all men and all things; hidden in the One, he sees nothing of anything.

36. The person who has not consciously invested his intelligence and intellect with the image of our Lord Jesus Christ, the heavenly one, man and God, is still but flesh and blood. He cannot perceive spiritual glory solely through his intelligence, just as those blind from birth cannot know the sun's light solely through their intelligence.

37. Whoever hears, sees and feels through his intelligence will know the meaning of what has just been said, because he already bears the image of the heavenly one (cf. 1 Cor. 15 : 49) and has attained that perfect manhood which is the fullness of Christ (cf. Eph. 4 : 13). Such a person can also guide God's flock aright in the way of His commandments. But if someone does not understand what has been said, it is clear that the perceptive organs of his soul are neither purified nor in good health, and that it would be better for him to be led than to lead others at their peril.

38. He who looks upon his teacher and guide as if he were God cannot call him into question. If he thinks and says that he can, he should know that he deceives himself, being ignorant of the attitude of holy men towards God.

39. If you believe that your life and death are in the hands of your spiritual guide you will never contradict him. Ignorance of this engenders contenticusness, and this brings about spiritual and eternal death.

40. Before the accused receives his sentence, he is given an opportunity to speak in his own defence before the judge about what he has done; but once the facts have been established and the judge has given his verdict, the accused can say nothing, whether important or trivial, to those who execute his punishment.

41. Before a monk has entered this court and has revealed what he has in his heart, he may perhaps argue with his spiritual guide, either out of ignorance or because he thinks he can keep things about himself hidden. But after he has revealed and sincerely confessed his thoughts, he cannot argue with the man who, after God, will be his judge and master until death. For when a monk has once entered this court and laid bare the secrets of his heart, he will know from the start – if he has any understanding at all – that he deserves a thousand deaths. He will believe that through humility and obedience he can be saved from all punishment and chastisement, if indeed he has truly grasped the nature of this mystery.

42. If you keep these things indelibly in mind, your heart will never rebel when you are disciplined or admonished or criticized. But whoever falls victim to the evils of contentiousness and disbelief with respect to his spiritual father and teacher is while yet living dragged down pitifully into the depths of Hades. Being disobedient and a son of perdition he becomes the dwelling-place of satan and all his unclean brood.

43. I exhort you, who are under obedience, to meditate on these things constantly and to make every effort not to plunge into these infernal evils of which I have spoken. Entreat God fervently each day with these words: 'God and Lord of all, master of everything that has breath and soul, who alone canst cure me, hear my prayer, abject as I am. Root out of me and destroy through the inspiration of Thy Holy Spirit the serpent that dwells in me. Make me worthy, poor though I am and bereft of virtue, of falling with tears at the feet of my spiritual father. Move his holy soul to have mercy on me; and, Lord, bestow humility on my heart and give me such thoughts as befit a sinner who has resolved to repent before Thee. Do not abandon for ever a soul that has once submitted and has confessed to Thee, that has chosen and honoured Thee above all the world. Thou knowest that I wish to be saved, even if my bad habits hinder me. But to Thee, O Lord, are possible all things that are impossible to men' (cf. Luke 18 : 27).

44. Those who with fear and trembling have laid a good foundation

of faith and hope in the court of devotion; who have planted their feet firmly on the rock of obedience to their spiritual father; who listen to his counsel as if it came from the mouth of God; and who with humility of soul build all this on the basis of obedience – such people will succeed immediately. They will achieve that great and primary task of denying themselves. For to fulfil the will of another and not one's own entails not only the denial of one's own soul, but also mortification towards the whole world.

45. The demons rejoice when a person argues with his spiritual father, but angels marvel at him when he humbles himself to the point of death. For then he performs God's work, making himself like the Son of God who was obedient to His Father unto death, the death on the cross (cf. Phil. 2 : 8).

46. Contrition of heart, when excessive and untimely, troubles and darkens the mind, destroying the soul's humility and pure prayer, and paining the heart. This induces a hardening to the point of total insensibility; and by means of this the demons reduce spiritual people to despair.

47. As you are a monk, such things may happen to you. If they do, you may still feel a great desire and eagerness for perfection, longing to fulfil all God's commandments and not wanting to err or sin even by uttering a single idle word (cf. Matt. 12 : 36), or to fall short of the saints of old in the practice of virtue, in spiritual knowledge and in contemplation. But then you may find yourself hampered by someone who sows tares of despondency. He tries to prevent you from climbing to such heights of holiness by discouraging you with various thoughts. For instance, he will tell you that it is impossible for you to be saved and to keep every single one of God's commandments while you live in this world. When this happens you should sit down in a solitary place by yourself, collect yourself, concentrate your thoughts and give good counsel to your soul, saying: 'Why, my soul, are you dejected, and why do you trouble me? Put your hope in God, for I will give thanks to Him; for my salvation lies not in my actions but in God (cf. Ps. 42 : 5). Who will be vindicated by actions done according to the law (cf. Gal. 2 : 16)? No living person will be vindicated before God (cf. Ps. 143 : 2). Yet by virtue of my faith in God I hope that in His ineffable mercy He will give me salvation. Get behind me, satan (cf. Matt. 4 : 10; 16 : 23). I worship the Lord my God (cf. Matt. 4 : 10; Luke 4 : 8) and serve Him from my youth; for He is able to save me simply

through His mercy. Go away from me. The God who created me in His image and likeness will reduce you to impotence.'

48. The only thing God requires of us is that we do not sin. But this is achieved, not by acting according to the law, but by carefully guarding the divine image in us and our supernal dignity. When we thus live in our natural state, wearing the resplendent robe of the Spirit, we dwell in God and God dwells in us. Then we are called gods by adoption and sons of God, sealed by the light of the knowledge of God (cf. Ps. 4 : 6. LXX).

49. Bodily listlessness and torpor, which affect the soul as a result of our laziness and negligence, not only make us abandon our normal rule of prayer, but also darken the mind and fill it with despondency. Then blasphemous and cowardly thoughts arise in the heart. Indeed, the person tempted by the demon of listlessness cannot even enter his usual place of prayer; he grows sluggish, and absurd thoughts directed against the Creator of all things arise in his mind. Aware of the cause of all this and why it has happened to you, resolutely enter your normal place of prayer and, falling down before the God of love, ask with a compunctive and aching heart, full of tears, to be freed from the weight of listlessness and from your pernicious thoughts. If you knock hard and insistently, this release will soon be given to you.

50. The person who has attained purity of heart has triumphed over cowardice. The person still in the process of being purified sometimes overcomes it and sometimes is overcome by it. The person not even engaged in spiritual warfare is either completely unaware that he is the ally of his own passions and of the demons and that he is sick with pride and presumption, thinking he is something when he is not; or else he is the slave and servant of cowardice, trembling like a baby and fearing fear where, for those who fear the Lord, there is no fear (cf. Ps. 14 : 5. LXX) nor any occasion for cowardice.

51. Whoever fears the Lord will not fear the sickly attacks of demons or the threats of evil people. Like a flame or a burning fire, he goes about day and night through dark and hidden places, and instead of fleeing from the demons he makes them flee from him, so as not to be scorched by the flaming rays of divine fire that pour from him.

52. Whoever goes in the fear of God is not afraid when surrounded by evil men, for he has the fear of God within him and wears the invincible armour of faith. This gives him strength to do all things, even those that seem to most people difficult or impossible. Like a giant

among monkeys or a roaring lion among dogs and foxes, he is resolute in the Lord, unnerving his enemies with the constancy of his purpose and filling their minds with terror; for he wields God's wisdom like a rod of iron (cf. Ps. 2 : 9).

53. Not only the hesychast, living alone, or the monk under obedience, but also the abbot, the spiritual director of many, and even a monk charged with specific duties, need to be detached and completely free from all worldly cares. For if we are not detached, we transgress the commandment of God which says, 'Do not be anxious about your life, what you will eat or drink, or what you will wear; for it is the heathen who worry about all these things' (Matt. 6 : 25, 32). And again, 'Take care that your heart is not weighed down by dissipation, drunkenness and worldly cares' (Luke 21 : 34).

54. A person full of anxiety about worldly things is not free: he is dominated and enslaved by this anxiety, whether it is about himself or about others. But he who is free from such things is untroubled by worldly concerns, whether they relate to himself or to others; and this is so, even if he is a bishop, abbot or priest. However, he will not be idle, or neglect even the most insignificant and trivial details; but all he does he will do for the glory of God, accomplishing everything in his life without anxiety.

55. Do not pull down your own house because you want to build a house for your neighbour. Think how exhausting and difficult the task will be. Otherwise you may make your decision only to find that, having destroyed your own house, you lack the strength to build a house for someone else.

56. Unless you are completely detached from worldly affairs and possessions, do not voluntarily assume responsibility for such things. Otherwise you may become caught up in them and, instead of receiving the reward for your services, may find yourself accused of theft and sacrilege. But if your abbot compels you to act as a steward, be like someone who holds in his hands a flaming fire; and if you ward off the attacks of your own evil thoughts through repentance and confession, you will be kept unharmed through the prayers of your superior.

57. Unless you have become dispassionate you cannot know what dispassion is, and will not believe that a dispassionate person exists anywhere on earth. For unless someone has first denied himself, readily giving his blood for the sake of a life that is truly blessed, how

can he imagine that anyone else has done this in order to attain the state of dispassion? It is the same with someone who thinks that he possesses the Holy Spirit while in fact he possesses nothing of the kind. When he hears about the workings of the Spirit in those who do possess Him, he refuses to believe that there is anyone in our generation who is energized and motivated by the Holy Spirit, or who consciously and experientially enjoys the vision of Him, in the same way as Christ's apostles and the saints from the beginning of the world. For each judges whether his neighbour's condition is virtuous or vicious according to his own state.

58. A dispassionate soul is one thing, a dispassionate body is another. For the soul, when dispassionate, sanctifies the body with its own luminosity and with the radiance of the Holy Spirit. But bodily dispassion by itself confers no benefit on the person who possesses it.

59. A person who is raised by the king from extreme poverty to wealth, who is invested by him with high office and a splendid uniform and commanded to stand in his presence, will be full of devotion for the king and will revere him as his benefactor. He will be fully aware of his splendid robes, of his high office and the wealth he has been given. Similarly, if a monk has truly withdrawn from the world and its affairs and has come to Christ, if he is fully conscious of his calling and has been raised to the heights of spiritual contemplation through the practice of the commandments, then he will look unwaveringly on God and be well aware of the change that has taken place in him. He will see the grace of the Spirit always illuminating him – the grace that is called a garment, the royal purple or, rather, that is Christ Himself, if it is indeed true that those who believe in Christ are clothed in Christ (cf. Gal. 3 : 27).

60. Many read the Holy Scriptures and hear them read. But few can grasp their meaning and import. For some what is said in the Scriptures is impossible, for others it is altogether beyond belief. Some again interpret them wrongly: they apply things said about the present to the future, and things said about the future to the past or else to what happens daily. In this way they reveal a lack of true judgment and discernment in things both human and divine.

61. We, the faithful, should look upon all the faithful as one single being, and should consider that Christ dwells in each of them. We should have such love for each of them that we are willing to lay down our lives for him. Nor should we ever think or say that anyone is evil:

we should look on everyone as good, as I have already said. Even should you see someone overwhelmed by some passion, execrate, not him, but the passions that fight against him. And if he is mastered by desires and prepossessions, have even greater compassion for him; for you too may be tempted, subject as you are to the same fluctuations of beguiling materiality.

62. A person false through hypocrisy, or culpable because of his actions, or easily shattered by some passion, or who lapses slightly through negligence, must not be left in the company of those who are working together in harmony. On the contrary he must be excluded from their society as still corrupt and reprobate. Otherwise at some crucial moment he might break their chain of union, causing division where there should be none and distress both to those who are at the head of the chain – for they will be grieved for those who follow after them – and to those at the tail of the chain, who will suffer because they are cut off from those in front of them.

63. Earth thrown on a fire puts it out. Similarly, worldly concerns and attachment to even the smallest and most insignificant thing quell the fervour initially burning in our hearts.

64. If you are pregnant with the fear of death you will feel disgust for all food and drink and smart clothing. You will not even find pleasure in eating bread or drinking water. You will give your body only what it needs to keep alive; and you will not only renounce all self-will, but at the discretion of those to whom you are obedient you will become the servant of all.

65. The person who from fear of punishment hereafter has placed himself as a slave in the hands of his spiritual fathers will not choose, even if commanded to do so, relief for his heart's suffering or deliverance from the bonds of his fear. Nor will he listen to those who out of friendship, or flattery, or in virtue of their authority, encourage him to seek such relief and freedom. On the contrary, he will choose what increases his suffering and heightens his fear, and will look with love on whatever helps another to inflict these things on him. Moreover, he will endure as though he never expected to be released; for hope of deliverance lightens one's burden, and this is harmful for someone who is repenting fervently.

66. Fear of punishment hereafter and the suffering it engenders are beneficial to all who are starting out on the spiritual way. Whoever imagines that he can make a start without such suffering and fear, and

without someone to inflict them, is not merely basing his actions on sand but thinks that he can build in the air without any foundations at all; and this of course is utterly impossible. Indeed, the suffering is the source of nearly all our joy, while the fear breaks the grip of all our sins and passions, and the one who inflicts these things brings us not death but eternal life.

67. He who does not attempt to evade the suffering engendered by the fear of eternal punishment, but accepts it wholeheartedly, and even adds to it as he can, will rapidly advance into the presence of the King of kings. And as soon as he has beheld the glory of God, however obscurely, his bonds will be loosed: fear, his tormenter, will leave him, and his heart's suffering will be turned to joy. It will become a spring from which unceasing tears will flow visibly and which will fill him spiritually with peace, gentleness and inexpressible sweetness, as well as with courage and the capacity to submit to God's commandments freely and unreservedly. This is something impossible for those who are still beginners, for it is the characteristic of such as are in the middle of their spiritual journey. As for the perfect, this spring becomes a light within their hearts, suddenly changed and transformed as they are.

68. The person inwardly illumined by the light of the Holy Spirit cannot endure the vision of it, but falls face down on the earth and cries out in great fear and amazement, since he has seen and experienced something that is beyond nature, thought or conception. He becomes like someone suddenly inflamed with a violent fever: as though on fire and unable to endure the flames, he is beside himself, utterly incapable of controlling himself. And though he pours forth incessant tears that bring him some relief, the flame of his desire kindles all the more. Then his tears flow yet more copiously and, washed by their flow, he becomes even more radiant. When, totally incandescent, he has become like light, then the saying is fulfilled, 'God is united with gods and known by them',[1] in the sense perhaps that He is now united to those who have joined themselves to Him, and revealed to those who have come to know Him.

69. 'Let no one deceive you with vain words' (Eph. 5 : 6), and let us not deceive ourselves: before we have experienced inward grief and

---

[1] St Gregory of Nazianzos, *Oration* 45,3 (*P.G.* xxxvi, 628A). Cf. Ps. 82 : 6; John 10 : 34.

tears there is no true repentance or change of mind in us, nor is there any fear of God in our hearts, nor have we passed sentence on ourselves, nor has our soul become conscious of the coming judgment and eternal torments. Had we accused ourselves and realized these things in ourselves, we would have immediately shed tears; for without tears our hardened hearts cannot be mollified, our souls cannot acquire spiritual humility, and we cannot be humble. If we do not attain such a state we cannot be united with the Holy Spirit. And if we have not been united with the Holy Spirit through purification, we cannot have either vision or knowledge of God, or be initiated into the hidden virtues of humility.

70. Those who simulate virtue and who, because of the sheepskin of the monastic habit, appear to be one thing outwardly but are something else inwardly – steeped perhaps in iniquity, jealousy, ambition, and foul pleasures – are revered by most people as saintly and dispassionate; for in most people the soul's eye is unpurified, and so they cannot recognize these imposters by their fruits (cf. Matt. 7 : 15–16). Those, on the other hand, who are full of devoutness, virtue and simplicity of heart, and who are truly saints, are judged by most people to be like other men; and they pass them by with disdain, counting them as nothing.

71. The garrulous and ostentatious man is thought by these people to be a spiritual master; but the quiet man, careful not to waste words, they regard as uncouth and inarticulate.

72. The arrogant, sick with diabolic pride, reject anyone inspired by the Holy Spirit as if this saintly man were himself arrogant and filled with pride; for his words strike them like blows, yet do not move them to compunction. But whoever uses his inborn talents or education to spin long phrases, and who tells lies to people about their salvation, is welcomed by them and praised to the skies; and so no one among them is able to see the situation as it is and judge it accordingly.

73. 'Blessed are the pure in heart,' says God, 'for they shall see God' (Matt. 5 : 8). But purity of heart cannot be realized through one virtue alone, or through two, or ten; it can only be realized through all of them together, as if they formed but a single virtue brought to perfection. Even so the virtues cannot by themselves purify the heart without the presence and inner working of the Spirit. For just as the bronzesmith demonstrates his skill through his tools, but cannot make anything without the activity of fire, so a man using the virtues as tools

can do everything, given the presence of the fire of the Spirit; but without this presence these tools remain useless and ineffective, not removing the stain that befouls the soul.

74. Through holy baptism we are granted remission of our sins, are freed from the ancient curse, and are sanctified by the presence of the Holy Spirit. But we do not as yet receive the perfection of grace, as described in the words of Scripture, 'I will dwell in them, and move in them' (2 Cor. 6 : 16); for that is true only of those who are steadfast in faith and have demonstrated this through what they do. If after we have been baptized we gravitate towards evil and foul actions, we lose the sanctification of baptism completely. But through repentance, confession and tears we receive a corresponding remission of our former sins and, in this way, sanctification accompanied by the grace of God.

75. Through repentance the filth of our foul actions is washed away. After this, we participate in the Holy Spirit, not automatically, but according to the faith, humility and inner disposition of the repentance in which our whole soul is engaged. In addition, we must also have received complete remission of our sins from our spiritual father. For this reason it is good to repent each day, in accordance with the commandment that tells us to do this; for the words, 'Repent, for the kingdom of heaven has drawn near' (Matt. 3 : 2), indicate that the act of repentance is unending.

76. The grace of the Holy Spirit is given as a pledge to souls that are betrothed to Christ; and just as without a pledge a woman cannot be sure that her union with her man will take place, so the soul will have no firm assurance that it will be joined for all eternity with its Lord and God, or be united with Him mystically and inexpressibly, or enjoy His unapproachable beauty, unless it receives the pledge of His grace and consciously possesses Him within itself.

77. Just as an engagement is not binding unless the documents of the contract bear the signatures of trustworthy witnesses, so the illumination of grace is dependent upon the practice of the commandments and the actualization of the virtues. What witnesses are to a contract, the virtues and the practice of the commandments are to spiritual betrothal: through them everyone who is going to be saved secures the consummation of the pledge.

78. It is as if the contract were written through the practice of the commandments and then signed and sealed by the virtues. Only then

does Christ, the bridegroom, give His ring – the pledge of the Holy Spirit – to the soul that is His bride-to-be.

79. Before the marriage the bride-to-be receives nothing but the pledge given by her future husband; she waits until after the marriage to receive the dowry that has been agreed upon and the gifts promised with it. So the Church – the bride-to-be composed of all the faithful – and the soul of each of us first receive from Christ, the bridegroom-to-be, only the pledge of the Spirit. The eternal blessings and the kingdom of heaven are given subsequent to this earthly life, though both the Church and the individual soul have the assurance of them through the pledge they have received, in which, as in a mirror, what has been agreed is disclosed and confirmed by their Lord and God.

80. If the bridegroom-to-be is delayed abroad or kept away by other business, and puts off the marriage for a while, and if the bride-to-be, indignant, rejects his love, erasing or tearing up the document that contains the pledge, she immediately loses all right to what she expected from him. The same is true where the soul is concerned. For if a person engaged in spiritual warfare should say 'How long must I suffer?' and begin to evade the rigour of the ascetic life and, as it were, to erase or tear up the contract through neglect of the commandments and by abandoning the constant task of repentance, then at once he forfeits completely the pledge given and his hope in God.

81. Should the bride-to-be transfer her love from the man to whom she is affianced to another, sharing his bed, whether publicly or not, not only does she not receive anything of what her betrothed had promised her, but she may rightly expect the censure and punishment of the law. The same is true in our own case. If someone shifts the love he has for Christ, his betrothed, to the desire for some other thing, whether openly or in secret, and his heart is possessed by that thing, he will become hateful and abhorrent to Christ, and unworthy of being united with Him. For it is written, 'I love them that love me' (Prov. 8 : 17).

82. Each of us should be able to understand from these signs whether or not he has received the pledge of the Spirit from Christ, our Lord and Betrothed. If he has received it, he should strive to retain it; and if he has not yet been privileged to receive it, he should strive through good works and actions, and through fervent repentance, to receive it, and then to keep it through the practice of the commandments and the acquisition of the virtues.

83. The roof of a house rests on its foundations and walls; correspondingly the foundations themselves are laid in the manner required for them to serve as support for the roof. A roof cannot stand without foundations, and foundations without a roof serve no living or practical purpose. Similarly, God's grace is preserved through the practice of the commandments, while the practice of the commandments is as it were the foundation for the divine gift. The grace of the Spirit will not remain with us without the practice of the commandments, nor will the practice of the commandments serve any useful purpose without the grace of God.

84. A house left without a roof through the neglect of the builder is not only useless, but brings ridicule on the builder. Similarly, a person who has laid foundations through the practice of the commandments, and has raised walls through the acquisition of the higher virtues, remains incomplete, and an object of pity to the perfect, if he does not receive the grace of the Spirit in the form of contemplation and spiritual knowledge. He will have been denied this grace for one of two reasons: either he has failed to repent; or, daunted by the serried ranks of the virtues as by a boundless forest, he may have overlooked one of them – one that may seem trivial to us, but is indispensable if the house of the virtues is to be completed, since without it that house cannot be roofed by the grace of the Spirit.

85. The Son of God, God Himself, came down to earth in order to reconcile us, His enemies, to His Father, and to unite us consciously to Himself through His holy and coessential Spirit. How, then, can someone who lacks this grace of the Spirit achieve any other form of grace? Certainly he has not been reconciled to Christ, nor has he been united to Christ through participation in the Spirit.

86. The person who participates in the Holy Spirit is freed from impassioned desires and sensual pleasures, but he is not divorced from his natural bodily needs. In virtue of his deliverance from the bonds of impassioned desire and his union with immortal tenderness and glory, he strives unflaggingly to attain the heights, to dwell there with God, and not to lose even for a moment his vision of God and his insatiable delight. But because he is fastened to the body and to corruption, he is dragged down and pulled along by them, and is turned towards earthly things. His distress at this must be as great, I imagine, as that of a sinner's soul when it is separated from the body.

87. For someone who loves the body, mortal life, sensual pleasure,

and the material world, separation from them is death; but for someone who loves holiness, God, the immaterial world and virtue, true death is for the mind to be separated from them even briefly. If the eyes of a person who can see sensible light are closed for an instant or covered by someone else, he suffers and is distressed and cannot bear it, especially if he was looking at something important or unusual. But if someone is illumined by the Holy Spirit and, whether asleep or awake, sees spiritually those blessings that 'the eye has not seen, and the ear has not heard, and man's heart has not grasped' (1 Cor. 2 : 9), and 'that angels long to glimpse' (1 Pet. 1 : 12), how much more will he suffer and be tormented if he is torn away from the vision of these things? For this will seem to him like death, a veritable exclusion from eternal life.

88. Many have called the eremitic life blessed, others, the communal or coenobitic life. Others again have described in this way leadership of the faithful, or the counselling, teaching and administration of churches. All of these are activities that provide people with nourishment in body and soul. But for my part I would not judge any one of them to be better than the others, nor would I say that one merits praise and another censure. But in every case, whatever our work or activity, it is the life led for God and according to God that is most blessed.

89. Man's material life is based upon a variety of sciences and skills, each person practising one or another of them and making his contribution. Thus, by giving and taking from one another, men satisfy their natural bodily needs. One can see the same thing among spiritual people, where one person pursues one virtue while another follows another path. But all are moving towards a single goal.

90. The goal of all who pursue the spiritual path is to do the will of Christ, their God, to be reconciled with the Father through communion in the Spirit, and so to achieve their salvation. For only in this way is the soul's salvation attained. And if it is not attained, our labour is fatuous and our work vain. Every path of life is pointless that does not lead the person pursuing it to this consummation.

91. The person who, totally forsaking the world, retires to the mountains as though in pursuit of stillness and who then showily writes to those in the world, blessing some and praising and flattering others, is like someone who, after divorcing a foul and slatternly whore of a wife and going off to a distant land to expunge even his memory of

her, then forgets why he came there and longs to write to those living with that whore, and sullied by her, even deeming them happy. If not bodily, at least in heart and in intellect he shares their passions, inasmuch as he deliberately condones their commerce with that woman.

92. Those who purify their senses and hearts from every evil desire while living in the world indeed deserve praise and are surely blessed. Correspondingly, those who dwell in mountains and caves, but who pursue human praise and blessing, deserve censure and rejection. In the eyes of God, diviner of our hearts, they are adulterers. For the person who wants his life and name and ascetic practice to be known in the world prostitutes himself in God's sight, as, according to David, the Jewish people once did (cf. Ps. 106 : 39).

93. Whoever renounces the world and worldly things with unhesitating faith in God believes that the Lord is compassionate and merciful and that He receives those who come to Him in repentance. But he knows, too, that God honours His servants with dishonour, enriches them with the utmost poverty, and glorifies them by means of insults and scorn, making them through death participants and inheritors of eternal life. Through such trials the servant of God is impelled like a panting hart to the deathless fountain (cf. Ps. 42 : 1); and through them he climbs upwards, as though up a ladder on which angels ascend and descend (cf. Gen. 28 : 12; John 1 : 51) in order to help those who are mounting. God is enthroned above, observing the strength of our intention and diligence, not because He enjoys seeing us struggle, but because He wishes, compassionate as He is, to give us our reward as if it were something He owed us.

94. The Lord never allows those who come to Him unhesitatingly to fall completely. When He sees them faltering He helps them in their efforts, stretching a hand of power down to them and drawing them up to Himself. He works with them visibly and invisibly, consciously and unconsciously, until, having climbed every step of the ladder, they draw near Him, wholly united with Him in His wholeness and forgetting all that is earthly. Whether they are there with Him in the body or out of the body, I cannot tell (cf. 2 Cor. 12 : 2); but they dwell with Him and enjoy His ineffable blessings.

95. It is right for us to place the yoke of Christ's commandments on our shoulders from the start; and we should not resist or hang back. On the contrary, we should walk straight ahead wholeheartedly

obedient to them, making ourselves in truth the new paradise of God, until the Son comes to dwell in us with the Father through the Holy Spirit. Then, when He totally indwells us and is our master, whomever of us He commands and whatever ministry He entrusts us with, we will take it in hand and carry it out sedulously, as seems best to Him. But we must not seek this ministry prematurely, or consent to accept it when given by men; but we must persevere in the commandments of our Lord and God and await His orders.

96. If, after we have committed ourselves to some form of ministry within the Church and have performed it honourably, the Spirit should then direct us to some other ministry or work or activity, we should not resist. For God does not want us to be idle, but neither does He want us to be confined for ever to the first work in which we engaged. On the contrary, He wants us to advance, moving always towards the realization of something better, acting in accordance with His will and not our own.

97. Whoever strives to mortify his own will should follow the will of God; and in the place of his own will he should put God's will, planting it in himself and grafting it into his heart. Moreover, he should carefully observe whether what he has planted has put down deep roots, whether what he has grafted has healed over so as to make a single tree, and whether it has grown and flowered and borne good, sweet fruit in such a way that he no longer recognizes the earth into which the seed was sown or the stock onto which the graft was made, so incomprehensible and miraculous is the life-bearing tree that has grown up.

98. If through fear of God you cut off your own will – inexplicably, for you do not know how this happens – God will give you His will. You will keep it indelibly in your heart, opening the eyes of your mind so that you recognize it; and you will be given the strength to fulfil it. The grace of the Holy Spirit operates these things: without it, nothing is accomplished.

99. If you have received the remission of all your sins, either through confession or through putting on the holy and angelic habit, this will be a great source of love, thanksgiving and humility for you. For not only have you been spared the countless punishments that you deserved, but you have been granted sonship, glory and the kingdom of heaven. Bear this in mind and continually meditate on it, taking care never to dishonour Him who honoured you and has forgiven you ten

thousand sins; glorify and honour Him in all you do, so that in return He will glorify you even more – you whom He has honoured above all visible creation and has called His true friend.

100. As the soul is more precious than the body, so man endowed with intelligence excels the whole world. When you contemplate the grandeur of the created things with which the world is filled, do not think that they are more precious than you are; but keeping in mind the grace that has been given you, and aware of the value of your deiform soul, celebrate the God who has honoured you above all visible things.

101. Let us consider how we should glorify God. We cannot glorify Him in any way other than that in which He was glorified by the Son; for in the same way as the Son glorified the Father, the Son in turn was glorified by the Father. Let us, then, diligently use these same means to glorify Him who allows us to call Him 'our Father in heaven', so that we may be glorified by Him with the glory that the Son possesses with the Father prior to the world (cf. John 17 : 5). These means are the cross, or death to the whole world, the afflictions, the trials and the other sufferings undergone by Christ. If we endure them with great patience, we imitate Christ's sufferings; and through them we glorify our Father and God, as His sons by grace and as coheirs of Christ.

102. A soul not consciously and completely free from ties and attachments to the visible world is not able to endure serenely the calamities and ravages with which both men and demons assail it. Bound by its attachment to human concerns, it is lacerated by the loss of material things, suffers when deprived of possessions, and is full of distress when its body is afflicted.

103. A person who has delivered his soul from its ties with and desires for sensible things, and has bound it to God, will not only scorn property and possessions, accepting their loss painlessly, as if they belonged to others and were not his own; he will also endure bodily distress with joy and gratitude. In the words of St Paul, he sees the outward self perishing, but the inward self being renewed day by day (cf. 2 Cor. 4 : 16). Otherwise it is impossible joyfully to bear the afflictions permitted by God, for this requires perfect knowledge and spiritual wisdom. He who lacks these things walks at all times in the darkness of ignorance and hopelessness, totally incapable of beholding the light of patience and benediction.

104. Anyone who thinks himself intelligent because of his scholarly

or scientific learning will never be granted insight into divine mysteries unless he first humbles himself and becomes a fool (cf. 1 Cor. 3 : 18), discarding both his presumption and the knowledge that he has acquired. But if he does this and with unhesitating faith allows himself to be led by those wise in divine matters, he will enter with them into the city of the living God. Guided and illumined by the divine Spirit, he will see and learn what others cannot ever see or learn. He will then be taught by God (cf. John 6 : 45).

105. Those taught by God will be regarded as fools by the disciples of such as are wise in the wisdom of this world. But in fact it is the worldly-wise that are fools, spouting an inane secular wisdom, the stupidity of which God has demonstrated (cf. 1 Cor. 1 : 20) and which Scripture condemns as material, unspiritual, devilish, filled with strife and malice (cf. Jas. 3 : 15). Since these people are blind to the divine light, they cannot see the marvels it contains; they regard as deluded those who dwell in that light and see and teach others about what is within it. On the contrary, it is they themselves that are deluded, not having tasted the ineffable blessings of God.

106. Even now, living in our midst, there are people who are dispassionate and saintly, filled with divine light; who have so mortified whatever in them pertains to the earth (cf. Col. 3 : 5), freeing it from all impurity and impassioned desire, that not only do they themselves not think or act maliciously, but even when drawn in this direction by another they are unwavering in their dispassion. Those who accuse these saints of folly, and who do not believe them when in the wisdom of the Spirit they teach about divine matters, would have recognized them had they understood the sacred writings that are read and sung daily. For if they possessed a mature knowledge of the Holy Scriptures they would have believed in the blessings spoken of and bestowed on us by God. But because out of self-conceit and negligence they do not share in these blessings, in their unbelief they slander those who do share in them and who teach others about them.

107. For this reason those filled with grace and perfect in spiritual knowledge and wisdom will meet and see people living in the world only in order to benefit them in some way through reminding them of God's commandments or by doing good; there is a chance that some will listen, understand, and be persuaded. For those not led by the Spirit of God walk in darkness and do not know where they are going

(cf. John 12 : 35) or what are the obstacles that make them stumble. Yet perhaps one day they may recover from their presumption and accept the true teaching of the Holy Spirit; learning about the will of God in all its purity and integrity, they may repent, carry out this will and receive some share in spiritual grace. But if these holy people cannot in this way benefit those living in the world, they return to their cells, lamenting the hardness of heart they have encountered; and they pray day and night for the salvation of such as are still in darkness. To those who dwell constantly with God and are more than abundantly filled with every blessing, this is the only thing that causes sadness.

108. What is the purpose of the Incarnation of the Divine Logos which is proclaimed throughout the Scriptures, about which we read and which yet we do not recognize? Surely it is that He has shared in what is ours so as to make us participants of what is His. For the Son of God became the Son of man in order to make us human beings sons of God, raising us up by grace to what He is by nature, giving us a new birth in the Holy Spirit and leading us directly into the kingdom of heaven. Or, rather, He gives us the grace to possess this kingdom within ourselves (cf. Luke 17 : 21), so that not merely do we hope to enter it but, being in full possession of it, we can affirm: 'Our life is hid with Christ in God' (Col. 3 : 3).

109. Baptism does not take away our free will or freedom of choice, but gives us the freedom no longer to be tyrannized by the devil unless we choose to be. After baptism it is in our power either to persist willingly in the practice of the commandments of Christ, into whom we were baptized, and to advance in the path of His ordinances, or to deviate from this straight way and to fall again into the hands of our enemy, the devil.

110. Whoever after baptism deliberately submits to the will of the devil and carries out his wishes, estranges himself – to adapt David's words – from the holy womb of baptism (cf. Ps. 58 : 3). None of us can be estranged or alienated from the nature with which we are created. We are created good by God – for God creates nothing evil – and we remain unchanging in our nature and essence as created. But we do what we choose and want, whether good or bad, of our own free will. Just as a knife does not change its nature, but remains iron whether used for good or for evil, so we, as has been said, act and do what we want without departing from our own nature.

111. To be merciful to just one person will not save you, but to scorn just one person will send you to the fire (cf. Matt. 18 : 10). The words, 'I was hungry' and 'I was thirsty' (Matt. 25 : 35), were spoken with reference not merely to a single occasion or to a single day, but to the whole of our life. Thus our Lord and God has declared that He accepts from His servants food, drink, clothing and so on, not once only but always and in all things.

112. Even though we may have been charitable to a hundred people, if there were others from whom we turned away when they asked for food and drink and we could have given it to them, we will be judged by Christ as having refused Him nourishment. For Christ, whom we nourish in the humblest of people, is in all those to whom we refused our charity.

113. He who today gives to all everything they need and tomorrow, though still in the position to act in a similar way, neglects some of his fellow beings and allows them to perish of hunger, thirst or cold, has scorned and allowed to die Him who said, 'Inasmuch as you have done it to the least of these My kindred, you have done it to Me' (Matt. 25 : 40).

114. Christ takes on the appearance of each of the poor and assimilates Himself to all of them so that no one who believes in Him will be arrogant towards his fellow being. On the contrary, he will look on his fellow being and his neighbour as his God, regarding himself as least of all in comparison just as much with his neighbour as with his Creator, honouring his neighbour as if he were his Creator, and exhausting his all in his service, just as Christ our God poured out His blood for our salvation.

115. We who have been commanded to regard our neighbour as ourself (cf. Lev. 19 : 18; Luke 10 : 27) should do so not for one day only, but for our whole life. Similarly, we who have been told to give to all who ask (cf. Matt. 5 : 42) are told to do this for our whole life. And if we would like others to do good to us, we should ourselves act in the same way towards them (cf. Matt. 7 : 12).

116. Whoever regards his neighbour as himself cannot bear to possess more than his neighbour. On the other hand, if he has more and does not give unstintingly until he himself becomes as poor as his neighbour, he fails to fulfil the Lord's commandment. And if someone wishes to give to all who ask, but rejects one of them while he still has a penny or a scrap of bread, or if he does not act towards his neighbour

as he would like other people to act towards him, he too is failing to fulfil the Lord's commandment. Similarly if you provide for even the humblest of the poor, and give him drink, and clothe him, and so on, but ignore a single person whom you know to be hungry and thirsty, you will be regarded as having ignored Christ our God when He was hungry and thirsty.

117. This may seem extremely severe, and you may well say to yourself: 'Who can do all this? Who can care and provide for everyone, and not ignore anyone?' But let us listen to what St Paul explicitly states: 'For the love of Christ impels us to pronounce this judgment: that, since one has died for all, therefore all have died' (2 Cor. 5 : 14).

118. Just as the more comprehensive commandments contain within themselves all the more particular commandments, so the more comprehensive virtues contain in themselves the more particular virtues. For he who sells what he has and distributes it to the poor (cf. Matt. 19 : 21), and who once and for all becomes poor himself, has fulfilled at once all the more particular commandments: he no longer has to give alms to the person who asks him for them, nor does he have to refrain from rejecting the man who wishes to borrow from him (cf. Matt. 5 : 42). So, too, someone who prays continuously (cf. 1 Thess. 5 : 17) has in this act included everything and is no longer obliged to praise the Lord seven times a day (cf. Ps. 119 : 164), or in the evening, in the morning, and at noonday (cf. Ps. 55 : 17): he has already done all that we do by way of prayer and psalmody according to the regulations and at specific times and hours. Similarly, he who has acquired consciously within himself the Teacher of spiritual knowledge (cf. Ps. 94 : 10) has gone through all Scripture, has gained all that is to be gained from reading, and will no longer have need to resort to books. How is this? The person who is in communion with Him who inspired those who wrote the Divine Scriptures, and is initiated by Him into the undivulged secrets of the hidden mysteries, will himself be an inspired book to others – a book containing old and new mysteries and written by the hand of God; for he has accomplished all things and in God, the principle of perfection, he rests from all his labours.

119. Emission of semen in sleep may be produced by many factors. It may be due to gluttony, or self-esteem, or the envy of the demons. It may occur after long vigils when the body is sluggish and ready for sleep. It may happen because of the fear that it may happen, especially

if one is a priest due to celebrate the Liturgy, or intends to receive holy communion: filled with anxious thoughts that this might happen, one falls asleep only to have it happen. This, too, is brought about by the envy of the demons. Or it may be that after seeing a lovely face during the day, one then recalls it mentally, and falls asleep full of unchaste thoughts which one fails to repel because of one's sluggishness: thus one lapses while asleep, or even while lying awake in bed. Or certain individuals – negligent, as I see it – may sit and talk, perhaps impassionately, perhaps not, about things involving the passions; then, when they go to bed, they turn those things over in their minds, drop off to sleep while thinking about them, and come under their spell during sleep. It may even happen during the conversation itself, one person being perverted by another. We should therefore always be attentive to ourselves and reflect on the prophet's words: 'I have set the Lord always before me, because He is at my right hand, so that I shall not be shaken' (Ps. 16 : 8); and we should not listen to such talk. Often even those engrossed in prayer are physically aroused, as I have stated in the text on prayer.[1]

120. Brother, at the beginning of your renunciation of the world, try hard to implant in yourself noble virtues, so that you become useful to the community and so that the Lord may finally exalt you. Do not try to be familiar with the abbot, as we have already said elsewhere, or request any honour from him. Do not seek friendship with the senior members of the community, and do not hang about their cells; for if you do, not only will the passion of self-esteem begin to take root in you, but you will be disliked by the superior. Why this is so will be clear if you think about it. Sit peacefully in your cell, whatever it is like. If someone wants to contact you, do not spurn him on the grounds that he disturbs your devotions. Provided that you meet him with the consent of your spiritual father, you will come to no harm, even if the visitor has been sent to you by the enemy. But if you see that no good comes from the meeting, you should follow the path that is of profit to you.

121. At all times you should fear God, and every day you should examine yourself to see what good things you have done and what bad things. And you should forget what was good, lest you succumb to the passion of self-esteem. But where what was bad is concerned you should weep, confess, and pray intensely. This self-examination should

---

[1] It is not clear to what text this refers.

take place as follows: when the day has ended and evening has come, ask yourself how, with God's help, you have passed the day. Did you judge anyone, speak harshly of anyone, or offend anyone? Did you look impassionately at anyone, or did you disobey your superior with regard to your duties and neglect them? Did you become angry with anyone, or occupy your mind with useless things while in church? Or, overcome by lethargy, did you leave church or depart from your rule of prayer? When you see that you are guiltless on all counts – which is impossible, for 'no one is free from stain, not even for a single day of his life' (cf. Job 14 : 4–5. LXX), and 'who will boast that his heart is pure?' (cf. Prov. 20 : 9) – then cry out to God, full of tears: 'Lord, forgive me all my sins, in thought or act, conscious or unwitting.' For we offend in many ways, and do not know it.

122. Each day you should reveal all your thoughts to your spiritual father; and you should accept with complete confidence what he says to you, as if it came from the mouth of God. Do not speak of any of this to anyone else, saying: 'When I asked my spiritual father such and such a thing, he said this or that; was that good counsel or not? And what should I do to heal myself?' Words like these display lack of trust in your spiritual father and injure the soul. Mostly they occur in the case of beginners.

123. You should look on all who are in the monastery as saints and regard only yourself as a sinner and as the least of all, thinking that on that day all will be saved and you alone will be punished. And when you are in church reflecting about these things, weep bitter tears of compunction, taking no account of those who will be shocked by this or mock such behaviour. But if you see that as a result of this you are slipping into self-esteem, leave the church and weep in secret, returning as soon as you can to your place. This is particularly valuable in the case of beginners, especially during the six psalms,[1] the psalter, the readings, and the Divine Liturgy. Be careful not to condemn anyone, but keep it in mind that all who see your distress will think that you are a great sinner and will pray for your salvation. If you think of this at all times and carry it out constantly, you will be greatly helped, attracting to yourself God's grace and becoming a participant in His divine blessings.

[1] Six unvarying psalms are read daily at the start of matins (*orthros*): Psalms 3, 38, 63, 88, 103 and 143.

124. Do not visit the cell of anyone except the abbot, and this rarely. Even if you want to ask the abbot about some thought, do this in church. After the service return at once to your cell; from there go to carry out your duties. After compline, prostrate yourself before the abbot's door, ask for his prayers, and then, head down, hurry silently back to your cell. For it is better to repeat the Trisagion prayer[1] once with attention before going to bed than to pass a four-hour vigil in idle talk. Where there are compunction and spiritual grief, there is also divine illumination; when this is present in you, listlessness and sickness are dispelled.

125. Do not permit yourself to feel special love for anyone, in particular for a novice, even if his way of life seems excellent, and much more so if it is suspect. Generally such love, even if initially spiritual, changes into an impassioned love, and results in useless afflictions. This tends to happen especially to those engaged in spiritual warfare, as one may learn through humility and constant prayer. This is not the right occasion for me to speak about these matters in detail, but he who has understanding will understand.

126. Be a stranger to every brother in the monastery – and even more to all whom you know in the world. Love everyone equally and look on all those devoutly engaged in spiritual warfare as saints. For those who are negligent, as we ourselves are, we must pray intensely; but nevertheless, as I said above, we should regard all as saints, and should strive through inward grief to be purified of our passions, so that, illumined by grace, we may look on all as equals and attain the blessing of those who are pure in heart (cf. Matt. 5 : 8).

127. Brother, regard perfect withdrawal from the world first as the complete mortification of your own will; in the second place regard it as detachment from and abjuration of parents, family and friends.

128. In the third place you must divest yourself of all that belongs to you and give it to the poor, in accordance with the words, 'Sell all you have and give it to the poor' (Matt. 19 : 21). Then you must forget all with whom you enjoyed a particular relationship of love, whether physical or spiritual.

129. You must confess all the secrets of your heart, all that you have done from your infancy until this very hour, to your spiritual father or to the abbot as if to God himself, the diviner of hearts and

[1] The prayer 'Holy God, Holy Strong, Holy Immortal, have mercy on us'.

minds. Do this in the knowledge that John baptized with the baptism of repentance and that all came to him confessing their sins (cf. Matt. 3 : 6). As a result of this your soul will experience great joy and your conscience will find relief, in accordance with the words of the Prophet: 'First declare your sins, so that you may be set free' (cf. Isa. 43 : 26).

130. Be fully persuaded that after your entry into the monastery your parents and all your friends are dead; and regard solely God and the abbot as your father and mother. Never ask anything of parents or friends on account of some bodily need. If in their concern they send you something, accept it and be grateful for their solicitude, but give whatever they send to the guest-house or to the hospital. Do this with humility; for it is not a sublime but an insignificant act.

131. Do everything good with humility, keeping in mind Him who said, 'When you have done everything, say, "We are useless servants; we have only done what was our duty" ' (Luke 17 : 10).

132. Take care never to receive communion while you have anything against anyone, even if this is only a hostile thought. Not until you have brought about reconciliation through repentance should you communicate. But you will learn this, too, through prayer.

133. You should be ready each day to receive all kinds of afflictions, regarding them as your release from many sins; and you should thank God for them. Through them you may acquire a close and unimpeachable communion with God, in accordance with St Paul's words: 'Afflictions produce patient endurance; patient endurance, strength of character; and strength of character, hope; and hope does not disappoint' (Rom. 5 : 3–5). For the things that 'the eye has not seen, and the ear has not heard, and man's heart has not grasped' (1 Cor. 2 : 9) – these things belong, according to the infallible promise, to those who, with the help of God's grace, patiently endure affliction. Without God's grace we can of course do nothing.

134. Have nothing material in your cell, not even a needle, except for a rush mat, your sheepskin, your cloak, and whatever else you wear. If possible, do not have a stool there. There is much to be said on this matter; but let him who has understanding understand.

135. Again, do not ask the abbot for any appurtenances other than those prescribed; and take these only when he calls you and himself gives them to you. Resist any thought of exchanging them for others. Accept them as they are with thanksgiving, as if they had been given by

God, and manage with them. It is not permitted to buy others. You should wash your outer garment twice a year if it becomes dirty; and, like some unknown beggar, you should ask your brother in all humility for something to wear until it has been washed and dried in the sun. Then you should return what you have borrowed with thanks. You should do the same with your cloak and any other clothing.

136. Perform the various duties assigned to you as well as you can; in your cell persevere in prayer with compunction, attentiveness and constant tears. You should not think that because you have worked exceptionally hard today you should reduce your prayer on account of bodily exhaustion. For however greatly you exert yourself in performing your duties, you should be aware that you have lost something of great value if you deprive yourself of prayer. For this is in fact the case.

137. You should arrive first at the church services, especially matins and the Liturgy, and leave last, unless forced to do otherwise.

138. You should be completely obedient to your abbot, from whom you received the tonsure, and should fulfil his orders uncritically until your death, even if they seem impossible to you. In this way you will imitate Him who was obedient 'to the point of death, even death on the cross' (Phil. 2 : 8). You should obey in everything not only the abbot, but all the brotherhood, and whoever is in charge of the various tasks that have to be done; and if you are told to do something beyond your power, make a prostration and ask forgiveness. Should this be refused, remember that 'the kingdom of heaven is entered forcibly, and those who force themselves take possession of it' (Matt. 11 : 12); and apply force to yourself.

139. Whoever with a contrite heart prostrates himself before the entire brotherhood as a person of no account, utterly inconspicuous, a nonentity, and who lives in this way throughout his life, will receive, I declare, the gift of insight, and will foretell many things about the future with the help of God's grace. Such a person will also grieve for the faults of others; moreover, he will be undistracted by attachment to material things, since the intensity of his love for what is divine and spiritual will not permit him to stumble because of them. There is nothing marvellous about foretelling things of the future: often, indeed, it is prompted by the demons, as he who has understanding will understand. But if a person begins to hear confessions, he may perhaps be deprived of these gifts, since he will then be busied with the examination of other people's thoughts. If, on the other hand, out of

great humility he stops hearing confessions and giving counsel, he may again recover his previous gift of insight. But God alone has knowledge of these things; as for myself, constrained by fear I dare not speak of them.

140. You should always direct your intellect towards God, whether asleep or awake, eating or talking, engaged in your handiwork or in any other activity. Thus you will fulfil the saying of the prophet, 'I have set the Lord always before me' (Ps. 16 : 8). Reckon yourself a greater sinner than anyone else. For if you persist in this state of recollectedness, illumination will enter your mind like a ray of light. And the more you aspire to such illumination, attentive and undistracted, striving and tearful, the more clearly it will shine. When it shines, it is loved; and when it is loved, it purifies; and as it purifies, it makes one godlike, enlightening one and teaching one to distinguish good from evil. But, my brother, much hard work is needed, and God's help, before this radiance indwells totally in your soul and illumines it as the moon illumines the darkness of the night. You must also pay attention to the thoughts of arrogance and presumption which attack you, and not condemn anyone when you see him doing something wrong. For when the demons see the soul freed from passions and temptations through the indwelling of grace and the resulting state of peace, they attack it through such thoughts. But help comes from God. Let your inward grief be continuous and your tears unquenchable. Yet take care not to harm yourself because of your great joy and compunction: recognize that they are the result not of your own labour but of God's grace. Otherwise they may be taken from you and, when you urgently seek them again in prayer, you will not be able to recover them. You will then know what a gift it is that you have lost. May we never, O Lord, be deprived of Thy grace.

Yet if this does happen to you, my brother, cast your weakness before the Lord and, standing up, stretch forth your hands and pray, saying, 'Lord, have mercy on me a sinner, abject and weak as I am; and grant me Thy grace, not allowing me to be tested beyond my capacity. See, Lord, to what despondency and bad thoughts my sins have led me. Lord, even if I wish to I cannot measure the loss of Thy benediction, brought about by the demons and my own presumption. I know that the demons range themselves against those who zealously fulfil Thy will. But since I daily do what they want, how is it that I am afflicted by them? I am tried constantly by my own sins. Yet now, Lord, if it is Thy

will and to my benefit, let Thy grace enter Thy servant once again, so
that, aware of it, I may rejoice with tears and compunction, illumined
by its eternal radiance. Guard me from unclean thoughts, from
everything evil, from the sins I commit daily in word or act,
consciously or unwittingly. May I be given the confidence to call upon
Thee freely, O Lord, from amidst all the afflictions that I suffer daily at
the hands of men and demons; and, cutting off my own will, may I be
mindful of the blessings stored up for those that love Thee. For Thou
hast said, Lord, that he who asks receives, that he who seeks finds, and
that the door will be opened to whoever knocks' (cf. Matt. 7 : 8). In
addition to saying these and other things that God puts into your mind,
persevere in prayer, not allowing yourself to grow slack through
listlessness. And God in His love will not abandon you.

141. Persevere until the end in the cell initially allotted to you by
your superior. If you are troubled because of its age or dilapidation,
make a prostration before your superior and humbly mention the
matter to him. If he hears you sympathetically, rejoice; if not, give
thanks anyway, remembering our Lord who had nowhere to lay His
head (cf. Matt. 8 : 20). For if you disturb the superior about this a
second time, then a third and fourth time, insolence will result, then
lack of trust, and finally disdain. So if you want to lead a quiet and
peaceful life, do not ask your superior for any bodily comfort. For it
was not to this that you dedicated yourself when originally making
your monastic vows; but you consented to be despised and scorned
by all, in accordance with our Lord's commandment, and to endure
manfully. If you want to maintain your trust in and love for your
superior, and to look on him as a saint, make sure of these three
things: that you do not ask him for any comfort; that you do not
take any liberties when speaking with him; and that you do not keep
visiting him, as some do, on the grounds that he helps them. This is
not perseverance, but human failing. On the other hand, I do not
condemn the practice of not hiding from him any distractive thought
that comes into your mind; for if you maintain this practice you will
pass over the sea of life smoothly and will regard your spiritual
father, whatever he may be like, as a saint. Should you approach him
in church in order to question him about a distractive thought, but
find that someone else has anticipated you for the same purpose, or
for some other reason, and that you are therefore ignored for a short
while, do not take it amiss or think anything hostile; stand by

yourself with hands folded until the other person has finished and you are called forward. The fathers often act in this way, perhaps deliberately, testing us and releasing us from sins we have committed.

142. You should observe the great Lenten fast by eating every third day (not counting Saturdays and Sundays), unless there is a major feast. During the other two main fasts – before Christmas and before the Feast of the Dormition – you should eat every other day. On the remaining days of the year you should eat once only, except on Saturday and Sunday and on feast days; but do not eat to repletion.

143. Strive to become for the whole community a good example of every virtue: of humility, gentleness, active compassion, obedience even in the least of things, freedom from anger, detachment, unpossessiveness and compunction, guilelessness and uninquisitiveness, of simplicity and estrangement from the world. Visit the sick, console the distressed, and do not make your longing for prayer a pretext for turning away from anyone who asks for your help; for love is greater than prayer. Show sympathy towards all, do not be arrogant or over-familiar, do not find fault with others, or ask for anything from the abbot or from those in charge of various monastic tasks; be respectful towards all priests, attentive in prayer, frank and loving towards everyone; and do not ransack the Scriptures for the sake of glory. Prayer accompanied by tears and illumination given by grace will teach you how to accomplish all this.

Whoever it may be who seeks your assistance and asks for your guidance, with great humility and self-effacement give advice as God's grace inspires you about the different forms of holy action, using your own life as the model but referring to it as though it were that of someone else. And do not reject anyone who seeks your help with regard to some distractive thought, but listen to his sins, whatever they may be, weeping and praying for him; for this, too, is a sign of love and perfect compassion. Do not repel someone who comes to you on the grounds that you might be harmed by hearing what he has to say: with the help of God's grace, you will not be harmed in any way. So that no one else may be scandalized, you should speak in some secluded place. Being human, you may be attacked by some distractive thought; but if God's grace is present in you, such a thing will not happen to you. In any case, we are taught to seek not our own good but that of others, so that they may be saved (cf. 1 Cor. 10 : 24, 33).

As we have already said, you should keep your life free from worldly concerns and possessions. You may recognize that grace is active within you when you truly feel that you are a greater sinner than all other men. How this happens, not I, but only God can say.

144. When keeping vigil you should read for two hours, pray for two hours with tears and compunction, go through whatever you choose of your own rule of prayer, and repeat, if you wish, the twelve psalms,[1] Psalm 119, and the prayer of St Eustratios.[2] Do this when the nights are long. When they are shorter, abbreviate the sequence of prayers and readings in accordance with the strength given you by God. For without Him nothing good is accomplished: as the prophet says, 'The steps of a man are guided by the Lord' (Ps. 37 : 23. LXX). And our Saviour Himself has said, 'Without Me you can do nothing' (John 15 : 5).

Never go to communion without tears.

145. You should eat what is put in front of you, no matter what it is; and take wine with uncomplaining self-restraint. If because of sickness you are having your meals by yourself, eat raw vegetables with olives. But if one of the brethren should send you something to eat, receive it with humility and thanks, as if you were a guest, and eat some of it, whatever it may be, sending what is left over to another brother, poor and pious. Should someone invite you to a meal, partake of all that is put in front of you, but eat only a little, maintaining your self-control in accordance with the commandment. Then, having stood up and bowed before him as though you were destitute and a stranger, thank him, saying, 'May God give you your reward, holy father.' Be careful to say nothing else, even though it might possibly be of help.

146. If some brother, badly upset by the abbot, or the steward, or by someone else, should come to you, encourage him in this way: 'Believe me, brother, this has happened in order to test you; for the same thing has happened to me in various ways, and because of my

---

[1] In the Russian usage these are Psalms 27, 32, 34, 38, 39, 40, 41, 70, 71, 77, 102 and 143: see S.N. Schoinas (ed.), *Varsanuphios and John of Gaza: Questions and Answers* (in Greek) (Volos, 1960), p. 69, n.1.

[2] Read at the midnight office on Saturday.

faint-heartedness I was grieved. But once I realized that these things occur in order to test us, I have endured them gratefully. You should do the same now, and be glad for such trials.' Even if he then begins to abuse you, still do not turn away from him, but console him in whatever way God's grace enables you to do so. We have to distinguish between many different situations. According to your knowledge of your brother's state and his thoughts, talk to him, and do not let him go away unhealed.

147. If one of the brethren falls ill and you visit him only after some time, first send him a message: 'Holy father, I learnt about your illness only today, and I ask your forgiveness.' Then go and see him; and, after making a prostration and receiving his blessing, say to him: 'How has God helped you, holy father?' Then, sitting down with your hands folded, be silent. Even if there are others visiting him at the same time, be careful not to say anything either about the Scriptures or about his health, especially when not asked, so that you will not be troubled afterwards. For this is what happens generally to the more simple brethren.

148. If you are having a meal with your brethren, eat unhesitatingly of what is presented to you, whatever it may be. If, however, you have been told not to eat fish or some other food, and it is offered to you, should the person who gave you the order be close at hand, go to him and request him to let you partake; but should he not be present, or if you know that he would not give his permission, and at the same time you do not wish to offend your hosts, tell him what you have done after you have eaten, and ask his forgiveness. If you are unwilling to do either of these things, it is better for you not to visit your brethren. For in this way you will be the gainer in two respects: you will escape the demon of self-esteem, and at the same time spare them offence and distress. If the foods offered to you are on the rich side, keep to your rule; yet even in this case it is better to take a little of everything. In short, when you are invited somewhere, apply the principle laid down by St Paul: 'Eat all that is set before you without raising questions of conscience' (cf. 1 Cor. 10 : 25).

149. If one of the brethren knocks on your door while you are praying in your cell, open it for him and sit down and talk with him humbly, provided he proposes a topic of conversation that has some positive purpose. If he is distraught, do what you can, through word or act, to rally him. But when he has gone, close your door and take up

your prayer again, and complete it. To comfort those who visit you is a form of reconciliation. But you should not act in this way with regard to non-monks; in their case you should complete your prayer and then speak with them.

150. If, while you are praying, you feel frightened, or hear some noise, or if a light shines around you, or something else happens, do not be troubled, but concentrate all the more fully on your prayer. Demonic disturbances, alarms and excursions occur so that you will lose heart and give up your prayer; then, if this happens regularly, you will fall into the demons' power. But if as you pray another light, beyond description, appears to you, and your soul is filled with joy, and you feel a desire for higher things, and tears of compunction flow, know that this is a divine visitation and succour. Should this state continue for a long time, recapture your intellect in case something more happens to you because of the anguish of your tears, and submit it to some physical activity, thereby humbling yourself. If it is your enemies that are trying to frighten you, take care not to abandon your prayer. Be as the child who, frightened by some hobgoblin, dispels his terror by flying into the arms of his mother or father: resort to God through prayer and you will find that you escape the fear which the demons provoke.

151. If, while you are sitting in your cell, one of the brothers comes to you and asks about carnal warfare, do not turn him away. But with compunction help him, using what God's grace has given you and what you have yourself learnt through your own experience; and then dismiss him. As he leaves, however, make a prostration before him and say, 'Believe me, brother, I have hope that through God's love this war you wage will end; only do not give in or relax.' When he has gone, stand up, recall his struggle and, lifting your hands with tears towards God, pray with all your heart for your brother, saying, 'O Lord God, who do not desire the death of a sinner, act as You know how and as will benefit this brother.' And God, who knows your brother's faith in you, and your compassion born of love, and the genuineness of your prayer on his behalf, will diminish this warfare for him.

152. All those things, brother, help you to acquire compunction. They should be carried out with a contrite heart, patience, and thanksgiving. They will cause you to shed tears, cleansing you of your passions, and will bring you to the kingdom of heaven. 'For the kingdom of heaven is entered forcibly, and those who force themselves

take possession of it' (Matt. 11 : 12). If you can accomplish these things you will leave your former way of life completely behind, and may even be freed from the attacks of distractive thoughts. For darkness gives way to light, and a shadow to the sun. But should someone at the start of the spiritual path neglect these things, growing sluggish in thought and full of curiosity, he will be deprived of grace. Then, falling a victim to evil passions, he will come to know his own weakness and be filled with fear. Yet the person who successfully accomplishes these things should realize that this is the result not of his own efforts but of God's grace. He should purify himself first, in accordance with the saying, 'First purify yourself and then speak to Him who is pure.' For he who through many tears has purified his intellect and has received the illumination of the divine light – light that would grow no less even if everyone received it – will dwell spiritually in the age to come.

153. St Symeon the New Theologian was once asked what a priest ought to be like, and he replied as follows:

'I am not worthy to be a priest; but I know very well what someone who is to celebrate the sacred mysteries of God should be like. In the first place, he should be chaste, not only in body but also in soul, and he should be free of all sin. Secondly, he should be humble both in his external manner and in the inner state of his soul. Then, when he stands before the holy altar, while gazing with his physical eyes on the holy gifts, spiritually – and with total certainty – he should perceive the Godhead. Moreover, his heart should be consciously aware of Him who is invisibly present and dwelling in the gifts, so that he may offer the petitions with confidence; and when, like a friend speaking to a friend, he says, 'Our Father, who art in heaven, hallowed be Thy name' (Matt. 6 : 9), the way in which he recites the prayer will show that he has dwelling within him the true Son of God, together with the Father and the Holy Spirit. I have seen such priests. Forgive me, fathers and brethren.'

He also spoke the following words, as if about someone else, thereby concealing himself so as to avoid human adulation, even though because of his love for others he felt at the same time compelled to reveal himself:

'A certain priest-monk, who had full confidence in me as his friend, once told me this: "I have never celebrated the Liturgy without seeing the Holy Spirit, just as I saw Him come upon me when I was ordained and the metropolitan said the prayer while the service-book rested on my head." When I asked him how he saw it at that time, and in what form, he said: "Undifferentiated and without form, except as light. At first I was astonished, beholding what I had never beheld before; and as I was asking myself what it might be, the light said to me, its voice heard only by the intellect: 'Thus have I appeared to all the prophets and apostles, and to those who are now the saints and the elect of God; for I am the Holy Spirit of God.' " To Him be glory and power through all the ages. Amen.'

Attributed to St Symeon the New Theologian:
The Three Methods of Prayer

INTRODUCTORY NOTE

The short work that follows, also known by the title *Method of Sacred Prayer and Attentiveness*, recommends a psychosomatic technique to be used in combination with the invocation of the name of Jesus. From at least the fourteenth century onwards it has been attributed to St Symeon the New Theologian, but since 1927 serious doubts have been expressed about the authorship. Fr Irénée Hausherr, noting the parallels between this text and the treatise *On Watchfulness and the Guarding of the Heart* by Nikiphoros the Monk, in which a closely similar psychosomatic technique is described in somewhat fuller detail,[1] concludes that Nikiphoros is the author of both works.[2] It is in fact unlikely that Nikiphoros wrote *The Three Methods of Prayer*, ascribed to Symeon.[3] The traditional attribution to the New Theologian may contain at least an element of truth; if not by Symeon himself, *The Three Methods* perhaps emanated from the circle of his disciples. For the time being the question of its precise date and provenance remains open. St Makarios and St Nikodimos provide only a modern Greek paraphrase of the work, and we have therefore

---

[1] See below, pp. 205–6.

[2] *La méthode d'oraison hésychaste* (*Orientalia Christiana* ix, 2 [36]: Rome, 1927), pp. 133–4. Archbishop Basil (Krivocheine), *In the Light of Christ: Saint Symeon the New Theologian*, p. 79, n. 1, rejects the attribution to Symeon, but says nothing about Nikiphoros as the possible author of *The Three Methods*.

[3] See Antonio Rigo, 'Niceforo l'Esicasta (XIII sec.): alcune considerazioni sulla vita e sull'opera', in Olivier Raquez (ed.), *Amore del Bello: Studi sulla Filocalia* (Magnano, 1991), pp. 87–93.

based our translation on the critical edition of the original text made by Hausherr.[1]

The central theme in *The Three Methods* is the need to guard the heart. The first two methods of prayer described by the author are in his view defective, and indeed potentially dangerous, precisely because they neglect the need for such guarding. It should always be remembered that, when the word 'heart' is used in this and many other texts, it signifies not merely the emotions and affections but the spiritual centre of the human person viewed as a unified whole; the heart, as the author states here, is 'where all the powers of the soul reside'.[2] To assist us in guarding the heart, the author of *The Three Methods* proposes a psychosomatic technique involving three features: first, a particular bodily posture, with the chin resting on the chest and the gaze directed towards the navel (other fourteenth-century texts speak of fixing the gaze on the place of the heart rather than on the navel); secondly, control over the breathing, so that its pace is slowed down; thirdly, inner exploration by the intellect, which searches for the place of the heart. All of this, so it seems, is meant to precede rather than to accompany the recitation of the Jesus Prayer; it is intended as a preliminary exercise to assist our concentration before we embark on the actual invocation of the Holy Name.

Modern Western writers have compared this psychosomatic technique with certain methods used in Yoga and in Sufism, but the parallels should not be exaggerated.[3] The author of *The Three Methods* places the technique in a specifically Christological context: its purpose is to prepare us for 'the invocation of Jesus Christ'.[4] Any such technique is certainly to be employed with prudence, and its misuse can inflict grave damage on a person's physical and mental health. Significantly *The Three Methods* emphasizes the importance of obedience to a spiritual father who can act, in this and in all matters, as our 'unerring guide'.[5] Almost all teachers in the Orthodox Church today likewise insist that anyone wishing to embark on the psychosomatic technique should do so only under the personal guidance of an

[1] In *La méthode d'oraison hésychaste*, pp. 150–72.

[2] See pp. 72–3, and compare the Glossary (p. 431).

[3] See Bishop Kallistos (Ware), 'Praying with the body: the hesychast method and non-Christian parallels', in *Sobornost incorporating Eastern Churches Review* 14:2 (1992), pp. 6–35.

[4] See p. 73.

[5] See below, p. 69.

experienced master. The Jesus Prayer can be practised in its fullness without the use of any physical method at all. Nevertheless the technique outlined here is theologically defensible, resting as it does on a sound doctrine of the human person. As St Gregory Palamas points out,[1] and as the opening paragraph of *The Three Methods* clearly states, man is a unity of body and soul; the body is an essential aspect of our total personhood, and so it is not to be neglected or ignored but used dynamically in the task of prayer.

[1] See below, p. 332–8.

The Three Methods of Prayer

There are three methods of prayer and attentiveness, by means of which the soul is either uplifted or cast down. Whoever employs these methods at the right time is uplifted, but whoever employs them foolishly and at the wrong time is cast down. Vigilance and prayer should be as closely linked together as the body to the soul, for the one cannot stand without the other. Vigilance first goes on ahead like a scout and engages sin in combat. Prayer then follows afterwards, and instantly destroys and exterminates all the evil thoughts with which vigilance has already been battling, for attentiveness alone cannot exterminate them. This, then, is the gate of life and death. If by means of vigilance we keep prayer pure, we make progress; but if we leave prayer unguarded and permit it to be defiled, our efforts are null and void.

Since, then, as we said, there are three methods of attentiveness and prayer, we should explain the distinctive features of each, so that he who aspires to attain life and wishes to set to work may with firm assurance select what suits him best; otherwise through ignorance he may choose what is worse and forfeit what is better.

THE FIRST METHOD OF PRAYER

The distinctive features of the first method of prayer are these. When a person stands at prayer, he raises hands, eyes and intellect heavenwards, and fills his intellect with divine thoughts, with images of celestial beauty, of the angelic hosts, of the abodes of the righteous. In brief, at the time of prayer he assembles in his intellect all that he has heard from Holy Scripture and so rouses his soul to divine longing as he gazes towards heaven, and sometimes he sheds tears. But when someone prays in this way, without him realizing it his heart grows proud and exalted, and he regards what is happening to him as the effect of divine grace and entreats God to allow him always to be engaged in this activity. Such assumptions, however, are signs of delusion, because the good is not good when it is not done in the right way.

If, then, such a person is pursuing a life of stillness and seclusion, he will almost inevitably become deranged. And even if this does not happen to him, it will be impossible for him to attain a state of holiness or dispassion. Those who adopt this method of prayer have also been deluded into thinking that they see lights with their bodily eyes, smell sweet scents, hear voices, and so on. Some have become completely possessed by demons and wander from place to place in their madness. Others fail to recognize the devil when he transforms himself into an angel of light (cf. 2 Cor. 11 : 14); and, putting their trust in him, they continue in an incorrigible state of delusion until their death, refusing to accept the counsel of anyone else. Still others, incited by the devil, have committed suicide, throwing themselves over a precipice or hanging themselves.

Indeed, who can describe all the various forms of deception employed by the devil? Yet from what we have said any sane person can understand the kind of harm that may result from this first method of attentiveness. Even if someone who has adopted this method may perhaps avoid the evils we have mentioned because he lives in a community – for it is solitaries who are especially subject to them – none the less he will pass his entire life without making any progress.

THE SECOND METHOD OF PRAYER

The second form of prayer is this. A person withdraws his intellect from sensory things and concentrates it in himself, guards his senses, and collects all his thoughts; and he advances oblivious of the vanities of this world. Sometimes he examines his thoughts, sometimes pays attention to the words of the prayer he is addressing to God, and sometimes drags back his thoughts when they have been taken captive; and when he is overcome by passion he forcefully strives to recover himself.

One who struggles in this way, however, can never be at peace or win the crown of victory. He is like a person fighting at night: he hears the voices of his enemies and is wounded by them, but he cannot see clearly who they are, where they come from, and how and for what purpose they assail him. Such is the damage done to him because of the darkness in his intellect. Fighting in this manner, he cannot ever escape his noetic enemies, but is worn out by them. For all his efforts he gains nothing. Falsely imagining that he is concentrated and attentive, he falls victim unawares to self-esteem. Dominated and mocked by it, he despises and criticizes others for their lack of attentiveness. Imagining that he is capable of becoming the shepherd of sheep, he is like the blind man who undertakes to lead the blind (cf. Matt. 15 : 14).

Such are the characteristics of the second method of prayer, and every one striving after salvation can see what harm it does. Yet this second method is better than the first, just as a moonlit night is better than a night that is pitch-dark and starless.

THE THIRD METHOD OF PRAYER

Let us now begin to speak about the third method of prayer, which is truly astonishing and hard to explain. For those ignorant of it, it is not only difficult to understand but virtually incredible, and there are very few to be found who practise it. It seems to me that it has deserted us along with the virtue of obedience. For it is the love of obedience that delivers us from entanglement with this evil world, rendering us free from anxiety and impassioned craving. It makes us wholehearted and unflagging in pursuit of our aim – provided, of course, that we find an unerring guide. For if through obedience you make yourself dead to every worldly and bodily attachment, how can anything transient enslave your intellect? If you entrust all the care of your soul and body to God and to your spiritual father, no longer living for yourself or desiring the good opinion of others, what anxiety can distract you?

This third method, then, destroys the invisible wiles of the demons, with which as with ropes they seek to drag down the intellect into all manner of devious thoughts. Set at liberty, the intellect wages war with its full strength, scrutinizing the thoughts insinuated by the enemy and with masterful dexterity expelling them, while the heart in its purity offers prayers to God. This is the beginning of a life of true seclusion, and those who fail to make such a beginning exhaust themselves in vain.

The starting-point of this third method of prayer is not to gaze upwards, to raise one's hands aloft, to concentrate one's thoughts and to call down help from heaven. These, as we said, are the marks of the first form of delusion. Nor does it begin, as the second method does, by keeping guard over the senses with the intellect, while failing to observe the enemies who attack from within. In such a case, a person is struck by the demons instead of striking them; when wounded he is unaware of it; taken captive, he cannot retaliate against his captors. His enemies constantly attack him, from behind and even face to face, and fill him with self-esteem and arrogance.

If you desire to embark on this light-giving and joyful task, begin as follows. You must first practise exact obedience, as described above, and so act always with a pure conscience; for without obedience it is impossible for your conscience to be pure. And you must keep your conscience pure in three respects: first, with respect to God; second, with respect to your spiritual father; and third, with respect to other people and to material things. With respect to God you must keep your conscience pure by refraining from doing anything that conflicts with the worship due to Him. With respect to your spiritual father do everything he tells you to do, neither more nor less, and be guided by his purpose and will. With respect to other people, you must keep your conscience pure by not doing to them anything that you hate (cf. Tobit 4 : 15) and that you do not want them to do to you. With respect to material things, you must take care not to misuse them, whether food, drink or clothing. In brief, do everything as if you were in the presence of God, so that your conscience does not rebuke you in any way.

Having cleared the ground and indicated in a preliminary way the true character of attentiveness, let us now speak clearly and concisely about its characteristics. True and unerring attentiveness and prayer mean that the intellect keeps watch over the heart while it prays; it

should always be on patrol within the heart, and from within – from
the depths of the heart – it should offer up its prayers to God. Once it
has tasted within the heart that the Lord is bountiful (cf. Ps. 34 : 8.
LXX), then the intellect will have no desire to leave the heart, and it
will repeat the words of the Apostle Peter, 'It is good for us to be here'
(Matt. 17 : 4). It will keep watch always within the heart, repulsing
and expelling all thoughts sown there by the enemy. To those who
have no knowledge of this practice it appears extremely harsh and
arduous; and indeed it is oppressive and laborious, not only to the
uninitiated, but also to those who, although genuinely experienced,
have not yet felt the delight to be found in the depths of the heart. But
those who have savoured this delight proclaim with St Paul, 'Who will
separate us from the love of Christ?' (Rom. 8 : 35).

Our holy fathers hearkened to the Lord's words, 'Out of the heart
proceed evil thoughts, murders, adulteries, unchastity, thefts, perjur-
ies, blasphemies; these are the things that defile a man' (Matt.
15 : 19–20); and they also hearkened to Him when He enjoins us to
cleanse the inside of the cup so that the outside may also be clean (cf.
Matt. 23 : 26). Hence they abandoned all other forms of spiritual
labour and concentrated wholly on this one task of guarding the heart,
convinced that through this practice they would also possess every
other virtue, whereas without it no virtue could be firmly established.
Some of the fathers have called this practice stillness of the heart,
others attentiveness, others the guarding of the heart, others watchfulness and rebuttal, and others again the investigation of thoughts and
the guarding of the intellect. But all of them alike worked the earth of
their own heart, and in this way they were fed on the divine manna (cf.
Exod. 16 : 15).

Ecclesiastes is referring to this when he says, 'Rejoice, O young
man, in your youth; and walk in the ways of your heart' (Eccles.
11 : 9), blameless, expelling anger from your heart; and 'if the spirit
of the ruler rises up against you, do not desert your place' (Eccles.
10 : 4), by 'place' meaning the heart. Similarly our Lord also says,
'Out of the heart proceed evil thoughts' (Matt. 15 : 19), and 'Do not
be distracted' (Luke 12 : 29). And again, 'Strait is the gate and narrow
is the way that leads to life' (Matt. 7 : 14). Elsewhere He also says,
'Blessed are the poor in spirit' (Matt. 5 : 3); that is to say, blessed are
those who are destitute of every worldly thought. St Peter says
likewise, 'Be watchful, be vigilant, because your adversary, the devil,

walks about like a roaring lion, seeking whom he may devour' (1 Pet. 5 : 8). And St Paul writes very plainly to the Ephesians about the guarding of the heart, 'We do not wrestle against flesh and blood' (Eph. 6 : 12), and so on. And our holy fathers have also spoken in their writings about guarding the heart, as those who wish can see for themselves by reading what St Mark the Ascetic, St John Klimakos, St Hesychios the Priest, St Philotheos of Sinai, St Isaiah the Solitary and St Varsanuphios, and the entire book known as *The Paradise of the Fathers*,[1] have to say about the subject.

In short, if you do not guard your intellect you cannot attain purity of heart, so as to be counted worthy to see God (cf. Matt. 5 : 18). Without such watchfulness you cannot become poor in spirit, or grieve, or hunger and thirst after righteousness, or be truly merciful, or pure in heart, or a peacemaker, or be persecuted for the sake of justice (cf. Matt. 5 : 3–10). To speak generally, it is impossible to acquire all the other virtues except through watchfulness. For this reason you must pursue it more diligently than anything else, so as to learn from experience these things, unknown to others, that I am speaking to you about. Now if you would like to learn also about the method of prayer, with God's help I will tell you about this too, in so far as I can.

Above all else you should strive to acquire three things, and so begin to attain what you seek. The first is freedom from anxiety with respect to everything, whether reasonable or senseless – in other words, you should be dead to everything. Secondly, you should strive to preserve a pure conscience, so that it has nothing to reproach you with. Thirdly, you should be completely detached, so that your thoughts incline towards nothing worldly, not even your own body.

Then sit down in a quiet cell, in a corner by yourself, and do what I tell you. Close the door, and withdraw your intellect from everything worthless and transient. Rest your beard on your chest, and focus your physical gaze, together with the whole of your intellect, upon the centre of your belly or your navel. Restrain the drawing-in of breath through your nostrils, so as not to breathe easily, and search inside yourself with your intellect so as to find the place of the heart, where

---

[1] The title *Paradise* is applied in particular to the *Lausiac History* of Palladius, but also more broadly to any work on Egyptian monasticism, such as the *Historia Monachorum in Aegypto* or the *Apophthegmata*. Cf. the Syriac collection compiled by Ânân-Îshô, *The Paradise or Garden of the Holy Fathers*, E.T., E.A. Wallis Budge (2 vols, London, 1907).

all the powers of the soul reside. To start with you will find there darkness and an impenetrable density. Later, when you persist and practise this task day and night, you will find, as though miraculously, an unceasing joy. For as soon as the intellect attains the place of the heart, at once it sees things of which it previously knew nothing. It sees the open space within the heart and it beholds itself entirely luminous and full of discrimination. From then on, from whatever side a distractive thought may appear, before it has come to completion and assumed a form, the intellect immediately drives it away and destroys it with the invocation of Jesus Christ. From this point onwards the intellect begins to be full of rancour against the demons and, rousing its natural anger against its noetic enemies, it pursues them and strikes them down. The rest you will learn for yourself, with God's help, by keeping guard over your intellect and by retaining Jesus in your heart. As the saying goes, 'Sit in your cell and it will teach you everything.'[1]

Question: Why cannot the monk attain perfection by means of the first and second form of keeping guard?

Answer: Because he does not embark on them in the proper order. St John Klimakos likens these methods to a ladder, saying, 'Some curtail their passions; others practise psalmody, persevering most of the time in this; others devote themselves to prayer; and others turn their gaze to the depths of contemplation. When examining this question let us use the analogy of a ladder.'[2] Now those who want to ascend a ladder do not start at the top and climb down, but start at the bottom and climb up. They ascend the first step, then the second, and so the rest in turn. In this way we can ascend from earth to heaven. If, then, we wish to attain the perfect stature of the fulness of Christ, like children who are growing up we must start to climb the ladder set before us, until progressing step by step we reach the level of a full-grown man and then of an old man.

The first age in the monastic state is to curtail the passions. This is the stage of beginners.

The second rung or stage whereby a person grows up spiritually from adolescence to youth is assiduously to practise psalmody. For when the passions have been curtailed and laid to rest, psalmody brings

---

[1] *Apophthegmata*, alphabetical collection, Moses 6; E.T., Sister Benedicta Ward, *The Sayings of the Desert Fathers: The Alphabetical Collection* (2nd ed., London/Oxford, 1981), p. 139.

[2] St John Klimakos, *The Ladder of Divine Ascent*, Step 27 (*P.G.* lxxxviii, 1105C); E.T., p. 266.

delight to the tongue and is welcomed by God, since it is not possible to sing to the Lord in a strange land (cf. Ps. 137 : 4), that is to say, from an impassioned heart. This is the mark of those who are beginning to make progress.

The third rung or stage in life, marking the spiritual transition from youth to manhood, is to persevere in prayer. This is the stage of those who are already well advanced. Prayer differs from psalmody just as the full-grown man differs from the youth and the adolescent, according to the scheme that we are following.

In addition there is a fourth rung or stage in spiritual life, that of the old man with grey hairs. This signifies undeviating absorption in contemplation, and this is the state of the perfect. So the journey is complete and the top of the ladder has been reached.

Since this is the way in which matters have been appointed and arranged by the Spirit, it is not possible for a child to grow up to manhood and to attain old age except by mounting the first rung of the ladder and so climbing up to perfection by the four steps in succession.

For someone who desires spiritual rebirth, the first step towards the light is to curtail the passions, that is to say, to guard the heart; for it is impossible otherwise to curtail the passions. The next stage is to devote oneself to psalmody; for when the passions have been curtailed and laid to rest through the heart's resistance against them, longing for intimate union with God inflames the intellect. Strengthened by this longing the intellect repulses all distractive thoughts that encircle the heart, attempting to get in, and it rebuffs them through attentiveness. So it applies itself assiduously to the second stage, that of attentiveness and prayer. This then stirs up the evil spirits, and the blasts of passion violently agitate the depths of the heart. But through the invocation of the Lord Jesus Christ they are utterly routed and all the tumult melts like wax in the fire. But though they have been driven out of the heart the demons continue to disturb the intellect externally through the senses. However, because they can only trouble it superficially, the intellect soon regains its serenity; none the less, it can never be completely free from the attacks of the demons. Such freedom is to be found only among those who have attained full manhood – who are totally detached from everything visible and who devote themselves unceasingly to giving attention to the heart. After that, those who have achieved attentiveness are raised little by little to the wisdom of old age, that is to say, they ascend to contemplation; and this is the stage of the perfect.

Thus if you practise all this in due sequence, completing each phase at the right time, your heart will first be cleansed of the passions, and you will then be able to concentrate wholly on psalmody; you will be able to wage war against the thoughts that are roused by the senses and disturb the surface of the intellect and you will gaze heavenwards, if need be, alike with your physical and your spiritual eyes, and will pray in true purity. Yet you should gaze upwards only occasionally because of the enemies that lie in ambush in the air.

God asks only this of us, that our heart be purified through watchfulness. As St Paul says, if the root is holy, so also will the branches and the fruit be holy (cf. Rom 11 : 16). But if without following the sequence of which we have spoken you raise eyes and intellect to heaven in the hope of envisaging noetic realities you will see fantasies rather than the truth. Because our heart is still unpurified, as we have said many times, the first and the second methods of attentiveness do not promote our progress. When we build a house we do not put on the roof before laying the foundations – this is impossible. We first lay the foundations, then build the house, and finally put on the roof. We must do the same in relation to spiritual matters. First we must lay the spiritual foundations of the house, that is to say, we must watch over the heart and curtail the passions arising from it. Then we must build the walls of the spiritual house, that is to say, through the second form of attentiveness we must repulse the turbulence of the evil spirits that fight us by means of the external senses, and must free ourselves as quickly as possible from their attacks. Then we must put on the roof, that is to say, detach ourselves entirely from all things and give ourselves wholly to God. In this way we complete our spiritual house in Christ Jesus our Lord, to whom be glory throughout all the ages. Amen.

NIKITAS STITHATOS

Introductory Note

Nikitas Stithatos, the disciple and biographer of St Symeon the New Theologian, is far less well known to us than St Symeon himself.[1] Born around the beginning of the eleventh century, at an early age (c. 1020) Nikitas entered the monastery of Studios at Constantinople, and here he remained as a monk for the rest of his life, being ordained in due course to the priesthood. His personal contact with the New Theologian cannot have lasted very long, for the latter died in 1022. Before his death St Symeon commissioned Nikitas to make copies of his writings; and some years later, as a result of a vision in which the saint appeared to him, Nikitas prepared an edition of Symeon's works which was widely circulated. He acquired the *sobriquet* 'Stithatos', meaning 'the Courageous', because of his outspoken opposition during the early 1040s to the illicit relations of the Emperor Constantine IX Monomachos with his mistress Skliraina. At the time of the confrontation between Cardinal Humbert and Patriarch Michael Kiroularios of Constantinople in 1054, Nikitas wrote in defence of the Orthodox Church against the Latins. It is possible that he became abbot of the Studios monastery in his extreme old age, at some point in the period 1076–92. The date of his death is unknown.

In addition to his polemical works against the Latins and his biography of St Symeon, Nikitas wrote theological treatises on the soul, on paradise, and on the correlation between the angelic and the ecclesiastical hierarchies.[2] The three Centuries of texts included in *The Philokalia* deal respectively, so the titles indicate, with the three main stages on the spiritual way: the practice of the commandments (*praktiki*), the contemplation of the inner essences of created things (*physiki*), and 'theology' or the knowledge of God (*gnosis*). Here Nikitas

[1] On the life and writings of Nikitas, see A. Solignac in *Dictionnaire de Spiritualité* xi (1981), cols 224–30.

[2] Edited by J. Darrouzès in *Sources chrétiennes* 81 (Paris, 1961).

is following the classic triadic pattern devised by Evagrios of Pontos[1] and used by, among many others, St Maximos the Confessor.[2] But in fact the contents of the Centuries do not correspond at all exactly to these titles, and Nikitas includes in each Century material relating to all three stages on the spiritual journey. While employing most frequently the Evagrian-Maximian scheme, Nikitas occasionally combines this with the somewhat different sequence proposed by St Dionysios the Areopagite, in which the three stages are described as the purgative, the illuminative and the mystical (III, 41–4). Elsewhere he adopts the threefold classification found in St Isaac the Syrian: carnal, psychic and spiritual (II, 3–7).

Although his style is more complex and his approach more abstract than are those of St Symeon the New Theologian, Nikitas shares in common with his master many dominant themes. There are frequent references to the divine light (II, 2, 5, 43, 45, etc.), but at the same time Nikitas places more emphasis than does his master upon St Dionysios the Areopagite's symbolism of divine darkness (I, 1, 42; II, 50–1; III, 39, 53). Like St Symeon, Nikitas underlines the role of the spiritual father (I, 35; II, 10, 53–4) and maintains that a life of holiness is always possible, whatever a person's outward situation; it is not necessary to withdraw physically into the desert (I, 72), for the true 'flight from the world' is the inner renunciation of our self-will (I, 2, 75–6). Faithful to the example set by the New Theologian, Nikitas insists that those initiated into the divine mysteries must then act as 'missionaries', telling others about the gifts of grace which they have received (II, 96; III, 13, 27–8, etc.); and he agrees with St Symeon the Studite that love for others is higher than prayer (II, 76).

One theme in particular that Nikitas derives from St Symeon the New Theologian is the vital significance of tears and compunction (katanyxis) within the spiritual life. The two are commonly mentioned together, although a distinction is also drawn between them (I, 71). A modern reader might easily assume that both of these things are primarily negative and penitential in character, but this is to misunderstand Nikitas' viewpoint. Following St John Klimakos,[3] he

---

[1] See The Philokalia, vol. i (London and Boston, 1979), p. 57; and compare the Glossary, 'Contemplation'.

[2] See The Philokalia, vol. ii (London and Boston, 1981), pp. 64, 90.

[3] See The Ladder of Divine Ascent, Step 7 passim, and also the Introduction to the E.T., pp. 23–7.

is careful to distinguish two types of tears: those that produce 'an acrid and painful feeling', and the 'joyous tears' that are full of 'delight and a sense of jubilation'. The first are caused by repentance and inner grief, the second by compunction (I, 69–70). By the same token compunction has also a bitter-sweet character: it is linked with repentance and contrition (II, 92; III, 81), but at the same time it brings sweetness, joy and light, so that Nikitas speaks of the 'intoxication' and the healing 'oil' of compunction (II, 39, 68), and describes it as a spring from Eden, a shower of rain from the Holy Spirit (II, 44; III, 84). Tears and compunction, then, are caused not just by a realization of our own sinfulness, but also and much more fundamentally by a grateful and tender recognition of God's forgiving love.

In his basic approach, Nikitas Stithatos remains always positive, although never blandly optimistic. Our human nature is essentially good, and sanctity is nothing else than a return through grace to our natural state (I, 15; II, 12, 66). The material world is likewise intrinsically good and beautiful, and forms a sacrament of God's presence, a means of ascent to the divine realm: 'Recognize the delightfulness of the Lord from the beauty of creation . . . in purity ascending to the Creator through the beauty of His creatures' (I, 74, 90).

On the Practice of the Virtues:
One Hundred Texts

1. Those who have passed the mid-point of the first stage of the spiritual path, and who have attained the triad of mystical theology, are prompted to write in a profitable manner by, it seems to me, four factors inherent in the faith, hope and love that constitute the perfect triad of the virtues. The first is the freedom – that is to say, the dispassion – of soul, which as a result of ascetic practice raises the aspirant to the contemplation of the spiritual essences of the created world and then inducts him into the divine darkness of theology. The second is the purity of intellect that arises from prayer and tears, a purity that gives birth to the consciousness of grace and from which streams of intellection flow. The third is the indwelling of the Holy Trinity within us, which produces in each of those undergoing purification the bountiful illumination of the Spirit, revealing to them the mysteries of the kingdom of heaven and disclosing the treasures of God hidden in the soul. The fourth is the constraint which as a result of God's threatening words is imposed upon all who have received the talent of the consciousness of spiritual knowledge; for God says, 'You wicked, slothful servant, you should have deposited My money with the bankers, and then when I came I would have received My capital with interest' (Matt. 25 : 26–27). It was certainly because of this that David in great fear wrote, 'Behold, I will not seal my lips, as Thou, O Lord, knowest. I have not hidden Thy righteousness within my heart; I have declared Thy truth and Thy salvation; I have not concealed Thy mercy and Thy truth from the great congregation' (Ps. 40 : 9–10).

2. A life in harmony with God begins with complete flight from the world. 'Flight from the world' means the denial of the soul's desires and the transformation of the mundane will. Reverting in this way to

the will of God, from being worldlings we become spiritual: dead to
the fallen self and to the world, we are quickened in soul and spirit in
Christ.

3. When a soul has true esteem for God, deeply-rooted faith
combined with detachment from visible things, and an ascetic practice
free from all self-love, it possesses, to use Solomon's phrase, a
'threefold cord' (Eccles. 4 : 12), not easily broken by the spirits of
wickedness.

4. In faith we hope to receive reward for our labours, and on this
account we readily endure the hardship of practising the virtues. But
when we experience the pledge of the Holy Spirit, we are winged with
love towards God.

5. To be troubled by unclean thoughts does not mean that we are
already of the devil's party. But when the soul becomes slack, when the
intellect, because of our dissolute and unruly life, is filled with turbid
and obscure images, and when our practice of the virtues lapses
because of our laxity in meditation and prayer, then, even if not
actively engaged in evil, we are ranked among those who deliberately
crawl in sensual pleasures.

6. As soon as the bridle of the higher senses is removed, our
passions at once revolt and the baser, more slavish senses are stirred
into action; for when these latter in their mindlessness are loosed from
the bonds of self-control, their habit is to light upon the sources of the
passions and to feed on them as upon poisonous weeds. And the longer
the laxity continues, the more they do this. For such being their
natural appetite they cannot refrain from indulging it once they are
free to do so.

7. Among the senses, sight and hearing possess a certain noetic
quality and are more intelligent and masterful than the other three
senses, taste, smell and touch, which are mindless and gross, and wait
on the higher senses. For we first see and hear, and then, through the
agency of the mind, we lay hold of what is before us and, smelling it,
finally taste it. Thus taste, smell and touch are more animal-like or,
quite simply, baser and more slavish than sight and hearing. The more
gluttonous and ruttish animals, both tame and wild, are especially
afflicted by them, and day and night either fill themselves with food or
indulge in copulation.

8. If you refer the activities of the outer senses back to their inner
counterparts – exposing your sight to the intellect, the beholder of the

light of life, your hearing to the judgment of the soul, your taste to the discrimination of the intelligence, your sense of smell to the understanding of the intellect, and relating your sense of touch to the watchfulness of the heart – you will lead an angelic life on earth; while being and appearing as a man among men, you will also be an angel coexisting with angels and spiritually conscious in the same way as they are.

9. Through the intellect, beholder of the light of divine life, we receive knowledge of God's hidden mysteries. Through the soul's faculty of judgment we winnow in the light of this knowledge the thoughts that arise within the heart, distinguishing the good from the bad. Through the discrimination of the intelligence we savour our conceptual images. Those that spring from a bitter root we transform into sweet nourishment for the soul, or else we reject them entirely; those that spring from a virtuous and vigorous stock we accept. In this way we take every thought captive and make it obey Christ (cf. 2 Cor. 10 : 5). Through the understanding of the intellect we smell the spiritual unguent of the grace of the Holy Spirit, our hearts filled with joy and gladness. Through the watchfulness of the heart we consciously perceive the Spirit, who refreshes the flame of our desire for supernal blessings and warms our spiritual powers, numbed as they have been by the frost of the passions.

10. Just as in the body there are five senses – sight, hearing, taste, smell and touch – so in the soul there are five senses: intellect, reason, noetic perception, intuitive knowledge, and cognitive insight. These are united in three psychic activities: intellection, ratiocination, and noetic perception. By means of intellection we apprehend spiritual intentions, by means of ratiocination we interpret them, and through noetic perception we grasp the images of divine insight and spiritual knowledge.

11. If your intellect clearly distinguishes the intentions of its thoughts and in its purity gives its assent only to those that are divine; if your reason can interpret the physical movements of the whole of visible creation – that is to say, can clearly elucidate the inner essences of things; if noetically you can perceive heavenly wisdom and spiritual knowledge: then through the light of the Sun of righteousness you have transcended all sense-perception and have attained what lies beyond it, and you savour the delight of things unseen.

12. The intellect comprises four principal faculties: judgment,

sagacity, noetic apprehension, perspicacity. If you conjoin these with
the four principal virtues of the soul, linking restraint of soul to the
judgment of the intellect, sound understanding to sagacity, righteousness to noetic apprehension, and courage to perspicacity, you build for
yourself a two-fold fiery heaven-coursing chariot that will protect you
against the three major principalities and powers of the mustered
passions: avarice, self-indulgence and love of praise.

13. To master the mundane will of the fallen self you have to fulfil
three conditions. First, you have to overcome avarice by embracing the
law of righteousness, which consists in merciful compassion for one's
fellow beings; second, you have to conquer self-indulgence through
prudent self-restraint, that is to say, through all-inclusive self-control;
and, third, you have to prevail over your love of praise through sagacity
and sound understanding, in other words through exact discrimination
in things human and divine, trampling such love underfoot as
something cloddish and worthless. All this you have to do until the
mundane will is converted into the law of the spirit of life and liberated
from domination by the law of the outer fallen self. Then you can say, 'I
thank God that the law of the spirit of life has freed me from the law
and dominion of death' (cf. Rom. 8 : 2).

14. If you aspire to the spuriousness of human praise as though it
were something authentic, wallow in self-indulgence because of your
soul's insatiability, and through your greed entwine yourself with
avarice, you will either make yourself demonic through self-conceit
and arrogance, or degenerate into bestiality through the gratification
of belly and genitals, or become savage to others because of your gross
inhuman avarice. In this way your faith in God will lapse, as Christ said
it would when you accept human praise (cf. John 5 : 44); you will
abandon self-restraint and purity because your lower organs are
unsatedly kindled and succumb to unbridled appetence; and you will
be shut out from love because you minister solely to yourself and do
not succour your fellow beings when they are in need. Like some
polymorphic monster compounded thus out of multifarious self-
antagonistic parts, you will be the implacable enemy of God, man and
the animals.

15. If when aroused and active a man's incensive, appetitive and
intelligent powers spontaneously operate in accordance with nature,
they make him wholly godlike and divine, sound in his actions and
never in any way dislodged from nature's bedrock. But if, betraying his

own nature, he follows a course that is contrary to nature, these same powers will turn him, as we have said, into a polymorphic monster, compounded of many self-antagonistic parts.

16. Our incensive power lies between the appetitive and intelligent aspects of our soul; for both of them it serves as a weapon, whether it is acting in a way that accords with or is contrary to nature. When our desire and intelligence, in a way that accords with nature, aspire to what is divine, then our incensiveness is for both of them a weapon of righteousness wielded solely against the hissing serpent that would persuade them to indulge in fleshly pleasures and to relish men's praise. But when we fail to act according to nature and direct our desire and intelligence to what is contrary to nature, transferring attention from what is divine to purely human matters, then our incensive power becomes a weapon of iniquity in the service of sin, and we use it to attack and fight against those who would restrain the passions and appetites of the other powers of our soul. Thus, whether we are engaged in ascetic practice or are contemplatives and theologians, when we act according to nature we prove ourselves to be among the faithful members of the Church, and when we act contrary to nature we become bestial, savage and demonic.

17. Unless through the labour of repentance and assiduous ascetic practice we first restore the soul's powers to the state in which they were when God originally formed Adam and breathed into him the breath of life (cf. Gen. 2 : 7), we will never be able to know ourselves; nor will we be able to acquire a disposition that is master of the passions, free from arrogance, not over-curious, guileless, simple, humble, without jealousy or malice, and that takes every thought captive and makes it obey Christ (cf. 2 Cor. 10 : 5). Nor will our soul be enkindled with God's love, never transgressing the bounds of self-control, but content with what is given to it and longing for the serenity of the saints. And if we do not achieve such a state we can never acquire a heart that is gentle, peaceful, free from anger, kind, uncontentious and filled with mercy and joy; for our soul will be divided against itself and because of the turbulence of its powers will remain impervious to the rays of the Spirit.

18. If we do not regain the beauty of our original high estate, continually renewing the impress of the image of Him who created us in His likeness (cf. Gen. 1 : 26–27), but instead distance ourselves from Him through the disparity of our qualities, how can we ever enter

into union with Him? How can we enter into union with Him who is
light when we have blotted out the light and have embraced its
opposite? And if we are not united to Him from whom we have
received the source of our being, and through whom we have come
into existence from things that are not and have been made pre-
eminent over things that are; and if, because of our unlikeness to our
Creator we are severed from Him, where will we be cast? This will be
clear to those who can see, even if I am silent.

19. So long as we have the raw material of the passions within
ourselves and, instead of repudiating it, deliberately nurture it, the
passions will prevail over us, deriving their strength from us. But when
we cast this raw material out, cleansing our hearts with the tears of
repentance and abhorring the deceitfulness of visible things, then we
share in the presence of the Paraclete: we see God in eternal light and
are seen by Him.

20. Those who have broken the bonds of worldly sense-perception
are free from all servitude to the senses: they live solely in the Spirit,
communing with Him, impelled by Him, and brought through Him in
some measure into union with the Father and the Logos who are one in
essence with Him; and so they become a single spirit with God, as St
Paul says (cf. 1 Cor. 6 : 17). Not only are they exempt from the
dominion of the demons but they actually fill them with terror, since
they share in the divine fire and are in fact called fire.

21. Our sense of touch is not partial in the sense that its activity is
restricted to one part of the body, as is that of the other senses; it is a
general, all-over sense belonging to the whole body. Thus if while still
addicted to the lubricity of things we touch some object unnecessarily,
passion-charged thoughts perturb the intellect; but if, after renouncing
such addiction and rising above the realm of sense, we touch
something in accordance with a need inherent in our nature, then our
sense of touch has no tendency to seduce the soul's organs of
perception.

22. When the intellect is established in the realm of what is beyond
nature, the senses, assuming their natural role, commune dispassionately with the springs of the passions; they seek out only their
underlying essences and natures, unerringly distinguishing their
activities and qualities while not being addicted to them or adventitiously attracted by them in a manner that is contrary to nature.

23. Spiritual struggles and labours generate gladness in the soul,

so long, that is, as the passions have been stilled; for what is difficult for those who are still dominated by the senses is easy and even delightful for an aspiring soul that through its holy exertions has acquired a longing for God and is smitten with desire for divine knowledge. For the sense-dominated, the labours and struggles for virtue, opposed as they are to bodily ease and indulgence in sensual pleasure, are difficult and seem very harsh, for in such people the brackish taste of pleasure has not yet been washed away by the flow of tears. But the soul that abominates pain-inducing pleasure and has rejected comfort along with the self-love of the body, feels the need for and embraces such labour and struggles. One thing alone distresses it: slackness in its labours and indolence in its struggles. Thus what for those still dominated by the senses is the source of bodily content is for the soul that aspires to what is divine a cause of distress. And what for the aspiring soul is a cause of spiritual gladness is for the sense-dominated the cause of pain and anguish.

24. Ascetic toil is initially painful for all those newly engaged in spiritual warfare; but for those exercised in the growth of virtue and who have reached the mid-point of their path, such toil is pleasurable and produces a strange sense of relief. When the mortal will of the flesh is swallowed up by the immortal life (cf. 2 Cor. 5 : 4) conferred through the indwelling of the Holy Spirit in those truly striving towards the perfection of virtue, they are filled with unspeakable joy and gladness, for a pure spring of tears has opened within them, and streams of sweet compunction flow down on them from above.

25. If you wish to advance to the frontiers of virtue and to find unerringly the path that leads to God, do not allow your eyes to sleep or let your eyelids droop or give rest to your brow (cf. Ps. 132 : 4) until, with your soul riven by toil and tears, you have attained the land of dispassion and have entered into the sanctuary of the knowledge of God. For then, aloof from all that is below, in your great thirst you will have climbed like a stag to the high mountains of contemplation and through God's personalized Wisdom you will have descried the ultimate reaches of human life.

26. For those newly engaged in spiritual warfare the swift path to the recovery of virtue consists in the silencing of the lips, the closure of the eyes and the stopping of the ears; for once the intellect has achieved this kind of intermission and has sealed off the external entrances to itself, it begins to understand itself and its own activities.

It immediately sets about interrogating the ideas swimming in the noetic sea of its thought, trying to discern whether the concepts that irrupt into the mind's crucible are pure, alloyed with no bitter seed, and conferred by an angel of light, or whether they are tares, hybridized, trashy, emanating from the devil. Standing thus like a masterful sovereign in the midst of its thoughts, judging them and separating the better from the worse, the intellect accepts those that are well-tested in the fire of the Spirit and saturated with divine water, absorbing them into its actions and practice and storing them up in its spiritual treasure-house; for by these thoughts it is nourished, strengthened and filled with light. The other thoughts it casts into the depths of oblivion, eradicating their bitterness. This is the work only of someone who has spiritually embarked upon the path that leads unerringly to the heavens and to God, and who has stripped off the lugubrious cloak of the dark passions.

27. Once the soul has divested itself of malice and of its futile propensity to cheap arrogance, and through the indwelling of the Paraclete has adorned the heart with simplicity and innocence, it will immediately be restored to God and to itself. And since it has now passed beyond the hellish pits of incredulity and malevolence, it will unhesitatingly accept what it hears and sees as trustworthy and true.

28. Deep-rooted faith is pre-eminent among the virtues, since such faith strips the soul of doubt and rids it completely of self-love. For nothing so prevents someone newly engaged in spiritual warfare from practising the commandments as this pernicious vice of self-love. It even prevents the progress of those well advanced on the spiritual path, for it suggests illnesses to them and malignant bodily ailments, so that their ardour wanes and they are persuaded to give up ascetic toil on the grounds that in their susceptible state it is dangerous. Self-love is inane amity for the body, which ends by making the monk a lover of himself – of his own soul and body – and so estranges him from God and from God's kingdom, in accordance with the gospel phrase, 'He who loves his life will destroy it' (John 12 : 25).

29. He who diligently begins to practise God's commandments, and with ardent longing shoulders the light yoke of asceticism (cf. Matt. 11 : 30), does not spare his body's health, or flinch at virtue's harsh demands, or shrink from exertion, or heed the laziness and negligence of others. Rather, whatever the hardship, he fervently ploughs the furrow of the virtues, attending only to himself and to the

commandments of God. Each day with tears he tills and sows the land of the living (cf. Ps. 126 : 5) until the first shoots of dispassion germinate within him, wax into divine knowledge, bear the grain of the Logos and fructify in His righteousness.

30. Nothing, I think, so promotes the soul's swift progress as faith – not just faith in God and in His only-begotten Son, but faith that is deeply rooted. With this faith we believe in the truth of Christ's promises, made and kept in readiness for those who love Him (cf. 1 Cor. 2 : 19), just as we also believe in the truth of the threats and the infernal punishments prepared for the devil and his accomplices (cf. Matt. 25 : 41). This faith inspires the striving soul with the hope that it will attain the state of the saints, their blessed dispassion, climbing the heights of their holiness and becoming a coheir with them of God's kingdom. With such assurance the soul assiduously and unwaveringly augments its practice of the commandments, imitating the labours of the saints and pursuing their perfection by means of similar struggles.

31. The external appearance of the face changes in accordance with the inner state of the soul: whatever the soul's noetic activity, it will be reflected in the face. Disposed and changed according to the thoughts within the soul, the face brightens when the heart rejoices in the upsurge of good thoughts and in its meditation on God, but is downcast and glum when the heart is embittered by unnatural thoughts. In both cases, what is happening is quite evident to those in whom the soul's organs of perception are well trained. Either it is a change brought about by 'the right hand of the Most High' (Ps. 77 : 10. LXX), and this is obvious to them because it is something familiar and dear to them whereby they are reborn in the Spirit and become light and salt to others near them (cf. Matt. 5 : 13–14); or else it is a change brought about by the discord of evil powers and the tumult of our thoughts, and this too is evident to them, since they resist such change, the impress of the image of the Son of God within them having been burnished to the highest degree by the rays of divine grace.

32. A soul receives either blessings or penalties and punishment according to its inner activities. If it concerns itself with things divine and tills the ground of humility, tears fall on it like rain from heaven, and it cultivates love for God, faith and compassion for others. And when in this way the soul is renewed in the beauty of Christ's image, it becomes a light to others; attracting their attention with the rays of its virtue, it inspires them to glorify God. But if the soul devotes itself to

mundane and merely human matters, stirring and agitating the fetid
waters of sin, it nourishes hatred and repels what is good and beautiful.
Deformed in this way according to the mundane, ugly image of fallen
man, it becomes a thing of darkness to others; and through its evil talk
and depravity it corrupts immature and fickle souls, inducing them to
blaspheme God. Thus the soul receives its reward according to the
state it is in when death overtakes it.

33. If you husband evil thoughts your face will be morose and
sullen; your tongue will be incapable of praising God and you will be
surly towards others. But if you husband in your heart what is
deathless and holy, your face will radiate joy and gladness, you will lift
up your voice in prayer and be most gentle in speech. Thus it will be
quite clear to all whether you are still subject to unclean passions and
to the law of the mundane will, or whether you are free from such
servitude and live according to the law of the Spirit. In the words of
Solomon, 'A glad heart makes the face radiant; but a doleful heart
makes it sullen' (cf. Prov. 15 : 13).

34. Passions acted out can be cured by action. Dissipation,
sensuality, gluttony and a dissolute, profligate life produce a passion-
charged state of soul and impel it to unnatural actions. On the other
hand, restraint and self-control, ascetic labour and spiritual struggle
translate the soul from its passion-charged state to a state of dispassion.

35. If after strenuous ascetic labour you receive great gifts from
God on account of your humility, but are then dragged down and
handed over to the passions and to the chastisement of the demons,
you must know that you have exalted yourself, have thought much of
yourself, and have disparaged others. And you will find no cure for or
release from the passions and demons that afflict you unless you make
use of a good mediator and through humility and awareness of your
limitations you repent and return to your original state. Such humility
and self-knowledge lead all who are firmly rooted in virtue to look
upon themselves as the lowest of created things.

36. In the eyes of God and of those who live a Christ-like life, to act
with passion because of one's dissolute character and to take pride in
one's virtues through a spirit of self-conceit are each as evil as the
other. In the first case it is shameful even to speak of the things that
those enslaved to the passions do in secret (cf. Eph. 5 : 12); in the
second case the self-vaunting of the heart is an abomination to God.
The dissolute person alienates himself from God, for he is 'flesh' (cf.

Gen. 6 : 3), while the person who takes pride in his virtue is unclean in God's sight because of his self-conceit.

37. A passion is not the same thing as a sinful act: they are quite distinct. A passion operates in the soul, a sinful act involves the body. For example, love of pleasure, avarice and love of praise are three particularly noxious passions of the soul; but unchastity, greed and wrong-doing are sinful acts of the flesh. Lust, anger and arrogance are passions of the soul produced when the soul's powers operate in a way that is contrary to nature. Adultery, murder, theft, drunkenness and whatever else is done through the body, are sinful and noxious actions of the flesh.

38. The three most general passions are self-indulgence, avarice and love of praise; and three are the ranks of men that fight against them and overcome them: those newly embarked on the spiritual path, those in mid-course, and those who have attained its goal.

39. The battle waged by those in the three stages of the spiritual path against these three principles and powers of the prince of this world is not one and the same, but at each stage the battle is different. At each stage there is a different way of fighting against these passions, and each way makes lawful and natural use of the power of righteous indignation.

40. If it is but recently that you have embarked on the struggle for holiness and ranked yourself against the passions, you must battle unremittingly and through every kind of ascetic hardship against the spirit of self-indulgence. You must waste your flesh through fasting, sleeping on the ground, vigils and night-long prayer; you must bring your soul into a state of contrition through thinking on the torments of hell and through meditation on death; and you must through tears of repentance purge your heart of all the defilement that comes from coupling with impure thoughts and giving your assent to them.

41. When you approach the mid-point of the initial stage of the spiritual path you will experience the first form of dispassion, and through it the strain of your exertions against the spirit of self-indulgence will be eased. Your eyes opened, you will begin to perceive the inner nature of things, and will now take up the weapons of faith against the spirit of perfidious avarice. You will exalt your intellect through meditation on things divine and quicken your thought with the inner essences of the created world, elucidating their true nature.

In faith you will lead your soul from what is visible to the heights of the invisible, assured that God, who brings all things from non-existence into existence, provides for all that He has created. In this way your whole aspiration will be directed towards life in God.

42. When through contemplation and dispassion you have passed the half-way mark of the spiritual journey and have transcended the deceitfulness of worldly sense-perception, you will now enter the divine darkness of theology, guided by the consciousness of spiritual knowledge and by God's personalized Wisdom. It is at this point that with the strength of humility you raise your weapons against the spirit of self-glory and the love of praise. Your soul will be spurred by holy revelations and painlessly you will pour forth tears; you will be humbled in your will through the recognition of human weakness, and exalted by intimations of divine knowledge.

43. By means of fasting, vigils, prayer, sleeping on the ground, bodily labours and the amputation of our desires through humility of soul, we inactivate the spirit of self-indulgence. We overcome it through tears of repentance and, shackling it with self-control, render it immobile and ineffective; for we are now among those proficient in spiritual warfare.

44. Repulsing and finally slaying the spirit of avarice with the weapons of faith and 'the sword of the Spirit, which is the word of God' (Eph. 6 : 17), we now approach, thanks to the consciousness of Wisdom, the contemplation of the inner essences of created beings. Illumined with the consciousness of spiritual knowledge, we pass beyond the lowly region of visible things and attain the realms of love, rich in God-inspired hope.

45. Winged by dispassion and humility, and inspired by the Holy Spirit, we enter the sphere of mystical theology and the abyss of the knowledge of God's mysteries. The spirit of self-glory is now consumed in the lightning of divine thought and doctrine. Weeping and filled with compunction we perceive the consummation of things human, and scatter that spirit's minions, who attack us through presumption, self-esteem and arrogance.

46. He who wholeheartedly hates and renounces 'the desire of the fallen self, the desire of the eyes, and the false pretentions of this life' (1 John 2 : 16) – that whole 'world of iniquity' (Jas. 3 : 6) through the love of which we become the enemies of God (cf. Jas. 4 : 4) – has crucified the world to himself and himself to the world: he has

destroyed in his flesh the enmity between God and his soul, and has made peace between the two (cf. Eph. 2 : 15). For he who has died to these things through effacing the will of the flesh has reconciled himself to God. He has eradicated the enmity of this world by obliterating sensual pleasure through a life crucified to the world, and has embraced friendship with Jesus. He is no longer God's enemy because of his love for the world, but is a friend of God, crucified to the world and able to say, 'The world is crucified to me, and I to the world' (Gal. 6 : 14).

47. God deserts those engaged in spiritual warfare for three reasons: because of their arrogance, because they censure others, and because they are so cock-a-hoop about their own virtue. The presence of any of these vices in the soul prompts God to withdraw; and until they are expelled and replaced by radical humility, the soul will not escape just punishment.

48. It is not only passion-charged thoughts that sully the heart and defile the soul. To be elated about one's many achievements, to be puffed up about one's virtue, to have a high idea of one's wisdom and spiritual knowledge, and to criticize those who are lazy and negligent – all this has the same effect, as is clear from the parable of the publican and the pharisee (cf. Luke 18 : 10–14).

49. Do not imagine that you will be delivered from your passions, or escape the defilement of the passion-charged thoughts which these generate, while your mind is still swollen with pride because of your virtues. You will not see the courts of peace, your thoughts full of lovingkindness, nor, generous and calm in heart, will you joyfully enter the temple of love, so long as you presume on yourself and on your own works.

50. If your soul is allured by comeliness of body and usurped by the passion-imbued thoughts that it seems to evoke, do not assume that such comeliness is the cause of your agitated and impassioned state. The cause lies hidden in your soul, and it is your soul's passionate disposition and evil habits that, as a magnet attracts iron, attracts to itself such impurity from the beauty it perceives. For all things are created by God and all, as He Himself says, are 'wholly good and beautiful' (Gen. 1 : 31), providing no ground at all for impugning His creation.

51. Just as seasickness is due, not to the sea's nature, but to the already existing disorder of the body's humours, so the soul's

confusion and turmoil are due, not to the beauty of countenance in the person that it perceives, but to its pre-existing evil disposition.

52. The soul's apprehension of the nature of things changes in accordance with its own inner state. Thus when its spiritual organs of perception operate in a way that accords with nature and the intellect unerringly penetrates to the inner essences of things, clearly and cogently elucidating their nature and function, then it perceives things and persons and every material body as they are according to nature, and is aware that no seed of impurity or vitiation lies hidden within them. But when its powers operate in a way that is contrary to nature, and are in a state of self-antagonism, it perceives things likewise in a way that is not in accord with nature; their natural beauty does not exalt it to an understanding of their Maker, but because of its own impassioned proclivities engulfs it in self-destruction.

53. If while you are engaged in ascetic labour and hardship God withdraws from you because of some bodily lapse, or lapse of tongue or thought, do not take this to be strange or untoward. The lapse is yours and due to yourself. Had you not yourself first indulged in some new-fangled, overweening and obnoxious thought about yourself, or had you not in arrogance treated someone disdainfully or criticized him for his human weakness, you would have recognized your own fallibility and God in His righteous judgment would not have withdrawn from you. Learn from this not to judge (cf. Matt. 7 : 1), not to think too highly of yourself (cf. Rom. 12 : 3), and not to look down on others (cf. 1 Cor. 4 : 6).

54. When you have fallen into the depths of wickedness, do not despair of your recall, even if you have been brought down to the nethermost reaches of hell. For if through the practice of the virtues you have already established your ascetic life on a firm basis, God will not forget your former labours and hardships even if the stones of virtue you have set in place should be shaken to the ground by the most impassioned of vices. Only you must bring to Him a heart full of contrition for your lapse, and you must 'remember the days of old' (cf. Ps. 143 : 5), recalling your fall with deep sorrow before Him. He will then swiftly visit you as you tremble at His words (cf. Isa. 66 : 2), and invisibly will touch the eyes of your grieving heart, recognizing the basis of virtue you have already established through your labours; and together with fervour of spirit He will give you strength that is greater and more perfect than your former strength. In this way the house of

virtue, patiently built up but then destroyed through the devil's malice, will in a spirit of humility be restored more splendidly than before as His eternal dwelling-place.

55. Everything that brings disgrace upon us, whether prompted by man or demons, occurs through God's just judgment in order to humble the overweening vanity of our soul. For God, the helmsman of our lives, wishes that we should always be humble and have not an exaggerated but a modest view of ourselves (cf. Rom. 12 : 3); that we should not have great ideas about ourselves, but should look to Christ and imitate, so far as we can, His blessed humility; for He was 'gentle and humble in heart' (Matt. 11 : 29). He who for our sake endured a disgraceful, unjust death desires us to be like this, for there is nothing so dear to Him or that in its true virtue so fully accords with Him – nothing so apt to raise us from the dunghill of the passions – as gentleness and humility and love for our fellow beings. If these are not present with us as we cultivate the virtues, all our labour is in vain and all our ascetic endeavours are useless and unacceptable.

56. Those newly embarked on the ascetic life are assisted in the practice of the commandments and in their escape from evil by fear of punishment. But in those who through virtue have advanced to the contemplation of God's glory this fear is followed by another fear – a pure fear (cf. Ps. 19 : 9) – which, because it is caused by love, fills them with great dread. This helps them to stand unshaken in their love for God, instilling in them terror at falling away from such love. If beginners in spiritual warfare lapse, but then repent and recover, they are filled once more with the first fear, accompanied now by auspicious hope. But when those who have attained the heights of contemplation fall from them as a result of the devil's malice, they do not at once recover the second kind of fear. A grey mist and a palpable darkness (cf. Exod. 10 : 21) envelop them, and they are filled with despondency, pain and bitterness, together with their earlier fear of punishment. And if the Lord of hosts did not curtail those days of unbearable pain, none who fall from the heights of contemplation would be rescued (cf. Matt. 24 : 22).

57. When our soul is freed from the persistent importunities of impassioned thoughts, and the flame that torments the flesh dies away, we should recognize that the Holy Spirit is actively present within us, disclosing that our past sins are forgiven and bestowing dispassion on us. But so long as we are still aware of the constant

importunity of such thoughts and our lower organs are enkindled as a result, we may be sure that the sweet fragrance of the Spirit is far from our soul, and that our soul is wholly subject to the unbroken bonds of the passions and the senses.

58. 'I have seen under the sun', remarked the sage (cf. Eccles. 1 : 3; 9 : 11), 'a man who thought he was intelligent, who though mortal presumed on his own works and had a high opinion of his own human, worldly and psychic wisdom. Because of this not only did he look down on simple men, but he ridiculed the divinely-appointed Christian teachers and mocked them on account of their peculiar form of speech, their deliberate eschewing of the polished diction of academics, and the lack of rhythmical dexterity in their writings. To such a man, ignorant that God prefers clarity of thought to well-turned phrases or sonorous words, I would commend the maxims: "Better a living dog than a dead lion" (Eccles. 9 : 4), and "Better a poor and wise child than an old and foolish king, who no longer knows how to pay attention" ' (Eccles. 4 : 13. LXX).

59. Blasphemy is a frightful passion, difficult to combat, for its origin lies in the arrogant mind of satan. It troubles all who live in virtue and in accord with God, but especially those advancing in prayer and in the contemplation of things divine. Hence we must guard the senses with great diligence, and reverence all the awe-inspiring mysteries of God, the holy images and holy words, and watch out for the attacks of this spirit. For it lies in wait for us while we pray and chant, and when we are inattentive it discharges through our lips curses against ourselves and strange blasphemies against God the Most High, introducing them into the verses of the psalms and into the words of our prayers. When it brings some such thing to our lips or sows it in our minds, we should turn against it the words of Christ and say, 'Get behind me, satan, full of every foul odour and condemned to eternal fire; may your blasphemy fall upon your own head' (cf. Luke 4 : 8; Matt. 25 : 41). Then, concentrating our thoughts, we should at once occupy our intellect with some other matter, either divine or human, and with tears raise it towards God; and so with God's assistance we will be relieved of the burden of blasphemy.

60. Dejection is a passion that corrupts soul and body, affecting even the marrow of one's bones – I mean that cosmic dejection induced by the transitoriness of things and often resulting in death. The sorrow prompted by God, however, is extremely salutary,

enabling one patiently to endure hardships and trials. It is a source of compunction for those struggling and thirsting for God's righteousness (cf. Matt. 5 : 6), and nourishes their heart with tears. In such people is the saying of David fulfilled, 'Thou shalt feed us with the bread of tears and give us tears to drink in great measure' (Ps. 80 : 5) – the wine of compunction.

61. Sorrow prompted by God is an excellent tonic for those parts of the soul corrupted by evil actions, and it restores them to their natural state. It dissolves through tears the storm-clouds of passion and sin and dispels them from the soul's spiritual firmament, so that at once a clear sky appears in the thoughts of our intellect, the sea of the mind grows calm, gladness rises in the heart and a change comes over our face. When this is now seen by those skilled in discerning our inner state from our outward appearance, they will exclaim, as did David, 'This change is from the right hand of the Most High' (Ps. 77 : 10. LXX).

62. Do not keep company with those who enkindle in you suspicions about your fellow beings, for such suspicions are false, destructive and utterly deceitful. They are ploys through which the demons try to engulf the souls of those progressing in virtue. For there is only one way in which the demons can thrust them into the pit of perdition and active sin, and that is by persuading them to harbour evil suspicions about the outward behaviour and inner state of their neighbour. By this means the demons contrive to have them condemned along with the world, in the manner indicated by St Paul's phrase, 'If we would judge ourselves, we would not be judged; but when we are judged, we are chastened by the Lord, so that we should not be condemned with the world' (1 Cor. 11 : 31–32).

63. When because of our laxity we allow the demons to beguile us with suspicious thoughts about other people – that is to say, when we fail to control the abduction of our eyes – then they incite us to pronounce judgment on others, sometimes even those who are perfect in virtue. If someone is affable, with a cheerful, smiling face, we think him prone to pleasure and the passions; and we assume that anyone who looks downcast and sullen is filled with arrogance and anger. But we ought not to concern ourselves with people's appearance. Everyone is likely to judge wrongly in this respect; for men have various characters, temperaments and bodily features, the true assessment and study of which pertain only to those in whom the spiritual eye of the

soul has been cleansed through deep compunction, who are filled with the boundless light of divine life, and to whom it has been given to know the mysteries of the kingdom of God (cf. Matt. 13 : 11).

64. When we act basely in obedience to our fallen self, we serve the soul's appetitive and incensive powers in a way that is contrary to nature. We defile the flesh with the noxious flux of sin, darken the soul with embittered anger and estrange ourselves from the Son of God. We should therefore cleanse the stain deriving from the body's intrinsic serosity with floods of heartfelt tears. In this way the body soiled by sensual indulgence on account of its natural serosity will, because of our remorse, in its turn be purified through the natural flow of tears; and we will dispel with the luminosity of compunction and the sweetness of a godlike love the cloud that darkens our soul because of our embittered anger. Thus we shall once again be united with Him from whom we had been estranged.

65. Just as the stain produced by sensual indulgence presupposes a satanic desire to fulfil the shabby act it involves, so the purification that comes from our remorse presupposes heartfelt longing for the grief and tears which purification demands. In accordance with God's supernal goodness and providence, we expel and purge sensual indulgence through grief, and the flesh's baneful serosity through the flow of tears. In this way we expunge the imprint of vilifying actions from the intellect and squalid images from the soul, disclosing ever more fully the splendour of its natural beauty.

66. Prompted by the devil, the libertine reaps fleshly pleasure, and his ugly actions induce self-pollution. Prompted by the Holy Spirit, the man of God reaps joy of soul, and his acts of beauty induce purification through tears, rebirth and union with God.

67. There are in us two natural fluids which come from the same source in our being: semen and our tears. Through the first we may sully our soul's garment, through the second we may cleanse it again. The stain that comes from our being has to be washed away with the tears that come from the same source. Otherwise it is impossible for us to cleanse this self-generated defilement.

68. The discordant soul, prompted by what is base, always acts in a manner that ends up in some fleeting pleasure; but the soul purged of vicious habits labours to attain enduring bliss. It is marvellous how the second form of pleasure restrains the first, mollifying the pain engendered by self-indulgence.

69. Sometimes the flow of tears produces an acrid and painful feeling in the heart's organ of spiritual perception, sometimes it induces delight and a sense of jubilation. Thus when through repentance we are in the process of cleansing ourselves from the poison and stain of sin and, enkindled by divine fire, hot tears of repentance flow from us, and when our conscience is as it were smitten by the heart's anguish, then we experience this acrid feeling and painfulness both spiritually and perceptibly. But when we have been largely cleansed by such tears and have attained freedom from the passions, then – refreshed by the divine Spirit, our heart pure and tranquil – we are filled with inexpressible tenderness and delight by the joyous tears provoked by compunction.

70. Tears of repentance are one thing, tears that flow because of divine compunction another. The first are like a river in spate that sweeps away all the bastions of sin; the second are to the soul like rain or snow to a field, making it yield a bountiful crop of spiritual knowledge.

71. Tears are not the same thing as compunction, and there is a great difference between them. Tears come from the transformation of our manner of life and the remembrance of our past lapses, as if fire and boiling water were purifying the heart. Compunction descends from above as the divine dew of the Spirit, comforting and refreshing the soul that has but recently entered with fervour into the depths of humility and attained the contemplation of the unapproachable light, crying out with joy as David cried, 'We went through fire and water; and Thou hast brought us out into a place where the soul is refreshed' (Ps. 66 : 12. LXX).

72. I have heard people say that one cannot achieve a persistent state of virtue without retreating far into the desert, and I was amazed that they should think that the unconfinable could be confined to a particular locality. For the state of virtue is the restitution of the soul's powers to their former nobility and the convergence of the principal virtues in an activity that accords with nature. Such a state is not achieved adventitiously, by external influences; it is implanted within us at our creation by virtue of our endemic divine and spiritual consciousness; and when we are impelled by this inner consciousness in accordance with our true nature we are led into the kingdom of heaven which, in our Lord's words, is 'within us' (cf. Luke 17 : 21). Thus the desert is in fact superfluous, since we can enter the kingdom

simply through repentance and the strict keeping of God's commandments. Entry into the kingdom can occur, as David states, 'in all places of His dominion'; for he says, 'In all places of His dominion bless the Lord, O my soul' (Ps. 103 : 22).

73. If you are in the ranks of the imperial army, fighting together with others under the command of generals and captains, and yet you fail to do anything noble or bold in battle against the enemy or even put a single one of them to flight, how will you be able to fight alone among so many enemies or perform any feat of brilliant strategy, inexperienced as you are in warfare? And if this is impossible in human affairs, it is all the more so where things divine are concerned. If you flee into the desert, how will you recognize the attacks of the demons, the open and covert assaults of the passions? How will you be able to attack them yourself, unless you have first been well trained in thwarting your own will by dwelling with a group of brethren under a leader experienced in such invisible and spiritual warfare? And if you are incapable of fighting even on your own behalf, then it is clearly inconceivable that you should do so on behalf of others and teach them how to defeat their invisible enemies.

74. Expunge from yourself the disgrace of negligence and the ignominy of disdaining God's commandments. Dispel self-love and battle with your fallen self unsparingly. Seek out the judgments of the Lord and His testimonies. Scorn glory and dishonour. Hate the titillating appetites of the body. Avoid overeating, because this enkindles your lower organs. Embrace poverty and hardship. Resist the passions. Introvert your senses towards your soul. Inwardly assent to the doing of what is more noble. Be deaf to human affairs. Expend all your strength in practising the commandments. Mourn, sleep on the ground, fast, endure hardship, be still and, last of all, know, not the things around you, but yourself. Transcend the lowly state of visible things. Open your spiritual eye to the contemplation of God and recognize the delightfulness of the Lord from the beauty of creation. And when you descend from these heights of contemplation, speak to your brethren about eternal life and the mysteries of God's kingdom. This is the purpose of flight from men through the strictest asceticism, and the ultimate goal of the life of solitude.

75. If you wish to see the blessings 'that God has prepared for those who love Him' (1 Cor. 2 : 9), then take up your abode in the desert of the renunciation of your own will and flee the world. What world?

The world of the lust of the eyes, of your fallen self (cf. 1 John 2 : 16), the presumptuousness of your own thoughts, the deceit of things visible. If you flee from this world, then light will dawn for you, you will see the life that is in God, and the medicine of your soul – that is, tears – will swiftly well up in you. You will experience the change brought about by 'the right hand of the Most High' (Ps. 77 : 10), and from that time the 'plague' of the passions will not 'come near your dwelling' (Ps. 91 : 10). In this way, living in the world and among people, you will be like a man living in the desert and seeing no one. If you do not flee the world in such a manner, you will gain nothing as regards the perfecting of virtue and union with God simply by flight from the visible world.

76. To become a monk does not mean to abandon men and the world, but to renounce the will of the flesh, to be destitute of the passions. If it was once said to a great spiritual master, 'Flee men and you will be saved', it was said in precisely this spirit;[1] for even after he fled, he dwelt among men and lived in inhabited regions along with his disciples. But because he so assiduously fled in a spiritual sense at the same time as he fled visibly, he suffered no harm from being with other men. And another great monk cried as he came out of a meeting, 'Flee, my brethren!' And when asked what he meant by this, he pointed to his mouth.[2]

77. Living together in one place is safer than living alone. The sacred words of Jesus our God bear witness to the necessity of living together; for He says, 'Where two or three are gathered together in My name, I am in the midst of them' (Matt. 18 : 20). Likewise Solomon speaks about the danger of living alone when he says, 'Alas for him who is alone when he falls; for he has no one to help him up' (Eccles. 4 : 10). And David calls those who praise God in love and concord blessed when he says, 'Blessed is the people that sing aloud together' (Ps. 89 : 15); and he commends life in community, saying: 'Behold, how good and pleasant it is for brethren to dwell together' (Ps. 133 : 1). And among the disciples of our Lord there was but a single soul and a single heart (cf. Acts 4 : 32); and even God's incarnation did not take place in the wilderness, but in inhabited areas and among

[1] *Apophthegmata*, alphabetical collection, Arsenios 1; E.T., p. 9.
[2] *Apophthegmata*, alphabetical collection, Makarios 16; E.T., p. 131.

sinful men. Thus we have need of the concord of communal life. Isolation is treacherous and full of danger.

78. 'Offensive provocations have to come,' said the Lord, 'but alas for him through whom such provocation comes!' (Matt. 18 : 7). The monk who loses his sense of reverence and behaves insolently, without awe for God, in the company of his brethren scandalizes many of the more simple among them. He does this by his acts, bearing and bad habits, and by his words and vicious talk. He corrupts their souls and undermines their probity.

79. If you keep God's commandments you will not become a stumbling-block to others, for there will be nothing offensive or provocative in you. 'Great peace have they who love Thy law, and for them there is no stumbling-block' (Ps. 119 : 165. LXX). Rather they are light, salt and life, in conformity with the Lord's words, 'You are the light of the world, and the salt of the earth' (cf. Matt. 5 : 13–14). Light, because they are virtuous in life, lucid in speech, and wise in thought; salt, because they are rich in divine knowledge and strong in the wisdom of God; life, because through their words they bring to life those slain by the passions, raising them up from the pit of despair. Through the light of their righteous works they shine before men and illumine them; with the sweet astringency of their words they brace those softened by sluggishness and free them from the putrescence of the passions; and by the life present in what they say they give life to souls deadened by sin.

80. The passion of self-esteem is a three-pronged barb heated and forged by the demons out of vanity, presumption and arrogance. Yet those who dwell under the protection of the God of heaven (cf. Ps. 91 : 1) detect it easily and shatter its prongs; for through their humility they rise above such vices and find repose in the tree of life.

81. While you are progressing in virtue this unclean and wily demon of self-esteem may attack you and predict that you will have a throne in heaven, reminding you of all your labour, extolling it above that of others, and even suggesting that you are capable of guiding souls. If this happens, and you have been given power from on high to enable you to do so, seize hold of him spiritually and do not let him escape. Once you have caught him, consider what unworthy act of yours has provoked his attack; and confronting him with this act, say to him: 'Are those who behave in this way worthy of ascending to such privileged heights, and do you regard them as qualified to guide souls

and lead them to salvation in Christ? Tell me, for I shall be silent.' Since he will have nothing to say to you in reply, out of shame he will disappear like smoke and will no longer greatly trouble you. And even if you have not done or said anything unworthy of the transcendent life you have embraced, yet compare yourself with the commandments and the sufferings of the Lord, and you will find that you fall as short of perfection as a basinful of water falls short of the sea. For man's righteousness is as far from the righteousness of God as the earth is in size from the heavens or a flea from a lion.

82. He who has been deeply smitten by the love of God will find that his bodily strength is not equal to his desire, for there are no limits to the ascetic labour in which he yearns to engage. He is like someone consumed by thirst, and the fire of his desire is insatiable. He longs to labour night and day, but is thwarted by his body's lack of strength. I think that Christ's martyrs were not aware of the pain they suffered precisely because they were overpowered by such an enormous passion. Mastering themselves through their burning love for God, they could not have their fill of the torments inflicted on them, and felt that their desire to suffer was never assuaged.

83. He who in any way compares himself with his fellow ascetics or with the brethren who live with him is unaware that he deceives himself and treads a path alien to God. Either he does not know himself or he has deviated from the path that leads heavenwards. But by following this path in modesty of mind, those more spiritually advanced surmount the devil's ploys and, winged by dispassion and adorned with humility, they attain the heights of spiritual illumination.

84. If you are puffed up and full of presumption you will never be illumined by compunction or attain the grace of humility. It is through this that the light of God's wisdom is bestowed on those with contrite hearts, in accordance with the words, 'In Thy light shall we see light' (Ps. 36 : 9). On the contrary, you will be swaddled in the night of the passions, in which all the beasts in the forest of man's nature prowl around, and in which the clamorous whelps of presumption – by which I mean the demons of self-esteem and unchastity – seek whom they may devour and dispatch into the maw of despair (cf. Ps. 104 : 20–21; 1 Pet. 5 : 8).

85. For the man who lives as most men, prompted by the spirit of presumption, this present life becomes a sea embroiled by the powers of evil; the noetic aspect of his soul is flooded with the brine of sensual

pleasure, its triple powers assailed by the fierce waves of the passions. The ship of his soul, and its rudder, are shattered by carnal self-indulgence; the intellect, his pilot, sinks into the depths of sin and spiritual death; and he is engulfed in a slough of despondency. Only the deep calm of humility can quell those malignant waves, and only under the gentle flow of tears can the brine of sensual pleasures be changed into the luminosity of compunction.

86. If you have enslaved yourself to bodily pleasure and indulgence to the point of repletion, you will need a corresponding measure of ascetic labour and hardship. Thus one form of repletion will counter another, pain will counter pleasure, bodily labour will counter bodily ease, and you will enjoy unmeasured felicity and repose, delighting in the fragrance of purity and chastity, and relishing the indescribable savour of the deathless fruits of the Spirit. In a similar way we apply cleansing unguents to the stains on our clothing when they have penetrated so deeply that we cannot wear it any longer.

87. To those newly engaged in spiritual warfare illness is salutary, for it contributes to reducing and subduing the ebullience of the flesh. It greatly debilitates the flesh and attenuates the soul's materialistic propensities, while at the same time it invigorates and braces the soul, in accordance with St Paul's words, 'When I am weak, then I am strong' (2 Cor. 12 : 10). Yet the benefits that it brings to beginners are equalled by the harm that it does to those who have progressed in the labours of virtue and have now transcended the world of the senses and entered into the realm of spiritual contemplation. It hinders their devotion to things divine and coarsens their soul's consciousness with distress and affliction, darkening it with despondency and drying up its compunction in the drought of its suffering. Paul knew this well when, attentive to himself in conformity with the law of discrimination, he said, 'I discipline my body through hardship and bring it into subjection through healing remedies, lest after preaching to others I myself should be cast away' (cf. 1 Cor. 9 : 27).

88. It often happens that illness occurs as a result of an irregular and unbalanced regimen, as when those proficient in spiritual warfare fast or extend their ascetic labours excessively and indiscreetly, or when they become prone to gluttony and repletion, the enemies of nature. Thus self-control is necessary both for those who are newly embarked on the spiritual path and for those who, now beyond mid-course, aspire to the higher reaches of contemplation; for self-control

is the mother of health, the friend of purity and the beloved consort of humility.

89. Dispassion is of two kinds and takes two main forms in those well advanced on the spiritual path. They attain the first kind of dispassion when they have become adept in the practice of the virtues. This dispassion, arising in various ways as a result of their toil in practising the commandments, at once mortifies the passions and cuts off the impulses of the fallen self; at the same time it induces the powers of the soul to act in a way that accords with nature, and restores the intellect to conscious meditation on things divine. Subsequently, when they embark on the contemplation of the inner essences of created things, they attain in their wisdom the second and more perfect kind of dispassion. Bringing inner stillness to their thoughts, this dispassion raises them to a state of intellectual peace, making their intellect visionary and prophetic to the highest degree: visionary in matters divine, in insight into supernal realities, and in the disclosure of God's mysteries; prophetic in matters human, destined to happen in the distant future. In both these forms of dispassion one and the same Spirit is at work (cf. 1 Cor. 12 : 11): through the first He controls and sustains, through the second He dispenses the freedom of eternal life.

90. When you approach the frontiers of dispassion – attaining a right view of God and the nature of things, and according to your growth in purity ascending to the Creator through the beauty of His creatures – you will be illumined by the Holy Spirit. Entertaining kindly feelings about all men and always thinking good of all, you will look on all as pure and holy and will rightly esteem things both human and divine. You will desire none of the material things that men seek but, divesting yourself of worldly sense-perception by means of the intellect, you will ascend towards heaven and towards God, free from all impurity and from every form of servitude, aware in spirit only of God's blessings and His beauty. Thus, full of reverence and joy, and in indescribable silence, you will dwell in the divine realm of God's blessed glory, all your senses transformed, and at the same time you will live spiritually among men like an angel in a material body.

91. Five senses characterize the ascetic life: vigilance, meditation, prayer, self-control and stillness. Once you have linked your five outward senses to them, joining sight to vigilance, hearing to meditation, smell to prayer, taste to self-control and touch to stillness,

you will swiftly purify your soul's intellect: refining it by means of them, you will make it dispassionate and visionary.

92. A dispassionate intellect is one that has gained control over its own passions and risen above both dejection and joy. It is neither subject to bouts of depression nor ebullient with high spirits, but is joyful in affliction, restrained when cheerful, and temperate in all things.

93. The demons rage violently against those who are progressing in contemplation, lying in wait for them night and day. Through fellow-ascetics they provoke formidable trials, while through their own direct action they terrify them with noises. Even when they are asleep they attack them, grudging them any rest. They harass them in various ways, even though they cannot injure those who have surrendered themselves to God. If an angel of the Lord God did not protect them, they could not escape the demons' attack and the snares of death.

94. If you are energetically struggling to practise the virtues, watch out for the ploys of the pernicious demons. The more you advance towards the heights of virtue and the more divine light increases in your prayers, and the closer you come to revelations and ineffable visions through the Spirit, the more they will gnash their teeth as they see you mounting towards heaven, and craftily spread their many nets of iniquity through the intellectual firmament. For not only will the demons of lust and anger, flesh-avid and bestial, breathe on you, but with acrid malice the demons of blasphemy will also rise up against you. In addition, the visible and invisible powers and principalities that wing through the air, in naked fancy changing themselves into strange and frightening forms, will batten on you and do you as much harm as they can. But if, with the eye of your intellect vigilant, you devote yourself to the spiritual work of prayer and to contemplation of the inner essences of God's creation, you will not be frightened by their 'arrow that flies by day' (Ps. 91 : 5), nor will they be able to invade your inner sanctuary; for like darkness they will be repulsed by the light that is in you and consumed in divine fire.

95. The spirits of evil are extremely frightened of the grace of the divine Spirit, especially when it is abundantly present in us or when we have been cleansed through meditation and pure prayer. Not daring to invade our inner sanctuary when we are illumined from that source, they try to alarm and trouble us by means of fantasies, fearful noises and meaningless screams, so as to divert us from vigil and prayer. They

do not spare us even when we allow ourselves a little sleep on the ground: begrudging us the slightest rest from our labours, they set upon us and dash sleep from our eyes with some commotion or other, thinking by such means to make our life more difficult and painful.

96. As we can learn from experience, the spirits of darkness seem to take on a subtle bodily form. This may be an illusion that they produce by deceiving our senses, or it may be that they are condemned to take such a form as the result of their age-old fall. In any case, they impetuously intertwine themselves with the struggling soul as our servile body draws it towards sleep. This seems to me to be a kind of testing for a soul that has but recently transcended the body's low estate: it provides an opportunity for the incensive and virile aspect of the soul to prove its mettle by reacting with wrath and violence against the demons that threaten it so formidably. The soul smitten with intense love for God and braced by the principal virtues will not only oppose the demons with righteous indignation, but will actually strike back at them – if, that is, having become so entirely earth-bound as a result of their fall from the primal divine light, they do have a perceptible appearance.

97. Before intermeshing with the soul and defeating it, the demons often disturb the soul's organs of perception and snatch sleep from our eyes. Yet the soul filled with manly courage by the Holy Spirit will pay no heed to the bitter fury of their attack, but will dispel their fantasies and put them to flight solely by means of the life-giving sign of the cross and the invocation of Jesus our God.

98. If you have embarked on the task of despoiling the hostile spirits through the practice of the virtues, see that you are thoroughly armed with the weapons of the Spirit. Are you aware of who it is you want to despoil? They are enemies, to be sure, but noetic and fleshless, while you are still doing battle with the body under the King of the spirits and our God. You must realize that they will fight against you more bitterly than before and that there will be many who will deploy their tricks against you. If, then, you fail to notice them and to strip them of their spoils they will take you prisoner, filling your soul with great bitterness; or else they will subject you to evil and distressing temptations, acting as a grievous thorn in your flesh (cf. 2 Cor. 12 : 7).

99. A good spring does not produce turbid, foul-smelling water, redolent of worldly matter; nor can a heart that is outside the kingdom

of heaven gush with streams of divine life, giving out the sweet savour
of spiritual myrrh. 'Does a spring from the same opening gush with
sweet water and bitter? Can the fig tree bear olives, or an olive tree
acorns?' (cf. Jas. 3 : 11–12). In the same way a single spring in the
heart cannot produce simultaneously both good and bad images.
Rather, 'a good man out of the good treasure-house of his heart brings
forth that which is good; and an evil man out of the evil treasure-house
of his heart brings forth that which is evil', as the Lord has said (Luke
6 : 45).

100. Just as it is impossible without oil and flame for a lamp to
burn and thus to give light to those in the house, so it is impossible
without the divine fire and Spirit for a soul to speak clearly about
divine matters and to illumine others. For every perfect gift bestowed
on the devout soul 'is from above . . . from the Father of lights, in
whom there is no variableness or shadow due to change' (Jas. 1 : 17).

On the Inner Nature of Things and on the Purification of the Intellect: One Hundred Texts

1. Love for God begins with detachment from things human and visible. Purification of heart and intellect marks the intermediate stage, for through such purification the eye of the intellect is spiritually unveiled and we attain knowledge of the kingdom of heaven hidden within us (cf. Luke 17 : 21). The final stage is consummated in an irrepressible longing for the supranatural gifts of God and in a natural desire for union with God and for finding one's abode in Him.

2. Where there is intense longing for God, noetic labour, and participation in the unapproachable light, there too the soul's powers will be at peace, the intellect will be purified, and the Holy Trinity will dwell within us; for it is written, 'He who loves Me will fulfil My teaching, and My Father will love him, and We will come to him and take up Our abode in him' (John 14 : 23).

3. Our teaching recognizes three modes of living: the carnal, the psychic and the spiritual. Each of these is characterized by its own particular attitude to life, distinctive to itself and dissimilar to that of the others.

4. The carnal mode of life is one wholly devoted to the pleasures and enjoyments of this present life, and has nothing to do with the psychic and spiritual modes of life, and does not even have any wish to acquire them. The psychic mode, which is situated on the borderline between evil and virtue, is preoccupied with the care and strengthening of the body and with men's praise; it not only repudiates the labours required for virtue, but also rejects carnal indulgence. It avoids both virtue and vice but for opposite reasons: virtue because this requires toil and discipline; vice because that would entail forfeiting

men's praise. The spiritual mode of life, on the other hand, has nothing in common with these two other modes, and on this account is not implicated in the evil that pertains to either: it is entirely free in every way from both the one and the other. Invested with the wings of love and dispassion, it soars above them both, doing nothing that is forbidden and not being hamstrung by evil.

5. Those who pursue the carnal mode of life and in whom the will of the flesh is imperious – who are, quite simply, carnal – are not able to conform to God's will (cf. Rom. 8 : 8). Their judgment is eclipsed and they are totally impervious to the rays of divine light: the engulfing clouds of the passions are like high walls that shut out the resplendence of the Spirit and leave them without illumination. Their soul's senses maimed, they cannot aspire to God's spiritual beauty and see the light of the true life and so transcend the lowliness of visible things. It is as if they had become beasts conscious only of this world, with the dignity of their intelligence fettered to things sensory and human. They strive only for what is visible and corruptible, on this account fighting among themselves and even sacrificing their lives for such things, avid for wealth, glory and the pleasures of the flesh, and regarding the lack of any of these things as a disaster. To such people applies the prophetic statement that comes from God's own mouth: 'My Spirit shall not remain in these men, for they are flesh' (Gen. 6 : 3. LXX).

6. Those who pursue the psychic mode of life and are therefore called 'psychic' are like the mentally defective whose limbs do not function properly. They never exert themselves on behalf of virtue or in the practice of God's commandments, and they refrain from acting reprehensibly simply in order to gain the esteem of other people. They are completely under the sway of self-love, nurse of the destructive passions, and they seek out whatever fosters physical health and pleasure. They repudiate all tribulation, effort and hardship embraced for the sake of virtue, and they cosset our enemy the body more than they should. Through such life and behaviour their passion-imbued intellect grows cloddish and becomes impervious to the divine and spiritual realities whereby the soul is plucked from the world of matter and soars into the noetic heaven. This happens to them because they are still possessed by the spirit of matter, love themselves, and choose to do what they themselves want. Void of the Holy Spirit, they have no share in His gifts. As a result they exhibit no godly fruit – love for God and for their fellow-men – no joy in the midst of poverty and

tribulation, no peace of soul, no deeply-rooted faith, no all-embracing self-control. Neither do they experience compunction, tears, humility or compassion, but they are altogether filled with conceit and arrogance. Hence they are totally incapable of plumbing the depths of the Spirit, for there is no guiding light in them to open their intellect to the understanding of the Scriptures (cf. Luke 24 : 45); indeed, they cannot endure even to hear other people talking about such things. St Paul was quite right when he said that 'the psychic man cannot grasp spiritual things: they are folly to him; he is unaware that the law is spiritual and must be discerned spiritually' (cf. 1 Cor. 2 : 14).

7. Those who 'cleave to the Spirit' (Gal. 5 : 25) and are totally committed to the spiritual life live in accordance with God's will, dedicated to Him as were the Nazirites (cf. Num. 6 : 2–8; Judg. 13 : 5). At all times they labour to purify their soul and to keep the Lord's commandments, expending their blood in their love for Him. They purify the flesh through fasts and vigils; they refine the heart's dross with tears; they mortify their materialistic tendencies through ascetic hardship; they fill the intellect with light through prayer and meditation, making it translucid; and by renouncing their own wills they sunder themselves from passionate attachment to the body and adhere solely to the Spirit. As a result everyone recognizes them as spiritual, and rightly refers to them as such. As they approach the state of dispassion and love, they ascend to the contemplation of the inner essences of created things; and from this they acquire the knowledge of created being that is bestowed by the hidden wisdom of God (cf. 1 Cor. 2 : 7) and given only to those who have risen above the body's low estate. Thus it is that when they have passed beyond all sensory experience of this world and have entered with an illumined mind into the realms that are above sense-perception, their intelligence is enlightened and they utter righteous words from a pure heart in the midst of the Church of God and the great congregation of the faithful (cf. Ps. 40 : 9–10). For other people they are salt and light, as the Lord says of them: 'You are the light of the world and the salt of the earth' (cf. Matt. 5 : 13–14).

8. 'Devote yourselves to stillness and know that I am God' (Ps. 46 : 10). This is the voice of the divine Logos and is experienced as such by those who put the words into practice. Thus once you have renounced the turmoil and frightening vanity of life you should in stillness scrutinize yourself and the inner reality of things with the

utmost attentiveness and should seek to know more fully the God within yourself, for His kingdom is within us (cf. Luke 17 : 21). Yet even if you do this over a long period of time it will be difficult for you to erase the imprint of evil from your soul and to restore it wholly to its Creator in all its primal beauty.

9. Since we are so greatly imbued with the poison of evil we are in a correspondingly great need of the cleansing fire of repentant tears and voluntary ascetic labour. For we are purged of the stains of sin either through embracing such labour willingly or through afflictions that come unsought. If we first engage in voluntary ascetic labour, we will be spared the unsought afflictions; but if we fail to cleanse 'the inside of the cup and the dish' (cf. Matt. 23 : 26) through ascetic labour, the afflictions will restore us to our original state with a greater harshness. So the Creator has ordained.

10. If you do not enter the way of renunciation in the right spirit – if, that is to say, from the start you refuse to accept a teacher and guide but, regarding yourself as an adept, rely on your own judgment – you will make a mockery of the religious life and in turn will be mocked by what happens to you.

11. Just as you cannot know exactly the causes and cures of bodily afflictions without great medical experience and skill, so you cannot know those of psychic afflictions without great spiritual training and practice. The diagnosis of bodily illnesses is a tricky business and only a few are truly versed in it; but the diagnosis of psychic illnesses is far more tricky. The soul is superior to the body, and correspondingly its afflictions are greater and harder to understand than those of the body, which is visible to all.

12. The principal and primary virtues were co-created with man as part of his nature. From them the rivers of all the other virtues are filled as from four well-heads, and they water the city of God, which is the heart cleansed and refreshed by tears. If you keep these four principal virtues impregnable to the spirits of malice, or if they fall but you raise them up again through the travails of repentance, you will build yourself a royal palace in which the King of All may make His abode (cf. John 14 : 23), lavishly bestowing His lofty gifts on those who have thus prepared the ground.

13. Life is short, the age to come is long, and little the length of our present existence. Man, this great but petty being, to whom the scant present has been allotted, is weak. Time is scant, man weak, but the

contest set before him, with its prize, is great, even if it is full of thorns and puts our trivial life at risk.

14. God does not wish the labours of those well advanced on the spiritual path to go untested, but wants them to be well tried. Consequently He casts upon them the fire of temptation and withdraws for a short time the grace given them, allowing the tranquillity of their thoughts to be perturbed for a while by the spirits of malice. In this manner He sees which way the soul will turn, and whether it will favour its own Creator and Benefactor or the senses of this world and the lure of pleasure. Depending on their proclivity He will either augment His grace in them as they advance in love of Him, or lash them with temptation and tribulation if they indulge in worldly thoughts and actions, continuing this until they come to hate the unstable whirl of visible things and with tears wash away the bitterness of its pleasures.

15. When the peace of your thoughts is disturbed by the spirits of malice, then those huntsmen – the flesh-loving demons – will at once assault your swiftly-mounting intellect with the fiery arrows of desire (cf. Eph. 6 : 16). As a result its upward motion is thwarted and it succumbs to unseemly, corrupt impulses; the flesh licentiously begins to revolt against the spirit, through titivation and incitement seeking to drag the intellect down into the pit of pleasure. And if the Lord of hosts did not curtail those days and grant His servants the strength to endure, 'no flesh would be saved' (cf. Matt. 24 : 22).

16. The highly experienced and wily demon of unchastity is for some a pitfall, for others a well-merited scourge, for others a test or trial of soul. He is a pitfall for those newly engaged in spiritual warfare, who still bear the ascetic yoke slackly and negligently; a scourge for those who have advanced midway along the path of virtue but then relax in their efforts; a test or trial for those who on the wings of the intellect have already entered the sphere of contemplation and who now aspire to the more perfect form of dispassion. Each category is thus divinely guided in the way that suits it best.

17. The demon of unchastity is a pitfall for those who live the ascetic life perfunctorily. It kindles their limbs with sensual desire and suggests ways of carrying out the will of the flesh even without intercourse with other flesh, something of which it is shameful even to speak or think (cf. Eph. 5 : 12). Such people defile the flesh (cf. Jude 8) and devour the fruits of bitter pleasure, blinding themselves and

deservedly slipping from the higher realms. If they wish for healing, they will find it in the fervour of repentance and the tearful compunction that flows from it. This will make them flee from evil and will cleanse their soul from its impurity, making it an heir of God's mercy. In his wisdom Solomon referred to this cryptically when he said, 'Healing puts an end to great offences' (cf. Eccles. 10 : 4. LXX).

18. This demon is a well-merited scourge for those who through the practice of the virtues have attained the first degree of dispassion and are now progressing to what lies beyond this and is more perfect. For when out of sluggishness they slacken the tension of their ascetic practice and deviate, albeit slightly, towards unguarded preoccupation with the sensible world, longing to involve themselves in human affairs, then, as a result of God's great goodness towards them, this demon acts as scourge: it begins to assail those who deviate in this way with thoughts tainted by carnal desire. Unable to bear this, they swiftly revert to their stronghold of intense ascetic practice and attentiveness, performing with ever greater eagerness and even more strenuously the tasks that will save them. In His bounteousness, God does not wish the soul that has reached this stage to turn completely to the world of the senses; on the contrary, He wants it to progress continuously and to embrace zealously ever more perfect works, so that no plague will come near its dwelling (cf. Ps. 91 : 10. LXX).

19. Through God's economy, this same demon is a test, a thorn and a trial for those who, having attained the first, aspire to the second degree of dispassion. So long as the demon troubles them, they recall the weakness of their nature and do not become conceited because of the 'abundance of the revelations' (2 Cor. 12 : 7) that they have received through contemplation. Rather, keenly aware of the law that wars against the law of the intellect (cf. Rom. 7 : 23), they repudiate even the passion-free recollection of sin, lest by recalling it they re-experience the defilement it engenders and thereby let the eye of the intellect lapse from the heights of contemplation.

20. Only those who through the Spirit have been privileged to receive the life-quickening deadness of the Lord (cf. 2 Cor. 4 : 10) in their limbs and thoughts can keep their intellect untroubled even by the passion-free memory of sin. Their flesh is dead to sin, while through the righteousness that is in Christ Jesus they have enriched their spirit with life (cf. Rom. 8 : 10). Those who through their consciousness of wisdom have received the intellect of Christ will also

experience the untroubled life-quickening deadness that comes from knowledge of God.

21. The spirit of desire and anger is liable to invade souls but recently purified. To do what? To shake down the fruits of the Holy Spirit burgeoning within them. For the joy of freedom produces a certain confusion in such souls; they tend to exalt themselves over others because of their great freedom and the richness of their gifts, and also to think that they have attained this great palace of peace through their own strength and understanding. Hence the Wisdom that orders all things for good, and seeks always to attract these souls to itself by means of its gifts and to keep them unshaken in their humility, withdraws from them slightly and so permits this spirit of desire and anger to attack them. Plunged as a result into the fear of falling, they once more keep guard over blessed humility; and, recognizing that they are bound to flesh and blood, they search in accordance with their true nature for the inner stronghold where by the power of the Holy Spirit they can sustain themselves unharmed.

22. The vehemence of our trials and temptations depends upon the degree to which we are debilitated by the passions and infected by sin; and the bitter cup of God's judgment varies accordingly. If the nature of the sin within us is such that it is easily treated and cured – if, that is to say, it consists of thoughts that are self-indulgent or worldly – then the Healer of our souls in His compassion adds but a mild dose of wormwood to the cup of trial and temptation He administers, since these are merely human ailments by which we are afflicted. But if the sin is deep-seated and hard to cure – a lethal infection of pretentious arrogant thoughts – then in the keenness of His wrath He gives us the cup undiluted, so that, dissolved and refined in the fire of successive trials and the humility they induce, the sickness may be removed from our soul and we may wash away our brackish thoughts with tears, thus presenting ourselves pure in the light of humility to our Healer.

23. Those engaged in spiritual warfare can escape from the cycle of trial and temptation only by recognizing their weakness, and regarding themselves as strangers to righteousness and unworthy of any solace, honour, or repose. God, the doctor of our souls, wishes us to be always humble and modest, detached from our fellow-men and imitators of His sufferings. For He was 'gentle and humble in heart' (Matt. 11 : 29), and wants us to pursue the path of His commandments with a similar gentleness and humility of heart.

24. Humility is not achieved by means of a scraggy neck, squalid hair, or filthy, ragged and unkempt clothing, to which the generality of men ascribe the sum total of this virtue. It comes from a contrite heart and a spirit of self-abasement. As David said, 'God will not scorn a contrite spirit, and a contrite and humble heart' (cf. Ps. 51 : 19. LXX).

25. To speak humbly is one thing, to act humbly is another, and to be inwardly humble is something else again. Through all manner of hardship and through the outward labours of virtue those engaged in spiritual warfare can attain the qualities of speaking and acting humbly, for these qualities require no more than bodily effort and discipline. But because the soul of such people often lacks inner stability, when temptation confronts them they are easily shaken. Inward humility, on the other hand, is something exalted and divine, bestowed through the indwelling of the Paraclete only on those who have passed the midpoint of the spiritual way – who have, that is to say, through acting in all humility traversed the rigorous path of virtue.

26. The soul is so distressed and oppressed when inner humility like a weighty stone has penetrated its depths, that it loses all its strength because of the tears which it uncontrollably sheds; while the intellect, cleansed of every defiling thought, attains like Isaiah to the vision of God. Under that divine influence it too confesses, 'How abject I am – I am pierced to the heart; because I am a man of unclean lips, and I dwell among a people of unclean lips; and my eyes have seen the King, the Lord of hosts' (Isa. 6 : 5).

27. When the ability to speak humbly is firmly established within you, then you will no longer indulge in boastful talk; when you act spontaneously in humbleness of heart, then you will cease from humble speech, whether superficial or profound; and when you are enriched by God with inner humility then both humility of outward action and humility of the tongue will no longer have any place in you. It is as St Paul said: 'But when that which is perfect comes, that which is partial is done away with' (1 Cor. 13 : 10).

28. Genuine humility of speech is as remote from genuine humility of action as East is from West. And as heaven surpasses earth, or the soul the body, so the inner humility given to the saints through the Holy Spirit excels genuine humility of action.

29. Do not readily assume that someone who in outward appearance and dress, and in manner of speech, seems to be humble is

actually humble at heart; and do not assume – unless you have put it to the test – that someone who speaks exaltedly of high things is full of boastfulness and vanity. For 'you shall know them by their fruits' (Matt. 7 : 16).

30. The fruits of the Holy Spirit are love, joy, peace, goodness, long-suffering, kindness, faith, gentleness, self-control (cf. Gal. 5 : 22–23). The fruits of the spirit of evil are hatred, worldly despondency, restlessness of soul, a troubled heart, guile, inquisitiveness, negligence, anger, lack of faith, envy, gluttony, drunkenness, abusiveness, censoriousness, the lust of the eyes (cf. 1 John 2 : 16), vanity and pretentiousness of soul. By these fruits you may know the tree (cf. Matt. 12 : 33), and in this way you will certainly recognize what kind of spirit you have to deal with. An even clearer indication of these things is given by the Lord Himself when He says, 'A good man out of the good treasury of his heart brings forth good things; and an evil man out of the evil treasury of his heart brings forth evil things' (Matt. 12 : 35). For as the tree, so is the fruit.

31. God dwells in those in whom the fruits of the Holy Spirit are evident and, whether they speak of lowly or exalted things, from them flows, full of wisdom and knowledge, the unsullied spring of the Logos. Those who display the fruits and gifts not of the Holy Spirit but of the spirit of evil are on the other hand benighted with ignorance of God and swarm with the passions and hostile spirits; and this is so whether they speak and dress humbly, or whether they speak exaltedly, wear fine clothes, and bear themselves with an outward show of pomp.

32. Truth is not evinced by looks, gestures or words, and God reposes not in these things but in a contrite heart, a humble spirit and a soul illumined by the knowledge of God. Sometimes we see someone speaking to all comers in an outwardly obsequious and humble manner, while inwardly he pursues the praise of men and is filled with self-conceit, guile, malice and rancour. And there are times when we see someone fighting for righteousness outwardly with lofty words of wisdom, taking a stand against falsehood or the transgression of God's laws, and looking only to the truth, while within he is all modesty, humility, and love for his fellow-men. Sometimes also we see such a person glorying in the Lord after the manner of St Paul, who when he gloried in the Lord said, 'I will glory in my infirmities' (2 Cor. 12 : 9).

33. God looks not at the outward form of what we say or do, but at

the disposition of our soul and the purpose for which we perform a visible action or express a thought. In the same way those of greater understanding than others look rather to the inward meaning of words and the intention of actions, and unfalteringly assess them accordingly. Man looks at the outward form, but God looks on the heart (cf. 1 Sam. 16 : 7).

34. God has judged it right that from generation to generation His prophets and friends should be equipped by the Spirit for the building up of His Church (cf. Eph. 4 : 11–13). For since the old serpent still devastates men's souls by spewing the poison of sin into their ears, how could He who fashioned our hearts one by one (cf. Ps. 33 : 15) not raise the needy from the earth of humility and lift them from the dunghill of the passions (cf. Ps. 113 : 7), assisting His inheritance with 'the sword of the Spirit which is the word of God' (Eph. 6 : 17)? Rightly, then, do those who begin with humility, and deny themselves, rise to the heights of spiritual knowledge, receiving from on high the teachings of wisdom through the power of God, so that they may proclaim the Gospel of salvation to His Church.

35. 'Know thyself': this is true humility, the humility that teaches us to be inwardly humble and makes our heart contrite. Such humility you must cultivate and guard. For if you do not yet know yourself you cannot know what humility is, and have not yet embarked truly on the task of cultivating and guarding. To know oneself is the goal of the practice of the virtues.

36. If having achieved a state of purity you advance to the knowledge of the essences of created beings, you will have fulfilled the injunction, 'Know thyself'. If on the other hand you have not yet attained a knowledge of the inner essences of creation and of things both divine and human, you may know what is outside and around you, but you will still be totally ignorant of your own self.

37. What I am is not at all the same as that which characterizes me; nor is what characterizes me the same as that which relates to my situation; nor is what relates to my situation the same as that which is external to me. In each case the one is distinct from the other. What I am is an image of God manifest in a spiritual, immortal and intelligent soul, having an intellect that is the father of my consciousness and that is consubstantial with the soul and inseparable from it. That which characterizes me, and is regal and sovereign, is the power of intelligence and free will. That which relates to my situation is what I

may choose in exercising my free will, such as whether to be a farmer, a merchant, a mathematician or a philosopher. That which is external to me is whatever relates to my ambitions in this present life, to my class status and worldly wealth, to glory, honour, prosperity and exalted rank, or to their opposites, poverty, ignominy, dishonour and misfortune.

38. When you know yourself you cease from all outward tasks undertaken with a view to serving God and enter into the very sanctuary of God, into the noetic liturgy of the Spirit, the divine haven of dispassion and humility. But until you come to know yourself through humility and spiritual knowledge your life is one of toil and sweat. It was of this that David cryptically spoke when he said, 'Toil lies before me until I enter the sanctuary of God' (Ps. 73 : 16–17. LXX).

39. To know yourself means that you must guard yourself diligently from everything external to you; it means respite from worldly concerns and cross-examination of the conscience. Once you come to know yourself a kind of suprarational divine humility suddenly descends upon the soul, bringing contrition and tears of fervent compunction to the heart. Acted upon in this way you regard yourself as earth and ashes (cf. Gen. 18 : 27), and as a worm and no man (cf. Ps. 22 : 6). Indeed, because of this overwhelming gift of God, you think you are unworthy of even this wormlike form of life. If you are privileged to remain in this state for some time you will be filled with a strange, unspeakable intoxication – the intoxication of compunction – and will enter into the depths of humility. Rapt out of yourself, you take no account of food, drink or clothing beyond the minimum needed; for you are as one who has experienced the blessed change that comes from 'the right hand of the Most High' (Ps. 77 : 10. LXX).

40. Humility is the greatest of the virtues. If as a result of sincere repentance it is implanted in you, you will also be given the gift of prayer and self-control, and will be freed from servitude to the passions. Peace will suffuse your powers, tears will cleanse your heart, and through the abiding presence of the Holy Spirit you will be filled with tranquillity. When you have attained this state, your consciousness of the knowledge of God will grow lucid and you will begin to contemplate the mysteries of the kingdom of heaven and the inner essences of created things. The more you descend into the depths of the Spirit, the more you plumb the abyss of humility. Correspondingly

you gain greater knowledge of your own limitations and recognize the weakness of human nature; at the same time your love for God and your fellow beings waxes until you think that sanctification flows simply from a greeting or from the proximity of those with whom you live.

41. Nothing so inspires the soul with longing for God and love for one's fellow beings as humility, compunction and pure prayer. Humility shatters the spirit and engenders tears, while by making us aware of the shortness of human life it teaches us to know the frailty of our limitations. Compunction purifies the intellect of materiality, illumines the eye of the heart, and makes the soul completely radiant. Pure prayer binds the whole person to God, making us share the life of the angels, allowing us to taste the sweetness of the immortal blessings of God, and bestowing on us the treasures of the great mysteries. Enkindling us with love, it gives us the courage to lay down our life for our friends (cf. John 15 : 13), for we have transcended the body's low estate.

42. Protect the pledge of enriching humility that has been entrusted to you, for in it are stored the hidden treasures of love and the pearls of compunction. In it, too, the King, Christ our God, reposes as on a golden throne, bestowing the gifts of the Holy Spirit on those it nourishes and giving them His great glories: consciousness of His divine knowledge, His ineffable wisdom, the vision of supernal realities, the prevision of human realities, the life-quickening deadness induced by dispassion, and union with Himself, so that we co-reign with Him in the kingdom of God the Father. For this accords with the petition He made to the Father, when He said on our behalf, 'Father, I desire that those whom Thou hast given Me should be with Me wherever I am' (John 17 : 24).

43. If while striving to practise the commandments you suddenly feel an inexpressible secret joy that strangely and unaccountably transforms you, alleviates the body's weight and puts from your mind all thought of food, sleep and the other necessities of nature, then you must know that all this is because God has come to dwell within you, inducing in you a life-quickening deadness and here and now raising you to the angelic state. The operative power behind this blessed life is humility; its mother and nurse, holy compunction; its friend and sister, the contemplation of the divine light; its throne, dispassion; its consummation, God the Holy Trinity.

44. Once you have achieved this lofty state you cannot be constrained by sensory attachment to things. You are not distracted by any of the delectations of this life, nor do you regard some people as holy and others as unholy; but just as God makes the rain fall and the sun shine equally on the just and on the unjust, on the evil and on the good (cf. Matt. 5 : 45), so you irradiate love and diffuse its rays to all men. Pregnant though you are with love for everything, yet your heart feels no distress or, rather, you are distressed and straitened because you cannot help others as much as you would wish. As from Eden, from you flows another spring of compunction, divided into the four streams of humility, chastity, dispassion and undistracted prayer; and it waters the face of God's entire spiritual creation (cf. Gen. 2 : 10).

45. Those who have not tasted the sweetness of the tears of compunction and are ignorant of its grace and of how it operates, think that such tears differ in no way from those shed for the dead; and they invent all manner of specious reasons and pretexts for thinking this, such as might naturally occur to us. But when what was haughty in our intellect inclines towards humility, and when the soul has closed its eyes to the deceitfulness of visible things and aspires solely to the contemplation of the immaterial, primal light, repudiating all that derives from sense perception and receiving the grace bestowed by the Spirit, then as water from a spring tears at once gush from it and sweeten its senses, filling the mind with all manner of joy and divine light. More than this, they shatter the heart and make the intellect humble in its contemplation of the higher world. These things cannot happen to those who lament and mourn in another way.

46. Without the deepest humility you cannot release the spring of tears within you, nor can you be humble without the compunction that is quickened through the abiding presence of the Spirit. For humility engenders compunction and compunction engenders humility through the Holy Spirit. It is as if these were strung together by a single grace, linked by the unbreakable bond of the Spirit.

47. The light that enters the soul through the agency of the divine Spirit is liable to withdraw as a result of our laxity, negligence or perfunctoriness in matters of food or speech. Carelessness over what we eat and an unstable diet, as well as an uncontrolled tongue and unguarded eyes, will naturally drive the light from the soul and plunge us into darkness. And once we are filled with darkness all the beasts in the wild places of our heart and our whelp-like passion-imbued

thoughts rove raucously through it, seeking to feed on our impassioned proclivities and to despoil the treasure garnered in us by the Spirit (cf. Ps. 104 : 20–21). But the self-control that is truly dear to us and the prayer that makes us angels not only prevent such things from ranging through the soul; they also preserve unquenched the light of the Spirit that encircles the intellect, pacify the heart and liberate the pure spring of divine compunction, opening the soul to the love of God and binding it through joy and virginity entirely to Christ.

48. There is nothing so kindred to the divine Logos as the soul's purity and chasteness. Their mother is a devout all-embracing self-control; and the father of this is fear. For once fear has changed to longing and is imbued with desire for things divine, it makes the soul not only fearless and full of love for God, but also the very mother of the divine Logos.

49. Once impregnated by fear, the soul becomes through repentance pregnant with the Logos of divine judgment: the birth-pangs of hell encompass it, heartfelt anguish and travail afflict it as it reflects on the retribution due for the evil it has done. Then, having through copious tears and labours gestated in the mind's womb the Spirit of salvation it has conceived, it brings it forth into the world of the heart. Thus liberated from the pangs of hell and the anguish of judgment, the soul is joyously filled with longing for the blessings in store for it; purity and chasteness attend on it and, spurred by intense desire, unite it with God. Through this union it experiences an ineffable delight and sheds the sweet pleasureful tears of compunction. Exempt from the ordinary forms of perception and as though in ecstasy following the Bridegroom, it cries voicelessly, 'I pursue Thee in the fragrance of Thy myrrh; tell me, O Thou whom my soul loves, where Thou feedest Thy flock, where Thou givest it rest. In the noon-day of pure contemplation? Let me not be rejected from the flock of the righteous. With Thee are the illuminations of the great mysteries' (cf. Song of Songs 1 : 4–7). Once the Bridegroom has led the soul into the sanctuary of His hidden mysteries, He will initiate it with wisdom into the contemplation of the inner essences of created things.

50. Do not say in your heart, it is now impossible for me to acquire a virginal purity, for I have succumbed in so many ways to the seduction and delirium of the body. For once the soul engages fervently and strenuously in the labours of repentance and we shed tears of compunction, then the prison-house is razed to the ground,

the fire of the passions is extinguished, we are spiritually reborn through the abiding presence of the Paraclete, and once again the soul becomes a palace of purity and virginity. God, who is above nature, descends with light and ineffable joy into the soul and sits on the heights of its intellect as upon a throne of glory, bestowing peace on all its inner powers and saying: 'Peace be with you, peace from hostile passions. I give you My peace, so that you may act according to your true nature. I leave My peace with you, so that you may be perfected into what is beyond nature' (cf. John 14 : 27). Through His threefold gift of peace He heals the soul's three powers, brings it into triadic perfection and unites it with Himself. Thus He refashions it and makes it at one stroke wholly virginal, good and beautiful through the fragrance of the myrrh of purity. Then he says to it, 'Arise. Come near to me, dove of loveliness, through the practice of the virtues; for behold, the storm of the passions has passed. The downpour of sensual pleasure-laden thoughts is over, it has gone its way. The flowers of the virtues, redolent with intellections, have appeared in the soil of your heart (cf. Song of Songs, 2 : 10–12). Arise, come near to Me in the knowledge gleaned from the contemplation of the essences of created beings. Come, my dove, on your own wing into the over-canopying darkness of mystical theology, to the faith rooted rock-like in Me, your God.'

51. Blessed in my eyes is the man who, changed through the practice of the virtues, transcends the encompassing walls of the passion-embroiled state and rises on the wings of dispassion – wings silver-toned with divine knowledge (cf. Ps. 68 : 13) – to the spiritual sphere in which he contemplates the essences of created things, and who from there enters the divine darkness of theology where in the life of blessedness he ceases from all outward labours and reposes in God. For he has become a terrestrial angel and a celestial man; he has glorified God in himself, and God will glorify him (cf. John 13 : 31–32).

52. 'Great peace have they who love God's law, and for them there is no stumbling-block' (cf. Ps. 119 : 165). For not all things congenial to men accord with God; and some things that do not appear good are seen, by those who know the inner essences of things and events, to be by nature most excellent.

53. It behoves us to die to the world and live in Christ. Otherwise we cannot be spiritually born anew – and, as the Lord says, 'Unless you

are born anew, you cannot enter the kingdom of heaven' (cf. John
3 : 3). Such a rebirth comes through obedience to a spiritual father;
for if we do not first become pregnant with the seed of the Logos
through the teaching of such a father and through him become
children of God, we cannot be spiritually reborn. For in this way the
twelve were born of one, that is, of Christ; and the seventy were born
of the twelve and were made children of God the Father, according to
our Lord's words, 'You are the children of My heavenly Father' (cf.
Matt. 5 : 45). Thus St Paul, too, says to us, 'For though you have ten
thousand instructors, you have not many fathers; I have begotten you;
be imitators of me' (cf. 1 Cor. 4 : 15–16).

54. If you are not obedient to a spiritual father in imitation of the
Son who was obedient to the Father even unto death and the cross (cf.
Phil. 2 : 8), you cannot be spiritually born anew. If you do not
become the beloved son of a holy father, and if you have not been born
anew in the Logos and the Spirit, how will you yourself become a holy
father and give birth to holy children who conform to the holiness of
their father? And if this does not happen – well, 'the tree is known by
its fruit' (cf. Matt. 12 : 33).

55. Lack of faith is evil, the most diabolic issue of diabolic avarice
and envy. And if it is evil, how much the more so is the avarice that
gives birth to it. For avarice impels men to love money more than they
love Christ, to esteem what is material more highly than God, to
worship creation rather than the Creator, and to pervert God's truth
into a lie (cf. Rom. 1 : 25). If this disease is so evil that it can be called
a second idolatry (cf. Col. 3 : 5), what exorbitance of evil will the soul
willingly sick with such a disease not surpass?

56. If you aspire to friendship with Christ, you will hate money and
the gluttonous love of money; for money lures towards itself the mind
of whoever loves it and diverts it from love for Jesus, a love which, I
think, is expressed not in words but in action, in the carrying out of His
commandments (cf. John 14 : 15). If, alas, what you want is money,
you will hoard away as much of it as you can, setting this desire for
money above love for Christ, and regarding wealth as a gain and not as
the greatest disaster that can befall you. You should realize, however,
that money is in fact disastrous to you, and the disaster will be all the
greater because you will also lose your true wealth, God, without
whom the life of salvation is impossible.

57. If you love money you do not love Christ; if you do not love

Christ, but love money, think to whose likeness that tyrant will reduce you: it will make you like the disciple who was unfaithful, who appeared to be a friend but was a traitor, who acted viciously towards the Master of All, and who fell miserably from both faith and love, plunging into the depths of despair. Fear his example and listen to my counsel: spurn money and love for money, so that you may gain the love of Christ. If not, well, you know the place prepared for those who have fallen.

58. If you are not called by God to a high status, never try to attain it through money or human support or by demanding it, even if you know you can help others. For if you do, three things lie in wait for you, and of them one will surely happen: either God's anger and wrath will fall upon you in the form of diverse assaults and misfortunes – for not only men but virtually the whole of creation will turn on you, and your life will be full of anguish; or your enemies will gain the upper hand and expel you from your position in deep disgrace; or you will die before your time, cut off from this present life.

59. You cannot be indifferent to both fame and disgrace, or rise above pleasure and pain, unless you are enabled by grace to perceive the upshot of all worldly preoccupations. For when you realize that the resultant of fame, pleasure, indulgence, wealth and prosperity is naught, since death and decay await them, then you will recognize the blatant vanity of all things worldly and will turn your eyes to the consummation of things divine. You will cleave to the realities that truly exist and cannot perish; and, making these things your own, you will rise above pain and pleasure: above pain in that you have defeated that which in your soul loves pleasure, fame and money; above pleasure, in that you have become impervious to worldly sensations. Thus you are the same whether you are honoured or scorned, attacked by bodily pain or endued with bodily ease. In all things you will give thanks to God and you will not be cast down.

60. Those who have attained spiritual maturity can also analyse the impulsions and proclivities of the soul, and can guide and guard their inner state, on the basis of dreams. For bodily impulsions and the images in our intellect depend upon our inner disposition and preoccupations. If your soul hankers after pleasure and material things, you will dream about acquiring possessions and having money, about the female figure and sexual intercourse – all of which leads to the soiling and defilement of soul and body. If you are haunted by images

of greed and avarice, you will see money everywhere, will get hold of it, and will make more money by lending it out at interest and storing the proceeds in the bank, and you will be condemned for your callousness. If you are hot-tempered and vicious, images of poisonous snakes and wild beasts will plague you and overwhelm you with terror. If you are full of self-esteem, you will dream of popular acclaim and mass-meetings, government posts and high office; and even when awake you will imagine that these things, which as yet you lack, are already yours, or soon will be. If you are proud and pretentious, you will see yourself being carried along in a splendid coach and even sometimes airborne, while everyone trembles at your great power. Similarly, if you are devoted to God, diligent in the practice of the virtues, scrupulous in the struggle for holiness and with a soul purged of material preoccupations, you will see in sleep the outcome of events and awe-inspiring visions will be disclosed to you. When you wake from sleep you will always find yourself praying with compunction and in a peaceful state of soul and body, and there will be tears on your cheeks, and on your lips words addressed to God.

61. The images that visit us during sleep are either dreams, or visions, or revelations. To the category of dreams belongs everything in the image-forming faculty of the intellect that is mutable – all that makes it confused and subject to constantly altering states. We have nothing to gain from such images and if we are sensible we should ignore them – indeed, they disappear of their own accord as soon as we awake. Visions on the other hand are constant; the one does not change into another, but they remain imprinted upon the intellect unforgettably for many years. Those that disclose the upshot of things to come, and assist the soul by inspiring it with compunction and the sight of fearful wonders, make the beholder reflective and strike him with awe on account of their constancy and their fearsome nature. Hence they are treated with great seriousness by those skilled in spiritual matters. Revelations occur when the purified and illumined soul is able to contemplate in a way that transcends normal sense-perception. They have the force of things and thoughts miraculous and divine, initiating us into the hidden mysteries of God, showing us the outcome of our most important problems and the universal transformation of things worldly and human.

62. The first category – that of dreams – pertains to materialistic sensually-minded people who worship their belly (cf. Phil. 3 : 19) and

are brash in their over-indulgence. Their dissolute, passion-polluted mode of life darkens their intellect, and they are mocked and spellbound by the demons. The second category – that of visions – pertains to those well advanced on the spiritual path, who have cleansed the soul's organs of perception. Beneficially assisted by things visible they ascend to the ever-increasing apprehension of things divine. The third category – that of revelations – pertains to those who are perfect, who are energized by the Holy Spirit, and whose soul through mystical prayer is united to God.

63. Things seen in sleep are true and imprinted on the spiritual intellect in the case, not of everyone, but only of those whose intellect is purified, who have cleansed the soul's organs of perception and who are advancing toward the contemplation of the inner essences of created things. Such people do not worry about day-to-day matters, nor are they troubled about this present life. Through long fasts they have acquired an all-embracing self-control and through exertion and hardship they have attained the sanctuary of God, the spiritual knowledge of created being and the wisdom of the higher world. Their life is the life of angels and is hidden in God (cf. Col. 3 : 3), their progress is based upon holy stillness and on the prophets of God's Church. It is of them that God has spoken through Moses, when He said, 'If there be a prophet among you, I will appear to him in his sleep and will speak to him in a vision' (cf. Num. 12 : 6); and through Joel, when He said, 'And it will come to pass after these things that I will pour out My spirit upon all flesh; and your sons and your daughters shall prophesy, your old men shall dream dreams and your young men shall see visions' (Joel 2 : 28).

64. Stillness is an undisturbed state of the intellect, the calm of a free and joyful soul, the tranquil unwavering stability of the heart in God, the contemplation of light, the knowledge of the mysteries of God, consciousness of wisdom by virtue of a pure mind, the abyss of divine intellections, the rapture of the intellect, intercourse with God, an unsleeping watchfulness, spiritual prayer, untroubled repose in the midst of great hardship and, finally, solidarity and union with God.

65. If the soul, its powers disordered, is still at war with itself and has not yet become receptive to the divine rays; if it is still enslaved to the will of the flesh and without peace; and if its battle with the rebellious passions has but recently come to an end, it needs to

preserve strict silence, so that with David it too can say: 'But I, as a deaf man, heard not; and I was as a dumb man who does not open his mouth' (Ps. 38 : 13). It should always be full of grief and should walk sorrowfully along the road of Christ's commandments; for it is still afflicted by the enemy and awaits the coming of the Paraclete, through whom it will receive the prize of true freedom for its compunction and cleansing tears.

66. If you generate the honey of the virtues in stillness, you will through struggle and self-discipline transcend the lowly estate of man's fallen condition and by overcoming your presumption you will restore the soul's powers to their natural state. Your heart purified by tears, you will now become receptive to the rays of the Spirit, will clothe yourself in the incorruption of the life-quickening deadness of Christ (cf. 1 Cor. 15 : 53; 2 Cor. 4 : 10), and will receive the Paraclete in tongues of fire in the upper room of your stillness (cf. Acts 2 : 3). You will then be under an obligation to speak unreservedly of the wonderful works of God (cf. Acts 2 : 11) and to 'declare His righteousness in the great congregation' (cf. Ps. 40 : 10), for you will have received inwardly the law of the Spirit (cf. John 7 : 38; Rom. 8 : 2); otherwise, like the wicked servant who hid the talent of his own master, you will be cast into eternal fire (cf. Matt. 25 : 30). Thus it was with David, when he washed away his sin through repentance and received once more the gift of prophecy; unable to conceal the blessings that he had received, he said to God, 'Behold, I will not seal my lips, as Thou, O Lord, knowest. I have not hidden Thy righteousness within my heart; I have declared Thy truth and Thy salvation; I have not concealed Thy mercy and Thy truth from the great congregation' (Ps. 40 : 9–10).

67. An intellect totally purged of impurities is like a star-filled sky that illumines the soul with lucid intellections; and the Sun of righteousness (cf. Mal. 4 : 2) shines within it, enlightening the world with divine knowledge. Cleansed in this way, the consciousness brings forth from the depths of wisdom the creative principles of things and the transparent revelations of what is hidden, and in their pure and unalloyed state it sets them before the intellect, so that it knows the depth, height and breadth of the knowledge of God (cf. Eph. 3 : 18). When the intellect has interiorized these principles and revelations and made them part of its own nature, then it will elucidate the profundities of the Spirit to all who possess God's Spirit within

themselves, exposing the guile of the demons and expounding the mysteries of the kingdom of heaven.

68. Bodily desires and the impulses of the flesh are checked by self-control, fasting and spiritual struggle. Psychic ferments and the overweeningness of the heart are allayed by the reading of the Divine Scriptures and humbled by constant prayer, while compunction like oil assuages them altogether.

69. Nothing so puts you in communion with God and unites you with the divine Logos as pure noetic prayer, when you pray undistractedly in the Spirit, your soul cleansed by tears, mellowed by compunction and illumined by the light of the Spirit.

70. Quantity is very important in the prayerful recitation of psalms, provided that it is accompanied by perseverance and attentiveness; but the quality of our recitation is what gives life to the soul and makes it fruitful. Quality in psalmody and prayer consists in praying with the Spirit and with the intellect (cf. 1 Cor. 14 : 15). We pray with the intellect when, as we say prayers and recite psalms, we perceive the meaning hidden in the Holy Scriptures and thence garner in the heart a harvest of ever more exalted divine thoughts. Rapt spiritually by these thoughts into the regions of light, the soul shines with a clear radiance, is further purified, rises wholly to the heavens, and beholds the beauty of the blessings held in store for the saints. Out of ardent longing for these blessings, tears – the fruit of prayer – at once flow from our eyes, induced by the light-creating energy of the Spirit, their taste so sweet that in experiencing them one may even forget to eat. This is the fruit of prayer, begotten through the quality of their psalmody in the soul of those who pray.

71. Where the fruit of the Spirit is present in a person, prayer is of a like quality; and where there is such quality, quantity in the recitation of psalms is excellent. Where there is no spiritual fruit, the quality is sapless. If the quality is arid, quantity is useless: even if it disciplines the body, for most people there is no gain to be got from it.

72. As you pray and sing psalms to the Lord, watch out for the guile of the demons. Either they deceive us into saying one thing instead of another, snatching the soul's attention and turning the verses of the psalms into blasphemies, so that we say things that we should not say; or, when we have started with a psalm, they cause us to skip to the end of it, distracting the intellect from what lies between; or else they make us return time and again to the same verse, through absent-

mindedness preventing us from going on to what comes next; or, when we are in the middle of a psalm, they suddenly blank out the intellect's memory of the sequence of the verses, so that we cannot even remember what verse of the psalm it was that we were saying, and thus we repeat it once more. This they do to make us neglectful and listless, and to deprive us of the fruits of our prayer by persuading us that we cannot go on because of the lateness of the hour. We should persevere strongly, however, and continue the psalm more slowly, so that through contemplation we may reap the profit of prayer from the verses and become rich with the light of the Holy Spirit that fills the souls of those who pray.

73. If something like this happens to you when you are 'singing with understanding' (cf. Ps. 47 : 7), do not become cursory or listless. Do not opt for bodily rest rather than the soul's profit, justifying this on the grounds that the hour is late. But when you realize that your intellect has become distracted, stop the recitation; and although you may be near the end of the psalm, bravely go back to the beginning, diligently resume it, and recite it over again, even if, because of distraction, you have to repeat this process several times in a single hour. If you do this the demons, unable to bear your patient perseverance and your ardour, will be put to shame and will leave you.

74. Unceasing prayer is prayer that does not leave the soul day or night. It consists not in what is outwardly perceived – outstretched hands, bodily stance, or verbal utterance – but in our inner concentration on the intellect's activity and on mindfulness of God born of unwavering compunction; and it can be perceived noetically by those capable of such perception.

75. You can devote yourself constantly to prayer only when your thoughts are mustered under the command of the intellect, delving in profound peace and reverence into the depths of God and seeking therein to taste the sweet waters of contemplation. When this peace is not present, such prayer is impossible. Only when your soul's powers are pacified through spiritual knowledge can you attain constant prayer.

76. If while you are singing a song of prayer to God, one of your brethren knocks at the door of your cell, do not opt for the work of prayer rather than that of love and ignore your brother, for so to act would be alien to God. God desires love's mercy, not the sacrifice of prayer (cf. Hos. 6 : 6). Rather, put aside the gift of prayer and speak

with healing love to your brother. Then with tears and a contrite heart once more offer your gift of prayer to the Father of the spiritual powers, and a righteous spirit will be renewed within you (cf. Matt. 5 : 23–24; Ps. 51 : 10, 17).

77. The mystery of prayer is not consummated at a certain specific time or place. For if you restrict prayer to particular times or places, you will waste the rest of the time in vain pursuits. Prayer may be defined as the intellect's unceasing intercourse with God. Its task is to engage the soul totally in things divine, its fulfilment – to adapt the words of St Paul (cf. 1 Cor. 6 : 17) – lies in so wedding the mind to God that it becomes one spirit with Him.

78. Even though you have died to your worldly self, and even though life has been generated in your soul by the Holy Spirit and God has granted you supernal gifts, you should still not leave your mind unoccupied. Accustom it to think continually on your past sins and the torments of hell, and regard yourself as one condemned. If you concern yourself with these things and look on yourself in this way, you will preserve a contrite spirit and within you a spring of compunction will flow with divine grace. God will have regard for your heart and will support it with His Spirit.

79. Controlled fasting, accompanied by vigils, meditation and prayer, quickly brings you to the frontiers of dispassion. At this point your great humility releases the spring of tears within you and you burn with love for God. When you have reached this state, you enter the peace of the Spirit that transcends every dauntless intellect (cf. Phil. 4 : 7) and through love you are united to God.

80. No king so rejoices over his glory and kingdom, or so exults in his power, as does a monk over the dispassion of his soul and over his tears of compunction. For the king's jubilation will wither with his kingdom, while the monk will be accompanied for limitless ages by the blessed dispassion and the joy he has attained. He moves like a wheel among men during this present life, touching only lightly the earth and the things upon it – and then simply because his bodily needs demand it; his intellect ascending through this circling movement entirely into the celestial sphere, in his beginning is his end; and, crowned with humility, he bears in himself the fruits of grace. His table is replete with the contemplation of the essences of created things, his drink is from the cup of Wisdom and his repose is in God.

81. If you willingly engage in the labours of virtue and zealously

pursue the ascetic path, you will be granted great gifts by God. As you approach the halfway mark, you will receive divine revelations and visions, and the greater your struggles the more full of light and wisdom you will become. At the same time, the greater the heights of contemplation you reach, the more you will provoke the destructive envy of the demons, for they cannot bear to see a human being attain an angelic nature. Hence they will deceitfully attack you with thoughts of presumption. But if you perceive their wiliness and, admonishing yourself, take refuge in the stronghold of humility, you will escape the havoc of pride and enter the haven of salvation. Failing this, and abandoned by God, you will be given over to punitive spirits; and because you did not willingly put yourself to the test, they will chastise you against your will. Carnal and pleasure-loving, full of guile and rage, these spirits will cruelly humiliate you with their attacks until you recognize your own weakness and, stricken with grief, free yourself from the rack, saying with David: 'It is good for me that Thou hast humiliated me, so that I may learn Thy commandments' (Ps. 119 : 71. LXX).

82. God does not want us always to be humiliated by the passions and to be hunted down by them like hares, making Him alone our rock and refuge (cf. Ps. 104 : 18); otherwise He would not have affirmed, 'I have said, you are gods; and all of you are children of the Most High' (Ps. 82 : 6). But He wants us to run as deer on the high mountains of His commandments (cf. Ps. 104 : 18. LXX), thirsting for the life-creating waters of the Spirit (cf. Ps. 42 : 1). For, they say, it is the deer's nature to eat snakes; but by virtue of the heat they generate through being always on the move, they strangely transform the snakes' poison into musk and it does them no harm. In a similar manner, when passion-imbued thoughts invade our mind we should bring them into subjection through our ardent pursuit of God's commandments and the power of the Spirit, and so transform them into the fragrant and salutary practice of virtue. In this way we can take every thought captive and make it obey Christ (cf. 2 Cor. 10 : 5). For the celestial world must be filled, not with people who are materialistic and imperfect, but with those who are spiritual and perfect – those who have advanced to the stature of perfect manhood in the fullness of Christ (cf. Eph. 4 : 13).

83. A person who keeps turning round and round on the same spot and does not want to make any spiritual progress is like a mule that

walks round and round a well-head operating a water-wheel. Always to be battling with your carnal proclivities and to be concerned only with disciplining the body through various forms of ascetic labour is to mistake God's purpose and unwittingly to inflict great damage on yourself. 'The gain to be derived from bodily discipline is but limited', says St Paul (1 Tim. 4 : 8) – at any rate as long as the earth-bound will of the flesh has not been swallowed up in tears of repentance, as long as the life-quickening deadness of the Spirit has not supervened in our body, and the law of the Spirit does not reign in our mortal flesh. But true devotion of soul attained through the spiritual knowledge of created things and of their immortal essences is as a tree of life within the spiritual activity of the intellect: it is 'profitable in all things' (cf. 1 Tim. 4 : 8) and everywhere, bestowing purity of heart, pacifying the soul's powers, giving light to the intellect and chastity to the body, and conferring restraint, all-embracing self-control, humility, compunction, love, holiness, heavenly knowledge, divine wisdom, and the contemplation of God. If, then, as a result of great spiritual discipline you have attained such perfection of true devotion you will have crossed the Red Sea of the passions and will have entered the promised land, from which flow the milk and the honey of divine knowledge (cf. Exod. 3 : 8), the inexhaustible delight of the saints.

84. If you persist in acting in a manner that is one-sided and of but limited profit and do not choose to do what is beneficial in every way, you still – in conformity to God's high decree – eat coarse bread in the sweat of your brow (cf. Gen. 3 : 19). Your soul feels no appetite for the spiritual manna and the honey that flows for Israel from the cloven rock (cf. Deut. 32 : 13; Ps. 81 : 16). If, however, you have heard the words, 'Arise, let us go hence' (John 14 : 31); if, in answer to the Master's call, you lay aside assiduous labour and stop eating the bread of pain, repudiating merely material perception and tasting the bowl of God's wisdom, then you will know that Christ is the Lord; for, having fulfilled the law of the commandments through ministering to the divine Logos, you will have ascended into the upper chamber and will be awaiting the coming of the Paraclete (cf. Acts 2 : 1–4).

85. We must ever progress according to the ranks and rungs of a life dedicated to wisdom and rise assiduously towards the higher world, always advancing towards God and never static in our aspiration towards supernal beauty. We must advance from ascetic practice to the contemplation of the essences of created beings, and

thence to the mystical knowledge of the divine Logos. There we may relinquish all external forms of bodily discipline, since we will have risen above the body's lowly state and will have been granted the lucidity of true discrimination. If we have not yet been granted that lucidity we will not know how to take the next step and pursue what is more perfect. We will be in an even worse condition than those 'in the world'; for many of them do not set any limit to their ambitions, and do not halt in their ascent, until they have reached the highest rank of all; and only then do they rest satisfied.

86. Cleansed through fervent ascetic labour, the soul is illumined by divine light and begins little by little to perceive the natural beauty which God originally bestowed on it and to expand in love for its Creator. And as through its purification the rays of the Sun of righteousness grow more lucid in it, and as its natural beauty is increasingly revealed to it and recognized, so in order to become yet more pure it extends its ascetic practice. In this way it acquires a clear vision of the glory of the gift it has received, regains its former nobility and restores to its Creator His own image pure and unalloyed. And it continues to add to its labours until it has cleansed itself of every stain and impurity and is privileged to contemplate and commune with God.

87. 'Open my eyes and I will perceive the wonders of Thy law' (Ps. 119 : 18). So he who is still bedarkened by his earth-bound will cries out to God. For the ignorance of the worldly mind, all murk and obscurity, blots out the soul's vision, so that it cannot grasp things either divine or human; it cannot perceive the rays of divine light or enjoy the blessings that 'the eye has not seen, and the ear has not heard, and man's heart has not grasped' (1 Cor. 2 : 9). But when through repentance its vision has been restored, it sees these things clearly, hears them with understanding and intuits them intellectually. Not only this, but it also assimilates more exalted things which, prompted by these intellections, arise in its heart; and, having tasted their sweetness, its knowledge grows more lucid. It can then, in the light of God's wisdom, explain to all the nature of the divine blessings 'that God has prepared for those who love Him' (1 Cor. 2 : 9); and it exhorts all to follow the path of struggle and tears in order to share in them.

88. Scripture enumerates seven gifts of the Spirit, beginning with wisdom and ending with the divine fear of the Spirit; for it speaks of

'the spirit of wisdom, the spirit of understanding, the spirit of counselling, the spirit of strength, the spirit of divine knowledge, the spirit of reverence, the spirit of the fear of God' (cf. Isa. 11 : 2). But we for our part should begin with the fear that purifies – that is to say, with the fear of punishment; in this way, first repudiating evil and through repentance expunging the squalor of sin, we may attain the pure fear of the Spirit. Having once attained it, we may lay aside all our struggles for virtue.

89. If you begin with fear of judgment and through tears of repentance advance towards purity of heart, you will first be filled with wisdom, since, as it is written, fear is 'the beginning of wisdom' (Prov. 1 : 7). You will then be filled simultaneously with the spirit of understanding and of counselling, and this will enable you to resolve matters in the way that is best for yourself. Having reached this stage through the practice of the commandments, you then advance to the spiritual apperception of created being and receive the most exact comprehension of things divine and human. Thereafter, entirely transformed into a tabernacle of holiness, you ascend to the citadel of love and are made perfect. At once the pure fear of the Spirit lays hold of you, so that you may guard the treasure of the kingdom of heaven of which you have become the repository. Such fear possesses great saving power; for when you have been exalted to the pinnacle of God's love it makes you fearful and full of disquiet lest you lapse from this love and are cast once more into the terrible fear of punishment.

90. The reading of the Scriptures means one thing for those who have but recently embraced the life of holiness, another for those who have attained the middle state, and another for those who are moving rapidly towards perfection. For the first, the Scriptures are bread from God's table, strengthening their hearts (cf. Ps. 104 : 15) in the holy struggle for virtue and filling them with forcefulness, power and courage in their battle against the spirits that activate the passions, so that they can say, 'For me Thou hast prepared a table with food against my enemies' (Ps. 23 : 5). For the second, the Scriptures are wine from God's chalice, gladdening their hearts (cf. Ps. 104 : 15) and transforming them through the power of the inner meaning, so that their intellect is raised above the letter that kills and led searchingly into the depths of the Spirit (cf. 2 Cor. 3 : 6; 1 Cor. 2 : 10). In this way they are enabled to discover and give birth to the inner meaning, so that fittingly they can exclaim, 'Thy chalice makes me drunk as with

the strongest wine' (Ps. 23 : 5. LXX). Finally, for those approaching perfection the Scriptures are the oil of the Holy Spirit (cf. Ps. 104 : 15), anointing the soul, making it gentle and humble through the excess of the divine illumination they bestow, and raising it wholly above the lowliness of the body, so that in its glory it may cry, 'Thou hast anointed my head with oil' (Ps. 23 : 5) and 'Thy mercy shall follow me all the days of my life' (Ps. 23 : 6).

91. So long as we dedicate ourselves to God through keeping the commandments in the sweat of our brow, and in this way diminish the passions of the flesh, the Lord sups with us at the table of His gifts on the heart-strengthening daily bread that is cultivated through the practice of the virtues. But when by attaining dispassion we hallow His name (cf. Matt. 6 : 9), and He Himself reigns in all the faculties of our soul, having brought under control and pacified what was in a state of schism – having, that is to say, subjected our lower consciousness to our higher consciousness – and when in this way His will is done in us as it is in heaven (cf. Matt. 6 : 10), then He drinks with us in His kingdom – which is now actively present within us – an inconceivable new drink (cf. Mark 14 : 25), the drink of the wisdom of the Logos mingled with compunction and the knowledge of the great mysteries. And once we have become partakers of the Holy Spirit, transformed through the renewing of our intellect (cf. Rom. 12 : 2), then as God He will dine with us as gods: for He renders immortal what He has made His own.

92. When the unbridled water of the intellect's passion-charged thoughts has been bridled through the abiding presence of the Holy Spirit, and the brine-bitter abyss of indecent images and desires has been brought into subjection through self-control and meditation on death, then the divine spirit of repentance begins to blow and the waters of compunction pour forth; and our God and Master, channelling them into the basin of repentance, washes our spiritual feet, making them worthy to walk in the courts of His kingdom.

93. The Logos of God, having taken flesh and given our nature subsistence in Himself, becoming perfect man, entirely free from sin, has as perfect God refashioned our nature and made it divine. As Logos of the primal Intellect and God, He has united Himself to our intelligence, giving it wings so that it may conceive divine, exalted thoughts. Because He is fire, He has with true divine fire steeled the incensive power of the soul against hostile passions and demons.

Aspiration of all intelligent being and slaker of all desire, He has in His deep-seated love dilated the appetitive aspect of the soul so that it can partake of the blessings of eternal life. Having thus renewed the whole man in Himself, He restores it in an act of re-creation that leaves no grounds for any reproach against the Creator-Logos.

94. Performing in Himself the sacred mystery of our re-creation, the Logos offered Himself up on our behalf through His death on the cross, and He continually offers Himself up, giving His immaculate body to us daily as a soul-nourishing banquet, so that by eating it and by drinking His precious blood we may through this participation consciously grow in spiritual stature. Communicating in His body and blood and refashioned in a purer form, we are united to the twofold divine-human Logos in two ways, in our body and in our deiform soul; for He is God incarnate whose flesh is the same in essence as our own. Thus we do not belong to ourselves, but to Him who has united us to Himself through this immortal meal and has made us by adoption what He Himself is by nature.

95. If, then, tested in the labours of virtue and purified by tears, we come forward and eat of this bread and drink of this cup, the divine-human Logos in His gentleness is commixed with our two natural faculties, with our soul and body; and as God incarnate, one with us in essence as regards our human nature, He totally refashions us in Himself, wholly deifying us through divine knowledge and uniting us with Himself as His brothers, conformed to Him who is God coessential with the Father. If, however, we are defiled with the materiality of the passions and soiled with sin, He visits us with His natural sin-devouring fire, igniting and consuming us entirely, and cutting us off from life, not because in His goodness He wishes to do this, but because He is constrained to do it by our indifference and lack of spiritual perception.

96. Invisibly the Lord draws near to all who by practising the virtues have begun to travel the path of His commandments, and He keeps them company even though they are as yet imperfect in understanding and still unsure as to the true nature of virtue. Rightly are the eyes of their soul impeded, so that they do not recognize their own progress even though the Lord accompanies them, co-operates with them in their efforts to be liberated from the passions, and assists them in the attainment of every form of virtue. For although they advance in the struggle for holiness, and through humility approach

the state of dispassion, the Logos does not want them to come to a halt, exhausted by their labours; rather He wishes them to advance still further and to rise to the state of contemplation. Thus, having nourished them in moderation on the bread of tears, He blesses them with the light of compunction and opens their intellect so that they can understand the profundities of Holy Scripture and thus perceive the nature and inner essence of everything that exists. At this point He abruptly withdraws from them so that they will be put on their mettle and will seek more zealously to learn what is meant by the spiritual knowledge of things and what is the exaltation that it brings. Prompted thus to pursue this knowledge more diligently, they become ministers of the Logos in a yet higher way and proclaim to all the resurrection consummated through the practice of the virtues and the contemplation of the Logos (cf. Luke 24 : 13–35).

97. The Logos justifiably rebukes the tardiness of those who drag out their time in the practice of the virtues and do not wish to advance beyond this and rise to the higher state of contemplation. 'Fools and slow of heart,' He calls them (Luke 24 : 25) – slow to place their trust in Him who can reveal the meaning of the contemplation of the inner principles of the created world to all who spiritually explore the depths of the Spirit. For not to wish to progress from the initial struggles to those that are more advanced, and to pass from the 'exterior' or literal meaning of Holy Scripture to its inner or spiritual meaning, is a sign of the sluggish soul, one with no taste for spiritual profit and extremely resentful about its own advancement. Such a soul, since its lamp has gone out, will not only be told to go and buy oil from those that sell it; but, finding the bridal chamber closed to it, it will also hear the words, 'Go away, I do not know you or whence you come' (cf. Matt. 25 : 9, 12).

98. When the Logos of God enters a fallen soul – as He entered the city of Bethany (cf. John 11 : 17) – in order to resurrect its intellect, sin-slain and buried under the corruption of the passions, then sound understanding and justice, plunged into grief by the intellect's death, come as mourners to meet Him, and they say, 'Hadst Thou been here with us, guarding and keeping watch, our brother intellect would not have died because of sin' (cf. John 11 : 32). Then justice will anxiously tend the Logos through the practice of the virtues and will want to prepare a menu of various kinds of hardship; but sound understanding, laying aside all other concerns and ascetic endeavours,

will devote itself solely to spiritual labour, cleaving to the spiritual discourse of the Logos and attentive to the intellections arising from its contemplation of Him. Thus although the Logos acknowledges justice and its efforts to nourish Him generously through various forms of practical activity, He still rebukes it for always being anxious about so many outward labours and for engaging in what is of but limited profit (cf. 1 Tim. 4 : 8). One thing only is needed in order to serve the Logos, and that is the subjection, through the labours of virtue, of the lower consciousness to the higher consciousness, and the transformation of the soul's earth-bound propensity into spiritual aspiration. Sound understanding, however, the Logos praises, and unites with Himself in a manner that accords with His nature, for it has chosen 'the better portion' – the knowledge of the Spirit whereby, transcending things human, it penetrates into the depths of the Divine. Here to its great profit it procures the pearl of the Logos (cf. Matt. 13 : 45–46), beholds the hidden treasures of the Spirit (cf. Matt. 13 : 44), and is filled with an inexpressible joy that will not be taken away from it (cf. Luke 10 : 38–42).

99. The intellect that has been slain by the passions and again brought to life by the indwelling presence of the divine Logos has thrown off the grave-stone of torpid insensibility and has been freed from the shroud of sin and from corrupting thoughts by the servants of the Logos, fear of punishment and ascetic labour. Having tasted the light of eternal life, it is released into dispassion (cf. John 11 : 38–43). Henceforward it enthrones itself over the senses and, having in purity celebrated the mystery of initiation, consorts with Christ the Logos, rising with Him from the earth to heaven, and reigning with Him in the kingdom of God the Father, all its desires quenched.

100. The restitution that will be consummated in the age to come after the dissolution of the body becomes clearly evident even now, through the inspiration and inner activity of the Spirit, in those who have truly striven, have traversed the midpoint of the spiritual path, and been made perfect according to 'the measure of the stature of the fullness of Christ' (Eph. 4 : 13). Their joy is eternal, in eternal light, and their blessedness is of that final state. For ceaseless joy possesses the hearts of those who in this present life are rightly fighting the spiritual fight, and the gladness of the Holy Spirit embraces them – a gladness which, according to our Lord's words, will not be taken away from them (cf. Luke 10 : 42). Thus he who in this present life is

privileged to experience the abiding presence of the Paraclete, and through the cultivation of the virtues delights in His fruits and is enriched by His divine gifts, is filled with joy and with all love, for fear has entirely left him. Joyously is he released from the bonds of the body and joyously he transcends the world of visible things, being already freed from his sensory attachment to them. He reposes in the inexpressible joy of the light in which dwell all who rejoice (cf. Ps. 87 : 7. LXX), even if his body often experiences pain at its dissolution and at the severing of its union with the soul, and suffers in various ways, as a woman does during a difficult childbirth.

On Spiritual Knowledge, Love and the Perfection of Living: One Hundred Texts

1. God is dispassionate Intellect, beyond every intellect and beyond every form of dispassion. He is Light and the source of blessed light. He is Wisdom, Intelligence and spiritual Knowledge, and the giver of wisdom, intelligence and spiritual knowledge. If on account of your purity these qualities have been bestowed on you and are richly present in you, then that within you which accords with the image of God has been safely preserved and you are now a son of God guided by the Holy Spirit; for 'all who are guided by the Spirit of God are sons of God' (Rom. 8 : 14).

2. Those who through ascetic practice cleanse themselves 'from all pollution of the flesh and spirit' (2 Cor. 7 : 1) receive the gifts of the Holy Spirit and so become vessels of immortal reality. Having attained this level they are filled with the light of glory. Their hearts now serene and at peace, they utter blessed words, and God's wisdom – knowledge of things divine and human – flows from their lips, while their intelligence undisturbed interprets the profundities of the Holy Spirit. Once they have been united with God and have experienced a blessed transformation, the law is no longer binding on such people (cf. Gal. 5 : 23).

3. He who wholeheartedly and assiduously directs himself towards God attains such virtue of soul and body that he becomes a mirror of the divine image. He is so commixed with God, and God with him, that each reposes in the other. Because of the richness of the gifts of the Spirit that he has received, henceforth he is and appears to be an image of divine blessedness and god by adoption, God being the perfector of his perfection.

4. Only in ignorance would one claim that man is created in the image of God with respect to the organic structure of his body. He is in

the image by virtue of the spiritual nature of his intellect, which is not circumscribed by the dead weight of the body. Since the divine nature is outside every created being and all material grossness, it is not circumscribed, but is unlimited and incorporeal, beyond substance and all condition, without qualities, impalpable, unquantifiable, invisible, immortal, incomprehensible and totally beyond our grasp. Similarly, the spiritual nature given to us by God is uncircumscribed and outside the material grossness of this world, and so is incorporeal, invisible, impalpable, incomprehensible, and an image of His immortal and eternal glory.

5. Since God, as sovereign King of all, is primordial Intellect, He possesses within Himself His Logos and His Spirit, coessential and coeternal with Him. He is never without the Logos and the Spirit because the divine nature is one and indivisible; nor is He to be confused with Them, for the three hypostases in God are distinct and unconfusable. Hence in naturally begetting the Logos from His essence, the Father is not severed from Him, since He is Himself indivisible. The coeternal Logos, not severed from His Begetter, possesses the Spirit, who proceeds eternally from the Father (cf. John 15 : 26) and shares with the Logos the same unoriginate nature. For the nature of both Logos and Spirit is one and undivided, even though by virtue of the distinction of hypostases the one God is divided into persons and is glorified as the Trinity of Father, Son and Holy Spirit. Yet the persons, since They constitute one nature and one God, are never separated from the coeternal essence and nature. Observe, then, an image of this trihypostatic and single divine nature in man, who is created by this nature and is the image of it, not according to his visible self but according to his spiritual self, not according to what is mortal and perishable in him but according to what is immortal and ever the same.

6. God is Intellect and transcends the creatures that in His Wisdom He has created; yet He also changelessly begets the Logos as their dwelling-place, and, as Scripture says (cf. John 14 : 26), sends the Holy Spirit to endow them with power. He is thus both outside everything and within everything. Similarly, man participates in the divine nature, and according to his spiritual self – that is to say, as a spiritual, incorporeal and immortal soul – is an image of God, and possesses an intellect which naturally begets consciousness from its essence; and by virtue of all this he maintains the power of the body.

He is thus both outside matter and visible things and within them. And just as the Father who created man is inseparable from the other two hypostases – that is, from the Logos and the Spirit – so man's soul is indivisible from his intellect and his consciousness, for they are of one nature and essence – an essence uncircumscribed by the body.

7. Since the Deity is worshipped in the three hypostases of Father, Son and Holy Spirit, the image formed by Him – man, that is – also subsists in a tripartite division, worshipping God, the Creator of all things out of things that are not, with soul, intellect and consciousness. Thus, things by nature coeternal and coessential within God are also intrinsic to and coessential with His image. They constitute the divine image in us and through them I am an image of God, even though I am a composite of clay and divine image.

8. The image of God is one thing, and that which is contemplated in the image is another. For the image of God is the noetic soul, the intellect and the consciousness, which form one indivisible nature. What is contemplated in the image is that which is sovereign, royal and self-determinative. Thus the glory of the intellect is one thing, its dignity is another, its being in the image of God is another, and its being in His likeness is another (cf. Gen. 1 : 26). The glory of the intellect is its power of ascent, its constant movement upwards, its acuity, purity, understanding, wisdom and immortality. The dignity of the intellect lies in its intelligence, its royal and sovereign nature, and its power of self-determination. Its being in the image of God resides in the self-subsistence of soul, intellect and consciousness and in their coessentiality, indivisibility and inseparability. For intellect and consciousness belong to the incorporeal, immortal, divine and noetic soul; these three are coessential and coeternal, and can never be divided or separated from each other. The intellect's being in the likeness of God resides in its justice, truthfulness, love, sympathy and compassion. When these qualities are energized and guarded in a person, that which is in the image and likeness of God is clearly manifest in him; he acts, that is to say, in accordance with nature and enjoys a higher dignity than others.

9. The tripartite deiform soul possesses two aspects, the one noetic and the other passible. The noetic aspect, being in the image of the soul's Creator, is not conditioned by the senses, is invisible to them and is not limited by them, since it is both outside them and within them. It is by virtue of this aspect that the soul communicates with spiritual and

divine powers and, through the sacred knowledge of created beings, ascends naturally to God as to its archetype, thus entering into the enjoyment of His divine nature. The passible aspect is split up among the senses and is subject to passions and prone to self-indulgence. It is by virtue of this aspect that the soul communicates with the world that is perceptible to the senses and that fosters nutrition and growth; and in this way it breathes the air, experiences cold and heat, and receives sustenance for self-preservation, life, growth and health. Since the passible aspect is modified by what it comes into contact with, it is sometimes incited by impulses contrary to nature and develops disordered desires; at other times it is provoked and carried away by mindless anger, or is subject to hunger and thirst, to sorrow and pain, and finally to physical dissolution; it luxuriates in self-indulgence, but shrinks back from affliction. Thus it is rightly called the passible aspect of the soul, since it is to be found in the company of the passions. When the noetic aspect of the soul holds sway and this mortal aspect is swallowed up by the Logos of life (cf. 2 Cor. 5 : 4), then the life of Jesus is also manifested in our mortal flesh (cf. 2 Cor. 4 : 11), producing in us the life-quickening deadness of dispassion, and conferring the incorruption of immortality in response to our spiritual aspiration.

10. Prior to His creation of all things out of nothing, the Creator possessed in Himself the knowledge and the intrinsic principles and essences of all that He brought into existence, for He is sovereign over the ages and has foreknowledge of them all. Correspondingly, when in His own image He fashioned man as the sovereign of creation, He endowed him with the knowledge and the intrinsic principles and essences of all created things. Thus through his creation man possesses the dry and cold qualities of the body's gastric fluid from the earth, the warm and moist qualities of blood from air and fire, the moist and cold qualities of phlegm from water, the power of growth from plants, the power of nutrition from zoophytes, his passible aspect from the animals, his spiritual and noetic aspect from the angels, and finally, in order to exist and live, his immaterial breath – his incorporeal and immortal soul, understood as intellect, consciousness and the power of the Holy Spirit – from God.

11. God created us in His image and likeness (cf. Gen. 1 : 26). We are in His likeness if we possess virtue and understanding; for 'His virtue covered the heavens, and the earth was full of His understand-

ing' (cf. Hab. 3 : 3). The virtue of God is His justice, holiness and truth: as David says, 'Thou art just, O Lord, and Thy truth is round about Thee' (cf. Ps. 89 : 8. LXX); and again, 'The Lord is just and holy' (cf. Ps. 145 : 17). We are also in the likeness of God if we possess uprightness and goodness, for 'good and upright is the Lord' (Ps. 25 : 8); or if we are conscious of wisdom and spiritual knowledge, for these are within Him and He is called Wisdom and Logos; or if we possess holiness and perfection, since He Himself said, 'You must be perfect, as your heavenly Father is perfect' (Matt. 5 : 48), and, 'You must be holy, for I am holy' (Lev. 11 : 44; 1 Pet. 1 : 16); or if we are humble and gentle, for it is written, 'Learn from Me, for I am gentle and humble in heart, and you will find rest for your souls' (Matt. 11 : 29).

12. Since our intellect is an image of God, it is true to itself when it remains among the things that are properly its own and does not divagate from its own dignity and nature. Hence it loves to dwell among things proximate to God, and seeks to unite itself with Him, from whom it had its origin, by whom it is activated, and towards whom it ascends by means of its natural capabilities; and it desires to imitate Him in His compassion and simplicity. Such an intellect even begets the Logos, and it recreates like new heavens the souls akin to it, strengthening them in the patient practice of the virtues; and it bestows life on them through the spiritual power of its counsel, providing them with the strength to resist destructive passions. If, then, it truly imitates God, it becomes itself also a creator both of the noetic world and of the macrocosm, and clearly hears God's words, 'He who extracts what is precious from what is vile will be as My mouth' (cf. Jer. 15 : 19).

13. He who staunchly adheres to those activities of the intellect which accord with its nature and affirms the dignity of the intelligence, is kept unsullied by material preoccupations, is invested with gentleness, humility, love and compassion, and is illumined by the Holy Spirit. His attention focussed on the higher spheres of contemplative activity, he is initiated into the hidden mysteries of God, and through his words of wisdom he lovingly ministers to those who are capable of learning about these things. In this way he does not use his talent solely for his own benefit, but also shares its benediction with his fellow-men.

14. Exalt the One over the dyad – the single over the dual – and

free its nobility from all commerce with dualism, and you will consort immaterially with immaterial spirits; for you will yourself have become a noetic spirit, even though you appear to dwell bodily among other men.

15. Once you have brought bondage to the dyad into subjection to the dignity and nature of the One, you will have subjected the whole of creation to God; for you will have brought into unity what was divided and will have reconciled all things.

16. So long as the nature of the powers within us is in a state of inner discord and is dispersed among many contrary things, we do not participate in God's supranatural gifts. And if we do not participate in these gifts, we are also far from the mystical eucharist of the heavenly sanctuary, celebrated by the intellect through its spiritual activity. When through assiduous ascetic labour we have purged ourselves of the crudity of evil and have reconciled our inner discord through the power of the Spirit, we then participate in the ineffable blessings of God, and worthily concelebrate the divine mysteries of the intellect's mystical eucharist with God the Logos in His supracelestial and spiritual sanctuary; for we have become initiates and priests of His immortal mysteries.

17. Our fallen self desires in a way that opposes our spiritual self, our spiritual self in a way that opposes our fallen self (cf. Gal. 5 : 17); and in this relentless warfare between the two each strives for victory and control over the other. This contrariety within us is also called 'discord', 'turning point', 'balance' and 'twofold struggle'; and if the intellect tips the balance towards an act of human passion the soul is split asunder.

18. So long as we are reft by the turmoil of our thoughts, and so long as we are ruled and constrained by our fallen self, we are self-fragmented and cut off from the divine Monad, since we have not made our own the riches of its unity. But when our mortality is swallowed up by the unifying power of the Monad and acquires a supranatural detachment, when the intellect becomes master of itself, illumined by its wisdom-engendering intellections, then the soul, in sacred embrace with the One, is freed from discord and becomes a unity: enfolded into the divine Monad, it is unified in a godlike simplicity. Such is the nature of the soul's restoration to its original state and such our renewal in a state yet more exalted.

19. Ignorance is terrible and more than terrible, a truly palpable

darkness (cf. Exod. 10 : 21). Souls suckled on ignorance are tenebrous, their thought is fragmented, and they are cut off from union with God. Its upshot is inanity, since it makes the whole person mindless and insensate. Waxing gross, it plunges the soul into the depths of hell, where there is every kind of punishment and pain, distress and anguish. Conversely, divine knowledge is luminous and endlessly illuminating: souls in which it has been engendered because of their purity possess a godlike radiance, for it fills them with peace, serenity, joy, ineffable wisdom and perfect love.

20. Simple and unified, the presence of divine light gathers within itself the souls that participate in it and converts them to itself, uniting them with its own unity, and perfecting them with its own perfection. It leads them to descry the depths of God, so that they contemplate the great mysteries and become initiates and mystagogues. Aspire, then, to be purified utterly through ascetic labour, and you will see these mysteries dear to God – of which I have spoken – actually at work within you.

21. The rays of primordial Light that illumine purified souls with spiritual knowledge not only fill them with benediction and luminosity; they also, by means of the contemplation of the inner essences of created things, lead them up to the noetic heavens. The effects of the divine energy, however, do not stop here; they continue until through wisdom and through knowledge of indescribable things they unite purified souls with the One, bringing them out of a state of multiplicity into a state of oneness in Him.

22. We must first purge ourselves of the vicious materiality prompted in us by the demons – this is the stage of purification; then, through the stage of illumination, we must make our spiritual eyes lucid and ever light-filled, and this is accomplished by means of the mystical wisdom hidden in God. In this way we ascend to the cognition of sacred knowledge, which through the intelligence imparts things new and old to those who have ears to hear. Then we in our turn must pass on to others images and intimations of this knowledge, conveying its hidden meaning to the purified while withholding it from the profane, lest holy things be given to dogs, or the pearl of the Logos be cast before swine-like souls that would defile it (cf. Matt. 7 : 6).

23. When you become aware of increasing ardency in your inner faith and love for God, then you should know that you are bringing Christ to birth within yourself, and that it is He who exalts your soul

above terrestrial and visible things and prepares a dwelling-place for it in heaven. When you perceive that your heart is replete with joy, and poignantly longs for God's unutterable blessings, then you should realize that you are activated by the divine Spirit. And when you sense that your intellect is full of ineffable light and the intellections of supernal Wisdom, then you should recognize that the Paraclete is present in your soul, disclosing the treasures of the kingdom of heaven hidden within you; and you should guard yourself strictly as a palace of God and as a dwelling-place of the Spirit.

24. Guardianship of the hidden treasure of the Spirit consists in that state of detachment from human affairs which is properly termed stillness. When through purity of heart and joyful compunction this stillness kindles a yet fiercer longing for God's love, it releases the soul from the bonds of the senses and impels it to embrace the life of freedom. Recalled to its natural state, the soul reorientates its powers, restoring them to their original condition. Thus it is evident that none of the evil that afflicts us as a result of our deviation and lapse from the divine image may be imputed to God, who creates only what is good.

25. It is stillness, full of wisdom and benediction, that leads us to this holy and godlike state of perfection – when, that is, it is practised and pursued genuinely. If an apparent hesychast has not attained this eminence and perfection, his stillness is not yet this noetic and perfect stillness. Indeed, until he has attained this eminence, he will not even have stilled the inner turbulence of the anarchic passions. All he will have is a body consisting of teguments, vents and cavities, and wasted by a disordered and deluded mind.

26. Souls that have attained total purity, and have reached the heights of wisdom and spiritual knowledge, resemble the Cherubim. By virtue of their unmediated cognition they draw close to the source of all beauty and goodness, and in this way they are directly and fully initiated into the vision of secret things. Among the spiritual powers it is said that only the Cherubim are illuminated in this direct manner by the source of divinity itself and thus possess this vision in the highest degree.[1]

27. Among the highest angelic powers, some are more ardent and clear-sighted in their devotion to the divine realities around which they

---

[1] See St Dionysios the Areopagite, *The Celestial Hierarchy* vii, 1 (*P.G.* iii, 205B).

unceasingly circle; others are more contemplative, gnostic and imbued with wisdom, this being the divine state that impels them unceasingly to circle around these realities. Similarly, angel-like souls are ardent and clear-sighted in their devotion to the divine realities, as well as wise, gnostic and exalted in mystical contemplation. Potentially and actually they too unceasingly circle around things divine, firmly rooted in them alone. Immutably receptive of divine illuminations, and thus participating in Him who truly is, they also unstintingly communicate His irradiance and grace to others through their teaching.

28. God is Intellect and the activating agent of everything. All intellects have both their permanent abode and their eternal mobility in this primary Intellect. Such is the experience of all whose activity is not adulterated by materiality but is pure and unsullied as a result of sacred ascetic labour. They experience this when, ardent with divine love, they communicate to each other and to themselves the illumination bestowed on them by the Divinity, generously transmitting to others the wisdom of God's mysteries concealed within it; and in this way they unceasingly extol the divine love that inspires them.

29. Souls whose intelligence has been freed from material preoccupation, and in whom the self-warring appetitive and incensive aspects have been restored to harmony and harnessed to their heaven-bound well-reined chariot, both revolve around God and yet stand fixedly. They revolve incessantly around God as the centre and cause of their circular movement. They stand steadfast and unwavering as fixed points on the circumference of the circle, and cannot be diverted from this fixed position by the sense-world and the distraction of human affairs. This is therefore the perfect consummation of stillness, and it is to this that stillness leads those who truly achieve it, so that while moving they are stationary, and while steadfast and immobile they move around the divine realities. So long as we do not experience this we can only be said to practise an apparent stillness, and our intellect is not free from materiality and distraction.

30. When through great diligence and effort we recover the original beauty of the intelligence, and through the abiding presence of the Holy Spirit participate in supernal wisdom and knowledge, we can then perceive things as they are by nature and hence can recognize that the source and cause of all things is itself wise and beautiful. We see that we cannot hold it in any way responsible for the evil that destroys created things when they deviate towards what is base. When we are

so deflected and dragged downwards, we are sundered from the
pristine beauty of the Logos and forfeit our deification, while the evil
that has invaded us disfigures us into its own obtuse and witless form.

31. When through the practice of the virtues we attain a spiritual
knowledge of created things we have achieved the first stage on the
path of deification. We achieve the second stage when – initiated
through the contemplation of the spiritual essences of created things –
we perceive the hidden mysteries of God. We achieve the third stage
when we are united and interfused with the primordial light. It is then
that we reach the goal of all ascetic and contemplative activity.

32. By means of these three stages all intellects are brought, in a
way that accords with their own nature, into unity with themselves
and with Him who truly is. They can then illumine their fellow-
intellects, initiating them into divine realities, through celestial wisdom
perfecting them as spirits already purified, and uniting them with
themselves and with the One.

33. Deification in this present life is the spiritual and truly sacred
rite in which the Logos of unutterable wisdom makes Himself a sacred
offering and gives Himself, so far as is possible, to those who have
prepared themselves. God, as befits His goodness, has bestowed this
deification on beings endowed with intelligence so that they may
achieve the union of faith. Those who as a result of their purity and
their knowledge of things divine participate in this dignity are
assimilated to God, 'conformed to the image of His Son' (Rom.
8 : 29) through their exalted and spiritual concentration upon the
divine. Thus they become as gods to other men on earth. These others
in their turn, perfected in virtue by purification through their divine
intelligence and through sacred intercourse with God, participate
according to their proficiency and the degree of their purification in
the same deification as their brethren, and they commune with them
in the God of unity. In this way all of them, joined together in the
union of love, are unceasingly united with the one God; and God, the
source of all holy works and totally free from any indictment because
of His work of creation, abides in the midst of gods (cf. Ps. 82 : 1.
LXX), God by nature among gods by adoption.

34. You cannot be assimilated to God and participate in His
ineffable blessings – in so far as this is possible – unless you first
through fervent tears and through the practice of Christ's sacred
commandments strip away the interposing foulness and disfigurement

of sin. If you want spiritually to taste the sweetness and delight of things spiritual you must renounce all mundane sense-experience, and in your aspiration for the blessings held in store for the saints you must devote yourself to the contemplation of the inner reality of created beings.

35. Assimilation to God, conferred upon us through intense purification and deep love for God, can be maintained only through an unceasing aspiration towards Him on the part of the contemplative intellect. Such aspiration is born within the soul through the persistent stillness produced by the acquisition of the virtues, by ceaseless and undistracted spiritual prayer, by total self-control, and by intensive reading of the Scriptures.

36. We must strive not only to bring the soul's powers into a state of peace, but also to acquire a longing for spiritual serenity. For through the pacifying of our thoughts every aspiration for what is good is strengthened, while divine heaven-sent dew heals and revives the heart wounded by Spirit-enkindled celestial fire.

37. Once a soul deeply wounded by divine longing has experienced the balm of God's noetic gifts, it cannot remain static or fixed in itself, but will aspire to rise ever further towards heaven. The higher it rises through the Spirit and the further it penetrates into the depths of God, the more it is consumed by the fire of desire; and it explores in all their immensity the yet deeper mysteries of God, anxious to attain the blessed light where every intellect is rapt out of itself and where – its goal achieved – it reposes in heartfelt joy.

38. When you come to participate in the Holy Spirit and recognize His presence through a certain ineffable energy and fragrance within yourself – this fragrance even spreading over the surface of your body – you can no longer be content to remain within the bounds of the created world. On the contrary, having experienced the noble conversion wrought by the 'right hand of the Most High' (Ps. 77 : 10. LXX), you forget food and sleep, transcend bodily needs, ignore physical repose and, after spending the whole day in ascetic toil, are yet unaware of stress or duress, of hunger, thirst, sleep, or of any other physical need. For with unutterable joy God's love is poured out invisibly into your heart (cf. Rom. 5 : 5). Wrapped the whole night in an illumination of fire, you accomplish spiritual work through the body and feast on the immortal fruits of the noetic paradise. It was into this paradise that St Paul, too, was caught up when he heard the

inexpressible words which no one is permitted to hear (cf. 2 Cor. 12 : 4) if still attached to the sense-world of visible things.

39. Once the body has been fired in the furnace of ascetic practice and tempered by the water of tears, it is no longer dulled by hardship, for it is now exempt from outward labours and ceases from the great toil they demand. Immersed in the silence and serenity of inward peace, it becomes full of a new power, a new vigour, a new spiritual strength. When the soul works hand in hand with such a body – one, that is to say, whose state transcends the need for bodily discipline – it changes its physical labours into spiritual warfare. It promptly begins to perform spiritual work, and guards in itself the immortal fruits of the noetic paradise, where the rivers of godlike intellection have their source, and where stands the tree of divine knowledge (cf. Gen. 2 : 9–10), bearing the fruits of wisdom, joy, peace, kindness, goodness, long-suffering and ineffable love (cf. Gal. 5 : 22). Working assiduously in this manner and guarding what it harvests, the soul goes out of the body and enters into the darkness of mystical theology. It leaves everything behind, not held back by anything belonging to the visible world; and, united with God, it ceases from toil and grief.

40. Those engaged in spiritual warfare confront the question of which in us is the more noble: the visible or the intelligible? If it is the visible, there is nothing in us more to be preferred or desired than what is corruptible, nor is the soul more noble than the body. If it is the intelligible then we must recognize that 'God is spirit, and those who worship Him must worship in spirit and in truth' (John 4 : 24). Thus once the soul is firmly established in spiritual work, freed from the downward pull of the body and rendered entirely spiritual through union with what is superior to it, then bodily discipline is superfluous.

41. There are three stages on the spiritual path: the purgative, the illuminative and finally the mystical, through which we are perfected. The first pertains to beginners, the second to those in the intermediate stage, and the third to the perfect. It is through these three consecutive stages that we ascend, growing in stature according to Christ and attaining 'mature manhood, the measure of the stature of the fullness of Christ' (Eph. 4 : 13).

42. The purgative stage pertains to those newly engaged in spiritual warfare. It is characterized by the rejection of the materialistic self, liberation from material evil, and investiture with the regenerate self, renewed by the Holy Spirit (cf. Col. 3 : 10). It involves hatred of

materiality, the attenuation of the flesh, the avoidance of whatever incites the mind to passion, repentance for sins committed, the dissolving with tears of the bitter sediment left by sin, the regulation of our life according to the generosity of the Spirit, and the cleansing through compunction of the inside of the cup (cf. Matt. 23 : 26) – the intellect – from every defilement of flesh and spirit (cf. 2 Cor. 7 : 1), so that it can then be filled with the wine of the Logos that gladdens the heart of the purified (cf. Ps. 104 : 15), and can be brought to the King of the celestial powers for Him to taste. Its final goal is that we should be forged in the fire of ascetic struggle, scouring off the rust of sin, and steeled and tempered in the water of compunction, so that sword-like we may effectively cut off the passions and the demons. Reaching this point through long ascetic struggle, we quench the fire within us, muzzle the brute-like passions, become strong in the Spirit instead of weak (cf. Heb. 11 : 33–34), and like another Job conquer the tempter through our patient endurance.

43. The illuminative stage pertains to those who as a result of their struggles have attained the first level of dispassion. It is characterized by the spiritual knowledge of created beings, the contemplation of their inner essences and communion in the Holy Spirit. It involves the intellect's purification by divine fire, the noetic opening of the eyes of the heart, and the birth of the Logos accompanied by sublime intellections of spiritual knowledge. Its final goal is the elucidation of the nature of created things by the Logos of Wisdom, insight into divine and human affairs, and the revelation of the mysteries of the kingdom of heaven (cf. Luke 8 : 10). He who has reached this point through the inner activity of the intellect rides, like another Elijah (cf. 2 Kgs. 2 : 11), in a chariot of fire drawn by the quaternity of the virtues; and while still living he is raised to the noetic realm and traverses the heavens, since he has risen above the lowliness of the body.

44. The mystical and perfective stage pertains to those who have already passed through all things and have come to 'the measure of the stature of the fullness of Christ' (Eph. 4 : 13). It is characterized by the transcending of the sphere of demonic powers and of all sublunar things, by our attaining to the higher celestial ranks, approaching the primordial light and plumbing the depths of God through the Spirit. It involves immersing our contemplative intellect in the inner principles of providence, justice and truth, and also the interpretation of the

arcane symbolism, parables and obscure passages in Holy Scripture. Its final goal is our initiation into the hidden mysteries of God and our being filled with ineffable wisdom through union with the Holy Spirit, so that each becomes a wise theologian in the great Church of God, illuminating others with the inner meaning of theology. He who has reached this point through the deepest humility and compunction has, like another Paul, been caught up into the third heaven of theology, and has heard indescribable things which he who is still dominated by the sense-world is not permitted to hear (cf. 2 Cor. 12 : 4); and he experiences unutterable blessings, such as no eye has seen or ear heard (cf. 1 Cor. 2 : 9). He becomes a steward of God's mysteries (cf. 1 Cor. 4 : 1), for he is God's mouthpiece, and through words he communicates these mysteries to other people; and in this he finds blessed repose. For he is now perfected in the perfect God, united in the company of other theologians with the supreme angelic powers of the Cherubim and Seraphim, in whom dwells the principle of wisdom and spiritual knowledge.

45. Human life is divided into two forms, while its goals are subsumed under three categories. One form is social and within the world, the other is solitary and transcends the world. Social life is characterized either by self-restraint or by insatiability; the solitary life is subdivided into three modes: the practice of the virtues, the spiritual cognition of created beings, and the indwelling of supranatural energy. Social life may be characterized by justice, in which case it accords with nature, or by injustice, in which case it is contrary to nature. The solitary life either aspires towards its goal in accordance with monastic precept and rule, and – perfected in a manner that transcends nature – attains the Infinite; or else it is prompted by presumption and so is balked of its purpose, debases the mind, and fails to attain perfection.

46. The Spirit is light, life and peace. If consequently you are illumined by the Spirit your own life is imbued with peace and serenity. Because of this you are filled with the spiritual knowledge of created beings and the wisdom of the Logos; you are granted the intellect of Christ (cf. 1 Cor. 2 : 16); and you come to know the mysteries of God's kingdom (cf. Luke 8 : 10). Thus you penetrate into the depths of the Divine and daily from an untroubled and illumined heart you utter words of life for the benefit of others; for you yourself are full of benediction, since you have within you Goodness itself that utters things new and old (cf. Matt. 13 : 52).

47. God is Wisdom, and by deifying through the spiritual knowledge of created beings those who live in the Logos and in Wisdom He unites them with Himself through light and makes them gods by adoption. Since God has created all things out of nothing through Wisdom, He directs and administers all that is in the world through Wisdom, and likewise in Wisdom brings about the salvation of all who turn towards Him and draw near to Him. Similarly, whoever as a result of his purity has been enabled to participate in the highest Wisdom always as an image of God acts in Wisdom, and in Wisdom carries out the divine will. Withdrawing himself from what is external and multiple, each day he raises his intelligence anagogically through the knowledge of unutterable things to a life that is truly angelic. Having unified his own life as far as possible, he unites himself with the angelic powers that move in a unified way around God, and under their good guidance is elevated to the first Principle and Cause.

48. Once you have united yourself through the higher Wisdom with the angelic powers and have thereby been united with God, through love of Wisdom you enter into communion with all men, since you have achieved God's likeness. Through divine power you sever those so disposed from their attachment to what is external and multiple, and as an imitator of God you concentrate them in spirit, elevating them as you are elevated to a unified life through wisdom, spiritual knowledge and the illumination of divine mysteries, until they come to contemplate the glory of the unique primordial light. When you have united them with the essences and orders that surround God, you induct them – wholly irradiated by the Spirit – to the unity of God Himself.

49. Linked to the four cardinal virtues there is a group of eight natural and general virtues. Each cardinal virtue is accompanied by two virtues from the second category, thus composing a triad. Sound understanding is accompanied by spiritual knowledge and wise contemplation; justice by discrimination and sympathetic understanding; courage by patience and firm resolution; self-restraint by purity and virginity. From the throne of the intellect, in His wisdom God presides like an architect and mystagogue over these twelve virtues divided into triads, and sends out the Logos to create them within us. From their underlying principles the Logos takes the substance of each of the virtues and creates in the soul a numinous noetic world. He places sound understanding in the soul like a star-filled sky from which

two great luminaries – divine knowledge and contemplation of spiritual
essences – irradiate it with their light. He makes justice its firm
foundation, rich like the earth with every kind of sustenance. He puts
self-restraint within it as the air, cooling and refreshing it with a life free
from all impurity. He sets courage like a sea around the weakness of our
nature, enabling us to undermine the strongholds and citadels of the
enemy. In thus establishing this world the Logos fills the soul with the
power of the Holy Spirit, so as to maintain it in unceasing noetic activity
and in indissoluble and enduring unity. As the Psalmist expresses it, 'By
the Logos of the Lord are the heavens established, and all their power
lies in the Spirit that comes from Him' (Ps. 33 : 6. LXX).

50. Our spiritual growth corresponds to the different stages in the
life of our Lord Jesus Christ. While we are infants in need of milk (cf.
Heb. 5 : 12) we are suckled on the milk of the introductory virtues
acquired through bodily discipline; yet this is of but limited profit (cf.
1 Tim. 4 : 8) to us once we begin to grow in virtue and gradually leave
our infancy behind. When we attain adolescence and are nourished by
the solid food of the contemplation of the spiritual essences of things –
for our soul's organs of perception are now well attuned (cf. Heb.
5 : 14) – it may be said that we increase in stature and in grace (cf.
Luke 2 : 52), and sit among the elders (cf. Luke 2 : 46), disclosing to
them things hidden in the depths of darkness (cf. Job 12 : 22). When
we have reached 'mature manhood, the measure of the stature of the
fullness of Christ' (Eph. 4 : 13), we proclaim to all the meaning of
repentance, teach others about the kingdom of heaven (cf. Matt.
4 : 17) and press on towards the Passion (cf. Luke 12 : 50). For this
is the ultimate goal of everyone who has reached perfection in the
practice of the virtues: after passing through all the different ages of
Christ he finally undergoes the trials that Christ suffered on the cross.

51. So long as we are learning the basic principles of bodily
discipline, watching ourselves carefully when we taste food, or touch
things, or gaze at beautiful objects, or listen to music, or smell
fragrances, we are under guardians and trustees; for we are still infants,
even though we are also heirs and lords of all that belongs to the
Father. But when the time of such training is over and we have attained
dispassion, the Logos is born within us as a result of our purity of mind,
and He submits to the law of the Spirit, so that He may redeem us who
are under the law of the will of the flesh and may grant us the status of
sonship. When this has taken place, the Spirit cries in our hearts,

'Abba! Father!', making this status known to us and revealing to us our intimate communion with the Father. And He abides in us and converses with us as sons and heirs of God through Christ, free from servitude to the senses (cf. Gal. 4 : 1–6).

52. For those who like Peter have advanced in faith, and like James have been restored in hope, and like John have achieved perfection in love, the Lord ascends the high mountain of theology and is transfigured (cf. Matt. 17 : 1). Through the disclosure and expression of His pure teaching He shines upon them as the sun, and with the intellections of His unutterable wisdom He becomes radiant with light. They see the Logos standing between Moses and Elijah – between law and prophecy – promulgating the law and teaching it to them, and at the same time revealing to them through vision and prophecy the depths and the hidden treasures of wisdom. The Holy Spirit overshadows them like a luminous cloud, and from the cloud they hear the voice of mystical theology, initiating them into the mystery of the tri-hypostatic Divinity and saying, 'This is My beloved, the Logos of perfection made manifest, in whom I take delight. Become for Me perfect sons in the perfect Spirit' (cf. Matt. 17 : 1–5).

53. A soul that disdains everything unspiritual and that is wholly wounded by love for God undergoes a strange divine ecstasy. Having clearly grasped the inner nature and essence of created beings, as well as the upshot of matters human, it cannot bear to be imprisoned or circumscribed by anything. On the contrary, surpassing its own limitations, rebelling against the fetters of the senses and transcending all creatureliness, it penetrates the divine darkness of theology in unutterable silence and – to the degree that grace permits – it perceives in the intellective light of inexpressible wisdom the beauty of Him who truly is. Reverentially entering ever more deeply into intellective contemplation of that beauty, it savours, in loving awe, the fruits of immortality – the visionary intellections of the Divine. Never withdrawing from these back into itself, it is able to express perfectly their magnificence and glory. Activated, as it were, in a strange way by the Spirit, it experiences this admirable passion in unspeakable joy and silence; yet how it is activated, or what it is that impels it, and is seen by it, and secretly communicates to it unutterable mysteries, it cannot explain.

54. If you sow tears of compunction in yourself for the sake of righteousness you will gather a harvest of life – inexpressible joy (cf. Ps.

126 : 5). If you search out the Lord and patiently wait for Him until the firstlings of His righteousness grow in you, you will reap a rich crop of divine knowledge. The light of wisdom will illuminate you and you will become a lamp of eternal light illuminating all men. You will not be grudging towards yourself or your fellow beings, hiding under the cloak of envy the light of wisdom given to you (cf. Matt. 5 : 15); but in the assembly of the faithful you will utter good words for the edification of many, explaining things hidden since the beginning of the world – all that you have heard from above, prompted by the divine Spirit, all that you have come to understand through the contemplation of the inner nature of created beings, and all that your fathers have told you (cf. Ps. 78 : 2–3. LXX).

55. The practice of God's commandments will lead the spiritual contestant to such heights that on the day when he becomes perfect in virtue he will be filled with quiet delight and will reign with a pure mind in Zion. The mountains – the spiritual principles of the virtues – will flow with milk, nourishing him as he reposes in the sanctuary of dispassion, and all the stream-beds of Judah – his faith and spiritual knowledge – will flow with water, with doctrines, parables and the arcane symbols of things divine. As from the house of God a fountain of ineffable wisdom will flow from his heart and will water the valley of dry reeds – all those, that is to say, who have been withered by the aridity and heat of the passions (cf. Joel 3 : 18. LXX). Then he will experience in himself the true fulfilment of the Lord's words, 'Rivers of living water will flow from the heart of him who believes in Me' (John 7 : 38).

56. For those who fear Me, says God, the Sun of righteousness will rise with healing in its wings. They will go forth from the prison-house of the passions and, loosed from the bonds of sin, they will leap like calves. On the day when God restores them they will tread the wicked and the demons under their feet like ashes; for they will be exalted by all the virtues and because of their wisdom and spiritual knowledge they will be made perfect through communion in the Spirit (cf. Mal. 4 : 2–3).

57. If on the mountain above the plain of this world and within the Church of Christ you raise the standard of new spiritual knowledge and cry aloud, as the prophet says (cf. Isa. 13 : 2), with the wisdom given to you by God, exhorting and teaching your brethren – opening their mind to the divine Scriptures so that they understand the

wonderful gifts of God, and encouraging them to practise His commandments – do not fear those who envy you the power of your words and distort every text of divine Scripture; for they are people swept empty and ready to be occupied by the demons (cf. Matt. 12 : 44). God will write what you say in the book of the living (cf. Rev. 3 : 5) and no harm will befall you from such men, just as no harm befell Peter from Simon Magus (cf. Acts 8 : 9–24). On the contrary, when you see such people trying to put obstacles in your way, you should say with the prophet: 'Behold, my God is my salvation and I will trust in Him; I will be saved by Him and will not be afraid; for the Lord is my glory and my praise, and He has become my salvation; and I shall not cease proclaiming His glorious deeds throughout the world' (cf. Isa. 12 : 2, 4. LXX).

58. When you perceive that the passions are no longer active within you, and when because of your humility tears of compunction flow from your eyes, then you must know that the kingdom of God has come upon you and that you have become pregnant with the Holy Spirit. And when you perceive the Spirit moving and speaking in your heart, inciting you to proclaim in the great congregation the saving power and truth of God (cf. Ps. 40 : 10), do not keep your lips sealed for fear of provoking the envy of bigoted men; but as Isaiah counsels (cf. Isa. 30 : 8), sit and write on a tablet, what the Spirit says to you, so that it may endure in times to come and for ever. For the envious are a rebellious people, lying sons who cannot be trusted (cf. Isa. 30 : 9). They do not want to be told that the Gospel is still effective and makes us friends of God and prophets. On the contrary, they say to the prophets and teachers of the Church: 'Do not proclaim God's wisdom to us'; and to the visionaries who perceive the spiritual essences of things, they say, 'Do not tell us about that, but speak and proclaim to us another deceit such as the world loves, and free us from the prophecy of Israel' (cf. Isa. 30 : 10). Pay no attention to their malice and their words; for even the deaf will eventually hear your message, divinely inspired as it is for the profit of many, and those blinded by life's opacity and the fog of sin will see the light of your words. The poor in spirit will exult in them, and those in despair will be filled with gladness; through your words those spiritually astray will attain understanding, those who revile you will learn obedience to the utterances of the Spirit, and inarticulate tongues will be taught to speak of peace (cf. Isa. 29 : 18–19, 24. LXX).

59. Blessed is he, says Isaiah, who sows the seeds of his teaching in Zion – that is, in the Church of God – and who begets spiritual children in the heavenly Jerusalem of the firstborn (cf. Isa. 31 : 9. LXX). For according to Scripture such a man may conceal his words for a while, and may himself be hidden as if by flowing water; but in the end he will be revealed in Zion – in the Church of the faithful – as a glorious river flowing in a land thirsty for the waters of his wisdom. Then those beguiled by the envious will listen to his words, the heart of those spiritually weak will give heed, and no longer will the servants of envy enjoin silence when in his devotion he gives good counsel, instead of declaiming the inanities of the wise fools of this world. For his heart has not been occupied with empty thoughts, with ways of doing evil and telling lies in God's sight, thus misleading hungry souls and leaving the souls of the thirsty unsatisfied (cf. Isa. 32 : 2–6. LXX). For this reason his words will endure and many will profit from them, even though the spiteful and malicious do not believe this to be so.

60. He who dwells in a cave high up on a great rock will be sated with the bread of spiritual knowledge and made drunk with the cup of wisdom, and hence his counsel will be trustworthy. He will see a king arrayed in glory and he will gaze on a distant land. His soul will meditate on wisdom and he will proclaim to all men the eternal abode that embraces all and everything.

61. The Lord's teaching is heard by all who fear Him; He gives them an ear with which to hear, and an instructed tongue so that they know when they too must speak (cf. Isa. 50 : 4–5. LXX). Who but He sets at naught the prudent and the wise of this world and shows their wisdom to be folly, yet confirms the words of His servants (cf. Isa. 44 : 25–26. LXX)? He it is that in His glory does new and astonishing things: He makes a highway of humility and gentleness in the barren and arid heart, and opens rivers of ineffable wisdom in the parched and desiccated mind, giving water to the chosen people that He made His own, so that they may declare His virtues (cf. Isa. 43 : 20–21. LXX). He marches at the head of those who love and fear Him, razes the mountains of the passions, shatters the brazen gates of ignorance, and opens the doors of the knowledge of God, revealing to them its obscure, secret and invisible treasures, so that they may know that He is the Lord their God, who calls them by their name, 'Israel' (cf. Isa. 45 : 1–3. LXX).

62. Who is this that strikes terror into the sea of the passions and

quells its waves? It is the Lord of hosts, who delivers those that love Him from the danger of sin and pacifies the turbulence of their thoughts, who puts His words into their mouth (cf. Jer. 1 : 9) and protects them under the shadow of His hands – the shadow within which He established the heaven and made firm the earth. He it is who gives to those who fear Him an instructed tongue (cf. Isa. 50 : 4) and an understanding ear, so that they may hear His voice and proclaim His commandments to the house of Jacob, to the Church of the faithful. Those who lack eyes to see the rays of the Sun of righteousness, and ears to hear of God's glory, are sunk in the darkness of total ignorance, of empty hope and vain words. Not one of them speaks justly or judges truly; for they have put their trust in vanities and their words are vacuous. They conceive envy and beget spite and malice (cf. Isa. 59 : 4. LXX), for their ears are obdurate and deaf. On account of this they revile the word of God's knowledge and refuse to listen to it.

63. What wisdom is there in those filled with pangs of envy against their fellow beings? By what right do the malicious claim, in the words of Jeremiah, that 'we are wise and the law of the Lord is with us' (Jer. 8 : 8), when they are consumed with jealousy against those who have received the grace of the Spirit in the form of wisdom and divine knowledge? But the false knowledge of the scribes and the wise men of this world – of those who have lost the path of true knowledge – is altogether valueless. For this reason the worldly-wise, void of the wisdom of the Paraclete, founder in confusion: they see the sons of fishermen rich in the wisdom of God and they quail at the power of their words; but at the same time they are entangled in the nets of their own concepts and reasoning, for they have rejected true wisdom and truly divine knowledge.

64. Why are these creatures of malice consumed with jealousy against those rich in the grace of the Spirit, against those blessed with a tongue of fire like the pen of a ready scribe (cf. Ps. 45 : 1)? Have they not spurned the source of divine wisdom? Had they walked in the way of God, they would have dwelt in the peace of dispassion for ever. They would have learnt where they could find sound understanding, strength, clear judgment, spiritual knowledge of created beings, length of days, life, light for the eyes and wisdom yoked with peace. They would have learnt who finds the dwelling-place of Wisdom and who enters into her storehouses (cf. Bar. 3 : 13–15), and how God issues a command through the prophet to those initiated into His

teaching, and says, 'Let the prophet to whom things have been revealed in sleep declare his vision, and having heard My teaching let him proclaim it faithfully' (cf. Jer. 23 : 28); as He also says, 'Write in a book all the words I have spoken to you' (Jer. 37 : 2. LXX). Had they themselves chosen this path, they would not be consumed with jealousy against those who do choose it.

65. Yet if the Ethiopian can change his skin or the leopard his spots (cf. Jer. 13 : 23), these same bantlings of malice can also speak and devise what seems good, well versed as they are in evil. With the heel they trip up their fellow men, their ways being ways of treachery and deception, even with regard to their friends. They lie because lying and quackery are what they are trained in (cf. Jer. 9 : 4–5. LXX). So if on account of your intelligence and spiritual knowledge you become a butt for their jealousy and deceit, you must be wary: appeal to God in the words of Jeremiah, saying, 'O Lord, remember me and visit me and free me from those who persecute me with their malice. Although it is Thy will to test me for a long time, in Thy forbearance do not reject me. See how those who repudiate Thy sacred knowledge have derided me. Consume them in their jealousy, and Thy teaching will be a joy to me and the delight of my heart. I have not sat in the company of those who spurn Thy knowledge, but have feared the presence of Thy hand, and sat alone because I was filled with bitterness by their envy.' When you say this you will hear the response: ' "This I know well. But if you set him who has gone astray on his right path, I will re-establish you among My friends; you will stand before Me; and if you extract what is precious from what is vile, you will be as My mouth. I will deliver you from these malicious people who plague you", says the Lord God of Israel' (cf. Jer. 15 : 15–21. LXX).

66. Let these malicious sages hear the conclusion of the whole matter (cf. Eccles. 12 : 13). By their labours were God's Nazirites cleansed cleaner than snow; their lives were whiter than milk, their wisdom was more lambent than the sapphire (cf. Lam. 4 : 7. LXX), their words purer than a pearl. Those who delight in worldly knowledge have been utterly destroyed by the departure of the Spirit. Those nourished on profane wisdom are swathed in the dung of ignorance (cf. Lam. 4 : 5. LXX): they are shackled in fetters, their tongue is pinioned to their larynx and they are mute. For they have rejected the true wisdom and knowledge of the Holy Spirit, not wanting to attain it through ascetic labour.

67. God who fells the lofty tree and raises the lowly tree, who desiccates green wood and make dry wood burgeon (cf. Ezek. 17 : 24), is also the God who opens the mouth of His servants in the midst of a great assembly (cf. Ezek. 29 : 21. LXX), and enables them to proclaim the Gospel with full power (cf. Ps. 68 : 12. LXX). For wisdom, understanding and strength are His; and just as He changes times and seasons, so He gives to souls that seek Him and desire Him sovereignty over the passions; He converts them from one life to another, bestowing wisdom on the wise in spirit and sound understanding on those endowed with intelligence. He reveals deep hidden things to those who explore His depths and initiates them into the meaning concealed in obscure symbolism. For the light of wisdom and spiritual knowledge dwells in Him and He gives it to whom He wishes (cf. Dan. 2 : 21–22).

68. If you patiently carry out the commandments in accordance with your outer and your inner self, and look only to the glory of God, you will be given the honour of heavenly knowledge, peace of soul and incorruptibility; for you carry out, and do not simply hear, the law of grace (cf. Jas. 1 : 25). God will not condemn your knowledge, since your actions will bear witness to it. On the contrary, He will glorify it through the words of knowledge spoken by those who by virtue of His wisdom shine as beacons in the Church of the faithful; for God is 'impartial' (Rom. 2 : 11). If on the other hand your endeavours are prompted by selfish ambition and you reject the teachings of those inspired by the Holy Spirit, trusting in your own understanding and in the deceptive words of those clad merely in the outward forms of piety and incited by a vainglorious and hedonistic spirit, then you will be filled with affliction and anguish, with envy, anger and animosity (cf. Rom. 2 : 8–9). Such will be the immediate reward for your delusion, and such at your death – when God judges the secrets of men and renders to each according to his actions (cf. Rom. 2 : 6) – will be the sentence for your mutually self-accusing, self-defending thoughts.

69. 'He is not a real Jew who is one outwardly,' says St Paul, 'nor is true circumcision something external and physical; he is a Jew who is one inwardly, and real circumcision is a matter of the heart, spiritual and not literal' (Rom. 2 : 28–29). Similarly, you are not perfect in wisdom and spiritual knowledge because you give an outward and voluble appearance of being so; and you are proficient in virtue, not

because you adopt extreme forms of bodily and outward ascetic practice, but because you dedicate yourself to hidden spiritual work. You are wise and perfect in knowledge when you speak from a pure unsullied heart through the Spirit of God, not when you repeat things according to the letter. Then 'you will receive praise not from men but from God' (Rom. 2 : 29), since you will be unknown to men or else envied by them, and beloved and known only by God and those inspired by God's Spirit.

70. If carrying out the law does not make you pure in the sight of God (cf. Gal. 2 : 16), then neither will ascetic struggle and labour alone perfect you in God's sight. We do indeed receive our grounding in virtue and check the activity of the passions through ascetic practice; but we are not initiated into the fullness of Christ through that alone. What, then, brings us to perfection? An ingrained faith in God, the 'faith that makes real the things for which we hope' (Heb. 11 : 1), the faith whereby Abel offered to God a better sacrifice than Cain and was commended as righteous (cf. Heb. 11 : 4), and whereby Abraham obeyed when he was called to go out and sojourn in the promised land (cf. Heb. 11 : 8). It is such faith that fills those assiduous in the search for truth with great aspiration for the exalted gifts of God, and leads them to the spiritual knowledge of created beings; and it pours into their hearts the inexhaustible treasures of the Spirit, enabling them to bring thence new and old mysteries of God (cf. Matt. 13 : 52) and to reveal them to the needy. He who is blessed with such faith is initiated by love into the knowledge of God, and has entered into God's rest, having ceased from all his labours as God did from His (cf. Heb. 4 : 10).

71. If God once swore to non-believers that they would never enter into His rest – and it was on account of their lack of faith that they could not do so (cf. Heb. 3 : 18–19) – how can mere bodily discipline, in the absence of faith, enable us to enter the rest of dispassion and the perfection of spiritual knowledge? We do in fact see many who because of this are unable to enter and to rest from their labours. We must therefore be wary lest we possess an evil, unbelieving heart (cf. Heb. 3 : 12), and because of this are thwarted of rest and perfection, in spite of our great labours. Otherwise we will be ceaselessly involved in the toils of the ascetic life and will always eat the bread of sorrow (cf. Ps. 127 : 2). If a sabbath rest awaits us – the rest of dispassion and of perfect gnosis – let us through faith strive to enter into it, and not fall

short of it because of our unbelief in the same way as those mentioned in the Bible (cf. Heb. 4 : 9–11).

72. Since we are endowed with senses, intelligence and intellection, we too ought to offer a tithe from ourselves to God (cf. Heb. 7 : 2). As beings endowed with senses we ought to perceive sensory things in the right way, through their beauty elevating ourselves to the Creator and referring back to Him our true knowledge of them. As intelligent beings we ought to speak correctly about divine and human matters. As noetic beings we ought unerringly to apprehend what pertains to God and eternal life, to the kingdom of heaven and the mysteries of the Spirit hidden within it. In this way how we perceive, speak and apprehend will conform to God, and will be genuinely true and divine, constituting a sacred offering to God.

73. The tithe that we offer to God is in the true sense the soul's Passover – its passing beyond, that is to say, every passion-embroiled state and all mindless sense-perception. In this Passover the Logos is offered up in the contemplation of the spiritual essences of created beings; He is eaten in the bread of spiritual knowledge; and His precious blood is drunk in the chalice of ineffable wisdom. Thus he who has fed upon and celebrated this Passover makes a sacred offering within himself of the Lamb who effaces the world's sin (cf. John 1 : 29); and he will no longer die but, in the Lord's words, 'will live eternally' (John 6 : 58).

74. If you have been raised above dead actions you are resurrected with Christ. And if you are resurrected with Christ through spiritual knowledge, and Christ no longer dies, then you will not be overcome by the death of ignorance. For the death which you have now died to sin, prompted by an impulse in accordance with nature, you have died once for all; but the life you now live you live in God through the freedom of the Holy Spirit, who has raised you above the dead actions of sin (cf. Rom. 6 : 9–11). Thus you will no longer live according to the flesh, in a fallen worldly state, for you will have died to the mortal members of your body and to worldly matters. On the contrary, Christ will live in you (cf. Gal. 2 : 20), for you will be guided by the grace of the Holy Spirit, not enslaved to the law of your outer unregenerate self; and your members will be weapons of righteousness consecrated to God the Father (cf. Rom. 6 : 13).

75. He who has freed his members from servitude to the passions, and has consecrated them to the service of righteousness (cf. Rom.

6 : 19), has risen above the law of his fallen self and has begun to share in the sanctification of the Holy Spirit. Sin will no longer dominate him, since he is free in the freedom and the law of the Spirit. Serving righteousness has an effect altogether different from that of servitude to sin. The latter inevitably leads to the destruction of the soul's noetic power, while the former leads to the eternal life hidden in Christ Jesus our Lord (cf. Col. 3 : 3).

76. So long as you live according to your fallen impulses you are dominated by your fallen mortal self. But once you die to the world, you are set free from this domination (cf. Rom. 7 : 2). We cannot die to the world unless we die to the mortal aspects of ourselves. We die to these when we become participants in the Holy Spirit. We know ourselves to be participants in the Holy Spirit when we offer to God fruits worthy of the Spirit: love for God with all our soul and genuine love for our fellow beings; joy of heart issuing from a clear conscience; peace of soul as a result of dispassion and humility; generosity in our thoughts, long-suffering in affliction and times of trial, kindness and restraint in our behaviour, deep-rooted unwavering faith in God, gentleness springing from humble-mindedness and compunction, and complete control of the senses. When we bear such fruits for God, we escape from the domination of our mortal self; and there is no law condemning and punishing us for the death-purveying fruits we produced while still living in an unregenerate state. Once we have risen with Christ above dead actions the freedom of the Spirit releases us from the law of our fallen self (cf. Rom. 7 : 4–6).

77. Those who, having passed through the 'washing of regeneration' (Tit. 3 : 4), possess the firstfruits of the Spirit, and who preserve them unimpaired, are deeply afflicted by the burden of their fallen self; and they long for their adoption as sons through the full gift of the Paraclete, so that their body may be freed from servitude to corruption (cf. Rom. 8 : 23). Indeed, the Spirit helps them in their natural weaknesses and intercedes for them 'with sighs too deep for words' (Rom. 8 : 26); for they have conformed their will to God and are filled with the hope of experiencing in their mortal flesh the 'revelation of the sons of God' (Rom. 8 : 19), the life-quickening death of Jesus (cf. 2 Cor. 4 : 10). In this way they too will be called sons of God, for they will be guided by the Holy Spirit, will be freed from servitude to the fallen self, and will attain 'the glorious liberty of the children of God' (Rom. 8 : 21), for

whom, since they love God, 'all things work together for their good' (Rom. 8 : 28).

78. Divine Scripture is to be interpreted spiritually and the treasures it contains are revealed only through the Holy Spirit to the spiritual. Hence the unspiritual man cannot receive the revelation of these treasures (cf. 1 Cor. 2 : 14). The ceaseless flow of his own thoughts makes it impossible for him to understand or listen to anything said by someone else. For he lacks the Spirit of God, that searches the depths of God (cf. 1 Cor. 2 : 10) and knows the things of God. He possesses only the material spirit of the world, full of jealousy and envy, of strife and discord; and for this reason he thinks it foolish to enquire into the sense and meaning of the written word. Unable to understand that everything in divine Scripture concerning things divine and human is to be interpreted spiritually, he mocks those who do interpret it in this way. Calling such people not 'spiritual', or 'guided by the Spirit', but 'anagogical', he twists and distorts their words and their divine intellections as much as he can, like the notorious Demas (cf. 2 Tim. 4 : 10). The spiritual man does not behave in this manner; on the contrary, inspired by the Holy Spirit, he discerns all things, but he himself cannot be called to account by anyone. For he has the intellect of Christ, and that no one can teach (cf. 1 Cor. 2 : 15–16).

79. Since the day of judgment will be one of fire, what each of us has done, as St Paul says, will be tested by fire (cf. 1 Cor. 3 : 13). Thus, if what we have built up is of an incorruptible nature, it will not be destroyed by fire; and not only will it not be consumed, but it will be made radiant, totally purified of whatever small amount of filth may adhere to it. But if the work with which we have burdened ourselves consists of corruptible matter, it will be consumed and burnt up and we will be left destitute in the midst of the fire (cf. 1 Cor. 3 : 13–15). Incorruptible and imperishable actions are the following: tears of repentance, acts of charity, compassion, prayer, humility, faith, hope, love and whatever else is done in a spirit of devotion. Even while we are still alive such actions help to build us up into a holy temple of God (cf. Eph. 2 : 21–22), while when we die they accompany us and remain incorruptibly with us for ever. The actions which are consumed by the fire are well known to all: self-indulgence, vainglory, avarice, hatred, envy, theft, drunkenness, abusiveness, censoriousness, and anything else of a base nature to which our appetites or incensive

power prompts us to give bodily expression. Such actions pollute us even while we are still living and consumed by the fire of desire; and when we are wrenched away from the body, they accompany us but do not survive. On the contrary, they are destroyed and leave their perpetrator in the midst of the fire, to be punished immortally for all eternity.

80. If through humility and prayer you have been initiated into the spiritual knowledge of God, this means that you are known by God and enriched by Him with an authentic knowledge of His supranatural mysteries. If you are tainted with conceit, you have not been so initiated, but are governed by the spirit of this material world. Thus, even if you imagine that you know something, in fact you know nothing about things divine in the way you ought to (cf. 1 Cor. 8 : 2). If, however, you love God and regard nothing as more precious than love for God and for your fellow being, you will also know the depths of God and the mysteries of His kingdom in the way that someone inspired by the Holy Spirit must know them. And you are known by God (cf. 1 Cor. 8 : 3), for you are a true worker in the paradise of His Church, out of love doing God's will – that is to say, converting others, making the unworthy worthy through the understanding given you by the Holy Spirit, and keeping your actions inviolate through humility and compunction.

81. All of us were baptized into Christ through water and the Holy Spirit, and we all eat the same spiritual food and drink the same spiritual drink; yet, though this food and drink are Christ Himself, God finds no delight in most of us (cf. 1 Cor. 10 : 4–5). For many of those faithful and diligent in ascetic practice and bodily discipline have mortified and emaciated their bodies; but because they lacked the compunction that comes from a contrite and virtuous state of mind, and the compassion that springs from love for their fellow beings as well as for themselves, they have remained bereft of the fullness of the Holy Spirit, remote from the spiritual knowledge of God. Their mind's womb is sterile and their intelligence without salt or illumination.

82. What the Logos seeks from the Nazirites is not simply to ascend Mount Sinai through ascetic practice or to be purified before ascending and to wash their clothes and to abstain from intercourse with a woman (cf. Exod. 19 : 14–15). It is also to see, not the rearward parts of God (cf. Exod. 33 : 23), but God Himself in His glory rejoicing in them, bestowing on them the tables of spiritual

knowledge, and sending them out to instruct His people (cf. Exod. 32 : 15).

83. The Logos does not take all His servants and disciples with Him when He reveals His hidden and greater mysteries; He takes only those to whom an ear has been given and whose eye has been opened and in whom a new tongue has been trained to speak clearly. Taking such people with Him and separating them from the others – even though the latter are likewise His disciples – He ascends Mount Tabor, the mountain of contemplation, and is transfigured before them (cf. Matt. 17 : 2). He does not yet initiate them into the mysteries of the kingdom of heaven, but shows them the glory and resplendence of the Divinity. And through the light that He gives He makes their life and intelligence shine like the sun in the midst of the Church of the faithful. He transforms their intellections into the whiteness and purity of the brightest light, and puts in them His own intellect, and sends them out to proclaim things new and old (cf. Matt. 13 : 52) for the edification of His Church.

84. Many have cultivated their own fields with great diligence and have sown pure seed in them, cutting away the thorn-bushes and burning the thistles on the fire of repentance; but because God did not water these fields with the compunction-born rain of the Holy Spirit, they did not yield anything. Parched as they were they did not bring forth the rich grain of the knowledge of God. Thus even if they did not perish through a total dearth of the divine Logos, they certainly died poor in the knowledge of God and with hands empty, having provided themselves with but scant nourishment for the divine banquet.

85. When someone says something that edifies his fellow beings, he speaks out of the goodness stored up in his heart, since he himself is good, as the Lord confirms (cf. Luke 6 : 45). No one can devote himself to theology and speak about what pertains to God unless so empowered by the Holy Spirit; and no one when inspired by the Spirit of God says anything contrary to faith in Christ (cf. 1 Cor. 12 : 3). But he says only what is edifying, only what leads others to God and His kingdom and restores them to their original nobility, bringing them to salvation and uniting them to God. And if 'the manifestation of the Spirit is given to each to the degree that is profitable' (1 Cor. 12 : 7), this means that anyone enriched with the wisdom of God and blessed with spiritual knowledge is inspired by the divine Spirit and is a storehouse of the inexhaustible treasures of God.

86. No one baptized into Christ and believing in Him is left without a share in the grace of the Spirit, so long as he has not succumbed to any diabolic influence and defiled his faith with evil actions, or does not live slothfully and dissolutely. Provided he has preserved unextinguished the firstfruits of the Holy Spirit, which he received from holy baptism, or, if he has extinguished them, has rekindled them through acts of righteousness, he cannot but receive from God the fullness of this grace. He may after worthily engaging in spiritual combat be blessed through the plenitude of the Spirit with the consciousness of God's wisdom and so become a teacher in the Church; or he may through the same Spirit be given knowledge of God's mysteries and so come to understand the mysteries of the kingdom of heaven; or from the same Spirit he may acquire deep-rooted faith in God's promises, as Abraham did (cf. Gen. 15 : 6; Rom. 4 : 3). He may receive the gift of healing, so that he can cure diseases; or of spiritual power, so that he can expel demons and perform miracles; or of prophecy, so that he can foresee and predict things of the future; or of the ability to distinguish between spirits, so that he can discern who is speaking in the Spirit of God and who is not; or of the interpretation of various tongues, or of helping the weary, or of governing God's flocks and His people, or of love for all men and the gifts of grace that go with it, long-suffering, kindness and the rest (cf. 1 Cor. 12 : 8–10, 28). If you are bereft of all these qualities, there is no way in which I can call you a believer or number you among those who have 'clothed themselves in Christ' through divine baptism (cf. Gal. 3 : 27).

87. If you possess love, you feel no jealousy or envy. You are not boastful, carried away by reckless pride. Nor do you put on airs with anyone. Nor do you act shamefully towards your fellow beings. You seek, not simply what is to your own advantage, but what also benefits your fellow beings. You are not quickly provoked by those who are angry with you. You are not resentful if wrong is done to you, nor do you rejoice if your friends act unjustly, though you do rejoice with them over the truth of their righteousness. You put up with disagreeable eventualities. You believe all things in simplicity and innocence, and hope to receive everything promised to us by God. You patiently endure all trials, never rendering evil for evil. And, labourer of love that you are, you never waver in your love for your fellow beings (cf. 1 Cor. 13 : 4–8).

88. Of those granted the grace of the Holy Spirit in the form of various gifts, some are still immature and imperfect with regard to

these gifts, while others are mature and perfect, enjoying them in their fullness. The first, by increasing their efforts to practise the divine commandments, augment the spiritual gifts they have received so that they are filled with yet greater gifts, leaving those of immaturity behind. The mature and the perfect, having attained the summit of God's love and knowledge, cease from exercising partial gifts, whether of prophecy, or of distinguishing between spirits, or of helping, or of governing, and so on (cf. 1 Cor. 12 : 28). Once you have entered the palace of love you no longer know in part the God who is love (cf. 1 Cor. 13 : 9) but, conversing with Him face to face, you understand Him fully even as you yourself are fully understood by Him (cf. 1 Cor. 13 : 12).

89. If in your aspiration for spiritual gifts you have pursued and laid hold of love, you cannot content yourself with praying and reading solely for your own edification. If when you pray and psalmodize you speak to God in private you edify yourself, as St Paul says. But once you have laid hold of love you feel impelled to prophesy for the edification of God's Church (cf. 1 Cor. 14 : 2–4), that is, to teach your fellow men how to practise the commandments of God and how they must endeavour to conform to God's will. For of what benefit can it be to others if, while charged with their guidance, you always converse with yourself and God alone through prayer and psalmody, and do not also speak to those in your charge, whether through the revelation of the Holy Spirit, or out of knowledge of the mysteries of God, or by exercising the prophetic gift of foresight, or by teaching the wisdom of God (cf. 1 Cor. 14 : 6)? For which of your disciples will prepare for battle against the passions and the demons (cf. 1 Cor. 14 : 8) if he does not receive clear instructions from you either in writing or by word of mouth? Truly, if it is not in order to edify his flock that the shepherd seeks to be richly endowed with the grace of teaching and the knowledge of the Spirit, he lacks fervour in his quest for God's gifts. By merely praying and psalmodizing inwardly with your tongue – that is, by praying in the soul – you edify yourself, but your intellect is unproductive (cf. 1 Cor. 14 : 14), for you do not prophesy with the language of sacred teaching or edify God's Church. If Paul, who of all men was the most closely united with God through prayer, would have rather spoken from his fertile intellect five words in church for the instruction of others than ten thousand words of psalmody in private (cf. 1 Cor. 14 : 19), surely those who have responsibility for others

have strayed from the path of love if they limit the shepherd's ministry solely to psalmody and reading.

90. He who has given us being by miraculously uniting and sustaining the two contrary aspects of our nature, material substratum and spiritual essence, has also given us the capacity for well-being, which we can realize by means of His wisdom and spiritual knowledge. Thus through spiritual knowledge we may perceive the hidden treasures of the kingdom of heaven that He discloses to us, and through wisdom we may make known to our fellow-men the riches of His supernal goodness and the blessings of eternal life which He has prepared for the joy of those who love Him (cf. 1 Cor. 2 : 9).

91. He who has risen above the threats and promises of the three laws and has entered into the life which is not subject to law has himself become the law of the Church and is not ruled by law. The life that is free is not subject to law, and therefore transcends all physical necessity and change. He who has attained such a life is as if liberated from his fallen unregenerate self, and through his participation in the Spirit he becomes incandescent. Purged of all within him that is imperfect (cf. 1 Cor. 13 : 9–10), he is united wholly with Christ, who transcends all nature.

92. If you embrace the knowledge of the primordial Intellect, who is the origin and consummation of all things, infinite in Himself, and existing both within all things and outside them, then you will know how to live as a solitary either by yourself or with other solitaries. For you will suffer no loss of perfection through being on your own, and no loss of solitude through being with others. On the contrary, you will be the same everywhere and alone among all. You will initiate in others their movement towards a life of solitude and will embody the highest perfection of virtue that they set before themselves.

93. The unconfused union and conjunction of soul and body constitutes, when maintained in harmony, a single reality, whether on the visible level or in their inner being. When not harmonious, there is civil war in which each side desires victory. But when the intelligence takes control, it at once puts an end to the jealousy and establishes concord, conforming the entire soul–body reality to its inner being and the Spirit.

94. Of the three main aspects of our being, the first rules the others and is not ruled by them, the second both rules and is ruled, the third does not rule but is ruled. Thus when the ruling aspect falls under the

domination of either of those aspects which are ruled, that which is by nature free becomes the servant of what are by nature servants; it loses its rightful pre-eminence and nature, and this provokes great discord among the three leading powers of the soul. So long as there is this discord among them, all things are not yet made subject to the divine Logos (cf. Heb. 2 : 8). But when the ruling aspect governs the others and brings them under its own direction and control, then the discordant elements, united into one and becoming concordant, are led peacefully to God. And when all is subjected to the Logos, He delivers the kingdom to God the Father (cf. 1 Cor. 15 : 24).

95. When the five senses are subject to the four principal virtues and maintain their obedience, they enable the body, composed of the four elements, tranquilly to fulfil the round of life. When the body is thus disposed, the soul's powers are not in a state of discord; the passible aspect of the appetitive and incensive powers is united with the power of the intelligence, and the intellect assumes its natural sovereignty. It makes the four principal virtues its chariot and the five subservient senses its seat. And once it has subdued the imperious and unregenerate self, the intellect is seized and borne heavenward in its four-horsed chariot and, led before the King of the ages, is crowned with the crown of victory and rests from its long endeavour.

96. For those who with the support of the Spirit have entered the fullness of contemplation, a chalice of wine is made ready, and bread from a royal banquet is set before them. A throne is prepared for their repose and silver for their wealth. Close at hand is a treasure-house of pearls and precious stones, and untold riches are bestowed upon them. Because of the promptness with which they act, their ascetic life renders them visionary and prepares them to be brought into the presence, not of sluggards, but of the King.

97. Is the kingdom of heaven already given in this life to all those advanced on the spiritual way, or is it given to them after the dissolution of the body? If in this life, our victory is unassailable, our joy inexpressible, and our path to paradise unimpeded: we are directly present in the divine East (cf. Gen. 2 : 8). But if it is given only after death and dissolution, we should ask that our departure from this life may take place without fear; we should learn what the kingdom of heaven is, what the kingdom of God is, and what paradise is, and how the one differs from the other; also what the nature of time is in each of them, and whether we enter all three, and how and when and after

how much time. If you enter the first while you are still alive and in the flesh you will not fail to enter the other two.

98. The world above is as yet incomplete, and awaits its fulfilment from the first-born of Israel – from those who see God; for it receives its completion from those who attain the knowledge of God. Once it is complete, and has brought to an end the lower world of believers and unbelievers, it constitutes a single congregation, allocating to each member his appointed place, and separating out what cannot be reconciled. It draws to itself the origins and ends of all other worlds and, itself unlimited, it sets bounds to them. It is not affected or limited by any other principle, as something that is under constraint. For it is ever-active, in such a way that it is never self-confined or extended beyond its own limits. It is the sabbath rest of other worlds and of every other principle and activity.

99. The nine[1] heavenly powers sing hymns of praise that have a threefold structure, as they stand in threefold rank before the Trinity, in awe celebrating their liturgy and glorifying God. Those who come first – immediately below Him who is the Source and Cause of all things and from whom they take their origin – are the initiators of the hymns and are named thrones, Cherubim and Seraphim. They are characterized by a fiery wisdom and a knowledge of heavenly things, and their supreme accomplishment is the godly hymn of El, as the Divinity is called in Hebrew. Those in the middle rank, encircling God between the first triad and the last, are the authorities, dominions and powers. They are characterized by their ordering of great events, their performance of wondrous deeds and working of miracles, and their supreme accomplishment is the Trisagion: Holy, Holy, Holy (cf. Isa. 6 : 3; Rev. 4 : 8). Those nearest to us, superior to us but below the more exalted ranks, are the principalities, archangels and angels. They are characterized by their ministrative function, and their supreme accomplishment is the sacred hymn Alleluia (cf. Rev. 19 : 1). When our intelligence is perfected through the practice of the virtues and is elevated through the knowledge and wisdom of the Spirit and by the divine fire, it is assimilated to these heavenly powers through the gifts of God, as by virtue of its purity it draws towards itself the particular characteristic of each of them. We are assimilated to the third rank through the ministration and performance of God's commandments.

[1] Reading *ennas* in place of *henas*.

We are assimilated to the second rank through our compassion and
solidarity with our fellow-men, as well as through our ordering of
matters great and divine, and through the activities of the Spirit. We
are assimilated to the first rank through the fiery wisdom of the Logos
and through knowledge of divine and human affairs. Perfected in this
way, and rewarded with the gifts that belong by nature to the heavenly
powers, our intelligence is united through them with the God of the
Decad, for it offers to Him from its own being the finest of all the
offerings that can be made by the tenth rank.

100. God is both Monad and Triad; He begins with the Monad and,
as Decad, He completes Himself through a cyclic movement.[1] Thus

---

[1] *The Decad*

In Pythagorean theory, the number ten is figurative of the Source of All. In this connection it is
the sum of the first four numbers, $1 + 2 + 3 + 4$, the Tetractys. These numbers first exist as
the simple Monad, Dyad, Triad and Tetrad. Their squares (viz. 1, 4, 9 and 16) are the
foundation of form and hence of manifestation.

In Jewish esoteric theory, as formulated in the Kabbalah, the number ten is most directly
connected with the Sefiroth, the metaphysical 'numbers' or 'numerations' of the ten principal
aspects of God. They form a tenfold hierarchy or concatenation, and are to the mystical
tradition of Judaism what the Ten Commandments are to the Torah, as the exoteric law. In
this respect they represent the spiritual archetypes not only of the Decalogue but also of all the
revelations of the Torah. They are the principal determinations or eternal causes of all things.
Thus the decad constitutes the intellections by which God, the 'cause of causes', makes
Himself known to Himself and operates His universal manifestation. It is the divine Unity in so
far as it reveals itself, in one intelligible mode or another, in the multiplicity of creation. It is in
this sense that it can be described as that in which or through which God 'completes' Himself.
At the same time, the existential multiplicity and separativeness of things is limited and
transitory, for, thanks to the universal concatenation, they return to the principial Unity, the
supreme Source of All, from which they came. This consummates the cyclic movement
through which God, as a decad, completes Himself. Yet the decad itself is figurative, and does
not imply that God has any specific number of attributes, since He is beyond all measurement
and numeration, and is infinite both in His hidden Essence and in His revealed qualities.

Nikitas Stithatos' decad has affinities with the decads of both the foregoing theories,
although it cannot be identified with either. It has its roots in the conception of the celestial
hierarchy or concatenation formulated by St Dionysios the Areopagite. This hierarchy
constitutes a threefold structure, each level of which consists of three orders or ranks (τάξεις)
of celestial intelligences, giving a total of nine such interlocking and mutually participating
orders. The function of the lowest of these orders, that of the angels, has two aspects. The first
is to transmit the divine grace and illumination, which it has received from God through the
mediation of the orders above it, to the order below it, the human order, that taken as a whole
thus represents the tenth order; the second is to convert the human intelligence, the 'finest of
all the offerings' that can be made by this human order, so that it mounts upward and stage by
stage returns, again through the mediation of the celestial hierarchy, to a state of union with its
divine Source and in this way achieves its divinization. This double mediation, descending and
ascending, constitutes the cyclic movement spoken of in the final text above.

He contains within Himself the origins and ends of all things. He is outside everything, since He transcends all things. To be within Him you must embrace the inner essences and possess a spiritual knowledge of created beings. Then while standing outside all things you will dwell within all things and know their origins and ends; for you will have attained a spiritual union with the Father through the Logos and will have been perfected in the Spirit. May the sovereignty of this all-perfect, indivisible and coessential Trinity, worshipped in Father, Son and Holy Spirit, and glorified in one nature, kingdom and power of Divinity, prevail throughout the ages. Amen.

THEOLIPTOS, METROPOLITAN OF PHILADELPHIA

Introductory Note

In the past the full significance of Theoliptos in the development of
fourteenth-century Orthodox theology has been underestimated,
largely because most of his writings remain still unpublished.[1] The
texts included in *The Philokalia* represent no more than a small part of
his total output. Born at Nicaea around 1250, Theoliptos was at first
married, but at an early age he separated from his wife and became a
monk. He suffered imprisonment because of his firm opposition to the
union between the Orthodox Church and the Church of Rome,
promulgated at the Council of Lyons (1274) and upheld by the
Emperor Michael VIII Palaiologos. Following Michael's death, Theoliptos was elevated to the see of Philadelphia in 1284, and held the
position of metropolitan there for nearly forty years. He led the heroic
defence of the city against Turkish attack in 1310, and died in 1322. He
was widely respected as a spiritual father, and his work in this sphere is
known to us above all through his letters of direction to the nun Irene-
Evlogia Choumnaina, abbess of the double monastery of Christ
Philanthropos Sotir in Constantinople. St Gregory Palamas, who in his
early years was a disciple of Theoliptos, in the *Triads* singles him out for
mention as one of the leading teachers of hesychasm who lived 'in our

---

[1] For a good survey of Theoliptos' life and writings, with full references to the earlier studies
by S. Salaville and V. Laurent, see Marie-Hélène Congourdeau, in *Dictionnaire de Spiritualité* xv
(1990), cols 446–59. On his spirituality, see Antonio Rigo, 'Nota sulla dottrina ascetico-
spirituale di Teolepto Metropolita di Filadelfia (1250/51–1322)', *Rivista di Studi Bizantini e
Neoellenici*, n.s. xxiv (1987), pp. 165–200. In English, consult Demetrios J. Constantelos,
'Mysticism and Social Involvement in the Later Byzantine Church: Theoleptos of Philadelphia
– a Case Study', *Byzantine Studies/Etudes Byzantines* vi (1979), pp. 83–94; Robert E. Sinkewicz,
'Church and Society in Asia Minor in the late Thirteenth Century: the Case of Theoleptos of
Philadelphia', in M. Gervers and R.J. Bikhazi (eds), *Conversion and Continuity: Indigenous
Christian Communities in Islamic Lands, Eighth to Eighteenth Centuries* (Toronto, 1989). Critical
editions of Theoliptos' works are being prepared by R.E. Sinkewicz and Angela Hero.

own day', and describes him as 'an authentic theologian and a trustworthy visionary of the truth of God's mysteries'.[1]

The main text included here, *On Inner Work in Christ and the Monastic Profession*, was addressed by Theoliptos to Irene-Evlogia, but in the manuscript used by St Makarios and St Nikodimos all the expressions originally in the feminine have been changed to the masculine. In our translation we have taken account of alternative readings supplied by Fr Sévérien Salaville.[2] *On Inner Work in Christ* is a brief but comprehensive survey of the monastic vocation, offering practical advice on the outward ordering of daily life – on behaviour in church and the refectory, on conversations within the community and with outside persons, on psalmody, spiritual reading, work and sleep – but dealing above all with inner prayer. Theoliptos draws a close parallel between monastic life and the sacrament of baptism.[3] He is apophatic in his approach, emphasizing the need to lay aside 'all representational images', thereby attaining 'an ignorance surpassing all knowledge'.[4] He refers several times to the invocation of the name of Jesus, and briefly mentions illumination by the divine light.[5] Here, drawing on earlier tradition, he anticipates the themes taken up by Palamas later in the fourteenth century.

[1] *Triads* I, ii, 12: see below, p. 341.
[2] 'Formes ou méthodes de prière d'après un byzantin du 14ᵉ siècle, Théolepte de Philadelphie', *Echos d'Orient* xxxix (1940), pp. 1–25.
[3] See. p. 178.
[4] See p. 181.
[5] See pp. 182, 184, 189.

On Inner Work in Christ and the Monastic Profession

The monastic profession is a lofty and fruitful tree whose root is detachment from all corporeal things, whose branches are freedom from passionate craving and total alienation from what you have renounced, and whose fruit is the acquisition of virtue, a deifying love, and the uninterrupted joy that results from these two things; for, as St Paul says, the fruit of the Spirit is love, joy, peace and the other things he mentions (cf. Gal. 5 : 22).

Flight from the world is rewarded by refuge in Christ. By 'world' I mean here attachment to sensory things and to worldly proclivities. If you detach yourself from such things through knowledge of the truth you are assimilated to Christ, acquiring a love for Him that allows you to put aside all worldly matters and to purchase the precious pearl, that is to say, Christ Himself (cf. Matt. 13 : 46).

You put on Christ through the baptism of salvation (cf. Gal. 3 : 27), being thus washed clean, illumined with spiritual grace and restored to your original nobility. But what happened then as a result of your weakness of will? Through over-attachment to the world you subverted your likeness to God, through coddling the flesh you rendered the divine image within you powerless, and with passion-embroiled thoughts you beclouded your soul's mirror so that Christ, the spiritual Sun, can no longer manifest Himself in it.

Now, however, you have transfixed your soul with the fear of God. You have recognized the world's benighted abnormity and the mental dissipation and vain distraction which it generates, and you have been wounded by a longing for stillness. Obedient to the precepts 'Seek peace and pursue it' (Ps. 34 : 14) and 'Return to your rest, O my soul' (Ps. 116 : 7), you have sought to bring peace to your thoughts. You have therefore resolved to regain the nobility that you received through grace at baptism, but jettisoned by your own free choice through your self-indulgence in the world; and accordingly you have entered this sacred school and set to work, donning the venerable habit of repentance and vowing courageously to remain in the monastery until death.

This is now the second covenant you have made with God. The first you made when you originally entered into this life; the second, as you swiftly approach its close. Then through the profession of the true faith you were numbered among Christ's flock; now you are united to Him through repentance. Then you found grace; now you have contracted an obligation. Then, still a little child, you were not aware of the honour conferred on you, although later, as you grew up, you began to appreciate the greatness of the gift and restrained your tongue accordingly. Now, having reached complete understanding, you fully recognize the significance of the vow you are taking. Beware lest you fail to fulfil this promise as well, and are cast, like some shattered pot, into the outer darkness where there is weeping and gnashing of teeth (cf. Matt. 8 : 12). No path other than that of repentance leads to salvation.

Listen to what David promises you: 'You have made the Most High your refuge' (Ps. 91 : 9) and, if on the model of Christ you choose a life of tribulation, 'no plague will come near you' (Ps. 91 : 10) – no evil, that is to say, will be inflicted on you because of your worldly life. Now that you have chosen to repent, you will not be shadowed by avidity, self-indulgence, self-glorification, self-display or sensual dissipation. Distraction of the mind, captivity of the intellect, the levity of successive thoughts, and every other kind of deliberate prevarication and confusion – from all such aberrations you will be set free. Nor will you be constrained by the love of parents, brothers and sisters, relatives, friends and acquaintances, and you will not waste time in pointless meetings and talks with them.

If you thus give yourself soul and body to the religious life, no scourge of anguish will afflict you (cf. Ps. 91 : 10), nor will distress pierce your heart or darken your countenance. Distress is muted in those who have renounced the life of pleasure and are free from attachment to the things that I have mentioned, for Christ reveals Himself to the striving soul and bestows ineffable joy on the heart. No worldly delight or suffering can take away this spiritual joy, for holy meditation, the mindfulness of God that brings salvation, divine thoughts and words of wisdom nourish and protect everyone engaged in spiritual warfare. That is why such a person treads upon all mindless desire and headstrong anger as upon an asp or basilisk, quelling pleasure as though it were a snake and wrath as though it were a lion (cf. Ps. 91 : 13. LXX). This is because he has transferred all his hope from men and from worldly things to God, has been enriched with divine knowledge and always calls spiritually upon God to come to his aid. As the Psalmist writes, 'Because he has set his hope on Me, I will deliver him; I will protect him, because he has known My name. He shall call upon Me, and I will answer him: not only will I deliver him from those who afflict him, but I will also glorify him' (cf. Ps. 91 : 15–16).

Do you see the struggles of those who lead a godly ascetic life, and the rewards granted them? Then put your calling into action without more ado. Just as you have secluded yourself bodily, rejecting worldly things, so likewise seclude yourself in soul by subjecting also the thoughts of all such things. You have changed your outward clothing; make your monastic profession into a reality. You have separated yourself from crowds of strangers; distance yourself also from the few who are related to you by birth. If you do not put an end to delusions prompted by external things, you will not overcome those that ambush you from within. If you do not triumph over those who fight against you with visible means, you will not repulse your invisible enemies. But when you have quelled both external and inner distraction, your intellect will rise to spiritual labour and spiritual discourse. In the place of conventional dealings with relatives and friends you will follow the ways of virtue; and instead of filling your soul with vain words born of worldly contacts, you will illumine and fill it with understanding through meditating upon the meaning of Holy Scripture.

To give free rein to the senses is to shackle the soul, to shackle the senses is to liberate it. When the sun sets, night comes; when Christ leaves the soul, the darkness of the passions envelops it and incorporeal predators tear it asunder. When the visible sun rises, animals retreat into their lairs; when Christ rises in the heaven of the praying mind, worldly preoccupations and proclivities abscond, and the intellect goes forth to its labour – that is, to meditate on the divine – until the evening (cf. Ps. 104 : 19–23). Not that the intellect limits its fulfilment of the spiritual law to any period of time or performs it according to some measure; on the contrary, it continues to fulfil it until it reaches the term of this present life and the soul departs from the body. That is what is meant in the Psalms when it is said, 'How I have loved Thy law, O Lord; it is my meditation all the day long' (Ps. 119 : 97) – where 'day' means the whole course of one's present life.

Suspend, then, your gossip with the outer world and fight against the thoughts within until you find the abode of pure prayer and Christ's dwelling-place. Thus you will be illumined and mellowed by His knowledge and His presence, enabled to experience tribulation for His sake as joy and to shun worldly pleasure as you would bitter poison.

Winds rouse the sea's waves, and until they drop the waves will not subside and the sea will not grow calm. Similarly, if you are not careful evil spirits will rouse in your soul memories of parents, brothers and sisters, relatives, acquaintances, banquets, celebrations, theatres and various other images of pleasure; and they will incite you to seek for happiness in visual, vocal and corporeal things, so that you waste not only the present moment but also the time that you sit alone in your cell, in bringing to mind what you have seen and spoken about. Preoccupied in this way with memories of his worldly activities, the monk's life passes profitlessly: he is like a man who retreads his own footsteps in the snow.

If we continue to nourish the demons, when will we slay them? If we let our mind dwell on actions and thoughts related to meaningless friendships and habits, when will we mortify the will of the flesh? When will we live the Christ-like life to which we have committed ourselves? The foot's imprint in the snow dissolves when the sun shines or when it begins to rain. Mind-embedded memories of self-indulgence whether in thought or act are effaced when as the result of prayer and tears of compunction Christ rises in the heart. But when will the monk who does not practise what he has professed expunge passion-imbued memories from his mind?

Moral virtues pertaining to the body are effectuated when you give up commerce with the world. Holy images and thoughts are imprinted on the soul when you efface memories of previous actions by frequent prayer and fervent compunction. Heartfelt contrition and the illumination that comes from constant mindfulness of God excise evil memories like a razor.

Copy the wisdom of the bees: when they become aware of an encircling swarm of wasps, they remain inside their hive and so escape the attacks with which they are threatened. Wasps signify commerce with the world: avoid such commerce at all costs, stay in your cell, and there try to re-enter the innermost citadel of the soul, the dwelling-place of Christ, where you will truly find the peace, joy and serenity of Christ the spiritual Sun – gifts that He irradiates and with which He rewards the soul that receives Him with faith and devotion.

Sitting in your cell, then, be mindful of God, raising your intellect above all things and prostrating it wordlessly before Him, exposing your heart's state to Him, and cleaving to Him in love. For mindfulness of God is the contemplation of God, who draws to Himself the intellect's vision and aspiration, and illumines the intellect with His own light. When the intellect turns toward God and stills all representational images of created things, it perceives in an imageless way, and through an ignorance surpassing all knowledge its vision is illumined by God's unapproachable glory. Although not knowing, because what it perceives is beyond all knowledge, nevertheless the intellect does know through the truth of Him who truly is and who alone transcends all being. Nourishing its love on the wealth of goodness that pours forth from God, and fulfilling thereby its own nature, it is granted blessed and eternal repose.

Such are the characteristics of true mindfulness of God. Prayer is the mind's dialogue with God, in which words of petition are uttered with the intellect riveted wholly on God. For when the mind unceasingly repeats the name of the Lord and the intellect gives its full attention to the invocation of the divine name, the light of the knowledge of God overshadows the entire soul like a luminous cloud.

Concentrated mindfulness of God is followed by love and joy: 'I remembered God, and I rejoiced', writes the Psalmist (Ps. 77 : 3. LXX). Pure prayer is followed by divine knowledge and compunction: again the Psalmist writes, 'On whatever day I call upon Thee, behold, I shall know that Thou art my God' (Ps. 56 : 9. LXX); and, 'The offering acceptable to God is a contrite spirit' (Ps. 51 : 17). When intellect and mind stand attentive before God in fervent supplication, compunction of the soul will ensue. When intellect, intelligence and spirit prostrate themselves before God, the first through attentiveness, the second through invocation, and the third through compunction and love, the whole of your inner self serves God; for 'You shall love your God with all your heart' (Deut. 6 : 5; Matt. 22 : 37).

You should take particular notice of this lest, though you think you are praying, you wander far from prayer, and accomplish nothing. This is what happens during the chanting of psalms when the tongue utters the words of the verses while the intellect is carried away elsewhere and is dispersed among passion-charged thoughts and other things, with the result that comprehension of the psalms goes by the board. The same thing also happens where the mind is concerned. Time and again, when the mind repeats the words of the prayer the intellect does not keep it company and does not fix its attention on God, to whom our words of prayer are being addressed; imperceptibly it is turned aside by one thought or another. The mind says the words as usual, but the intellect lapses from the knowledge of God. As a result, the soul is devoid of understanding and devotion, since the intellect is fragmented by fantasies, distracted by what has enticed it away or by what it has deliberately chosen.

When there is no conscious understanding of prayer and when the suppliant does not put himself in the presence of Him whom he invokes, how can the soul be gladdened? How can a heart find joy when it only pretends to pray but lacks true prayer? 'The hearts of those who seek the Lord will rejoice' (cf. Ps. 105 : 3). To seek the Lord is to prostrate yourself with your whole mind and with great fervour before God and to expel every worldly thought with the knowledge and love of God that spring from pure and unremitting prayer.

In order to clarify the nature of the vision born in the intellect as a result of the mindfulness of God and the status of the mind during pure prayer, I shall use the analogy of the bodily eye and tongue. What the pupil is to the eye and utterance is to the tongue, mindfulness is to the intellect and prayer is to the mind. Just as the eye, when it receives the visual impression of an object, makes no sound, but acquires knowledge of what is seen through the experience of sight, so it is with the intellect: when through its mindfulness of God it is lovingly assimilated to Him, cleaving to Him experientially and in the silence of direct and unalloyed intellection, it is illumined by divine light and receives a pledge of the radiance in store for it. Or again, as the tongue when it speaks reveals to the hearer the hidden disposition of the intellect, so the mind, when it repeats frequently and ardently the brief words of the prayer, reveals the soul's petition to the all-knowing God. Persistence in prayer and unceasing contrition of heart enkindle God's compassion for man and call down the riches of salvation; for 'God will not despise a broken and a contrite heart' (Ps. 51 : 17).

Another illustration which may lead you to an understanding of pure prayer is that of the earthly king. When you approach a king, you stand before him bodily, entreat him orally, and fix your eyes upon him, thus drawing to yourself his royal favour. Act in the same manner, whether in church or in the solitude of your cell. When in God's name you gather together with the brethren, present yourself bodily to God and offer Him psalms chanted orally; and likewise keep your intellect attentive to the words and to God Himself, aware of who it is that your intellect addresses and entreats. For when the mind devotes itself to prayer actively and with purity, the heart is granted inexpressible peace and a joy which cannot be taken away. Again, when you sit alone in your cell, cleave to this mental prayer with watchful intellect and contrite spirit. Then on account of your watchfulness the grace of contemplation will descend upon you, knowledge will dwell in you by virtue of your prayer, and wisdom will repose in you because of your compunction, banishing mindless pleasure and replacing it with divine love.

Believe me; I tell the truth. If in all your activity you cleave inseparably to the mother of blessings, prayer, then prayer itself will not rest until it has shown you the bridal chamber and has led you within, filling you with ineffable glory and joy. By removing every impediment, prayer smooths the path of virtue and renders it easy for those who pursue it.

Consider now the effects of mental prayer. Dialogue with God destroys passion-imbued thoughts, while the intellect's concentration on God dispels worldly preoccupations. Compunction of soul repels affection for the flesh, and the prayer born from ceaseless invocation of the divine name reveals itself as the concordance and union of intellect, intelligence and soul; for 'where two or three are gathered together in My name, I am in the midst of them' (Matt. 18 : 20). Thus by re-collecting the powers of the soul dispersed by the passions, and by uniting them to one another and to itself, prayer assimilates the tripartite soul to the one God in three hypostases.

By first removing the ugliness of sin from the soul through the practice of virtue, and then through sacred knowledge renewing the divine beauty imprinted upon it, prayer presents the soul to God. At once the soul recognizes its Creator, for 'on whatever day I call upon Thee, behold, I shall know that Thou art my God' (Ps. 56 : 9. LXX); and in turn it is known by God, for 'the Lord knows those that are His'

(2 Tim. 2 : 19). It knows God because of the purity of His image within it, for every image leads one back to its original; and it is known by God because its likeness to God has been restored through the practice of the virtues. Thus it is by means of the virtues that the soul knows God and is known by God.

The person who courts the favour of a king does so in one of three ways. He either entreats his possible benefactor with words, or stands silently before him, or throws himself at his feet. Pure prayer, uniting to itself intellect, intelligence and spirit, invokes the divine name with the intelligence; with the intellect it concentrates its unwavering attention on God whom it invokes; and with the spirit it manifests compunction, humility, and love. In this way it entreats the unoriginate Trinity – Father, Son, and Holy Spirit – the one God.

Just as variety in food stimulates the appetite, so the varied forms of virtue awaken the activity of the intellect. Thus while you travel the path of the mind, repeat again and again the words of the prayer, hold converse with the Lord, cry out ceaselessly, and do not give up, praying frequently and imitating the boldness of the widow who managed to prevail upon the inexorable judge (cf. Luke 18 : 1–5). Then you will walk in the path of the Spirit, impervious to sensual desires, the flow of your prayer unbroken by worldly thoughts, and you will become a temple of God, praising Him undistractedly. If you pray in the mind in this way you will be granted the privilege of attaining mindfulness of God and will penetrate the innermost sanctuary of the intellect, mystically contemplating the Invisible and alone celebrating in solitude God alone in the unity of divine knowledge and in outpourings of love.

When you see yourself, therefore, growing sluggish in prayer, take up a book and by paying careful attention to what you read absorb its meaning. Do not read through the words in a cursory fashion, but examine them with depth of understanding and treasure their meaning. Then meditate on what you have read, so that your mind in comprehending it is mellowed and it remains unforgotten. Thus will your ardour for reflection on things divine be kindled, for 'a fire shall be kindled during my meditation' (Ps. 39 : 3. LXX). Just as you have to chew food before you can savour its taste, so you have to ruminate in your soul on holy texts before they enrich and gladden the mind: as the Psalmist says, 'How sweet Thy words are in my throat' (Ps. 119 : 103). Learn by heart the words of the Gospels and the sayings of the blessed fathers, and study their lives diligently, so that you may meditate on these things during the night. In this way when your mind grows listless in prayer you can refresh it by reading and meditating on sacred texts and rekindle its appetite for prayer.

When chanting psalms, do this in a low voice, with your intellect fully attentive: do not allow any phrase to go uncomprehended. Should anything escape your understanding, begin the verse again, and repeat this as many times as necessary, until your intellect grasps what is being said. For the intellect can attend to the chanting and simultaneously can recollect God. You may learn this from everyday experience: you can meet and speak with someone and also focus your eyes on him. Similarly, you can chant psalms and focus on God through recollectedness.

Do not neglect prostration. It provides an image of man's fall into sin and expresses the confession of our sinfulness. Getting up, on the other hand, signifies repentance and the promise to lead a life of virtue. Let each prostration be accompanied by a noetic invocation of Christ, so that by falling before the Lord in soul and body you may gain the grace of the God of souls and bodies.

To dispel sleep and indolence while practising mental prayer you may occupy your hands with some quiet task, for this, too, contributes to the ascetic struggle. All such tasks when accompanied by prayer quicken the intellect, banish listlessness, give youthful vigour to the soul, and render the intellect more prompt and eager to devote itself to mental work.

When the wooden sounding-board[1] is struck, leave your cell, your eyes lowered and your mind anchored in mindfulness of God. When you have entered the church and taken your place in the choir, do not indulge in idle talk with the monk next to you or let your intellect be distracted by vain thoughts. Secure your tongue with the chanting of psalms and your mind with prayer. After the dismissal, go back to your cell and begin the tasks prescribed for you by your rule.

When you enter the refectory, do not look round to see how much food your brethren are eating and so fragment your soul with ugly suspicions. Look only at what lies before you; with your mouth eat

---

[1] The *simantron*, a plank of wood used in monasteries to summon the community to services.

your food, with your ears listen to what is being read, and with your soul pray. Nourishing body and spirit in this way, with your whole being you may truly praise Him who 'satisfies your desire with blessings' (Ps. 103 : 5. LXX). Then rise and enter your cell with dignity and silence, and like an industrious bee make virtue your labour of love. When you work with the brethren, let your hands do the work while your lips keep silence, and let your intellect be mindful of God. Should someone be prompted to speak idle words, to restore order rise and make a prostration.

Repulse evil thoughts and do not let them penetrate the heart and settle there; for when passion-imbued thoughts persist they bring the passions themselves to life and are the death of the intellect. As soon as you sense that they are attacking you, try to destroy them with the arrow of prayer. If they go on importuning you to be let in, confusing your mind, now withdrawing, now assailing you again, you may be sure that a prevenient desire for them on your part is giving them strength. Because the soul's free will has been overcome in this way, they now have a lawful claim against it, and so they perturb and pester it. Hence you should expose them through confession, for evil thoughts take to flight as soon as they are denounced. Just as darkness recedes when light shines, so the light of confession dispels the darkness of impassioned thoughts. The vanity and self-indulgence that provided an opening for such thoughts are destroyed by the shame felt in confessing them and by the hardship of the penance imposed. Evil thoughts flee in confusion when they find the mind already free from passions as a result of continuous, truly contrite prayer.

When a spiritual athlete tries by means of prayer to cut off the thoughts that agitate him, he is successful for a while and, wrestling and fighting, controls his mental distraction. But he is not delivered completely, because he is still attached to the things that cause these disturbing thoughts – to bodily comfort, that is to say, and to worldly ambition. It is for this reason, indeed, that he is reluctant to confess his thoughts. Thus he is not at peace, for he himself keeps hold of what properly belongs to his enemies. If you retain someone else's goods, will not the rightful owner claim them back from you? And if you do not surrender what you wrongfully possess, how can you escape from your adversary? But when the spiritual athlete, strengthened by mindfulness of God, willingly humiliates and ill-treats his mortal self, and confesses his thoughts without shame, the enemy withdraws at once, and the mind – now free – enjoys ceaseless prayer and uninterrupted meditation on things divine.

Reject completely every suspicion about someone else that rises in your heart, because it destroys love and peace. But accept with courage any calamity that comes from without, since it provides an opportunity for exercising the patience that leads to salvation, the patience that bestows an abiding-place and repose in heaven.

If you pass your days in this manner, you will spend this present life in good heart, glad in the expectation of blessedness; and at death you will leave this world with confidence and be translated to the place of repose that the Lord has prepared for you, granting you as a reward for your present labours the privilege of reigning with Him in His kingdom. To Him be all glory, honour and worship, as also to His unoriginate Father, and to His all-holy, blessed and life-quickening Spirit, now, for ever, and through all the ages. Amen.

Texts

1. When the intellect turns away from external things and concentrates on what is within, it is restored to itself; it is united, that is to say, to the principle of its own consciousness, and through this principle naturally inherent in its own substance it devotes itself entirely to prayer. By means of prayer it ascends with all its loving power and affection to the knowledge of God. Then sensual desire vanishes, every pleasure-inciting sense becomes inert, and the delectable things of earth cease to have any attraction. For once the soul has put behind it all that pertains and is endemic to the body, it pursues the beauty of Christ, engaging in works of devotion and of mental purity. It sings aloud, 'The virgins that follow Him shall be brought to the King' (cf. Ps. 45 : 14. LXX). With Christ's image ever before it, it exclaims, 'I have set the Lord always before me, for He is at my right hand' (Ps. 16 : 8). It cleaves to Christ with love and cries, 'Lord, all my desire is before Thee' (Ps. 38 : 9). It continually contemplates Christ, uttering the words, 'My eyes are ever towards the Lord' (Ps. 25 : 15). Discoursing with Christ in pure prayer it is filled with delight and joy, in accordance with the Psalmist's words, 'My discourse with Him will be full of delight, I will rejoice in the Lord' (Ps. 104 : 34). For God welcomes the discourse born of prayer, and when He is lovingly invoked and called to our aid, He bestows inexpressible joy on the beseeching soul. For when the soul brings God to mind in the discourse of prayer, it is gladdened by the Lord: again as the Psalmist says, 'I remembered God and was gladdened' (Ps. 77 : 4. LXX).

2. Spurn the senses and you will quell sensual pleasure. Spurn mental fantasies of delectation and you will quell self-indulgent thoughts. For when the intellect remains free from fantasy and image, not permitting itself to be shaped or stamped either by the taints of sensual pleasure or by thoughts full of desire, then it is in a state of

simplicity; and transcending all sensory and intelligible realities, it concentrates its vision on God. Its sole activity is to invoke the Lord's name in the depth of itself with continuous recollectedness, as a child repeats the name of his father: as it is said in the Scriptures, 'I will invoke the name of the Lord before you' (Exod. 33 : 19). And as Adam, moulded by God's hand from dust, became through divine spiration a living soul, so the intellect moulded by the virtues and repeatedly invoking the Lord with a pure mind and an ardent spirit, is divinely transformed, quickened and deified through knowing and loving God.

3. If through sincere, continual prayer you stand aloof from desire for earthly things, if you repose not with sleep but through abandoning concern with everything except God, being steadfastly rooted solely in mindfulness of God, you will establish in yourself, like another helpmate, love for God. For the cry of the prayer that rises from within you releases divine love; and divine love awakens the intellect, revealing to it what is hidden. Then the intellect, united with love, gives birth to wisdom, and through wisdom proclaims the esoteric meaning of things. For the divine Logos, invoked in the cry of the prayer that rises from within you, lays hold of the noetic power of the intellect as though it were Adam's rib and fills it with divine knowledge; and in its place, bringing to perfection your inner state, He confers the gift of virtue. Next He vivifies light-generating love and brings it to the enraptured intellect as it sleeps a sleep free from all desire for anything earthly. Love appears as another helpmate to the intellect liberated from mindless attachment to sensory things; it is because of this that it awakens the intellect, now in a state of purity that permits it to embrace the words of wisdom. Then the intellect, gazing on love and filled with delight, speaks at length to others, disclosing to them the hidden dimensions of virtue and the unseen operations of divine knowledge (cf. Gen. 2 : 18, 21–23).

4. Stand aloof from all things sensory, abjuring the law of your unregenerate self, and the spiritual law will be engraved on your mind. As, according to St Paul, the spiritually awakened do not implement the desire of the flesh (cf. Gal. 5 : 16), so he who stands aloof from the senses and from sensory things – stands aloof, that is to say, from the world and the flesh – is energized by the Spirit and meditates on the things of the Spirit. One can learn of this from God's relationship with Adam prior to the fall.

5. If you struggle to keep the commandments, persisting in the paradise of prayer and cleaving to God through continuous recollection of Him, then God will release you from the self-indulgent proclivities of the flesh, from all sensory impulsion and from all forms engraved upon your thought; and rendering you dead to the passions and to sin He will make you a participant in divine life. A sleeping person looks like one dead so far as his bodily activity is concerned, and yet he is alive thanks to the co-operation of his soul. Similarly if you abide in the Spirit you are dead to the world and the flesh, but you live according to the spontaneity of the Spirit.

6. If you grasp the meaning of what you chant you will acquire knowledge. From such knowledge you will attain understanding. From understanding springs the practice of what you know. From practice you will reap abiding spiritual knowledge. Experiential spiritual knowledge gives rise to true contemplation. From true contemplation is born wisdom, filling the firmament of the mind with refulgent words of grace and elucidating what is hidden to the uninitiated.

7. First the intellect seeks and finds, and then it is united to what it has found. The searching is effectuated by means of the intelligence, the union by means of love. The search by means of the intelligence is undertaken for the sake of truth, the union by means of love is consummated for the sake of sanctity.

8. If you transcend the flow of temporal things and detach yourself from desire for what is transient, you will not notice mundane objects or crave for the delectable things of earth. On the contrary, supernal visions will be disclosed to you and you will contemplate celestial beauty and the blessedness of unfading realities. To the person who hankers after material things and who steeps himself in sensual pleasure, the heavens are closed, since his spiritual eyes are shrouded; but he who scorns material things and who repudiates them exalts his intellect and perceives the glory of eternal realities and the luminosity of the saints. Such a person is filled with divine love and becomes a temple of the Holy Spirit; he aspires to do God's will and is guided by the Spirit of God, being granted divine sonship, blessed by God and conforming to Him. 'For all who are guided by the Spirit of God are sons of God' (Rom. 8 : 14).

9. For as long as you live do not abandon prayer even for a single day on the excuse of illness. Heed St Paul, who says, 'When I am weak, then I am strong' (2 Cor. 12 : 10). If you act in this spirit, your profit

will be greater, and the prayer – grace assisting – will soon make you well. Wherever the Spirit brings solace, illness and listlessness are short-lived.

NIKIPHOROS THE MONK

Introductory Note

Nikiphoros the Monk, often known as Nikiphoros the Hesychast or the Athonite, lived in the second half of the thirteenth century. He was born in Italy, so St Gregory Palamas tells us,[1] and was originally a Roman Catholic. But, rejecting what Palamas terms the 'kakodoxy' of the Latin West, he travelled to the Byzantine Empire, where he embraced the Orthodox faith, becoming a monk on the Holy Mountain of Athos. Here he dwelt in 'quietness and stillness', according to Palamas – presumably this means that he lived in a small hermitage, not in a fully-organized cenobium – and eventually he withdrew to the 'most isolated parts' of the mountain. Like Theoliptos of Philadelphia, he was fiercely opposed to the unionist policy of Michael VIII,[2] and he has himself left an account of the imprisonment and exile that he suffered in consequence during 1276–7.[3] Probably he died before 1300.

The present work, *On Watchfulness and the Guarding of the Heart*, is mentioned by Palamas, who writes: 'Seeing that many beginners were incapable of controlling the instability of their intellect, even to a limited degree, Nikiphoros proposed a method whereby they could restrain to some extent the wanderings of the fantasy.'[4] The 'method' in question is closely similar to the psychosomatic technique recommended in *The Three Methods of Prayer*, attributed to St Symeon the New Theologian.[5] Nikiphoros is sometimes styled the 'inventor' of this bodily 'method', but Palamas does not actually assert this. It is more

---

[1] See *Triads*, I, ii, 12 (cf. below, p. 341); II, ii, 2–3. Compare Daniel Stiernon, in *Dictionnaire de Spiritualité* xi (1981), cols 198–203; Antonio Rigo, 'Niceforo l'Esicasta (XIII sec.): alcune considerazioni sulla vita e sull'opera', in Olivier Raquez (ed.), *Amore del Bello: Studi sulla Filocalia* (Magnano, 1991), pp. 81–119.

[2] See above, p. 175.

[3] Edited by V. Laurent and J. Darrouzès, *Dossier grec de l'union de Lyon (1273–1277)* (*Archives de l'Orient Chrétien* 16: Paris, 1976), pp. 486–507; cf. pp. 82–8.

[4] *Triads* II, ii, 2.

[5] See above, pp. 72–3.

probable that the 'method' had long been traditional on the Holy Mountain and elsewhere, handed down orally from teacher to disciple, and that Nikiphoros – along with the author of *The Three Methods* – did no more than provide the first written descriptions of this technique.

The main theme of the work *On Watchfulness* is the need to return into oneself, to descend with the intellect into the depths of the heart, and to seek there the hidden treasure of the inner kingdom. After a short anthology of texts, underlining the importance of keeping guard over the intellect, Nikiphoros concludes by suggesting the physical 'method' as a practical way of 'entering the heart' and so achieving this state of spiritual watchfulness. As in *The Three Methods*, the psychosomatic technique, so it seems, is to be practised before actually commencing the Jesus Prayer. Nikiphoros insists that it is highly desirable to have personal direction from an 'unerring guide', but then recommends the 'method' for those who cannot find such a spiritual director. Most modern Orthodox writers adopt a different view, and consider it dangerous to use this technique except under the immediate instruction of an experienced teacher.

St Gregory Palamas concedes that Nikiphoros has written 'in a simple and unsophisticated manner'.[1] Statements about making the intellect descend into the heart, Palamas insists, are not to be interpreted literally, for our mental faculties are not located spatially inside the physical heart 'as in a container'.[2] But there is none the less the genuine correlation – what has sometimes been termed a relationship of 'analogy-participation' – between our physical modalities and our mental or spiritual state: 'After the fall our inner being naturally adapts itself to outward forms.'[3] Nikiphoros was therefore correct, Palamas concludes, in suggesting specific ways whereby our bodily energies can be harnessed to the work of prayer.

---

[1] *Triads*, II, ii, 3.

[2] *Triads* I, ii, 3 (see p. 334).

[3] *Triads* I, ii, 8 (see p. 338). For the phrase 'analogy-participation' see J.-A. Cuttat, *The Encounter of Religions: A Dialogue between the West and the Orient, with an Essay on the Prayer of Jesus* (New York/Tournai, 1960), pp. 92–3.

On Watchfulness and the Guarding of the Heart

If you ardently long to attain the wondrous divine illumination of our Saviour Jesus Christ; to experience in your heart the supracelestial fire and to be consciously reconciled with God; to dispossess yourself of worldly things in order to find and possess the treasure hidden in the field of your heart (cf. Matt. 13 : 44); to enkindle here and now your soul's flame and to renounce all that is only here and now; and spiritually to know and experience the kingdom of heaven within you (cf. Luke 17 : 21): then I will impart to you the science of eternal or heavenly life or, rather, a method that will lead you, if you apply it, painlessly and without toil to the harbour of dispassion, without the danger of being deceived or terrified by the demons. Terror of this kind we experience only when through disobedience we estrange ourselves from the life I am about to describe. This was the fate of Adam when he violated God's commandments: associating with the serpent and trusting him, he was sated by him with the fruits of deceit (cf. Gen. 3 : 1–6), and thus wretchedly plunged himself and all those who came after him into the pit of death, darkness and corruption.

You should, then, return; or – to put it more truly – let us return, brethren, to ourselves, rejecting once and for all with disgust the serpent's counsel and our deflection to what is base. For we cannot be reconciled with God and assimilated to Him unless we first return or, rather, enter into ourselves, in so far as this lies within our power. For the miracle consists in tearing ourselves away from the distraction and vain concerns of the world and in this way relentlessly seizing hold of the kingdom of heaven within us.

That is why the monastic life has been called the art of arts and the science of sciences. For this holy discipline does not procure us what is corruptible, so that we divert our intellect from higher to lower things and completely stifle it. On the contrary it offers us strange, indescribable blessings, that 'the eye has not seen, and the ear has not heard, and man's heart has not grasped' (1 Cor. 2 : 9). Henceforward 'we wrestle not against flesh and blood but against principalities, against powers, against the rulers of the darkness of this world' (Eph. 6 : 12). If, then, this present age is one of darkness, let us flee from it. Let us flee from it in our thoughts so that we may have nothing in common with the enemy of God. For if you choose to be a friend of this present age you are an enemy of God (cf. Jas. 4 : 4). And who can help an enemy of God?

Let us therefore imitate our fathers and like them let us seek the treasure within our hearts. And when we have found it let us hold fast to it with all our might, both cultivating and guarding it (cf. Gen. 2 : 15); for this is what we were commanded to do from the beginning. And if another Nikodimos should appear and begin to argue, saying, 'How can anyone enter into his own heart and work or dwell in it?' – as the original Nikodimos, doubting the Saviour, said, 'How can someone who is old enter the second time into his mother's womb and be born?' (John 3 : 4) – let him in his turn hear the words, 'The Spirit blows where He wants to' (John 3 : 8). If we are full of disbelief and doubt about the practice of the ascetic life, how shall we enjoy the fruits of contemplation? For it is practice that initiates us into contemplation.

Doubters of this kind cannot be convinced without written evidence. Hence for the benefit of many I will include in this discourse passages from the lives of the saints and from their writings: reading them should dispel all doubt. I will begin at the beginning with St Antony the Great, and then continue with his successors, selecting and setting forth their words and actions as best I can, so as to confirm what I have been saying.

FROM THE LIFE OF OUR HOLY FATHER ANTONY

Once two brothers were on their way to visit St Antony, but on the journey their water gave out and one of them died and the other was near to dying. Unable to go any further, he too lay down on the ground

and awaited death. But Antony, seated on the mountain, called two
monks who happened to be with him and said to them urgently, 'Take
a jar of water and go as fast as you can along the road leading to Egypt:
two men were on their way here, but one has just died and the other
will also die if you don't hurry. This was revealed to me as I was
praying.' The monks set off; and finding the one man dead they buried
him, while they revived the other with water and brought him to the
elder. It was about a day's journey off. Should you ask why Antony did
not speak before the first man died, I would say that the question is
inapt: the decision about death rested not with Antony but with God,
and He allowed the first man to die and sent a revelation to St Antony
about the second. The miracle happened to St Antony, and to him
alone, because while seated on the mountain he kept his heart
watchful, and so the Lord showed him what was happening a long way
off.[1]

Do you see how through watchfulness of heart St Antony was able
to perceive God and to acquire the power of clairvoyance? For it is in
the heart that God manifests Himself to the intellect, first – according
to St John Klimakos – as fire that purifies the lover and then as light
that illumines the intellect and renders it godlike.[2]

FROM THE LIFE OF ST THEODOSIOS THE CENOBIARCH

St Theodosios was so deeply wounded by the sweet arrow of love, and
was held so fast in love's fetters, that he fulfilled in actual practice the
exalted commandment, 'You shall love the Lord your God with all
your heart, and with all your soul, and with all your mind' (Matt.
22 : 37). Such a state can be attained only by so concentrating the
soul's natural powers that they aspire to nothing other than the
Creator alone. So great were these spiritual energies in his soul that
when exhorting someone he often inspired awe; yet when giving

[1] St Athanasios of Alexandria, The Life of St Antony 59 (P.G. xxvi, 928B–929A); E.T., R.C.
Gregg (The Classics of Western Spirituality: New York, 1980). p. 75.
[2] Cf. St John Klimakos, The Ladder of Divine Ascent, Step 28 (P.G. lxxxviii, 1137C); E.T.,
p. 280.

rebukes he was always gentle and tender. Who else could talk with so many people and be of such service to them, or could so concentrate their senses and turn them inwards that in the midst of tumult they lived with greater serenity than did those in the desert? Who else could remain just the same whether among crowds or dwelling alone? It was by thus concentrating the senses and turning them inwards that the great Theodosios came to be wounded by love for the Creator.[1]

FROM THE LIFE OF ST ARSENIOS

St Arsenios made it a rule never to discuss things in writing and never to send letters. This was not out of weakness or incapacity – how could it have been, seeing that he could speak eloquently with as much ease as others displayed when speaking in a normal way? But it was due to his long habit of silence and his dislike of self-display. For the same reason he took great care when in church or at any other gathering not to look at other people or to be seen by them; he would stand behind a column or some other obstruction and hide himself from view, remaining unseen and not mixing with others. This holy man and earthly angel acted like this because he too wanted to keep a strict watch on himself and to concentrate his intellect inwardly so that he could raise himself towards God without impediment.[2]

FROM THE LIFE OF ST PAUL OF MOUNT LATROS

Although the divine Paul always lived in the mountains and in desert places, and shared his solitude and his food with wild animals, there were nevertheless times when he went down to the Lavra[3] in order to visit the brethren. He counselled them, exhorting them not to be fainthearted and not to neglect the assiduous practice of the virtues,

[1] Cf. Theodore of Petra, *The Life of St Theodosios*: ed. H. Usener (Leipzig, 1890), pp. 16–17, 47–8.

[2] Cf. *Apophthegmata*, alphabetical collection, Arsenios 42; E.T., pp. 18–19.

[3] A monastic settlement. Usually the term refers to a loosely organized collection of individual cells; less frequently it means a fully integrated community.

but to persevere with all attentiveness and discrimination in their efforts to live according to the Gospels and in their courageous fight against the spirits of evil. He also taught them a method by which they could expunge ingrained passion-imbued dispositions as well as counteract new seeds of passion.[1]

You see how this holy father teaches his uninitiated disciples a method through which they could ward off the attacks of the passions? This method was none other than the art of keeping watch over the intellect, for it is only by keeping such watch that we can ward off the passions.

FROM THE LIFE OF ST SAVVAS

When St Savvas saw that a monk had thoroughly mastered the rules of monastic conduct, and was already able to keep watch over his intellect and fight off demonic thoughts – had indeed banished from his mind all memory of worldly things – then, if this monk was physically weak and ill, St Savvas allowed him to have a cell in the Lavra. But if such a monk was vigorous and in good health, he told him to build his own cell.[2]

Do you see how the divine Savvas, too, required his disciples to keep watch over the intellect and only then permitted them to dwell by themselves in their own cells? What are we doing who idly sit in our cells without even knowing whether there is such an art as keeping watch over the intellect?

FROM THE LIFE OF ABBA AGATHON

One of the brethren asked Abba Agathon which is the better, bodily asceticism or the guarding of our inner state. The elder replied: 'Man is

[1] Cf. *The Life of St Paul the Younger of Mount Latros* 20: ed. H. Delehaye, *Analecta Bollandiana* 11 (1892), pp. 57–8.

[2] Cf. Cyril of Skythopolis, *The Life of St Savvas* 28: ed. E. Schwartz (*Texte und Untersuchungen* 49:2: Leipzig, 1939), p. 113; E.T., R.M. Price and J. Binns (*Cistercian Studies Series* 114: Kalamazoo, 1991), p. 122.

like a tree: bodily asceticism is the leaves, the guarding of our inner state the fruit. Since, according to the Scriptures, "every tree that fails to produce good fruit is cut down and thrown into the fire" (Matt. 3 : 10), it is clear that all our efforts should be devoted to producing the fruit, that is, to keeping watch over our intellect. But we also need the shelter and canopy of the leaves – bodily asceticism.'[1]

How astonishing it is that this saint denounced those who fail to learn how to keep watch over the intellect and who boast only of their bodily asceticism: every tree, he said, which does not produce fruit – by which is meant keeping watch over the intellect – but only has leaves, that is, bodily asceticism, is cut down and thrown into the fire. How terrible, father, is your verdict.

FROM ABBA MARK'S LETTER TO NICOLAS

If, my son, you wish to acquire within yourself your own lamp of noetic light and spiritual knowledge, so as to walk without stumbling in the dark night of this age; and if you wish your steps to be ordered by the Lord, delighting in the way of the Gospel – that is, desiring with ardent faith, with zeal and prayer, to practise the commandments of the Gospel – then I will show you a wonderful spiritual method to help you achieve this. It does not call for bodily exertion, but requires spiritual effort, control of the intellect, and an attentive understanding, assisted by fear and love of God. Through this method you can easily put to flight the cohorts of the enemy. If, then, you wish to triumph over the passions, enter within yourself through prayer and with the help of God. Descend into the depths of the heart, and search out the three powerful giants – forgetfulness, sloth and ignorance – which enable the rest of the evil passions to infiltrate into the self-indulgent soul, and to live, energize and flourish there. Then through strict attentiveness and control of the intellect, together with help from above, you will track down these evil giants, about which most people are ignorant; and so you will be able to free yourself from them by means of strict attentiveness and prayer. For when, through the action

[1] *Apophthegmata*, alphabetical collection, Agathon 8; E.T., p. 21.

of grace, zeal for true knowledge, for mindfulness of God's words and for genuine concord is diligently planted and cultivated in the heart, then the last traces of forgetfulness, ignorance and sloth are expunged from it.[1]

Observe how admirably different spiritual teachings concur, and how clearly they explain the meaning of prayer.

FROM ST JOHN KLIMAKOS

A hesychast is one who strives to enshrine what is bodiless within the temple of the body, paradoxical though this may sound. A hesychast is one who says, 'I sleep but my heart is watchful' (Song of Songs 5 : 2). Close the door of your cell to the body, the door of your tongue to speech, and your inner gate to evil spirits. Ascend into a watchtower – if you know how to – and observe how and when and whence, and in what numbers and what form, the robbers try to break in and steal your grapes. When the watchman grows weary he stands up and prays; then he sits down again and manfully resumes the same task. Guarding against evil thoughts is one thing, keeping watch over the intellect is another. The latter differs from the former as much as east from west, and is far more difficult to attain. Where thieves see royal weapons at the ready they do not attack the place lightly. Similarly, spiritual robbers do not lightly try to plunder the person who has enshrined prayer within his heart.[2]

Do you see how these words reveal the wonderful inner work of this great father? We, on the other hand, walk in darkness and as though in some midnight brawl tread these soul-saving words of the Spirit underfoot, spurning them as though wilfully deaf. But now in the passages that follow see what the fathers set down for us as guidance in the attaining of watchfulness.

---

[1] St Mark the Ascetic, Letter to Nicolas the Solitary 12–13 (P.G. lxv, 1048C–1049D); E.T., The Philokalia, vol. i, pp. 158–9.

[2] St John Klimakos, The Ladder of Divine Ascent, Steps 27 and 26 (P.G. lxxxviii, 1097B, 1100AB, 1029B, 1088A); E.T., pp. 239–40, 258, 262, 263.

FROM ST ISAIAH THE SOLITARY

When a man severs himself from evil, he gains an exact understanding of all the sins he has committed against God; for he does not see his sins unless he severs himself from them with a feeling of revulsion. Those who have reached this level pray to God with tears, and are filled with shame when they recall their evil love of the passions. Let us therefore pursue the spiritual way with all our strength, and God in His great mercy will help us. And if we have not guarded our hearts as our fathers guarded theirs, at least in obedience to God let us do all we can to keep our bodies sinless, trusting that at this time of spiritual dearth He will grant mercy to us together with His saints.[1]

Here then this great father encourages those who are very weak, saying that, even if we have not guarded our hearts as the fathers have done, let us at least keep our bodies free from sin, as God demands, and He will be merciful to us. Great is the compassion and sympathy of such a father.

FROM ST MAKARIOS THE GREAT

The most important task for an ascetic is to enter into his heart, to wage war against satan, to hate him, and to battle with him by wrestling against the thoughts he provokes. If you keep your body outwardly chaste and pure, but inwardly are adulterous where God is concerned and profligate in your thoughts, then you gain nothing from keeping your body chaste. For it is written, 'Whoever looks at a woman with lust has already committed adultery with her in his heart' (Matt. 5 : 28). In other words, you can fornicate through the body, and you also fornicate when your soul communes with satan.[2]

---

[1] St Isaiah the Solitary (Abba Isaias), *Logos* xvii, 6 and *Logos* xxi, 10: ed. Avgoustinos Monachos (Jerusalem, 1911), pp. 108–9, 132; E.T., *The Philokalia*, vol. i, p. 25.

[2] Cf. *Spiritual Homilies* (Collection II) xxvi, 12–13: ed. H. Dörries, E. Klostermann and M. Kroeger (*Patristische Texte und Studien* 4: Berlin, 1964), pp. 210–11; E.T., A.J. Mason (London, 1921), p. 191.

This great father seems to contradict the words of St Isaiah quoted above. Yet this is not the case, for St Makarios exhorts us also to guard our body in the way that God requires. But he asks us to keep pure not only our body but our spirit as well. Thus he too enjoins what the Gospel commandments stipulate.

FROM ST DIADOCHOS

He who dwells continually within his own heart is detached from the attractions of this world, for he lives in the Spirit and cannot know the desires of the flesh. Such a man henceforward patrols the fortress of the virtues, posting them as watchmen at all the gates. The assaults of the demons are now ineffective against him.[1]

Rightly does the saint say that the assaults of the demons are now ineffective – ineffective, that is, when we dwell in the depth of our own hearts, and the more so the longer we dwell there. But I lack time to cite here extracts from all the fathers, so I will add one or two more and bring this work to a close.

FROM ST ISAAC THE SYRIAN

Strive to enter the shrine within you and you will see the shrine of heaven, for the one is the same as the other and a single entrance permits you to contemplate both. The ladder leading to that kingdom is hidden within you, that is, within your soul: cleanse yourself from sin and there you will find the steps by which to ascend.[2]

[1] St Diadochos of Photiki, *On Spiritual Knowledge* 57: ed. E. des Places (*Sources chrétiennes* 5: 2nd ed. revised, Paris, 1966), pp. 117–18; E.T., *The Philokalia*, vol. i, p. 270.

[2] St Isaac the Syrian (Isaac of Nineveh), *Ascetical Homilies*, Greek translation, ed. Nikiphoros Theotokis and Joachim Spetsieris (Athens, 1895), p. 127; E.T., A.J. Wensinck (Amsterdam, 1923), p. 8; E.T., Holy Transfiguration Monastery (Boston, 1984), p. 11.

FROM ST JOHN OF KARPATHOS

A great effort and much toil are needed in prayer before we can reach a state in which our mind is no longer troubled, and so attain the inward heaven of the heart where Christ dwells. As St Paul says, 'Do you not realize that Christ dwells within you, unless you are worthless?' (cf. 2 Cor. 13 : 5).[1]

FROM ST SYMEON THE NEW THEOLOGIAN

After the devil and his demons had brought about man's exile from paradise and from God by making him transgress, they found they could inwardly derange – to a greater or lesser extent – anyone's reason whenever they wanted to. The only defence against this is the ceaseless mindfulness of God, for if such mindfulness is stamped on the heart through the power of the cross it will render our thought steadfast and unshakeable. This is a state to which the spiritual contest of every Christian who enters the arena of Christ's faith should lead, if he is not to struggle in vain. For it is to achieve this state that God's athlete embraces all the various forms of ascetic practice. He embraces them so as to call down God's mercy upon him, that Christ may restore him to his original status and may be set as a seal on his mind. This accords with St Paul's words, 'My little children, for you I again bear the pangs of birth, until Christ is formed in you' (Gal. 4 : 19).[2]

Have you grasped, brethren, that there is a spiritual art or method swiftly leading whoever pursues it to dispassion and the vision of God? Are you convinced that every external form of asceticism is regarded by God as the foliage of a fruitless tree and will be of no benefit to the

[1] St John of Karpathos, *For the Encouragement of the Monks in India* 52; E.T., *The Philokalia*, vol. i, p. 310.

[2] This passage is not to be found in the published writings of St Symeon the New Theologian. See Rigo, 'Niceforo l'Esicasta', op. cit., p. 94.

soul that is not capable of guarding the intellect? Let us then strive not to die fruitless, and thereafter repent to no purpose.

Question: From what has been said we have learned not only of the practice of those who live in accordance with God's will but also that there is a certain form of action that speedily frees the soul from passions and unites it to love for God, and that everyone who engages in spiritual warfare must adopt this form. About these things we have no doubt and are quite convinced. But we are anxious to know what exactly attentiveness is and how we may acquire it, for of this we are altogether ignorant.

Response: In the name of our Lord Jesus Christ who said, 'Without Me you can do nothing' (John 15 : 5), having invoked His help and assistance, I will do my best to show you what attentiveness is and how, if God wills, it may be attained.

FROM NIKIPHOROS HIMSELF

Some of the saints have called attentiveness the guarding of the intellect; others have called it custody of the heart, or watchfulness, or noetic stillness, and others something else. All these expressions indicate one and the same thing, just as 'bread' and 'a round' or 'a slice' do; and you should read them in this sense. As to what attentiveness itself is and what its characteristics are, this you can now learn in more detail.

Attentiveness is the sign of true repentance. It is the soul's restoration, hatred of the world, and return to God. It is rejection of sin and recovery of virtue. It is the unreserved assurance that our sins are forgiven. It is the beginning of contemplation or, rather, its presupposition, for through it God, descrying its presence in us, reveals Himself to the intellect. It is serenity of intellect or, rather, the repose bestowed on the soul through God's mercy. It is the subjection of our thoughts, the palace of the mindfulness of God, the stronghold that enables us patiently to accept all that befalls. It is the ground of faith, hope and love. For if you do not have faith you cannot endure the outward afflictions that assail you; and if you do not bear them gladly you cannot say to the Lord, 'Thou art my helper and my refuge' (Ps.

91 : 2). And if the Most High is not your refuge you will not lay up His love in your heart.

Most if not all of those who attain this greatest of gifts do so chiefly through being taught. To be sure, a few without being taught receive it directly from God through the ardour of their endeavour and the fervour of their faith; but what is rare does not constitute the norm. That is why we should search for an unerring guide, so that under his instruction we may learn how to deal with the shortcomings and exaggerations suggested to us by the devil whenever we deviate left or right from the axis of attentiveness. Since such a guide will himself have been tested through what he has suffered, he will be able to make these things clear to us and will unambiguously disclose the spiritual path to us so that we can follow it easily. If you have no such guide you must diligently search for one. If, however, no guide is to be found, you must renounce worldly attachments, call on God with a contrite spirit and with tears, and do what I tell you.

You know that what we breathe is air. When we exhale it, it is for the heart's sake, for the heart is the source of life and warmth for the body. The heart draws towards itself the air inhaled when breathing, so that by discharging some of its heat when the air is exhaled it may maintain an even temperature. The cause of this process or, rather, its agent, are the lungs. The Creator has made these capable of expanding and contracting, like bellows, so that they can easily draw in and expel their contents. Thus, by taking in coolness and expelling heat through breathing, the heart performs unobstructed the function for which it was created, that of maintaining life.

Seat yourself, then, concentrate your intellect, and lead it into the respiratory passage through which your breath passes into your heart. Put pressure on your intellect and compel it to descend with your inhaled breath into your heart. Once it has entered there, what follows will be neither dismal nor glum. Just as a man, after being far away from home, on his return is overjoyed at being with his wife and children again, so the intellect, once it is united with the soul, is filled with indescribable delight.

Therefore, brother, train your intellect not to leave your heart quickly, for at first it is strongly disinclined to remain constrained and circumscribed in this way. But once it becomes accustomed to remaining there, it can no longer bear to be outside the heart. For the kingdom of heaven is within us (cf. Luke 17 : 21); and when the intellect concentrates its attention in the heart and through pure prayer searches there for the kingdom of heaven, all external things become abominable and hateful to it. If, then, after your first attempts you enter through your intellect into the abode of the heart in the way that I have explained, give thanks and glory to God, and exult in Him. Continually persevere in this practice and it will teach you what you do not know.

Moreover, when your intellect is firmly established in your heart, it must not remain there silent and idle; it should constantly repeat and meditate on the prayer, 'Lord Jesus Christ, Son of God, have mercy on me', and should never stop doing this. For this prayer protects the intellect from distraction, renders it impregnable to diabolic attacks, and every day increases its love and desire for God.

If, however, in spite of all your efforts you are not able to enter the realms of the heart in the way I have enjoined, do what I now tell you and with God's help you will find what you seek. You know that everyone's discursive faculty is centred in his breast; for when our lips are silent we speak and deliberate and formulate prayers, psalms and other things in our breast. Banish, then, all thoughts from this faculty – and you can do this if you want to – and in their place put the prayer, 'Lord Jesus Christ, Son of God, have mercy on me', and compel it to repeat this prayer ceaselessly. If you continue to do this for some time, it will assuredly open for you the entrance to your heart in the way we have explained, and as we ourselves know from experience.

Then, along with the attentiveness you have so wished for, the whole choir of the virtues – love, joy, peace and the others (cf. Gal. 5 : 22) – will come to you. Through the virtues all your petitions will be answered in Christ Jesus our Lord, to whom with the Father and the Holy Spirit be glory, power, honour and worship now and always and throughout the ages. Amen.

ST GREGORY OF SINAI

Introductory Note

Orthodox mystical theology in the mid-fourteenth century possesses as its crowning glory the two Gregories: St Gregory of Sinai and St Gregory Palamas.[1] Although they were on the Holy Mountain of Athos at the same time, it is uncertain how far they were in personal contact.[2] Gregory of Sinai was born, probably around 1265 (but the date is uncertain), near Klazomenai, on the western shores of Asia Minor. Taken prisoner as a young man in a Turkish raid, after being ransomed he went to Cyprus, where he entered the first grade of the monastic life, becoming a rasophore. Next he travelled to Sinai, where he received full monastic profession. From here he went to Crete, where – according to his disciple and biographer Patriarch Kallistos I – he learnt from a monk called Arsenios about the 'guarding of the intellect, true watchfulness and pure prayer': in other words, he was initiated into that tradition of inner prayer – including the Jesus Prayer – to which the writings in *The Philokalia* bear witness.

After this St Gregory moved to Mount Athos, perhaps around the turn of the century, where he remained for the next twenty-five years. Like Nikiphoros the Monk,[3] he chose to live not in one of the large cenobia but in a secluded hermitage, settling in the *skete* of Magoula, not far from the monastery of Philotheou. Turkish incursions forced him to leave Athos around 1325–8, although he returned there briefly during the 1330s. He played no direct part in the hesychast dispute which broke out around 1335, and in which his namesake St Gregory Palamas was deeply involved; probably it was by deliberate choice that

---

[1] On St Gregory of Sinai, see Kallistos Ware, 'The Jesus Prayer in St Gregory of Sinai', *Eastern Churches Review* 4 : 1 (1972), pp. 3–22; David Balfour, *Saint Gregory the Sinaïte: Discourse on the Transfiguration* (offprint from the periodical *Theologia*: Athens, 1983).

[2] See David Balfour, 'Was St Gregory Palamas St Gregory the Sinaïte's Pupil?', *St Vladimir's Theological Quarterly* xxviii (1984), pp. 115–30. Balfour answers this question with an emphatic 'yes', but many of his arguments remain speculative.

[3] See p. 192.

he avoided controversy and polemics. But there can be no doubt that his own theological standpoint, although less explicitly developed, agrees fundamentally with that of Palamas on all essential points. This is confirmed by the *Discourse on the Transfiguration*, recently edited by David Balfour, in which the Sinaite clearly speaks of the light of Tabor as divine and uncreated. The last years of his life were spent in the remote wilderness of Paroria, in the Strandzha Mountains on the border between the Byzantine Empire and Bulgaria, where he enjoyed the patronage of John Alexander, Tsar of Bulgaria. Here he gathered round him a large group of disciples, both Greeks and Slavs, and here he died on 27 November 1346.[1]

St Makarios and St Nikodimos have included five works by the Sinaite in *The Philokalia*. Since their titles vary widely in the manuscripts and they are cited in different ways by modern writers, it will be helpful to list them here, giving first the titles used in our translation, and then the Latin titles used in Migne:

(I) *On Commandments and Doctrines, Warnings and Promises; on Thoughts, Passions and Virtues, and also on Stillness and Prayer: One Hundred and Thirty-Seven Texts*; Migne: *Capita valde utilia per acrostichidem* (*P.G.* cl, 1240–1300). In the Greek original, the initial letters of each text form an acrostic, spelling out the title of the work. The subject matter, as the title indicates, is extremely varied; the work is concerned mainly with ascetic practice rather than inner prayer.

(II) *Further Texts*; Migne: *Alia Capita* (*P.G.* cl, 1300–4). Seven texts, forming a short supplement to (I).

(III) *On the Signs of Grace and Delusion, Written for the Confessor Longinos: Ten Texts*; Migne: *De quiete et oratione* (*P.G.* cl, 1304–12). In this and the two following works, St Gregory discusses more particularly inner prayer, especially the Jesus Prayer, as well as indicating how to distinguish between experiences that come from God and those emanating from the demons or the fallen self. Nothing is known about the Longinos to whom this third treatise is addressed, but he was presumably one of Gregory's monastic colleagues or disciples. Gregory terms him σημειοφόρος, which means literally

---

[1] For the decisive influence of Gregory of Sinai's disciples upon the Slav world, see Dimitri Obolensky, *The Byzantine Commonwealth: Eastern Europe, 500–1453* (London, 1971), pp. 301–8, 336–43; Anthony-Emil N. Tachiaos, 'Gregory Sinaites' legacy to the Slavs: Preliminary Remarks', *Cyrillomethodianum* vii (1983), pp. 113–65.

'standard-bearer', 'ensign'; in Christian authors, it can signify a confessor for the faith or a miracle-worker. Perhaps Longinos, like Theoliptos of Philadelphia and Nikiphoros the Monk, suffered for the Orthodox faith under the unionist Emperor Michael VIII.

(IV) *On Stillness: Fifteen Texts*; Migne: *De quietudine et duobis orationis modis* (*P.G.* cl, 1313–29). This work contains a lengthy section on psalmody (§§ 5–9). The manuscripts disagree concerning the recipient, who is variously named 'Joachim the Vigilant', 'Niphon the Hesychast', 'brother Philotheos of the same mountain of Sinai'. It is extremely unlikely that Gregory wrote this work while still at Sinai, before being initiated into inner prayer by the monk Arsenios; but it is of course possible that, while on Athos or at Paroria, he continued to maintain contact with monks whom he had met at Sinai. All three of these persons are otherwise unknown to us, but clearly they are monks.

(V) *On Prayer: Seven Texts*; Migne: *Quomodo oporteat sedere hesychastam ad orationem nec cito assurgere* (*P.G.* cl, 1329–45). This includes a section on food (§ 6). No name of any addressee is mentioned in the manuscripts. The work has a warm and friendly tone and was obviously intended for a real individual, who is said to be advanced in years (§ 6). Gregory is forthright in his demands, but speaks to the recipient in respectful and encouraging terms.[1]

None of these works contains any indication of date or place, and so it is impossible to say at what point in St Gregory's career they were composed; but from their tone it seems likely that they were written towards the end of his life, either during his last years on Athos or at Paroria. Clearly he had a monastic audience in mind, and was writing for hesychasts dwelling alone or in hermitages rather than for cenobites in large, fully organized communities.

Patriarch Kallistos, in his *Life* of St Gregory, emphasizes the Sinaite's austerity in his earlier years and his radiant joy and lovingkindness at the end of his life. Both of these characteristics are evident in the texts that follow. The daily programme that Gregory proposes for the

---

[1] In our translation of works (I) and (II) we have used the Greek text printed in *The Philokalia*, which is reproduced without change in Migne. For works (III)–(V) we have been able to consult a preliminary draft of the forthcoming critical edition of Gregory of Sinai, in course of preparation by Dr Hans-Veit Beyer of the Kommission für Byzantinistik attached to the Austrian Academy of Sciences in Vienna. We look forward eagerly to its eventual publication.

hesychast is daunting in its severity (I, 99, 101),[1] and he is strict and
uncompromising in his analysis of delusion (I, 131–2, 135; III, 10; V, 7),
in his warnings about the coming judgment (I, 34–40), his strictures
upon the passions (I, 62–5, 70–9, 110), and his demand for total
humility (I, 115, 117). But he speaks also about the 'warmth of heart'
which marks 'the beginning of prayer' (IV, 10), and about the
exultation, rapture and ecstasy to which, by God's grace, the inner
pilgrimage of the hesychast eventually leads (I, 58–9, 113, 118; III, 3, 5,
9). True to the apophatic tradition of inner prayer, the Sinaite requires
a resolute 'shedding' of images and thoughts (I, 118; III, 3; IV, 9; V, 7),[2]
yet he allows an important place to feelings – although without
any trace of sentimental emotionalism. Although he is deliberately
reticent when referring to the transfiguring vision of the divine light (I,
23, 116, 118), and is careful to warn the reader against the ever-
present danger of delusion by false visions of light (III, 3; IV, 10),[3] it is
evident that he stands in the same spiritual tradition as St Symeon the
New Theologian and St Gregory Palamas.

In his teaching upon inner prayer, the Sinaite assigns a central place
to the invocation of the name of Jesus. This is to be practised 'under
spiritual guidance' (III, 3; cf. IV, 15), that is to say, under the
immediate direction of an experienced spiritual father. Gregory
recommends the psychosomatic technique, but provides no detailed
instructions; probably he considered that these were best supplied
orally and on a personal basis by each spiritual guide to his immediate
disciples. Whereas Nikiphoros and *The Three Methods* seem to regard
the technique as a preliminary exercise, preceding the actual invocation, Gregory's language suggests that the control of the breathing is to
be simultaneous with the recitation of the Prayer, although he does not
explain exactly how the two are to be co-ordinated (IV, 2; V, 1).
Although endorsing the use of the bodily technique, he sees it as
limited in value (V, 3, 7). He allows a certain flexibility as regards the
precise formula of prayer that is to be employed, but he discourages
the hesychast from making constant changes in the wording: 'For

[1] In references to Gregory's writings, the number of the work is given first in Roman
numerals, followed by the number of the section in Arabic figures. Thus I, 99 signifies *On
Commandments and Doctrines*, text 99.

[2] On prayer as 'the shedding of thoughts', see Evagrios, *On Prayer* 71; E.T., *The Philokalia*, vol.
i, p. 64.

[3] Cf. St Diadochos of Photiki, *On Spiritual Knowledge* 36; E.T., *The Philokalia*, vol. i, p. 263.

plants which are frequently transplanted do not put down roots' (IV, 2; cf. V, 2).[1]

Of particular interest is the way in which St Gregory connects the Jesus Prayer with the sacrament of baptism. Prayer, he states, is 'baptism made manifest' (I, 113; cf. I, 129). The aim of the Jesus Prayer, as of all prayer, is to reveal in a conscious and dynamically active way 'the energy of the Holy Spirit, which we have already mystically received in baptism' (III, 3). Through the invocation of the Holy Name, we are enabled to pass from the stage when baptismal grace is present in our hearts merely in a hidden and unconscious manner, to the point of full awareness at which we experience the activity of this grace directly and consciously. While emphasizing the indwelling presence of Christ through baptism, Gregory does not make any explicit connection between the Jesus Prayer and the eucharist, as we might have expected him to do. But in other contexts he does employ eucharistic imagery, speaking of prayer as an inner liturgy celebrated in the sanctuary of the heart, and likening the soul to a 'noetic altar' on which the Lamb of God is offered in mystical sacrifice (I, 112; cf, I, 43).[2]

---

[1] In the manuscripts of Gregory's works there are many minor variations in the formulae given for the Jesus Prayer, and it is impossible to be sure exactly what words Gregory recommended. Scribes naturally substituted the forms with which they were personally familiar.

[2] See Michel van Parys, 'La Liturgie du Coeur selon saint Grégoire le Sinaïte', Irénikon li (1973), pp. 312–37.

On Commandments and Doctrines, Warnings and Promises; on Thoughts, Passions and Virtues, and also on Stillness and Prayer: One Hundred and Thirty-Seven Texts

1. You cannot be or become spiritually intelligent in the way that is natural to man in his pre-fallen state unless you first attain purity and freedom from corruption. For our purity has been overlaid by a state of sense-dominated mindlessness, and our original incorruption by the corruption of the flesh.

2. Only those who through their purity have become saints are spiritually intelligent in the way that is natural to man in his pre-fallen state. Mere skill in reasoning does not make a person's intelligence pure, for since the fall our intelligence has been corrupted by evil thoughts. The materialistic and wordy spirit of the wisdom of this world may lead us to speak about ever wider spheres of knowledge, but it renders our thoughts increasingly crude and uncouth. This combination of well-informed talk and crude thought falls far short of real wisdom and contemplation, as well as of undivided and unified knowledge.

3. By knowledge of truth understand above all apprehension of truth through grace. Other kinds of knowledge should be regarded as images of intellections or the rational demonstration of facts.

4. If you fail to receive grace it is because of your lack of faith and your negligence; if you find it again it is because of your faith and your diligence. For faith and diligence always conduce to progress, while their opposites do the reverse.

5. To be utterly senseless is like being dead, and to be blind in intellect is like not seeing physically. To be utterly senseless is to be deprived of life-giving energizing power; to be blind in intellect is to be

deprived of the divine light by which a man can see and be seen by God.

6. Few men receive both power and wisdom from God. Through power we partake of divine blessings; through wisdom we manifest them. This participation and this communication to others is a truly divine gift, beyond man's unaided capacity.

7. A true sanctuary, even before the life to come, is a heart free from distractive thoughts and energized by the Spirit, for all is done and said there spiritually. If we do not attain such a state in this life, we may because of our other virtues be a stone fit for building into the temple of God; but we will not ourselves be a temple or a celebrant of the Spirit.

8. Man is created incorruptible, without bodily humours, and thus he will be when resurrected. Yet he is not created either immutable or mutable, since he possesses the power to choose at will whether to be subject to change or not. But the will cannot confer total immutability of nature upon him. Such immutability is bestowed only when he has attained the state of changeless deification.

9. Corruption is generated by the flesh. To feed, to excrete, to stride about and to sleep are the natural characteristics of beasts and wild animals; acquiring these characteristics through the fall, we have become beast-like, losing the natural blessings bestowed on us by God. We have become brutal instead of spiritually intelligent, ferine instead of godlike.

10. Paradise is twofold – sensible and spiritual: there is the paradise of Eden and the paradise of grace. The paradise of Eden is so exalted that it is said to extend to the third heaven. It has been planted by God with every kind of sweet-scented plant. It is neither entirely free from corruption nor altogether subject to it. Created between corruption and incorruption, it is always rich in fruits, ripe and unripe, and continually full of flowers. When trees and ripe fruit rot and fall to the ground they turn into sweet-scented soil, free from the smell of decay exuded by the vegetable-matter of this world. That is because of the great richness and holiness of the grace ever abounding there. The river Ocean, appointed always to irrigate paradise with its waters, flows through the middle of it. On leaving paradise, it divides into four other rivers, and flowing down to the Indians and Ethiopians brings them soil and fallen leaves. Their fields are flooded by the united rivers of Pison and Gihon until these

divide again, the one watering Libya and the other the land of Egypt (cf. Gen. 2 : 8–14).

11. It is said that when the world was first created it was not subject to flux and corruption. According to Scripture it was only later corrupted and 'made subject to vanity' – that is, to man – not by its own choice but by the will of Him to whom it is subject, the expectation being that Adam, who had fallen into corruption, would be restored to his original state (cf. Rom. 8 : 20–21). For by renewing man and sanctifying him, even though in this transient life he bears a corruptible body, God also renewed creation, although creation is not yet freed from the process of corruption. This deliverance from corruption is said by some to be a translation to a better state, by others to require a complete transmutation of everything sensory. Scripture generally makes simple and straightforward statements about matters that are still obscure.

12. People who have received grace are as if impregnated and with child by the Holy Spirit; but they may abort the divine seed through sinning, or divorce themselves from God through intercourse with the enemy lurking within them. It is the turbulence of the passions that aborts grace, while the act of sinning deprives us of it altogether. A passion- and sin-loving soul, shorn of grace and divorced from God, is the haunt of passions – not to say of demons – in this world and the next.

13. Nothing so converts anger into joy and gentleness as courage and mercy. Like a siege-engine, courage shatters enemies attacking the soul from without, mercy those attacking it from within.

14. Many who practise the commandments think they are following the spiritual path. But they have not yet reached the city, and in fact remain outside it. For they travel foolishly, deviating unawares from the straight highway into side-roads, not realizing how close the vices are to the path of virtue. For the true fulfilment of the commandments demands that we do neither too little nor too much but simply pursue a course acceptable to God and in accordance with His will. Otherwise we labour in vain and do not make straight the paths of the Lord (cf. Isa. 40 : 3). For in everything we do we must be clear about the goal we are pursuing.

15. To be on the spiritual path means seeking the Lord in your heart through fulfilling the commandments. For when you listen to John the Baptist crying in the wilderness, 'Prepare the way of the Lord,

make His paths straight' (Matt. 3 : 3), you must understand that he is referring to the commandments and their fulfilment both in the heart and in actions. It is impossible to 'make straight' the path of the commandments and to act rightly unless your heart too is straight and upright.

16. When Scripture speaks of rod and staff (cf. Ps. 23 : 4), you should take these to signify in the prophetic sense judgment and providence, and in the moral sense psalmody and prayer. For when we are chastened by the Lord with the rod of correction (cf. 1 Cor. 11 : 32), this is so that we may learn how to mend our ways. And when we chasten our assailants with the rod of dauntless psalmody, we become established in prayer. Since we thus wield the rod and the staff of spiritual action, let us not cease to chasten and be chastened until we are wholly in the hands of providence and escape judgment both now and hereafter.

17. The essence of the commandments is always to give precedence to the one that embraces them all: mindfulness of God, as stipulated in the phrase, 'Always be mindful of the Lord your God' (cf. Deut. 8 : 18). Our failure or success in keeping the commandments depends on such mindfulness, for it is this that forgetfulness first destroys when it shrouds the commandments in darkness and strips us of every blessing.

18. Those engaged in spiritual warfare regain their original state by practising two commandments – obedience and fasting; for evil has infiltrated our human condition by means of their opposites. Those who keep the commandments out of obedience return to God more quickly. Others who keep them by means of fasting and prayer return more slowly. Obedience befits beginners, fasting those in the middle way, who have attained a state of spiritual enlightenment and self-mastery. To observe genuine obedience to God when practising the commandments is something only very few can do, and proves difficult even for those who have attained a state of self-mastery.

19. According to St Paul, it is characteristic of the Spirit of life to act and speak in the heart, while a literal, outwardly correct observance of things characterizes the fallen unregenerate person (cf. Rom. 8 : 2; 2 Cor. 3 : 6). The Spirit of life frees the intellect from sin and death, whereas a literal, outwardly correct observance imperceptibly turns us into pharisees, since we then act only in an external bodily

sense and practise the commandments merely in order to be seen doing so (cf. Matt. 23 : 5).

20. The whole complex of the commandments united and knit together in the Spirit (cf. Eph. 4 : 16) has its analogue in man, whether his state is perfect or imperfect. The commandments are the body. The virtues – established inner qualities – are the bones. Grace is the soul that lives and vivifies, energizing the vital power of the commandments just as the soul animates the body. The degree of negligence or diligence with which a man tries to attain to Christ's stature reveals what stage he has reached. Alike in this world and in the next, it indicates whether he is in his spiritual infancy or has achieved maturity.

21. If you want the body of the commandments to flourish, you must zealously desire the pure spiritual milk of maternal grace (cf. 1 Pet. 2 : 2); for it is on this milk of grace that you must suckle yourself if you wish to increase your stature in Christ. Wisdom yields fervour from her breasts as milk that helps you to grow; but to nourish the perfect she gives them the honey of her purifying joy. 'Honey and milk are under your tongue' (Song of Songs 4 : 11): by 'milk' Solomon means the Spirit's nurturing and maturing power, while by 'honey' he means the Spirit's purificatory power. St Paul likewise refers to the differing functions of these powers when he says, 'I have fed you as little children with milk and not with meat' (cf. 1 Cor. 3 : 2).

22. To try to discover the meaning of the commandments through study and reading without actually living in accordance with them is like mistaking the shadow of something for its reality. It is only by participating in the truth that you can share in the meaning of truth. If you search for the meaning without participating in the truth and without having been initiated into it, you will find only a besotted kind of wisdom (cf. 1 Cor. 1 : 20). You will be among those whom St Jude categorized as 'psychic' or worldly because they lack the Spirit (cf. Jude 19), boast as they may of their knowledge of the truth.

23. The physical eye perceives the outward or literal sense of things and from it derives sensory images. The intellect, once purified and re-established in its pristine state, perceives God and from Him derives divine images. Instead of a book the intellect has the Spirit; instead of a pen, mind and tongue – 'my tongue is a pen', says the Psalmist (cf. Ps. 45 : 1); and instead of ink, light. So plunging the mind into the light that it becomes light, the intellect, guided by the Spirit, inscribes the

inner meaning of things in the pure hearts of those who listen. Then it grasps the significance of the statement that the faithful 'shall be taught by God' (cf. Isa. 54 : 13; John 6 : 45), and that through the Spirit God 'teaches man knowledge' (Ps. 94 : 10).

24. The efficacy of the commandments depends on faith working directly in the heart. Through faith each commandment kindles and activates the soul's illumination. The fruits of a true and effective faith are self-control and love, its consummation God-given humility, the source and support of love.

25. A right view of created things depends upon a truly spiritual knowledge of visible and invisible realities. Visible realities are objects perceived by the senses, while invisible realities are noetic, intelligent, intelligible and divine.

26. Orthodoxy may be defined as the clear perception and grasp of the two dogmas of the faith, namely, the Trinity and the Duality. It is to know and contemplate the three Persons of the Trinity as distinctively and indivisibly constituting the one God, and the divine and human natures of Christ as united in His single Person – that is to say, to know and profess that the single Son, both prior and subsequent to the Incarnation, is to be glorified in two natures, divine and human, and in two wills, divine and human, the one distinct from the other.

27. Three unaltering and changeless properties typify the Holy Trinity: unbegottenness, begottenness and procession. The Father is unbegotten and unoriginate; the Son is begotten and also unoriginate; the Holy Spirit proceeds from the Father through the Son, as St John of Damaskos says,[1] and is equally coeternal.

28. Grace-imbued faith, energized by the Spirit through our keeping of the commandments, alone suffices for salvation, provided we sustain it and do not opt for a dead and ineffectual faith rather than for a living effective faith in Christ. To embody and give life to an effective faith in Christ is all we need to do as believers. But nowadays we who call ourselves orthodox believers have in our ignorance imbibed not the faith imbued with grace but a faith that is merely a matter of words, dead and unfeeling.

29. The Trinity is simple unity, unqualified and uncompounded. It is three-in-one, for God is three-personed, each person wholly

---

[1] *On the Orthodox Faith* i, 8 (*P.G.* xciv, 821C, 833A): ed. B. Kotter (*Patristische Texte und Studien* 12: Berlin, 1973), § 8, pp. 26, 30–31.

interpenetrating the others without any loss of distinct personal identity.

30. God reveals and manifests Himself in all things in a threefold manner. In Himself He is undetermined; but through the Son in the Holy Spirit He sustains and watches over all things. And wherever He expresses Himself, none of the three Persons is manifest or to be perceived apart from or without the other two.

31. In man there is intellect, consciousness and spirit. There is neither intellect without consciousness nor consciousness without spirit: each subsists in the others and in itself. Intellect expresses itself through consciousness and consciousness is manifested through the spirit. In this way man is a dim image of the ineffable and archetypal Trinity, disclosing even now the divine image in which he is created.

32. When the divine fathers expound the doctrine of the supra-essential, holy and supranatural Trinity, they illustrate it by saying that the Father truly corresponds to the intellect, the Son to consciousness and the Holy Spirit to the spirit. Thus they bequeath to us the dogma of one God in three Persons as the hallmark of the true faith and the anchor of hope. For, according to Scripture, to apprehend the one God is the root of immortality, and to know the majesty of the three-personed Monad is complete righteousness (cf. Wisd. 15 : 3). Again, we should read what is said in the Gospel in the same way: eternal life is to know Thee the only true God in three Persons, and Him whom Thou hast sent, Jesus Christ, in two natures and two wills (cf. John 17 : 3).

33. Chastisements differ, as do the rewards of the righteous. Chastisements are inflicted in hell, in what Scripture describes as 'a dark and gloomy land, a land of eternal darkness' (Job 10 : 21–22. LXX), where sinners dwell before the judgment and whither they return after judgment is given. For can the phrases, 'Let sinners be returned to hell' (Ps. 9 : 17. LXX), and 'death will rule over them' (Ps. 49 : 14. LXX), refer to anything other than the final judgment visited upon sinners, and their eternal condemnation?

34. Fire, darkness, the worm and the nether world correspond to ubiquitous self-indulgence, total tenebrific ignorance, all-pervasive lecherous titivation, and the fearfulness and foul stench of sin. Already even now they can be seen to be active, as foretastes and firstfruits of hell's torments, in sinners in whose souls they have taken root.

35. Passion-embroiled states are foretastes of hell's torments, just

as the activity of the virtues is a foretaste of the kingdom of heaven. We must realize that the commandments are activities producing effects, and that virtues are states, just as vices that have taken root are also states.

36. Requitals correspond to our deserts, even if many people think they do not. To some, divine justice gives eternal life; to others, eternal chastisement. Each will be requited according to his actions – according to whether he has passed through this present life in a virtuous or in a sinful manner. The degree or quality of the requital will accord with the state induced in each by either the passions or the virtues, and the differing effects these have had.

37. Lakes of fire (cf. Rev. 19 : 20) signify self-indulgent souls. In these lakes the stench of the passions, like fetid bogs, nourishes the sleepless worm of dissipation – the unbridled lusts of the flesh – as it also nourishes the snakes, frogs and leeches of evil desire, the loathsome and poisonous thoughts and demons. A soul in such a state already in this life receives a foretaste of the chastisement to come.

38. As the firstfruits of future chastisement are secretly present in the souls of sinners, so the foretaste of future blessings is present and experienced in the hearts of the righteous through the activity of the Spirit. For a life lived virtuously is the kingdom of heaven, just as a passion-embroiled state is hell.

39. The coming night of which Christ speaks (cf. John 9 : 4) is the complete inertia of hell's darkness. Or, interpreted differently, it is antichrist, who is, and is called, both night and darkness. Or alternatively, according to the moral sense, it is our daily negligence which, like a dark night, deadens the soul in insensate sleep. For just as the night makes all men sleep and is the image of the lifelessness of death, so the night of hell's darkness deadens and stupefies sinners with the sottishness of pain.

40. Judgment upon this world (cf. John 12 : 31) is synonymous with ungodly lack of faith; for 'he who lacks faith is already judged' (John 3 : 18). It is also a providential visitation restraining us or turning us back from sin, and likewise a way of testing whether by inner disposition we incline towards good or evil actions; for according to the Psalmist, 'The wicked are estranged from the womb' (Ps. 58 : 3). Thus God manifests His judgment either because of our lack of faith, or to discipline us, or to test which way our actions gravitate. Some He chastens, to others He is merciful; on some He bestows

crowns of glory, others He visits with the torments of hell. Those whom He chastens are the utterly godless. Those to whom He shows mercy possess faith, but at the same time they are negligent, and it is for this reason that they are compassionately chastised. Those consummate either in virtue or in wickedness receive their rewards accordingly.

41. If our human nature is not kept pure or else restored to its original purity by the Holy Spirit, it cannot become one body and one spirit in Christ, either in this life or in the harmonious order of the life to come. For the all-embracing and unifying power of the Spirit does not complete the new garment of grace by sewing on to it a patch taken from the old garment of the passions (cf. Matt. 9 : 16).

42. Every person who has been renewed in the Spirit and has preserved this gift will be transformed and embodied in Christ, experiencing ineffably the supranatural state of deification. But he will not hereafter be one with Christ or be engrafted into His body unless in this life he has come to share in divine grace and has embodied spiritual knowledge and truth.

43. The kingdom of heaven is like the tabernacle which was built by God, and which He disclosed to Moses as a pattern (cf. Exod. 25 : 40); for it too has an outer and an inner sanctuary. Into the first will enter all who are priests of grace. But into the second – which is noetic – will enter only those who in this life have attained the divine darkness of theological wisdom and there as true hierarchs have celebrated the triadic liturgy,[1] entering into the tabernacle that Jesus Himself has set up, where He acts as their consecrator and chief Hierarch before the Trinity, and illumines them ever more richly with His own splendour.

44. By 'many dwelling-places' (John 14 : 2) the Saviour meant the differing stages of spiritual ascent and states of development in the other world; for although the kingdom of heaven is one, there are many different levels within it. That is to say, there is place for both heavenly and earthy men (cf. 1 Cor. 15 : 48) according to their virtue, their knowledge and the degree of deification that they have attained. 'For there is one glory of the sun, and another glory of the moon, and another glory of the stars, for one star differs from another star in

---

[1] The worship, that is to say, of the three aspects of man that mirror the Trinity: intellect, consciousness and spirit (see above, §§ 31–2).

glory' (1 Cor. 15 : 41); and yet all of them shine in a single divine firmament.

45. You partake of angelic life and attain an incorruptible and hence almost bodiless state when you have cleansed your intellect through tears, have through the power of the Spirit resurrected your soul even in this life, and with the help of the Logos have made your flesh – your natural human form of clay – a resplendent and fiery image of divine beauty. For bodies become incorruptible when rid of their natural humours and their material density.

46. The body in its incorruptible state will be earthy, but it will be without humours or material density, indescribably transmuted from an unspiritual body into a spiritual body (cf. 1 Cor. 15 : 44), so that it will be in its godlike refinement and subtleness both earthy and heavenly. Its state when it is resurrected will be the same as that in which it was originally created – one in which it conforms to the image of the Son of Man (cf. Rom. 8 : 29; Phil. 3 : 21) through full participation in His divinity.

47. The land of the gentle (cf. Ps. 37 : 11) is the kingdom of heaven. Or else it is the theandric state of the Son, which we have attained or are in the process of attaining, having through grace been reborn as sons of God into the new life of the resurrection. Or again, the holy land is our human nature when it has been divinized or, it may be, the land purified according to the measure of those dwelling in it. Or, according to another interpretation, it is the land granted as an inheritance (cf. Numb. 34 : 13) to those who are truly saints, the untroubled and divine serenity and the peace that transcends the intellect (cf. Phil. 4 : 7) – the land wherein the righteous dwell quietly and unmolested.

48. The promised land is dispassion, from which spiritual joy flows like milk and honey (cf. Exod. 13 : 5).

49. The saints in heaven hold inner converse together, communicating mystically through the power of the Holy Spirit.

50. If we do not know what we are like when God makes us, we shall not realize what sin has turned us into.

51. All who have received the fullness of the perfection of Christ in this life are of equal spiritual stature.

52. Rewards correspond to labours. But their quantity or quality – that is to say, their measure – will be shown by the position and state in heaven of those who receive them.

53. According to Scripture the saints, the sons of Christ's resurrection, through incorruption and deification will become intellects, that is to say, equal to the angels (cf. Luke 20 : 36).

54. It is said that in the life to come the angels and saints ever increase in gifts of grace and never abate their longing for further blessings. No lapse or veering from virtue to vice takes place in that life.

55. A person is perfect in this life when as a pledge of what is to come he receives the grace to assimilate himself to the various stages of Christ's life. In the life to come perfection is made manifest through the power of deification.

56. If by passing through the different stages of spiritual growth you become perfect in virtue during this life, you will attain a state of deification in the life hereafter equal to that of your peers.

57. It is said that true belief is knowledge or contemplation of the Holy Spirit. It is also said that scrupulous discernment in matters of dogma constitutes full knowledge of the true faith.

58. Rapture means the total elevation of the soul's powers towards the majesty of divine glory, disclosed as an undivided unity. Or again rapture is a pure and all-embracing ascent towards the limitless power that dwells in light. Ecstasy is not only the heavenward ravishing of the soul's powers; it is also complete transcendence of the sense-world itself. Intense longing for God – there are two forms of it – is a spiritual intoxication that arouses our desire.

59. As just remarked, there are two main forms of ecstatic longing for God: one within the heart and the other an enravishment taking one beyond oneself. The first pertains to those who are still in the process of achieving illumination, the second to those perfected in love. Both, acting on the intellect, transport it beyond the sense-world. Such longing for the divine is truly a spiritual intoxication, impelling natural thoughts towards higher states and detaching the senses from their involvement with visible things.

60. The source and ground of our distractive thoughts is the fragmented state of our memory. The memory was originally simple and one-pointed, but as a result of the fall its natural powers have been perverted: it has lost its recollectedness in God and has become compound instead of simple, diversified instead of one-pointed.

61. We recover the original state of our memory by restoring it to

its primal simplicity, when it will no longer act as a source of evil and destructive thoughts. For Adam's disobedience has not only deformed into a weapon of evil the soul's simple memory of what is good; it has also corrupted all its powers and quenched its natural appetite for virtue. The memory is restored above all by constant mindfulness of God consolidated through prayer, for this spiritually elevates the memory from a natural to a supranatural state.

62. Sinful acts provoke passions, the passions provoke distractive thoughts, and distractive thoughts provoke fantasies. The fragmented memory begets a multiplicity of ideas, forgetfulness causes the fragmentation of the memory, ignorance leads to forgetfulness, and laziness to ignorance. Laziness is spawned by lustful appetites, appetites are aroused by misdirected emotions, and misdirected emotions by committing sinful acts. A sinful act is provoked by a mindless desire for evil and a strong attachment to the senses and to sensory things.

63. Distractive thoughts arise and are activated in the soul's intelligent faculty, violent passions in the incensive faculty, the memory of bestial appetites in the desiring faculty, imaginary forms in the mind, and ideas in the conceptualizing faculty.

64. The irruption of evil thoughts is like the current of a river. We are provoked to sin by such thoughts, and when as a result of this we give our assent to sin our heart is overwhelmed as though by a turbulent flood.

65. By the 'deep mire' (Ps. 69 : 2) understand slimy sensual pleasure, or the sludge of lechery, or the burden of material things. Weighed down by all this the impassioned intellect casts itself into the depths of despair.

66. Scripture often calls thoughts motives for actions, just as it also calls these motives mental images and, conversely, calls mental images motives. This is because the point of departure for such actions, although in itself immaterial, is embodied through them and changed into a particular visible form. Thus the sin that is provoked is identified and named according to its external manifestation.

67. Distractive thoughts are the promptings of the demons and precursors of the passions, just as such promptings and mental images are also the precursors of particular actions. There can be no action, either for good or evil, that is not initially provoked by the particular thought of that action; for thought is the impulse, non-

visible in form, that provokes us to act at all, whatever the action may
be.

68. The raw material of actions generates neutral thoughts, while
demonic provocation begets evil thoughts. Thus when they are
compared it is clear that there is a difference between motives and
thoughts that accord with nature and those which are either contrary
to nature or supranatural.

69. Thoughts in different classes of people are equally prone to
change, thoughts that accord with nature becoming either thoughts
contrary to nature or, alternatively, becoming thoughts that transcend
nature. Occasions for these changes are provided, in the case of evil-
minded people, by thoughts suggested by material things; whereas in
the case of those who are materially-minded they are provided by
demonic provocation. Similarly, in the case of saints, it is thoughts that
accord with nature that provide the occasion for this change, such
thoughts generating thoughts that transcend nature. For the motivat-
ing occasions and grounds for these changes of the various types of
thought into their congenerate types are fourfold: material, demonic,
natural and supranatural.

70. Occasions give rise to distractive thoughts, thoughts to
fantasies, fantasies to the passions, and the passions give entry to the
demons. It is as if there were a certain cunningly devised sequence and
order among the disordered spirits, one thing following and derived
from another. But no one thing in the sequence is self-operative: each
is prompted and activated by the demons. Fantasy is not wrought into
an image, passion is not energized, without unperceived hidden
demonic impulsion. For even though satan has fallen and is shattered,
he is still stronger than we are and exults over us because of our sloth.

71. The demons fill our minds with images; or, rather, they clothe
themselves in images that correspond to the character of the most
dominant and active passion in our soul, and in this way they provoke
us to give our assent to that passion. For the demons use the state of
passion as an occasion for stirring up images. Thus, whether we are
awake or asleep, they visit us with varied and diverse imaginings. The
demons of desire turn themselves sometimes into pigs, sometimes
into donkeys, sometimes into fiery stallions avid for copulation, and
sometimes – particularly the demons of licentiousness – into Israelites. The demons of wrath turn themselves sometimes into gentiles
and sometimes into lions. The demons of cowardice take on the form

of Ishmaelites, those of licentiousness the form of Idumaeans, and those of drunkenness and dissipation the form of Hagarenes. The demons of greed appear sometimes as wolves and sometimes as leopards, those of malice assume the form sometimes of snakes, sometimes of vipers, and sometimes of foxes, those of shamelessness the form of dogs and those of listlessness the form of cats. Finally there are the demons of lechery, that turn sometimes into snakes and sometimes into crows and jackdaws. Carnal-minded demons, particularly those dwelling in the air, transform themselves into birds. Our fantasy transmutes the images of the demons in a threefold manner corresponding to the tripartite nature of the soul: into birds, wild animals and domestic animals, that correspond respectively to the desiring, incensive and intelligent aspect of the soul. For the three princes of the passions are always ready to wage war on these three powers of the soul. Whatever the passion that dominates the soul, they assume a form that corresponds to it and thus they insinuate themselves into us.

72. The demons of sensual pleasure often attack us in the form of fire and coals. For the spirits of self-indulgence kindle the soul's desiring faculty, while they also confuse the intelligence and plunge it into darkness. The chief cause of lustful burning and mental confusion and beclouding lies in the sensuality of the passions.

73. The night of the passions is the darkness of ignorance. Or alternatively the night is the state which begets the passions, where the prince of darkness rules, and where the beasts of the field, the birds of the air and the creeping things of the earth have their dwelling, these being allegorical terms for the roving spirits that seek to lay hold of us in order to devour us (cf. Ps. 104 : 20).

74. Some distractive thoughts precede the activity of the passions and others follow it. Such thoughts precede fantasies, while passions are sequent to fantasies. The passions precede demons, while demons follow the passions.

75. The cause and origin of the passions is the misuse of things. Such misuse results from perversion of our character. Perversion expresses the bias of the will, and the state of our will is tested by demonic provocation. The demons thus are permitted by divine providence to demonstrate to us the specific state of our will.

76. The lethal poison of the sting of sin is the soul's passion-charged state. For if by your own free choice you allow yourself to be

dominated by the passions you will develop a firm and unchanging propensity to sin.

77. The passions are variously named. They are divided into those pertaining to the body and those pertaining to the soul. The bodily passions are subdivided into those that involve suffering and those that are sinful. The passions that induce suffering are further subdivided into those connected with disease and those connected with corrective discipline. The passions pertaining to the soul are divided according to whether they affect the incensive, appetitive or intelligent aspect of the soul. Those connected with the intelligence are subdivided into those affecting the imagination and those affecting the understanding. Of these some are the result of the deliberate misuse of things; others we suffer against our will, out of necessity, and for these we are not culpable. The fathers have also called them concomitants and natural idiosyncrasies.

78. The passions that pertain to the body differ from those that pertain to the soul; those affecting the appetitive faculty differ from those affecting the incensive faculty; and those of the intelligence differ from those of the intellect and the reason. But all intercommunicate, and all collaborate, the bodily passions with those of the appetitive faculty, passions of the soul with those of the incensive faculty, passions of the intelligence with those of the intellect, and passions of the intellect with those of the reason and of the memory.

79. The passions of the incensive faculty are anger, animosity, shouting, bad temper, self-assertion, conceit, boastfulness, and so on. The passions of the appetitive faculty are greed, licentiousness, dissipation, insatiateness, self-indulgence, avarice and self-love, which is the worst of all. The passions of the flesh are unchastity, adultery, uncleanliness, profligacy, injustice, gluttony, listlessness, ostentation, self-adornment, cowardice and so on. The passions of the intelligence are lack of faith, blasphemy, malice, cunning, inquisitiveness, duplicity, abuse, backbiting, censoriousness, vilification, frivolous talk, hypocrisy, lying, foul talk, foolish chatter, deceitfulness, sarcasm, self-display, love of popularity, day-dreaming, perjury, gossiping and so on. The passions of the intellect are self-conceit, pomposity, arrogance, quarrelsomeness, envy, self-satisfaction, contentiousness, inattentiveness, fantasy, fabrication, swaggering, vainglory and pride, the beginning and end of all the vices. The passions of the reason are dithering, distraction, captivation, obfuscation, blindness, abduction,

provocation, connivance in sin, bias, perversion, instability of mind and similar things. In short, all the unnatural vices commingle with the three faculties of the soul, just as all the virtues naturally coexist within them.

80. How eloquent is David when he speaks to God in ecstasy, saying, 'Thy knowledge is too wonderful for me; I cannot attain to it' (cf. Ps. 139 : 6), for it exceeds my feeble knowledge and my powers. How incomprehensible, indeed, is even this flesh in the way it has been constituted: it too is triadic in every detail, and yet a single harmony embraces its limbs and parts; in addition it is graced by the numbers seven and two which, according to mathematicians, signify time and creation. Thus it, too, when perceived according to the laws at work in creation, is to be seen as an organ of God's glory manifesting His triadic magnificence.

81. The laws of creation are the qualities investing wholes compounded of energized parts – qualities also known as generic differences, since they invest many different composites constituted from identical properties. Or again the natural law is the potential power to energize inherent in each species and in each part. As God does with respect to the whole of creation, so does the soul with respect to the body: it energizes and impels each member of the body in accordance with the energy intrinsic to that member. At this point it must be asked why the holy fathers sometimes say that anger and desire are powers pertaining to the body and sometimes that they are powers pertaining to the soul. Assuredly, the words of the saints never disagree if they are carefully examined. In this case, both statements are true, if correctly understood in context. For indescribably body and soul are brought into being in such a way that they coexist. The soul is in a state of perfection from the start, but the body is imperfect since it has to grow through taking nourishment. The soul by virtue of its creation as a deiform and intellective entity possesses an intrinsic power of desire and an intrinsic incensive power, and these lead it to manifest both courage and divine love. For senseless anger and mindless desire were not created along with the soul. Nor originally did they pertain to the body. On the contrary, when the body was created it was free from corruption and without the humours from which such desire and uncontrollable rage arise. But after the fall anger and desire were necessarily generated within it, for then it became subject to the corruption and gross materiality of the instinct-driven

animals. That is why when the body has the upper hand it opposes the will of the soul through anger and desire. But when what is mortal is made subject to the intelligence it assists the soul in doing what is good. For when characteristics that do not originally pertain to the body but have subsequently infiltrated into it become entangled with the soul, man becomes like an animal (cf. Ps. 49 : 20), since he is now necessarily subject to the law of sin. He ceases to be an intelligent human being and becomes beast-like.

82. When God through His life-giving breath created the soul deiform and intellective, He did not implant in it anger and desire that are animal-like. But He did endow it with a power of longing and aspiration, as well as with a courage responsive to divine love. Similarly when God formed the body He did not originally implant in it instinctual anger and desire. It was only afterwards, through the fall, that it was invested with these characteristics that have rendered it mortal, corruptible and animal-like. For the body, even though susceptive of corruption, was created, as theologians will tell us, free from corruption, and that is how it will be resurrected. In the same way the soul when originally created was dispassionate. But soul and body have both been defiled, commingled as they are through the natural law of mutual interpenetration and exchange. The soul has acquired the qualities of the passions or, rather, of the demons; and the body, passing under the sway of corruption because of its fallen state, has become akin to instinct-driven animals. The powers of body and soul have merged together and have produced a single animal, driven impulsively and mindlessly by anger and desire. That is how man has sunk to the level of animals, as Scripture testifies, and has become like them in every respect (cf. Ps. 49 : 20).

83. The principle and source of the virtues is a good disposition of the will, that is to say, an aspiration for goodness and beauty. God is the source and ground of all supernal goodness. Thus the principle of goodness and beauty is faith or, rather, it is Christ, the rock of faith, who is principle and foundation of all the virtues. On this rock we stand and on this foundation we build every good thing (cf. 1 Cor. 3 : 11). Christ is the capstone (cf. Eph. 2 : 20) uniting us with Himself. He is the pearl of great price (cf. Matt. 13 : 46): it is this for which the monk seeks when he plunges into the depths of stillness and it is this for which he sells all his own desires through obedience to the commandments, so that he may acquire it even in this life.

84. The virtues are all equal and together reduce themselves to one, thus constituting a single principle and form of virtue. But some virtues – such as divine love, humility and divine patience – are greater than others, embracing and comprising as they do a large number or even all of the rest. With regard to patience the Lord says, 'You will gain possession of your souls through your patient endurance' (Luke 21 : 19). He did not say 'through your fasting' or 'through your vigils'. I refer to the patience bestowed by God, which is the queen of virtues, the foundation of courageous actions. It is patience that is peace amid strife, serenity amid distress, and a steadfast base for those who acquire it. Once you have attained it with the help of Christ Jesus, no swords and spears, no attacking armies, not even the ranks of demons, the dark phalanx of hostile powers, will be able to do you any harm.

85. The virtues, though they beget each other, yet have their origin in the three powers of the soul – all except those virtues that are divine. For the ground and principle of the four cardinal virtues, both natural and divine – sound understanding, courage, self-restraint and justice, the progenitors of all the other virtues – is the divine Wisdom that inspires those who have attained a state of mystical prayer. This Wisdom operates in a fourfold manner in the intellect. It activates not all the four virtues simultaneously, but each one individually, as is appropriate and as it determines. It activates sound understanding in the form of light, courage as clear-sighted power and ever-moving inspiration, self-restraint as a power of sanctification and purification, and justice as the dew of purity, joy-inducing and cooling the arid heat of the passions. In every one who has attained the state of perfection it activates each virtue fully, in the appropriate form.

86. The pursuit of the virtues through one's own efforts does not confer complete strength on the soul unless grace transforms them into an essential inner disposition. Each virtue is endowed with its own specific gift of grace, its own particular energy, and thus possesses the capacity to produce such a disposition and blessed state in those who attain it even when they have not consciously sought for any such state. Once a virtue has been bestowed on us it remains unchanged and unfailing. For just as a living soul activates the body's members, so the grace of the Holy Spirit activates the virtues. Without such grace the whole bevy of the virtues is moribund; and in those who appear to have attained them, or to be in the way of attaining them, solely through

their own efforts they are but shadows and prefigurations of beauty, not the reality itself.

87. The cardinal virtues are four: courage, sound understanding, self-restraint and justice. There are eight other moral qualities, that either go beyond or fall short of these virtues. These we regard as vices, and so we call them; but non-spiritual people regard them as virtues and that is what they call them. Exceeding or falling short of courage are audacity and cowardice; of sound understanding are cunning and ignorance; of self-restraint are licentiousness and obtuseness; of justice are excess and injustice, or taking less than one's due. In between, and superior to, what goes beyond or what falls short of them, lie not only the cardinal and natural virtues, but also the practical virtues. These are consolidated by resolution combined with probity of character; the others by perversion and self-conceit. That the virtues lie along the midpoint or axis of rectitude is testified to by the proverb, 'You will attain every well-founded axis' (Prov. 2 : 9. LXX). Thus when they are all established in the soul's three faculties in which they are begotten and built up, they have as their foundation the four cardinal virtues or, rather, Christ Himself. In this way the natural virtues are purified through the practical virtues, while the divine and supranatural virtues are conferred through the bounty of the Holy Spirit.

88. Among the virtues some are practical, others are natural, and others are divine and conferred by the Holy Spirit. The practical virtues are the products of our resolution, the natural virtues are built into us when we are created, the divine virtues are the fruits of grace.

89. Just as the virtues are begotten in the soul, so are the passions. But the virtues are begotten in accordance with nature, the passions in a mode contrary to nature. For what produces good or evil in the soul is the will's bias: it is like the joint of a pair of compasses or the pivot of a pair of scales: whichever way it inclines, so it will determine the consequences. For our inner disposition is capable of operating in one way or another, since it bears within itself both virtue and vice, the first as its natural birthright, the second as the result of the self-incurred proclivity of our moral will.

90. Scripture calls the virtues 'maidens' (cf. Song of Songs 1 : 3) because through their close union with the soul they become one with it in spirit and body. In the same way as a girl's beauty is emblematic of her love, the presence of these holy virtues expresses our inner purity and saintliness. Grace habitually gives to divine things an outward form

that accords with their inner nature, at the same time unerringly moulding those receptive to it in a way that corresponds to this nature.

91. There are eight ruling passions: gluttony, avarice and self-esteem – the three principal passions; and unchastity, anger, dejection, listlessness and arrogance – the five subordinate passions. In the same way, among the virtues opposed to these there are three that are all-embracing, namely, total shedding of possessions, self-control and humility, and five deriving from them, namely, purity, gentleness, joy, courage, and self-belittlement – and then come all the other virtues. To study and recognize the power, action and special flavour of each virtue and vice is not within the competence of everyone who wishes to do so; it is the prerogative of those who practise and experience the virtues actively and consciously and who receive from the Holy Spirit the gifts of cognitive insight and discrimination.

92. Virtues either energize in us or are energized by us. They energize in us by being present in us when it is appropriate, when they will, for as long as they will and in whatever manner they will. We energize them ourselves according to our resolve and the moral state of our capabilities. But they energize in us by virtue of their own essence, whereas we energize them merely in an imitative way, by modelling our moral conduct upon them. For all our actions are but typifications of the divine archetypes; and few indeed are those who participate concretely in noetic realities before they enjoy the eternal blessings of the life to come. In this life we mainly activate and make our own not the virtues themselves but their reflections and the ascetic toil they require.

93. According to St Paul (cf. Rom. 15 : 16), you 'minister' the Gospel only when, having yourself participated in the light of Christ, you can pass it on actively to others. Then you sow the Logos like a divine seed in the fields of your listeners' souls. 'Let your speech be always filled with grace', says St Paul (Col. 4 : 6), 'seasoned' with divine goodness. Then it will impart grace to those who listen to you with faith. Elsewhere St Paul, calling the teachers tillers and their pupils the fields they till (cf. 2 Tim. 2 : 6), wisely presents the former as ploughers and sowers of the divine Logos and the latter as the fertile soil, yielding a rich crop of virtues. True ministry is not simply a celebration of sacred rites; it also involves participation in divine blessings and the communication of these blessings to others.

94. Oral teaching for the guidance of others has many forms,

varying in accordance with the diverse ways in which it is put together from different sources. These sources are four in number: instruction, reading, ascetic practice, and grace. For just as water, while essentially the same, changes and acquires a distinctive quality according to the composition of the soil under it, so that it tastes bitter, or sweet, or brackish, or acidic, so oral teaching, coloured as it is by the moral state of the teacher, varies accordingly in the way it operates and in the benefits it confers.

95. Oral teaching is something to be enjoyed by all intelligent beings. But just as there are many different kinds of food, so the recipient of this teaching experiences its pleasure in a variety of ways. Instruction moulds the moral character; teaching by reading is like 'still waters' that nourish and restore the soul (cf. Ps. 23 : 2); teaching through ascetic practice is like 'green pastures', strengthening it (cf. Ps. 23 : 2); while teaching imparted through grace is like a cup that intoxicates it (cf. Ps. 23 : 5. LXX), filling it with unspeakable joy, or else it is like oil that exhilarates the face and makes it radiant (cf. Ps. 104 : 15).

96. Strictly speaking the soul possesses these various forms of teachings within itself as part of its own life; but when it learns about them through listening to others it becomes conscious of them, provided it listens with faith and provided the teacher teaches with love, speaking of the virtues without vanity or self-esteem. Then the soul is disciplined by instruction, nourished by reading, graciously escorted to her wedding by the deeply-rooted teaching that derives from ascetic practice, and receives the illuminative teaching of the Holy Spirit as a bridegroom who unites her to Himself and fills her with delight. 'Every word that proceeds out of the mouth of God' (Matt. 4 : 4) denotes the words that, inspired by the Holy Spirit, issue from the mouths of the saints – an inspiration granted not to all but only to those who are worthy. For although all intelligent beings take pleasure in knowledge, very few are those in this world who are consciously filled with joy by the wisdom of the Spirit; most of us only know and participate through the power of memory in the images and reflections of spiritual wisdom, for we do not yet with full awareness partake of the Logos of God, the true celestial bread. But in the life to come this bread is the sole food of the saints, proffered in such abundance that it is never exhausted, depleted, or immolated anew.

97. Without spiritual perception you cannot consciously experi-

ence the delight of divine things. If you dull your physical senses you make them insensible to sensory things, and you neither see, hear nor smell, but are paralysed or, rather, half-dead; similarly, if through the passions you deaden the natural powers of your soul you make them insensible to the activity of the mysteries of the Spirit and you cannot participate in them. If you are spiritually blind, deaf and insensible you are as dead: Christ does not live in you, and you do not live and act in Christ.

98. The physical senses and the soul's powers have an equal and similar, not to say identical, mode of operation, especially when they are in a healthy state; for then the soul's powers live and act through the senses, and the life-giving Spirit sustains them both. A man is truly ill when he succumbs to the generic malady of the passions and spends his whole time in the sickroom of inertia. When there is no satanic battle between them, making them reject the rule of the intellect and of the Spirit, the senses clearly perceive sensory things, the soul's powers intelligible things; for when they are united through the Spirit and constitute a single whole, they know directly and essentially the nature of divine and human things. They contemplate with clarity the *logoi*, or inward essences of these things, and distinctly perceive, so far as is possible, the single source of all things, the Holy Trinity.

99. He who practises hesychasm must acquire the following five virtues, as a foundation on which to build: silence, self-control, vigilance, humility and patience. Then there are three practices blessed by God: psalmody, prayer and reading – and handiwork for those weak in body. These virtues which we have listed not only embrace all the rest but also consolidate each other. From early morning the hesychast must devote himself to the remembrance of God through prayer and stillness of heart, praying diligently in the first hour, reading in the second, chanting psalms in the third, praying in the fourth, reading in the fifth, chanting psalms in the sixth, praying in the seventh, reading in the eighth, chanting psalms in the ninth, eating in the tenth, sleeping in the eleventh, if need be, and reciting vespers in the twelfth hour. Thus fruitfully spending the course of the day he gains God's blessings.

100. Like a bee one should extract from each of the virtues what is most profitable. In this way, by taking a small amount from all of them, one builds up from the practice of the virtues a great honeycomb overflowing with the soul-delighting honey of wisdom.

101. Now hear, if you will, how it is best to spend the night. For the

night vigil there are three programmes: for beginners, for those midway on the path, and for the perfect. The first programme is as follows: to sleep half the night and to keep vigil for the other half, either from evening till midnight or from midnight till dawn. The second is to keep vigil after nightfall for one or two hours, then to sleep for four hours, then to rise for matins and to chant psalms and pray for six hours until daybreak, then to chant the first hour, and after that to sit down and practise stillness, in the way already described. Then one can either follow the programme of spiritual work given for the daylight hours, or else continue in unbroken prayer, which gives a greater inner stability. The third programme is to stand and keep vigil uninterruptedly throughout the night.

102. Now let us say something about food. A pound of bread is sufficient for anyone aspiring to attain the state of inner stillness. You may drink two cups of undiluted wine and three of water. Your food should consist of whatever is at hand – not whatever your natural craving seeks, but what providence provides, to be eaten sparingly. The best and shortest guiding rule for those who wish to live as they should is to maintain the threefold all-embracing practices of fasting, vigilance and prayer, for these provide a most powerful support for all the other virtues.

103. Stillness requires above all faith, patience, love with all one's heart and strength and might (cf. Deut. 6 : 5), and hope. For if you have faith, even though because of negligence or some other fault you fail to attain what you seek in this life, you will on leaving this life most certainly be vouchsafed the fruit of faith and spiritual struggle and will behold your liberation, which is Jesus Christ, the redemption and salvation of souls, the Logos who is both God and man. But if you lack faith, you will certainly be condemned on leaving this world. In fact, as the Lord says, you are condemned already (cf. John 3 : 18). For if you are a slave to sensual pleasure, and want to be honoured by other people rather than by God (cf. John 5 : 44), you lack faith, even though you may profess faith verbally; and you deceive yourself without realizing it. And you will incur the rebuke: 'Because you did not receive Me in your heart but cast Me out behind your back, I too will reject you' (cf. Ezek. 5 : 11). If you possess faith you should have hope, and believe in God's truth to which the whole of Scripture bears witness, and confess your own weakness; otherwise you will inescapably receive double condemnation.

104. Nothing so fills the heart with contrition and humbles the soul as solitude embraced with self-awareness, and utter silence. And nothing so destroys the state of inner stillness and takes away the divine power that comes from it as the following six universal passions: insolence, gluttony, talkativeness, distraction, pretentiousness and the mistress of the passions, self-conceit. Whoever commits himself to these passions plunges himself progressively into darkness until he becomes completely insensate. But if he comes to himself again and with faith and ardour makes a fresh start, he will once more attain what he seeks, especially if he seeks it with humility. Yet if through his negligence even one of the passions that we have mentioned gets a hold on him once more, then the whole host of evils, including pernicious lack of faith, moves in and attacks him, devastating his soul till it becomes like another city of Babylon, full of diabolical turmoil and confusion (cf. Isa. 13 : 21). Then the last state of the person to whom this happens is worse than his first (cf. Matt. 12 : 45), and he turns into a violent enemy and defamer of those pursuing the path of hesychasm, always whetting his tongue against them like a sharp double-edged sword.

105. Once the waters of the passions, like a turbid and chaotic sea, have flooded the soul's state of stillness, there is no way of crossing over them except in the light swift-winged barque of self-control and total poverty. For when because of our dissipation and enslavement to materiality the torrents of the passions inundate the soil of the heart, they deposit there all the filth and sludge of evil thoughts, befouling the intellect, muddying the reason, clogging the body, and slackening, darkening and deadening soul and heart, depriving them of their natural stability and responsiveness.

106. Nothing so makes the soul of those striving to advance on the spiritual path sluggish, apathetic and mindless as self-love, that pimp of the passions. For whenever it induces us to choose bodily ease rather than virtue-promoting hardship, or to regard it as positive good sense not willingly to burden ourselves with ascetic labour, especially with respect to the light exertions involved in practising the commandments, then it causes the soul to relax its efforts to attain a state of stillness, and produces in it a strong, irresistible sense of indolence and slackness.

107. If you are feeble in practising the commandments yet want to expel your inner murkiness, the best and most efficient physic is

trustful unhesitating obedience in all things. This remedy, distilled from many virtues, restores vitality and acts as a knife which at a single stroke cuts away festering sores. If, then, in total trust and simplicity you choose this remedy out of all alternatives you excise every passion at once. Not only will you reach the state of stillness but also through your obedience you will fully enter into it, having found Christ and become His imitator and servitor in name and act.

108. Unless your life and actions are accompanied by a sense of inner grief you cannot endure the incandescence of stillness. If with this sense of grief you meditate – before they come to pass – on the many terrors that await us prior to and after death you will achieve both patience and humility, the twin foundations of stillness. Without them your efforts to attain stillness will always be accompanied by apathy and self-conceit. From these will arise a host of distractions and day-dreams, all inducing sluggishness. In their wake comes dissipation, daughter of indolence, making the body sluggish and slack and the intellect benighted and callous. Then Jesus is hidden, concealed by the throng of thoughts and images that crowd the mind (cf. John 5 : 13).

109. The torments of conscience in this life or the life to come are experienced with full awareness not by everyone but only by those who in this world or the next are deprived of divine glory and love. Such torment is like a fearful torturer punishing the guilty in various ways, or like a sharp sword striking with pitiless indignation and reproach. Once our conscience is active, what some call righteous indignation and others natural wrath is roused in three ways – against the demons, against our nature and against our own soul; for such indignation or wrath impels us to sharpen our conscience like a keen-bladed sword against our enemies. If this righteous indignation triumphs and subjects sin and our unregenerate self to the soul, then it is transmuted into the loftiest courage and leads us to God. But if the soul enslaves itself to sin and our unregenerate self, then this righteous indignation turns against it and torments it mercilessly, for it has enslaved itself to its enemies by its own free will. Thus enslaved, the soul commits terrible crimes, for its state of virtue is lost and it has alienated itself from God.

110. Of all the passions, lechery and listlessness are especially harsh and burdensome, for they oppress and debilitate the unhappy soul. And as they are inter-related and intertwined they are difficult to fight against and to overcome – in fact by our own efforts alone we cannot

defeat them. Lechery burgeons in the soul's appetitive aspect and by nature embraces indiscriminately both soul and body, since the total pleasure it generates spreads through all our members. Listlessness, once it has laid hold of our intellect and like bindweed has enlaced our soul and body, makes us slothful, enfeebled and indolent. Even before we have attained the blessed state of dispassion these two passions are expelled, though not finally defeated, whenever through prayer our soul receives from the Holy Spirit a power that releases it from tension, producing strength and profound peace in the heart, and solacing us with stillness. Lechery is the pleasure that includes all other forms of sensual indulgence, their source, mistress and queen; and its crony, sloth, is the invincible chariot bearing Pharaoh's captains (cf. Exod. 14 : 7). Through these two – lechery and sloth – the seeds of the passions are sown in our unhappy lives.

111. Noetic prayer is an activity initiated by the cleansing power of the Spirit and the mystical rites celebrated by the intellect. Similarly, stillness is initiated by attentive waiting upon God, its intermediate stage is characterized by illuminative power and contemplation, and its final goal is ecstasy and the enraptured flight of the intellect towards God.

112. Prior to the enjoyment of the blessings that transcend the intellect, and as a foretaste of that enjoyment, the noetic activity of the intellect mystically offers up the Lamb of God upon the altar of the soul and partakes of Him in communion. To eat the Lamb of God upon the soul's noetic altar is not simply to apprehend Him spiritually or to participate in Him; it is also to become an image of the Lamb as He is in the age to come. Now we experience the manifest expression of the mysteries; hereafter we hope to enjoy their very substance.

113. For beginners prayer is like a joyous fire kindled in the heart; for the perfect it is like a vigorous sweet-scented light. Or again, prayer is the preaching of the Apostles, an action of faith or, rather, faith itself, 'that makes real for us the things for which we hope' (Heb. 11 : 1), active love, angelic impulse, the power of the bodiless spirits, their work and delight, the Gospel of God, the heart's assurance, hope of salvation, a sign of purity, a token of holiness, knowledge of God, baptism made manifest, purification in the water of regeneration, a pledge of the Holy Spirit, the exultation of Jesus, the soul's delight, God's mercy, a sign of reconciliation, the seal of Christ, a ray of the noetic sun, the heart's dawn-star, the confirmation of the Christian

faith, the disclosure of reconciliation with God, God's grace, God's wisdom or, rather, the origin of true and absolute Wisdom; the revelation of God, the work of monks, the life of hesychasts, the source of stillness, and expression of the angelic state. Why say more? Prayer is God, who accomplishes everything in everyone (cf. 1 Cor. 12 : 6), for there is a single action of Father, Son and Holy Spirit, activating all things through Christ Jesus.

114. Had Moses not received the rod of power from God, he would not have become a god to Pharaoh (cf. Exod. 7 : 1) and a scourge both to him and to Egypt. Correspondingly the intellect, if it fails to grasp the power of prayer, will not be able to shatter sin and the hostile forces ranged against it.

115. Those who say or do anything without humility are like people who build in winter or without bricks and mortar. Very few acquire humility and know it through experience; and those who try to talk about it are like people measuring a bottomless pit. And I who in my blindness have formed a faint image of this great light am rash enough to say this about it: true humility does not consist in speaking humbly, or in looking humble. The humble person does not have to force himself to think humbly, nor does he keep finding fault with himself. Such conduct may provide us with an occasion for humility or constitute its outward form, but humility itself is a grace and a divine gift. The holy fathers teach that there are two kinds of humility: to regard oneself as lower than everyone else, and to ascribe all one's achievement to God. The first is the beginning, the second the consummation.

Those who seek humility should bear in mind the three following things: that they are the worst of sinners, that they are the most despicable of all creatures since their state is an unnatural one, and that they are even more pitiable than the demons, since they are slaves to the demons. You will also profit if you say this to yourself: how do I know what or how many other people's sins are, or whether they are greater than or equal to my own? In our ignorance you and I, my soul, are worse than all men, we are dust and ashes under their feet. How can I not regard myself as more despicable than all other creatures, for they act in accordance with the nature they have been given, while I, owing to my innumerable sins, am in a state contrary to nature. Truly animals are more pure than I, sinner that I am; on account of this I am the lowest of all, since even before my death I have made my bed in hell. Who is not fully aware that the person who sins is worse than the demons, since he is their thrall and their slave, even in this life sharing their murk-mantled prison? If I am mastered by the demons I must be inferior to them. Therefore my lot will be with them in the abyss of hell, pitiful that I am. You on earth who even before your death dwell in that abyss, how do you dare delude yourself, calling yourself righteous, when through the evil you have done you have defiled yourself and made yourself a sinner and a demon? Woe to your self-deception and your delusion, squalid cur that you are, consigned to fire and darkness for these offences.

116. According to theologians, noetic, pure, angelic prayer is in its power wisdom inspired by the Holy Spirit. A sign that you have attained such prayer is that the intellect's vision when praying is completely free from form and that the intellect sees neither itself nor anything else in a material way. On the contrary, it is often drawn away even from its own senses by the light acting within it; for it now grows immaterial and filled with spiritual radiance, becoming through ineffable union a single spirit with God (cf. 1 Cor. 6 : 17).

117. We are led and guided towards God-given humility by seven different qualities, each of which generates and complements the others: silence, humbleness in thought, in speech, in appearance, self-reproach, contrition and looking on oneself as the least of men. Silence consciously espoused gives birth to humbleness in thought. Humbleness in thought produces three further modes of humility, namely, humbleness in speech, bearing oneself in a simple and humble way, and constant self-belittlement. These three modes give birth to contrition; this arises within us when God allows us to suffer temptations – when, that is, we are disciplined by providence and humbled by the demons. Contrition readily induces the soul to feel the lowest and least of all, and the servant of all. Contrition and looking on oneself as the least of all bring about the perfect humility that is the gift of God, a power rightly regarded as the perfection of all the virtues. It is a state in which one ascribes all one's achievements to God. Thus the first factor leading to humility is silence, from which humbleness of thought is born. This gives birth to the three further modes of humility. These three generate the single quality of contrition. The quality of contrition gives birth to the seventh mode, the primal humility of regarding oneself as the least of men, which is also called providential humility. Providential humility confers the true and God-given humility that is

perfect and indescribable. Primal humility comes thus: when you are abandoned, overcome, enslaved and dominated by every passion, distractive thought and evil spirit, and can find no help in doing good works, or in God, or in anything at all, so that you are ready to fall into despair, then you are humbled in everything, are filled with contrition and regard yourself as the lowest and least of all things, the slave of all, and worse even than the demons, since you are dominated and vanquished by them. This is providential humility. Once acquired, through it God bestows the ultimate humility. This is a divine power that activates and accomplishes all things. With its aid a man always sees himself as an instrument of divine power, and through it he accomplishes the miraculous works of God.

118. Because we are now mastered by the passions and succumb to a host of temptations we cannot in our age attain those states that characterize sanctity – I mean real spiritual contemplation of the divine light, an intellect free from fantasy and distraction, the true energy of prayer ceaselessly flowing from the depths of the heart, the soul's resurrection and ascension, divine rapture, the soaring beyond the limits of this world, the mind's ecstasy in spirit above all things sensory, the ravishment of the intellect above even its own powers, the angelic flight of the soul impelled by God towards what is infinite and utterly sublime. The intellect – especially in the more superficial among us – tends to picture these states prematurely to itself, and in this way it loses even the slight stability God has given it and becomes altogether moribund. Hence we must exercise great discrimination and not try to pre-empt things that come in their own good time, or reject what we already possess and dream of something else. For by nature the intellect readily invents fantasies and illusions about the high spiritual states it has not yet attained, and thus there is no small danger that we may lose what has already been given to us and destroy our mind through repeated self-deception, becoming a day-dreamer and not a hesychast.

119. Faith, like active prayer, is a grace. For prayer, when activated by love through the power of the Spirit, renders true faith manifest – the faith that reveals the life of Jesus. If, then, you are aware that such faith is not at work within you, that means your faith is dead and lifeless. In fact you should not even speak of yourself as one of the 'faithful' if your faith is merely theoretical and is not actualized by the practice of the commandments or by the Spirit. Thus faith must be

evidenced by progress in keeping the commandments, or it must be actualized and translucent in what we do. This is confirmed by St James when he says, 'Show me your faith through your works and I will show you the works that I do through my faith' (cf. Jas. 2 : 18). In saying this he makes it clear that grace-inspired faith is evidenced by the keeping of the commandments, just as the commandments are actualized and made translucent by grace-inspired faith. Faith is the root of the commandments or, rather, it is the spring that feeds their growth. It has two aspects – that of confession and that of grace – though it is essentially one and indivisible.

120. The short ladder of spiritual progress – which is at the same time both small and great – has five rungs leading to perfection. The first is renunciation, the second submission to a religious way of life, the third obedience to spiritual direction, the fourth humility, and the fifth God-imbued love. Renunciation raises the prisoner from hell and sets him free from enslavement to material things. Submission is the discovery of Christ and the decision to serve Him. As Christ Himself said, 'He who serves Me, follows Me; and where I am he who serves Me will also be' (cf. John 12 : 26). And where is Christ? In heaven, enthroned at the right hand of the Father. Thus he who serves Christ must be in heaven as well, his foot placed ready to climb up; indeed, before he even begins to ascend by his own efforts he is already raised up and ascending with Christ. Obedience, put into action through the practice of the commandments, builds a ladder out of various virtues and places them in the soul as rungs by which to ascend (cf. Ps. 84 : 5. LXX). Thence the spiritual aspirant is embraced by humility, the great exalter, and is borne heavenwards and delivered over to love, the queen of the virtues. By love he is led to Christ and brought into His presence. Thus by this short ladder he who is truly obedient swiftly ascends to heaven.

121. The quickest way to ascend to the kingdom of heaven by the short ladder of the virtues is through effacing the five passions hostile to obedience, namely, disobedience, contentiousness, self-gratification, self-justification and pernicious self-conceit. For these are the limbs and organs of the recalcitrant demon that devours those who offer false obedience and consigns them to the dragon of the abyss. Disobedience is the mouth of hell; contentiousness its tongue, whetted like a sword; self-gratification its sharp teeth; self-justification its gullet; and self-conceit, that sends one to hell, is the vent that evacuates its all-

devouring belly. If through obedience you overcome the first of these – disobedience – you cut off all the rest at a stroke, and with a single swift stride attain heaven. This is the truly ineffable and inconceivable miracle wrought by our compassionate Lord: that through a single virtue or, rather, a single commandment, we can ascend straightway to heaven, just as through a single act of disobedience we have descended and continue to descend into hell.

122. Man is like another or second world – a new world, as he is called by St Paul when he states, 'Whoever is in Christ is a new creation' (2 Cor. 5 : 17). For through virtue man becomes a heaven and an earth and everything that a world is. Every quality and mystery exists for man's sake, as St Gregory of Nazianzos says.[1] Moreover, if, as St Paul affirms, our struggle is not against creatures of flesh and blood, but against the potentates and rulers of the darkness of this world, against the spirits of evil in the celestial realms of the prince of the air (cf. Eph. 2 : 2; 6 : 12), it follows that those who secretly fight against us inhabit the world of our psychic powers, which is like another great world of nature. For the three princes that oppose us in our struggle attack the three powers of the soul; and it is precisely where we have made progress, and in areas that we have laboured to develop, that they launch their assault.

Thus the dragon, the prince of the abyss, whose strength is manifest in the loins and the belly – organs of our soul's appetitive power – sallies forth against those who strive to keep their attention in their hearts; and through the lust-loving giant of forgetfulness he hurls at them the whole battery of his fiery darts (cf. Eph. 6 : 16). Desire being for him like another sea and abyss, he plunges into it, coils his way through it, and stirs it up, making it foam and boil. In this way he inflames it with sexual longing and inundates it with sensual pleasure; but this does not slake it, for it is insatiable.

The prince of this world (cf. John 12 : 31), who campaigns against the soul's incensive power, attacks those striving to attain practical virtue. With the help of the giant of sloth, he continually ranges his forces against us and engages us in a spiritual contest with every trick of passion he can devise. As though in the theatre or stadium of some other world, he wrestles with all who stand up against him with

---

[1] *Oration* 39, 20 (*P.G.* xxxvi, 360A).

courage and endurance; sometimes he wins, sometimes he is defeated, and so he either disgraces us or gains us crowns of glory in the sight of the angels.

The prince of the air (cf. Eph. 2 : 2) attacks those whose minds are absorbed in contemplation, deluding them with fantasies; for supported by the evil spirits of the air he attacks the soul's intellectual and spiritual power. Through the giant of ignorance he clouds the aspiring mind as though it were an intellectual heaven, disrupting its composure, craftily insinuating into it vague fantastic images of evil spirits and their metamorphoses, and producing fear-inspiring similitudes of thunder and lightning, tempests and alarums. These three princes, assisted by the three giants, attack the three powers of our soul, each waging war against the particular power that corresponds to him.

123. These demons were once celestial intelligences; but, having fallen from their original state of immateriality and refinement, each of them has acquired a certain material grossness, assuming a bodily form corresponding to the kind of action allotted to it. For like human beings they have lost the delights of the angels and have been deprived of divine bliss, and so they too, like us, now find pleasure in earthly things, becoming to a certain extent material because of the disposition to material passions which they have acquired. We should not be surprised at this, for our own soul, created intellectual and spiritual in the image of God, has become bestial, insensate and virtually mindless through losing the knowledge of God and finding pleasure in material things. Inner disposition changes outward nature, and acts of moral choice alter the way that nature functions. Some evil spirits are material, gross, uncontrollable, passionate and vindictive. They hunger for material pleasure and indulgence as carnivores for flesh. Like savage dogs and like those possessed they devour and relish rotten food; and their delight and habitation are coarse, fleshy bodies. Others are licentious and slimy. They creep about in the pool of desire like leeches, frogs and snakes. Sometimes they assume the form of fish, delighting in their brackish lubricity. Slippery and flaccid, they swim in the sea of drunkenness, rejoicing in the humectation of mindless pleasures. In this manner they constantly stir up waves of impure thoughts, and storms and tempests in the soul. Others are light and subtle, since they are aerial spirits, and agitate the soul's contemplative power, provoking strong winds and fantasies. They deceive the soul by

appearing sometimes in the form of birds or angels. They fill one's memory with the forms of people one knows. They pervert and deform the contemplative vision of those pursuing the path of holiness who have not yet attained the state of purity and inner discrimination; for there is nothing spiritual but that they can secretly transform themselves into it in the imagination. They too arm themselves according to our spiritual state and degree of progress, and substituting illusion for truth and fantasy for contemplation they take up their abode within us. It is to these evil spirits that Scripture refers when it speaks of beasts of the field, birds of the air and things that creep on the ground (cf. Hos. 2 : 18).

124. There are five ways in which the passions may be aroused in us and our fallen self may wage war against our soul. Sometimes our fallen self misuses things. Sometimes it seeks to do what is unnatural as though it were natural. Sometimes it forms warm friendship with the demons and they provide it with arms against the soul. Sometimes under the influence of the passions it falls into a state of civil war, divided against itself. Finally, if the demons have failed to achieve their purpose in any of the ways just mentioned, God may permit them in their malice to wage war against us in order to teach us greater humility.

125. The main causes of warfare – arising in us through every kind of object or situation – are three: our inner disposition, the misuse of created things and, by God's leave, the malice and onslaught of the demons. As the fallen self rises in protest against the soul, and the soul against the fallen self (cf. Gal. 5:17), so in the same way our inner disposition and our mode of acting make the passions of the fallen self war against the soul, and the valiant powers of the soul wage war against the fallen self. And sometimes our enemy, shameless as he is, has the audacity to fight against us in his own person, without cause or warning. Thus, my friend, do not let this blood-loving leech bleed your arteries, and then spit out the blood he has sucked from you. Do not glut the snake and the dragon, and then you will easily trample on the insolence of the lion and the dragon (cf. Ps. 91 : 13). Lament until you have stripped off the passions and clothed yourself in your heavenly dwelling-place (cf. 2 Cor. 5 : 2), and are refashioned according to the likeness of Jesus Christ, who made you in His image (cf. Col. 3 : 10).

126. Those completely given over to the pursuits of the flesh and

full of self-love are always slaves to sensual pleasure and to vanity. Envy, too, is rooted in them. Consumed by malice and embittered by their neighbour's blessings, they calumniate good as bad, calling it the fruit of deceit. They do not accept things of the Spirit or believe in them; and because of their lack of faith they cannot see or know God. Such people, due to this same blindness and lack of faith, on the last day will justly hear spoken to them the words, 'I know you not' (Matt. 25 : 12). For the questing believer must either believe when he hears what he does not know, or come to know what he believes; and he must teach to others what he has come to know and abundantly multiply the talent entrusted to him. But if he disbelieves what he does not know, and vilifies what he does not understand, and teaches what he has not learnt, envying those who teach things from practical experience, his lot will surely be to suffer punishment with those consumed by 'the gall of bitterness' (Acts 8 : 23).

127. According to the wise, a true teacher is he who through his all-embracing cognitive insight comprehends created things concisely, as if they constituted a single body, establishing distinctions and connections between them according to their generic difference and identity, so as to indicate which possess similar qualities. Or he may be described as one who can truly demonstrate things apodictically. Or again, a true spiritual teacher is he who distinguishes and relates the general and universal qualities of created things – classified as five in number, but compounded in the incarnate Logos – in accordance with a particular formulation that embraces everything. But his apodictic skill is not a matter of mere verbal dexterity, like that of profane philosophers, for he is able to enlighten others through the contemplative vision of created things manifested to him by the Holy Spirit.

A true philosopher is one who perceives in created things their spiritual Cause, or who knows created things through knowing their Cause, having attained a union with God that transcends the intellect and a direct, unmediated faith. He does not simply learn about divine things, but actually experiences them. Or again, a true philosopher is one whose intellect is conversant equally with ascetic practice and contemplative wisdom. Thus the perfect philosopher or lover of wisdom is one whose intellect has attained – alike on the moral, natural and theological levels – love of wisdom or, rather, love of God. That is to say, he has learnt from God the principles of ascetic practice (moral philosophy), an insight into the spiritual causes of created things (natural philosophy), and a precise contemplative understanding of doctrinal principles (theology).

Or again, a teacher initiated into things divine is one who distinguishes principial beings from participative beings or beings that have no autonomous self-subsistent reality; he adduces the essences of principial beings from beings that exist through participating in them, and, inspired by the Holy Spirit, he perceives the essences of principial beings embodied in participative beings. In other words, he interprets what is intelligible and invisible in terms of what is sensible and visible, and the visible sense-world in terms of the invisible and suprasensory world, conscious that what is visible is an image of what is invisible, and that what is invisible is the archetype of what is visible. He knows that things possessing form and figure are brought into being by what is formless and without figure, and that each manifests the other spiritually; and he clearly perceives each in the other and conveys this perception in his teaching of the truth. His knowledge of the truth, with all its sun-like radiance, is not expressed in anagogical or allegorical form; on the contrary, he elucidates the true underlying principles of both worlds with spiritual insight and power, and expounds them forcibly and vividly. In this way the visible world becomes our teacher and the invisible world is shown to be an eternal divine dwelling-place manifestly brought into being for our sake.

A divine philosopher is he who through ascetic purification and noetic contemplation has achieved a direct union with God, and is a true friend of God, in that he esteems and loves the supreme, creative and true wisdom above every other love, wisdom and knowledge. A student of spiritual knowledge, though not properly speaking a philosopher (even though reflected wisdom has unnoticed appropriated the name of philosophy, as St Gregory of Nazianzos points out) is he who esteems and studies God's wisdom mirrored in His creation, down to the least vestige of it; but he does this without any self-display or any hankering after human praise and glory, for he wishes to be a lover of God's wisdom in creation and not a lover of materialism.

An interpreter of sacred texts adept in the mysteries of the kingdom of God is everyone who after practising the ascetic life devotes himself to the contemplation of God and cleaves to stillness. Out of the treasury of his heart he brings forth things new and old (cf. Matt. 13 : 52), that is, things from the Gospel of Christ and the Prophets, or from the New and Old Testaments, or doctrinal teachings and rules of ascetic practice, or themes from the Apostles and from the Law. These are the mysteries new and old that the skilled interpreter brings forth when he has been schooled in the life of holiness.

An interpreter is one proficient in the practice of the ascetic life and still actively engaged in scriptural exegesis. A divine teacher is one who mediates, in accordance with the laws governing the natural world, the spiritual knowledge and inner meanings of created things and, inspired by the Holy Spirit, elucidates all things with the analytic power of his intelligence. A true philosopher is one who has attained, consciously and directly, a supranatural union with God.

128. Those who write and speak and who wish to build up the Church, while lacking the inspiration of the Holy Spirit, are 'psychic' or worldly people void of the Spirit, as St Jude observes (cf. Jude 19). Such people come under the curse which says, 'Woe to those who are wise in their own sight, and esteem themselves as possessors of knowledge' (Isa. 5 : 21); for they speak from themselves and it is not the Spirit of God that speaks in them (cf. Matt. 10 : 20). For those who speak what are simply their own thoughts before they have attained purity are deluded by the spirit of self-conceit. It is to them that Solomon refers when he says, 'I knew a man who regarded himself as wise; there is more hope for a fool than for him' (Prov. 26 : 12. LXX); and again, 'Do not be wise in your own sight' (Prov. 3 : 7). St Paul himself, filled with the Spirit, endorses this when he says, 'We are not qualified to form any judgment on our own account; our qualification comes from God' (2 Cor. 3 : 5), and, 'As men sent from God, we speak before God in the grace of Christ' (2 Cor. 2 : 17). What people say when they speak on their own account is repellent and murksome, for their words do not come from the living spring of the Spirit, but are spawned from the morass of their own heart, a bog infested with the leeches, snakes and frogs of desire, delusion and dissipation; the water of their knowledge is evil-smelling, turbid and torpid, sickening to those who drink it and filling them with nausea and disgust.

129. 'We are the body of Christ', says St Paul, 'and each of us is one of its members' (cf. 1 Cor. 12 : 27). And elsewhere he says, 'You are one body and one spirit, even as you have been called' (Eph. 4 : 4). For 'as the body without the spirit is dead' (Jas. 2 : 26) and insensate, so if you have been deadened by the passions through neglecting the commandments after your baptism the Holy Spirit and the grace of

Christ cease to operate in you and to enlighten you; for though you possess the Spirit, since you have faith and have been regenerated through baptism, yet the Spirit is quiescent and inactive within you because of the deadness of your soul.

Although the soul is one and the members of the body are many, the soul sustains them all, giving life and movement to those that can be animated. Should some of them have withered because of some disease and become as if dead and inert, yet they are still sustained by the soul, even in their lifeless and insensate state. Similarly, the Spirit of Christ is present with integral wholeness in all who are members of Christ, activating and generating life in all capable of participating in it; and in His compassion He still sustains even those who through some weakness do not actively participate in the life of the Spirit. In this way each of the faithful participates, by virtue of his faith, in adoption to sonship through the Spirit; but should he grow negligent and fail to sustain his faith he will become inert and benighted, deprived of Christ's life and light. Such is the state of each of the faithful who, though a member of Christ and possessing the Spirit of Christ, fails to activate this Spirit within himself and so is stagnant, incapable of participating positively in the life of grace.

130. The principal forms of contemplation are eight in number. The first is contemplation of the formless, unoriginate and uncreated God, source of all things – that is, contemplation of the one Triadic Deity that transcends all being. The second is contemplation of the hierarchy and order of the spiritual powers. The third is contemplation of the structure of created beings. The fourth is contemplation of God's descent through the incarnation of the Logos. The fifth is contemplation of the universal resurrection. The sixth is contemplation of the dread second coming of Christ. The seventh is contemplation of age-long punishment. The eighth is contemplation of the kingdom of heaven. The first four pertain to what has already been manifested and realized. The second four pertain to what is in store and has not yet been manifested; but they are clearly contemplated by and disclosed to those who through grace have attained great purity of intellect. Whoever without such grace attempts to descry them should realize that far from attaining spiritual vision he will merely become the prey of fantasies, deceived by and forming illusions in obedience to the spirit of delusion.

131. Here something must be said about delusion, so far as this is

possible; for, because of its deviousness and the number of ways in which it can ensnare us, few recognize it clearly and for most it is almost inscrutable. Delusion manifests itself or, rather, attacks and invades us in two ways – in the form of mental images and fantasies or in the form of diabolic influence – though its sole cause and origin is always arrogance. The first form is the origin of the second and the second is the origin of a third form – mental derangement. The first form, illusory visions, is caused by self-conceit; for this leads us to invest the divine with some illusory shape, thus deceiving us through mental images and fantasies. This deception in its turn produces blasphemy as well as the fear induced by monstrous apparitions, occurring both when awake and when asleep – a state described as the terror and perturbation of the soul. Thus arrogance is followed by delusion, delusion by blasphemy, blasphemy by fear, fear by terror, and terror by a derangement of the natural state of the mind. This is the first form of delusion, that induced by mental images and fantasies.

The second form, induced by diabolic influence, is as follows. It has its origin in self-indulgence, which in its turn results from so-called natural desire. Self-indulgence begets licentiousness in all its forms of indescribable impurity. By inflaming man's whole nature and clouding his intelligence as a result of its intercourse with spurious images, licentiousness deranges the intellect, searing it into a state of delirium and impelling its victim to utter false prophecies, interpreting the visions and discourses of certain supposed saints, which he claims are revealed to him when he is intoxicated and befuddled with passion, his whole character perverted and corrupted by demons. Those ignorant of spiritual matters, beguiled by delusion, call such men 'little souls'. These 'little souls' are to be found sitting near the shrines of saints, by whose spirit they claim to be inspired and tested, and whose purported message they proclaim to others. But in truth they should be called possessed by the demons, deceived and enslaved by delusion, and not prophets foretelling what is to happen now and in the future. For the demon of licentiousness himself darkens and deranges their minds, inflaming them with the fire of spiritual lust, conjuring up before them the illusory appearance of saints, and making them hear conversations and see visions. Sometimes the demons themselves appear to them and convulse them with fear. For having harnessed them to the yoke of Belial, the demon of licentiousness drives them on to practise their deceits, so that he may keep them captive and enslaved until death, when he will consign them to hell.

132. Delusion arises in us from three principal sources: arrogance, the envy of demons, and the divine will that allows us to be tried and corrected. Arrogance arises from superficiality, demonic envy is provoked by our spiritual progress, and the need for correction is the consequence of our sinful way of life. The delusion arising solely from envy and self-conceit is swiftly healed, especially when we humble ourselves. On the other hand, the delusion allowed by God for our correction, when we are handed over to satan because of our sinfulness, God often permits to continue until our death, if this is needed to efface our sins. Sometimes God hands over even the guiltless to the torment of demons for the sake of their salvation. One should also know that the demon of self-conceit himself prophesies in those who are not scrupulously attentive to their hearts.

133. All the faithful are truly anointed priests and kings in the spiritual renewal brought about through baptism, just as priests and kings were anointed figuratively in former times. For those anointings were prefigurations of the truth of our anointing: prefigurations in relation not merely to some of us but to all of us. For our kingship and priesthood is not of the same form or character as theirs, even though the symbolic actions are the same. Nor does our anointing recognize any distinction in nature, grace or calling, in such a way that those anointed essentially differ one from the other: we have but one and the same calling, faith and ritual. The true significance of this is that he who is anointed is pure, dispassionate and wholly consecrated to God now and for ever.

134. If your speech is full of wisdom and you meditate on understanding in your heart (cf. Ps. 49 : 3), you will disclose in created things the presence of the divine Logos, the substantive Wisdom of God the Father (cf. 1 Cor. 1 : 24); for in created things you will perceive the outward expression of the archetypes that characterize them, and thus through your active living intelligence you will speak wisdom that derives from the divine Wisdom. And because your heart will be illuminated by the power of the transfiguring understanding on which you meditate in your spirit, you will be able through this understanding to instruct and illuminate those who listen with faith.

135. Today's great enemy of truth, drawing men to perdition, is

delusion. As a result of this delusion, tenebrous ignorance rules the souls of all those sunk in lethargy and alienates them from God. Such people are as if unaware that there exists a God who gives us rebirth and illumination, or they assume that we can believe in Him and know Him only in a theoretical way and not through our actions, or else they imagine that He has revealed Himself only to the people of former times and not to us also; and they pretend that the scriptural texts about God are applicable only to the original authors, or to others, but not to themselves. Thus they blaspheme the teaching about God, since they repudiate true knowledge inspired by devotion to God, and read the Scriptures only in a literal, not to say Judaic, manner; denying the possibility that man even in this life can be resurrected through the resurrection of his soul, they choose to remain in the grave of ignorance. Delusion consists of three passions: lack of faith, guile and sloth. These generate and support each other: lack of faith sharpens the wits of guile, and guile goes hand in hand with sloth, which expresses itself outwardly in laziness. Or conversely, sloth may beget guile – did not the Lord say, 'You cunning and lazy servant' (Matt. 25 : 26)? – and guile mothers lack of faith. For if you are full of guile you lack faith, and if you lack faith you stand in no awe of God. From such lack of faith comes sloth, which begets contempt; and when you are full of contempt you scorn all goodness and practise every kind of wickedness.

136. Complete dogmatic orthodoxy consists in a true doctrine about God and an unerring spiritual knowledge of created things. If you are orthodox in this way you should glorify God thus: Glory to Thee, Christ our God, glory to Thee, because for our sake Thou, the divine Logos who transcends all things, becamest man. Great is the mystery of Thine incarnation, Saviour: glory to Thee.

137. According to St Maximos the Confessor there are three motives for writing which are above reproach and censure: to assist one's memory, to help others, or as an act of obedience.[1] It is for the last reason that most spiritual writings have been composed, at the humble request of those who have need of them. If you write about spiritual matters simply for pleasure, fame or self-display, you will get your deserts, as Scripture says (cf. Matt. 6 : 5, 16), and will not profit

---

[1] *On Love* ii, 94; E.T., *The Philokalia*, vol. ii, p. 81.

from it in this life or gain any reward in the life to come. On the contrary, you will be condemned for courting popularity and for fraudulently trafficking in God's wisdom.

Further Texts

1. Everyone baptized into Christ should pass progressively through all the stages of Christ's own life, for in baptism he receives the power so to progress, and through the commandments he can discover and learn how to accomplish such progression. To Christ's conception corresponds the foretaste of the gift of the Holy Spirit, to His nativity the actual experience of joyousness, to His baptism the cleansing force of the fire of the Spirit, to His transfiguration the contemplation of divine light, to His crucifixion the dying to all things, to His burial the indwelling of divine love in the heart, to His resurrection the soul's life-quickening resurrection, and to His ascension divine ecstasy and the transport of the intellect into God. He who fails to pass consciously through these stages is still callow in body and spirit, even though he may be regarded by all as mature and accomplished in the practice of virtue.

2. Christ's Passion is a life-quickening death to those who have experienced all its phases, for by experiencing what He experienced we are glorified as He is (cf. Rom. 8 : 17). But indulgence in sensual passions induces a truly lethal death. Willingly to experience what Christ experienced is to crucify crucifixion and to put death to death.

3. To suffer for Christ's sake is patiently to endure whatever happens to us. For the envy which the innocent provoke is for their benefit, while the Lord's schooling tests us so as to bring about our conversion, since it opens our ears when we are guilty. That is why the Lord has promised an eternal crown to those who endure in this manner (cf. Jas. 1 : 12). Glory to Thee, our God; glory to Thee, Holy Trinity; glory to Thee for all things.

ON PASSION-IMBUED CHANGE

4. Listlessness – a most difficult passion to overcome – makes the body sluggish. And when the body is sluggish, the soul also grows sluggish. When both have become thoroughly lax, self-indulgence induces a change in the body's temperament. Self-indulgence incites the appetite, appetite gives rise to pernicious desire, desire to the spirit of revolt, revolt to dormant recollections, recollection to imaginings, imagining to mental provocation, provocation to coupling with the thought provoked, and coupling to assent. Such assent to a diabolic provocation leads to actual sinning, either through the body or in various other ways. Thus we are defeated and thus we lapse.

ON BENEFICENT CHANGE

5. In whatever work we engage patience gives birth to courage, courage to commitment, commitment to perseverance, and perseverance to an increase in the work done. Such additional labour quells the body's dissolute impulses and checks the desire for sensual indulgence. Thus checked, desire gives rise to spiritual longing, longing to love, love to aspiration, aspiration to ardour, ardour to self-galvanizing, self-galvanizing to assiduousness, assiduousness to prayer, and prayer to stillness. Stillness gives birth to contemplation, contemplation to spiritual knowledge, and knowledge to the apprehension of the mysteries. The consummation of the mysteries is theology, the fruit of theology is perfect love, of love humility, of humility dispassion, and of dispassion foresight, prophecy and foreknowledge. No one possesses the virtues perfectly in this life, nor does he cut off evil all at once. On the contrary, by small increases of virtue evil gradually ceases to exist.

ON MORBID DEFLUXIONS

Question: In how many ways do morbid defluxions take place, whether sinful or sinless?

6. *Answer*:   Sinful defluxions take place in three ways: through fornication, through self-abuse, and through consent to pernicious thoughts. Sinless defluxions take place in seven ways: through the urine, through eating solid or stimulating foods, through drinking too much chill water, through the sluggishness of the body, through excessive tiredness, and through all kinds of demonic fantasy. In veterans in the ascetic life they generally take place through the first five of the ways we have just mentioned. In those who have attained the state of dispassion, the fluid only issues mixed with urine, because on account of their ascetic labours their inner ducts have in some way become porous and they have been given the grace of a divine energy, purificatory and sanctifying – the grace of continence. The last form of defluxion – that prompted by demonic fantasy during sleep – pertains both to those still under the domination of the passions and to those suffering from weakness. But since this is involuntary it is free from sin, as the holy fathers tell us.

By divine dispensation the person who has attained the state of dispassion experiences from time to time a sinless propulsion, while the remaining fluid is consumed by divine fire. The person still engaged in the ascetic life and so under various forms of constraint experiences a discharge that is innocuous. The person still under the sway of the passions experiences a natural discharge and an unnatural discharge, the first prompted by diabolic fantasy during sleep and the second by diabolic fantasy to which assent has been given while he is awake. The first is innocuous, the second is sinful and liable to penance.

In those who have attained the state of dispassion the propulsion and the bodily discharge constitute a single action through which by divine dispensation surplus fluid is expelled through the urine while the rest is consumed by divine fire, as already stated. In those midway along the ascetic path there are said to be six general ways of innocuous defluxion through which the body is cleansed and freed from the corruptive fluid formed naturally and unavoidably in it. These are prompted by solid or stimulating foods, by drinking cold water, by sluggishness of the body, by torpor resulting from excessive labour, and finally by the malice of demons. In the weak and those newly engaged in the ascetic life there are similarly six ways, all embroiled with the passions. They are prompted by gluttony, by back-biting, by censoriousness, by self-esteem, by demonic fantasy during sleep and assent to it while awake, and finally by the aggressive malice of demons. Yet even these have in God's providence a double purpose: first, they cleanse human nature from corruption, from the surplus matter it has absorbed, and from impulse-driven appetites; and, second, they train the person engaged in the spiritual struggle to be humble and attentive, and to restrain himself in all things and from all things.

7. He who dwells in solitude and depends on charity for his food must accept alms in seven ways. First, he must ask only for what is needful. Secondly, he must take only what is needful. Thirdly, he must receive whatever is offered to him as if from God. Fourthly, he must trust in God and believe that He will recompense the giver. Fifthly, he must apply himself to keeping the commandments. Sixthly, he must not misuse what is given to him. Seventhly, he must not be stingy but must give to others and be compassionate. He who conducts himself thus in these matters experiences the joy of having his needs supplied not by man but by God.

On the Signs of Grace and Delusion, Written for the Confessor Longinos: Ten Texts

1. As the great teacher St John Chrysostom states,[1] we should be in a position to say that we need no help from the Scriptures, no assistance from other people, but are instructed by God; for 'all will be taught by God' (Isa. 54 : 13; John 6 : 45), in such a way that we learn from Him and through Him what we ought to know. And this applies not only to those of us who are monks but to each and every one of the faithful: we are all of us called to carry the law of the Spirit written on the tablets of our hearts (cf. 2 Cor. 3 : 3), and to attain like the Cherubim the supreme privilege of conversing through pure prayer in the heart directly with Jesus. But because we are infants at the time of our renewal through baptism we do not understand the grace and the new life conferred upon us. Unaware of the surpassing grandeur of the honour and glory in which we share, we fail to realize that we ought to grow in soul and spirit through the keeping of the commandments and so perceive noetically what we have received. On account of this most of us fall through indifference and servitude to the passions into a state of benighted obduracy. We do not know whether God exists, or who we are, or what we have become, although through baptism we have been made sons of God, sons of light, and children and members of Christ. If we are baptized when grown up, we feel that we have been baptized only in water and not by the Spirit. And even though we have been renewed in the Spirit, we believe only in a formal, lifeless and ineffectual sense, and we say we are full of doubts.

Hence because we are in fact non-spiritual we live and behave in a non-spiritual manner. Should we repent, we understand and practise

---

[1] *Homilies on Matthew* 1, 1 (*P.G.* lvii, 13).

the commandments only in a bodily way and not spiritually. And if after many labours a revelation of grace is in God's compassion granted to us, we take it for a delusion. Or if we hear from others how grace acts, we are persuaded by our envy to regard that also as a delusion. Thus we remain corpses until death, failing to live in Christ and to be inspired by Him. According to Scripture, even that which we possess will be taken away from us at the time of our death or our judgment because of our lack of faith and our despair (cf. Matt. 25 : 29). We do not understand that the children must be like the father, that is to say, we are to be made gods by God and spiritual by the Holy Spirit; for 'that which is born of the Spirit is spirit' (John 3 : 6). But we are unregenerate, even though we have become members of the faith and heavenly, and so the Spirit of God does not dwell within us (cf. Gen. 6 : 3). Because of this the Lord has handed us over to strange afflictions and captivity, and slaughter flourishes, perhaps because He wishes to correct evil, or cut it off, or heal it by more powerful remedies.

2. With the help of God, then, who inspires those who declare good tidings (cf. Ps. 68 : 11. LXX), we must first examine how one finds Christ or, rather, how one is found by Him, since we already possess and have received Him through baptism in the Spirit: as St Paul says, 'Do you not realize that Jesus Christ dwells within you?' (2 Cor. 13 : 5). Then we must ask how to advance or, simply, how to retain what we have discovered. The best and shortest course is for us to give a brief summary of the whole spiritual journey from start to finish, long though it is. Many, indeed, have been so exhausted by their efforts to discover what they were looking for that, on finding the starting-point, they have remained content with this, and have not tried to advance further. Encountering obstacles and turning aside unawares from the true path, they think that they are on the right track when actually they are veering profitlessly off course. Others, on reaching the halfway point of illumination, have then grown slack, wilting before reaching the end; or they have reverted through their slipshod way of life, and have become beginners again. Yet others, on the point of attaining perfection, have grown inattentive and self-conceited, relapsing to the state of those in the middle way or even of beginners. Beginners, those in the middle way and the perfect have each their distinctive characteristic: for the first it is activity, for the second illumination, for the third purification and resurrection of the soul.

ON HOW TO DISCOVER THE ENERGY OF THE HOLY SPIRIT

3. The energy of the Holy Spirit, which we have already mystically received in baptism, is realized in two ways. First – to generalize – this gift is revealed, as St Mark tells us,[1] through arduous and protracted practice of the commandments: to the degree to which we effectively practise the commandments its radiance is increasingly manifested in us. Secondly, it is manifested to those under spiritual guidance through the continuous invocation of the Lord Jesus, repeated with conscious awareness, that is, through mindfulness of God. In the first way, it is revealed more slowly, in the second more rapidly, if one diligently and persistently learns how to dig the ground and locate the gold. Thus if we want to realize and know the truth and not to be led astray, let us seek to possess only the heart-engrafted energy in a way that is totally without shape or form, not trying to contemplate in our imagination what we take to be the figure or similitude of things holy or to see any colours or lights. For in the nature of things the spirit of delusion deceives the intellect through such spurious fantasies, especially at the early stages, in those who are still inexperienced. On the contrary, let our aim be to make the energy of prayer alone active in our hearts, for it brings warmth and joy to the intellect, and sets the heart alight with an ineffable love for God and man. It is on account of this that humility and contrition flow richly from prayer. For prayer in beginners is the unceasing noetic activity of the Holy Spirit. To start with it rises like a fire of joy from the heart; in the end it is like light made fragrant by divine energy.

4. There are several signs that the energy of the Holy Spirit is beginning to be active in those who genuinely aspire for this to happen and are not just putting God to the test – for, according to the Wisdom of Solomon, 'It is found by those who do not put it to the test, and manifests itself to those who do not distrust it' (cf. Wisd. 1 : 2). In some it appears as awe arising in the heart, in others as a tremulous sense of jubilation, in others as joy, in others as joy mingled with awe, or as tremulousness mingled with joy, and sometimes it manifests itself

---

[1] St Mark the Ascetic, *On Baptism* (P.G. lxv, 1001B).

as tears and awe. For the soul is joyous at God's visitation and mercy, but at the same time is in awe and trepidation at His presence because it is guilty of so many sins. Again, in some the soul at the outset experiences an unutterable sense of contrition and an indescribable pain, like the woman in Scripture who labours to give birth (cf. Rev. 12 : 2). For the living and active Logos – that is to say, Jesus – penetrates, as the apostle says, to the point at which soul separates from body, joints from marrow (cf. Heb. 4 : 12), so as to expel by force every trace of passion from both soul and body. In others it is manifest as an unconquerable love and peace, shown towards all, or as a joyousness that the fathers have often called exultation – a spiritual force and an impulsion of the living heart that is also described as a vibration and sighing of the Spirit who makes wordless intercession for us to God (cf. Rom. 8 : 26). Isaiah has also called this the 'waves' of God's righteousness (cf. Isa. 48 : 18), while the great Ephrem calls it 'spurring'. The Lord Himself describes it as 'a spring of water welling up for eternal life' (John 4 : 14) – He refers to the Spirit as water – a source that leaps up in the heart and erupts through the ebullience of its power.

5. You should know that there are two kinds of exultation or joyousness: the calm variety (called a vibration or sighing or intercession of the Spirit), and the great exultation of the heart – a leap, bound or jump, the soaring flight of the living heart towards the sphere of the divine. For when the soul has been raised on the wings of divine love by the Holy Spirit and has been freed from the bonds of the passio⟨ns⟩ ⟨…⟩ h⟨…⟩ higher realm even before death, seeking t⟨o⟩ ⟨sep⟩arate itself from its burden. This is also known as a stirring of the spirit – that is to say, an eruption or impulsion – as in the text, 'Jesus was stirred in spirit and, deeply moved, He said, "Where have you laid him?"' (cf. John 11 : 34). David the Psalmist indicates the difference between the greater and the lesser exultation when he declares that the mountains leap like rams and the little hills like lambs (cf. Ps. 114 : 6). He is referring of course to those who are perfect and to beginners, for physical mountains and hills, lacking animal life, do not actually leap about.

6. Divine awe has nothing to do with trepidation – by which I mean, not the tremulousness induced by joy, but the trepidation induced by wrath or chastisement or the feeling of desertion by God. On the contrary, divine awe is accompanied by a tremulous sense of

jubilation arising from the prayer of fire that we offer when filled with awe. This awe is not the fear provoked by wrath or punishment, but it is inspired by wisdom, and is also described as 'the beginning of wisdom' (Ps. 111 : 10). Awe may be divided into three kinds, even though the fathers speak only of two: the awe of beginners, that of the perfect, and that provoked by wrath, which should properly be called trepidation, agitation or contrition.

7. There are several kinds of trembling. That of wrath is one, that of joy is another, and that of the soul's incensive power, when the heart's blood is over-heated, is another, that of old age is another, that of sin or delusion is another, and that of the curse which was laid on the human race because of Cain is another (cf. Gen. 4 : 11–15). In the early stages of spiritual warfare, however, it sometimes but not always happens that the trembling induced by joy and that induced by sin contend with one another. The first is the tremulous sense of jubilation, when grace refreshes the soul with great joyfulness accompanied by tears; the second is characterized by a disordered fervour, stupor and obduracy that consume the soul, inflame the sexual organs, and impel one to assent through the imagination to erotic physical obscenities.

ON THE DIFFERENT KINDS OF ENERGY

8. In every beginner two forms of energy are at work, each affecting the heart in a distinct way. The first comes from grace, the second from delusion. St Mark the Ascetic corroborates this when he says that there is a spiritual energy and a satanic energy, and that the beginner cannot distinguish between them.[1] These energies in their turn generate three kinds of fervour, the first prompted by grace, the second by delusion or sin, and the third by an excess of blood. This last relates to what St Thalassios the Libyan calls the body's temperament,[2] the balance and concord of which can be achieved by appropriate self-control.

[1] On Those who Think that They are Made Righteous by Works 28; E.T., The Philokalia, vol. i, p. 127.
[2] On Love iii, 35; E.T., The Philokalia, vol. ii, p. 321.

ON DIVINE ENERGY

9. The energy of grace is the power of spiritual fire that fills the heart
with joy and gladness, stabilizes, warms and purifies the soul,
temporarily stills our provocative thoughts, and for a time suspends
the body's impulsions. The signs and fruits that testify to its
authenticity are tears, contrition, humility, self-control, silence,
patience, self-effacement and similar qualities, all of which constitute
undeniable evidence of its presence.

ON DELUSION

10. The energy of delusion is the passion for sin, inflaming the soul
with thoughts of sensual pleasure and arousing phrenetic desire in the
body for intercourse with other bodies. According to St Diadochos it is
entirely amorphous and disordered,[1] inducing a mindless joy,
presumption and confusion, accompanied by a mood of ill-defined
sterile levity, and fomenting above all the soul's appetitive power with
its sensuality. It nourishes itself on pleasure, aided and abetted by the
insatiable belly; for through the belly it not only impregnates and
enkindles our whole bodily temperament but also acts upon and
inflames the soul, drawing it to itself so that little by little the
disposition to self-indulgence expels all grace from the person thus
possessed.[2]

[1] *On Spiritual Knowledge* 33: ed. des Places, p. 103; E.T., *The Philokalia*, vol. i, p. 262.
[2] Here the Greek text as given in *The Philokalia* comes to an end, but it seems to be
incomplete. Several manuscripts contain a continuation, dealing at greater length with the
'energy of delusion': for the Greek text (with English translation), see D. Balfour, *Saint Gregory
the Sinaïte: Discourse on the Transfiguration*, op. cit., pp. 109–14.

On Stillness: Fifteen Texts

TWO WAYS OF PRAYER

1. There are two modes of union or, rather, two ways of entering into the noetic prayer that the Spirit activates in the heart. For either the intellect, cleaving to the Lord (cf. 1 Cor. 6 : 17), is present in the heart prior to the action of the prayer; or the prayer itself, progressively quickened in the fire of spiritual joy, draws the intellect along with it or welds it to the invocation of the Lord Jesus and to union with Him. For since the Spirit works in each person as He wishes (cf. 1 Cor. 12 : 11), one of these two ways we have mentioned will take precedence in some people, the other in others. Sometimes, as the passions subside through the ceaseless invocation of Jesus Christ, a divine energy wells up in the heart, and a divine warmth is kindled; for Scripture says that our God is a fire that consumes the passions (cf. Deut. 4 : 24; Heb. 12 : 29). At other times the Spirit draws the intellect to Himself, confining it to the depths of the heart and restraining it from its usual distractions. Then it will no longer be led captive from Jerusalem to the Assyrians, but a change for the better brings it back from Babylon to Zion, so that it says with the Psalmist, 'It is right to praise Thee, O God, in Zion, and to Thee shall our vows be rendered in Jerusalem' (Ps. 65 : 1. LXX), and 'When the Lord brought back the prisoners to Zion' (Ps. 126 : 1), and 'Jacob will rejoice and Israel will be glad (Ps. 53 : 6). The names Jacob and Israel refer respectively to the ascetically active and to the contemplative intellect which through ascetic labour and with God's help overcomes the passions and through contemplation sees God, so far as is possible. Then the intellect, as if invited to a rich banquet and replete with divine joy, will sing, 'Thou hast prepared a table before me in the face of the demons and passions that afflict me' (cf. Ps. 23 : 5).

THE BEGINNING OF WATCHFULNESS

2. 'In the morning sow your seed', says Solomon – and by 'seed' is to
be understood the seed of prayer – 'and in the evening do not withhold
your hand', so that there may be no break in the continuity of your
prayer, no moment when through lack of attention you cease to pray;
'for you do not know which will flourish, this or that' (Eccles. 11 : 6).
Sitting from dawn on a seat about nine inches high, compel your
intellect to descend from your head into your heart, and retain it there.
Keeping your head forcibly bent downwards, and suffering acute pain
in your chest, shoulders and neck, persevere in repeating noetically or
in your soul 'Lord Jesus Christ, have mercy'. Then, since that may
become constrictive and wearisome, and even galling because of the
constant repetition – though this is not because you are constantly
eating the one food of the threefold name, for 'those who eat Me', says
Scripture, 'will still be hungry' (Eccles. 24 : 21) – let your intellect
concentrate on the second half of the prayer and repeat the words 'Son
of God, have mercy'. You must say this half over and over again and
not out of laziness constantly change the words. For plants which are
frequently transplanted do not put down roots. Restrain your
breathing, so as not to breathe unimpededly; for when you exhale, the
air, rising from the heart, beclouds the intellect and ruffles your
thinking, keeping the intellect away from the heart. Then the intellect
is either enslaved by forgetfulness or induced to give its attention to all
manner of things, insensibly becoming preoccupied with what it
should ignore. If you see impure evil thoughts rising up and assuming
various forms in your intellect, do not be startled. Even if images of
good things appear to you, pay no attention to them. But restraining
your breathing as much as possible and enclosing your intellect in your
heart, invoke the Lord Jesus continuously and diligently and you will
swiftly consume and subdue them, flaying them invisibly with the
divine name. For St John Klimakos says, 'With the name of Jesus lash
your enemies, for there is no more powerful weapon in heaven or on
earth.'[1]

3. Isaiah the Solitary is one of many who affirm that when praying

[1] *The Ladder of Divine Ascent*, Step 21 (P.G. lxxxviii, 945C); E.T., p. 200.

you have to restrain your breath. Another author says that you have to control your uncontrollable intellect, impelled and dispersed as it is by the satanic power which seizes hold of your lax soul because of your negligence after baptism, bringing with it other spirits even more evil than itself and thus making your soul's state worse than it was originally (cf. Matt. 12 : 45). Another writer says that in a monk mindfulness of God ought to take the place of breathing, while another declares that the love of God acts as a brake on his out-breathing. St Symeon the New Theologian tells us, 'Restrain the drawing-in of breath through your nostrils, so as not to breathe easily';[1] St John Klimakos says, 'Let mindfulness of Jesus be united to your breathing, and then you will know the blessings of stillness.'[2] St Paul affirms that it is not he who lives but Christ in him (cf. Gal. 2 : 20), activating him and inspiring him with divine life. And the Lord, taking as an example the blowing of the physical wind, says, 'The Spirit blows where He wishes' (John 3 : 8). For when we were cleansed through baptism we received in seed-like form the foretaste of the Spirit (cf. 2 Cor. 1 : 22) and what St James calls the 'implanted Logos' (Jas. 1 : 21), embedded and as it were consolidated in us through an unparticipable participation; and, while keeping Himself inviolate and undiminished, He deifies us in His superabundant bounty. But then we neglected the commandments, the guardians of grace, and through this negligence we again fell into the clutches of the passions, filled with the afflatus of the evil spirits instead of the breath of the Holy Spirit. That is why, as the holy fathers explain, we are subject to lassitude and continually enervated. For had we laid hold of the Spirit and been purified by Him we would have been enkindled by Him and inspired with divine life, and would speak and think and act in the manner that the Lord indicates when He says, 'For it is not you that speak but the Spirit of My Father that speaks in you' (cf. Matt. 10 : 20). Conversely, if we embrace the devil and are mastered by him, we speak and act in the opposite manner.

4. 'When the watchman grows weary,' says St John Klimakos, 'he stands up and prays; then he sits down again and courageously resumes the same task.'[3] Although St John is here referring to the intellect and

---

[1] *The Three Methods of Prayer* (see above, p. 72).

[2] *The Ladder of Divine Ascent*, Step 27 (*P.G.* lxxxviii, 1112C); E.T., p. 270.

[3] Ibid., Step 27 (*P.G.* lxxxviii, 1100B); E.T., p. 263.

is saying that it should behave in this manner when it has learnt how to guard the heart, yet what he says can apply equally to psalmody. For it is said that when the great Varsanuphios was asked about how one should psalmodize, he replied, 'The Hours and the liturgical Odes are church traditions, rightly given so that concord is maintained when there are many praying together. But the monks of Sketis do not recite the Hours, nor do they sing Odes. On their own they practise manual labour, meditation and a little prayer. When you stand in prayer, you should repeat the Trisagion and the Lord's Prayer. You should also ask God to deliver you from your fallen selfhood. Do not grow slack in doing this; your mind should be concentrated in prayer all day long.'[1] What St Varsanuphios wanted to make clear is that private meditation is the prayer of the heart, and that to practise 'a little prayer' means to stand and psalmodize. Moreover, St John Klimakos explicitly says that to attain the state of stillness entails first total detachment, secondly resolute prayer – this means standing and psalmodizing – and thirdly, unbroken labour of the heart, that is to say, sitting down to pray in stillness.[2]

DIFFERENT WAYS OF PSALMODIZING

5. Why do some teach that we should psalmodize a lot, others a little, and others that we should not psalmodize at all but should devote ourselves only to prayer and to physical exertion such as manual labour, prostrations or some other strenuous activity? The explanation is as follows. Those who have found grace through long, arduous practice of the ascetic life teach others to find it in the same way. They do not believe that there are some who through cognitive insight and fervent faith have by the mercy of God attained the state of grace in a short time, as St Isaac, for instance, recognizes. Led astray by ignorance and self-conceit they disparage such people, claiming that anything different from their own experience is delusion and not the operation of grace. They do not know that 'it is easy for God to enrich

---

[1] *Questions and Answers*, § 74 (143): ed. S.N. Schoinas, pp. 68–9.
[2] *The Ladder of Divine Ascent*, Step 27 (*P.G.* lxxxviii, 1109B); E.T., p. 268.

a poor man suddenly' (Eccles. 11 : 21), and that 'wisdom is the principal thing; therefore acquire wisdom', as Proverbs says, referring to grace (4 : 7). Similarly St Paul is rebuking the disciples of his time who were ignorant of grace when he says, 'Do you not realize that Jesus Christ dwells within you, unless you are worthless?' (cf. 2 Cor. 13 : 5) – unless, that is to say, you make no progress because of your negligence. Thus in their disbelief and arrogance they do not acknowledge the exceptional qualities of prayer activated in some people by the Spirit in a special way.

6. *Objection*: Tell me, if a person fasts, practises self-control, keeps vigils, stands, makes prostrations, grieves inwardly and lives in poverty, is this not active asceticism? How then do you advocate simply the singing of psalms, yet say that without ascetic labour it is impossible to succeed in prayer? Do not the activities I mention constitute ascetic labour?

Answer: If you pray with your lips but your mind wanders, how do you benefit? 'When one builds and another tears down, what do they gain but toil?' (Eccles. 34 : 23). As you labour with your body, so you must labour with your intellect, lest you appear righteous in the body while your heart is filled with every form of injustice and impurity. St Paul confirms this when he says that if he prays with his tongue – that is, with his lips – his spirit or his voice prays, but his intellect is unproductive: 'I will pray with my spirit, and I will also pray with my intellect' (cf. 1 Cor. 14 : 14–15). And he adds, 'I would rather speak five words with my intellect than ten thousand with my tongue' (cf. 1 Cor. 14 : 19). St John Klimakos, too, indicates that St Paul is speaking here about prayer when he says in his chapter on prayer, 'The great practitioner of sublime and perfect prayer says, "I would rather speak five words with my intellect." '[1] There are many other forms of spiritual work, yet not one in itself is all-sufficient; but prayer of the heart, according to St John Klimakos, is pre-eminent and all-embracing, the source of the virtues and catalyst of all goodness.[2] 'There is nothing more fearful than the thought of death,' says St Maximos, 'or more wonderful than mindfulness of God,'[3] indicating

---

[1] Ibid., Step 28 (*P.G.* lxxxviii, 1133A); E.T., p. 276.

[2] Ibid., Step 28 (*P.G.* lxxxviii, 1129B); E.T., p. 274.

[3] Ilias the Presbyter, *A Gnomic Anthology* iii, 12; E.T., *The Philokalia*, vol. iii (London & Boston, 1984), p. 48. This work is sometimes attributed to St Maximos the Confessor (ibid., p. 32).

the supremacy of this activity. But some do not even wish to know that
we can attain a state of active grace in this present life, so blinded and
weak in faith are they because of their ignorance and obduracy.

7. In my opinion, those who do not psalmodize much act rightly,
for it means that they esteem moderation – and according to the sages
moderation is best in all things. In this way they do not expend all the
energy of their soul in ascetic labour, thus making the intellect
negligent and slack where prayer is concerned. On the contrary, by
devoting but little time to psalmodizing, they can give most of their
time to prayer. On the other hand, when the intellect is exhausted by
continuous noetic invocation and intense concentration, it can be
given some rest by releasing it from the straitness of silent prayer and
allowing it to relax in the amplitude of psalmody. This is an excellent
rule, taught by the wisest men.

8. Those who do not psalmodize at all also act rightly, provided
they are well advanced on the spiritual path. Such people have no need
to recite psalms; if they have attained the state of illumination, they
should cultivate silence, uninterrupted prayer and contemplation.
They are united with God and have no need to tear their intellect away
from Him and so to throw it into confusion. As St John Klimakos says,
'One under monastic obedience falls when he follows his own will,
while the hesychast falls when he is interrupted in his prayer.'[1] For
the hesychast commits adultery in his intellect when he sunders it from
its mindfulness of God: it is as if he were being unfaithful to his true
spouse and philandering with trivial matters.

To impart this discipline to others is not always possible. But it can
be taught to simple uneducated people who are under obedience to a
spiritual father, for such obedience, thanks to the humility that goes
with it, can partake of every virtue. Those, however, who are not
under this kind of obedience should not be taught it, regardless of
whether they are unlearned people or educated: they may easily be
deluded, because people who are a law unto themselves cannot avoid
being conceited, and the natural result of conceit is delusion, as St Isaac
says. Yet some people, unaware of the harm which will result, counsel
anybody they happen to meet to practise this discipline alone, so that
their intellect may grow accustomed to being mindful of God and may
come to love it. But this is not possible, especially for those not under

[1] *The Ladder of Divine Ascent*, Step 27 (P.G. lxxxviii, 1112C); E.T., p. 270.

obedience. For, because of their negligence and arrogance, their intellect is still impure and has not first been cleansed by tears; and so, instead of concentrating on prayer, they are filled with images of shameful thoughts, while the unclean spirits in their heart, panic-struck by the invocation of the dread name of the Lord Jesus, howl for the destruction of the person who scourges them. Thus if you hear about or are taught this discipline, and want to practise it, but are not under spiritual direction you will experience one of two things: you will either force yourself to persist, in which case you fall into delusion and will fail to attain healing; or you will grow negligent, in which case you will never make any progress during your whole life.

9. I will add this from my own small experience. When you sit in stillness, by day or by night, free from random thoughts and continuously praying to God in humility, you may find that your intellect becomes exhausted through calling upon God and that your body and heart begin to feel pain because of the intense concentration with which you unceasingly invoke the name of Jesus, with the result that you no longer experience the warmth and joy that engender ardour and patience in the spiritual aspirant. If this is the case, stand up and psalmodize, either by yourself or with a disciple who lives with you, or occupy yourself with meditation on some scriptural passage or with the remembrance of death, or with manual labour or with some other thing, or give your attention to reading, preferably standing up so as to involve your body in the task as well.

When you stand and psalmodize by yourself, recite the Trisagion and then pray in your soul or your intellect, making your intellect pay attention to your heart; and recite two or three psalms and a few penitential *troparia* but without chanting them: as St John Klimakos confirms, people at this stage of spiritual development do not chant.[1] For 'the suffering of the heart endured in a spirit of devotion', as St Mark puts it,[2] is sufficient to produce joy in them, and the warmth of the Spirit is given to them as a source of grace and exultation. After each psalm again pray in your intellect or soul, keeping your thoughts from wandering, and repeat the Alleluia. This is the order established

---

[1] Ibid., Step 7 (*P.G.* lxxxviii, 813A); E.T., p. 143. A *troparion* is a short stanza in rhythmic prose, occurring in the service books.

[2] *On Those who Think that They are Made Righteous by Works* 131; E.T., *The Philokalia*, vol. i, p. 136.

by the holy fathers Varsanuphios, Diadochos and others. And as St Basil the Great says, one should vary the psalms daily to enkindle one's fervour and to prevent the intellect from getting bored with having to recite always the same things. The intellect should be given freedom and then its fervour will be quickened.[1] If you stand and psalmodize with a trusted disciple, let him recite the psalms while you guard yourself, secretly watching your heart and praying. With the help of prayer ignore all images, whether sensory or conceptual, that rise up from the heart. For stillness means the shedding of all thoughts for a time, even those which are divine and engendered by the Spirit; otherwise through giving them our attention because they are good we will lose what is better.

10. So, lover of God, attend with care and intelligence. If while engaged in spiritual work you see a light or a fire outside you, or a form supposedly of Christ or of an angel or of someone else, reject it lest you suffer harm. And do not pay court to images, lest you allow them to stamp themselves on your intellect. For all these things that externally and inopportunely assume various guises do so in order to delude your soul. The true beginning of prayer is the warmth of heart that scorifies the passions, fills the soul with joy and delight, and establishes the heart in unwavering love and unhesitating surety. The holy fathers teach that if the heart is in doubt about whether to accept something either sensory or conceptual that enters the soul, then that thing is not from God but has been sent by the devil. Moreover, if you become aware that your intellect is being enticed by some invisible power either from the outside or from above, do not trust in that power or let your intellect be so enticed, but immediately force it to continue its work.[2]

What is of God, says St Isaac, comes of itself, without you knowing when it will come. Our natural enemy – the demon who operates in the seat of our desiring power – gives the spirit-forces various guises in

---

[1] Cf. *Longer Rules* xxxvii, 5 (*P.G.* xxxi, 1016C); E.T. by W.K.L. Clarke, *The Ascetic Works of Saint Basil* (London, 1925), p. 209.

[2] Here most manuscripts add: 'Unceasingly cry out: "Lord Jesus Christ, Son of God, have mercy", and do not allow yourself to retain any concept, object, thought or form that is supposedly divine, or any sequence of argument or any colour, but concentrate solely on the pure, simple, formless remembrance of Jesus. Then God, seeing your intellect so strict in guarding itself in every way against the enemy, will Himself bestow pure and unerring vision upon it and will make it participate in God and share in all other blessings.'

our imagination. In this way he substitutes his own unruly heat for spiritual warmth, so that the soul is oppressed by this deceit. For spiritual delight he substitutes mindless joy and a muggy sense of pleasure, inducing self-satisfaction and vanity. Thus he tries to conceal himself from those who lack experience and to persuade them to take his delusions for manifestations of spiritual joy. But time, experience and perspicacity will reveal him to those not entirely ignorant of his wiles. As the palate discriminates between different kinds of food (cf. Eccles. 36 : 18,19), so the spiritual sense of taste clearly and unerringly reveals everything as it truly is.

11. 'Since you are engaged in spiritual warfare,' says St John Klimakos, 'you should read texts concerned with ascetic practice. Translating such texts into action makes other reading superfluous.'[1] Read works of the fathers related to stillness and prayer, like those of St John Klimakos, St Isaac, St Maximos, St Neilos, St Hesychios, Philotheos of Sinai, St Symeon the New Theologian and his disciple Stithatos, and whatever else exists of writers of this kind. Leave other books for the time being, not because they are to be rejected, but because they do not contribute to your present purpose, diverting the intellect from prayer by their narrative character. Read by yourself, but not in a pompous voice, or with pretentious eloquence or affected enunciation or melodic delectation, or, insensibly carried away by passion, as if you are wanting to please an audience. Do not read with inordinate avidity, for in all things moderation is best, nor on the other hand in a rough, sluggish or negligent manner. On the contrary, read reverently, gently, steadily, with understanding, and at an even pace, your intellect, your soul and your reason all engaged. When the intellect is invigorated by such reading, it acquires the strength to pray harder. But if you read in the contrary manner – as I have described it above – you cloud the intellect and make it sluggish and distracted, so that you develop a headache and grow slack in prayer.

12. Continually take careful note of your inner intention: watch carefully which way it inclines, and discover whether it is for God and for the sake of goodness itself and the benefit of your soul that you practise stillness or psalmodize or read or pray or cultivate some virtue. Otherwise you may unknowingly be ensnared and prove to be an ascetic in outward appearance alone while in your manner of life and

[1] *The Ladder of Divine Ascent*, Step 27 (P.G. lxxxviii, 1116C); E.T., p. 272.

inner intention you are wanting to impress men, and not to conform to God. For the devil's traps are many, and he persistently and secretly watches the bias of our intention, without most of us being aware of it, striving imperceptibly to corrupt our labour so that what we do is not done in accordance with God's will. But even if he attacks and assaults you relentlessly and shamelessly, and even if he distracts the bias of your will and makes it waver in spite of your efforts to prevent it, you will not often be caught out by him so long as you keep yourself steadfastly intent on God. If again in spite of your efforts you are overcome through weakness, you will swiftly be forgiven and praised by Him who knows our intentions and our hearts. There is, however, one passion – self-esteem – that does not permit a monk to grow in virtue, so that though he engages in ascetic labours in the end he remains barren. For whether you are a beginner, or midway along the spiritual path, or have attained the stage of perfection, self-esteem always tries to insinuate itself, and it nullifies your efforts to live a holy life, so that you waste your time in listlessness and day-dreaming.

13. I have also learnt this from experience, that unless a monk cultivates the following virtues he will never make progress: fasting, self-control, keeping vigil, patient endurance, courage, stillness, prayer, silence, inward grief and humility. These virtues generate and protect each other. Constant fasting withers lust and begets self-control. Self-control enables us to keep vigils, vigils beget patient endurance, endurance courage, courage stillness, stillness prayer, prayer silence, silence inward grief, and grief begets humility. Or, going in the reverse order, you will find how daughters give birth to mothers – how, that is to say, humility begets inward grief, and so on. In the realm of the virtues there is nothing more important than this form of mutual generation. The things opposite to these virtues are obvious to all.

14. Here we should specify the toils and hardships of the ascetic life and explain clearly how we should embark on each task. We must do this lest someone who coasts along without exerting himself, simply relying on what he has heard, and who consequently remains barren, should blame us or other writers, alleging that things are not as we have said. For it is only through travail of heart and bodily toil that the work can properly be carried out. Through them the grace of the Holy Spirit is revealed. This is the grace with which we and all Christians are endowed at baptism but which through neglect of the commandments

has been stifled by the passions. Now through God's ineffable mercy it awaits our repentance, so that at the end of our life we may not because of our barrenness hear the words 'Take the talent from him', and 'What he thinks he has will be taken away from him' (cf. Matt. 25 : 28–29), and may not be sent to hell to suffer endlessly in Gehenna. No activity, whether bodily or spiritual, unaccompanied by toil and hardship bears fruit; 'for the kingdom of heaven is entered forcibly,' says the Lord, 'and those who force themselves take possession of it' (Matt. 11 : 12), where 'forcibly' and 'force' relate to the body's awareness of exertion in all things.

Many for long years may have been preoccupied with the spiritual life without exerting themselves, or may still be preoccupied with it in this way; but because they do not assiduously embrace hardships with heartfelt fervour and sense of purpose, and have repudiated the severity of bodily toil, they remain devoid of purity, without a share in the Holy Spirit. Those who practise the spiritual life, but do so carelessly and lazily, may think that they make considerable efforts; but they will never reap any harvest because they have not exerted themselves and basically have never experienced any real tribulation. A witness to this is St John Klimakos, who says, 'However exalted our way of life may be, it is worthless and bogus if our heart does not suffer.'[1] Sometimes when we fail to exert ourselves we are in our listlessness carried away by spurious forms of distraction and plunged into darkness, thinking we can find rest in them when that is impossible. The truth is that we are then bound invisibly by unloosable cords and become inert and ineffective in everything we do, for we grow increasingly sluggish, especially if we are beginners. For those who have reached the stage of perfection everything is profitable in moderation. St Ephrem also testifies to this when he says, 'Persistently suffer hardships in order to avoid the hardship of vain sufferings.' For unless, to use the prophet's phrase, our loins are exhausted by the weakness induced through the exertions of fasting, and unless like a woman in childbirth we are afflicted with pains arising from the constriction of our heart, we will not conceive the Spirit of salvation in the earth of our heart (cf. Isa. 21 : 3; 26 : 18). Instead, all we will have to boast about is the many profitless years we have spent in the wilderness, lazily cultivating stillness and imagining that we are

---

[1] Ibid., Step 7 (*P.G.* lxxxviii, 816A); E.T., p. 144.

somebody. At the moment of our death we will all know for certain what is the outcome of our life.

15. No one can learn the art of virtue by himself, though some have taken experience as their teacher. For to act on one's own and not on the advice of those who have gone before us is overweening presumption – or, rather, it engenders such presumption. If the Son does nothing of His own accord, but does only what the Father has taught Him (cf. John 5 : 19–20), and the Spirit will not speak of His own accord (cf. John 16 : 3), who can think he has attained such heights of virtue that he does not need anyone to initiate him into the mysteries? Such a person is deluded and out of his mind rather than virtuous.[1] One should therefore listen to those who have experienced the hardships involved in cultivating the virtues and should cultivate them as they have – that is to say, by severe fasting, painful self-control, steadfast vigils, laborious genuflexions, assiduous standing motionless, constant prayer, unfeigned humility, ceaseless contrition and compunctive sorrow, eloquent silence, as if seasoned with salt (cf. Col. 4 : 6), and by patience in all things. You must not be always relaxing or pray sitting down, before it is the proper time to do so, or before age or sickness compels you. For, as Scripture says, 'You will nourish yourself on the hardships of your practice of the virtues' (cf. Ps. 128 : 2. LXX); and, 'The kingdom of heaven is entered forcibly' (Matt. 11 : 12). Hence those who diligently strive day by day to practise the virtues that we have mentioned will with God's help gather in the harvest at the appropriate time.

---

[1] Many manuscripts omit all that follow the words '. . . rather than virtuous', and give a much shorter alternative ending: 'He therefore who seeks to traverse the path of perfection unerringly and to be entrusted with the guidance of other souls must obey those who have experienced the hardships of the ascetic life and must follow a guide. An unerring guide is one whose life is founded on the testimony of the Holy Scriptures.'

On Prayer: Seven Texts

HOW THE HESYCHAST SHOULD SIT FOR PRAYER AND NOT RISE AGAIN TOO QUICKLY

1. Sometimes – and most often – you should sit on a stool, because it is more arduous; but sometimes, for a break, you should sit for a while on a mattress. As you sit be patient and assiduous, in accordance with St Paul's precept, 'Cleave patiently to prayer' (Col. 4 : 2). Do not grow discouraged and quickly rise up again because of the strain and effort needed to keep your intellect concentrated on its inner invocation. It is as the prophet says: 'The birth-pangs are upon me, like those of a woman in travail' (Isa. 21 : 3). You must bend down and gather your intellect into your heart – provided it has been opened – and call on the Lord Jesus to help you. Should you feel pain in your shoulders or in your head – as you often will – endure it patiently and fervently, seeking the Lord in your heart. For 'the kingdom of God is entered forcibly, and those who force themselves take possession of it' (Matt. 11 : 12). With these words the Lord truly indicated the persistence and labour needed in this task. Patience and endurance in all things involve hardship in both body and soul.

HOW TO SAY THE PRAYER

2. Some of the fathers advise us to say the whole prayer, 'Lord Jesus Christ, Son of God, have mercy', while others specify that we say it in two parts – 'Lord Jesus Christ, have mercy', and then 'Son of God, help me' – because this is easier, given the immaturity and feebleness of our

intellect. For no one on his own account and without the help of the Spirit can mystically invoke the Lord Jesus, for this can be done with purity and in its fullness only with the help of the Holy Spirit (cf. 1 Cor. 12 : 3). Like children who can still speak only falteringly, we are unable by ourselves to articulate the prayer properly. Yet we must not out of laziness frequently change the words of the invocation, but only do this rarely, so as to ensure continuity. Again, some fathers teach that the prayer should be said aloud; others, that it should be said silently with the intellect. On the basis of my personal experience I recommend both ways. For at times the intellect grows listless and cannot repeat the prayer, while at other times the same thing happens to the voice. Thus we should pray both vocally and in the intellect. But when we pray vocally we should speak quietly and calmly and not loudly, so that the voice does not disturb and hinder the intellect's consciousness and concentration. This is always a danger until the intellect grows accustomed to its work, makes progress and receives power from the Spirit to pray firmly and with complete attention. Then there will be no need to pray aloud – indeed, it will be impossible, for we shall be content to carry out the whole work with the intellect alone.

HOW TO MASTER THE INTELLECT IN PRAYER

3. No one can master the intellect unless he himself is mastered by the Spirit. For the intellect is uncontrollable, not because it is by nature ever-active, but because through our continual remissness it has been given over to distraction and has become used to that. When we violated the commandments of Him who in baptism regenerates us we separated ourselves from God and lost our conscious awareness of Him and our union with Him. Sundered from that union and estranged from God, the intellect is led captive everywhere; and it cannot regain its stability unless it submits to God and is stilled by Him, joyfully uniting with Him through unceasing and diligent prayer and through noetically confessing all our lapses to Him each day. God immediately forgives everything to those who ask forgiveness in a spirit of humility and contrition and who ceaselessly invoke His holy name. As the

Psalmist says, 'Confess to the Lord and call upon His holy name' (cf. Ps. 105 : 1). Holding the breath also helps to stabilize the intellect, but only temporarily, for after a little it lapses into distraction again. But when prayer is activated, then it really does keep the intellect in its presence, and it gladdens it and frees it from captivity. But it may sometimes happen that the intellect, rooted in the heart, is praying, yet the mind wanders and gives its attention to other things; for the mind is brought under control only in those who have been made perfect by the Holy Spirit and who have attained a state of total concentration upon Christ Jesus.

HOW TO EXPEL THOUGHTS

4. In the case of a beginner in the art of spiritual warfare, God alone can expel thoughts, for it is only those strong in such warfare who are in a position to wrestle with them and banish them. Yet even they do not achieve this by themselves, but they fight against them with God's assistance, clothed in the armour of His grace. So when thoughts invade you, in place of weapons call on the Lord Jesus frequently and persistently and then they will retreat; for they cannot bear the warmth produced in the heart by prayer and they flee as if scorched by fire. St John Klimakos tells us, 'Lash your enemies with the name of Jesus',[1] because God is a fire the cauterizes wickedness (cf. Deut. 4 : 24; Heb. 12 : 29). The Lord is prompt to help, and will speedily come to the defence of those who wholeheartedly call on Him day and night (cf. Luke 18 : 7). But if prayer is not yet activated in you, you can put these thoughts to flight in another manner, by imitating Moses (cf. Exod. 17 : 11–12): rise up, lift hands and eyes to heaven, and God will rout them. Then sit down again and begin to pray resolutely. This is what you should do if you have not yet acquired the power of prayer. Yet even if prayer is activated in you and you are attacked by the more obdurate and grievous of the bodily passions – namely, listlessness and lust – you should sometimes rise up and lift your hands for help against them. But you should do this only seldom, and then sit down again, for

---

[1] *The Ladder of Divine Ascent*, Step 21 (P.G. lxxxviii, 945C); E.T., p. 200.

there is a danger of the enemy deluding you by showing you some illusory form of the truth. For only in those who are pure and perfect does God keep the intellect steadfast and intact wherever it is, whether above or below, or in the heart.

HOW TO PSALMODIZE

5. Some say that we should psalmodize seldom, others often, others not at all. You for your part should not psalmodize often, for that induces unrest, nor yet not at all, for that induces indolence and negligence. Instead you should follow the example of those who psalmodize from time to time, for moderation in all things is best, as the ancient Greeks tell us. To psalmodize often is appropriate for novices in the ascetic life, because of the toil it involves and the spiritual knowledge it confers. It is not appropriate for hesychasts, since they concentrate wholly upon praying to God with travail of heart, eschewing all conceptual images. For according to St John Klimakos, 'Stillness is the shedding of thoughts',[1] whether of sensible or of intelligible realities. Moreover, if we expend all our energy in reciting many psalms, our intellect will grow slack and will not be able to pray firmly and resolutely. Again according to St John Klimakos, 'Devote most of the night to prayer and only a little of it to psalmody.'[2]

You, too, should do the same. If you are seated and you see that prayer is continuously active in your heart, do not abandon it and get up to psalmodize until in God's good time it leaves you of its own accord. Otherwise, abandoning the interior presence of God, you will address yourself to Him from without, thus passing from a higher to a lower state, provoking unrest and disrupting the intellect's serenity. Stillness, in accordance with its name, is maintained by means of peace and serenity; for God is peace (cf. Eph. 2 : 14) beyond all unrest and clamour. Our psalmody, too, should accord with our mode of life, and be angelic, not unspiritual and secular. For to psalmodize with clamour

---

[1] Ibid., Step 27 (P.G. lxxxviii, 1112A); E.T., p. 269.
[2] Ibid., Step 27 (P.G. lxxxviii, 1116C); E.T., p. 272.

and a loud voice is a sign of inner turbulence. Psalmody has been given to us because of our grossness and indolence, so that we may be led back to our true state.

As for those not yet initiated into prayer – this prayer which, according to St John Klimakos, is the source of the virtues[1] and which waters, as plants, the faculties of the soul – they should psalmodize frequently, without measure, reciting a great variety of psalms; and they should not desist from such assiduous practice until they have attained the state of contemplation and find that noetic prayer is activated within them. For the practice of stillness is one thing and that of community life is another. 'Let each persist in that to which he is called' (1 Cor. 7 : 24) and he will be saved. It was on account of this that I hesitated to write to you, for I know that you live among those still weak. If someone's experience of praying derives from hearsay or reading he will lose his way, for he lacks a guide. According to the fathers, once you have tasted grace you should psalmodize sparingly, giving most of your time to prayer. But if you find yourself growing indolent you should psalmodize or read patristic texts. A ship has no need of oars when a fair wind swells the sails and drives it lightly across the salt sea of the passions. But when it is becalmed it has to be propelled by oars or towed by another boat.

To gainsay this, some point to the holy fathers, or to certain living persons, saying that they kept all-night watches psalmodizing the whole time. But, as we learn from Scripture, not all things can be accomplished by everyone, for some lack diligence and strength. As St John Klimakos says, 'Small things may not always seem so to the great, and great things may not seem altogether perfect to the small.'[2] Everything is easy for the perfect; and not everyone, either now or in former times, remains always a probationer, nor does everyone travel along the same road or pursue it to the end. Many have passed from the life of ascetic labour to the life of contemplation, laying aside outward practices, keeping the sabbath according to the spiritual law, and delighting in God alone. They are replete with divine fare, and the grace that fills them does not permit them to psalmodize or to meditate on anything else; for the time being they are in a state of ecstasy, having attained, if only in part and as a foretaste, the ultimate

---

[1] Ibid., Step 28 (P.G. lxxxviii, 1129B); E.T., p. 274.
[2] Ibid., Step 26 (P.G. lxxxviii, 1033B); E.T., p. 242.

desire of all desires. Others have been saved through pursuing the life
of ascetic labour until their death, awaiting their reward in the life to
come. Some have received conscious assurance of salvation at their
death, or else after death they have given off a fragrant odour as
testimony to their salvation. Like all other Christians they had received
the grace of baptism, but because of the distraught and ignorant state
of their intellects they did not participate in it mystically while still
alive. Others excel in both psalmody and prayer and spend their lives
in this manner, richly endowed with ever-active grace and not
impeded by anything. Yet others, being unlettered and restricting
themselves solely to prayer, have persevered in stillness until the end of
their lives; and in doing this they have done well, uniting themselves as
single individuals with God alone. To the perfect, as we said, all things
are possible through Christ who is their strength (cf. Phil. 4 : 13).

HOW TO PARTAKE OF FOOD

6. What shall I say about the belly, the queen of the passions? If you
can deaden or half-deaden it, do not relent. It has mastered me,
beloved, and I worship it as a slave and vassal, this abettor of the
demons and dwelling-place of the passions. Through it we fall and
through it – when it is well-disciplined – we rise again. Through it we
have lost both our original divine status and also our second divine
status, that which was bestowed on us when after our initial
corruption we are renewed in Christ through baptism, and from which
we have lapsed once more, separating ourselves from God through our
neglect of the commandments, even though in our ignorance we exalt
ourselves. We think that we are with God, but it is only by keeping the
commandments that we advance, guarding and increasing the grace
bestowed upon us.

As the fathers have pointed out, bodies vary greatly in their need for
food. One person needs little, another much to sustain his physical
strength, each according to his capacity and habit. A hesychast,
however, should always eat too little, never too much. For when the
stomach is heavy the intellect is clouded, and you cannot pray
resolutely and with purity. On the contrary, made drowsy by the
effects of too much food you are soon induced to sleep; and as you

sleep the food produces countless fantasies in your mind. Thus in my opinion if you want to attain salvation and strive for the Lord's sake to lead a life of stillness, you should be satisfied with a pound of bread and three or four cups of water or wine daily, taking at appropriate times a little from whatever victuals happen to be at hand, but never eating to satiety. In this way you will avoid growing conceited, and by thanking God for everything you will show no disdain for the excellent things He has made. This is the counsel of those who are wise in such matters. For those weak in faith and soul, abstinence from specific types of food is most beneficial; St Paul exhorts them to eat herbs (cf. Rom. 14 : 2), for they do not believe that God will preserve them.

What shall I say? You are old, yet have asked for a rule, and an extremely severe one at that. Younger people cannot keep to a strict rule by weight and measure, so how will you keep to it? Because you are ill, you should be entirely free in partaking of food. If you eat too much, repent and try again. Always act like this – lapsing and recovering again, and always blaming yourself and no one else – and you will be at peace, wisely converting such lapses into victories, as Scripture says. But do not exceed the limit I set down above, and this will be enough, for no other food strengthens the body as much as bread and water. That is why the prophet disregarded everything else and simply said, 'Son of man, by weight you will eat your bread and by measure you will drink water' (cf. Ezek. 4 : 16).

There are three degrees of eating: self-control, sufficiency and satiety. Self-control is to be hungry after having eaten. Sufficiency is to be neither hungry nor weighed down. Satiety is to be slightly weighed down. To eat again after reaching the point of satiety is to open the door of gluttony, through which unchastity comes in. Attentive to these distinctions, choose what is best for you according to your powers, not overstepping the limits. For according to St Paul only the perfect can be both hungry and full, and at the same time be strong in all things (cf. Phil. 4 : 12).

ON DELUSION AND OTHER SUBJECTS

7. I wish you to be fully informed about delusion, so that you can guard yourself against it and not do great harm to yourself through

ignorance, and lose your soul. For our free will easily veers towards keeping company with the demons, especially when we are inexperienced and still under their sway. Around beginners and those who rely on their own counsel the demons spread the nets of destructive thoughts and images, and open pits into which such people fall; for their city is still in the hands of the workers of iniquity, and in their impetuosity they are easily slain by them. It is not surprising that they are deceived, or lose their wits, or have been and still are deluded, or heed what is contrary to truth, or from inexperience and ignorance say things that should not be said. Often some witless person will speak about truth and will hold forth at length without being aware of what he is saying or in a position to give a correct account of things. In this way he troubles many who hear him and by his inept behaviour he brings abuse and ridicule on the heads of hesychasts. It is not in the least strange that beginners should be deceived even after making great efforts, for this has happened to many who have sought God, both now and in the past.

Mindfulness of God, or noetic prayer, is superior to all other activities. Indeed, being love for God, it is the chief virtue. But a person who is brazen and shameless in his approach to God, and who is over-zealous in his efforts to converse with Him in purity and to possess Him inwardly, is easily destroyed by the demons if they are given licence to attack him; for in rashly and presumptuously striving prematurely to attain what is beyond his present capacity, he becomes a victim of his own arrogance. The Lord in His compassion often prevents us from succumbing to temptation when He sees us aspiring over-confidently to attain what is still beyond our powers, for in this way He gives each of us the opportunity of discovering his own presumption and so of repenting of his own accord before making himself the butt of demons as well as of other people's ridicule or pity. Especially is this the case when we try to accomplish this task with patience and contrition; for we stand in need of much sorrow and lamentation, of solitude, deprivation of all things, hardship and humility, and – most important of all for its marvellous effects – of guidance and obedience; for otherwise we might unknowingly reap thorns instead of wheat, gall instead of sweetness, ruin instead of salvation. Only the strong and the perfect can continuously fight alone with the demons, wielding against them the sword of the Spirit, which is the teaching of God (cf. Eph. 6 : 17). The weak and beginners escape death by taking refuge in flight, reverently and with fear withdrawing from the battle rather than risking their life prematurely.

For your part, if you are rightly cultivating stillness and aspiring to be with God, and you see something either sensory or noetic, within or without, be it even an image of Christ or of an angel or of some saint, or you imagine you see a light in your intellect and give it a specific form, you should never entertain it. For the intellect itself naturally possesses an imaginative power and in those who do not keep a strict watch over it it can easily produce, to its own hurt, whatever forms and images it wants to. In this way the recollection of things good or evil can suddenly imprint images on the intellect's perceptive faculty and so induce it to entertain fantasies, thus making whoever this happens to a daydreamer rather than a hesychast.

Be careful, therefore, not to entertain and readily give assent to anything even if it be good, before questioning those with spiritual experience and investigating it thoroughly, so as not to come to any harm. Always be suspicious of it and keep your intellect free from colours, forms and images. For it has often happened that things sent by God to test our free will, to see which way it inclines and to act as a spur to our efforts, have in fact had bad consequences. For when we see something, whether with mind or senses – even if this thing be from God – and then readily entertain it without consulting those experienced in such matters, we are easily deceived, or will be in the future, because of our gullibility. A novice should pay close attention solely to the activity of his heart, because this is not led astray. Everything else he must reject until the passions are quietened. For God does not censure those who out of fear of being deluded pay strict attention to themselves, even though this means that they refuse to entertain what He sends them until they have questioned others and made careful enquiry. Indeed, He is more likely to praise their prudence, even though in some cases He is grieved.

Yet you should not question everyone. You should go only to one, to someone who has been entrusted with the guidance of others as well, who is radiant alike in his life and in his words, and who although poor makes many rich (cf. 2 Cor. 6 : 10). For people lacking spiritual experience have often done harm to foolish questioners, and for this they will be judged after death. Not everyone is qualified to guide others: only those can do so who have been granted divine discrimination – what St Paul calls the 'discrimination of spirits'

(1 Cor. 12 : 10) – enabling them to distinguish between bad and good with the sword of God's teaching (cf. Eph. 6 : 17). Everyone possesses his own private knowledge and discrimination, whether inborn, pragmatic or scientific, but not all possess spiritual knowledge and discrimination. That is why Sirach said, 'Be at peace with many, but let your counsellors be one in a thousand' (Eccles. 6 : 6). It is hard to find a guide who in all he does, says or thinks is free from delusion. You can tell that a person is undeluded when his actions and judgment are founded on the testimony of divine Scripture, and when he is humble in whatever he has to give his mind to. No little effort is needed to attain a clear understanding of the truth and to be cleansed from whatever is contrary to grace, for the devil – especially in the case of beginners – is liable to present his delusions in the forms of truth, thus giving his deceit a spiritual guise.

If, then, you are striving in stillness to attain a state of pure prayer, you must journey with great trepidation and inward grief, questioning those with spiritual experience, accepting their guidance, always lamenting your sins, and full of distress and fear lest you should be chastised or should fall away from God and be divorced from Him in this life or the next. For when the devil sees someone leading a penitent life, he retreats, frightened of the humility that such inward grief engenders. But if, with a longing that is satanic rather than authentic, you are presumptuous enough to imagine that you have attained a lofty state, the devil will easily trap you in his nets and make you his slave. Thus the surest guard against falling from the joy of prayer into a state of conceit is to persevere in prayer and inward grief, for by embracing a solace-filled grief you keep yourself safe from harm. Authentic prayer – the warmth that accompanies the Jesus Prayer, for it is Jesus who enkindles fire on the earth of our hearts (cf. Luke 12 : 49) – consumes the passions like thorns and fills the soul with delight and joyfulness. Such prayer comes neither from right or left, nor from above, but wells up in the heart like a spring of water from the life-quickening Spirit. It is this prayer alone that you should aspire to realize and possess in your heart, always keeping your intellect free from images, concepts and thoughts. And do not be afraid, for He who says, 'Take heart; it is I; be not afraid' (Matt. 14 : 27), is with us – He whom we seek and who protects us always. When we invoke God we must be neither timid nor hesitant.

If some have gone astray and lost their mental balance, this is because they have in arrogance followed their own counsels. For when you seek God in obedience and humility, and with the guidance of a spiritual master, you will never come to any harm, by the grace of Christ who desires all to be saved (cf. 1 Tim. 2 : 4). Should temptation arise, its purpose is to test you and to spur you on; and God, who has permitted this testing, will speedily come to your help in whatever way He sees fit. As the holy fathers assure us, a person who lives an upright and blameless life, avoiding arrogance and spurning popularity, will come to no harm even if a whole host of demons provoke him with countless temptations. But if you are presumptuous and follow your own counsel you will readily fall victim to delusion. That is why a hesychast must always keep to the royal road. For excess in anything easily leads to conceit, and conceit induces self-delusion. Keep the intellect at rest by gently pressing your lips together when you pray, but do not impede your nasal breathing, as the ignorant do, in case you harm yourself by building up inward pressure.

There are three virtues connected with stillness which we must guard scrupulously, examining ourselves every hour to make sure that we possess them, in case through unmindfulness we are robbed of them and wander far away from them. These virtues are self-control, silence and self-reproach, which is the same thing as humility. They are all-embracing and support one another; and from them prayer is born and through them it burgeons.

Grace begins to operate in people during prayer in different ways, for, as the apostle says, the Spirit distributes Himself as He wills in a variety of modes, and is perceived and known correspondingly (cf. Heb. 2 : 4). Elijah the Tishbite serves here as an example for us (cf. 1 Kgs. 19 : 11–12). In some the Spirit appears as a whirlwind of awe, dissolving the mountains of the passions and shattering the rocks of our hardened hearts, so that our worldly self is transpierced and mortified. In others the Spirit appears as an earthquake, that is to say as a sense of inward jubilation or what the fathers more clearly define as a sense of exultation. In others He is manifested inwardly as a fire that is non-material yet real; for what is unreal and imaginary is also non-existent. Finally, in others – particularly in those well advanced in prayer – God produces a gentle and serene flow of light. This is when Christ comes to dwell in the heart, as St Paul says (cf. Eph. 3 : 17), mystically disclosing Himself through the Holy Spirit. That is why God said to Elijah on Mount Horeb that the Lord was not in this or in that –

not in the particular actions He manifests Himself in to beginners – but
in the gentle flow of light; for it is in this that He attests the perfection
of our prayer.

Question: What should we do when the devil transforms himself
into an angel of light (cf. 2 Cor. 11 : 14) and tries to seduce us?

Answer: You need great discrimination in order to distinguish
between good and evil. So do not readily or lightly put your trust in
appearances, but weigh things well, and after testing everything
carefully cleave to what is good and reject what is evil (cf. 1 Thess.
5 : 21–2). You must test and discriminate before you give credence to
anything. You must also be aware that the effects of grace are self-
evident, and that even if the devil does transform himself he cannot
produce these effects: he cannot induce you to be gentle, or forbearing,
or humble, or joyful, or serene, or stable in your thoughts; he cannot
make you hate what is worldly, or cut off sensual indulgence and the
working of the passions, as grace does. He produces vanity, haughti-
ness, cowardice and every kind of evil. Thus you can tell from its
effects whether the light shining in your soul is from God or from
satan. The lettuce is similar in appearance to the endive, and vinegar to
wine; but when you taste them the palate discerns and recognizes the
differences between each. In the same way the soul, if it possesses the
power of discrimination, can distinguish with its noetic sense between
the gifts of the Holy Spirit and the illusions of satan.

ST GREGORY PALAMAS

Introductory Note

In the Calendar of the Orthodox Church, St Gregory Palamas (1296–1359)[1] – 'St Gregory of Thessaloniki', as he is usually termed in Orthodox texts – enjoys a particular prominence, since his memory is celebrated not only on the day of his death (14 November) but also on the second Sunday in Lent. The first Sunday in Lent, commemorating the definitive restoration of the holy ikons in 843 at the end of the iconoclast controversy, is known as 'the Sunday of Orthodoxy' or 'the Triumph of Orthodoxy'. If St Gregory's feast was assigned to the following Sunday, this means that his successful defence of the divine and uncreated character of the light of Tabor and his victory over the heretics of his time – Barlaam, Akindynos, Gregoras and others – were seen as a direct continuation of the preceding celebration, as nothing less than a renewed Triumph of Orthodoxy.

Born and brought up in Constantinople, St Gregory Palamas came from a distinguished family, closely linked with the imperial house; his father was a personal friend of the Emperor Andronikos II and tutor to the future Emperor Andronikos III. In his youth Gregory enjoyed for a time the spiritual guidance of Theoliptos of Philadelphia. After his father's death he gave up a promising secular career and around 1316, at the age of twenty, he travelled to Mount Athos with two of his brothers; at the same time his mother, with two of his sisters and many of their servants, entered convents in Thessaloniki. The next twenty years were passed by Gregory in monastic seclusion on the Holy Mountain, except for a six-year period when he left Athos because of

[1] On the life and theology of Palamas, the fundamental work remains the book of John Meyendorff, *A Study of Gregory Palamas* (London, 1964). Meyendorff's more popular study, *St Gregory Palamas and Orthodox Spirituality* (Crestwood, 1974), places Palamas in the broader context of Orthodox mystical theology from the fourth century onwards. For more recent bibliography, see the same author's article in *Dictionnaire de Spiritualité* xii (1983), cols 81–107. For selections from the *Triads* of Palamas, see Nicholas Gendle (tr.), *Gregory Palamas: The Triads* (*The Classics of Western Spirituality*: New York, 1983).

the danger of Turkish attacks and settled in a cave near Veroia. Apart
from a relatively short time spent in cenobia, he chose – like St
Gregory of Sinai – to follow the hesychast way of life in various small
hermitages. Palamas's normal programme was to spend five days of
each week in total solitude, joining his brethren for the Liturgy and
other services on Saturday and Sunday. Such was the preparation for
his future work as defender of the faith.

Around 1335–6 a new era commenced in St Gregory's life. For the
next fourteen years he became involved in what is often termed the
hesychast controversy. Initially his main opponent was a learned Greek
from southern Italy, Barlaam the Calabrian, who maintained that the
light seen by the hesychasts in prayer was not the uncreated light of the
Godhead but simply a created and physical radiance. He also ridiculed
the psychosomatic technique used by some of the monks, referring to
them as *omphalopsychoi*, 'navel-psychics', people who locate the soul in
the navel. Although, so far as his personal wishes were concerned.
Gregory would doubtless have preferred to remain in the stillness of
his hermitage, he felt obliged to come to the defence of the spiritual
tradition of the Holy Mountain and to act as spokesman for the monks.
This forced him to leave Athos and to settle in the imperial capital.
Gregory's standpoint was vindicated at the Council of Constantinople
in 1341, and Barlaam now withdrew to the west. Unfortunately this
did not mean the end of the controversy, which continued for another
six years (1341–7), chiefly because the theological points at issue
became entangled in politics. Gregory's main opponents during this
second period of the dispute were his former friend Gregory
Akindynos and the humanist scholar and statesman Nikiphoros
Gregoras. The doctrinal position upheld by Gregory was eventually
reaffirmed at two further councils held in Constantinople in 1347 and
1351, and since then it has remained the official teaching of the
Orthodox Church.

The final period in St Gregory's career began in 1347, when he was
consecrated Metropolitan of Thessaloniki, the second city of the
Byzantine Empire. Because of the unstable political situation, he could
not take possession of his see until 1350. As bishop he made strenuous
efforts to reconcile the members of his flock to each other, deeply
divided as they still were by the social and political conflicts of the
1340s. In his sermons he insisted upon the urgent need for social
righteousness, consistently supporting the poor and oppressed. His

preaching was also firmly sacramental: whereas the writings of Palamas to be found in *The Philokalia* make but few references to baptism and the eucharist, the balance is redressed by his pastoral homilies to the faithful of Thessaloniki. In 1354, while travelling by sea to Constantinople, he was taken captive by the Turks and spent a year as a prisoner in Asia Minor, where he took part in doctrinal discussions with the local Muslims. Following his death in 1359, a popular veneration for him sprang up almost immediately in Thessaloniki, in Constantinople and on the Holy Mountain, and only nine years later, in 1368, he was formally glorified as a saint.

The writings of St Gregory Palamas are extremely voluminous. A six-volume critical edition is in course of publication, prepared by Professor Panagiotis K. Christou, assisted by other scholars; five volumes have so far appeared (Thessaloniki, 1962–92). St Makarios and St Nikodimos included six works by Palamas in *The Philokalia*:

(1) *To the Most Reverend Nun Xenia* (Greek text, ed. P.K. Christou, vol. v, pp. 193–230). This was written around 1342–6, at a time when Palamas was suffering sharp persecution from his opponents, and he makes several allusions to his difficulties (§§ 3, 5, 6, 57). The work itself, however, is not an answer to his theological critics, but a statement of the traditional Orthodox teaching concerning the ascetic life, written at Xenia's request. It is the most substantial of Palamas's ascetic writings, and offers a general overview of his teaching about human nature, about death and the future life, about the passions and the virtues, and in particular about virginity and inward grief. Little is said concerning the higher stages of the spiritual way, but he refers briefly to the vision of divine light (§ 59) and to the uncreated character of the grace dwelling within the saints (§ 70). Nothing is known about the nun Xenia except that she had under her charge the daughters of 'the Great King', by which is probably meant the daughters of the late Emperor Andronikos III, who had died in 1341 (§ 7).

(2) *A New Testament Decalogue* (Greek text, ed. P.K. Christou, vol. v, pp. 251–60).[1] This was probably composed by St Gregory Palamas towards the end of his life, during his episcopate, perhaps in the autumn of 1355. It is a brief summary of Christian moral teaching,

---

[1] There is a previous English translation by S.A. Mousalimas in *The Greek Orthodox Theological Review* xxv (1980), pp. 297–305.

indicating how the Ten Commandments of the Mosaic Law are transformed within the life of the Church because of the incarnation. Addressed to the laity, it exemplifies St Gregory's pastoral concerns. Among other things he refers to the Orthodox teaching on ikons (§ 2), on spiritual fatherhood (§ 5), and on virginity and marriage (§ 6), but he does not discuss the specifically hesychast teaching concerning inner prayer.

(3) *In Defence of Those who Devoutly Practise a Life of Stillness* (= *Triads* I, ii: Greek text, ed. J. Meyendorff, *Défense des saints hésychastes* [*Spicilegium Sacrum Lovaniense* 30–31: Louvain, 1959], vol. i, pp. 75–101). This is a section of a much larger work, written by Palamas in defence of the hesychast tradition of prayer during 1337–9, chiefly in answer to the attacks of Barlaam the Calabrian. In the portion included in *The Philokalia*, Palamas's main concern is to uphold the legitimacy of the psychosomatic technique. The crouching posture adopted by the hesychast assists him in establishing a 'circular' movement within himself, so that his concentration is turned inward (§§ 5, 8). Slowing down the rhythm of the breathing also helps to hold in check the volatile and easily distracted intellect; but this control of the breathing is an exercise appropriate chiefly for 'beginners . . . recently embarked on the spiritual path', who may abandon it once they have advanced 'to a higher stage' (§ 7). Yet, while attaching only limited importance to the physical method, Gregory Palamas recognizes that it reflects a genuinely Christian doctrine of the human person, with the heart regarded symbolically as man's spiritual centre (§ 3). The body is God's creation, and we are to take full advantage of its Spirit-bearing potentialities; St Paul condemned, not the body itself, but only 'the body of this death' (§ 1).

(4) *Three Texts on Prayer and Purity of Heart* (Greek text, ed. P.K. Christou, vol. v, pp. 157–9). Here again St Gregory emphasizes the centrality of the heart (§ 5). In this brief work there is no specific reference to the concerns of the hesychast controversy, and it was perhaps written in the early 1330s, before the outbreak of the dispute.

(5) *Topics of Natural and Theological Science and on the Moral and Ascetic Life: One Hundred and Fifty Texts* (Greek text, ed. Robert E. Sinkewicz [Pontifical Institute of Mediaeval Studies, Studies and Texts 83: Toronto, 1988]). This important but difficult work has been variously dated: some place it at the end of St Gregory's life, others assign it to the years 1344–7, but most probably it was composed in

1349–50. It provides a comprehensive picture of his theology, constituting what Fr Meyendorff calls 'a sort of systematic *summa*'. It falls into two distinct parts:

(a) §§ 1–63: a general survey of the divine economy of creation and salvation:[1]

(1) The non-eternity of the cosmos: the world had an origin, and it will have a consummation (§§ 1–2).

(2) The celestial realm (§§ 3–7).

(3) The terrestrial realm (§§ 8–14).

(4) The natural human faculties: sense perception, the imaginative faculty, the intellect (§§ 15–20).

(5) Spiritual knowledge, and its superiority to Hellenic philosophy (§§ 21–29).

(6) Human nature, compared with that of the angels and the animals; the soul and its immortality (§§ 30–33).

(7) God the Holy Trinity and the Triadic image of God in the human person (§§ 34–40).

(8) The fallen state of man (§§ 41–63). Here St Gregory emphasizes that man is more perfectly in God's image than the angels (§§ 62–63; but cf. § 78).

(b) §§ 64–150: a refutation of false teachings concerning the divine light of Tabor and the uncreated energies of God. This is directed primarily against Akindynos rather than Barlaam, who at the time of writing had already withdrawn from the dispute and returned to Italy. St Gregory Palamas, supporting his argument with frequent quotations from the fathers, maintains that there is a distinction-in-unity between God's essence and His energies. The divine essence signifies God's absolute transcendence, and we humans will never participate in it, either in this life or in the age to come. The divine energies, on the other hand, permeate the entire creation, and we humans participate in them by grace (§§ 65, 78). Thus deification (*theosis*) and union with God signify union with God's energies, not His essence (§ 75). That which the energies effect and produce is created, but the divine energies themselves are supranatural, eternal and uncreated (§§ 72–73). The energies are Trinitarian, proceeding from all three persons at

[1] It has to be said that the cosmological aspects of this survey reflect very largely Palamas's own personal views and must not be taken to represent Christian cosmology as such. It should also be noted that Palamas's account of the thought of 'the Greek sages' makes it clear that he was not closely familiar with their works.

once (§§ 72, 112). They are not to be identified with the hypostasis of the Holy Spirit (§ 74). The threefold distinction within God between the one essence, the three hypostases, and the multiplicity of energies in no way destroys the divine unity, for God 'is indivisibly divided and is united dividedly, and yet in spite of this suffers neither multiplicity nor compositeness' (§ 81). The light which shone from Christ at the transfiguration on Tabor is not created, natural or physical, but it is the uncreated energies of God. It is this uncreated glory that the saints behold in prayer, and that will shine from Christ at the second coming. Thus, even when experienced in this present life, it is an eschatological glory, the eternal radiance of the age to come (§§ 74, 146–50).

(6) *The Declaration of the Holy Mountain* (also known as 'The Hagioritic Tome': Greek text, ed. P.K. Christou, vol. ii, pp. 567–78). This short statement of the hesychast standpoint, drafted by St Gregory Palamas in 1340, is of particular importance because it bears the signatures of leading Athonite monks and also of the local hierarch, the Bishop of Hierissos in Chalkidiki. This makes it clear that Palamas is expressing, not merely his own personal opinion, but the accepted teaching of the Holy Mountain. Palamas emphasizes the eschatological character of the divine light, which is a foretaste and anticipation of the glory of the age to come. The monks who bear witness to the uncreated light fulfil a prophetic role within the Church: just as the Old Testament prophets foretold Christ's first coming at the incarnation, so the monks as the prophets of the new covenant point forward to His second coming (*Prologue*). Here as elsewhere Palamas expresses a holistic vision of the human person: the body is glorified along with the soul (§ 4). Our *theosis* is in no sense merely symbolical or metaphorical: it is a genuine and specific reality, a pure gift of grace experienced even in this present life (§ 2).

To the Most Reverend Nun Xenia

1. Those who truly desire to live a monastic life find all talk troublesome, whether it is with people at large or with those living in the same way as themselves. For it breaks the continuity of their joyful intercourse with God and sunders, and sometimes shatters, that one-pointed concentration of the intellect which constitutes the inward and true monk. For this reason one of the fathers, when asked why he avoided people, answered that he could not be with God while associating with men.[1] Another father, speaking of these things from experience, affirms that not only talk with others but even the sight of them can destroy the steady quietude of mind possessed by those who practise stillness.

2. If you observe carefully you will find that even the thought of someone's approach, and the expectation of a visit and of having to talk, disrupt your mental tranquillity. If you write you burden your intellect with even more demanding worries. For if you are among those who are well advanced on the spiritual path and who through their soul's good health have attained God's love, then though this love will be active within you while you write, it will be so only indirectly and not unalloyed. But if you are one who still falls into many maladies and passions of the soul – and such in truth am I – and must continually cry out to God, 'Heal me, for I have sinned against Thee' (cf. Ps. 41 : 4), then it is unwise for you to leave off prayer before being healed and of your own accord to occupy yourself with something else. In addition, through your writings you converse also with those who are not present, and often what you write falls into the hands of others, sometimes of those whom you would not wish to read it, since writings usually survive the death of their author.

[1] *Apophthegmata*, alphabetical collection, Arsenios 13; E.T., p. 11.

3. For this reason many of the fathers who practised extreme stillness could not bear to write anything at all, although they were in a position to set forth great and profitable things. It is true that I myself, who totally lack the strict observance of the fathers, have the habit of writing, although only when some great need compels me to do so. Now, however, those who look upon certain of my writings with malicious eyes and seek to find in them grounds to do me wrong have made me more reluctant to write. Such people, according to St Dionysios,[1] are passionately attached to the component parts of letters, to meaningless penstrokes, to unfamiliar syllables and words – things that do not touch their power of noetic understanding. It is indeed witless, perverse and entirely inappropriate to want to understand divine things and yet to pay attention, not to the purpose of what is said, but to the words alone.

4. Yet I know that I have been justly censured, not because what I have written conflicts with the fathers – for by the grace of Christ I have been kept from doing this – but because I have written on things whereof I am unworthy, perhaps, like another Uzzah, trying through words to prevent the chariot of truth from overturning (cf. 2 Sam. 6 : 6–7). Yet my punishment was not a matter of divine wrath, but a fit measure of instruction. On account of this my adversaries were not permitted to get the better of me. Yet this, too, may have been due to my unworthiness, for, it seems, I was not worthy, or capable, of suffering anything on behalf of the truth, and so sharing joyfully in the sufferings of the saints. [5.] Indeed, was not St John Chrysostom, who while yet clothed with the body was united to the Church of the firstborn in the heavens, and who as no other truthfully, clearly and fluently wrote about holiness – was not he cut off from the Church and condemned to exile on the charge of holding and expounding the doctrines of Origen? And St Peter, the chief of the foremost choir of the Lord's disciples, says that unlearned and unstable people in his days distorted difficult passages in St Paul's epistles and brought destruction upon themselves as a result (cf. 2 Pet. 3 : 16).

6. I myself had intended to give up writing altogether because of the somewhat trivial attacks made upon me, even though those who attacked me have been synodically condemned. But now you, most reverend mother, through your constant requests in letters and

---

[1] St Dionysios the Areopagite, *On the Divine Names* iv, 11 (*P.G.* iii, 708C).

messages, have persuaded me once again to write words of counsel, though indeed you have no great need of counsel. For by the grace of Christ you have gained, together with old age, a venerable understanding, and for many years you have studied and applied the ordinances of the divine commandments, dividing your life in due measure between obedience and stillness. In this way you have wiped clean the tablet of your soul, so that it is capable of receiving and preserving whatever God writes on it. But the soul completely dominated by its desire for spiritual instruction is never sated.

7. It is because of this that Wisdom says of herself, 'Those who eat Me will still be hungry' (Eccles. 24 : 21); while the Lord, who has instilled this divine desire in the soul, says of Mary who chose 'what is best' that it will not be taken away from her (cf. Luke 10 : 42). But you perhaps may be in need of such words of instruction for the sake of the daughters of the Emperor who live under your guidance, and especially for the sake of the nun Synesis, who is of your own family and whom you have longed to espouse to Christ, the bestower of incorruption. And, indeed, you imitate Him in that, just as He truly assumed our form for our sakes, so you have now assumed the role of a novice who is in need of instruction. Therefore, although I am not rich in words, and particularly in such words as these, I shall repay the debt of Christian love from what I now possess, showing thus my good will as well as my obedience and my readiness to keep the commandment, 'Give to him that asks' (Matt. 5 : 42).

8. You must know, then, reverend mother – or rather, let the maidens who have chosen to live a godly life learn through you – that there is a death of the soul, though by nature the soul is immortal. This is made clear by the beloved disciple, St John the Theologian, when he says, 'There is sin that leads to death' and 'There is sin that does not lead to death' (1 John 5 : 16, 17). By death he certainly means here the death of the soul. And St Paul says, 'Worldly sorrowfulness produces death' (2 Cor. 7 : 10) – death, certainly, of the soul. Again, St Paul says, 'Awake, you who sleep, and arise from the dead, and Christ will give you light' (Eph. 5 : 14). From which 'dead' is one enjoined to arise? Clearly, from those who have been killed by 'sinful desires that wage war against the soul' (1 Pet. 2 : 11). Hence the Lord also described those who live in this vain world as 'dead', for when one of His disciples asked to be allowed to go and bury his father, He refused permission, and told him to follow Him, leaving the dead to

bury their dead (cf. Matt. 8 : 22). Here, then, the Lord clearly calls those living people 'dead', in the sense that they are dead in soul.

9. As the separation of the soul from the body is the death of the body, so the separation of God from the soul is the death of the soul. And this death of the soul is the true death. This is made clear by the commandment given in paradise, when God said to Adam, 'On whatever day you eat from the forbidden tree you will certainly die' (cf. Gen. 2 : 17). And it was indeed Adam's soul that died by becoming through his transgression separated from God; for bodily he continued to live after that time, even for nine hundred and thirty years (cf. Gen. 5 : 5). [10.] The death, however, that befell the soul because of the transgression not only crippled the soul and made man accursed; it also rendered the body itself subject to fatigue, suffering and corruptibility, and finally handed it over to death. For it was after the dying of his inner self brought about by the transgression that the earthly Adam heard the words, 'Earth will be cursed because of what you do, it will produce thorns and thistles for you; through the sweat of your brow you will eat your bread until you return to the earth from which you were taken: for you are earth, and to earth you will return' (Gen. 3 : 17–19. LXX).

11. Even though at the regeneration to come, in the resurrection of the righteous, the bodies of the godless and sinners will also be raised up, yet they will be given over to the second death, age-long chastisement, the unsleeping worm (cf. Mark 9 : 44), the gnashing of teeth, the outer, tangible darkness (cf. Matt. 8 : 12), the murky and unquenchable fire of Gehenna (cf. Matt. 5 : 22), in which, as the prophet says, the godless and sinners 'will be burned up together and there will be none to quench the flame' (Isa. 1 : 31). For this is the second death, as St John has taught us in the Revelation (cf. Rev. 20 : 14). Hark, too, to the words of St Paul, 'If you live in accordance with your fallen self, you will die, but if through the Spirit you extirpate the evil actions of your fallen self, you will live' (Rom. 8 : 13). Here he speaks of life and death in the age to be: life is the enjoyment of the everlasting kingdom, death age-long chastisement.

12. Thus the violation of God's commandment is the cause of all types of death, both of soul and body, whether in the present life or in that endless chastisement. And death, properly speaking, is this: for the soul to be unharnessed from divine grace and to be yoked to sin. This death, for those who have their wits, is truly dreadful and something to

be avoided. This, for those who think aright, is more terrible than the chastisement of Gehenna. From this let us also flee with all our might. Let us cast away, let us reject all things, bid farewell to all things: to all relationships, actions and intentions that drag us downward, separate us from God and produce such a death. He who is frightened of this death and has preserved himself from it will not be alarmed by the oncoming death of the body, for in him the true life dwells, and bodily death, so far from taking true life away, renders it inalienable.

As the death of the soul is authentic death, so the life of the soul is authentic life. [13.] Life of the soul is union with God, as life of the body is its union with the soul. As the soul was separated from God and died in consequence of the violation of the commandment, so by obedience to the commandment it is again united to God and is quickened. This is why the Lord says in the Gospels, 'The words I speak to you are spirit and life' (John 6 : 63). And having experienced the truth of this, St Peter said to Him, 'Thy words are the words of eternal life' (John 6 : 68). But they are words of eternal life for those who obey them; for those who disobey, this commandment of life results in death (cf. Rom. 7 : 10). So it was that the apostles, being Christ's fragrance, were to some the death-inducing odour of death, while to others they were the life-inducing odour of life (cf. 2 Cor. 2 : 16). [14.] And this life is not only the life of the soul, it is also the life of the body. Through resurrection the body is also rendered immortal: it is delivered not merely from mortality, but also from that never-abating death of future chastisement. On it, too, is bestowed everlasting life in Christ, free of pain, sickness and sorrow, and truly immortal.

The death of the soul through transgression and sin is, then, followed by the death of the body and by its dissolution in the earth and its conversion into dust; and this bodily death is followed in its turn by the soul's banishment to Hades. In the same way the resurrection of the soul – its return to God through obedience to the divine commandments – is followed by the body's resurrection and its reunion with the soul. And for those who experience it the consequence of this resurrection will be true incorruption and eternal life with God: they will become spiritual instead of non-spiritual, and will dwell in heaven as angels of God (cf. Matt. 22 : 30). [15.] As St Paul says, 'We shall be caught up in the clouds to meet the Lord in the air, and so we shall be with the Lord for ever' (1 Thess. 4 : 17).

The Son of God, who in His compassion became man, died so far as His body was concerned when His soul was separated from His body; but this body was not separated from His divinity, and so He raised up His body once more and took it with Him to heaven in glory. Similarly, when those who have lived here in a godly manner are separated from their bodies, they are not separated from God, and in the resurrection they will take their bodies with them to God, and in their bodies they will enter with inexpressible joy there where Jesus has preceded us (cf. Heb. 6 : 20) and in their bodies they will enjoy the glory that will be revealed in Christ (cf. 1 Pet. 5 : 1). Indeed, they will share not only in resurrection, but also in the Lord's ascension and in all divine life. But this does not apply to those who live this present life in an unregenerate manner and who at death have no communion with God. For though all will be resurrected, yet the resurrection of each individual will be in accordance with his own inner state (cf. 1 Cor. 15 : 23). He who through the power of the Spirit has extirpated his materialistic worldly proclivities in this life will hereafter live a divine and truly eternal life in communion with Christ. But he who through surrendering to his materialistic and worldly lusts and passions has in this life deadened his spiritual being will, alas, hereafter be co-judged with the devil, the *agent-provocateur* of evil, and will be handed over to unbearable and immeasurable chastisement, which is the second and final death.

16. Where did true death – the death that produces and induces in soul and body both temporal and eternal death – have its origin? Was it not in the realm of life? Thus was man, alas, at once banished from God's paradise, for he had imbued his life with death and made it unfit for paradise. Consequently true life – the life that confers immortality and true life on both soul and body – will have its origin here, in this place of death. If you do not strive here to gain this life in your soul, do not deceive yourself with vain hopes about receiving it hereafter, or about God then being compassionate towards you. For then is the time of requital and retribution, not of sympathy and compassion: the time for the revealing of God's wrath and anger and just judgment, for the manifestation of the mighty and sublime power that brings chastisement upon unbelievers. Woe to him who falls into the hands of the living God (cf. Heb. 10 : 31)! Woe to him who hereafter experiences the Lord's wrath, who has not acquired in this life the fear of God and so come to know the might of His anger, who

has not through his actions gained a foretaste of God's compassion! For the time to do all this is the present life. That is the reason why God has accorded us this present life, giving us a place for repentance. Were this not the case a person who sinned would at once be deprived of this life. For otherwise of what use would it be to him?

17. This is why no one should give way to despair, even though the devil finds various means by which to insinuate it not only into those who live carelessly but also into those who practise the ascetic life. If, then, the time of this life is time for repentance, the very fact that a sinner still lives is a pledge that God will accept whoever desires to return to Him. Free will is always part and parcel of this present life. And it lies within the power of free will to choose or to reject the road of life or the road of death that we have described above; for it can pursue whichever it wishes. Where, then, are the grounds for despair, since all of us can at all times lay hold of eternal life whenever we want to? [18.] Do you not perceive the grandeur of God's compassion? When we are disobedient He does not immediately condemn us, but He is longsuffering and allows us time for conversion. Throughout this period of longsuffering He gives us power to gain divine sonship if we so wish. Yet why do I say 'gain sonship'? He gives us power to be united with Him and to become one spirit with Him (cf. 1 Cor. 6 : 17).

If, however, during this period of longsuffering we pursue the opposite path and choose death rather than true life, God does not take away the power that He gave us. And not only does He not take it away, but He reminds us of it again and again. From the dawn till the dusk of this life, He goes round, as in the parable of the vineyard, seeking us out and inviting us to engage in the works of life (cf. Matt. 20 : 7–15). And who is it that calls us in this way and would engage us in His service? It is the Father of our Lord Jesus Christ, the God of all solace (cf. 2 Cor. 1 : 3). And who is the vineyard into which He calls us to work? The Son of God, who said, 'I am the vine' (cf. John 15 : 1). For, indeed, no one can come to Christ, as He Himself said in the Gospels, unless the Father draws him (cf. John 6 : 44). Who are the branches? We ourselves are. For directly afterwards Christ says, 'You are the branches, My Father is the vine-dresser' (cf. John 15 : 1, 5).

19. The Father, therefore, through the Son reconciles us to Himself, not taking into account our offences (cf. 2 Cor. 5 : 19); and

He calls us, not in so far as we are engaged in unseemly works, but in so far as we are idle; although idleness is also a sin, since we shall give an account even for an idle word (cf. Matt. 12 : 36). But, as I said, God overlooks former sins and calls us again and again. And what does He call us to do? To work in the vineyard, that is, to work on behalf of the branches, on behalf of ourselves. And afterwards – O the incomparable grandeur of His compassion! – He promises and gives us a reward for toiling on our own behalf. 'Come,' He says, 'receive eternal life, which I bestow abundantly; and as though in your debt I reward you in full for the labour of your journey and even for your very desire to receive eternal life from Me.'

20. Who does not owe the price of redemption to the Redeemer from death? Who will not give thanks to the Giver of Life? But He even promises to give us a reward as well, an inexpressible reward. 'I am come', He says, 'so that they may have life, and have it in all its fullness' (John 10 : 10). What is meant by 'in all its fullness'? He came not only to be and to live with us, but to make us His brethren and coheirs. This, it seems, is the reward granted 'in all its fullness' to those who hasten to the life-giving Vine and establish themselves as branches in it, who labour on behalf of themselves and who cultivate it on behalf of themselves. And what do they do? First, they cut away everything that is superfluous and that, instead of promoting, impedes the bearing of fruit worthy of the divine cellars. And what are these things? Wealth, soft living, vain honours, all things that are transitory and fleeting, every sly and abominable passion of soul and body, all the litter gathered while daydreaming, everything heard, seen and spoken that can bring injury to the soul. If you do not cut out these things and prune the heart's offshoots with great assiduity, you will never bear fruit fit for eternal life.

Married people can also strive for this purity, but only with the greatest difficulty. [21.] For this reason all who from their youth have by God's mercy glimpsed that eternal life with the mind's keen eye, and who have longed for its blessings, avoid getting married, since likewise in the resurrection, as the Lord said, people neither marry nor are given in marriage, but are 'as the angels of God' (Matt. 22 : 30). Therefore those who wish to become 'as the angels of God' will even in this present life, like the sons of the resurrection, rightly place themselves above bodily intercourse. Moreover, the occasion for sinning was first provided by the wife. Consequently those who do not wish ever to give the devil any way of catching hold of them should not marry.

22. If this body of ours is hard to harness and hard to lead towards virtue – if, indeed, we carry it about like an innate opposing force – why should we ever entrust ourselves to it, thereby increasing the difficulty we have in attaining a state of virtue by binding ourselves to many different bodies? How will the woman, who is tied by natural bonds to a husband, children and all her blood relations, possess that freedom for which she is enjoined to strive? How will she, when she has taken upon herself the care of so many, devote herself, free from care, to the Lord? How will she possess tranquillity when entangled with such a multitude?

23. For this reason she who is really a virgin – who models herself on Him who is virgin, who was born of a Virgin and who is the Bridegroom of the souls that live in true virginity – will shun not merely carnal wedlock but also worldly companionship, having renounced all kindred, so that like St Peter she can say boldly to Christ, 'We have left all and followed Thee' (Matt. 19 : 27). If an earthly bride leaves father and mother for the sake of a mortal bridegroom and cleaves to him alone, as Scripture says (cf. Gen. 2 : 24), what is untoward in a woman leaving her parents for the sake of an immortal Bridegroom and bridal chamber? How can she whose 'citizenship is in heaven' (Phil. 3 : 20) have kinship on the earth? How can she who is not an offspring of the flesh but of the Spirit (cf. John 1 : 13) have a fleshly father or mother or blood relative? How will she who has renounced the carnal life, and so as far as possible has spurned and continues to spurn her own body, entertain any relationship whatever to bodies that are not her own? And if, as they say, likeness leads to friendship and everything adheres to what is like itself, how can the virgin align herself with worldly loves and fall victim once again to the disease of self-adornment? 'Love of the world is hostility to God' (Jas. 4 : 4), says the apostle who is our bridal escort into the spiritual bridal chamber. Thus a virgin who reverts to worldly affections is not only in danger of separating herself from the immortal Bridegroom, but also of being at enmity with him.

Do not be astonished or distressed by the fact that no criticism is made in Scripture of women who live in wedlock, caring for the things of the world but not for the things of the Lord (cf. 1 Cor. 7 : 34), while at the same time those who have vowed themselves to virginity

are forbidden even to approach worldly things and are never allowed
to live in comfort. Yet St Paul also warns those who live in wedlock:
'The time is short; so let those who have wives live as though they had
none and those involved in worldly affairs as though they were not
involved' (1 Cor. 7 : 29, 31); and this, I think, is harder to accomplish
than the keeping of one's virginity. For experience shows that total
abstinence is easier than self-control in food and drink. And one might
justly and truly say that if someone is not concerned to save himself,
we have nothing to say to him, but if he is so concerned, then he should
know that a life led in virginity is more easily accomplished and less
laborious than married life.

24. Yet let us leave these matters and return, O virgin, bride of
Christ, branch of the Vine of life, to what was said above. The Lord
says, 'I am the vine, you are the branches. . . . My Father is the
vine-dresser . . . He prunes every branch in Me that bears fruit, so that
it may bring forth more fruit' (John 15 : 1, 2, 5). Reflecting on His
careful concern for yourself, recognize what fruit your virginity should
bear and how great is the Bridegroom's affection for you; and rejoice
the more and strive in return to be still more obedient to Him. Gold
that has been mixed with brass is called counterfeit, but brass that has
been smelted with gold dust appears brighter and more radiant than its
natural colour. Similarly, it is an honourable thing for married women
to long for you and the chastity of your way of life, but for you to yearn
for them brings dishonour upon you. For such a yearning returns you
to the world, first because though you have died to the world you still
want to have relations with those who live in the world and to share
their life, and second because being in contact with such persons leads
you to desire what they desire for themselves and their kindred, that is,
abundance in all things pertaining to this life – wealth, fame, glory, and
the delight that these things bring. In this way you will fall away from
your Bridegroom's will, for in the Gospels He clearly disparages such
things, saying, 'Woe to the rich, woe to those who mock, woe to those
who stuff themselves, woe to you when everyone speaks well of you'
(cf. Luke 6 : 24–26).

25. Why does He deplore such people? Is it not because their souls
are dead? What kinship can the bride of life have with the dead? What
communion with those who walk in the opposite direction? Wide and
broad is the way they travel; and unless they restrain themselves by
blending some aspects of your life with theirs, they will lapse into total

destruction. But you should enter through the strait and narrow gate, the way that leads to life (cf. Matt. 7 : 13–14). You cannot pass through this narrow gate and along this way while carrying a load of self-glory, or a cornucopia of self-indulgence, or the burden of money and possessions.

26. But when you hear that other path of life called 'broad', do not suppose it to be free of sorrow, for in fact it is filled with many oppressive misfortunes. He calls it 'broad' and 'wide' because there are many who pass along it (cf. Matt. 7 : 13), each bearing a heavy load of the rubbish of this fleeting material life. But yours is a narrow path, O virgin, not even wide enough for two together. None the less, many at first embroiled in the world have renounced it on the death of their spouses, emulating your supranatural way of life and choosing to journey along your path so as to share in its rewards. And St Paul enjoins us to honour such people, for with hope in God they persevere in supplication and prayer (cf. 1 Tim. 5 : 3, 5). Although the narrow way of life involves affliction, it also brings solace, confers the kingdom of heaven and fosters salvation. But on the broad path what is pleasant and what is grievous are both alike. For, as St Paul says, worldly sorrowfulness produces death, while 'godly sorrow produces a saving repentance that is not to be regretted' (2 Cor. 7 : 10).

27. It is for this reason that the Lord blesses the opposite of what the world calls blessed, saying, 'Blessed are the poor in spirit, for theirs is the kingdom of the heavens' (Matt. 5 : 3). In saying 'Blessed are the poor', why did He add 'in spirit'? So as to show that He blesses and commends humility of soul. And why did He not say, 'Blessed are those whose spirit is poor', thus indicating the modesty of their manner of thinking, but 'Blessed are the poor in spirit'? So as to teach us that poverty of body is also blessed and fosters the kingdom of heaven, but only when it is accomplished in accordance with the soul's humility, when it is united to it and originates from it. By calling the poor in spirit blessed He wonderfully demonstrated what is the root, as it were, and mainspring of the outward poverty of the saints, namely, their humility of spirit. For from our spirit, once it has embraced the grace of the gospel teaching, flows a wellspring of poverty that 'waters the whole face of our ground' (cf. Gen. 2 : 6), I mean our outward self, transforming us into a paradise of virtues. Such, then, is the poverty that is called blessed by God.

28. 'The Lord has given a concise saying upon the earth', as the

prophet observes (cf. Isa. 10 : 23. LXX). Having pointed out and
called blessed the root cause of voluntary and many-sided poverty, He
also teaches us in this single short saying about its many effects. For we
can choose to shed possessions, and to be frugal and abstinent, simply
in order to be praised by other people. In such a case we are not 'poor
in spirit'. Hypocrisy is born of self-conceit, and self-conceit is contrary
to being poor in spirit. But if you possess a contrite, lowly and humble
spirit you cannot but rejoice in outward simplicity and self-abasement,
because you will regard yourself as unworthy of praise, comfort,
prosperity and all such things. The poor man deemed blessed by God is
he who considers himself unworthy of these things. It is he who is
really poor, being poor in full measure. It was on this account that St
Luke also wrote, 'Blessed are the poor' (6 : 20), without adding 'in
spirit'. These are they who have hearkened to the Son of God,
following Him and assimilating themselves to him; for He said, 'Learn
of Me, for I am gentle and humble in heart, and you will find rest for
your souls' (Matt. 11 : 29). Hence 'theirs is the kingdom of heaven',
for they are 'joint-heirs with Christ' (Rom. 8 : 17).

29. The soul is tripartite and is considered as having three powers:
the intelligent, the incensive, and the appetitive. Because the soul was
ill in all three powers, Christ, the soul's Healer, began His cure with
the last, the appetitive. For desire unsatisfied fuels the incensive
power, and when both the appetitive and incensive powers are sick
they produce distraction of mind. Thus the soul's incensive power will
never be healthy before the appetitive power is healed; nor will the
intelligence be healthy until the other two powers are first restored to
health. [30.] If you examine things you will find that the first evil
offspring of the appetitive power is love of material possessions. For
the desires that help men to live are not blameworthy, as is clear from
the fact that they are with us from a very early age. Love of possessions,
however, comes a little later – although still in childhood – and in this
way it is evident that it does not have its ground in nature, but is a
matter of individual choice. St Paul rightly termed it the root of all evils
(cf. 1 Tim. 6 : 10), and the evils that it usually begets are
niggardliness, trickery, rapacity, thievery and, in short, greed in all its
forms, which St Paul called a second idolatry (cf. Col. 3 : 5). Even in
the case of evils that do not spring directly from it, greed nearly always
provides the fuel for their sustenance.

31. Such evils, begotten of the love for material things, are passions

of a soul that has no zeal for spiritual work. We can free ourselves more easily from passions that are a matter of our own volition than from those rooted in nature. It is disbelief in God's providence that makes it difficult for us to eradicate the passions that arise from our love of possessions, for such disbelief leads us to put our trust in material riches. 'It is easier', said the Lord, 'for a camel to go through the eye of a needle than for a rich man to enter into the kingdom of God' (Matt. 19 : 24). But if we trust in material riches, this means nothing to us; we long for worldly, perishable wealth, not for a kingdom that is heavenly and eternal. And even when we fail to acquire that wealth, the mere desire for it is extremely pernicious. For, as St Paul says, those who want to be rich fall into the temptations and snares of the devil (cf. 1 Tim. 6 : 9). Yet when wealth comes, it proves itself to be nothing, since its possessors, unless they are brought to their senses by experience, still thirst after it as though they lacked it. This love that is no love does not come from need; rather the need arises from the love. The love itself arises from folly, the same folly that led Christ, the Master of all, justly to describe as foolish the man who pulled down his barns and built greater ones (cf. Luke 12 : 18–20). [32.] How could such a person not be a fool when for the sake of things that cannot profit him – 'For a man's life does not consist in the abundance of the things that he possesses' (Luke 12 : 15) – he gives up what is most profitable of all? He fails to become a wise merchant, selling even necessities, so far as possible, and in this way adding to the capital of a truly bountiful and gainful form of commerce or husbandry – a husbandry, indeed, which even before the harvest time multiplies a hundredfold that which was sown, thus foreshowing that the profit to come and the harvest shortly to be reaped will be indescribable and unimaginable. And the curious thing is that the smaller the storerooms the seed comes from the larger will the harvest be.

Hence there is no justification in aspiring to become rich even for a good cause. The truth is that people are frightened of being poor because they have no faith in Him who promised to provide all things needful to those who seek the kingdom of God (cf. Matt. 6 : 33). It is this fear that spurs them, even when they are endowed with all things, and it prevents them from ever freeing themselves from this sickly and baneful desire. They go on amassing wealth, loading themselves with a worthless burden or, rather, enclosing themselves while still living in a most absurd kind of tomb. [33.] Dead men are simply buried in the earth, but the intellect of a living pinchpenny is buried in the dust and earth of gold. Further, for those whose senses are in a healthy state this grave smells worse than the normal one, and the more earth one throws on it, the stronger the smell grows. For the festering wound of wretched persons buried in this way spreads, and its stench rises up to heaven, even up to the angels of God and to God Himself. They have become loathsome and repulsive, stinking on account of their folly, as David puts it (cf. Ps. 38 : 5). Voluntary poverty – not undertaken to impress others – delivers men from this foul-smelling and deadly passion; and such poverty is precisely the 'poorness in spirit' that the Lord called blessed.

34. Yet a monk who has this passion cannot be obedient. If he persists in serving it diligently, there is a grave risk of him lapsing also into incurable maladies of the body. Gehazi in the Old Testament and Judas in the New Testament are sufficient examples of this. The first sprouted leprosy as evidence of his incurable soul (cf. 2 Kgs. 5 : 27), while the second hanged himself in the field of blood, and falling headlong he burst his belly and his intestines gushed out (cf. Acts 1 : 18). If, then, renunciation precedes obedience, how can it be the other way round? And if renunciation is the initial step in the monastic profession, how can anyone who has not first renounced material possessions succeed in any of the other struggles of monastic life? Moreover, if a monk is incapable of practising obedience, how will he be able to cultivate stillness by himself in a cell, devoting himself to solitude and persevering in prayer? But as the Lord says, 'Where your treasure is, there will your intellect be also' (Matt. 6 : 21). How, then, can you gaze noetically at Him who sits in heaven on the right hand of the divine Majesty (cf. Heb. 1 : 3) while you are still amassing treasure upon the earth? How will you inherit that kingdom which this passion entirely prevents you even from conceiving in your mind? 'Blessed', therefore, 'are the poor in spirit, for theirs is the kingdom of heaven.' Do you see how many passions the Lord has cut away with one beatitude?

35. Yet this is not all. If love for material things is the first offspring of evil desire, there is a second offspring which is even more to be shunned, and a third that is no less evil. What is the second? Self-flattery. We encounter this passion while we are still quite young, as a kind of prelude to the love for worldly things which we encounter later. Here I am referring to the self-flattery that expresses itself in the

beautification of the body through expensive clothing and so on. It is what the fathers call worldly vanity, to distinguish it from the other kind of vanity, which afflicts those noted for their virtue and is accompanied by self-conceit and hypocrisy, whereby the devil contrives to plunder and disperse our spiritual riches.

36. You can be completely healed from all these things if you become aware of divine glory and long for it while regarding yourself as unworthy of it, and if you patiently endure people's scorn while thinking you deserve it. In addition, you should esteem God's glory above your own, in conformity with the Psalmist's words, 'Not unto us, O Lord, not unto us, but unto Thy name give glory' (Ps. 115 : 2). And should you feel that you have done something praiseworthy, you should attribute it to God, proclaiming Him as its cause and gratefully praising Him for it and not yourself. In your rejoicing you will regard each virtue as a gift, and will not become conceited about it, since it is not your personal achievement; on the contrary, you will grow more humble, and night and day will fix your mental eyes on God, as the eyes of the handmaid – to use the Psalmist's words again – are fixed on the hands of her mistress (cf. Ps. 123 : 2). At the same time you will be full of fear lest, becoming separated from Him who alone confers goodness and preserves us in it, you are pulled down into the pit of evil; for this is what happens when you are enslaved to conceit and vanity. A great help in healing these passions is withdrawal from the world and living a life of solitude, keeping yourself to your cell. But you must be deeply aware of the frailty of your will and regard yourself as not strong enough to mix with other people. Yet what is this but the poverty in spirit that the Lord called blessed?

37. If you recognize the disgrace that such self-flattery brings upon you, you will spurn it with all your might. For by longing for men's praise you dishonour yourself through the very deeds you do in order to attain it. By caring about your appearance, by attaching great importance to the fame of your ancestors and to gaudy clothes and so on, you show that yours is still a puerile mind. For all these things are mere dust, and what is more despicable than dust? The nun who wears what she wears not simply for covering or warmth, but because it is gossamery and gaudy, not only proclaims the barrenness of her soul but also displays the indecency of a loose woman. She should listen rather to Him who says, 'They that wear fine clothing are to be found in royal palaces' (Matt. 11 : 8). But 'our citizenship is in heaven' (Phil.

3 : 20), as St Paul says. Let us not be cast out of heaven into the abodes of the 'ruler of the darkness of this world' (cf. Eph. 6 : 12) simply for the sake of foolish ostentation in our clothing.

38. This same thing happens to those who practise virtue in order to be praised by others. While they are called to be citizens of heaven, they 'degrade their glory to the dust' (Ps. 7 : 5), and make their dwelling there, thus drawing upon themselves the curse of the Psalmist. For their prayer does not rise to heaven, and their every endeavour falls to the earth, since it is not supported by the wings of divine love that raise aloft the works we do upon the earth. So although they labour they reap no reward. But why do I speak of reaping no reward? For indeed they bear fruit, only it is the fruit of shame, instability of thoughts, and distraction and turbulence of mind. For the Lord, as the Psalmist says, 'has scattered the bones of those who court popularity; they have been put to shame, because God has set them at naught' (Ps. 53 : 5. LXX).

This passion is the subtlest of all the passions, and for this reason the person who fights against it must not merely be on guard against coupling with it or avoid assenting to it, but he must regard the very provocation as assent and must shield himself from it. Only in this way can he narrowly escape speedy defeat. If through inward watchfulness he manages to do this, the provocation itself will become an occasion for compunction. But if he fails to do it, the provocation induces pride; and once a person has fallen a victim to pride it is hard, in fact impossible, to cure him, for such a fall is the same as the devil's. Yet even before this the passion for popularity brings such injury upon those it masters that it shipwrecks faith itself (cf. 1 Tim. 1 : 19). Our Lord confirms this when He says, 'How can you have faith in Me when you receive honour from one another and do not seek for the honour that comes from the only God?' (cf. John 5 : 44).

39. What have you to do with honour accorded by men or, rather, with the empty name of honour? Not only is such honour no honour at all, but it also deprives you of true honour. And not only this, but among other evils it also generates envy: envy that is potentially murder and that was the cause of the first murder (cf. Gen. 4 : 1–8) and then of the slaying of God (cf. Matt. 27 : 18). What, in fact, does this passion for human honour contribute to our nature? Does it sustain or protect it, or in any way restore or heal it when it has gone awry? No one could claim it does anything like that; and I think that

this alone is enough to show how baseless are the excuses made for its perversions. Should you examine things closely you will find that in a treacherous fashion the thirst for glory among men first provokes us to various kinds of villainy and then denounces us, shamelessly unmasking itself and disgracing even its own lovers. And yet the champions of profane Greek teachings dare to say that nothing in life can be achieved without it – an absurd delusion! [40.] But we Christians have not been taught thus, we who bear the name of Him who lovingly anointed our nature with His own and who watches over our actions. Turning to Him, we accomplish whatever is most excellent through Him and because of Him, doing all for the glory of God (cf. 1 Cor. 10 : 31) and having no desire at all to court popularity. In fact, we are positively displeasing to people, as St Paul, the most intimate initiate of our Lawmaker and Lawgiver, confirms when he says: 'If I still wanted to be popular I would not be the servant of Christ' (Gal. 1 : 10).

41. Let us now see whether the third offspring of evil desire is likewise destroyed by that poverty which the Lord called blessed. The third offspring of the desire of a sick soul is gluttony; and from gluttony arises every kind of carnal impurity. Yet why do we call this the third and last when it is implanted in us from our very birth? For not only this passion, but also the natural motions related to the begetting of children, can be detected in infants that are still at the breast. Why, then, do we place the disease of carnal desire at the end of the list? The reason is this: the passions to which it gives birth belong to us by nature, and natural things are not indictable; for they were created by God who is good, so that through them we can act in ways that are also good. Hence in themselves they do not indicate sickness of soul, but they become evidence of such sickness when we misuse them. When we coddle the flesh in order to foster its desires, then the passion becomes evil and self-indulgence gives rise to the carnal passions and renders the soul diseased.

The first victim of these passions is the intellect. Because the passions initially spring from the mind, the Lord says that the evil thoughts which defile us proceed from the heart (cf. Matt. 15 : 18–19). And prior to the Gospel the Law tells us, 'Be attentive to yourself, lest there arise some secret iniquity in your hearts' (Deut. 15 : 9. LXX). Yet though it is the intellect that initiates evil, none the less the images of sensory bodies that entice the intellect towards these bodies and incite it to misuse them are impressed on it from below, through the senses, and above all through the eyes, for the eyes can embrace a defiling object even from a distance. Eve, our primordial mother, is clear evidence of this: first she saw that the forbidden tree was 'comely to look upon and beautiful to contemplate', and then, assenting in her heart, she plucked and ate its fruit (cf. Gen. 3 : 6). [42.] So we were right when we said that yielding to the beauty of physical objects precedes and leads us to the degrading passions. Hence the fathers advise us not to look closely upon another's beauty or to find delectation in our own.

Before the mind becomes embroiled with them, the passions which are naturally implanted in children conduce not to sin but to the sustaining of nature. For this reason they are not at that stage evil. It is in the passion-charged intellect that the carnal passions arise initially, and so healing must begin with the intellect. You cannot extinguish a raging fire by slashing at it from above; but if you pull away the fuel from below, the fire will die down immediately. So it is with the passions of impurity. If you do not cut off the inner flow of evil thoughts by means of prayer and humility, but fight against them merely with the weapons of fasting and bodily hardship, you will labour in vain. But if through prayer and humility you sanctify the root, as we said, you will attain outward sanctity as well. This it seems to me is what St Paul counsels when he exhorts us to gird our loins with truth (cf. Eph. 6 : 14). One of the fathers has excellently interpreted this as signifying that when the contemplative faculty of the soul tightly girds the appetitive faculty it also girds the passions manifested through the loins and the genitals. The body, nevertheless, is in need of hardship and moderate abstention from food, lest it become unruly and more powerful than the intelligence. Thus all the passions of the flesh are healed solely by bodily hardship and prayer issuing from a humble heart, which indeed is the poverty in spirit that the Lord called blessed.

43. If, then, you yearn to be enriched with holiness – and without holiness no one will see the Lord (cf. Heb. 12 : 14) – you should abide in your own cell, enduring hardship and praying with humility. For the cell of one rightly pursuing the monastic life is a haven of self-restraint. But all that lies outside, and especially what is found in market places and at fairs, constitutes an obscene medley of ugly sounds and sights, drowning the wretched soul of the nun who exposes herself to them. One might also call this evil world a raging fire that devours those

who come into contact with it and burns up every virtue they possess. The fire that did not burn was found in the desert (cf. Exod. 3 : 2). Instead of in the desert, you should abide in your cell and hide yourself a little until the tempest of passion has passed over you. When it has passed, spending time outside your cell will do you no harm.

Then in truth you will be poor in spirit and will gain dominion over the passions and clearly be called blessed by Him who said, 'Blessed are the poor in spirit, for theirs is the kingdom of heaven.' [44.] How, indeed, can those not be called blessed who have absolutely no truck with material wealth and place all their trust in Him? Who wish to please only Him? Who with humility and the other virtues live in His presence? Let us, then, also become poor in spirit by being humble, by submitting our unregenerate self to hardship and by shedding all possessions, so that the kingdom of God may be ours, and we may fulfil our blessed aspirations by inheriting the kingdom of heaven.

The Lord has left us certain synoptic statements that express in a succinct manner the Gospel of our salvation, and one of these statements is the beatitude of which we have been speaking. By including so many virtues in that single phrase and excluding so many vices, the Lord has conferred His blessing on all those who through these virtues and through repentance prune the aspect of their souls that is vulnerable to passion. But this is not all; for in that phrase He also includes many other things, analogous not to pruning but rather to the activity of cold, ice, snow, frost and the violence of the wind – in a word, to the hardship that plants undergo in winter and summer by being exposed to the cold and heat, yet without which nothing upon earth can ever bear fruit. [45.] What are these things? The various trials and temptations that afflict us and that we must gladly endure if we are to yield fruit to the Husbandman of our souls. If we were to feel sorry for earthly plants and build a wall around them and put a roof over them and not allow them to suffer such hardships, then although we may prune and otherwise tend them assiduously, they will bear no fruit. On the contrary, we must let them endure everything, for then, after the winter's hardship, in springtime they will bud, blossom, adorn themselves with leaves and, covered with this bountiful foliage, they will produce young fruit. This fruit, as the sun's rays grow stronger, will thrive, mature and become ready for harvesting and eating. Similarly, if we do not courageously bear the burden of trial and temptation – even though we may practise all the other virtues – we will never yield fruit worthy of the divine wine-press and the eternal granaries. For it is through patient endurance of afflictions deliberately entered into and those that are unsought, whether they come upon us from without or assault us from within, that we become perfect. What happens naturally to plants as a result of the farmer's care and the changing seasons happens, if we so choose, to us, Christ's spiritual branches (cf. John 15 : 5), when as creatures possessing free-will we are obedient to Him, the Husbandman of souls.

Unless we bear with patience the afflictions that come to us unsought, God will not bless those that we embrace deliberately. For our love for God is demonstrated above all by the way we endure trials and temptations. [46.] First the soul has to surmount afflictions embraced willingly, thereby learning to spurn sensual pleasure and self-glory; and this in its turn will permit us readily to bear the afflictions that come unsought. If for the sake of poverty of spirit you spurn such pleasure and self-glory, and also regard yourself as deserving the more drastic remedy of repentance, you will be ready to bear any affliction and will accept any temptation as your due, and you will rejoice when it comes, for you will see it as a cleansing-agent for your soul. In addition, it will spur you to ardent and most efficacious prayer to God, and you will regard it as the source and protector of the soul's health. Not only will you forgive those who afflict you, but you will be grateful to them and will pray for them as for your benefactors. Thus you will not only receive forgiveness for your sins, as the Lord has promised (cf. Matt. 6 : 14), but you will also attain the kingdom of heaven and God's benediction, for you will be blessed by the Lord for enduring with patience and a spirit of humility till the end.

47. Having spoken briefly about spiritual pruning, I will now add something about the productiveness that results from it. After first calling blessed those who gain imperishable wealth because of their poverty in spirit, God, who alone is blessed, next makes those who grieve partakers of His own blessedness, saying, 'Blessed are those who grieve, for they will be consoled' (Matt. 5 : 4). [48.] Why did Christ thus join grief to poverty? Because it always coexists with it. But while sorrow over worldly poverty induces the soul's death, grief over poverty embraced in God's name induces the 'saving repentance that is not to be regretted' (2 Cor. 7 : 10). The first kind of poverty, being unsought, is followed by unwished-for grief; the second, being freely embraced, is followed by grief freely embraced. Because the grief here

called blessed is linked with the poverty embraced in God's name, necessarily issuing from it and depending on it as its cause, it too possesses a spiritual and voluntary character.

Let us see, then, how this blessed poverty begets blessed grief. [49.] In this single word 'poverty' four types of spiritual poverty are represented: poverty in body, poverty in our way of thinking, poverty in worldly goods, and poverty through trials and temptations that come upon us from without. But because you see me setting down these four types of poverty separately, do not conclude that they are to be practised separately. Each of them is to be implemented along with the others. Hence they are embraced by a single beatitude, which also discloses in a marvellous way what is, as it were, their root and mainspring, I mean, our spirit. For from our spirit, as has been said, once it has embraced the grace of the gospel teaching, there flows a wellspring of poverty that 'waters the whole face of our ground' (cf. Gen. 2 : 6), I mean our outward self, transforming us into a paradise of virtues.

There are, then, four types of spiritual poverty, and each gives birth to a corresponding kind of grief, as well as to a corresponding form of spiritual solace. [50.] In the first place, freely-embraced physical poverty and humility – and that means hunger, thirst, vigils and in general hardship and tribulation of body, as well as a reasonable restraint of the senses – begets not only grief, but also tears. For just as insensibility, callousness and hardness of heart develop as the result of ease, soft living and self-indulgence, so from a way of life marked by self-control and renunciation come contrition of heart and compunction, expelling all bitterness and generating a gentle gladness. It is said that without contrition of heart it is impossible to be free from vice; and the heart is rendered contrite by a triple form of self-control, in sleep, food and bodily ease. When through such contrition the soul is freed from vice and bitterness, it will certainly receive spiritual delight in their place. This is the solace on account of which the Lord calls those who grieve blessed. St John Klimakos, who has constructed for us the ladder of spiritual ascent, says: 'Thirst and vigil afflict the heart, and when the heart is afflicted, tears spring up. . . . He who has found this by experience will laugh'[1] – he will laugh with that blessed joyousness which springs from the solace that the Lord promised. Thus

---

[1] *The Ladder of Divine Ascent*, Step 6 (*P.G.* lxxxviii, 796B); E.T., p. 133.

from bodily poverty embraced out of love for God is born the grief that brings solace to those who experience it and fills them with blessing.

How, in the second place, does grief arise from a fear-dominated state of mind and a godly humility of soul? [51.] Self-reproach always coexists with humility of soul. Initially self-reproach strongly emphasizes the fear of torment, bringing before our eyes a frightening image in which all the various conflicting forms of hell are combined into one. Our fear is increased yet more as we reflect that these torments of hell are inexpressible, and so even worse than they have been painted, and – to add still further to the dismay – that they are unending. Heat, cold, darkness, fire, movement and immobility, bonds, terrors, and the biting of undying beasts are all brought together into this single condemnation; but all these things fail properly to convey the true horror of hell which – to use St Paul's words – 'man's mind has not grasped' (1 Cor. 2 : 9). [52.] What, then, is this profitless, unconsoling and endless grief experienced in hell? It is the grief stirred up in those who have sinned against God when they become aware of their offences. There, in hell, convicted of their sins, stripped of all hope of salvation or of any improvement in their condition, they feel yet greater anguish and grief because of the unsought reproof of their conscience. And this itself, and the everlasting nature of their grief, gives rise to yet another form of grief, and to another dreadful darkness, to unbearable heat and a helpless abyss of despondency. In this life, however, such grief is altogether beneficial, for God hearkens to it compassionately, so much so that He even came down and dwelt among us; and He promised consolation to those who grieve in this way, the consolation being Himself, since He is called, and He is indeed, a Comforter (cf. John 14 : 16).

Do you see what grief arises in a humble soul and the consolation that ensues? [53.] Indeed, self-reproach on its own, when lying for a protracted time upon the soul's thoughts like some intellectual weight, crushes and presses and squeezes out the saving wine that gladdens the heart of man (cf. Ps. 104 : 15), that is to say, our inner self. This wine is compunction (cf. Ps. 60 : 3. LXX). Together with grief compunction crushes the passions and, having freed the soul from the weight that oppresses it, fills it with blessed joy. That is the reason why Christ says, 'Blessed are those who grieve, for they will be consoled' (Matt. 5 : 4).

Thirdly, grief also arises from the shedding of possessions, that is to say, from poverty in worldly goods and in what we gather around us. This, we said, is to be conjoined with poverty in spirit, for it is only when all types of poverty are practised together that they are perfected and pleasing to God. Now listen attentively so as to learn how from such poverty in worldly goods grief is produced in us along with the consolation that grief confers. When a person bids farewell to all things, to both money and possessions, either casting them away or distributing them to the poor according to the commandment (cf. Luke 14 : 33), and weans his soul from anxiety about such things, he enables it to turn inwards to self-scrutiny, free now from all external attachments. [54.] And whenever the intellect withdraws itself from all material things, emerges from the turbulence they generate, and becomes aware of our inner self, then first of all it sees the ugly mask it has wrought for itself as a result of its divagations among worldly things, and it strives to wash it away through grief. When it has got rid of that uncouth guise, and the soul is no longer coarsely distracted by various cares and worries, then the intellect withdraws untroubled into its true treasure-house and prays to the Father 'in secret' (Matt. 6 : 6). And the Father first bestows upon it peace of thoughts, the gift which contains within it all other gifts. Then He makes it perfect in humility, which is begetter and sustainer of every virtue – not the humility that consists of words and postures easily taken by anyone who wishes, but that to which the Holy Spirit bears witness and which the Spirit Himself creates when enshrined in the depths of the soul. [55.] In such peace and humility, as in the secure enclosure of the noetic paradise, every tree of true virtue flourishes. At its heart stands the sacred palace of love, and in the forecourt of this palace blossoms the harbinger of the age to be, ineffable and inalienable joy.

The shedding of possessions gives birth to freedom from anxiety, this freedom to attentiveness and prayer, while attentiveness and prayer induce grief and tears. Grief and tears expunge passion-imbued predispositions. When these are expunged the path of virtue is made smooth, since the obstacles are removed, and the conscience is no longer full of reproach. As a consequence joy and the soul's blessed laughter break through. [56.] Then tears of tribulation are transformed into tears of delight, and the words of God become sweet to the palate and more sweet than honey to the mouth (cf. Ps. 119 : 103). Prayer changes from entreaty to thanksgiving, and meditation on the divine truths of faith fills the heart with a sense of jubilation and unimpeachable hope. This hope is a foretaste of future blessings, of which the soul even now receives direct experience, and so it comes to know in part the surpassing richness of God's bounty, in accordance with the Psalmist's words, 'Taste and know that the Lord is bountiful' (Ps. 34 : 8). For He is the jubilation of the righteous, the joy of the upright, the gladness of the humble, and the solace of those who grieve because of Him.

57. Yet does such solace extend no further than this? Are these the only gifts of the sacred betrothal? Will not the Bridegroom of such souls manifest Himself still more clearly to those who are perfected and cleansed by blessed grief, and who through the virtues are arrayed as brides? Undoubtedly He will. We are well aware that at this point certain people out of malice are ready to censure us, telling us, in effect, 'You are not to speak in the name of the Lord (cf. Jer. 11 : 21), and if you do we will repudiate your name as evil (cf. Luke 6 : 22), devising and spreading slanders and falsehoods about you.' But let us take no notice of these people, and let us now continue with what we were saying, believing in and affirming the teachings of the holy fathers, directing our attention to them and convincing others through them. For it is written, 'I believed, and so I have spoken' (Ps. 116 : 10). We also believe, and so we, too, will speak (cf. 2 Cor. 4 : 13).

58. When every shameful indwelling passion has been expelled and the intellect, as already indicated, has returned wholly to itself, converting at the same time the other powers of the soul – and when through cultivating the virtues it sets the soul in good order, ever advancing to a more perfect state, ascending through its active spiritual progress and with God's help cleansing itself more fully – then it not only expunges all imprints of evil but also rids itself of every accretion, however good it is or appears to be. [59.] And when it has transcended intelligible realities and the concepts, not unmixed with images, that pertain to them, and in a godly and devout manner has rejected all things, then it will stand before God deaf and speechless (cf. Ps. 38 : 13).

It is now that the intellect becomes simple matter in God's hands and is unresistingly recreated in the most sublime way, for nothing alien intrudes on it: inner grace translates it to a better state and, in an altogether marvellous fashion, illumines it with ineffable light, thus perfecting our inner being. And when in this manner 'the day breaks and the morning star rises in our hearts' (cf. 2 Pet. 1 : 19), then 'the true man' – the intellect – 'will go out to his true work' (cf. Ps. 104 : 23), ascending in the light the road that leads to the eternal mountains. In this light it miraculously surveys supramundane things, being either still joined to the materiality to which it was originally linked, or else separated from it – this depending on the level that it has attained. For it does not ascend on the wings of the mind's fantasy, for the mind always wanders about as though blind, without possessing an accurate and assured understanding either of sensory things not immediately present to it or of transcendent intelligible realities. Rather it ascends in very truth, raised by the Spirit's ineffable power, and with spiritual and ineffable apperception it hears words too sacred to utter (cf. 2 Cor. 12 : 4) and sees invisible things. And it becomes entirely rapt in the miracle of it, even when it is no longer there, and it rivals the tireless angelic choir, having become truly another angel of God upon earth. Through itself it brings every created thing closer to God, for it itself now participates in all things and even in Him who transcends all, inasmuch as it has faithfully conformed itself to the divine image.

60. For this reason St Neilos says, 'The intellect's proper state is a noetic height, somewhat resembling the sky's hue, which is filled with the light of the Holy Trinity during the time of prayer.' And again: 'If you wish to see the intellect's proper state, rid yourself of all concepts, and then you will see it like sapphire or the sky's hue. But you cannot do this unless you have attained a state of dispassion, for God has to co-operate with you and to imbue you with His co-natural light.'[1] And St Diadochos writes: 'Divine grace confers on us two gifts through the baptism of regeneration, one being infinitely superior to the other. The first gift is given to us at once, when grace renews us in the actual waters of baptism and cleanses all the lineaments of our soul, that is, the image of God in us, by washing away every stain of sin. The second – our likeness to God – requires our co-operation. When the intellect begins to perceive the Holy Spirit with full consciousness, we should realize that grace is beginning to paint the divine likeness over the divine image in us. . . . Our power of perception shows us that we are being formed into the divine likeness; but the perfecting of this likeness

[1] Evagrios of Pontos, *Skemmata* 4 and 2: ed. J. Muyldermans, 'Evagriana', *Le Muséon* 44 (1931), p. 374 [38]; cf. *P.G.* xl, 1244AB and lxxix, 1221B; *The Philokalia*, vol. i, p. 49.

we shall know only by the light of grace. But no one can acquire spiritual love unless he experiences fully and clearly the illumination of the Holy Spirit. If the intellect does not receive the perfection of the divine likeness through such illumination, although it may have almost every other virtue, it will still have no share in perfect love.'[1] [61.] And likewise St Isaac writes that during the time of prayer the intellect that has received grace sees its own purity to be 'like heaven's hue, which was also called the "place of God" by the council of the elders of Israel, when it was seen by them in the mountain' (cf. Exod. 24 : 9–10). Again, he says that 'prayer is purity of the intellect, and it is consummated when we are illumined in utter amazement by the light of the Holy Trinity'. He also speaks of 'the purity of the intellect upon and through which the light of the Holy Trinity shines at the time of prayer'.[2]

62. The intellect that has been accounted worthy of this light also transmits to the body that is united with it many clear tokens of the divine beauty, acting as an intermediary between divine grace and the grossness of the flesh and conferring on the flesh the power to do what lies beyond its power. This gives birth to a godlike, unmatched and stable state of virtue as well as to a disposition that has no or little inclination to sin. It is then that the intellect is illumined by the divine Logos who enables it to perceive clearly the inner essences – the *logoi* – of created things and on account of its purity reveals to it the mysteries of nature. In this way, through relationships of correspondence the perceiving and trusting intelligence is raised up to the apprehension of supranatural realities – an apprehension that the Father of the Logos communicates through an immaterial union. From this arise various other miraculous effects, such as visionary insight, the seeing of things future, and the experience of things happening afar off as though they were occurring before one's very eyes. But what is more important is that those blessed in this manner do not aspire to attain such powers. Rather it is as though one were to look at a ray of sunlight and at the same time perceive the small particles in the air, though this was not one's intention. So it is with those who commune directly with the

[1] *On Spiritual Knowledge* 89: ed. des Places, pp. 149–50; E.T., *The Philokalia*, vol. i, p. 288. Palamas has slightly abbreviated the passage, but in our translation we follow the original text of Diadochos.

[2] Cf. *Ascetical Homilies*, Greek translation, p. 140; E.T., Wensinck, p. 118; E.T., Holy Transfiguration Monastery, p. 121.

rays of divine light, which by nature reveal all things: according to their degree of purity they truly attain – albeit as something incidental – a knowledge of what is past, of what is present, and even of what is to come. But their main concern is the return of the intellect to itself and its concentration on itself. Or, rather, their aim is the reconvergence of all the soul's powers in the intellect – however strange this may sound – and the attaining of the state in which both intellect and God work together. In this way they are restored to their original state and assimilated to their Archetype, grace renewing in them their pristine and inconceivable beauty. To such a consummation, then, does grief bring those who are humble in heart and poor in spirit.

63. Since on account of our innate laziness such a consummation is beyond us, let us return to its foundation and say a little more about grief itself. Grief also accompanies every kind of unsolicited worldly poverty. For how can a person in need of money not be sorrowful, or he who hungers against his will or who suffers pain and dishonour? Such grief, indeed, lacks all consolation, the more so the more acute the poverty becomes, especially when the sufferer lacks true knowledge. For if you do not keep an intelligent control over sensual pleasures and pains but, rather, allow yourself to be dominated by them through the misuse of your intelligence, you wrongly and profitlessly multiply them, even causing yourself great injury. For thereby you give sure and self-accusing evidence that you do not firmly adhere to God's Gospel and to the prophets who preceded Him, and to those who came after Him and were His disciples and apostles. For these all teach that inexhaustible riches come through poverty, that ineffable glory comes through simplicity of life, that painless delight comes through self-control, and that through patiently enduring the trials and temptations that befall us we are delivered from the eternal tribulation and affliction held in store for those who choose an easy and soft life in this world instead of entering by the strait and narrow gate (cf. Matt. 7 : 14).

64. Rightly did St Paul say, 'Worldly sorrowfulness produces death' (2 Cor. 7 : 10), for from what we have said it is clear that such sorrow is sin leading to death. If the soul's true life is the divine light conferred, according to the fathers, through spiritual grief, then the death of the soul is an evil darkness induced in the soul through worldly sorrowfulness. It is with reference to this darkness that St Basil the Great says, 'Sin, which exists through the absence of the good,

takes the form of noetic darkness caused by acts of evil.'[1] [65.] And St Mark also says: 'If you are beset by evil thoughts, how can you see the reality of the sin concealed behind them? This sin wraps the soul in darkness and obscurity, and increases its hold upon us through our evil thoughts and actions. . . . If you fail to perceive this general process of sinning, when will you pray about it and be cleansed from it? And if you have not been cleansed, how will you find purity of nature? And if you have not found this, how will you behold the inner dwelling-place of Christ? . . . We should try to find that dwelling-place and knock with persistent prayer. . . . Not only ought we to ask and receive, but we should also keep safely what is given; for some people lose what they have received. A theoretical knowledge or chance experience of this may perhaps be gained by those who have begun to learn late in life or who are still young; but the constant and patient practice of these things is barely to be acquired even by devout and deeply experienced elders.'[2] St Makarios, possessor of divine knowledge, says the same, as do all the saints.

66. Just as this darkness derives its existence from all our various sins, so – as you will find if you examine it closely – worldly sorrowfulness is born of and dominated by all the passions. Such sorrowfulness is thus an image and a kind of firstfruit, prelude to and foretaste of the future endless grief that overwhelms those who do not choose for themselves the grief that the Lord called blessed. This grief not only brings spiritual solace and provides a foretaste of eternal joy, but it also stabilizes virtue and takes from the soul its disposition to fall into a lower state. For although you may become poor and humble yourself and strive to live with godlike simplicity, yet if you do not acquire grief as you advance along the spiritual path you can easily be changed and can readily return in thought to that which you have abandoned, desiring again what you initially renounced and thus making yourself a transgressor (cf. Gal. 2 : 18). But if you persist in your intention to live a life of blessed poverty, and devote your attention to it, you will give birth to this grief in yourself and will lose all tendency to regress, and will not wrongly want to return to what

---

[1] Cf. *On the Six Days of Creation* ii, 4–5 (*P.G.* xxix, 37CD, 40C, 41B); *God is not the Cause of Evils* 5 (*P.G.* xxxi, 341B).

[2] *On Those who Think that They are Made Righteous by Works* 224–5; E.T., *The Philokalia*, vol. i, pp. 145–6.

you have so well abandoned. [67.] For, as St Paul says, 'Godly sorrow produces in the soul a saving repentance which is not to be regretted (cf. 2 Cor. 7 : 10). Hence one of the fathers has said that 'grief both acts and protects'.

This is not the only gain that comes of grief, namely, that you virtually lose all disposition towards evil and do not regress to your former sins; it also makes former sins as though they never existed. For once you begin to grieve over them, God reckons them as unintentional, and there is no guilt in actions performed unintentionally. A person who grieves because of his poverty shows that he is not in this state through his own choice, and so – like those who want to be rich or are already rich – he falls into the snares of the devil (cf. 1 Tim. 6 : 9); and unless he changes and strives to escape these snares, he will be sent with the devil into eternal torment. On the other hand, if a person who has sinned against God continues to grieve over his sins, they will be justly regarded as unintentional, and along with those who have not sinned he will journey without stumbling on the path leading to eternal life.

68. This, then, is the profit of the initial stage of grief, which is painful inasmuch as it is conjoined with the fear of God. But in later stages it becomes in a wondrous manner wedded to love for God, and once you are conditioned by it you experience the tender and sacred solace of the Comforter's blessing. But to those who have not experienced this it is something virtually incomprehensible, since it cannot be described in words. For if one cannot explain the sweetness of honey to someone who has never tasted it, how can one describe the delight of God's joy and grace to those who have never experienced it? [69.] In addition, the initial stage of grief resembles something that appears to be almost unattainable – a kind of petition for betrothal to God. Thus those who grieve in their longing for the Bridegroom to whom they are not yet united utter as it were certain words of courtship, smiting themselves and calling upon Him with tears as though He were not present and perhaps might never be present. But the consummation of grief is pure bridal union with the Bridegroom. For this reason St Paul, after describing a married couple's union in one flesh as 'a great mystery', added, 'but I say this with respect to Christ and the Church' (Eph. 5 : 32). As they are one flesh, so those who are with God are one spirit, as St Paul clearly testifies elsewhere when he says that he who cleaves to the Lord is one spirit with Him (cf. 1 Cor.

6 : 17). [70.] What are we to say, then, of those who regard the grace that dwells in God's saints as created? Let them know that they blaspheme against the Spirit Himself who, in giving His grace, is united to the saints.

Let us add another still clearer example of what we are saying. The first stage of grief resembles the return of the prodigal son. For this reason it fills the mourner with dejection and leads him to employ these very words, 'Father, I have sinned against heaven and before Thee, and am no more worthy to be called Thy son' (Luke 15 : 21). But the consummation of grief resembles the moment when the heavenly Father runs out to meet him and embraces him. And when the son finds himself accepted with such inexpressible compassion and on account of it is filled with great joy and boldness, he receives the Father's embrace and embraces Him in return. Then, entering into the Father's house, he shares together in the feast of divine felicity.

71. Let us, then, in blessed poverty also fall down and weep before the Lord our God, so that we may wash away our former sins, make ourselves impervious to evil and, receiving the blessings and solace of the Comforter, may glorify Him and the unoriginate Father and the Only-begotten Son, now and always and throughout the ages. Amen.

A New Testament Decalogue

1. 'The Lord your God is one Lord' (cf. Deut. 6 : 4), revealed in the Father, Son and Holy Spirit: in the unbegotten Father; in the Son, who is begotten eternally, timelessly and impassibly as the Logos, and who through Himself anointed that which He assumed from us and so is called Christ; and in the Holy Spirit, who also comes forth from the Father, not begotten, but proceeding. This alone is God and alone is true God, the one Lord in a Trinity of hypostases, undivided in nature, will, glory, power, energy, and all the characteristics of divinity.

Him alone shall you love and Him alone shall you worship with all your mind and with all your heart and with all your strength. And His words and His commandments shall be in your heart so that you carry them out and meditate on them and speak of them both sitting and walking, lying down and standing up (cf. Deut. 6 : 5, 6, 7). And you shall remember the Lord your God always and fear Him alone (cf. Deut. 8 : 18; 6 : 13); and you shall not forget Him or His commandments, for thus shall He give you strength to do His will. For He requires nothing else from you except that you fear and love Him and walk in all His ways (cf. Deut. 10 : 12).

'He is your boast and He is your God' (cf. Deut. 10 : 21). When you hear of the impassible and invisible nature of the supramundane angels and of the wicked nature – wise, acute and extremely crafty in deceit – of him who fell away from that realm, do not think that any such being is equal with God. Seeing the greatness of the heaven and its manifold motions, the sun's brilliance, the shining of the moon, the bright twinkle of the stars, the beneficial breezes of the air, the broad back of sea and land, do not make a god of any of them. For all are servants and creations of the one God, brought forth from non-being by His Logos. 'For He spake and they came into being; He commanded and they were created' (Ps. 33 : 9. LXX). Him alone, therefore, the

Master and Creator of all, you should glorify as God and through love you should cleave to Him; before Him you should repent day and night for your deliberate and unintentional lapses. For 'He is compassionate and merciful, long-suffering and full of mercy' (Ps. 103 : 8) and eternally bountiful. He has promised and He actually gives a celestial, unending kingdom, a painless existence, an immortal life and unwaning light for the delight of those who revere and worship Him and who love and keep His commandments.

Yet God is also a 'jealous God' (Exod. 20 : 5), a just judge who takes terrible vengeance on those who dishonour Him, who disobey Him and who scorn His commandments, visiting them with eternal chastisement, unquenchable fire, unceasing pain, unconsolable affliction, a cloak of lugubrious darkness, an obscure and grievous region, piteous gnashing of teeth, venomous and sleepless worms – things He prepared for that first evil apostate together with all those deluded by him who became his followers, rejecting their Creator in their actions, words and thoughts.

2. 'You shall not make an image of anything in the heavens above, or in the earth below, or in the sea' (cf. Exod. 20 : 4), in such a way that you worship these things and glorify them as gods. For all are the creations of the one God, created by Him in the Holy Spirit through His Son and Logos, who as Logos of God in these latter times took flesh from a virgin's womb, appeared on earth and associated with men (cf. Baruch 3 : 37), and who for the salvation of men suffered, died and arose again, ascended with His body into the heavens and 'sat down on the right hand of the Majesty on High' (Heb. 1 : 3), and who will come again with His body to judge the living and the dead. Out of love for Him you should make, therefore, an ikon of Him who became man for our sakes, and through His ikon you should bring Him to mind and worship Him, elevating your intellect through it to the venerable body of the Saviour, that is set on the right hand of the Father in heaven.

In like manner you should also make ikons of the saints and venerate them, not as gods – for this is forbidden – but because of the attachment, inner affection and sense of surpassing honour that you feel for the saints when by means of their ikons the intellect is raised up to them. It was in this spirit that Moses made ikons of the Cherubim within the Holy of Holies (cf. Exod. 25 : 18). The Holy of Holies itself was an image of things supracelestial (cf. Exod. 25 : 40; Heb. 8 : 5), while the Holy Place was an image of the entire world. Moses called these things holy, not glorifying what is created, but through it glorifying God the Creator of the world. You must not, then, deify the ikons of Christ and of the saints, but through them you should venerate Him who originally created us in His own image, and who subsequently consented in His ineffable compassion to assume the human image and to be circumscribed by it.

You should venerate not only the ikon of Christ, but also the similitude of His cross. For the cross is Christ's great sign and trophy of victory over the devil and all his hostile hosts; for this reason they tremble and flee when they see the figuration of the cross. This figure, even prior to the crucifixion, was greatly glorified by the prophets and wrought great wonders; and when He who was hung upon it, our Lord Jesus Christ, comes again to judge the living and the dead, this His great and terrible sign will precede Him, full of power and glory (cf. Matt. 24 : 30). So glorify the cross now, so that you may boldly look upon it then and be glorified with it. And you should venerate ikons of the saints, for the saints have been crucified with the Lord; and you should make the sign of the cross upon your person before doing so, bringing to mind their communion in the sufferings of Christ. In the same way you should venerate their holy shrines and any relic of their bones; for God's grace is not sundered from these things, even as the divinity was not sundered from Christ's venerable body at the time of His life-quickening death. By doing this and by glorifying those who glorified God – for through their actions they showed themselves to be perfect in their love for God – you too will be glorified together with them by God, and with David you will chant: 'I have held Thy friends in high honour, O Lord' (Ps. 139 : 17. LXX).

3. 'You shall not take the name of the Lord your God in vain' (Exod. 20 : 7), swearing an oath falsely because of some worldly thing, or out of human fear, or shame, or for personal gain. For a false oath is a denial of God. For this reason you should not take an oath at all (cf. Matt. 5 : 34). Avoid oaths altogether, since through an oath a man forswears himself, and this estranges him from God and numbers him among the wrongdoers. If you are truthful in all your words, that will convey the certainty of an oath. Should you, however, bind yourself with an oath – something to be deprecated – you must fulfil it as a legal obligation, provided it involves something permitted by the divine law; but you should hold yourself at fault because you swore at

all, and by acts of mercy, supplication, grief and bodily hardship you should ask Christ's forgiveness, since He said you should not swear oaths. If, on the other hand, you take an oath that involves something that is unlawful, beware lest on account of your oath you do what is wrong and are numbered with Herod, the prophet-slayer (cf. Matt. 14 : 7–9). And when you have put that unlawful oath behind you, make it a rule never again to take an oath, and with tears ask more intensely for God's forgiveness, using the remedies already mentioned.

4. One day of the week you should 'keep holy' (Exod. 20 : 8): that which is called the Lord's day, because it is consecrated to the Lord, who on that day arose from the dead, disclosing and giving prior assurance of the general resurrection, when every earthly activity will come to an end. And you must not engage in any worldly activity that is not essential; and you must allow those who are under your authority and those who live with you to rest, so that together you may all glorify Him who redeemed us through His death and who arose from the dead and resurrected our human nature with Himself. You should bring to mind the age to come and meditate upon all the commandments and statutes of the Lord, and you should examine yourself to see whether you have transgressed or overlooked any of them, and you should correct yourself in all ways. On this day you should go to the temple of God and attend the services held there and with sincere faith and a clean conscience you should receive the holy body and blood of Christ. You should make a beginning of a more perfect life and renew and prepare yourself for the reception of the eternal blessings to come. For the sake of these same blessings you must not misuse material things on the other days of the week either; but on the Lord's day, so as to be constantly near to God, abstain from all activities except those which are absolutely necessary and which you have to perform in order to live. God thus being your refuge, you will not be distracted, the fire of the passions will not burn you, and you will be free from the burden of sin. In this way you will sanctify the sabbath, observing it by doing no evil deeds. To the Lord's day you should join the days dedicated to the great feasts, doing the same things and abstaining from the same things.

5. 'Honour your father and your mother' (Exod. 20 : 12), for it is through them that God has brought you into this life and they, after God, are the causes of your existence. Thus after God you should honour them and love them, provided that your love for them

strengthens your love for God. If it does not, flee from them, yet
without feelings of hatred. Should they actually be a hindrance to you –
especially with respect to the true and saving faith because they profess
some other faith – you should not merely flee from them, but also hate
them, and not them alone but all relatives and everyone else bound to
you by affection or other union, and, indeed, the very limbs of your
body and their appetites, and your body itself and its bond with the
passions. For 'if anyone does not hate his father and mother, and wife,
and children, and brothers and sisters, and even his own life, and if he
does not take up his cross and follow Me, he is not worthy of Me',
Christ said (cf. Luke 14 : 26–27; Matt. 10 : 37). Such is the way in
which you are to act towards your earthly parents and your friends and
brethren. But if they share your faith and do not hinder you in your
quest for salvation, you should honour and love them.

   If it is thus with natural fathers, how much more should you honour
and love those who are your spiritual fathers. For they have brought
you from a state of mere existence to a state of virtue and spiritual
health; they have transmitted to you the illumination of knowledge,
have taught you the revelation of the truth, have given you rebirth
through the water of regeneration and have instilled in you the hope of
resurrection and immortality, and of the eternal kingdom and
inheritance. In this way they have converted you from being unworthy
to being worthy of eternal blessings, have transformed you from an
earthly into a heavenly being, and have made you eternal instead of
temporal, a son and disciple not of a man, but of the God-man Jesus
Christ, who bestowed upon you the Spirit of adoption, and who told
you not to call anyone on earth your father or teacher, because you
have only one Father and Teacher, namely Christ (cf. Matt. 23 : 9–
10). You must, therefore, render all honour and love to your spiritual
fathers, since the honour rendered to them redounds to Christ and the
all-holy Spirit, in whom you received adoption, and to the heavenly
Father, 'from whom derives all fatherhood in heaven and on earth'
(Eph. 3 : 15). You should strive to have a spiritual father throughout
your life and to confess to him every sin and every evil thought and to
receive from him healing and remission. For they have been given the
power to bind and to unbind souls, and whatever they bind on earth
will be bound in heaven, and whatever they unbind on earth will be
unbound in heaven (cf. Matt. 18 : 18). This grace and power they
have received from Christ, and so you should obey them and not

gainsay them, lest you bring destruction upon your soul. For if a person who gainsays his natural parents in matters not interdicted by the divine law is – according to the law (cf. Exod. 21 : 17) – to be put to death, how will he who contradicts his spiritual fathers not expel the Spirit of God from himself and destroy his soul? For this reason be counselled by your spiritual fathers and obey them till the end, so that you may save your soul and inherit eternal and untarnished blessings.

6. 'You shall not be unchaste' (Exod. 20 : 14), lest instead of being united to Christ you become united to a prostitute (cf. 1 Cor. 6 : 15), severing yourself from the divine body, forfeiting the divine inheritance and throwing yourself into hell. According to the law (cf. Lev. 21 : 9), a daughter of a priest caught whoring is to be burnt, for she dishonours her father; how much more, then, does the person who defiles the body of Christ deserve endless chastisement. If you are capable of it, embrace the path of virginity, so that you may become wholly God's and may cleave to Him with perfect love, all your life devoting yourself undistractedly to the Lord and to what belongs to Him (cf. 1 Cor. 7 : 32), and in this way anticipating the life to come and living as an angel of God on earth. For the angels are characterized by virginity and if you cleave to virginity you emulate them with your body, in so far as this is possible. Or, rather, prior to them you emulate the Father who in virginity begot the Son before all ages, and also the virginal Son who in the beginning came forth from the virginal Father by way of generation, and in these latter times was born in the flesh of a virginal Mother; you likewise emulate the Holy Spirit who ineffably proceeds from the Father alone, not by way of generation, but by procession. Hence if you practise true chastity in soul and body you emulate God and are joined to Him in imperishable wedlock, embellishing every sensation, word and thought with virginal beauty.

If, however, you do not choose to live in virginity and have not promised God that you will do this, God's law allows you to marry one woman and to live with her alone and to hold her in holiness as your own wife (cf. 1 Thess. 4 : 4), abstaining entirely from other women. You can totally abstain from them if you shun untimely meetings with them, do not indulge in lewd words and stories and, as far as you can, avoid looking at them with the eyes of both body and soul, training yourself not to gaze overmuch upon the beauty of their faces. For 'whoever looks at a woman with lust has already committed adultery with her in his heart' (Matt. 5 : 28), and in this way he is impure before Christ who sees his heart; and the next step is that he commits shameless acts with his body also. But why do I speak of fornication and adultery and other natural abominations? For by looking overfondly on the beauty of bodies a person is dragged down unrestrainedly into lascivious acts contrary to all nature. Thus, if you cut away from yourself the bitter roots, you will not reap the deadly harvest but, on the contrary, you will gather the fruits of chastity and the holiness which it confers, and without which 'no one will see the Lord' (Heb. 12 : 14).

7. 'You shall not kill' (Exod. 20 : 15), lest you forfeit the adoption of Him who quickens even the dead, and because of your actions are adopted instead by the devil, who was 'a murderer from the beginning' (John 8 : 44). As murder results from a blow, a blow from an insult, an insult from anger, and we are roused to anger because someone else injures, hits or insults us, for this reason Christ told us not to stop anyone who took our coat from taking our shirt also (cf. Luke 6 : 29); and we must not strike back at him who strikes us, or revile him who reviles us. In this manner we will free from the crime of murder both ourself and him who does us wrong. Further, we will be forgiven our sins, since He says, 'Forgive and you will be forgiven' (cf. Matt. 6 : 14). But the person who speaks and acts evilly will be condemned to eternal chastisement. For Christ said, 'Whoever shall say to his brother "You fool" shall be guilty enough to go to the hell of fire' (Matt. 5 : 22). If, then, you can eradicate this evil, calling down upon your soul the benediction of gentleness, then glorify Christ, the teacher and ministrant of every virtue, without whom, as we have been taught, we can do nothing good (cf. John 15 : 5). But if you are unable to bridle your temper, censure yourself whenever you lose it, and repent before God and before anyone to whom you have spoken or have acted evilly. If you repent at the inception of sin you will not commit the sin itself; but if you feel no pang in committing minor offences you will through them fall into major transgressions.

8. 'You shall not steal' (Exod. 20 : 15), lest He who knows things secret increases your punishment because you have set Him at naught. Rather you should secretly give from what you have to those in need, so that you receive from God, who sees in secret, a hundred times more, as well as life eternal in the age to come (cf. Matt. 6 : 4; Mark 10 : 30).

9. 'You shall not accuse anyone falsely' (cf. Exod. 20 : 16), lest you

become like the devil, who falsely accused God to Eve and was cursed by God (cf. Gen. 3 : 14). Rather, you should conceal your neighbour's offence, unless by so doing others may be injured; and in this way you will imitate not Ham, but Shem and Japheth, and so like them receive the blessing (cf. Gen. 9 : 25–7).

10. 'You shall not covet anything belonging to your neighbour' (cf. Exod 20 : 17), neither his land, nor his money, nor his glory, nor anything that is his. For covetousness, conceived in the soul, produces sin; and sin, when committed, results in death (cf. Jas. 1 : 15). Refrain, then, from coveting what belongs to others and, so far as you can, avoid filching things out of greediness. Rather you should give from what you possess to whoever asks of you, and you should, as much as you can, be charitable to whoever is in need of charity, and you should not refuse whoever wants to borrow from you (cf. Matt. 5 : 42). Should you find some lost article, you should keep it for its owner, even though he is hostilely disposed towards you; for in this way you will change him and will overcome evil with good, as Christ commands (cf. Rom. 12 : 21).

If you observe these things with all your strength and live in accordance with them, you will store up in your soul the treasures of holiness, you will please God, you will be rewarded by God and by those who are godly, and you will inherit eternal blessings. May we all receive such blessings through the grace and compassion of our Lord, God and Saviour Jesus Christ, to whom with His unoriginate Father and the all-holy, bountiful and life-quickening Spirit are due all glory, honour and worship, now and ever and through all the ages. Amen.

In Defence of Those who Devoutly Practise a Life of Stillness

A QUESTION POSED TO HIM

You have done well, father, to quote the words of the saints regarding the subject of my query. For as I heard you resolve my difficulties, I marvelled at the clarity of the truth; but it also entered my mind that since – as you yourself said – every word fights with another word, there may be grounds for contradicting what you have said. Yet because I recognize that only by their fruits can we know things unquestionably, and because I have heard the saints saying exactly the same as you, I am no longer anxious on this score. Indeed, how can a man who is not convinced by the saints be worthy of credence? And how will such a person not reject also the God of the saints? For it is God who said with respect to the apostles and, through them, to the saints who succeeded them, 'He who rejects you, rejects Me' (Luke 10 : 16), which is to say that he rejects Truth itself. How, then, can the enemy of truth be accepted by those who seek the truth? Hence I entreat you, father, to listen as I recount each of the other points that I heard from those who pass their life in the pursuit of profane learning, and I beg you to tell me some of your thoughts on these matters, adding also what the saints say about them. For they maintain that we are wrong in striving to enclose our intellect within our body. Rather, they say, we should alienate it by any means possible from the body. They actively mock some of those among us, writing against us on the grounds that we counsel those newly embarked on the spiritual path to direct their gaze upon themselves and to draw their intellect into themselves by means of their breathing. Our critics claim that the intellect is not separate from the soul; and since it is not separate, they say, but included in the soul, how is it possible to reintroduce it into oneself? Further, they report us as saying that we intromit divine grace through the nostrils. As I have never heard any of those among us say this, I know that we are being misrepresented; and this has made me realize that their other charges are also malicious. People who fabricate false charges can also deal falsely with realities. Yet, father, I would ask you to teach me why we devote such care to inducing our intellect to come back into ourselves and do not think it wrong to enclose it within the body.

ANSWER

That it is not wrong for those who have chosen a life of self-attentiveness and stillness to strive to keep their intellect within their body.

1. Brother, do you not recall St Paul's statements, 'Our body is the temple of the Holy Spirit within us' (cf. 1 Cor. 6 : 19), and, 'We are the house of God' (cf. Heb. 3 : 6), as God Himself confirms when He says, 'I will dwell in them and walk in them, and I will be their God' (Lev. 26 : 12; 2 Cor. 6 : 16)? Since, then, the body is God's dwelling-place, what sane person would object to his intellect dwelling in it? And how was it that God established the intellect in the body to start with? Did He do so wrongly? These are the things we should say to the heretics, to those who declare that the body is evil and created by the devil. But we regard it as evil for the intellect to be caught up in material thoughts, not for it to be in the body, for the body is not evil. Hence everyone who devotes his life to God calls to Him as David did: 'My soul has thirsted for Thee, how often has my flesh longed for Thee' (Ps. 63 : 1), and: 'My heart and my flesh have rejoiced in the living God' (Ps. 84 : 2. LXX); and he says with Isaiah: 'My belly shall sound as a harp and my inward parts as a brazen wall that Thou hast restored' (cf. Isa. 16 : 11. LXX), and: 'Out of awe for Thee, O Lord, we are pregnant with the Spirit of Thy salvation' (Isa. 26 : 18. LXX). Filled with courage by this Spirit, we will not fall; but it is those who speak in a materialistic way, and who pretend that celestial words and citizenship are materialistic, that will fall.

Although St Paul called the body 'death' when he said, 'Who will deliver me from the body of this death?' (Rom. 7 : 24), this is simply because the materialistic, carnal mentality is bodylike, and so he rightly called it a body when comparing it to the spiritual and divine mind. Further, he did not say simply 'body' but 'death of the body'. Shortly before this he clarifies his meaning when he says that the flesh is not at fault, but the sinful impulse that infiltrates into the flesh because of the fall. 'I am sold', he says, 'into slavery under sin' (Rom. 7 : 14); but he who is sold is not a slave by nature. And again he says, 'I know that in me − that is, in my flesh − there dwells nothing good' (Rom. 7 : 18). Note that he does not say the flesh is evil, but that which dwells therein. Thus it is evil for this 'law that is in our bodily members, warring against the law of the intellect' (cf. Rom. 7 : 23)-to dwell in the body, not for the intellect to dwell there.

2. That is why we grapple with this 'law of sin' (Rom. 8 : 2) and expel it from our body, establishing in its place the surveillance of the intellect. Through this surveillance we prescribe what is fitting for every faculty of the soul and every member of the body. For the senses we prescribe what they should take into account and to what extent they should do so, and this exercise of the spiritual law is called self-control. To the aspect of the soul that is accessible to passion we impart the best of all dispositions, that of love; and we also raise the level of the intelligence by repelling whatever impedes the mind in its ascent towards God: this aspect of the law we call watchfulness. When through self-control we have purified our body, and when through divine love we have made our incensive power and our desire incentives for virtue, and when we offer to God an intellect cleansed by prayer, then we will possess and see within ourselves the grace promised to the pure in heart (cf. Matt. 5 : 8). Then, too, we will be able to affirm with St Paul: 'The God who said, "Out of darkness let light shine", has made this light shine in our hearts, to give us the illumination of the knowledge of God's glory in the Person of Jesus Christ' (2 Cor. 4 : 6). 'But we have', he says, 'this treasure in earthen vessels' (2 Cor. 4 : 7). Since, therefore, we carry as in earthen vessels − that is to say, in our bodies − the Father's Light in the Person of Jesus Christ, and so can experience the glory of the Holy Spirit, are we doing anything unworthy of the intellect's nobility if we retain it within our body? What person of spiritual insight − and, indeed, what person endowed with human intelligence, even though bereft of divine grace − would say such a thing?

3. Since our soul is a single entity possessing many powers, it utilizes as an organ the body that by nature lives in conjunction with it. What organs, then, does the power of the soul that we call 'intellect' make use of when it is active? No one has ever supposed that the mind resides in the finger-nails or the eye-lashes, the nostrils or the lips. But we all agree that it resides within us, even though we may not all agree as to which of our inner organs it chiefly makes use of. For some locate it in the head, as though in a sort of acropolis; others consider that its vehicle is the centremost part of the heart, that aspect of the heart that has been purified from natural life. We know very well that our intelligence is neither within us as in a container – for it is incorporeal – nor yet outside us, for it is united to us; but it is located in the heart as in its own organ. And we know this because we are taught it not by men but by the Creator of man Himself when He says, 'It is not that which goes into man's mouth that defiles him, but what comes out of it' (Matt. 15 : 11), adding, 'for thoughts come out of the heart' (Matt. 15 : 19). St Makarios the Great says the same: 'The heart rules over the whole human organism, and when grace takes possession of the pastures of the heart, it reigns over all a man's thoughts and members. For the intellect and all the thoughts of the soul are located there.'[1]

Our heart is, therefore, the shrine of the intelligence and the chief intellectual organ of the body. When, therefore, we strive to scrutinize and to amend our intelligence through rigorous watchfulness, how could we do this if we did not collect our intellect, outwardly dispersed through the senses, and bring it back within ourselves – back to the heart itself, the shrine of the thoughts? It is for this reason that St Makarios – rightly called blessed – directly after what he says above, adds: 'So it is there that we must look to see whether grace has inscribed the laws of the Spirit.'[2] Where? In the ruling organ, in the throne of grace, where the intellect and all the thoughts of the soul reside, that is to say, in the heart. Do you see, then, how greatly necessary it is for those who have chosen a life of self-attentiveness and stillness to bring their intellect back and to enclose it within their body, and particularly within that innermost body within the body that we call the heart?

---

[1] *Spiritual Homilies* (Collection II) xv, 20: ed. Dörries, Klostermann and Kroeger, p. 139; E.T., Mason, p. 116.

[2] Ibid.; E.T., p. 115.

4. If, as the Psalmist says, 'All the glory of the king's daughter is within' (Ps. 45 : 13. LXX), how shall we seek it somewhere without? And if, as St Paul says, 'God has sent forth His Spirit into our hearts, crying: "Abba Father" ' (cf. Gal. 4 : 6), how shall we not pray in union with the Spirit that is in our hearts? And if, as the Lord of the prophets and the apostles says, 'The kingdom of heaven is within us' (cf. Luke 17 : 21), how shall we not find ourselves outside the kingdom of heaven if we strive to alienate our intellect from what lies within us? 'An upright heart', says Solomon, 'seeks conscious awareness' (cf. Prov. 27 : 21. LXX), the awareness or perception which he elsewhere calls noetic and divine (cf. Prov. 2 : 5. LXX). It is to such awareness that the fathers urge all of us when they say: 'A noetic intellect assuredly acquires noetic awareness. Let us never cease from seeking for this, which is both in us and not in us.'[1] Do you not see that whether we wish to withstand sin, or to acquire virtue, or to gain the reward of the contest for virtue or, rather, the noetic awareness which is the pledge of the reward for virtue, we have to bring our intellect back into our body and into ourselves? On the other hand, to extract the intellect not from a materialistic manner of thought but from the body itself, in the hope that there, outside the body, it may attain noetic visions, is the worst of profane delusions, the root and source of every heresy, an invention of demons, a doctrine engendering folly and itself the result of dementedness. It is for this reason that those who speak by the inspiration of the demons are out of their wits and do not even comprehend what they say. But we, on the contrary, install our intellect not only within the body and the heart, but also within itself.

5. Those who claim that the intellect is never separate from the soul, but is always within it, assert consequently that it is not possible to reinstall it in this way. They are ignorant, it seems, that the essence of the intellect is one thing and its energy is another. Or, rather, although they know this, they deliberately side with the deceivers, making play with verbal equivocations. 'By not accepting the simplicity of spiritual teaching,' says St Basil the Great, 'these people whose wits are sharpened for disputation by dialectic pervert the power of the truth with the counter-arguments of spurious knowledge (cf. 1 Tim.

[1] St John Klimakos, *The Ladder of Divine Ascent*, Step 26 (*P.G.* lxxxviii, 1020A); E.T., p. 233.

6 : 20) and with sophistic plausibilities.'[1] Such inevitably is the
character of those who, without being spiritual, think themselves
competent to judge and give instruction in spiritual matters (cf. 1 Cor.
2 : 14–15). It should not have escaped them that the intellect is not
like the eye which sees other visible things but does not see itself. On
the contrary the intellect functions, first, by observing things other
than itself, so far as this is necessary; and this is what St Dionysios the
Great calls the intellect's 'direct movement'. Secondly, it returns to
itself and operates within itself, and so beholds itself; and this is called
by St Dionysios the intellect's 'circular movement'.[2] This is the
intellect's highest and most befitting activity and, through it, it even
transcends itself and is united with God. 'For the intellect,' writes St
Basil, 'when not dispersed outwardly' – note that it does go out from
itself; and so, having gone out, it must find a way to return inwards –
'returns to itself, and through itself ascends to God' in a way that is free
from delusion.[3] St Dionysios, the unerring beholder of noetic things,
also says that this circular movement of the intellect is not subject to
delusion.[4]

6. The father of error, ever desirous of seducing man from this
ascent and of leading him to that form of action which permits the
devil to insinuate his delusions, has not found until now, so far as we
know, a helper who with fair-sounding words would aid and abet him
in achieving this. But now, if what you tell me is correct, it seems that
he has discovered collaborators who write treatises which lead to this
very thing and who endeavour to persuade people, including those
who have embraced the sublime life of stillness, that during prayer it is
better to keep the intellect outside the body. They do not respect even
the definitive and unambiguous statement of St John Klimakos, who
with his words constructed the ladder leading to heaven: 'A hesychast
is one who tries to enshrine what is bodiless within his body.'[5] And
our spiritual fathers have rightly taught us things in harmony with this.
For if the hesychast does not enclose his intellect within his body, how
can he possess within himself the One who is invested with the body
and who as its natural form penetrates all structurally organized

---

[1] *Homily 12: On the Beginning of Proverbs* 7 (P.G. xxxi, 401A).
[2] St Dionysios the Areopagite, *On the Divine Names* iv, 9 (P.G. iii, 705A).
[3] *Letter* 2, 2 (P.G. xxxii, 228A).
[4] Loc. cit.
[5] *The Ladder of Divine Ascent*, Step 27 (P.G. lxxxviii, 1097B); E.T., p. 262.

matter? The determined exterior aspect of this matter – the material body – cannot enshrine the essence of the intellect until the material body itself truly lives by adopting a form of life appropriate to union with the intellect.

7. Do you see, brother, how St John has shown, not simply from the spiritual but even from a human point of view, how vital it is for those who seek to be true masters of themselves, and to be monks according to their inner self, to install or possess the intellect within the body? Nor is it out of place to teach beginners in particular to look within themselves and to bring their intellect within themselves by means of their breathing. For no one of sound judgment would prevent a person who has not yet achieved a true knowledge of himself from concentrating his intellect within himself with the aid of certain methods. Since the intellect of those recently embarked on the spiritual path continually darts away again as soon as it has been concentrated, they must continually bring it back once more; for in their inexperience they are unaware that of all things it is the most difficult to observe and the most mobile. That is why some teachers recommend them to pay attention to the exhalation and inhalation of their breath, and to restrain it a little, so that while they are watching it the intellect, too, may be held in check. This they should do until they advance with God's help to a higher stage and are able to prevent their intellect from going out to external things, to keep it uncompounded, and to gather it into what St Dionysios calls a state of 'unified concentration'.[1] This control of the breathing may, indeed, be regarded as a spontaneous consequence of paying attention to the intellect; for the breath is always quietly inhaled and exhaled at moments of intense concentration, especially in the case of those who practise stillness both bodily and mentally. Such people keep the Sabbath in a spiritual fashion and, so far as is possible, they rest from all personal activities; they strip their soul's powers free from every transient, fleeting and compound form of knowledge, from every type of sense-perception and, in general, from every bodily act that is under our sway, and, so far as they can, even from those not entirely under our sway, such as breathing.

8. In those who have made progress in stillness all these things

[1] On the Divine Names iv, 9 (P.G. iii, 705A).

come to pass without toil and anxious care, for of necessity they spontaneously follow upon the soul's perfect entry into itself. But where beginners are concerned none of them can be achieved without effort. Patient endurance is the fruit of love, for 'love patiently accepts all things' (1 Cor. 13 : 7), and teaches us to achieve such endurance by forcing ourselves so that through patience we may attain love; and this is a case in point. But what need is there to say anything more about this? Everyone possessing experience can but laugh when contradicted by those who lack experience; for such a person is taught not by argument but by the exertions he makes and the experience that comes from these exertions. It is from experience that we reap what is profitable, and it is experience that refutes the fruitless arguments of contentious braggarts.

A great teacher has said that after the fall our inner being naturally adapts itself to outward forms. When, then, someone is striving to concentrate his intellect in himself so that it functions, not according to the direct form of movement but according to the circular, delusion-free form, how could he not gain immensely if, instead of letting his gaze flit hither and thither, he fixes it upon his chest or his navel as upon a point of support? Outwardly curling himself – so far as is possible – into the form of a circle, in conformity with the mode of action that he tries to establish in his intellect, he also, through this same position of his body, sends into his heart the power of the intellect that is dispersed outwardly when his gaze is turned outward. If the power of the noetic demon resides in the navel of the belly, since there the law of sin exercises its dominion and provides him with fodder, why should we not establish there also the law of the intellect that, armed with prayer, contends against that dominion (cf. Rom. 7 : 23)? Then the evil spirit expelled through our baptism – 'the water of regeneration' (Tit. 3 : 5) – will not return with seven other spirits more wicked than himself and again take up residence in us, so that 'the last state is worse than the first' (Luke 11 : 26).

9. 'Be attentive to yourself,' says Moses (Deut. 15 : 9. LXX) – that is, to the whole of yourself, not to a few things that pertain to you, neglecting the rest. By what means? With the intellect assuredly, for nothing else can pay attention to the whole of yourself. Set this guard, therefore, over your soul and body, for thereby you will readily free yourself from the evil passions of body and soul. Take yourself in hand, then, be attentive to yourself, scrutinize yourself; or, rather, guard,

watch over and test yourself, for in this manner you will subdue your rebellious unregenerate self to the Spirit and there will never again be 'some secret iniquity in your heart' (Deut. 15 : 9). If, says, the Preacher, the spirit that rules over the evil demons and passions rises up against you, do not desert your place (cf. Eccles. 10 : 4) – that is to say, do not leave any part of your soul or body unwatched. In this way you will master the evil spirits that assail you and you will boldly present yourself to Him who examines hearts and minds (cf. Ps. 7 : 9); and He will not scrutinize you, for you will have already scrutinized yourself. As St Paul says, 'If we judged ourselves we would not be judged' (1 Cor. 11 : 31).

Then you will experience the blessing that David experienced, and you will say to God, 'Darkness will not be darkness with Thee and night shall be bright as day for me, for Thou hast taken possession of my mind' (cf. Ps. 139 : 12–13). It is as if David were saying that not only has God become the sole object of his soul's desire, but also that any spark of this desire in his body has returned to the soul that produced it, and through the soul has risen to God, hangs upon Him and cleaves to Him. For just as those who cleave to the perishable pleasures of the senses expend all the soul's desire in satisfying their fleshly proclivities and become so entirely materialistic that the Spirit of God cannot abide in them (cf. Gen. 6 : 3), so in the case of those who have elevated their intellect to God, and who through divine longing have attached their soul to Him, the flesh is also transformed, is exalted with the soul, communes together with the soul in the Divine, and itself likewise becomes the possession and dwelling-place of God, no longer harbouring any enmity towards Him or any desires that are contrary to the Spirit (cf. Gal. 5 : 17).

10. Which is the place – the flesh or the intellect – most expedient for the spirit of evil that rises up against us from below? Is it not the flesh, in which St Paul says that there is nothing good (cf. Rom. 7 : 18) until the law of life makes its habitation there? It is on account of this especially that the flesh must never escape our attention. How can it become our own? How can we avoid abandoning it? How can we repulse the devil's assault upon it – especially we who do not yet know how to contend spiritually with the spiritual forces of wickedness – unless we train ourselves to pay attention to ourselves also with respect to the outward positioning of the body? But why do I speak of those newly engaged in spiritual warfare when there are more perfect

people, not only after Christ's incarnation but also before it, who during prayer have adopted this outward positioning of the body and to whom the Deity readily hearkened? Elijah himself, pre-eminent among spiritual visionaries, leaned his head upon his knees, and having in this manner assiduously gathered his intellect into itself and into God he put an end to the drought that had lasted many years (cf. 1 Kgs. 18 : 42–45). But it seems to me, brother, that these men from whom you say you heard such slanders suffer from the illness of the Pharisees: they refuse to examine and cleanse the inside of the cup – that is to say, their heart – and not being grounded in the traditions of the fathers they try to assume precedence over everyone, as new teachers of the law (Matt. 23 : 25–26). They disdain the form of prayer that God vindicated in the case of the publican, and they exhort others who pray not to adopt it. For the Lord says in the Gospel that the publican 'would not even lift his eyes to heaven' (Luke 18 : 13). Those who when praying turn their gaze on themselves are trying to imitate the publican; yet their critics call them 'navel-psychics', with the clear intention of slandering them. For who among the people who pray in this way has ever said that the soul is located in the navel?

11. These critics, then, are evident calumniators; indeed, so far from healing those in error, they revile those who should be praised. They write not for the sake of truth and the life of stillness, but out of self-flattery; not in order to lead men towards spiritual watchfulness, but in order to draw them away from it. For they do all they can to discredit both the practice of hesychasm and those who engage in it in the appropriate manner. They would readily describe as belly-psychics those who said: 'The law of God is in the centre of my belly' (cf. Ps. 40 : 8. LXX), and: 'My belly shall sound as a harp and my inward parts as a brazen wall that Thou hast restored' (cf. Isa. 16 : 11. LXX). In general they slander all those who use corporeal symbols to represent, name and search out things noetic, divine and spiritual. Yet in spite of this they will inflict no injury on those whom they misrepresent or, rather, because of their attacks the saints will receive more blessings and still greater rewards in heaven, while their opponents will remain outside the sacred veils, unable to gaze upon even the shadows of the truth. It is, indeed, greatly to be feared that they will be punished eternally, for not only have they separated themselves from the saints, but they have also inveighed against them by their words.

12. You know the life of Symeon the New Theologian,[1] and how it was all virtually a miracle, glorified by God through supranatural miracles. You know also his writings, which without exaggeration one can call writings of life. In addition, you know of St Nikiphoros, how he passed many years in quietness and stillness and how he subsequently withdrew into the most isolated parts of the Holy Mountain of Athos and devoted himself to gathering texts of the holy fathers concerned with the practice of watchfulness, thus passing this practice on to us.[2] These two saints clearly teach those who have chosen this way of life the practices which, you report, are now under attack. But why do I refer to saints of past times? For shortly before our own day men of attested sanctity, recognized as endowed with the power of the Holy Spirit, have transmitted these things to us by their own mouths. You have heard of Theoliptos, whose name signifies 'inspired by God' and who is recognized in our days as an authentic theologian and a trustworthy visionary of the truth of God's mysteries – the bishop of Philadelphia or, rather, he who from Philadelphia as from a lampstand illumined the world.[3] You have heard also of Athanasios, who for not a few years adorned the patriarchal throne and whose tomb God has honoured;[4] and of Neilos of Italy, the emulator of the great Neilos; of Seliotis and Ilias, who were in no wise inferior to Neilos; and of Gabriel and Athanasios, who were endowed with the gift of prophecy.[5] You have certainly heard of all these men and of many others who lived before them, with them and after them, all of whom exhort and encourage those wishing to embrace this tradition – this tradition which the new doctors of *hesychia*, who have no idea of the life of stillness and who instruct not from experience but through spurious argument, try to repudiate, deform and disparage, all to no

[1] St Gregory Palamas presumably has in mind the *Life* of St Symeon the New Theologian, written by his disciple Nikitas Stithatos (see above, pp. 11, 76). The inclusion here of Symeon among the authorities who teach the 'physical method' indicates that, in Palamas's opinion, the treatise on *The Three Methods of Prayer* is a work of the New Theologian (see p. 64).

[2] On Nikiphoros the Monk and his treatise *On Watchfulness and the Guarding of the Heart*, see p. 192.

[3] On Theoliptos of Philadelphia, see pp. 175–6.

[4] Athanasios I, twice Patriarch of Constantinople (1289–93, 1303–9), reintroduced a primitive strictness in the monasteries and inspired a moral renewal among the Byzantine laity.

[5] By 'the great Neilos' Palamas probably means St Neilos of Ankyra (see *The Philokalia*, vol. i, p. 199). Neilos of Italy, Ilias and Athanasios were members of the Monastery of Mount Auxentios in Asia Minor during the late thirteenth century; Seliotis and Gabriel are otherwise unknown (see Meyendorff, *Grégoire Palamas: Défense des saints hésychastes*, i, pp. xli–xlii).

profit for their hearers. We, however, have spoken in person with some of these saints and they have been our teachers. Are we, then, to count as nothing these people who have been taught by experience and grace, and to submit ourselves to those who assume the role of teachers out of conceit and in a spirit of contention? This we will never, never do. And you, too, should turn away from them, wisely repeating to yourself the words of David, 'Bless the Lord, O my soul, and all that is within me bless His holy name' (Ps. 103 : 1). Guided by the fathers, take note how they urge us always to bring our intellect back into ourselves.

Three Texts on Prayer and Purity of Heart

1. Because the Deity is goodness itself, true mercy and an abyss of loving bounty – or, rather, He is that which embraces and contains this abyss, since He transcends every name that is named (cf. Eph. 1 : 21) and everything we can conceive – we can receive mercy only by union with Him. We unite ourselves to Him, in so far as this is possible, by participating in the godlike virtues and by entering into communion with Him through prayer and praise. Because the virtues are similitudes of God, to participate in them puts us in a fit state to receive the Deity, yet it does not actually unite us to Him. But prayer through its sacral and hieratic power actualizes our ascent to and union with the Deity, for it is a bond between noetic creatures and their Creator. Or at least this happens when our prayer, through its fervent compunction, transcends the passions and conceptual thoughts; for the intellect, while still passion-dominated, cannot be united to God. Thus so long as the intellect when praying remains in a passion-charged state, it will not obtain mercy; but to the extent that it can dispel distractive thoughts it will experience inward grief, and in so far as it experiences such grief it will partake of God's mercy. And if with humility it continues to savour this mercy it will transform entirely the aspect of the soul that is accessible to passion.

2. When the intellect's oneness becomes threefold, yet remains single, then it is united with the divine Triadic Unity, and it closes the door to every form of delusion and is raised above the flesh, the world and the prince of the world. As the intellect thus escapes the grip of these enemies, it finds itself in itself and in God; and for as long as it abides in this state it delights in the sense of spiritual jubilation that springs up within it. The intellect's oneness becomes threefold, yet remains single, when it reverts to itself and through itself ascends to God. The intellect's return to itself is its own self-guarding, while its

ascent to God is initiated through prayer, prayer that is succinct, although at times it may be more lengthy in form, which requires more effort. If you persist in concentrating your intellect in this way and in raising it up towards the Deity, and in forcibly restraining the mind's propensity to stray hither and thither, you will draw noetically close to God, will reap things ineffable, taste the age to come, and by noetic perception will know that the Lord is full of bounty, in accordance with the Psalmist's words, 'Taste and know that the Lord is bountiful' (Ps. 34 : 8). It is, perhaps, not very difficult for the intellect to find itself in the threefold state – for it itself to be, that is to say, both the guard, that which is guarded, and that which prays while it is keeping guard; but it is extremely difficult to persevere for a long time in this state that gives birth to things ineffable. For the effort involved in acquiring every other virtue is slight and altogether easy to sustain when compared with this. Hence many, unable to endure the self-constraint needed for acquiring the virtue of prayer, do not attain a plenitude of divine gifts; but those who do persist are rewarded with greater manifestations of divine aid, which sustain, support and joyfully carry them forward. Then what is difficult to accomplish is easily achieved, for they are invested with what one might call an angelic capacity, which empowers our human nature to commune with what lies beyond it. This accords with the words of the prophet, that those who persist will grow wings and will gain new strength (cf. Isa. 40 : 31).

3. The intellectual activity consisting of thought and intuition is called intellect, and the power that activates thought and intuition is likewise the intellect; and this power Scripture also calls the heart. It is because the intellect is pre-eminent among our inner powers that our soul is deiform. In those devoted to prayer, and especially to the single-phrased Jesus Prayer, the intellect's noetic activity is easily ordered and purified; but the power that produces this activity cannot be purified unless all the soul's other powers are also purified. For the soul is a single entity possessing many powers. Thus if one of its powers is vitiated the whole of it is defiled; for since the soul is single, the evil in one of its powers is communicated to all the rest. Now since each of the soul's powers produces a different energy, it is possible that with diligence one of these energies might be temporarily purified; but the power in question will not therefore be pure, since it communes with all the rest and so it remains impure rather than pure. Suppose, then,

that a person has purified his intellectual energy through diligence in prayer, and has been to a certain extent enlightened either by the light of knowledge or in addition by noetic illumination: if he considers himself for this reason to be pure he deceives himself and is utterly mistaken, and through his presumption he throws wide open a door into himself for the devil, who always strives to delude us human beings. But if he recognizes his heart's impurity, and is not filled with pride because of the partial degree of purity he has attained, but uses it as an aid, then he will see more clearly the impurity of the other powers of his soul and will progress in humility; his inward grief will grow and he will find suitable ways of healing each of his soul's powers. He will cleanse its moral aspect with the right kind of ascetic practice, its power of spiritual apperception with spiritual knowledge, its power of contemplation with prayer; and in this way he will attain perfect, true and enduring purity of heart and intellect – a purity that no one can ever experience except through perfection in the ascetic life, persistent practice, contemplation and contemplative prayer.

Topics of Natural and Theological Science and on the Moral and Ascetic Life: One Hundred and Fifty Texts

1. That the world has an origin nature teaches and history confirms, while the discoveries of the arts, the institution of laws and the constitution of states also clearly affirm it. We know who are the founders of nearly all the arts, the lawgivers and those who established states, and indeed we know what has been written about the origin of everything. Yet we see that none of this surpasses the account of the genesis of the world and of time as narrated by Moses. And Moses, who wrote about the genesis of the world, has so irrefutably substantiated the truth of what he writes through such extraordinary actions and words that he has convinced virtually the whole human race and has persuaded them to deride those who sophistically teach the contrary. Since the nature of this world is such that everything in it requires a specific cause in each instance, and since without such a cause nothing can exist at all, the very nature of things demonstrates that there must be a first principle which is self-existent and does not derive from any other principle.

2. That the world not only has an origin but also will have a consummation is affirmed by the fact that all things in it are contingent, and indeed it is partially coming to an end all the time. Moreover, sure and irrefutable assurance of this is furnished by the prophecy both of those inspired by God and of Christ Himself, the God of all; and not only the pious but also the impious must believe that what they say is true, since everyone can see that what they predicted about other things has proved correct. From them we learn that the world will not lapse entirely into non-being but, like our bodies and in a manner analogous to what will happen to us, it will be changed by the

power of the Holy Spirit, being dissolved and transformed into something more divine.

3. The ancient Greek sages say that the heavens revolve in accordance with the nature of the world soul, and that they teach justice and reason. What sort of justice? What kind of reason? For if the heavens revolve not by virtue of their own nature but by virtue of the nature of what they call the world soul, and if this world soul belongs to the entire world, how is it that the earth and the water and the air do not also revolve? Yet though in their opinion the soul is ever-moving, none the less the earth is stationary by nature, and so is water, which occupies the lower region, whereas the heavens, which occupy the upper region, are by nature ever in motion and move in a circle. But what is the character of this world soul by virtue of whose nature the heavens revolve? Is it endowed with intelligence? If so, it must be self-determining, and so it would not always move the celestial body in the same way, for what is self-determining moves differently at different times. And what trace of deiform soul do we observe in the lowermost sphere – the sphere of the earth – or in the elements most proximate to it, namely those of water, air, and even fire itself, for the world soul supposedly pertains to them as well? And again, how in their opinion are some things animate and others inanimate? And among inanimate things it turns out that not merely a few examples taken at random but every stone, every piece of metal, all earth, water, air and fire, moves by virtue of its own nature and not by virtue of a soul; for they admit that this is true even of fire. Yet if the soul is common to all, how is it that only the heavens move by virtue of the nature of this soul and not by virtue of their own nature? And how in their view can the soul that moves the celestial body be void of intelligence since according to them it is the source of our souls? But if it is void of intelligence it must be either sentient or vegetative. We observe, however, that no soul moves a body without the assistance of organs, and we cannot observe any such organ that specifically serves the earth, or the heavens, or any of the other element contained within them; for every organ is composed of various natures, while the elements severally, and above all the heavens, are simple and not composite. The soul is the actuality of a body possessing organs and having the potentiality for life; but the heavens, since they have no member or part that can serve as an organ, have no potentiality for life. How, then, can that which is incapable of life possibly have a soul? But

those who have become 'vain in their reasonings' have invented 'out of their foolish hearts' (Rom. 1 : 21) a world soul that does not exist, never has existed, and never will exist. Yet they claim that this soul is the demiurge and governor and controller of the entire sensible world and, further, that it is some sort of root and source of our souls or, rather, of every soul. Moreover, they say that it is born from the intellect, and that the intellect is other in substance than the supreme Intellect which they call God. Such doctrines are taught by those among them most proficient in wisdom and theology, but they are no better than men who deify wild beasts and stones. In fact their religiosity is much worse, for beasts, gold, stone and bronze are real things, even though they are among the least of creatures; but the star-bearing world soul neither exists, nor is it anything real, for it is nothing at all but the invention of an evil mind.

4. Since, they say, the celestial body must be in motion, and there is no place to which it can advance, it turns about itself and thus its 'advancement' is that of rotation. Well and good. So if there were a place, it would move upwards, like fire, and more so than fire since it is by nature lighter than fire. Yet this movement is due not to the nature of a soul but to that of lightness. Thus if the heavens' motion is rotational, and this motion exists by virtue of their own nature, and not that of the soul, then the celestial body revolves not by virtue of the nature of the soul but by virtue of its own nature. Hence it does not possess a soul, nor is there any such thing as a celestial or pancosmic soul. The only soul that possesses intelligence is the human soul, and this is not celestial, but supracelestial, not because of its location but because of its very nature, for its essence is noetic.

5. The celestial body does not move forward or upward. The reason for this is not that there is no place beyond it. For adjacent to the heavens and enclosed within them is the sphere of aether, and this too does not advance upward, not because there is no place to which it might proceed – for the breadth of the heavens embraces it – but because what is above is lighter. Hence, the heavens are by their own nature higher than the sphere of aether. It is not because there is no place higher that the heavens do not proceed upward, but because there is no body more subtle and light than they are.

6. No body is higher than the celestial body. Yet this is not to say that the region beyond the heavens does not admit a body, but only that the heavens contain every body and there is no other body

beyond. But if a body could pass beyond the heavens, which is our pious belief, then the region beyond the heavens would not be inaccessible. God, who fills all things and extends infinitely beyond the heavens, existed before the world, filling as He now fills the whole region of the world. Yet this did not prevent a body from existing in that region. Thus even outside of the heavens there is nothing to prevent the existence of a region, such as that which surrounds the world or as that which is in the world, in which a body could abide.

7. Since there is no such hindrance, how is it, then, that the celestial body does not move upwards, but turning back upon itself moves in a circular fashion? Because, as it is the lightest of bodies, it rises to the surface of all the others and is the highest of them all, as well as being the most mobile. Just as what is most compressed and most heavy is the lowest and most stationary, so what is more rarified and lightest is the highest and most mobile. Thus since the celestial body moves by nature above the level of all other bodies, and since by nature it is impossible for it to separate itself from those things on the surface of which it is located, and since those things on which it is located are spherical, it must encircle them unceasingly. And this it does not by virtue of the nature of a soul but by virtue of its own proper nature as a body, since it passes successively from place to place, which is the movement most characteristic of the highest bodies, just as a stationary state most characterizes the lowest bodies.

8. It may be observed that in the regions close about us the winds, whose nature it is to rise upwards, move about these regions without separating themselves from them and without proceeding further in an upward direction. This is not because there is no place for them to rise to, but because what is above the winds is lighter than they are. They remain on the surface of the regions above which they are situated because by nature they are lighter than those regions. And they move around those regions by virtue of their own nature and not that of a soul. I think that Solomon, wise in all things, intended to indicate this partial likeness that the winds bear to the celestial body when he applied the same kind of language to the winds as is used of it; for he wrote, 'The wind proceeds circle-wise, and returns on its own circuits' (Eccles. 1 : 6). But the nature of the winds round about us differs from the nature of higher bodies, in that the winds' motion is slower and they are more heavy.

9. According to the Greek sages, there are two opposing zones of

the earth that are temperate and habitable, and each of these is divided
into two inhabited regions, thus making four in all. Therefore they
assert that there are also four races of men upon the earth, and that
these are unable to have any contact with one another. There are,
according to these philosophers, men living in the temperate zone
lateral to us, who are separated from us by the torrid zone. And there
are people who dwell antipodal to these latter, living from their point
of view beneath the temperate zone and its inhabitants. In a similar
way there are those who dwell beneath us. The first they say are
opposite to us, while the second are antipodal and reversed. What
these sages did not realize is that only one tenth of the earth's sphere is
land, while the rest is almost entirely swallowed up by the abyss of the
waters.

10. You should realize that, apart from the region of the earth
which we inhabit, there is no other habitable land, since it is all
inundated by the waters of the abyss. You should also bear in mind that
(omitting aether) the four elements out of which the world is fashioned
balance one another equally, and that each of the elements has its own
sphere, the size of which is proportionate to its density, as Aristotle
also thinks. 'For', he says, 'there are five elements located in five
spherical regions, and the greater spheres always encompass the lesser:
water encompasses earth; air encompasses water; fire, air; and aether,
fire. This constitutes the world.'[1]

11. Aether is more translucent than fire, which is also called
'combustible matter', and fire is many times greater in volume than
air, and air than water, and water than earth which, as it is the most
compressed, is the least in volume of all the four elements under the
heavens. Since the sphere of water is many times greater in size than
that of earth, if the two spheres – that of water and that of earth – had
the same centre and the water was poured over the entire surface of
the earth, the water would not have left any part of the earth's surface
available for use by terrestrial animals, since it would have covered all
the soil and the earth's surface would have been everywhere at a
considerable depth beneath it. But since the waters do not entirely
swallow up earth's surface – for the dry land we inhabit is not covered
by them – the sphere of the waters must of necessity be eccentric to
the earth's sphere. Thus we must try to discover by how much it is

---

[1] Aristotle (attributed to), *On the World* 3 (393a).

eccentric and where its centre lies, whether above or beneath us. Yet it cannot be above us, since we see a part of the water's surface below us. Thus from our point of view the centre of the sphere of water is beneath the earth's centre. We have still to discover how far this centre is from the centre of the earth.

12. You can see how far from our viewpoint the centre of water's sphere lies beneath the centre of earth's sphere if you take into consideration that the surface of the water visible to us and beneath us – just as the ground we walk upon is beneath us – coincides almost exactly with the surface of the earth which we inhabit. But the habitable region of the earth is about one tenth of its circumference, for the earth has five zones, and we inhabit half of one of those five. Hence if you want to fit a sphere that encompasses the earth on to one that encompasses this tenth part of its surface you will find that the diameter of the exterior sphere is nearly twice as great as the diameter of the interior sphere, while its volume is eight times greater; and its centre will be situated at what is from our viewpoint the bottom extremity of the sphere of the earth. This is clear from the following diagram.

13. Let us represent the earth's sphere with a circle on the inside of which are the letters A, B, C, D; and around this let us draw another circle representing water's sphere, which touches the first circle at its highest point, and on the outside of this second circle let us write the letters E, F, G, H. It will be found that, from our point of view, the centre of the outer circle will lie on the circumference of the inner circle at its bottom extremity. And since the diameter of the outer circle is twice that of the inner circle, and since it can be demonstrated geometrically that the sphere whose diameter is twice that of another sphere is eight times the size of the latter, it follows that one eighth of the sphere of the element of water is contained by and merged with earth's sphere. It is for this reason that many springs of water gush forth from the earth and abundant, ever-flowing rivers issue from it, and the gulfs of many seas pour into it, and many lakes spread over it. There is scarcely any place on the earth where, if you dig, you will not find water flowing beneath.

14. As the above diagram and logic itself teach us, no region of the earth other than our own is inhabited. For just as the earth would be totally uninhabitable if both earth and water had the same centre, so, even more truly, if the water has its centre at what is from our point of

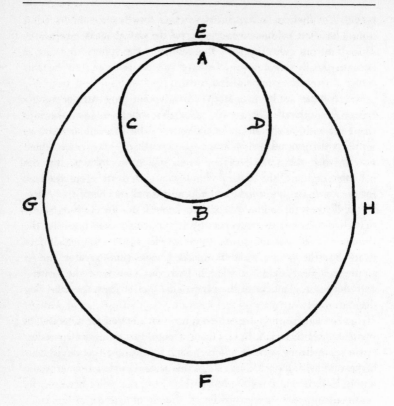

view the lowest extremity of the earth, all the other parts of the earth, apart from the region where we live which fits into the upper section of the water's sphere, must be uninhabitable since they are flooded by water. And since it has already been demonstrated that embodied deiform souls dwell only in the inhabited region of the earth, and that there is but one such region on the earth – the one in which we live – it follows that land animals not endowed with intelligence also dwell solely in this region.

15. Sight is formed from the manifold impressions of colours and shapes; smell from odours; taste from flavours; hearing from sounds; and touch from things that are rough or smooth on contact. The impressions that the senses receive come from bodies but, although corporeal, they are not bodies themselves. For they do not arise directly from bodies, but from the forms that are associated with

bodies. Yet they are not themselves these forms, since they are but impressions left by the forms; and so, like images, they are inseparably separated from these forms. This is particularly evident in the case of sight, especially when objects are seen in mirrors.

16. These sense impressions are in turn appropriated from the senses by the soul's imaginative faculty; and this faculty totally separates not the senses themselves but what we have called the images that exist within them from the bodies and their forms. It stores them up like treasures and brings them forward interiorly – now one and now another, each in its own time – for its own use even when there is no corresponding body present. In this way it sets before itself all manner of things seen, heard, tasted, smelt and touched.

17. In creatures endowed with intelligence this imaginative faculty of the soul is an intermediary between the intellect and the senses. For the intellect beholds and dwells upon the images received in itself from the senses – images separated from bodies and already bodiless – and it formulates various kinds of thought by means of distinctions, analysis and inference. This happens in various ways – impassionately or dispassionately or in a state between the two, both with and without error. From these thoughts are born most virtues and vices, as well as opinions, whether right or wrong. Yet not every thought that comes into the intellect has its origin in the images of things perceived or is connected with them. There are some thoughts that do not come within the scope of the senses, but are given to the thinking faculty by the intellect itself. As regards our thoughts, then, not every truth or error, virtue or vice has its origin in the imagination.

18. What is remarkable and deserving our attention is how beauty or ugliness, wealth or poverty, glory or ill repute – and, in short, either the noetic light that bestows eternal life or the noetic darkness of chastisement – enter the soul, becoming firmly established within it, from merely transitory and sensible things.

19. When the intellect enthrones itself on the soul's imaginative faculty and thereby becomes associated with the senses, it engenders a composite form of knowledge. For suppose you look at the setting sun and then see the moon follow it, illuminated in the small part turned towards the sun, and in the subsequent days you note that the moon gradually recedes and is illuminated more brightly until the opposite process sets in; and suppose you then see the moon draw closer from the other side and its light wane more and more until it disappears

altogether at the point at which it first received illumination; suppose
you take intellectual note of all this, having in your imagination the
images you have previously received and with the moon itself ever
present before your eyes, you will in this way understand from sense-
perception, imagination and intellection that the moon gets its light
from the sun, and that its orbit is much lower than the sun's and closer
to the earth.

20. As in this way we achieve knowledge of things pertaining to the
moon, so in a similar way we can achieve knowledge of things
pertaining to the sun – the solar eclipses and their nodes – as well as of
the parallaxes, intervals and varied configurations involving the
planets, and in short of all phenomena concerning the heavens. The
same holds true with regard to the laws of nature, and every method
and art, and in brief with regard to all knowledge acquired from the
perception of particulars. Such knowledge we gather from the senses
and the imagination by means of the intellect. Yet no such knowledge
can ever be called spiritual, for it is natural, things of the Spirit being
beyond its scope (cf. 1 Cor. 2 : 14).

21. Where can we learn anything certain and true about God,
about the world as a whole, and about ourselves? Is it not from the
teaching of the Holy Spirit? For this teaching has taught us that God is
the only Being that truly is – the only eternal and immutable Being –
who neither receives being from non-being nor returns to non-being;
who is Tri-hypostatic and Almighty, and who through His Logos
brought forth all things from non-being in six days or, rather, as Moses
states, He created them instantaneously. For we have heard him say,
'First of all God created heaven and earth' (Gen. 1 : 1). And He did
not create them totally empty or without any intermediary bodies at
all. For the earth was mixed with water, and each was pregnant with
air and with the various species of animals and plants, while the
heavens were pregnant with various lights and fires; and so with the
heavens and the earth all things received their existence. Thus first of
all God created the heavens and the earth as a kind of all-embracing
material substance with the potentiality of giving birth to all things. In
this way He rightly rebuts those who wrongly think that matter pre-
existed on its own as an autonomous entity.

22. After this initial creation, He who brings forth all things from
non-being proceeds as it were to embellish and adorn the world. In
six days He allotted its own proper and appropriate rank to each of

His creatures that together constitute His world. He differentiates each by command alone, as though bringing forth from hidden treasuries the things stored within, giving them form, and disposing and composing them harmoniously, with perfection and aptness, one to the other, each to all and all to each. Establishing the immovable earth as the centre He encircled it in the highest vault with the ever-moving heavens and in His great wisdom bound the two together by means of the intermediary regions. Thus the same world is both at rest and moving. For while the heavenly bodies encircle the earth in rapid and perpetual motion, the immovable body of the earth necessarily occupies the central position, its state of rest serving as a counter-balance to the heavens' mobility. In this way the pancosmic sphere does not change its position as it would if it were cylindrical.

23. Thus by assigning such positions to the two bodies that mark the boundaries of the universe – the earth and the heavens – the Master-craftsman both made fast and set in motion what one might call this entire and orderly world; and He further allotted what was fitting to each thing lying between these two limits. Some He placed on high, enjoining them to move in the upper regions and to revolve for all time round the uttermost boundary of the universe in a wise and ordered manner. Those are the light and active bodies capable of making bodies that lie beneath them fit and serviceable. They are most wisely set above the world's middle region so that they can sufficiently dispel the excessive coldness there and restrain their own excessive heat to its proper level. In some manner they also restrict the excessive mobility of the world's outermost bounds, for they have their own opposing movement and they hold that outermost region in place through their counter-rotation. At the same time they provide us with beneficial yearly changes of season, whereby we can measure temporal extension; and to those with understanding they supply knowledge of the God who has created, ordered and adorned the world. Hence He commanded those bodies in the upper region to dance round it in swift rotation for two reasons: to fill the entire universe with beauty and to furnish a variety of more specific benefits. He set lower down in the middle region other bodies of a heavy and passive nature that come into being and undergo change, that decompose and are recompounded, and that suffer alteration for a useful purpose. He established these bodies and their relationships to one another in an orderly manner

so that all things together could rightly be called 'cosmos', that is to say, that which is well-ordered.

24. In this manner the first of beings was brought forth into creation and after that another was brought forth, and after that still another, and so on, until last of all man was brought forth. So great was the honour and providential care which God bestowed upon man that He brought the entire sensible world into being before him and for his sake. The kingdom of heaven was prepared for him from the foundation of the world (cf. Matt. 25 : 34); God first took counsel concerning him, and then he was fashioned by God's hand and according to the image of God (cf. Gen. 1 : 26–27). God did not form the whole of man from matter and from the elements of this sensible world, as He did the other animals. He formed only man's body from these materials; but man's soul He took from things supracelestial or, rather, it came from God Himself when mysteriously He breathed life into man (cf. Gen. 2 : 7). The human soul is something great and wondrous, superior to the entire world; it overlooks the universe and has all things in its care; it is capable of knowing and receiving God, and more than anything else has the capacity of manifesting the sublime magnificence of the Master-Craftsman. Not only capable of receiving God and His grace through ascetic struggle, it is also able to be united in Him in a single hypostasis.

25. Here and in such things as these lie the true wisdom and the saving knowledge that procure for us the blessedness of heaven. What Euclid, Marinos or Ptolemy has been able to understand these truths? What Empedocleans, Socratics, Aristotelians and Platonists with their logical methods and mathematical demonstrations? Or, rather, what form of sense-perception has grasped such things, what intellect apprehended them? If the wisdom of the Spirit seemed something lowly to these philosophers of nature and their followers, this fact alone demonstrates its incomparable superiority. In much the same way as animals not endowed with intelligence are related to the wisdom of these men – or, if you wish, as children would consider the pastries they hold in their hands superior to the imperial crown and to all the knowledge of these philosophers – so are these philosophers in relation to the true and sublime wisdom and teaching of the Spirit.

26. To know God truly in so far as this is possible is incomparably superior to the philosophy of the Greeks, and simply to know what place man has in relation to God surpasses all their wisdom. For man

alone among all terrestrial and celestial beings is created in the image of his Maker, so that he might look to God and love Him and be an initiate and worshipper of God alone, and so that he might preserve his own beauty by his faith in God and his devotion and affection towards Him, and might know that whatever is found on earth and in the heavens is inferior to himself and is completely void of intelligence. This the Greek sages could never conceive of, and they dishonoured our nature and were irreverent towards God. 'They worshipped and served the creature rather than the Creator' (Rom. 1 : 25), attributing to the sense-perceptible yet insensate stars an intelligence in each case proportionate in power and dignity to its physical size. They wretchedly worshipped these things, called them greater and lesser gods, and committed the lordship of all things to them. Did they not thus shame their own souls, dishonouring and impoverishing them, and filling them with a truly noetic and chastising darkness by their preoccupation with a philosophy based on sense-objects?

27. To know that we have been created in God's image prevents us from deifying even the noetic world. 'Image' here refers not to the body but to the nature of the intellect. Nothing in nature is superior to the intellect, for if there were then it would constitute the divine image. Since, therefore, the intellect is what is best in us and this, even though it is in the divine image, is none the less created by God, why, then, is it difficult to understand or, rather, how is it not self-evident that the Creator of that which is noetic in us is also the Creator of everything noetic? Thus every noetic being, since it is likewise created in the image of God, is our fellow-servant, even if certain noetic beings are more honourable than us in that they possess no body and so more closely resemble the utterly bodiless and uncreated Nature. Or, rather, those noetic beings who have kept their rank and who maintain the purpose for which they were created deserve our homage and are far superior to us, even though they are fellow-servants. On the other hand, the noetic beings who did not keep their rank but rebelled and rejected the purpose for which they were created are totally estranged from those close to God, and they have fallen from honour. And if they attempt to drag us after them and to make us fall, they are not only worthless and disgraced but are also God's enemies and destructive and inimical to the human race.

28. Yet natural scientists, astronomers and those who boast of possessing universal knowledge are unable to understand anything of

what has just been said on the basis of their philosophy. Moreover, they have regarded the ruler of the noetic darkness and all the rebellious powers under him not only as superior to themselves but even as gods, and they have honoured them with temples, made sacrifices to them and submitted themselves to their ruinous oracles. In this way they were mocked exceedingly by the demons, through unholy sacred objects, through defiling purifications which only increased their accursed conceit, and through prophets and prophetesses who estranged them totally from the essential truth.

29. For a man to know God, and to know himself and his proper rank – a knowledge now possessed even by Christians who are thought to be quite unlearned – is a knowledge superior to natural science and astronomy and to all philosophy concerning such matters. Moreover, for our intellect to know its own infirmity, and to seek healing for it, is incomparably greater than to know and search out the magnitude of the stars, the principles of nature, the generation of terrestrial things and the circuits of celestial bodies, their solstices and risings, stations and retrogressions, separations and conjunctions and, in short, all the multiform relationships which arise from the many different motions in the heavens. For the intellect that recognizes its own infirmity has discovered where to enter in order to find salvation and how to approach the light of knowledge and receive the true wisdom that does not pass away with this present world.

30. Every spiritual and noetic nature, whether angelic or human, possesses life as its essence, whereby it continues immortal in its existence and does not admit dissolution. But the spiritual and noetic nature within us has life not only as its essence but also as its activity, since it quickens the body united to it. For this reason it is also called the body's life. And when it is called the life of the body, it is called life with reference to something else and is an activity of our nature; for when relative to something else it can never be called an essence in itself. The noetic nature of angels, however, does not possess life as an activity of this sort, because it did not receive an earthy body from God and was not united to it in such a way as to have a quickening power in regard to it. Yet their nature can admit opposites, that is, good and evil. This is confirmed by the fact that the wicked angels fell away because of their pride. Thus the angels are somehow composite, being formed of their essence and one of these contrary qualities of virtue or vice.

Hence it is evident that even angels do not have goodness as their essence.

31. The soul of each animal not imbued with intelligence is the life of the body that it animates; it does not possess life as essence, but as activity, since here life is relative and not something in itself. Indeed, the soul of animals consists of nothing except that which is actuated by the body. Thus when the body dissolves, the soul inevitably dissolves as well. Their soul is no less mortal than their body, since everything that it is relates and refers to what is mortal. So when the body dies the soul also dies.

32. The soul of each man is also the life of the body that it animates, and possesses a quickening activity in relation to something else, namely, to the body that it quickens. Yet the soul has life not only as an activity but also as its essence, since it is self-existent; for it possesses a spiritual and noetic life that is evidently different from the body's and from what is actuated by the body. Hence when the body dissolves the human soul does not perish with it; and not only does it not perish but it continues to exist immortally, since it is not manifest only in relation to something else, but possesses its own life as its essence.

33. The spiritual and noetic soul possesses life as essence, yet it can admit contraries, that is to say, good and evil. Thus it is evident that it does not have goodness as essence, nor evil either; both are as it were qualities and when either is present it is because the soul has chosen it. They are present, not with respect to place, but whenever the noetic soul, having received free will from its Creator, inclines to one or the other and wills to live in accordance with it. Hence the spiritual and noetic soul is somehow composite, but not on account of the activity mentioned above; for this activity is related to something else, namely, the body, and so does not by nature produce what is composite. Rather the soul is composite on account of its own essence and the presence in it of one of the two contrary qualities – good and evil – of which we have just spoken.

34. The supreme Intellect, the uttermost Good, the Nature which transcends life and divinity, being entirely incapable of admitting opposites in any way, clearly possesses goodness not as a quality but as essence. Hence everything that we can conceive of as good is to be found in It or, rather, the supreme Intellect both *is* that good and surpasses goodness. And everything that we can conceive of as being in the Intellect is good or, rather, is both goodness and a Goodness that

transcends goodness. Life, too, is to be found in It or, rather, the
Intellect is life; for life is good and the life that is in the Intellect is
goodness. And Wisdom is in It, or, rather, the Intellect is Wisdom; for
Wisdom is good and the Wisdom that is in the Intellect is goodness. It
is the same with eternity, blessedness and everything that we can
conceive of as good. There is no distinction between life and wisdom
and goodness and so on, for this Goodness embraces all these things
comprehensively, unitively and in utter simplicity, and we conceive of
It and call It Goodness by virtue of Its embracing every form of
goodness. Whatever goodness we can conceive of and ascribe to It is
one and true. Yet this Goodness is not only that which is truly
conceived of by those who perceive with an intellect imbued with
divine Wisdom and who speak of God with a tongue moved by the
Spirit; it is also ineffable and incomprehensible and transcends these
things, and is not inferior to the unitive and supranatural simplicity; for
absolute and transcendent Goodness is one. It is by virtue of this alone
– namely, that He is absolute and transcendent Goodness, possessing
goodness as His essence – that the Creator and Lord of Creation is both
intellectually perceived and described; and this solely on the basis of
His energies which are directed towards creation. Hence in no way
whatever does God admit what is contrary to goodness, since there is
nothing contrary where essence is concerned.

35. This absolute and transcendent Goodness is also the source of
goodness; and that which proceeds from It is likewise good and is
supremely good and cannot be lacking in perfect goodness. The
transcendently and absolutely perfect Goodness is Intellect; thus what
else could that which proceeds from It as from a source be except
Intelligence-content or Logos? But the divine Logos is not to be
understood in the same way as the human thought-form that we
express orally, for that proceeds not from the intellect but from a body
activated by the intellect; nor is it to be understood in the same way as
our human inner intelligence-principle, for this, too, is disposed within
us in such a way as to give birth to different forms of sound. Neither is
the divine Logos equivalent to the reasoning power in our mind, even
though this is soundless and operates entirely according to impulses
that are bodiless. For the reasoning *logos*, as a faculty dependent on us,
requires for its functioning successive moments of time, since it
emerges gradually, proceeding from an incomplete starting-point to its
complete conclusion. Rather, the divine Logos is similar to the *logos*

implanted by nature in our intellect, according to which we are made by the Creator in His own image and which constitutes the spiritual knowledge coexistent with the intellect. On the plane of the sublime Intellect of the absolute and transcendently perfect Goodness, wherein there is nothing imperfect, the divine Logos-Gnosis is indistinguishably whatever that Goodness is, except for the fact that it is derived from It. Thus the supreme Logos is also the Son, and is so described by us, in order that we may recognize Him to be perfect in a perfect and individual hypostasis, since He comes from the Father and is in no way inferior to the Father's essence, but is indistinguishably identical with Him, although not according to hypostasis; for His distinction as hypostasis is manifest in the fact that the Logos is begotten in a divinely fitting manner from the Father.

36. The Goodness, then, that issues by way of generation from the Source of noetic goodness is Logos. But no intelligent person could conceive of a Logos or Intelligence-content that is lifeless and without spirit. Hence the Logos, God from God, possesses the Holy Spirit that issues together with Himself from the Father. Yet the Holy Spirit is spirit not in the sense whereby the breath conjoined to the word issuing from our lips is spirit, for this is a body and is conjoined to our speech through bodily organs; nor is it spirit in the sense whereby that which accompanies, albeit bodilessly, our innate reasoning process is spirit, for that, too, entails a certain impulse of the intellect that accompanies our thought-process through successive intervals of time, and progresses from incompletion to completion. The Spirit of the supreme Logos is a kind of ineffable yet intense longing or *eros* experienced by the Begetter for the Logos born ineffably from Him, a longing experienced also by the beloved Logos and Son of the Father for His Begetter; but the Logos possesses this love by virtue of the fact that it comes from the Father in the very act through which He comes from the Father, and it resides co-naturally in Him. It is from the Logos's discourse with us through His incarnation that we have learned what is the name of the Spirit's distinct mode of coming to be from the Father and that the Spirit belongs not only to the Father but also to the Logos. For He says 'the Spirit of Truth, who proceeds from the Father' (John 15 : 26), so that we may know that from the Father comes not solely the Logos – who is begotten from the Father – but also the Spirit who proceeds from the Father. Yet the Spirit belongs also to the Son, who receives Him from the Father as the Spirit of

Truth, Wisdom and Logos. For Truth and Wisdom constitute a Logos that befits His Begetter, a Logos that rejoices with the Father as the Father rejoices in Him. This accords with the words that He spoke through Solomon: 'I was She who rejoiced together with Him' (Prov. 8 : 30). Solomon did not say simply 'rejoiced' but 'rejoiced together with'. This pre-eternal rejoicing of the Father and the Son is the Holy Spirit who, as I said, is common to both, which explains why He is sent from both to those who are worthy. Yet the Spirit has His existence from the Father alone, and hence He proceeds as regards His existence only from the Father.

37. Our intellect, because created in God's image, possesses likewise the image of this sublime Eros or intense longing – an image expressed in the love experienced by the intellect for the spiritual knowledge that originates from it and continually abides in it. This love is of the intellect and in the intellect and issues forth from it together with its innermost intelligence or *logos*. This is shown clearly by the fact that even those who are unable to perceive what lies deeply within themselves possess an insatiable desire for spiritual knowledge. Yet in the Archetype, in this absolutely and transcendently perfect Goodness, wherein there is nothing imperfect, the divine Eros is indistinguishably whatever that Goodness is, except for the fact that it is derived from It. Hence this intense longing is – and is called – the Holy Spirit and the other Comforter (cf. John 14 : 16), since He accompanies the Logos. Thus we know Him to be perfect in a perfect and individual hypostasis, in no way inferior to the Father's essence, but indistinguishably identical with the Son and the Father, although not according to hypostasis; for His distinction as hypostasis is manifest in the fact that He proceeds from God in a divinely fitting manner. Thus we worship one true and perfect God in three true and perfect hypostases – not, certainly, a threefold God but one who is simple. For Goodness is not something threefold, nor a triad of goodnesses. Rather, the most sublime Goodness is a holy, awe-inspiring and venerable Trinity flowing forth out of Itself into Itself without change and divinely established in Itself before the ages. The Trinity is without limits and is limited only by Itself; It limits all things, transcends all and permits no beings to be outside Itself.

38. The noetic and intelligent nature of angels also possesses intellect, and the thought-form (*logos*) that proceeds from the intellect, and the intense longing (*eros*) of the intellect for its thought-form.

This longing is likewise from the intellect and coexists eternally with the thought-form and the intellect, and can be called spirit since by nature it accompanies the thought-form. But this spirit in the case of angels is not life-generating, for it has not received from God an earthy body conjoined with it, and so it has not received the power to generate and sustain life. On the other hand the noetic and intelligent nature of the human soul has received a life-generating spirit from God since the soul is created together with an earthy body, and so by means of the spirit it sustains and quickens the body conjoined to it. This makes it clear to those who possess understanding that the spirit of man that quickens the body is noetic longing (*eros*), a longing that issues from the intellect and its thought-form, that exists in the thought-form and the intellect, and that possesses in itself both the thought-form and the intellect. Through the spirit the soul possesses such a natural union of love with its particular body that it never wants to abandon it, and it would never leave it at all if it was not forced to do so by some grave illness or affliction that assails it from without.

39. Since the noetic and intelligent nature of the human soul alone possesses intellect, thought-form and life-generating spirit, it alone – more so than the bodiless angels – is created by God in His image. This image the soul possesses inalienably, even if it does not recognize its own dignity, or think and live in a manner worthy of the Creator's image within it. After our forefather's transgression in paradise through the tree, we suffered the death of our soul – which is the separation of the soul from God – prior to our bodily death; yet although we cast away our divine likeness, we did not lose our divine image. Thus when the soul renounces its attachment to inferior things and cleaves through love to God and submits itself to Him through acts and modes of virtue, it is illuminated and made beautiful by God and is raised to a higher level, obeying His counsels and exhortations; and by these means it regains the truly eternal life. Through this life it makes the body conjoined to it immortal, so that in due time the body attains the promised resurrection and participates in eternal glory. But if the soul does not repudiate its attachment and submission to inferior things whereby it shamefully dishonours God's image, it alienates itself from God and is estranged from the true and truly blessed life of God; for as it has first abandoned God, it is justly abandoned by Him.

40. The triadic nature sequent to the supreme Trinity – that is to say, the human soul – has more than other natures been made by the

Trinity noetic, intelligent and spiritual. In this way it is created more than other natures in the image of the Trinity. Thus it ought to maintain its proper rank, be sequent to God alone, yoked to Him alone, and subject and obedient to Him alone. It ought to look only to Him and adorn itself with the constant mindfulness and contemplation of Him, and with most fervent and ardent love for Him. For by these means it is wondrously drawn back to itself or, rather, it draws to itself the mystical and ineffable glory of God's nature. Then the soul truly possesses the image and the likeness of God and is thereby made gracious, wise and divine. When this glory is manifestly present or when it approaches unnoticed, the soul now increasingly learns to love God more than itself and to love its neighbour as itself. From this it learns to know and preserve its own dignity and rank, and truly to love itself. On the other hand, 'He who loves injustice hates his own soul' (Ps. 11 : 5. LXX), and through tearing apart and crippling the image of God in himself he suffers in a way similar to the mentally deranged who pitifully rend their own flesh without being aware of it. Such a person unconsciously outrages and most wretchedly mutilates his innate beauty, mindlessly shattering the soul's triadic, supra-mundane and love-filled world. What can be more wrong-headed and pernicious than to refuse to remember, to refuse to gaze continually upon and love Him who created and adorned the soul with His own image, thus conferring the capacity for spiritual knowledge and love, as well as lavishing indescribable gifts and eternal life upon all who use this capacity aright.

41. The noetic serpent, the author of evil, is one of the beings inferior to our soul, as he is also far inferior to other creatures. He has now become an angel and herald of his own wickedness as a result of his wicked counsel to human beings. He is so much more base than and inferior to all other beings that he desired in his arrogance to become like the Creator in authority; and he was justly abandoned by God to the same degree that he himself had first abandoned God. So total was his defection from God that he became His opponent and adversary and manifest enemy. Thus if God is living Goodness and the Quickener of living things, clearly the devil is deadly and death-dealing evil. God possesses goodness as His essence and by nature does not admit of its opposite, that is, evil, so that whoever partakes of evil of any sort may not so much as draw near Him. How much more will He not drive as far as possible from Himself the creator and originator of evil and the

cause of it in others? The evil one possesses not evil but life as his essence, and hence he lives immortally. Yet his essence was capable of admitting evil since he was honoured with free will. Had he voluntarily accepted a subordinate status and cleaved to the everflowing Well-spring of goodness he would have partaken of true life. But since he deliberately gave himself over to evil, he was deprived of true life and was justly expelled from it, having himself abandoned it in the first place. Thus he became a dead spirit, not in essence – since death lacks substantial reality – but through his rejection of true life. Yet unsated in his pursuit of evil and adding more and more to his wretchedness, he made himself into a death-generating spirit, eagerly drawing man into communion with his own state of death.

42. The mediator and cause of death, twisted in character and inordinate in craftiness, once insinuated himself into a twisting serpent in God's paradise. He did not himself become a serpent (nor could he, except in an illusory form; and this he preferred not to adopt at that time, for fear of being detected); but, not daring an open confronta-tion, he chose a deceitful approach, trusting that by this means he would escape detection. Thus, having the visible aspect of a friend he could secretly insinuate the most hateful things, and by the extra-ordinary fact of his talking – for the visible serpent was not endowed with intelligence, nor did it previously appear capable of speaking – he could astonish Eve and draw her whole attention entirely to himself and by his devices make her easy to deal with. In this way he was able immediately to induce her to subject herself to what is inferior and so to enslave herself to things over which she was appointed to reign worthily, as she alone among visible beings had been honoured by God with intelligence and created in the image of the Creator. God permitted this so that man, seeing the counsel coming from a creature inferior to himself – and, indeed, how greatly is the serpent his inferior – might realize how completely worthless this counsel was and might rightly reject with indignation the idea of submitting to what was clearly inferior to him. In this way he would preserve his own dignity and at the same time, by obeying the divine commandment, would keep faith with the Creator. Thus he would have won an easy victory over the spirit that had fallen away from true life, and would have justly received blessed immortality and would abide eternally in life divine.

43. No being is superior to man so as to be in a position to advise

him and propose opinions and thus discern and provide what is fitting
for him. But this is the case only if man maintains his rank, knows
himself and knows, too, Him who alone is superior to him, observing
those things which he learns from God and resolutely accepting God's
counsel alone as regards anything proposed to him by others. For
although angels are superior to us in dignity, it is their task obediently
to execute God's designs respecting us; for they are ministers sent to
serve 'those who are to be the heirs of salvation' (Heb. 1 : 14) – not all
angels, of course, but only the beneficent angels who have kept their
own rank. The angels have received intellect, intelligence and spirit
from God, three co-natural qualities; and like us they should obey the
creative Intellect, Intelligence and Spirit. Although the angels are
superior to us in many ways, yet in some respects – as we have said and
as we will repeat – they fall short of us with regard to being in the
image of the Creator; for we, rather than they, have been created in
God's image.

44. The angels are ordained to serve the Creator effectively and
their appointed role is to be ruled by God. But they are not appointed
to rule over beings inferior to themselves unless they are sent to do so
by the Sovereign Ruler of all. Yet satan presumptuously yearned to
rule contrary to the will of the Creator, and when together with his
fellow apostate angels he forsook his proper rank he was rightly
abandoned by the true Source of life and illumination and clothed
himself in death and eternal darkness. But because man was appointed
not merely to be ruled by God but also to rule over all creatures upon
the earth, the arch-fiend looked upon him with malicious eyes and
made use of every ploy to deprive him of his dominion. Being unable to
use constraint, since he is prevented from doing this by the Sovereign
Ruler who created all intelligent nature free and self-determining, he
deceitfully suggested such counsel as would abolish man's dominion.
He beguiled him or, rather, persuaded him to disregard, disdain and
reject, and indeed to oppose and to act contrary to the commandment
and counsel given him by God. In this way he induced man to share in
his apostasy, and so to share also in his state of eternal darkness and
death.

45. St Paul has taught us that the soul endowed with intelligence
can be as if dead even though it possesses life as its being; for he writes,
'The self-indulgent widow is dead while still alive' (1 Tim. 5 : 6). He
could not have said worse than this about the present subject of our

discourse, namely, the soul endowed with intelligence. For if the soul deprived of the spiritual Bridegroom does not humble itself and mourn, and does not adopt the strait and grievous life of repentance, but is, on the contrary, profligate, sunk in sensual pleasure and self-indulgence, it is dead even while it lives and even though it is immortal in essence. It has the capacity for what is worse, death, and likewise for what is better, life. The apostle says that if a widow deprived of her earthly bridegroom lives self-indulgently, although alive in her body she is utterly dead in her soul. He also says elsewhere, 'Even when we were dead because of our sins God quickened us together with Christ' (Eph. 2 : 5). As St John says, 'There is sin that leads to death and there is sin that does not lead to death' (1 John 5 : 16–17). And the Lord Himself, in commanding a man to 'let the dead bury their own dead' (Matt. 8 : 22), made it clear that those involved in the funeral, although alive in body, were utterly dead in soul.

46. The ancestors of our race wilfully desisted from mindfulness and contemplation of God. They disregarded His commandment, made themselves of one mind with the dead spirit of satan and, contrary to the Creator's will, ate of the forbidden tree. Stripped of their resplendent and life-giving garments of supernal radiance, they became, alas, dead in spirit like satan. But since satan is not merely a dead spirit, but also brings death upon those who draw near him, and since those who shared in his deadness possessed a body through which the deadly counsel took effect, they transmitted those dead and death-dealing spirits of death to their own bodies. The human body would have immediately decomposed and returned to the earth whence it was taken (cf. Gen. 3 : 19), had it not been preserved by divine providence and power, patiently awaiting the decision of Him who brings about all things through His word alone. Without this decision nothing at all is accomplished, and it is always just. As the Psalmist says, 'The Lord is just and He loves justice' (Ps. 11 : 7. LXX).

47. Scripture tells us, 'God did not create death' (Wisd. 1 : 13). Rather, He impeded its inception in so far as this was fitting, and in so far as it was consistent with His justice to obstruct those to whom He Himself had given free will when He created them. For from the beginning God gave them a counsel that would lead to immortality, and so that they would be safeguarded as far as possible He made His life-generating counsel a commandment. He clearly foretold and forewarned that death would be the consequence of rejecting this

vivifying commandment, so that either through love or knowledge or fear they would protect themselves from the experience of death. For God loves, knows and has the power to effect what is profitable for every created being. If God only knew what is profitable but did not love it, He might have left unfinished what He knew to be good. Again, if He loved what is profitable but did not know it or was unable to accomplish it, perhaps against His will what He loved and knew would have remained unaccomplished. But since to the highest possible degree He loves, knows and is able to effect what is profitable for us, everything that comes to us from Him, even though it be without our wanting it, will certainly prove to be to our profit. On the other hand, it is greatly to be feared that whatever we engage in on our own initiative, as creatures endowed with free will, will prove to be unprofitable for us. When, however, God in His providence has plainly forbidden something, whether speaking directly, as He does in paradise and in the Gospel, or else speaking through the prophets, as He does to the Israelites, or through the apostles and their successors, as He does in the law of grace, it is clearly most unprofitable and destructive for us to desire and pursue it. And if someone proffers it to us and induces us to seek it, either by persuasive words or by enchanting us with apparent friendship, he is manifestly an enemy and hostile to our life.

48. Hence – whether out of love for Him who wants us to live (for why would God have created us as living creatures if He did not especially want us to live?), or because we recognize that He knows what is for our profit better than we do (and how could He who grants us knowledge and is the Lord of knowledge not know this incomparably better than we do?), or out of fear for His almighty power – we ought not to have been misled, lured and persuaded at that time into rejecting God's commandment and counsel; and the same now holds good with regard to those saving commandments and counsels which we later received. Just as now those who do not choose courageously to resist sin, and who set the divine commandments at nought, end up – if they do not renew their souls through repentance – by following a path that leads to inner and eternal death, so our two primal ancestors, by not resisting those who persuaded them to disobey, violated the commandment. Because of this the sentence previously proclaimed to them by Him who judges justly immediately took effect, so that as soon as they ate of the tree they died. At this they understood in

practice the meaning of the commandment which they had forgotten – the commandment of truth, love, wisdom and power – and they hid themselves in shame (cf. Gen. 3 : 7–8), perceiving themselves to be stripped of the glory that bestows on immortal spirits a more excellent life and without which the life of spiritual beings is believed to be and is indeed far worse than many deaths.

49. That it was not yet to our ancestors' benefit to eat of the tree is made clear by St Gregory of Nazianzos when he writes: 'The tree, in my vision of things, is divine contemplation, which only those established in a high degree of perfection can safely approach, while it is not good for those who are still immature and greedy in their desires, just as solid food is not good for those who are yet tender and have need of milk.'[1] But even if you do not want to refer that tree and its fruit anagogically to divine contemplation, it is not difficult, I think, to see that eating its fruit was of no benefit to our ancestors, since they were still immature. In my opinion they saw that the tree was the most attractive in paradise to look at and to eat from. But the food most pleasant to the senses is not truly and in every way good, nor is it always good, nor good for everyone. Rather it is good for those who can make use of it without being mastered by it, and then only when it is necessary and to the extent that it is necessary, and for the glory of Him who made it; but it is not good for those who are unable to make use of it in such a manner. It is on account of this, I think, that the tree was called the tree of the knowledge of good and evil (cf. Gen. 2 : 17). For only those fully established in the practice of divine contemplation and virtue can have concourse with things strongly attractive to the senses without withdrawing their intellect from the contemplation of God and from hymns and prayers to Him. Only such people can make these things the material and starting-point for raising themselves to God, and through this noetic movement towards God can totally master sensual pleasure. And even though the pleasure may be novel, and may be greater and more powerful because of its novelty, they will not allow their soul's intelligence to be overcome by that which is evil, even though at the time it is regarded as good by those totally captured and mastered by it.

50. Consequently our ancestors – who since they dwelt in the

---

[1] *Oration* 38, 12 (*P.G.* xxxvi, 324C); cf. Heb. 5 : 12–14.

sacred land of paradise should never have forgotten God – ought first
to have acquired more practice and, so to speak, schooling in simple,
genuine goodness and to have gained greater stability in the life of
contemplation. Being still in an imperfect and intermediate state – that
is to say, easily influenced, whether for good or evil, by whatever they
made use of – they should not have ventured on the experience of
things pleasant to the senses. They ought especially to have been on
their guard against things that by nature greatly allure and dominate
the senses and that seduce the entire intellect and give access to evil
passions, thus rendering plausible the originator and creator of these
passions. Now, after the devil, the cause of the passions is the
impassioned eating of the most delectable kinds of foods. For if, as
Scripture testifies, simply the sight of the tree was enough to make the
serpent an acceptable and trustworthy counsellor, how much more
would the taste of the fruit have the same effect? And if this is true for
the taste, how much more is it so for eating to repletion? Thus is it not
clear that it was not yet profitable for our ancestors to eat of that tree
through the senses? And because they did eat of it at the wrong time,
was it not necessary for them to be cast out of paradise, to prevent
them from making that divine land a council-chamber and workshop
of evil? And should they not have undergone bodily death immediately
after their transgression? But the Lord was long-suffering and patient
with them.

51. The soul's death sentence, brought into effect by man's
transgression, was in accord with the Creator's justice; for when our
forefathers forsook God and chose to do their own will, He abandoned
them, not subjecting them to constraint. And, for the reasons we have
stated above, God in His compassion had already forewarned them of
this sentence (cf. Gen. 2 : 17). But in the abyss of His wisdom and the
superabundance of His compassion he forbore and delayed in
executing the sentence of death upon the body; and when He did
pronounce it He relegated its execution to the future. He did not say to
Adam, 'Return whence you were taken', but 'You are earth, and to
earth you will return' (Gen. 3 : 19). Those who listen to these words
with intelligence can gather from them that God did not make death
(cf. Wisd. 1 : 13), neither that of the soul nor that of the body. He did
not originally give the command, 'Die on the day you eat of it'; on the
contrary, He said simply, 'You will die on the day you eat of it' (Gen.
2 : 17). Nor did He say, 'Return now to earth', but 'You will return'

(Gen. 3 : 19). This He said as a forewarning, but He then delayed its just execution, without prejudicing the eventual outcome.

52. Death was thus to become the lot of our forefathers, just as it lies in store for us who are now living, and our body was rendered mortal. Death is thus a kind of protracted process or, rather, there are myriads of deaths, one death succeeding the next until we reach the one final and long-enduring death. For we are born into corruption, and having once come into existence we are in a state of transiency until we cease from this constant passing away and coming to be. We are never truly the same, although we may appear to be so to those who do not observe us closely. Just as a flame that catches one end of a slender reed changes continually, and its existence is measured by the length of the reed, so we likewise are ever changing, and our measure is the length of life appointed to each of us.

53. That we should not be entirely ignorant of the superabundance of His compassion for us and the abyss of His wisdom, God deferred man's death, allowing him to live for a considerably longer time. From the first God shows that His discipline is merciful or, rather, that He delays a just chastisement so that we do not utterly despair. He also granted time for repentance and for a new life pleasing to Him, while through the succession of generations He eased the sorrow produced by death. He increased the human race with descendants so that initially the number of those being born would greatly exceed the number of those who died. In the place of one man, Adam, who became pitiable and impoverished through the sensible beauty of a tree, God brought forth many men who by means of things perceptible to the senses became blessedly enriched with divine wisdom, with virtue, with knowledge and divine favour: for example, Seth, Enos, Enoch, Noah, Melchisedec, Abraham, and those who were their contemporaries or who lived before them and after them, and who proved to be their equals, or nearly so. But there was no one among these great men who passed his life utterly free of sin, so that he might retrieve the defeat which our forefathers had suffered, heal the wound at the root of our race and be sufficient warranty for the sanctification, blessing and return to life of all who followed. God foreknew this; and during the course of time He chose out people from among the races and tribes who would produce that celebrated staff from which would blossom the Flower that was to accomplish the saving economy of our whole race (cf. Num. 17 : 8; Isa. 11 : 1).

54. O the depth of God's riches, wisdom and compassion (cf. Rom. 11 : 33)! Had there been no death and had our race not become mortal prior to death – for it is from a mortal root – we should not in fact have been enriched with the firstfruit of immortality, nor should we have been called into the heavens, nor would our nature have been enthroned 'above every principality and power' (Eph. 1 : 21) 'at the right hand of the Majesty in the heavens' (Heb. 8 : 1). Thus God in His wisdom, power and compassion knows how to change for the better the lapses we suffer as a result of our freely-willed perversion.

55. Many may blame Adam for being so easily persuaded by that wicked counsellor and for rejecting the divine commandment, thus becoming the agent of death for us all. Yet to wish to taste a deadly plant before actually doing so, and to desire to eat of such a plant after having learned by experience that it is deadly, are not the same thing. The man who drinks poison knowing that it is poison, and so wretchedly causes his own death, is more culpable than he who takes poison and so kills himself without knowing beforehand that it is poison. Therefore each of us is more culpable and guilty than Adam. But, you might ask, is that tree really within us? Do we still have a commandment from God forbidding us to eat from that tree? Perhaps exactly that same tree is not within us, yet the commandment of God is with us even now. And if we obey it, and try to lead our life in accordance with it, it frees us from punishment for all our sins, as well as from the ancestral curse and condemnation. But if we now reject it, and choose instead the provocation and counsel of the evil one, we cannot but fall away from the life and fellowship of paradise and be cast into the gehenna of everlasting fire with which we were threatened.

56. What, then, is the divine commandment now laid upon us? It is repentance, the essence of which is never again to touch forbidden things. We were expelled from the land of divine delight, we were justly shut out from God's paradise, and we have fallen into this pit where we are condemned to dwell together with dumb creatures without hope of returning – in so far as it depends on us – to the paradise we have lost. But He who initially passed a just sentence of punishment or, rather, justly permitted punishment to come upon us, has now in His great goodness, compassion and mercy descended for our sake to us. And He became a human being like us in all things except sin so that by His likeness to us He might teach us anew and rescue us; and He gave us the saving counsel and commandment of

repentance, saying: 'Repent, for the kingdom of heaven has drawn near' (Matt. 3 : 2). Prior to the incarnation of the Logos of God the kingdom of heaven was as far from us as the sky is from the earth; but when the King of heaven came to dwell amongst us and chose to unite Himself with us, the kingdom of heaven drew near to us all.

57. Since the Logos of God through His descent to us has brought the kingdom of heaven close to us, let us not distance ourselves from it by leading an unrepentant life. Let us rather flee the wretchedness of those who sit 'in darkness and the shadow of death' (Isa. 9 : 2). Let us acquire the fruits of repentance: a humble disposition, compunction and spiritual grief, a gentle and merciful heart that loves righteousness and pursues purity, peaceful, peace-making, patient in toil, glad to endure persecution, loss, outrage, slander and suffering for the sake of truth and righteousness. For the kingdom of heaven or, rather, the King of heaven – ineffable in His generosity – is within us (cf. Luke 17 : 21); and to Him we should cleave through acts of repentance and patient endurance, loving as much as we can Him who so dearly has loved us.

58. Absence of passions and the possession of virtue constitute love for God; for hatred of evil, resulting in the absence of passions, introduces in its place the desire for and acquisition of spiritual blessings. How could the lover and possessor of such blessings not love God above all, the Master who is Benediction itself, the only provider and guardian of every good thing? For in a special way such a person is in God, and by means of love he also bears God within himself, in accordance with the words, 'He who dwells in love dwells in God, and God in him' (1 John 4 : 16). Thus we can see both that love for God is begotten from the virtues and that the virtues are born of love. For this reason the Lord said at one point in the Gospel, 'He who has My commandments and keeps them is the one who loves Me' (John 14 : 21), and at another point, 'He who loves Me will keep My commandments' (cf. John 14 : 23). But without love the works of virtue are not praiseworthy or profitable to the man who practises them, and the same is true of love without works. St Paul makes this fully clear with reference to works when he writes to the Corinthians, 'If I do this and that, but have no love, it profits me nothing' (cf. 1 Cor. 13 : 1–3); and with reference to love the disciple especially beloved by Christ writes, 'Let us not love in word or tongue but in action and truth' (1 John 3 : 18).

59. The sublime and worshipful Father is the Father of Truth itself, that is, of the Only-begotten Son; and the Holy Spirit is a spirit of truth, as the Logos of truth proclaimed (cf. John 14 : 17). Those who worship the Father 'in Spirit and in Truth', and who believe accordingly, are activated by Them. As St Paul says, 'It is through the Spirit that we worship and pray' (cf. Rom: 8 : 26), while the Only-begotten Son of God says, 'No one comes to the Father except through Me' (John 14 : 6). Hence those who worship the supreme Father 'in Spirit and in Truth' are the true worshippers (John 4 : 23).

60. 'God is spirit, and those who worship Him must worship Him in spirit and in truth' (John 4 : 24) – that is to say, by conceiving the Incorporeal incorporeally. For thus they will truly behold Him everywhere in His spirit and His truth. Since God is spirit, He is incorporeal. That which is incorporeal is not situated in place, nor is it circumscribed by spatial boundaries. Thus he who claims that God must be worshipped in certain restricted places within the plenitude of heaven and earth neither speaks nor worships truly. As incorporeal, God is nowhere; as God, He is everywhere. For if there were a mountain or place or creature where God is not, He would be circumscribed by something. He is, therefore, everywhere, since He has no limit. But how can God be everywhere? As encompassed, not by a part, but by the whole? Assuredly not, for then once again He would be a body. Thus since He sustains and embraces everything, He is in Himself both everywhere and beyond everything, and is worshipped by His true worshippers in His Spirit and His Truth (cf. John 4 : 23).

61. Since angels and souls are incorporeal beings, they are not in a particular place, yet neither are they everywhere. They do not sustain all things, but themselves depend on Him who sustains them. Hence they, too, are in Him who sustains and embraces all things, and they are appropriately delimited by Him. The soul, since it sustains the body with which it is created, is everywhere in the body, although not in the sense of being located in a place or encompassed; but it itself sustains, encompasses and quickens the body, by virtue of the fact that it is in God's image.

62. Man is created more perfectly in God's image than the angels, both because he possesses in himself a sustaining and quickening power and because he has a capacity for sovereignty. There is within our soul's nature a governing and ruling faculty, and there is also that which is naturally subservient and obedient, namely, will, appetite,

sense-perception, and in general everything that is sequent to the intellect and that was created by God together with the intellect. And these things may be termed subservient even though, incited by a sin-loving disposition, we rebel not only against the all-ruling God but also against the ruling power inherent in our nature. God, then, by virtue of our capacity for sovereignty, has given us lordship over all the earth. But angels do not have a body joined to them and subject to their intellect. Angels that have fallen have acquired a noetic volition which is perpetually evil, while the good angels possess one that is perpetually good and has no need of a bridle. The evil one has no dominion upon earth which he has not stolen, and it is therefore evident that he was not created as ruler of the earth. The Ruler of All appointed the good angels to be overseers of the earth after our fall and our subsequent loss of rank, even though, due to God's compassion, the fall was not total. For, as Moses said in his *Ode*, God established boundaries for the angels when He divided the nations (cf. Deut. 32 : 8). This division took place after Cain and Seth, when Cain's descendants were called men and Seth's descendants were called the sons of God (cf. Gen. 6 : 2). From that time, it seems to me, the race from which the Only-begotten Son of God would take His flesh was foretokened by the differentiation of names.

63. As others have also pointed out, the threefold nature of our knowledge likewise demonstrates that we, to a greater extent than the angels, are created in God's image. Indeed, this knowledge is not only threefold but also encompasses every form of knowledge. We alone of all creatures have a faculty of sense-perception in addition to our noetic and rational faculties. Since this faculty is united to our reason we have invented multifarious arts, sciences and forms of knowledge. Only to man is it given to farm, to build and to produce from nothing – but not from absolute non-being, for this pertains only to God. Indeed, even in God's case scarcely anything that He effects in the world starts from nothing or utterly perishes, but when differently combined together things take a different form. In addition, by the gift of God it pertains to men alone both to make the invisible thought of the intellect audible by uniting it with the air and to write it down so that it may be seen with and through the body. God thus leads us to a steadfast faith in the abiding presence and manifestation of the supreme Logos in the flesh. But angels have no share whatsoever in any of these things.

64. Even though we still bear God's image to a greater degree than the angels, yet as regards the likeness of God we fall far short of them. This is especially true if we compare our present state with that of the good angels. Leaving aside other matters for the present, I shall simply say that perfection of the divine likeness is accomplished by means of the divine illumination that issues from God. There is, I think, no one who reads the divinely inspired Scriptures with diligence and understanding who does not know that the evil angels are deprived of this illumination and are therefore 'under darkness' (Jude 6), whereas the divine intellects are entirely filled with divine illumination and for this reason are called 'a secondary light' and 'an emanation of the Primal Light'.[1] As emanations of the First Light, the good angels also possess knowledge of sensible objects, though they do not apprehend these things by any physical faculty of perception, but know them by means of a divine power from which nothing present, past or future can be hidden.

65. Whoever partakes of this divine illumination, partakes of it to a certain degree; and to a proportionate degree he also possesses a spiritual knowledge of created things. All who assiduously study the writings of the divinely wise theologians know that the angels likewise partake of this illumination, and that it is uncreated but is not the divine essence. Yet those who hold the views of Barlaam and Akindynos think otherwise and blaspheme this divine illumination, obstinately affirming either that it is created or that it is the essence of God. And when they affirm it to be created, they deny that it is the light of the angels. But let the revealer of things divine, St Dionysios the Areopagite, concisely elucidate these three matters for us. 'The divine intellects,' he writes, 'move in a circular fashion, uniting themselves with the unoriginate and unending illuminations of the Beautiful and Good.'[2] It is clear to everyone that by divine intellects he means the good angels. And by referring to these illuminations in the plural, he distinguishes them from the divine essence, since this is single and is altogether indivisible; and by calling them unoriginate and endless, what else could he mean to say except that they are uncreated?

66. Through the fall our nature was stripped of this divine illumination and resplendence. But the Logos of God had pity upon

---

[1] St Gregory of Nazianzos, *Oration* 40, 5 (*P.G.* xxxvi, 364B).
[2] *On the Divine Names* iv, 8 (*P.G.* iii, 704D).

our disfigurement and in His compassion He took our nature upon Himself, and on Tabor He manifested it to His elect disciples clothed once again most brilliantly. As St John Chrysostom says, He shows what we once were and what we shall become through Him in the age to come, if we choose to live our present life as far as possible in accordance with His ways.[1]

67. Adam, before the fall, also participated in this divine illumination and resplendence, and because he was truly clothed in a garment of glory he was not naked, nor was he unseemly by reason of his nakedness. He was far more richly adorned than those who now deck themselves out with diadems of gold and brightly sparkling jewels. St Paul calls this divine illumination and grace our celestial dwelling when he says, 'For this we sigh, yearning to be clothed in our heavenly habitation, since thus clothed we will not be found naked' (2 Cor. 5 : 2). And St Paul himself received from God the pledge of this divine illumination and of our investiture in it on his way from Jerusalem to Damaskos (cf. Acts 9 : 3). As St Gregory of Nazianzos, surnamed the Theologian, has written, 'Before he was cleansed of his persecutions Paul spoke with Him whom he was persecuting or, rather, with a brief irradiation of the great Light.'[2]

68. The divine supraessentiality is never named in the plural. But the divine and uncreated grace and energy of God is indivisibly divided, like the sun's rays that warm, illumine, quicken and bring increase as they cast their radiance upon what they enlighten, and shine on the eyes of whoever beholds them. In the manner, then, of this faint likeness, the divine energy of God is called not only one but also multiple by the theologians. Thus St Basil the Great declares: 'What are the energies of the Spirit? Their greatness cannot be told and they are numberless. How can we comprehend what precedes the ages? What were God's energies before the creation of noetic reality?'[3] For prior to the creation of noetic reality and beyond the ages – for the ages are also noetic creations – no one has ever spoken or conceived of anything created. Therefore the powers and energies of the divine Spirit – even though they are said in theology to be multiple

[1] Cf. *Homilies on Matthew* 56, 4 (*P.G.* lviii, 554–5).

[2] *Oration* 39, 9 (*P.G.* xxxvi, 344B).

[3] *On the Holy Spirit* xix (49) (*P.G.* xxxii, 156D).

– are uncreated and are to be indivisibly distinguished from the single and wholly undivided essence of the Spirit.

69. The theologians affirm that the uncreated energy of God is indivisibly divided and multiple, as St Basil the Great has explained above. And since the divine and deifying illumination and grace is not the essence but the energy of God, for this reason it comes forth from God not only in the singular but in multiplicity as well. It is bestowed proportionately on those who participate in it, and corresponding to the capacity of those who receive it the deifying resplendence enters them to a greater or lesser degree.

70. Isaiah has said that these energies are seven in number, and for the Jews the number seven signifies a multiplicity. 'There shall come forth', he says, 'a rod out of the root of Jesse, and a flower shall come from it; and seven spirits shall rest upon Him: the spirit of wisdom, understanding, knowledge, reverence, counsel, strength and fear' (cf. Isa. 11 : 1–2). Those who hold the views of Barlaam and Akindynos dementedly maintain that these seven spirits are created; but this error we have refuted exhaustively in our *Refutation of Akindynos*. Moreover, referring to these energies of the Spirit, St Gregory of Nazianzos says, 'Isaiah likes to call the energies of the Spirit spirits.'[1] And Isaiah himself, the clarion voice of the prophets, not only distinguished them plainly from the divine essence by their number, but also indicated the uncreated nature of these divine energies by the words 'rest upon Him'. For to 'rest upon' is the privilege of a superior dignity. How, then, could those spirits that rest upon the humanity the Lord assumed from us have a created character?

71. Our Lord Jesus Christ cast out demons 'with the finger of God', according to Luke (11 : 20); but Matthew says 'by the Spirit of God' (12 : 28). St Basil explains that the finger of God is one of the Spirit's energies.[2] If one of these energies is the Holy Spirit, most certainly the others are as well, as St Basil also teaches us. Yet there are not for this reason many gods or many Spirits. These energies are processions, manifestations and natural operations of the one Spirit and in each case the operative agent is one. Yet the heterodox make the Spirit of God a created being seven times over when they assert that these energies are created. But let them be humiliated sevenfold, for

---

[1] *Oration* 41, 3 (*P.G.* xxxvi, 432C).
[2] St Basil (attributed to), *Against Eunomios* v (*P.G.* xxix, 716C–717A).

the prophet Zechariah calls these energies 'the seven eyes of the Lord that look upon all the earth' (4 : 10). And St John writes in Revelation, 'Grace be with you, and peace from God and from the seven spirits that are before His throne, and from Christ' (cf. Rev. 1 : 4–5), thus making it clear to the faithful that these are the Holy Spirit.

72. When God the Father preannounced through the prophet Micah the birth in the flesh of His Only-begotten Son, and wished to indicate also the unoriginate nature of Christ's divinity, He said: 'And His goings forth have been from the beginning, even from an eternity of days' (5 : 2. LXX). The holy fathers explain that these 'goings forth' are the energies of the Godhead, for the powers and energies are the same for Father, Son and Holy Spirit. Yet those who strive to vindicate the views of Barlaam and Akindynos proclaim these energies to be created. Let them, however, come to their senses, late though it is, and comprehend who it is that exists from the beginning, and who it is to whom David says: 'From eternity' – which has the same meaning as 'from an eternity of days' – 'and to eternity Thou art' (Ps. 89 : 2). Let them intelligently consider, if they will, that when God said through His prophet that these goings forth are from the beginning, He did not say that they came into being, or were made or created. And St Basil, inspired by the Spirit of God, said, not that the energies of the Spirit 'came into being', but that they existed 'prior to the creation of noetic reality' and 'beyond the ages'.[1] Only God is operative and all-powerful from eternity, and therefore He possesses pre-eternal operations and powers.

73. In obvious opposition to the saints, those who champion the views of Akindynos say that there is only one thing that is uncreated, namely, the divine nature, and that anything that is in any way distinguished from the divine nature is created. Hereby they declare the Father, Son and Holy Spirit to be created beings, for there is one and the same energy for the three, and that of which the energy is created cannot itself be uncreated. Thus that which is created is not God's energy – this is impossible – but what is effected and accomplished by the divine energy. This is why St John of Damaskos teaches that the energy, although distinct from the divine nature, is

---

[1] Cf. On the Holy Spirit xix (49) (P.G. xxxii, 156CD).

also an essential, that is to say, a natural activity of that nature.[1] Since, then, it is the property of the divine energy to create, as St Cyril has said,[2] how could this energy be something created, unless it was activated by another energy, and that energy in turn by still another, and so on *ad infinitum*? In this way we would always be looking for the uncreated source of the energy.

74. Because both the divine essence and the divine energy are everywhere inseparably present, God's energy is accessible also to us creatures; for, according to the theologians it is indivisibly divided, whereas the divine nature, they say, remains totally undivided. Thus St John Chrysostom says, 'A drop of grace filled all things with knowledge; through it miracles were wrought and sins forgiven.' Here, while indicating that this drop of grace is uncreated, he hastens to make it clear that it is an energy of God but not His essence. Further, in order to show how the divine energy differs both from the divine essence and from the hypostasis of the Spirit, he adds, 'I mean a part of the energy, for the Paraclete is not divided.'[3] Therefore God's grace and energy is accessible to each one of us, since it is divided indivisibly. But since God's essence is in every way indivisible, how could it be accessible to any created being?

75. Three realities pertain to God: essence, energy, and the triad of divine hypostases. As we have seen, those privileged to be united to God so as to become one spirit with Him – as St Paul said, 'He who cleaves to the Lord is one spirit with Him' (1 Cor. 6 : 17) – are not united to God with respect to His essence, since all the theologians testify that with respect to His essence God suffers no participation. Moreover, the hypostatic union is fulfilled only in the case of the Logos, the God-man. Thus those privileged to attain union with God are united to Him with respect to His energy; and the 'spirit', according to which they who cleave to God are one with Him, is and is called the uncreated energy of the Holy Spirit, but not the essence of God, even though Barlaam and Akindynos may disagree. Thus God prophesied through His prophet saying, 'I shall pour forth', not 'My Spirit', but 'of My Spirit upon the faithful' (cf. Joel 2 : 28. LXX).

---

[1] *On the Orthodox Faith* ii, 23 and iii, 15 (*P.G.* xciv, 949AB, 1048A): ed. Kotter, §§ 37, 59, pp. 93, 144.

[2] St Cyril of Alexandria, *Treasuries* 18 (*P.G.* lxxv, 312C).

[3] *On Psalm 44*, § 3 (*P.G.* lv, 186).

76. According to St Maximos, 'Moses and David, and whoever else became vessels of divine energy by laying aside the properties of their fallen nature, were inspired by the power of God';[1] and, 'They became living ikons of Christ, being the same as He is, by grace rather than by assimilation.'[2] He further says, 'The purity in Christ and in the saints is one.'[3] As the divine Psalmist chants, 'May the splendour of our God be upon us' (Ps. 90 : 17. LXX). For according to St Basil, 'Spirit-bearing souls, when illumined by the Spirit, both become spiritual themselves and shed forth grace upon others. From this comes foreknowledge of things future, understanding of mysteries, apprehension of things hidden, distribution of spiritual gifts, citizenship in heaven, the dance with the angels, unending joy, divine largesse, likeness to God, and the desire of all desires, to become god.'[4]

77. The angels excel men with respect to this grace, resplendence, and union with God. On this account they are secondary luminaries, ministers of the supreme resplendence. 'The noetic powers and ministering spirits are secondary lights and irradiations of the primal Light.'[5] The angels are 'the first luminous nature after the Primal Being, because they shine forth from It'.[6] 'An angel is a secondary light, an emanation or a communication of the Primal Light.'[7] 'The divine intellects move in a circular fashion, uniting themselves with the unoriginate and unending illuminations of the Beautiful and Good',[8] for 'God Himself and naught else is light for eternal beings';[9] 'What the sun is for sensory beings, God is for noetic beings. He is the primal and supreme light illumining all intelligent nature.'[10] As St John Chrysostom says, when you hear the prophet saying, 'I saw the Lord sitting upon a throne' (Isa. 6 : 1), understand that he saw not God's essence but His gift of Himself, and this even more obscurely than the supreme powers behold it.[11]

[1] *Disputation with Pyrrhos* (P.G. xci, 297A).
[2] *Ambigua* 21 (P.G. xci, 1253D).
[3] Cf. *To Marinos* (P.G. xci, 33A).
[4] *On the Holy Spirit* ix (23) (P.G. xxxii, 109C).
[5] St Gregory of Nazianzos, *Oration* 44, 3 (P.G. xxxvi, 609B).
[6] Id., *Oration* 45, 2 (P.G. xxxvi, 624C).
[7] Id., *Oration* 40, 5 (P.G. xxxvi, 364B).
[8] St Dionysios the Areopagite, *On the Divine Names* iv, 8 (P.G. iii, 704D).
[9] St Gregory of Nazianzos, *Oration* 44, 3 (P.G. xxxvi, 609C).
[10] Cf. id., *Oration* 40, 5 (P.G. xxxvi, 364B).
[11] Cf. *On Isaiah* 6, 1 (P.G. lvi, 68).

78. Every created nature is far removed from and completely foreign to the divine nature. For if God is nature, other things are not nature; but if every other thing is nature, He is not a nature, just as He is not a being if all other things are beings. And if He is a being, then all other things are not beings. And if you accept this as true also for wisdom, goodness, and in general all things that pertain to God or are ascribed to Him, then your theology will be correct and in accordance with the saints. God both is and is said to be the nature of all beings, in so far as all partake of Him and subsist by means of this participation: not, however, by participation in His nature – far from it – but by participation in His energy. In this sense He is the Being of all beings, the Form that is in all forms as the Author of form, the Wisdom of the wise and, simply, the All of all things. Moreover, He is not nature, because He transcends every nature; He is not a being, because He transcends every being; and He is not nor does He possess a form, because He transcends form. How, then, can we draw near to God? By drawing near to His nature? But not a single created being has or can have any communication with or proximity to the sublime nature. Thus if anyone has drawn close to God, he has evidently approached Him by means of His energy. In what way? By natural participation in that energy? But this is common to all created things. It is not, therefore, by virtue of natural qualities, but by virtue of what one achieves through free choice that one is close to or distant from God. But free choice pertains only to beings endowed with intelligence. So among all creatures only those endowed with intelligence can be far from or close to God, drawing close to Him through virtue or becoming distant through vice. Thus such beings alone are capable of wretchedness or blessedness. Let us strive to lay hold of blessedness.

79. When created beings are compared among themselves, some are said to be naturally akin to God and others alien. The noetic natures that are apprehended by the intellect alone are, so it is claimed, akin to the Divinity, whereas all natures subject to sense-perception are in every way alien to It; and those among them that are utterly bereft of soul and unmoving are the most remote of all. Thus, when compared among themselves, created beings are said to be naturally either akin or alien to God. Properly speaking, however, all of them in themselves are alien to Him by nature. Indeed, it is no more possible to say how distant noetic nature is from God than how remote sense-perception and the things of the realm of the senses are from noetic

beings. If we are, then, by nature so far removed from God, alas for us if we do not draw close to Him by freely choosing to act well and to conduct ourselves with probity.

80. The inspired and universal tongue of the divine theologians, St John of Damaskos, says in the second of his theological chapters: 'A man who would speak or hear anything about God should know with all clarity that in what concerns theology and the divine economy not all things are inexpressible and not all are capable of expression, and neither are all things unknowable nor are they all knowable.'[1] We know that those divine realities of which we desire to speak transcend speech, since such realities exist according to a principle that is transcendent. They are not outside the realm of speech by reason of some deficiency, but are beyond the conceptual power innate within us and to which we give utterance when speaking to others. For neither can our speech explain these realities by interpretation, nor does our innate conceptual power have the capacity to attain them of its own accord through investigation. Thus we should not permit ourselves to say anything concerning God, but rather we should have recourse to those who in the Spirit speak of the things of the Spirit, and this is the case even when our adversaries require some statement from us.

81. It is said that on the portals of Plato's academy were inscribed the words, 'Let no man enter who is ignorant of geometry.' A person incapable of conceiving and discoursing about inseparable things as separate is in every respect ignorant of geometry. For there cannot be a limit without something limited. But geometry is almost entirely a science of limits, and it even defines and extends limits on their own account, abstracted from that which they limit, because the intellect separates the inseparable. How, then, can a person who has never learnt to separate in his intellect a physical object from its attributes be able to conceive of nature in itself? For nature is not merely inseparable from the natural elements in which it inheres, but it cannot even exist at any time without them. How can he conceive of universals as universals, since they exist as such in particulars and are distinguished from them only by the intelligence and reason, being perceived intellectually as prior to the many particulars although in truth they can in no way exist apart from these many particulars? How shall he

---

[1] *On the Orthodox Faith* i, 2 (*P.G.* xciv, 792B): ed. Kotter, § 2, p. 8.

apprehend intellectual and noetic things? How shall he understand us when we say that each intellect also has thought and that each of our thoughts is our intellect? How shall he not ridicule us and accuse us of saying that each man possesses two or many minds?

If, then, someone is unable to speak or conceive of things indivisible as distinct, how will he be able to discuss or be taught anything of this sort concerning God, with respect to whom, according to the theologians, there are and are said to be many unions and distinctions? But although the unions pertaining to God prevail over and are prior to the distinctions, they do not abolish them nor are they at all impeded by them. The followers of Akindynos, however, cannot accept nor can they understand the indivisible distinction that exists in God, even when they hear us speaking – in harmony with the saints – of a divided union. For to God pertains both incomprehensibility and comprehensibility, though He Himself is one. The same God is incomprehensible in His essence, but comprehensible from what He creates according to His divine energies: according, that is, to His pre-eternal will for us, His pre-eternal providence concerning us, His pre-eternal wisdom with regard to us, and – to use the words of St Maximos – His infinite power, wisdom and goodness. But when Barlaam and Akindynos and those who follow in their footsteps hear us saying these things which we are obliged to say, they accuse us of speaking of many gods and many uncreated realities, and of making God composite. For they are ignorant of the fact that God is indivisibly divided and is united dividedly, and yet in spite of this suffers neither multiplicity nor compositeness.

82. St Paul, the mouth of Christ, the chosen vessel, the glorious chariot of the divine name, says, 'From the creation of the world the invisible realities of God, namely, His eternal power and divinity, may be perceived in created things by means of intellection' (Rom. 1 : 20). May, then, the essence of God be perceived in created things by means of intellection? Certainly not. This is the madness of Barlaam and Akindynos and, before them, the delusion of Eunomios.[1] For, prior to them but in the same manner, Eunomios in his discourses wrote that from created things we may comprehend nothing less than God's

---

[1] Eunomios (d. 394) was a leading member of the extreme Arian group known as the Anomoeans; his teaching was refuted by the Cappadocian Fathers.

essence itself. St Paul, however, is very far from teaching any such thing. For having just stated, 'What can be known of God is manifest' (Rom. 1 : 19), and having thus indicated that there exists something else beyond that which can be known about God and which He Himself has made manifest to all men of intelligence, he then adds: 'For from the creation of the world the invisible realities of God may be perceived in created things by means of intellection.' You may in this way learn what it is that is knowable about God. The holy fathers explain that what is unknowable in God is His essence, while what may be known is that which pertains to His essence, namely, goodness, wisdom, power, divinity and majesty. These St Paul also calls invisible, though they are perceived in created things by means of intellection. But how could these things, which pertain to God's essence and may be perceived in things created, be themselves created? Therefore the divine energy, intellected through created things, is both uncreated and yet not the essence. For the divine energy is referred to not only in the singular but also in the plural.

83. In refuting Eunomios, who claimed that the essence of God is revealed by created things, St Basil the Great writes that 'created things manifest wisdom, art and power, but not essence'.[1] Thus the divine energy made manifest by created things is both uncreated and yet not God's essence; and those who like Barlaam and Akindynos say that there is no difference between the divine essence and the divine energy are clearly Eunomians.

84. Most excellently does St Gregory of Nyssa, St Basil's bodily and spiritual brother, say in his refutation of Eunomios: 'When we perceive the beauty and grandeur of the wonders of creation, and from these and similar things derive other intellections concerning the Divinity, we interpret each of the intellections produced in us by its own distinctive name. "For from the grandeur and beauty of created things the Creator is contemplated by way of analogy" (Wisd. 13 : 5). We also call the Creator the Demiurge; Powerful, in that His power is sufficient to make His will reality; and Just, as the impartial Judge. Likewise the term God (*Theos*) we have taken from His providential and overseeing activity. In this manner, then, by the term God we have been taught about a certain partial activity of the divine nature, but we

---

[1] *Against Eunomios* ii, 32 (*P.G.* xxix, 648A).

have not attained an understanding of God's essence by means of this word.'[1]

85. St Dionysios the Areopagite, the most eminent theologian after the divine apostles, having clarified the distinction of the hypostases in God, says: 'The beneficent procession is a divine distinction, for the divine unity in a transcendently united manner multiplies and makes itself manifold through goodness.'[2] And a little further on he says: 'We call divine distinction the beneficial processions of the Thearchy. For in bestowing itself upon all beings and abundantly pouring forth participation in all good things, it is distinguished in its unity, multiplied in its oneness, and made manifold without ceasing to be one.'[3] Later he writes: 'These common and united distinctions – or, rather, these beneficent processions – of the whole Godhead we will try to praise to the best of our ability.'[4]

Thus St Dionysios shows clearly that there is also another distinction in God besides the distinction of the hypostases, and this distinction that is different from that of the hypostases he calls the distinction of the Godhead. For, indeed, the distinction of the hypostases is not a distinction pertaining to the Godhead. And he says that according to the divine processions and energies God multiplies Himself and makes Himself manifold, and he states in this respect that the procession may be spoken of both in the singular and in the plural. In regard to the distinction of the hypostases, however, the Deity certainly does not multiply Himself, nor as God is He subject to distinction. For us God is a Trinity, but not triple. St Dionysios also affirms that these processions and energies are uncreated, since he calls them divine and says that they are distinctions pertaining to the whole Godhead. He likewise says that the very Thearchy itself multiplies and makes Itself manifold according to these divine processions and energies, though not certainly by assuming anything external. Furthermore, this most sublime of the divine hymnologists promises to celebrate these processions; but he adds, 'to the best of our ability', in order to show that they transcend all celebration.

86. Having said that the beneficent procession is a divine

---

[1] *Against Eunomios* ii (xiiB) (*P.G.* xlv, 1105C–1108B): ed. W. Jaeger, vol. i (Leiden, 1960), pp. 396–7.

[2] *On the Divine Names* ii, 5 (*P.G.* iii, 641D–644A).

[3] Ibid., ii, 11 (649B).

[4] Ibid. (652A).

distinction, this same revealer of things divine adds: 'Yet the unconditioned communications are united with respect to the divine distinction.'[1] Here he groups together all the processions and energies of God and calls them communications. He says further that they are unconditioned, lest anyone should suppose that these communications are created effects such as the individual essence of each thing that exists, or the physical life of animals, or the reason and intellect inherent in rational and noetic beings. For how could these things be unconditioned in God and at the same time be created? And how could God's unconditioned processions and communications be created things, since the unconditioned communication is naturally inherent in the communicator, as we see in the case of light?

87. St Dionysios now goes on to celebrate these processions and energies with other godlike names, calling them participable principles and essential participable principles. In many places in his writings he shows them to be superior to existent things, and that they are the paradigms or exemplars of existent things, pre-existing in God by means of a supra-essential union. How, then, could they be created? He then tells us what these paradigms are, saying: 'We call paradigms the essence-forming *logoi* or inner principles of existent things; they unitedly pre-exist in God, and theology refers to them as the predeterminations and divine and sacred volitions that determine and create existent things. It is in accordance with them that the Supra-essential both predetermines and brings forth everything that is.'[2] How could the predeterminations and the divine volitions that create all existent things be themselves created? Is it not clear that those who maintain that these processions and energies are created degrade God's providence to the level of something created? For the energy that creates individual essence, life and wisdom, and in general makes and sustains created beings, is identical with the divine volitions and the divine participable principles and the gifts of supernal Goodness, the Cause of all.

88. The participable principle of absolute Being in no way participates in anything, as the great Dionysios also says. But the other participable principles, in that they are participable principles of existent things, also participate in nothing else whatsoever, for

---

[1] Op. cit., ii, 5 (*P.G.* iii, 644A).

[2] Op. cit., v, 8 (*P.G.* iii, 824C).

providence does not participate in providence, nor life in life. But in that they possess being they are said to participate in absolute Being, since without this they can neither exist nor be participated in, just as there can be no foreknowledge without knowledge. Thus, as essential participable principles, they are in no way created. Hence, according to St Maximos, they never began to be and they are seen to pertain to God in an essential manner, and there was never a time when they were not.[1] But when the followers of Barlaam impiously suppose that because life itself, goodness itself and so forth, share in the common denomination of existent things they are therefore created, they do not comprehend that although they are called existent things, they are also superior to existent things, as St Dionysios says.[2] Those who for this reason place the essential participable principles among created things could easily regard the Holy Spirit as created, whereas St Basil the Great says that the Spirit shares in names befitting the Divinity.[3]

89. Should someone claim that only absolute Being is a participable principle since it alone does not participate in anything but is solely participated in, whilst the other participable principles participate in it, he should know that he does not think aright with regard to the other participable principles. For living things or holy things or good things are said to live and to become holy and good by participation, not simply because they exist and participate in absolute Being, but because they partake of absolute life, holiness and goodness. But absolute life – and the same applies to other such realities – does not become absolute life by participation in some other absolute life. As absolute life, it is among those realities that are participated in, not among those that participate. How could that which does not participate in life, but is itself participated in by living things and quickens them, be something created? And one may say the same with regard to the other participable principles.

90. Let St Maximos now lend us his support. He writes in his *Scholia* that the providence creating existent things is identical with the processions of God. He says: 'The creative providences and good-nesses' – those that bestow individual essence, life and wisdom – 'are

[1] *Texts on Theology* ii, 48, 50; E.T., *The Philokalia*, vol. ii, pp. 123–4.
[2] *On the Divine Names* xi, 6 (P.G. iii, 953B–956B).
[3] *On the Holy Spirit* ix (22) (P.G. xxxii, 108A).

common to the tri-hypostatic differentiated Unity.'[1] By stating that these providences and goodnesses are many and distinct, he shows that they are not the essence of God, since that is one and altogether indivisible. But because they are common to the tri-hypostatic differentiated Unity, he shows us that they are not identical with the Son or the Holy Spirit, for neither the Son nor the Holy Spirit is an energy common to the three hypostases. Yet by stating that they are not only providences and goodnesses but are also creative, he shows them to be uncreated. For if this were not the case, then the creative power would itself be created by another creative power, and that in turn by another, and so on to the uttermost absurdity, not even stopping at infinity. Thus God's processions and energies are uncreated, and none of them is either divine essence or hypostasis.

91. In the incomparable superabundance of His goodness He who brought forth and adorned the universe established it as multiform. He willed that some things should simply possess being, while others should possess life in addition to being. Of these latter He willed that some should possess noetic life, that others should enjoy merely a sensible life, while others again should possess a life mingled of both. When this last category of beings had received from Him rational and noetic life, He willed that by the free inclination of their will towards Him they should achieve union with Him and thus live in a divine and supranatural manner, having been vouchsafed His deifying grace and energy. For His will is generation for things that exist, whether for those brought forth out of non-being, or for those being brought to a better state; and this takes place in diverse ways. Because of the diversity of the divine will with respect to existent things, the one providence and goodness of God – or, in other words, God's turning towards inferior beings by reason of His goodness – both is, and is thus called by the divinely wise theologians, many providences and goodnesses, for they are indivisibly divided and differentiated among divisible things. Thus one is called God's power of foreknowledge, and another His creative and sustaining power. Further, according to the great Dionysios, some bestow individual essence, some life, and some wisdom.[2] Now each of these powers is common to Father, Son and

---

[1] Scholia on the Divine Names of St Dionysios (P.G. iv, 221B).
[2] On the Divine Names ii, 5 (P.G. iii, 644A).

Holy Spirit, and in each good and divine volition with respect to us it is Father, Son and Holy Spirit that are its essence-bestowing, life-bestowing and wisdom-bestowing energy and power. These St Dionysios calls unconditioned and undiminishable communications, elevating them above all created things and teaching us that they inhere by nature in Him who communicates them.

92. Just as the sun without diminution communicates heat and light to those who participate in them, and itself possesses these qualities as its inherent and essential energies, so the divine communications, since they inhere without diminution in Him who bestows communion, are His natural and essential energies. Thus they are also uncreated. When the sun sets beneath the horizon and is no longer visible, not even a trace of its light remains; yet when it is visible, the eye that receives its light cannot but be mingled with it and united by it to the wellspring of light. The sun's warmth, however, and its effects which contribute to the generation and growth of sensible things, and to the manifold diversity of humours and qualities, do not desert these creatures, even when there is no contact with the sun through the sun's rays. In the same manner as indicated in this inadequate image taken from sensible reality, only those who aspire after the supernal and most divine light participate integrally in deifying grace and by it are united to God. All other beings are effects of the creative energy, brought forth from nothing by grace as a free gift but not illumined by grace, which is the same as God's resplendence.

93. This resplendence and deifying energy of God, that deifies those who participate in it, constitutes divine grace, but it is not the nature of God. This does not mean that God's nature is distant from those who have received grace – and this is Akindynos' ridiculous slander – for God's nature is everywhere; but it means that it is not participable, since no created thing, as we have already shown, is capable of participating in it. The divine energy and grace of the Spirit, being everywhere present and remaining inseparable from the Spirit, is imparticipable, as though absent, for those who on account of their impurity are unfit to participate in it. Just as faces, so it is said, are not reflected by every material, but only by such materials as possess smoothness and transparency, so the energy of the Spirit is not found in all souls, but only in those possessing no perversity or deviousness. Again, it is said that the Holy Spirit is present to all, but He manifests His power only in those who are purified from the passions, and does

not manifest it in those whose intellect is still confused by the defilement of sin.[1]

94. The light of the sun is inseparable from the sun's rays and from the heat which they dispense; yet for those who receive the rays but have no eyes the light is imparticipable and they sense only the heat coming from the rays. For those bereft of eyes cannot possibly perceive light. In the same way, but to a greater extent, no one who enjoys the divine radiance can participate in the essence of the Creator. For there is absolutely no creature that possesses the capacity to perceive the Creator's nature.

95. Here let St John, the Baptist of Christ, as well as St John who was more beloved by Christ than the other disciples, and St John Chrysostom, now bear witness with us that the participated divine energy is neither created nor the essence of God. St John the Evangelist does so by what he writes in his Gospel, the Forerunner and Baptist of Christ when he says: 'It is not by measure that the Spirit is given to Christ by God the Father' (cf. John 3 : 34). St John Chrysostom explains this passage when he states: 'Here "Spirit" means the energy of the Spirit. For all of us receive the energy of the Spirit by measure, but Christ possesses the Spirit's entire energy in full and without measure. But if His energy is without measure, how much more so is His essence.'[2] By calling the energy 'Spirit' – or, rather, the very Spirit of God – as the Baptist did, and by saying that the energy is without measure, Chrysostom showed its uncreated character. Again, by saying that we receive it by measure he indicated the difference between the uncreated energy and the uncreated essence of God. For no one ever receives the essence of God, not even if all men are taken collectively, each one receiving in part according to his degree of purity. Chrysostom then goes on to reveal another difference between the uncreated essence and the uncreated energy, for he says, 'If the energy of the Spirit is without measure, how much more so is His essence.'

96. If, according to the absurdities of Akindynos and those who share his views, the divine energy does not in any respect differ from the divine essence, then the act of creating, which is something that pertains to the energy, will not in any respect differ from the act of

---

[1] Cf. St Basil (attributed to), *On Isaiah* 3 (P.G. xxx, 121C–124A).
[2] *Homilies on John* 30, 2 (P.G. lix, 174).

begetting and the act of procession, which are things that pertain to the essence. But if the act of creating is not distinct from that of begetting and of procession, then created things will in no way differ from Him who is begotten and Him who is sent forth. But if this is the case – as according to these men it is – then both the Son of God and the Holy Spirit will in no way differ from creatures: all created things will be begotten and sent forth by God the Father, creation will be deified, and God will share His rank with creatures. For this reason St Cyril, affirming the distinction between God's essence and energy, says, 'The act of generation pertains to the divine nature, whereas the act of creating pertains to His divine energy.' Then he clearly underscores what he has affirmed by saying, 'Nature and energy are not identical.'[1]

97. If the divine essence does not in any respect differ from the divine energy, then the act of generation and of procession will in no respect differ from the act of creating. But God the Father creates through the Son in the Holy Spirit. Thus, in the view of Akindynos and his adherents, He also begets and sends forth through the Son in the Holy Spirit.

98. If the divine essence does not in any respect differ from the divine energy, then neither does it differ from the divine will. Thus the Son, who alone is begotten from the Father's essence, is according to these people also created from the Father's will.

99. If the divine essence does not in any respect differ from the divine energy, and if the holy fathers testify that God has many energies – for, as shown above, He has creative providences and goodnesses – then God also has many essences. This is a view that no member of the Christian race has ever uttered or entertained.

100. If the energies of God do not in any respect differ from the divine essence, then neither will they differ from one another. Therefore God's will is in no way different from His foreknowledge, and consequently either God does not foreknow all things – because He does not will all that occurs – or else He wills evil also, since He foreknows all. This means either that He does not foreknow all things, which is the same as saying that He is not God, or that He is not good, which is also the same as saying that He is not God. Thus God's

---

[1] St Cyril of Alexandria, *Treasuries* 18 (*P.G.* lxxv, 312C).

foreknowledge does differ from His will, and so both differ from the divine essence.

101. If the divine energies do not differ from one another, then God's creative power is not distinct from His foreknowledge. But in that case, since God began to create at a particular moment, He also began to foreknow at a particular moment. Yet if God did not have foreknowledge of all things before the ages how could He be God?

102. If God's creative energy does not differ in any respect from divine foreknowledge, then created things are concurrent with God's foreknowledge. Thus because God unoriginately has foreknowledge and what is foreknown is unoriginately foreknown, it follows that God creates unoriginately, and therefore that created things will have been created unoriginately. But how shall He be God if His creatures are in no way subsequent to Him?

103. If God's creative energy in no respect differs from His foreknowledge, then the act of creating is not subject to His will, since His foreknowledge is not so subject. In that case God will create, not by an act of volition, but simply because it is His nature to create. But how will He be God if He creates without volition?

104. God Himself is within Himself, since the three divine hypostases co-naturally and eternally cleave to one another and unconfusedly interpenetrate each other. Yet God is also in the universe and the universe is within God, the one sustaining, the other being sustained by Him. Thus all things participate in God's sustaining energy, but not in His essence. Hence the theologians say that divine omnipresence also constitutes an energy of God.

105. If we have conformed ourselves to God and have attained that for which we are created, namely, deification – for they say that God created us in order to make us partakers of His own divinity (cf. 2 Pet. 1 : 4) – then we are in God since we are deified by Him, and God is in us since it is He who deifies us. Thus we, too, participate in the divine energy – though in a different way from the universe as a whole – but not in the essence of God. Hence the theologians say that 'divinity' is also an appellation of the divine energy.

106. The supra-essential, supra-existential nature that transcends the Godhead and goodness, in that it is more than God and more than goodness, and so on, can be neither described nor conceived nor in any way contemplated, since it transcends all things and is surpassingly unknowable, being established by uncircumscribed power beyond the

supracelestial intelligences, and always utterly ungraspable and ineffable for all. Neither in the present age nor in the age to come is there any name with which it can be named, nor can the soul form any concept of it or any word express it; and there can be no contact with or participation in it, whether sensible or noetic, nor any imagining of it at all. Thus the theologians hold that the closest idea we can have of this nature is that of its perfect incomprehensibility attained by means of negation, or apophasis, since this nature is transcendentally privative of all that exists or can be expressed. Hence he who possesses knowledge of the truth beyond all truth, if he is to name it correctly, cannot legitimately call it either essence or nature. Yet it is the cause of all things and all things pertain to it and exist on its account; and it is prior to all things and in a simple and undetermined manner it precontains all things in itself. Thus it can be named loosely and inexactly from all things. Accordingly it can be called both essence and nature, though properly speaking we should name it the creative procession and energy whereby God creates individual essences; for the great Dionysios says that this is 'the proper theological name for the essence of Him who truly is'.[1]

107. One can find the term 'nature' applied also to natural attributes, both in the case of created beings and in the case of God. Thus St Gregory of Nazianzos says somewhere in his poems, 'It is the nature of my King to bestow blessedness.'[2] Now bestowing is not the nature of anything; it is, rather, the natural attribute of one who is beneficent. Similarly, with regard to fire one can say that its nature is to ascend upwards and to cast light upon those who behold it. Yet the motion in itself is not the nature of fire, nor is the production of light; rather its nature is the origin of the motion. Hence natural attributes are also called nature. This is confirmed by the great Dionysios when he says somewhere, 'It is the nature of the Good to bring forth and to save,'[3] meaning that these acts are attributes of the divine nature. Thus when you hear the fathers saying that God's essence is imparticipable, you should realize that they refer to the essence that does not depart from itself and is unmanifest. Again, when they say that it is participable, you should realize that they refer to the procession, manifestation and energy that are God's natural attributes.

---

[1] On the Divine Names v, 1 (P.G. iii, 816B).
[2] Dogmatic Poems iv, 83 (P.G. xxxvii, 422A).
[3] On the Divine Names iv, 19 (P.G. iii, 716C).

When you accept both statements in this sense you will be in agreement with the fathers.

108. Even the smallest portion of an essence possesses all that essence's powers. Thus a spark is both brilliant and illuminating, it melts and burns whatever comes close to it, it is self-moving by nature and rises upwards and, in brief, it is whatever fire is, of which it is a part. Similarly a drop of water possesses every quality that water has, of which it is a drop; and a nugget possesses whatever quality is possessed by the metal of which it is a fragment. Thus if we participate in the unmanifest essence of God, then, whether we participate in the whole of it or a part of it, we would be all-powerful, and in the same way each existent being would be all-powerful. But all-powerfulness is not a quality that even all mankind or all creation collectively possesses. St Paul shows this with abundant clarity when referring to those who share in the deifying gifts of the Spirit; for he testifies that not all the gifts of the Spirit belong to each individual. 'To one', he says, 'is given the quality of wisdom, to another the quality of knowledge, to another some other gift of the same Spirit' (cf. 1 Cor. 12 : 8). And St John Chrysostom clearly thwarts in advance the error of Barlaam and Akindynos when he says, 'A man does not possess all the gifts, lest he think that grace is nature.'[1] Yet no intelligent person would suppose that grace, here distinguished from the divine nature, is created, for obviously no one would be in any danger of supposing a created thing to be the nature of God. Moreover, the grace of the Spirit, though differing from the divine nature, is not separated from it; rather, it draws those privileged to receive it towards union with the Holy Spirit.

109. An essence has as many hypostases as there are partakers of it. We make as many hypostases of fire as the number of lamps we light from a single lamp. Yet if, as our opponents assert, God's essence is participated in, and is even participated in by everyone, this means that His essence is not tri-hypostatic, but multi-hypostatic. Who trained in the divine doctrine will not recognize this as the absurdity of the Messalians?[2] For the Messalians maintain that those who have

---

[1] Chrysostom (attributed to), *On the Holy Spirit* 3 (P.G. lii, 817).

[2] The Messalians or Euchites ('those who pray') – an ascetic movement originating in Syria during the second half of the fourth century – were accused by their opponents of believing that we can behold God's essence with our bodily eyes. Palamas was charged with Messalianism, but his standpoint is clearly different. On his view the divine light that is perceived by the saints through their bodily eyes is not the essence but the energies of God.

attained the height of virtue participate in the essence of God. Yet the followers of Akindynos in their zeal to surpass this blasphemy say that not only do certain people distinguished in virtue participate in the divine essence, but all beings in general participate in it; and they say this on the spurious pretext that the divine essence is everywhere present. But St Gregory of Nazianzos, eminent in theology, long ago refuted the dotty views of both the Messalians and the Akindynists when he said, 'He is "Christ", the Anointed, on account of His divinity; for it is the divinity that anoints His human nature. This anointing sanctifies the human nature not merely with an energy, as is the case with all others who are anointed, but with the presence of the whole of Him who anoints.'[1] With one voice the holy fathers have declared that the divinity dwells in those who are fittingly purified, but not as regards its nature. Thus a person does not participate in God either according to His essence or according to His hypostases, for neither of these can be in any way divided, nor can they be communicated to any one at all. Hence God is in this respect totally inaccessible to all, though indeed He is also everywhere present. But the energy and power common to the tri-hypostatic nature is variously and proportionately divided among those who participate in it, and is therefore accessible to those who are blessed with it. For, as St Basil says, 'the Holy Spirit is not participated in to the same degree by each person who receives Him; rather, He distributes His energy according to the faith of the participant; for though He is simple in essence, He is diverse in His powers.'[2]

110. That which is said to participate in something possesses a part of that in which it participates; for if it participates not in a part only but in the whole, then strictly speaking it does not participate in but possesses that whole. Hence, if the participant must necessarily participate in a part, what is participated in is divisible. But the essence of God is in every way indivisible, and therefore it is altogether imparticipable. On the other hand, the property of the divine energy is to be divisible, as the holy father St John Chrysostom frequently affirms.[3] Hence it is the divine energy that is participated in by those who have been privileged to receive deifying grace. Listen, then, once

---

[1] *Oration* 30, 21 (*Theological Oration* 4, 21) (*P.G.* xxxvi, 132B).
[2] *On the Holy Spirit* ix (22) (*P.G.* xxxii, 108C).
[3] E.g., *Homilies on John* 14, 1 (*P.G.* lix, 91–92); 30, 2 (*P.G.* lix, 174).

more to St John Chrysostom, as he clearly elucidates both these points, namely, that it is the energy that is indivisibly divided and also participated in, and not the imparticipable essence from which the divine energy proceeds. Citing the gospel words, 'Of His fullness we have all received' (John 1 : 16), he says, 'If in the case of fire, where what is divided is both essence and body, we both divide it and do not divide it, how much more so is this the case with respect to the energy, especially the energy of the unembodied essence?'[1]

111. Further, that which participates in something according to its essence must necessarily possess a common essence with that in which it participates and be identical to it in some respect. But who has ever heard that God and we possess in some respect the same essence? St Basil the Great says, 'The energies of God come down to us, but the essence remains inaccessible.'[2] And St Maximos also says, 'He who is deified through grace will be everything that God is, without possessing identity of essence.'[3] Thus it is impossible to participate in God's essence, even for those who are deified by divine grace. It is, however, possible to participate in the divine energy. 'To this does the measured light of truth here below lead me, to behold and experience the splendour of God,' states St Gregory of Nazianzos.[4] As the Psalmist says, 'May the splendour of our God be upon us' (Ps. 90 : 17. LXX). 'There is a single energy of God and the saints,' St Maximos clearly writes,[5] who was one of their number; they are 'living ikons of Christ, being the same as He is, by grace rather than by assimilation.'[6]

112. God is identical within Himself, since the three divine hypostases mutually coinhere and interpenetrate naturally, totally, eternally, inseparably, and yet without mingling or confusion, so that their energy is also one. This could never be the case among creatures. There are similarities among creatures of the same genus, but since each independent existence, or hypostasis, operates by itself, its energy is uniquely its own. The situation is different with the three divine hypostases that we worship, for there the energy is truly one and the

---

[1] Cf. Homilies on John 14, 1 (P.G. lix, 91–92).

[2] Letter 234, 1 (P.G. xxxii, 869AB).

[3] Cf. To Thalassios 22 (P.G. cx, 320A); Ambigua 41 (P.G. xci, 1308B).

[4] Oration 38, 11 (P.G. xxxvi, 324A).

[5] To Marinos (P.G. xci, 33A). Cf. Various Texts iv, 19; E.T., The Philokalia, vol. ii, p. 240; To Thalassios 59 (P.G. xc, 609A).

[6] Ambigua 21 (P.G. xci, 1253D).

same. For the activity of the divine will is one, originating from the
Father, the primal Cause, issuing through the Son, and made manifest
in the Holy Spirit. This is clear from the created effects, for it is from
the effects that we know every natural energy. Although they are
similar, different nests are made by different swallows, and different
pages are written by different scribes, though the materials used are
the same. But with the Father, Son and Holy Spirit it is not the case
that each one of the hypostases has His own particular effect. Rather,
all creation is the single work of the three. Thus we have been initiated
by the fathers to recognize from creation that the divine energy of the
three Persons whom we worship is one and the same, and that they do
not each possess an individual energy which merely resembles that of
the other two.

113. Since Father, Son and Holy Spirit unconfusedly and unmix-
edly interpenetrate one another, we know that they possess an activity
and energy that is strictly one and unique. The life or power that the
Father possesses in Himself is not different from that in the Son, since
the Son possesses the same life and power as the Father; and the same
can be said of the Son and the Holy Spirit. As for those who think that
the divine energy does not differ from the divine essence because our
life is nothing else but God Himself, and He Himself is pre-eternal life
not in relation to something else but in Himself, they are both ignorant
and heretics. They are ignorant because they have not yet learnt that
the supreme Trinity is none other than God Himself, and that the
supreme Unity is none other than God Himself, though this in no way
prevents the Unity from being distinguished from the Trinity. They are
heretics because they abolish both essence and energy, the one through
the other. For what is dependent on another is not essence; and what is
self-subsistent is not dependent on another. Thus if the essence and the
energy in no way differ from each other, they abolish each other, or,
rather, I should say that they expel from the number of the godfearing
those who say that there is no difference between them.

114. We, on the contrary, confess that the Son of God is our life as
regards cause and energy, and that He is also life in Himself absolutely
and independently of all; and we declare that He possesses both these
attributes uncreatedly. We likewise confess the same thing with
reference to the Father and the Holy Spirit. Thus this life of ours, that
as the cause of living things quickens us, is none other than Father, Son
and Holy Spirit. For our tri-hypostatic God is said to be our life as

being its cause. And when in theology the divine life is spoken of not as cause, nor in relation to something else, but absolutely and in itself, again it is not anything other than the Father and also the Son and the Holy Spirit. Such doctrines in no way give offence to those who affirm that God is uncreated, not only as regards His essence and hypostases, but also as regards the divine energy that is common to the three. We proclaim in our theology one God in three hypostases, possessing a single essence, power and energy, as well as whatever other realities pertain to the essence – realities that are called in Scripture assembly and fullness of divinity (cf. Col. 2 : 9), and are perceived and theologically declared to belong to each of the three holy hypostases.[1]

115. Those who reject this divine energy, saying sometimes that it is created, and sometimes that it differs in no respect from the divine essence, fabricate at other times a new heresy, teaching the doctrine that the sole uncreated energy is the only-begotten Son of the Father. In order to validate this view they appeal to the words of St Cyril: 'The life that the Father possesses in Himself is nothing other than the Son, and the life that is in the Son is nothing other than the Father. Thus He speaks the truth when He says, "I am in the Father and the Father is in Me" (John 14 : 11).'[2] Briefly and so far as we can we will now clarify the sense of the saint's words, and we will refute the impiety of those who in their undiscerning darkness oppose us. They wrongly maintain that the Son is not only unlike the Father, but is also posterior to the Father, because He possesses the faculty of life and life itself not by nature, but as something added from without, and by participation and adventitiously, and because He takes and receives life from the Father, according to the words of Scripture, 'For as the Father has life in Himself, so has He granted the Son also to have life in Himself' (John 5 : 26).

St Cyril counters those who interpret the text of the Gospel in such an impious way. 'God', he says, 'is called life by virtue of His energy, as the Quickener of living things. He is Himself the life of things that naturally live, since He is the Creator of nature, just as He is also the Bestower of grace on those who live in a divine manner. But God is also said to be life in Himself, not in relation to another, but independently

---

[1] Cf. St Athanasios of Alexandria (attributed to), *Homily on the Annunciation of the Mother of God* 2–3 (*P.G.* xxviii, 920BC).

[2] *Treasuries* 14 (*P.G.* lxxv, 244BC).

and in every way unconditionally.'[1] The divine Cyril wanted to show
that in neither of these two cases does the Son differ from the Father,
and that the fact that the Son receives something from the Father does
not indicate that He is posterior to the Father, or that where His
essence is concerned the Son is second to the Father in a temporal
sense. Thus among many other things St Cyril says, 'It is not as
receiving something that the Son possesses being, but as being He
receives something.' Then he adds in conclusion: 'Therefore, the fact
that the Son receives something from the Father does not mean that
where His essence is concerned the Son is second to the Father in a
temporal sense.'[2] Here, then, he does not accept that the life which
the Father has and which the Son receives from the Father is the divine
essence.

116. Further, the divine Cyril shows that although the Son of God
is said by virtue of His energy to be life in relation to living things, since
He quickens them and is called their life, yet not even in this is He
unlike the Father; rather, by nature He is their life and He quickens
them, just as the Father does. Then, continuing, St Cyril writes, 'If the
Son is not life by nature, how can He be speaking the truth when He
says, "He that believes in Me has eternal life" (John 6 : 47), and again,
"My sheep hear my voice, and I give them eternal life" (John 10 : 27–
28)?' Shortly after St Cyril writes, 'To those who believe in Him He
promises to give the life that belongs to and inheres in Him
substantially. How, then, is it possible to think that the Son did not
have this life but received it from the Father?'[3] They should be
ashamed, then, to say in their madness that, because this life is a natural
attribute of God, therefore it must be identical with God's essence. For
neither the Father, nor the Son, nor the Holy Spirit offers us believers
their essence. We must dismiss such impiety.

117. The great Cyril confutes in a similar way those who are
infected with Barlaam's disease when he says shortly afterwards, 'In
proceeding from the Father the Son takes with Him all that is by
nature the Father's. Now one of the Father's attributes is life.'[4] By the
words, 'one of the Father's attributes', he clearly demonstrates that the

[1] Not traced in St Cyril's works.
[2] *Treasuries* 14 (*P.G.* lxxv, 233BC).
[3] Ibid. (236BC).
[4] Ibid. (236C).

Father has many attributes. In the opinion of those who think that life is the essence of God, this must mean that God has many essences. Yet, apart from this impiety, to say that being and attribute are the same, except perhaps with regard to some particular relation, also displays excessive ignorance. And even more senseless is it to say that being and attributes – in other words, the one and what is more than one – are in no way different. For it is utterly and completely impossible and senseless to assert that something should be both one and many with respect to the same thing.

118. In stating, then, that life is one of the Father's attributes, the divine Cyril shows that in this passage, when referring to 'life', he does not mean the essence of God. But let us produce his exact words where he states that God has many attributes. For slightly later he says, 'Many excellent properties pertain to the Father, but the Son is not without them either.'[1] How could these many things that pertain to God be the divine essence? Wishing to indicate some of these excellent properties that pertain to the Father, he refers to the words of St Paul, 'To the immortal, invisible, and only wise God' (1 Tim. 1 : 17). Thus he shows even more clearly that none of God's attributes constitutes the essence. How, indeed, could immortality, invisibility, and in general all the things said of God privatively and apophatically, whether collectively or severally, be equated with the essence? For there is no essence unless there exists this or that definite object. If to the divine attributes described apophatically are added those that the theologians ascribe to God cataphatically, it is evident that none of them can be shown to disclose God's essence, even though when necessary we apply all the names of these attributes to the supra-essential Being that is absolutely nameless.

119. When attributes are in question, we necessarily ask what they pertain to. If they do not pertain to anything, they are not attributes, and it is wrong to call them such. But if the attributes pertain to any one thing, and if this is the essence, which according to our adversaries in no way differs from each one of the attributes and all of them together, then, since there are many attributes, the one essence will be many essences; and that thing which is one in essence will be many in essence, and therefore will have many essences. But if it is one and also has many essences, it is necessarily composite. Delivering his adherents

---

[1] Ibid. (240A).

from such impious and ignorant opinions, the divine Cyril says in his *Treasuries*: 'If that which pertains to God alone is inevitably also His essence, He will be composed of many essences. For there are many things that pertain by nature to God alone and to no other being. Indeed, the divine Scriptures call Him King, Lord, incorruptible, invisible, and say many thousands of other things about Him. If, then, each of His attributes is ranked with essence, how can the simple God not be composite? But this is a most absurd view to hold.'[1]

120. By many arguments St Cyril, wise in things divine, shows that even though the Son is life and is said to possess life as energy, since He quickens us and is the life of living things, still He is not on this account unlike the Father, for the Father, too, bestows life. He wanted also to show that even when the Son is said to be life and to have life not in relation to something else but altogether independently and absolutely, yet in this case also He will not be unlike the Father with respect to life. For when we call God our life, not in so far as He bestows life on us, but altogether independently and absolutely, then we are naming His essence on the basis of the energy that pertains to Him by nature, as we do also when we call Him wisdom, goodness, and so on. Wishing, then, to demonstrate this, St Cyril says: 'When we say that "the Father has life in Himself" (John 5 : 26), we are at the same time calling the Son life, for He is other than the Father only with respect to His hypostasis, but not with respect to life. For this reason there is no question of compositeness or twofoldedness in the Father. And again, when we say that the Son has life in Himself, and we mean life absolute, we are at the same time calling the Father life. For as the Father is life, not in relation to anything else, but independently and in Himself, the Father and the Son coinhere in one another, as the Son Himself said: "I am in the Father and the Father is in Me" (John 14 : 11).'[2] In this way, then, the divine Cyril demonstrates that the life that is in the Father – namely, the Son – is somehow both other and not other than the Father. But our opponents say that the life that is in the Father is in no way other than the Father and is entirely identical with Him since it is in no respect different. By proposing such things and affirming that this life is the Only-begotten Son of the Father, they necessarily range

---

[1] *Treasuries* 31 (P.G. lxxv, 444BC).
[2] Not traced in St Cyril's works.

themselves not with the doctrines of the venerable Cyril but with those of Sabellius.[1]

121. Do not the followers of Barlaam and Akindynos roundly condemn themselves when they claim that the divine Cyril contradicts himself? To affirm sometimes one thing, sometimes another, when both affirmations are true, is a distinguishing mark of every orthodox theologian. But to contradict oneself does not betoken an intelligent person. St Cyril quite rightly says that by nature the Son has life, which He gives to those who believe in Him. By this he shows that not only the essence of God – which no one receives – but also His natural energy is called life. This life has been received as a gift of grace by those whom He has quickened, and thus they themselves are able to save – that is to say, to render immortal in spirit – those who previously were not alive in spirit, and sometimes to restore people lifeless in one of their limbs or even in their whole body. How could St Cyril, who has demonstrated these things so excellently and clearly, subsequently assert, with the intention of denying what he has said about the divine energy, that only God's essence is called life? For this is what is senselessly maintained by those who now pervert or, rather, misrepresent, what St Cyril says.

122. Not just the Only-begotten Son of God but also the Holy Spirit is called energy and power by the saints, and this because the Son and the Spirit possess precisely the same powers and energies as the Father. For according to St Dionysios God is called power, 'as both possessing it originally in Himself and transcending all power'.[2] Therefore, whenever one of those two distinct hypostases, the Son and the Holy Spirit, is called power or energy, it is understood or expressed that He is so together with the Father. Thus St Basil the Great says, 'The Holy Spirit is a sanctifying power that possesses essence, existence and hypostatic subsistence.'[3] But in his writing about the Spirit he also shows that the energies of the Spirit are none of them self-subsistent, in this way clearly distinguishing them in turn from created things; for what come forth from the Spirit as created objects

<hr/>

[1] Sabellius the Libyan, who was active in Rome in the early third century, subscribed to the Modalist or Monarchian heresy. He regarded the Father, Son and Holy Spirit as modes or operations within the Godhead, not as genuinely distinct Persons or hypostases.

[2] *On the Divine Names* viii, 2 (*P.G.* iii, 889D).

[3] St Basil (attributed to), *Against Eunomios* v (*P.G.* xxix, 713B).

are independent existences, for God creates them as essences with specific qualities.

123. Apophatic theology does not contradict or confute cataphatic theology, but it shows that although statements made cataphatically about God are true and reverent, yet they do not apply to God as they might to us. For example, God possesses knowledge of existent things, and we, too, possess this in some cases. But we know things in so far as they exist and have come into existence, whereas God does not know them solely in this way, since He knows them just as well even prior to their coming into existence. Thus he who says that God does not know existent things as existent does not contradict him who says that God knows existent things and knows them as existent. There is also a cataphatic theology which has the force of apophatic theology, as when one says that all knowledge is affirmed of some object, namely, the thing known, while God's knowledge does not refer to any object. This is the same as saying God does not know existent things as existent, and He does not have knowledge of existent things – that is to say, does not have it as we do. In this way it can be said that in terms of His pre-eminence God does not exist. But he who asserts this in order to show that people who say God exists are not speaking correctly, clearly employs apophatic theology not in a way that connotes pre-eminence, but as though it connoted deficiency and signified in this case that God has absolutely no existence whatsoever. This is the uttermost impiety, of which, alas, those are guilty who by means of apophatic theology attempt to deny that God has both an uncreated essence and uncreated energy. We, however, embrace both modes of theology, since the one does not exclude the other – rather, by means of each we confirm ourselves in a sound way of thought.

124. I think a brief patristic quotation will be sufficient to confute utterly all the sophistries of Barlaam's followers and prove them to be sheer folly. St Gregory of Nazianzos says: 'The Unoriginate, the First Originate and the One who is with the First Originate, constitute one God. But the First Originate is not, because it is the First Originate, separated from the Unoriginate. For its origin is not its nature, any more than to be without origin is the nature of the other. These things pertain to the nature, but are not the nature itself.'[1] What, then? Shall we say that because origin and unoriginateness are not nature but

[1] *Oration* 42, 15 (P.G. xxxvi, 476A).

pertain to the nature that they are therefore created? Not unless we are out of our mind. And is God composite because origin and unoriginateness are uncreated and pertain to His nature? Certainly not; for though they pertain to His nature, they are yet distinct from it. But, as St Cyril and other fathers teach at length, if the natural attributes of God are identified with the nature, then the Divinity is composite.[1] Read through the writings against Eunomios by St Basil the Great and his brother, St Gregory of Nyssa, who fraternally shares his views. There you will find clearly that the followers of Barlaam and Akindynos are in agreement with Eunomios, and you will have ample refutations to use against them.

125. The Eunomians asserted that the Father and the Son did not have the same essence, and they came to this conclusion because they imagined that everything predicated of God is said with regard to His essence; and so they contentiously argued that because to beget and to be begotten are different, on this account there are also different essences. The Akindynists assert that it cannot be one and the same God who possesses both a divine essence and divine energy, because they imagine that everything predicated of God is essence; and so they contentiously argue that, if there is any difference between divine essence and energy, there are also many different gods. To refute both groups it is enough to show that not everything predicated of God is said with regard to His essence; it can be said relatively, that is, with relation to something that is not God's essence. For example, the Father is spoken of in relation to the Son, for the Son is not the Father. And God is called Lord in relation to the subject creation, for God is Lord over beings that are in time and in the eternal age, and also Lord over the ages themselves. But this dominion is an uncreated energy of God, distinct from His essence in that it is said in relation to something else, something which He Himself is not.

126. The Eunomians maintain that everything that is attributed to God is essence. In this way they conclude that unbegottenness is God's essence, thus degrading – so far as they can – the Son to the rank of a creature because He differs from the Father. Their purpose, they claim, is to avoid positing two Gods: the first, unbegotten, and the one who comes second after Him, begotten. In imitation of the Eunomians, the Akindynists maintain that everything that is attributed to God is

---

[1] Cf. *Treasuries* 31 (*P.G.* lxxv, 448D).

essence, and in this way they impiously degrade God's energy to the rank of creature – the energy that although inseparable from God nevertheless differs from His essence in that it originates from the essence and is participated in by created things; for, as St Dionysios says, 'All things participate in the providence that wells forth from the Godhead, the Cause of all.'[1] Their purpose, the Akindynists claim, is to avoid positing two Godheads: one, the tri-hypostatic essence that transcends name, cause, and participation; and the other, God's energy that proceeds from the essence, is participated in, and is named. They do not comprehend that, just as God the Father is called Father in relation to His own Son and fatherhood pertains to Him as an uncreated property, even though the name 'Father' does not betoken the essence, so likewise God possesses energy uncreatedly, even though energy differs from essence. When we speak of one Godhead, we speak of everything that God is, namely, both essence and energy. Consequently the Akindynists are the ones who impiously split God's single divinity into created and uncreated.

127. An accident is that which comes into existence and passes out of existence, and in this way we can conceive of inseparable attributes as well. From one point of view, a natural attribute is also an accident, since it increases and decreases, as, for instance, knowledge in the soul endowed with intelligence. But there is no such thing in God because He remains entirely changeless. For this reason nothing can be attributed to Him that is an accident. Yet not all things said of God betoken His essence. For what belongs to the category of relation is also predicated of Him, and this is relative and refers to relationship with something else, and does not signify essence. Such is the divine energy in God. For it is not essence, nor an accident, even though it is called a kind of accident by some theologians, who mean to say simply this, that it is in God and that it is not essence.

128. St Gregory of Nazianzos, when writing about the Holy Spirit, teaches us that, even though the divine energy is as it were also an accident, it is still seen to be in God without thereby making God composite. For he says, 'The Holy Spirit must either be ranked among beings that are self-existent or among those that are seen to be in another. Those skilled in such matters call the former essence and the latter accident. If the Holy Spirit were an accident, He would be an

---

[1] *The Celestial Hierarchy* iv, 1 (P.G. iii, 177C).

energy of God. For what else, or of whom else, could He be? And this avoids making God composite.'[1] He is clearly saying that if the Spirit is one of the things seen to be in God, and so is not essence, but is an accident and is called Spirit, He cannot be anything other than God's energy. This he indicated by saying, 'For what else, or of whom else, could He be?' In order to make it clear also that apart from energy nothing else – not quality, or quantity, or anything else of this kind – can be seen to be in God, he adds, 'And this avoids making God composite.' But how does the energy, though it is seen to be in God, not introduce composition into God? Because only God possesses completely impassible energy: He alone acts without being acted upon. He does not come into existence, nor does He change.

129. Slightly before this, in contrasting this energy with what is created, St Gregory also shows that he regarded it as uncreated. For he says, 'Of the wise men among ourselves, some have supposed the Spirit to be an energy, others a created thing, and still others God.'[2] By 'God' here he means the actual hypostasis; and by distinguishing the energy from what is created he clearly demonstrates that it is not created. Shortly afterwards he calls the energy an activity of God. How could God's activity not be uncreated? St John of Damaskos writes on this question: 'The energy is the dynamic and essential activity of the nature. That which possesses the capacity to energize is the nature from which the energy proceeds. That which is energized is the effect of the energy. That which energizes is what uses the energy, that is to say, the hypostasis.'[3]

130. In the same work St Gregory also says, 'If He is energy, then He will be energized but will not energize; and He will cease to exist once He has been energized.'[4] From this the followers of Akindynos conclude and declare that the divine energy is created. They do not understand that being energized can also be said of uncreated realities, as St Gregory shows when he says that if 'Father' is the name of an energy, 'then what the Father energizes will be the consubstantiality of the Son'.[5] And St John of Damaskos also says, 'Christ sat at the right

---

[1] *Oration* 31, 6 (*Theological Oration* 5, 6) (*P.G.* xxxvi, 140A).
[2] Op. cit. 5 (137C).
[3] *On the Orthodox Faith* iii, 15 (*P.G.* xciv, 1048A): ed. Kotter, § 59, p. 144.
[4] *Oration* 31, 6 (*Theological Oration* 5, 6) (*P.G.* xxxvi, 140A).
[5] *Oration* 29, 16 (*Theological Oration* 3, 16) (*P.G.* xxxvi, 96A).

hand of God, divinely energizing universal providence.'[1] Yet neither does the expression 'He rested' call in question the uncreated nature of the energy. For in creating God begins and ceases: as Moses says, 'God rested from all the works that He had begun to make' (Gen. 2 : 2). But the act of creating itself, with respect to which God begins and ceases, is a natural and uncreated energy of God.

131. After saying, 'The energy is the dynamic and essential activity of the nature', St John of Damaskos seeks to demonstrate that, according to St Gregory of Nazianzos, this energy is both actuated and ceases to act. For he adds, 'We should realize that the energy is an activity and is energized rather than energizes. As St Gregory the Theologian says in his homily on the Holy Spirit, "If He is energy, then He will be energized but will not energize; and He will cease to exist once He has been energized".'[2] Thus it is obvious that those who share the views of Barlaam and Akindynos, and who teach that the energy of which St Gregory here speaks is created, mindlessly degrade to the rank of a creature God's natural and essential energy. Yet St John of Damaskos, when he affirms that this energy is not only energized but also energizes, shows thereby that it is uncreated. That in this St John does not disagree with St Gregory I have made abundantly clear in my longer works.

132. In God the hypostatic properties are affirmed relatively one to the other. The hypostases differ from each other, but not with respect to essence. Sometimes God is also referred to in relation to creation. Yet God, the All-Holy Trinity, cannot be called Father in the same way that He is called pre-eternal, pre-unoriginate, great and good. For it is not each of the three hypostases that is the Father, but only one of them, from whom and to whom subsequent realities are referred. None the less, in relation to creation the Trinity can also be called the Father, because creation is the joint work of the Three, brought forth from absolute nothingness, and because our adoption as sons is achieved through the bestowal of the grace common to the Three. The scriptural texts, 'The Lord your God is one Lord' (cf. Deut. 6 : 4) and 'One is our Father in heaven' (cf. Matt. 6 : 9; 23 : 9), refer to the Holy Trinity as our one Lord and God, and also as our Father who

[1] *On the Orthodox Faith* iv, 1 (*P.G.* xciv, 1104A): ed. Kotter, § 74, p. 173.
[2] *On the Orthodox Faith* iii, 15 (*P.G.* xciv, 1048B): ed. Kotter, § 59, p. 145; citing St Gregory of Nazianzos, *Oration* 31, 6 (*P.G.* xxxvi, 140A).

through His grace confers on us a new birth. As we said, the Father is called Father only in relation to His coessential Son. In relation to both Son and Spirit He is called Principle, as He is also called Principle in relation to creation, but here in the sense that He is the Creator and Master of all creatures. Thus when the Father is called such things in relation to creation, the Son is also Principle, though they constitute not two Principles but one. For the Son is called Principle in relation to creation, as He is likewise called Master in relation to the created things subject to Him. Thus the Father and the Son, together with the Spirit, are – in relation to creation – one Principle, one Master, one Creator, one God and Father, one Provider and Overseer, and so on. Yet none of these properties constitute the essence, for if it was the essence it could not have been spoken of in relation to another.

133. States, conditions, places, times, and any other such thing are not literally but metaphorically predicated of God. But to create and to energize can in the truest sense be predicated of God alone; for only God creates. He does not come into existence nor with respect to His essence is He acted upon. He alone through all things creates each one. He alone creates from absolute nothingness, since He possesses energy that is all-powerful. With respect to this energy He can be referred to in relation to creation and possesses potentiality. For He Himself in His own nature is not capable of being affected by anything at all, but if He wishes He is capable of adding to His creations. For God in His essence to be capable of being affected, of possessing or acquiring something, would denote weakness. But for God through His energy to be capable of creating, and of possessing and adding to His creations whenever He wishes, is a token of divinely fitting and almighty power.

134. All existent things can be grouped into ten categories, namely, essence, quantity, quality, relation, place, time, activity, passivity, possession and dependence; and these ten categories apply likewise to everything subsequently seen to pertain to essence. But God is supra-essential essence, in which can be seen only relation and activity or creation, and these two things do not produce in His essence any composition or change. For God creates all things without being affected in His essence. He is Creator in relation to creation, and also its Principle and Master in that it has its origin in Him and is dependent on Him. But He is also our Father, since by grace He confers on us rebirth. Yet He is Father, too, in relation to the Son who is completely without any temporal beginning. The Son is Son in relation to the

Father, while the Spirit is the projection of the Father, coeternal with the Father and the Son, being of one and the same essence. Those who assert that God is only essence, with nothing to be seen in Him, fabricate a God who has neither creativity and energy nor relation. But if He whom they suppose to be God does not possess these properties, then He is neither active nor Creator, nor does He possess an energy; and neither is He Principle, Creator and Master, nor is He our Father by grace. For how could He be these things if relation and creativity are not to be envisaged in His essence? Furthermore, if relation is not to be envisaged in God's essence, the tri-hypostatic character of the Godhead is also abolished. But He who is not tri-hypostatic is not the Master of all or God. Thus those who hold the views of Barlaam and Akindynos are atheists.

135. God also possesses that which is not essence. Yet because it is not essence it is not on that account an accident. For that which not only does not pass away but which also neither admits nor induces in itself the slightest increase or decrease, cannot be included among accidents. But the fact that it is neither an accident nor essence does not mean that it has no existence: it exists and it truly exists. It is not an accident, because it is altogether changeless. But again it is not an essence, because it is not among those things that are self-subsistent. It is because of this that some theologians say that it is in a certain way an accident, by which they wish only to indicate that it is not essence. But because each hypostatic property and each of the hypostases is neither an essence nor an accident in God, is it on this account totally non-existent? Certainly not. In the same way, then, God's divine energy is neither an essence nor an accident, nor is it something utterly non-existent. To speak in accord with all the theologians: if God creates by will and not simply because it is His nature to do so, then to will is one thing and natural being is another. If this is so, it means that God's volition is other than the divine essence. Does it follow from this that because in God the will is other than the nature and is not an essence it therefore does not exist at all? Certainly not: it does exist and it pertains to God, who possesses not only essence but also a will with which He creates. One may if one wishes say that it is in a certain way an accident, since it is not an essence; yet neither is it in the strict sense an accident, since it does not produce any composition or alteration. Thus God possesses both essence and that which is not essence, even if it should not be called an accident, namely, the divine will and energy.

136. Unless an essence has an energy distinct from itself, it will entirely lack actual existence and will be a mere mental concept. For man as a general concept does not think, does not have opinions, does not see, does not smell, does not speak, does not hear, does not walk, does not breathe, does not eat and, in short, does not have an energy which is distinct from his essence, and which shows that he possesses an individual state of being. Thus man as a general concept entirely lacks actual existence. But when man possesses an inherent energy distinct from his essence, whether it be one or many or all of those activities we have mentioned, it is known thereby that he possesses an individual state of being and does not lack actual existence. And because these energies are observed not only in one or two or three but in a great number of individuals, it is clear that man exists in countless individual states of being.

137. According to the true faith of God's Church which by His grace we hold, God possesses inherent energy that makes Him manifest and is in this respect distinct from His essence. For He foreknows and provides for inferior beings; He creates, sustains, rules and transforms them according to His own will and knowledge. In this way it is clear that He possesses an individual state of being, and that He is not simply essence lacking actual existence. But since all these energies are to be seen not in one but in three Persons, God is known to us as one essence existing in three individual states of being or hypostases. But the followers of Akindynos, by asserting that God does not have inherent energy that makes Him manifest and is in this respect distinct from His essence, are saying that God does not possess an individual state of being, and they entirely deprive the tri-hypostatic Lord of actual existence. In this way they excel Sabellius the Libyan in heresy; for their total impiety is worse than his corrupt piety.

138. The energy of the three divine hypostases is one not in the sense that each has an energy similar to that of the others, as is the case with us, but in the sense of true numerical unity. This is something which those who hold the views of Akindynos are unable to accept. For they say that there is no common, uncreated energy pertaining to the three hypostases and that the hypostases are energies of one another, since according to them there is no common divine energy. Thus they are unable to affirm that the three hypostases possess a single energy, and by excluding now one, now another energy they again deprive the tri-hypostatic God of actual existence.

139. Because those diseased in soul with Akindynos's delusions say that the energy that is distinct from God's essence is created, they conclude that God's creative power is created. For it is impossible to act and create without an energy, just as it is impossible to exist without existence. Therefore, just as one cannot say that God's existence is created and at the same time affirm that His being is uncreated, so also one cannot say that God's energy is created and at the same time affirm that His power to act and create is uncreated.

140. According to those who hold the true faith – and contrary to Akindynos's nonsensical and impious ramblings – created things are not the energy of God, but they are the effects of the divine energy. For if the created things are the energy, either such things are uncreated – which is sheer folly, for it would mean that they exist before they are created – or else prior to created things God possesses no energy; and this is mere godlessness. For of course God is eternally active and all-powerful. Thus creatures are not God's energy, but things that (whatever the precise terminology employed) have been actualized and effected. But God's energy, according to the theologians, is uncreated and coeternal with God.

141. The energy is not known from the essence; but we do know from the energy that the essence exists, though we do not know what it is. Thus according to the theologians God's existence is known from His providence, not from His essence. Such, then, is the way in which energy can be distinguished from essence: the energy is that which makes known, while the essence is that whose existence is made known by the energy. The advocates of Akindynos's impiety, in their anxiety to persuade us that the divine energy in no way differs from the divine essence, abolish that which makes God known, and so end up by trying to convince us that we cannot know that God exists – since they at any rate have no knowledge of Him. But he who does not even know that God exists will be the most godless and stupid of men.

142. When the Akindynists say that, although God possesses an energy, it does not in any way differ from His essence, they attempt thus to cloak their own impiety and sophistically to mislead and deceive their hearers. Sabellius the Libyan likewise said that God the Father has a Son who differs in no way from the Father. But just as he was guilty of teaching that the Father is without a Son, since he denied their hypostatic distinction, so now these people are guilty of holding that God has no energy whatsoever, since they assert that the divine

energy in no way differs from the divine essence. If, indeed, there were
no difference between these two, God would possess no capacity for
creating and actuating, for according to the theologians it is impossible
to act without an energy, just as it is impossible to exist without
existence. For those who think rightly, there is also another fact which
indicates that there is a difference between the divine energy and the
divine essence. The energy actuates something else, not identical with
the one who acts. God actuates and makes created things, but He
Himself is uncreated. Further, a relationship is always affirmed in
relation to something else: son is spoken of in relation to father, but a
son is never father of his father. Therefore, as it is impossible for the
relationship not to differ in any way from the essence and for it to be
itself the essence instead of being in the essence, so likewise it is
impossible for the energy not to differ from the essence but to be the
essence, even though this may give offence to Akindynos.

143. St Basil the Great, when he writes of God in his *Syllogistic
Chapters*, says, 'The energy is neither the one who energizes nor that
which is energized. Therefore the energy is not to be confused with the
essence.'[1] St Cyril likewise affirms concerning God: 'To create
pertains to energy, to beget pertains to nature. But nature and energy
are not identical.'[2] And St John of Damaskos writes, 'Generation is an
operation of the divine nature, but the creation is an operation of the
divine will.'[3] And elsewhere he says clearly, 'Energy is one thing and
that which has the capacity to energize is another. For energy is the
essential activity of the nature. That which possesses the capacity to
energize is the nature from which the energy proceeds.'[4] The energy,
then, according to the holy fathers, differs in many ways from the
divine essence.

144. God's essence is entirely unnamable since it is also completely
incomprehensible. Therefore we name it on the basis of all its energies,
although with respect to the essence itself none of those names means
anything different from any other. For by each name and by all names
together nothing other is named except that which is hidden and
whose real identity is unknown to all. But with respect to the energies,

---

[1] Cf. St Basil (attributed to), *Against Eunomios* iv (*P.G.* xxix, 689C).
[2] *Treasuries* 18 (*P.G.* lxxv, 312C).
[3] Cf. *On the Orthodox Faith* i, 8 (*P.G.* xciv, 813A): ed. Kotter, § 8, p. 21.
[4] Op. cit., iii, 15 (*P.G.* xciv, 1048A): ed. Kotter, § 59, p. 144.

each of these names has a different significance, for we all know that the acts of creating, ruling, judging, providential guidance, and of God's adopting us as sons through His grace, are acts that differ from one another. Thus when the Akindynists say that these natural, divine energies are created because they differ both from one another and from the divine nature, what else are they doing except degrading God and making Him a creature? For things that are created, ruled, judged and so on, are creatures and not the Creator, the Ruler, and the Judge. And the same can be said of the acts of judging, ruling, and creating, which are acts that by nature pertain to God.

145. Just as the essence of God is altogether without name because according to the theologians it transcends all names, so it is also imparticipable in that according to them it transcends participation. Thus those who in our day disbelieve the teaching of the Spirit given through our holy fathers and who revile us when we agree with the fathers, say that if the divine energy differs from the divine essence, even though it is envisaged as wholly pertaining to God's essence, then either there will be many gods or the one God will be composite. They are unaware that it is not activating and energy but being acted upon and passivity that produce composition. God activates without in any way being acted upon or subject to change. Thus He is not composite on account of His energy. Furthermore, God also possesses relationship and is related to creation, as being its Principle and Master; but He is not on this account numbered among things that have come into existence. And how will there be many gods because of God possessing an energy, since the energy pertains to one God or, rather, since God Himself is both the divine essence and the divine energy? All this is clearly folly deriving from a demented state of mind.

146. The Lord said to His disciples, 'There are some standing here who will not taste death till they have seen the kingdom of God come with power' (Mark 9 : 1); and after six days He took Peter, James and John, and when they had ascended Mount Tabor He shone like the sun, and His clothes became white as light (cf. Matt. 17 : 1–2). When the disciples could look at it no longer or, rather, because they lacked the strength to gaze at the brightness, they fell prostrate to the earth (cf. Matt. 17 : 6). None the less, in accordance with the Saviour's promise they did see the kingdom of God, that divine and inexpressible light. St Gregory of Nazianzos and St Basil call this light 'divinity', saying that 'the light is the divinity manifested to the disciples on the

Mount',[1] and that it is 'the beauty of Him who is almighty, and His noetic and contemplatable divinity'.[2] St Basil the Great also says that this light is the beauty of God contemplated by the saints alone in the power of the divine Spirit; and again he writes, 'On the mountain Peter and the sons of thunder saw His beauty shining more brightly than the sun; and they were privileged to receive with their eyes a foretaste of His advent.'[3] St John of Damaskos as well as St John Chrysostom call that light a natural ray of the Divinity. The former writes, 'Because the Son was begotten unoriginately from the Father, He possesses the natural, unoriginate ray of the Divinity; and the glory of the Divinity becomes the glory of His body.'[4] And St John Chrysostom says, 'The Lord appeared upon the mountain more radiant than Himself because the Divinity revealed its rays.'[5]

147. This divine and inexpressible light, God's divinity and kingdom, the beauty and resplendence of the divine nature, the vision and delight of the saints in the age without end, the natural ray and glory of the Divinity – this the followers of Akindynos call an apparition and a creature. Further, they slanderously call ditheists those who refuse to blaspheme as they do against the divine light and who affirm God to be uncreated both in His essence and in His energy. But they should be ashamed, for though the divine light is uncreated, there is for us one God in one divinity, since, as has been shown above in many different ways, both the uncreated essence and the uncreated energy – that is, this divine grace and illumination – pertain to one God.

148. Because the followers of Akindynos at the Synod[6] audaciously asserted and strove to demonstrate that the divine light that shone from the Saviour on Tabor was an apparition and a creature, and because they did not change their views although they were frequently confuted, they were placed under a writ of excommunication and anathema. For they blaspheme God's economy in the flesh, and

[1] St Gregory of Nazianzos, *Oration 40*, 6 (*P.G.* xxxvi, 365A).

[2] St Basil the Great, *On Psalm 44*, § 5 (*P.G.* xxix, 400C).

[3] Ibid. (400CD).

[4] *Homily on the Transfiguration of Christ* 12 (*P.G.* xcvi, 564B): ed. B. Kotter (*Patristische Texte und Studien* 29: Berlin, 1988), pp. 449–50.

[5] Not traced in the works of Chrysostom.

[6] This probably refers to the Synod of Constantinople held in 1341, and perhaps also to the further Synod held there in 1347.

mindlessly say that God's divinity is created; and in this way – since the divinity of the three Persons is one and the same – they degrade the Father, the Son and the Holy Spirit themselves to the rank of a creature. And when they claim to worship an uncreated divinity, they plainly profess that there are two divinities in God, the one created and the other uncreated. In this manner they strive to surpass in impiety all the ancient heretics.

149. At other times these people contrive to conceal their heresy by saying that the light that shone on Tabor is both uncreated and also the essence of God, and in this they blaspheme in many ways. For since that light was seen by the apostles, these people perversely imagine that the essence of God is visible. Let them listen to him who says, 'No one has been in such a position as to see or disclose the essence and nature of God.'[1] Not only men but also the angels are unable to do so; for even the six-winged Cherubim cover their faces with their wings because of the surpassing brilliance of the illumination shining from the divine essence (cf. Isa. 6 : 2). God's supraessentiality has never appeared to anyone at any time. Thus when the followers of Akindynos identify it with the light of the Transfiguration, what they are asserting is that this light is entirely invisible, that not even the chosen apostles were able to see it on Mount Tabor, that the Lord did not truthfully promise them the sight of it, and that he who said, 'We saw His glory when we were with Him in the holy mount' (cf. John 1 : 14; 2 Pet. 1 : 18), and 'Peter and those with him stayed awake and saw His glory' (cf. Luke 9 : 32), did not speak the truth; nor did that other who says that Christ's especially beloved disciple 'saw disclosed upon the mountain the actual divinity of the Logos'.[2] Thus they saw, they truly saw that uncreated and divine effulgence, while God yet continued invisible in His supraessential hiddenness, although Barlaam and Akindynos and their followers may explode with indignation at this.

150. Whenever one asks the Akindynists who say that the light of the Divinity is the essence: 'Is, then, the essence of God visible?', they are forced to unmask their treachery. For they assert that this light is the essence, since through it the essence of God is manifest; thus God's essence can be seen by means of created things. So once again these

[1] St Gregory of Nazianzos, *Oration* 28, 19 (*Theological Oration* 2, 19) (*P.G.* xxxvi, 52B).
[2] St Symeon Metaphrastis, *Commentary on the Holy Apostle John* 1 (*P.G.* cxvi, 685D).

wretches assert that the light of the Lord's Transfiguration is a created thing. Yet that which is seen through created things is not God's essence but His creative energy. Therefore those who say that by means of creatures God's essence is seen speak irreligiously and in agreement with Eunomios, so prolific is the crop of their impiety. Thus we should shun them and their company, for their teaching is a soul-destroying and many-headed serpent, corrupting the true faith in a multitude of ways.

The Declaration of the Holy Mountain in Defence of Those who Devoutly Practise a Life of Stillness

(*Prologue*) The mysteries of the Mosaic law, once foreseen in the Spirit by the prophets alone, have now become doctrines known to all alike and openly proclaimed. Similarly the way of life according to the Gospel has also its own mysteries; and these are the blessings of the age to come which are promised to the saints, and which are now disclosed prophetically to those whom the Spirit accounts worthy, but only to a limited extent and as a pledge and a foretaste. If one of the Jews of old, lacking a proper spirit of reverence, were to hear the prophets proclaiming the Logos and the Spirit of God to be pre-eternal and coeternal with God, he might have stopped up his ears, supposing that he heard things forbidden to piety and opposed to what was openly confessed by true believers, namely, 'The Lord your God is one Lord' (cf. Deut. 6 : 4). Similarly a person today who without proper reverence hears of the mysteries of the Spirit that are known only by those who have been purified through virtue might react in the same way. Again, the fulfilment of the prophecies in the Old Testament showed the mysteries of that time to be concordant with what was later made manifest, so that now we believe in Father, Son and Holy Spirit, the tri-hypostatic Godhead, one simple, non-composite, uncreated, unseen, incomprehensible nature. Similarly, when in its own time the age to come is revealed according to the ineffable manifestation of the one God in three perfect hypostases, it will be clear that the present mysteries accord with all that is then made manifest.

Yet we must also take into account the fact that, although the tri-hypostatic nature of the Godhead – that is in no way destroyed by the principle of unity – was in later times revealed to the ends of the earth, it was also fully known to the prophets prior to the fulfilment of the things prophesied and was readily accepted by those who trusted in them. In the same manner, even at this present time we are not ignorant of the doctrines of the Christian confession, both those which are openly proclaimed and those which are mystically and prophetically revealed by the Spirit to such as are accounted worthy. These are persons who have been initiated by actual experience, who have renounced possessions, human glory and the ugly pleasures of the body for the sake of the evangelical life; and not only this, but they have also strengthened their renunciation by submitting themselves to those who have attained spiritual maturity in Christ. Through the practice of the life of stillness they devote their attention undistractedly to themselves and to God, and by transcending themselves through sincere prayer and by establishing themselves in God through their mystical and supra-intellectual union with Him they have been initiated into what surpasses the intellect. Others again have learnt about these things through their reverence, faith and love for such persons.

When, therefore, we hear the great Dionysios in his second epistle to Gaios referring to God's deifying gift as 'divinity and the source of divinity and goodness',[1] we conclude that the God who grants this grace to those worthy to receive it surpasses this divinity; for God does not suffer multiplicity, nor can we speak thus of two divinities. And St Maximos, when speaking about Melchisedec, writes that this deifying grace of God is 'uncreated', declaring it to be 'eternally existent, proceeding from the eternally existing God';[2] and elsewhere in many places he says it is a light, ungenerated and completely real, that is manifested to the saints when they become worthy of receiving it, though it does not come into being merely at that moment. He also calls this light 'the light of utterly inexpressible glory and the purity of angels'; while St Makarios calls it the nourishment of the bodiless, the glory of the divine nature, the beauty of the age to come, divine and celestial fire, inexpressible noetic light, foretaste and pledge of the Holy Spirit, the sanctifying oil of gladness.[3]

---

[1] Cf. St Dionysios the Areopagite, *Letter* 2 (P.G. iii, 1068A).

[2] *Ambigua* 10 (P.G. cxi, 1141AB).

[3] Cf. St Symeon Metaphrastis, *Paraphrase of the Homilies of St Makarios*, §§62, 70, 73, 74; E.T., *The Philokalia*, vol. iii, pp. 312, 315, 317–18.

1. If, then, anyone condemns as Messalians those who declare this deifying grace of God to be uncreated, ungenerated and completely real, and calls them ditheists, he must know – if indeed there is such a person – that he is an adversary of the saints of God, and that if he does not repent he excludes himself from the inheritance of the redeemed and falls away from Him who by nature is the one and only God professed by the saints. But if anyone believes, is persuaded by and concurs with the saints and does not 'make excuses to justify sin' (Ps. 141 : 4. LXX), and if although ignorant of the manner of the mystery he does not because of his ignorance reject what is clearly proclaimed, let him not refuse to enquire and learn from those who do possess knowledge. For he will find that there is nothing inconsistent either in the divine words and acts, especially with respect to those things that are most essential and without which nothing can stand firm, or in the sound doctrine that concerns ourselves, or in the mystery that is altogether divine.

2. If anyone declares that perfect union with God is accomplished simply in an imitative and relative fashion, without the deifying grace of the Spirit and merely in the manner of persons who share the same disposition and who love one another, and that the deifying grace of God is a state of our intellectual nature acquired by imitation alone, but is not a supranatural illumination and an ineffable and divine energy beheld invisibly and conceived inconceivably by those privileged to participate in it, then he must know that he has fallen unawares into the delusion of the Messalians. For if deification is accomplished according to a capacity inherent in human nature and if it is encompassed within the bounds of nature, then of necessity the person deified is by nature God. Whoever thinks like this should not attempt, therefore, to foist his own delusion upon those who stand on secure ground and to impose a defiled creed upon those whose faith is undefiled; rather he should lay aside his presumption and learn from persons of experience or from their disciples that the grace of deification is entirely unconditional, and there is no faculty whatever in nature capable of achieving it since, if there were, this grace would no longer be grace but merely the manifestation of the operation of a natural capacity. Nor, if deification were in accord with a natural capacity, would there be anything miraculous in it; for then deification would truly be the work of nature, not the gift of God, and a man would be able to be and to be called a God by nature in the full sense of

the words. For the natural capacity of every being is nothing other than the undeviating and natural disposition for active accomplishment. It is, indeed, incomprehensible how deification can raise the person deified outside or beyond himself if it is encompassed within the bounds of nature.[1]

The grace of deification is, therefore, above nature, virtue and knowledge and, according to St Maximos, all such things infinitely fall short of it. For all the virtue we can attain and such imitation of God as lies in our power does no more than fit us for union with the Deity, but it is through grace that this ineffable union is actually accomplished. Through grace God in His entirety penetrates the saints in their entirety, and the saints in their entirety penetrate God entirely, exchanging the whole of Him for themselves, and acquiring Him alone as the reward of their ascent towards Him; for He embraces them as the soul embraces the body, enabling them to be in Him as His own members.[2]

3. If anyone asserts that those who regard the intellect as seated in the heart or in the head are Messalians, let him know that he is misguidedly attacking the saints. For St Athanasios the Great says that the soul's intelligence resides in the head,[3] and St Makarios, who is in no way inferior, says that the intellect is active in the heart;[4] and nearly all the saints concur with them. When St Gregory of Nyssa writes that the intellect is neither within the body nor outside it for it is bodiless,[5] this does not contradict what all these other saints affirm; for they say that the intellect is in the body because it is united to it, and thus they state the same thing in a different fashion, not in the least disagreeing with St Gregory. For if someone says that the Logos of God once dwelt within a virginal and immaculate womb, out of ineffable divine compassion united there to our human substance, he does not contradict someone who maintains that whatever is divine is not contained within a place because it is unembodied.

[1] The last part of this paragraph is taken from St Maximos the Confessor, *Ambigua* 20 (*P.G.* xci, 1237B). See also *Various Texts* i, 75; E.T., *The Philokalia*, vol. ii, p. 181.

[2] Most of this paragraph is likewise from St Maximos: see *Ambigua* 7, 20, 41 (*P.G.* xci, 1076C, 1088C, 1237D–1240A, 1308B).

[3] Cf. *To the Monks Everywhere, on the Actions of the Arians* 70 (*P.G.* xxv, 776CD).

[4] Cf. *Spiritual Homilies* (Collection II) xv, 20: ed. Dörries, Klostermann and Kroeger, p. 139; E.T., Mason, p. 116.

[5] Cf. *On the Creation of Man* 15 (*P.G.* xliv, 177B).

4. If anyone maintains that the light which shone about the disciples on Mount Tabor was an apparition and a symbol of the kind that now is and now is not, but has no real being and is an effect that not only does not surpass comprehension, but is inferior to it, he clearly contends against the doctrines of the saints. For the saints both in hymns and in their writings call this light ineffable, uncreated, eternal, timeless, unapproachable, boundless, infinite, limitless, invisible to angels and men, archetypal and unchanging beauty, the glory of God, the glory of Christ, the glory of the Spirit, the ray of Divinity and so forth.[1] The flesh of Christ, it is said,[2] is glorified at the moment of its assumption and the glory of the Godhead becomes the body's glory. But this glory was invisible in His visible body to those unable to perceive that upon which even angels cannot gaze. Thus Christ was transfigured, not by the addition of something He was not, nor by a transformation into something He was not, but by the manifestation to His disciples of what He really was. He opened their eyes so that instead of being blind they could see. While He Himself remained the same, they could now see Him as other than He had appeared to them formerly. For He is 'the true light' (John 1 : 9), the beauty of divine glory, and He shone forth like the sun – though this image is imperfect, since what is uncreated cannot be imaged in creation without some diminution.

5. If anyone maintains that only God's essence is uncreated, while His eternal energies are not uncreated, and that as what energizes transcends all it activates, so God transcends all His energies, let him listen to St Maximos, who says: 'All immortal things and immortality itself, all living things and life itself, all holy things and holiness itself, all good things and goodness itself, all blessings and blessedness itself, all beings and being itself are manifestly works of God. Some began to be in time, for they have not always existed. Others did not begin to be in time, for goodness, blessedness, holiness and immortality have always existed.'[3] And again he says: 'Goodness, and all that is included in the principle of goodness, and – to be brief – all life, immortality, simplicity, immutability and infinity, and all the other qualities that

---

[1] Cf. the texts used at the Feast of the Transfiguration (6 August): Mother Mary and Archimandrite Kallistos Ware, *The Festal Menaion* (London, 1969), pp. 468–503.

[2] Cf. St John of Damaskos, *Homily on the Transfiguration of Christ* 12–13 (*P.G.* xcvi, 564B–565A): ed. Kotter, pp. 450–1.

[3] *Texts on Theology* i, 50; E.T., *The Philokalia*, vol. ii, p. 124.

contemplative vision perceives as substantively appertaining to God, are realities of God which did not begin to be in time. For non-existence is never prior to goodness, nor to any of the other things we have listed, even if those things which participate in them do in themselves have a beginning in time. All goodness is without beginning because there is no time prior to it: God is eternally the unique author of its being, and God is infinitely above all beings, whether participant or participable.'[1] It is clear, therefore, from what has been said that not everything which issues from God is subject to time. For there are some things issuing from God that are without beginning, without this in the least impairing the principle of the Triadic Unity, that alone is intrinsically without beginning, or God's supraessential simplicity. In the same way the intellect, which is the imperfect image of that transcendent indivisibility, is not in the least compound because of the variety of its inherent intellections.

6. If anyone does not acknowledge that spiritual dispositions are stamped upon the body as a consequence of the gifts of the Spirit that exist in the soul of those advancing on the spiritual path; and if he does not regard dispassion as a state of aspiration for higher things that leads a person to free himself from evil habits by completely spurning what is evil and to acquire good habits by espousing what is good, but considers it to be the deathlike condition of the soul's passible aspect, then, by adhering to such views, he inevitably denies that we can enjoy an embodied life in the world of incorruption that is to come. For if in the age to come the body is to share with the soul in ineffable blessings, then it is evident that in this world as well it will also share according to its capacity in the grace mystically and ineffably bestowed by God upon the purified intellect, and it will experience the divine in conformity with its nature. For once the soul's passible aspect is transformed and sanctified – but not reduced to a deathlike condition – through it the dispositions and activities of the body are also sanctified, since body and soul share a conjoint existence. As St Diadochos states, in the case of those who have abandoned the delights of this age in the hope of enjoying the blessings of eternity, the intellect, because of its freedom from worldly cares, is able to act with its full vigour and becomes capable of perceiving the ineffable goodness of God. Then according to the measure of its own progress it

[1] Op. cit., i, 48–9; E.T., pp. 123–4.

communicates its joy to the body too, and this joy which then fills both soul and body is a true recalling of incorruptible life.[1]

The intellect perceives one light, and the senses another. The senses perceive sensible light, which manifests sensory things as sensory. The light of the intellect is the spiritual knowledge inherent in intellection. Thus sight and intellect do not perceive the same light, but each operates to the limit of its nature in what is natural to it. When saintly people become the happy possessors of spiritual and supranatural grace and power, they see both with the sense of sight and with the intellect that which surpasses both sense and intellect in the manner that – to use the expression of St Gregory of Nazianzos – 'God alone knows and those in whom these things are brought to pass'.[2]

7. These things we have been taught by the Scriptures and have received from our fathers; and we have come to know them from our own small experience. Having seen them set down in the treatise of our brother, the most reverend Hieromonk Gregory, *In Defence of Those who Devoutly Practise a Life of Stillness*, and acknowledging them to be fully consistent with the traditions of the saints, we have adjoined our signature for the assurance of those who read this present document.

The Protos of the venerable monasteries on the Holy Mountain, Hieromonk Isaac.

The abbot of the venerable, imperial and sacred Lavra, Theodosios Hieromonk.

The signature of the abbot of the monastery of Iviron in his own language [*in Georgian*].

The abbot of the venerable and imperial monastery of Vatopedi, Hieromonk Ioannikios.

The signature of the abbot of the monastery of the Serbs in his own language [*in Slavonic*].

I, Philotheos, the least of hieromonks, being of the same mind, have undersigned.

Amphilochios, the least of hieromonks and the spiritual father of the venerable monastery of Esphigmenou.

I, Gerasimos, the lowly hieromonk, having seen and read what has here

[1] Cf. *On Spiritual Knowledge* 25: ed. des Places, p. 97; E.T., *The Philokalia*, vol. i, p. 259.
[2] *Oration* 28, 19 (*Theological Oration* 2, 19) (*P.G.* xxxvi, 52B).

been written with love for the truth, and having assented thereto, have undersigned.

I, Moses, the lowly elder and least of monks, being of the same mind, have undersigned.

Theodosios, the least of hieromonks and the spiritual father of Vatopedi.

The abbot of the sacred monastery of Koutloumousiou, Theostiriktos Hieromonk.

I, Gerontios of Maroula, the sinner, one of the council of elders of the venerable Lavra, being of the same mind, have undersigned.

Kallistos of Mouzalon, the least of monks.

I, the lowly and least of monks, Gregory of Stravolangado, and perhaps a hesychast, being of the same mind and opinion, have undersigned.

I, the elder from the Skete of Magoula and least of hieromonks, Isaias, being of the same mind, have undersigned.

Mark of Sinai, the least of monks.

Kallistos of the Skete of Magoula and least of hieromonks.

The signature of an elder and hesychast from Syria in his own language [in Arabic].

Sophronios, the least of monks.

Ioasaph, the least of monks.

I, Iakovos, the humble bishop of Hierissos and the Holy Mountain, who was reared on the traditions of the Holy Mountain and the fathers, testify that by the signatures of these select men the entire Holy Mountain has undersigned with one accord, and I myself, assenting to these things and putting my seal thereto, have undersigned. I add, furthermore, together with all the rest, that we shall have no communion with anyone who is not in agreement with the saints, as we are, and as were the fathers who immediately preceded us.

GLOSSARY

AGE (*αἰών – aeon*): the ensemble of cosmic duration. It includes the angelic orders, and is an attribute of God as the principle and consummation of all the centuries created by Him. The term is used more particularly in two ways:

(i) Frequently a distinction is made between the 'present age' and the 'age to come' or the 'new age'. The first corresponds to our present sense of time, the second to time as it exists in God, that is, to eternity understood, not as endless time, but as the simultaneous presence of all time. Our present sense of time, according to which we experience time as sundered from God, is the consequence of the loss of vision and spiritual perception occasioned by the fall and is on this account more or less illusory. In reality time is not and never can be sundered from God, the 'present age' from the 'age to come'. Because of this the 'age to come' and its realities must be thought of, not as non-existent or as coming into existence in the future, but as actualities that by grace we can experience here and now. To indicate this, the Greek phrase for these realities (*τὰ μέλλοντα – ta mellonta*) is often translated as 'the blessings held in store'.

(ii) Certain texts, especially in St Maximos the Confessor, also use the term *aeon* in a connected but more specific way, to denote a level intermediate between eternity in the full sense (*ἀϊδιότης – aïdiotis*) and time as known to us in our present experience (*χρόνος – chronos*). Where this is the case we normally employ the rendering 'aeon' instead of 'age'. There are thus three levels:

(a) eternity, the *totum simul* or simultaneous presence of all time and reality as known to God, who alone has neither origin nor end, and who therefore is alone eternal in the full sense;

(b) the aeon, the *totum simul* as known to the angels, and also to human persons who possess experience of the 'age to come':

although having no end, these angelic or human beings, since they are created, are not self-originating and therefore are not eternal in the sense that God is eternal;

(c) time, that is, temporal succession as known to us in the 'present age'.

APPETITIVE ASPECT OF THE SOUL, or the soul's desiring power (τὸ ἐπιθυμητικόν – to epithymitikon): one of the three aspects or powers of the soul according to the tripartite division formulated by Plato (see his Republic, Book iv, 434D–441C) and on the whole accepted by the Greek Christian Fathers. The other two are, first, the intelligent aspect or power (τὸ λογιστικόν – to logistikon: see Intelligent); and, second, the incensive aspect or power (τὸ θυμικόν – to thymikon), which often manifests itself as wrath or anger, but which can be more generally defined as the force provoking vehement feelings. The three aspects or powers can be used positively, that is, in accordance with nature and as created by God, or negatively, that is, in a way contrary to nature and leading to sin (q.v.). For instance, the incensive power can be used positively to repel demonic attacks or to intensify desire for God; but it can also, when not controlled, lead to self-indulgent, disruptive thought and action.

The appetitive and incensive aspects, in particular the former, are sometimes termed the soul's passible aspect (τὸ παθητικόν – to pathitikon), that is to say, the aspect which is more especially vulnerable to pathos or passion (q.v.), and which, when not transformed by positive spiritual influences, is susceptive to the influence of negative and self-destructive forces. The intelligent aspect, although also susceptible to passion, is not normally regarded as part of the soul's passible aspect.

ASSENT (συγκατάθεσις – synkatathesis): see Temptation.

ATTENTIVENESS (προσοχή – prosochi): see Watchfulness.

COMPUNCTION (κατάνυξις – katanyxis): in our version sometimes also translated 'deep penitence'. The state of one who is 'pricked to the heart', becoming conscious both of his own sinfulness and of the forgiveness extended to him by God; a mingled feeling of sorrow, tenderness and joy, springing from sincere repentance (q.v.).

CONCEPTUAL IMAGE (νόημα – noïma): see Thought.

CONTEMPLATION (θεωρία – theoria): the perception or vision of the intellect (q.v.) through which one attains spiritual knowledge (q.v.). It may be contrasted with the practice of the virtues (πρακτική –

praktiki) which designates the more external aspect of the ascetic life – purification and the keeping of the commandments – but which is an indispensable prerequisite of contemplation. Depending on the level of personal spiritual growth, contemplation has two main stages: it may be either of the inner essences or principles (q.v.) of created beings or, at a higher stage, of God Himself.

COUPLING (*συνδυασμός – syndyasmos*): *see* Temptation.

DELUSION (*πλάνη – plani*): *see* Illusion.

DESIRE, Desiring power of the soul: *see* Appetitive aspect of the soul.

DISCRIMINATION (*διάκρισις – diakrisis*): a spiritual gift permitting one to discriminate between the types of thought that enter into one's mind, to assess them accurately and to treat them accordingly. Through this gift one gains 'discernment of spirits' – that is, the ability to distinguish between the thoughts or visions inspired by God and the suggestions or fantasies coming from the devil. It is a kind of eye or lantern of the soul by which man finds his way along the spiritual path without falling into extremes; thus it includes the idea of discretion.

DISPASSION (*ἀπάθεια – apatheia*): among the writers of the texts here translated, some regard passion (q.v.) as evil and the consequence of sin (q.v.), and for them dispassion signifies passionlessness, the uprooting of the passions; others, such as St Isaiah the Solitary, regard the passions as fundamentally good, and for them dispassion signifies a state in which the passions are exercised in accordance with their original purity and so without committing sin in act or thought. Dispassion is a state of reintegration and spiritual freedom; when translating the term into Latin, Cassian rendered it 'purity of heart'. Such a state may imply impartiality and detachment, but not indifference, for if a dispassionate man does not suffer on his own account, he suffers for his fellow creatures. It consists, not in ceasing to feel the attacks of the demons, but in no longer yielding to them. It is positive, not negative: Evagrios links it closely with the quality of love (*agapi*) and Diadochos speaks of the 'fire of dispassion' (§ 17: in our translation, vol. i, p. 258). Dispassion is among the gifts of God.

ECSTASY (*'έκστασις – ekstasis*): a 'going out' from oneself and from all created things towards God, under the influence of *eros* or intense longing (q.v.). A man does not attain ecstasy by his own efforts, but is drawn out of himself by the power of God's love. Ecstasy implies a passing beyond all the conceptual thinking of the discursive reason (q.v.). It may sometimes be marked by a state of trance, or by a loss of normal consciousness; but such psychophysical accompaniments are in no way essential. Occasionally the term *ekstasis* is used in a bad sense, to mean infatuation, loss of self-control, or madness.

FAITH (πίστις – *pistis*): not only an individual or theoretical belief in the dogmatic truths of Christianity, but an all-embracing relationship, an attitude of love and total trust in God. As such it involves a transformation of man's entire life. Faith is a gift from God, the means whereby we are taken up into the whole theanthropic activity of God in Christ and of man in Christ through which man attains salvation.

FALLEN NATURE (παλαιὸς 'ἄνθρωπος – *palaios anthropos*): literally, the 'old man'. *See* Flesh, sense (ii).

FANTASY (φαντασία – *fantasia*): denoting the image-producing faculty of the psyche, this is one of the most important words in the hesychast vocabulary. As one begins to advance along the spiritual path one begins to 'perceive' images of things which have no direct point of reference in the external world, and which emerge inexplicably from within oneself. This experience is a sign that one's consciousness is beginning to deepen: outer sensations and ordinary thoughts have to some extent been quietened, and the impulses, fears, hopes, passions hidden in the subconscious region are beginning to break through to the surface. One of the goals of the spiritual life is indeed the attainment of a spiritual knowledge (q.v.) which transcends both the ordinary level of consciousness and the subconscious; and it is true that images, especially when the recipient is in an advanced spiritual state, may well be projections on the plane of the imagination of celestial archetypes, and that in this case they can be used creatively, to form the images of sacred art and iconography. But more often than not they will simply derive from a middle or lower sphere, and will have nothing spiritual or creative about them. Hence they correspond to the world of fantasy and not to the world of the imagination in the proper sense. It is on this account that the hesychastic masters on the whole take a negative attitude towards them. They emphasize the grave dangers involved in this kind of experience, especially as the very production of these images may be the consequence of demonic or diabolic activity; and they admonish those still in the early stages and not yet possessing spiritual discrimination (q.v.) not to be enticed and led captive by these illusory appearances, whose tumult may well overwhelm the mind. Their advice is to pay no attention to them, but to continue with prayer and invocation, dispelling them with the name of Jesus Christ.

FLESH (σάρξ – sarx): has various senses: (i) the human in contrast to the divine, as in the sentence, 'The Logos became flesh' (John 1 : 14); (ii) fallen and sinful human nature in contrast to human nature as originally created and dwelling in communion with God; man when separated from God and in rebellion against Him; (iii) the body in contrast to the soul. The second meaning is probably the most frequent. If the word is being employed in this sense, it is important to distinguish 'flesh' from 'body' (σῶμα – soma). When St Paul lists the 'works of the flesh' in Gal. 5 : 19–21, he mentions such things as 'seditions', 'heresy' and 'envy', which have no special connection with the body. In sense (ii) of the word, 'flesh' denotes the *whole* soul–body structure in so far as a man is fallen; likewise 'spirit' denotes the *whole* soul–body structure in so far as a man is redeemed. The soul as well as the body can become fleshly or 'carnal', just as the body as well as the soul can become spiritual. Asceticism involves a war against the flesh – in sense (ii) of the word – but not against the body as such.

GUARD OF THE HEART, OF THE INTELLECT (φυλακὴ καρδίας, νοῦ – phylaki kardias, nou): see Watchfulness.

HEART (καρδία – kardia): not simply the physical organ but the spiritual centre of man's being, man as made in the image of God, his deepest and truest self, or the inner shrine, to be entered only through sacrifice and death, in which the mystery of the union between the divine and the human is consummated. ' "I called with my whole heart", says the psalmist – that is, with body, soul and spirit' (John Klimakos, *The Ladder of Divine Ascent*, Step 28, translated by Archimandrite Lazarus [London, 1959], pp. 257–8). 'Heart' has thus an all-embracing significance: 'prayer of the heart' means prayer not just of the emotions and affections, but of the whole person, including the body.

ILLUSION (πλάνη – plani): in our version sometimes also translated 'delusion'. Literally, wandering astray, deflection from the right path; hence error, beguilement, the acceptance of a mirage mistaken for truth. Cf. the literal sense of sin (q.v.) as 'missing the mark'.

INCENSIVE POWER or aspect of the soul (θυμός – thymos; τὸ θυμικόν – to thymikon): see Appetitive aspect of the soul.

INNER ESSENCES OR PRINCIPLES (λόγοι – logoi): see Logos.

INTELLECT (νοῦς – nous): the highest faculty in man, through which – provided it is purified – he knows God or the inner essences or principles (q.v.) of created things by means of direct apprehension or spiritual perception. Unlike the *dianoia* or reason (q.v.), from which it must be carefully distinguished, the intellect does not function by formulating abstract concepts and then arguing on this basis to a conclusion reached through deductive reasoning, but it understands divine truth by means of immediate experience, intuition or 'simple cognition' (the term used by St Isaac the Syrian). The intellect dwells in the 'depths of the soul'; it constitutes the innermost aspect of the heart (St Diadochos, §§ 79, 88: in our translation, vol. i, pp. 280, 287). The intellect is the organ of contemplation (q.v.), the 'eye of the heart' (*Makarian Homilies*).

INTELLECTION (νόησις – noïsis): not an abstract concept or a visual image, but the act or function of the intellect (q.v.) whereby it apprehends spiritual realities in a direct manner.

INTELLIGENT (λογικός – logikos): the Greek term *logikos* is so closely connected with Logos (q.v.), and therefore with the divine Intellect, that to render it simply as 'logical' and hence descriptive of the reason (q.v.) is clearly inadequate. Rather it pertains to the intellect (q.v.) and qualifies the possessor of spiritual knowledge (q.v.). Hence when found in conjunction with 'soul' (*logiki psychi*), *logikos* is translated as 'deiform' or as 'endowed with intelligence'. Intelligence itself (τὸ λογικόν – to logikon; τὸ λογιστικόν – to logistikon; 'ο λογισμός – ho logismos) is the ruling aspect of the intellect (q.v.) or its operative faculty.

INTENSE LONGING ('έρως – eros): the word *eros*, when used in these texts, retains much of the significance it has in Platonic thought. It denotes that intense aspiration and longing which impel man towards union with God, and at the same time something of the force which links the divine and the human. As unitive love *par excellence*, it is not distinct from *agapi*, but may be contrasted with *agapi* in that it expresses a greater degree of intensity and ecstasy (q.v.).

INTIMATE COMMUNION (παρρησία – parrisia): literally, 'frankness', 'freedom of speech'; hence freedom of approach to God, such as

Adam possessed before the fall and the saints have regained by grace; a sense of confidence and loving trust in God's mercy.

JESUS PRAYER ('Ιησοῦ εὐχή – Iïsou evchi): the invocation of the name of Jesus, most commonly in the words, 'Lord Jesus Christ, Son of God, have mercy on me', although there are a number of variant forms. Not merely a 'technique' or a 'Christian mantra', but a prayer addressed to the Person of Jesus Christ, expressing our living faith (q.v.) in Him as Son of God and Saviour.

LOGOS (Λόγος – Logos): the Second Person of the Holy Trinity, or the Intellect, Wisdom and Providence of God in whom and through whom all things are created. As the unitary cosmic principle, the Logos contains in Himself the multiple logoi (inner principles or inner essences, thoughts of God) in accordance with which all things come into existence at the times and places, and in the forms, appointed for them, each single thing thereby containing in itself the principle of its own development. It is these logoi, contained principally in the Logos and manifest in the forms of the created universe, that constitute the first or lower stage of contemplation (q.v.).

MIND: see Reason.

NOETIC (νοητός – noïtos): that which belongs to or is characteristic of the intellect (q.v.). See also Intellection.

PASSION (πάθος – pathos): in Greek, the word signifies literally that which happens to a person or thing, an experience undergone passively; hence an appetite or impulse such as anger, desire or jealousy, that violently dominates the soul. Many Greek Fathers regard the passions as something intrinsically evil, a 'disease' of the soul: thus St John Klimakos affirms that God is not the creator of the passions and that they are 'unnatural', alien to man's true self (The Ladder of Divine Ascent, Step 26, translated by Archimandrite Lazarus [op. cit.], p. 211). Other Greek Fathers, however, look on the passions as impulses originally placed in man by God, and so fundamentally good, although at present distorted by sin (cf. St Isaiah the Solitary, § 1: in our translation, vol. i, p. 22). On this second view, then, the passions are to be educated, not eradicated; to be transfigured, not suppressed; to be used positively, not negatively (see Dispassion).

PRACTICE OF THE VIRTUES (πρακτική – praktiki): see Contemplation.

PREPOSSESSION (πρόληψις – prolipsis): see Temptation.

PROVOCATION (προσβολή – *prosvoli*): *see* Temptation.

REASON, mind (διάνοια – *dianoia*): the discursive, conceptualizing and logical faculty in man, the function of which is to draw conclusions or formulate concepts deriving from data provided either by revelation or spiritual knowledge (q.v.) or by sense-observation. The knowledge of the reason is consequently of a lower order than spiritual knowledge (q.v.) and does not imply any direct apprehension or perception of the inner essences or principles (q.v.) of created beings, still less of divine truth itself. Indeed, such apprehension or perception, which is the function of the intellect (q.v.), is beyond the scope of the reason.

REBUTTAL (ἀντιλογία – *antilogia*; ἀντίρρησις – *antirrisis*): the repulsing of a demon or demonic thought at the moment of provocation (q.v.); or, in a more general sense, the bridling of evil thoughts.

REMEMBRANCE OF GOD (μνήμη Θεοῦ – *mnimi Theou*): not just calling God to mind, but the state of recollectedness or concentration in which attention is centred on God. As such it is the opposite of the state of self-indulgence and insensitivity.

REPENTANCE (μετάνοια – *metanoia*): the Greek signifies primarily a 'change of mind' or 'change of intellect': not only sorrow, contrition or regret, but more positively and fundamentally the conversion or turning of our whole life towards God.

SENSUAL PLEASURE (ἡδονή – *hidoni*): according to the context the Greek term signifies either sensual pleasure (the most frequent meaning) or spiritual pleasure or delight.

SIN (ἁμαρτία – *hamartia*): the primary meaning of the Greek word is 'failure' or, more specifically, 'failure to hit the mark' and so a 'missing of the mark', a 'going astray' or, ultimately, 'failure to achieve the purpose for which one is created'. It is closely related, therefore, to illusion (q.v.). The translation 'sin' should be read with these connotations in mind.

SORROW (λύπη – *lypi*): often with the sense of 'godly sorrow' – the sorrow which nourishes the soul with the hope engendered by repentance (q.v.).

SPIRITUAL KNOWLEDGE (γνῶσις – *gnosis*): the knowledge of the intellect (q.v.) as distinct from that of the reason (q.v.). As such it is knowledge inspired by God, and so linked with contemplation (q.v.) and immediate spiritual perception.

STILLNESS (ἡσυχία – *hesychia*): from which are derived the words hesychasm and hesychast, used to denote the whole spiritual tradition represented in *The Philokalia* as well as the person who pursues the spiritual path it delineates (*see* Introduction, vol. i, pp. 14–16): a state of inner tranquillity or mental quietude and concentration which arises in conjunction with, and is deepened by, the practice of pure prayer and the guarding of heart (q.v.) and intellect (q.v.). Not simply silence, but an attitude of listening to God and of openness towards Him.

TEMPERAMENT (*κρᾶσις* – *krasis*): primarily the well-balanced blending of elements, humours or qualities in animal bodies, but sometimes extended to denote the whole soul–body structure of man. In this sense it is the opposite to a state of psychic or physical disequilibrium.

TEMPTATION (*πειρασμός* – *peirasmos*): also translated in our version as 'trial' or 'test'. The word indicates, according to context: (i) a test or trial sent to man by God, so as to aid his progress on the spiritual way; (ii) a suggestion from the devil, enticing man into sin.

Using the word in sense (ii), the Greek Fathers employ a series of technical terms to describe the process of temptation. (See in particular Mark the Ascetic, *On the Spiritual Law*, §§ 138–41, in vol. i of our translation, pp. 119–20; John Klimakos, *Ladder*, Step 15, translated by Archimandrite Lazarus [op. cit.], pp. 157–8; Maximos, *On Love*, i, §§ 83–84, in vol. ii of our translation, pp. 62–63; John of Damaskos, *On the Virtues and Vices*, also in vol. ii of our translation, pp. 337–8.) The basic distinction made by these Fathers is between the demonic *provocation* and man's *assent*: the first lies outside man's control, while for the second he is morally responsible. In detail, the chief terms employed are as follows:

(i) *Provocation* (*προσβολή* – *prosvoli*): the initial incitement to evil. Mark the Ascetic defines this as an 'image-free stimulation in the heart'; so long as the provocation is not accompanied by images, it does not involve man in any guilt. Such provocations, originating as they do from the devil, assail man from the outside independently of his free will, and so he is not morally responsible for them. His liability to these provocations is not a consequence of the fall: even in paradise, Mark maintains, Adam was assailed by the devil's provocations. Man cannot prevent provocations from assailing him; what does lie in his power, however, is to maintain constant watchfulness (q.v.) and so to reject each provocation as soon as it emerges into his consciousness – that is to say, at its first appearance as a thought in his mind or intellect (μονολόγιστος 'έμφασις – monologistos emphasis). If he does reject the provocation, the sequence is cut off and the process of temptation is terminated.

(ii) *Momentary disturbance* (παραρριπισμός – pararripismos) of the intellect, occurring 'without any movement or working of bodily passion' (see Mark, *Letter to Nicolas the Solitary*: in our translation, vol. i, p. 153). This seems to be more than the 'first appearance' of a provocation described in stage (i) above; for, at a certain point of spiritual growth in this life, it is possible to be totally released from such 'momentary disturbance', whereas no one can expect to be altogether free from demonic provocations.

(iii) *Communion* (όμιλία – homilia); *coupling* (συνδυασμός – syndyasmos). Without as yet entirely assenting to the demonic provocation, a man may begin to 'entertain' it, to converse or parley with it, turning it over in his mind pleasurably, yet still hesitating whether or not to act upon it. At this stage, which is indicated by the terms 'communion' or 'coupling', the provocation is no longer 'image-free' but has become a *logismos* or thought (q.v.); and a person is morally responsible for having allowed this to happen.

(iv) *Assent* (συγκατάθεσις – synkatathesis). This signifies a step beyond mere 'communion' or 'coupling'. No longer merely 'playing' with the evil suggestion, a person now resolves to act upon it. There is now no doubt as to his moral culpability: even if circumstances prevent him from sinning outwardly, he is judged by God according to the intention in his heart.

(v) *Prepossession* (πρόληψις – prolipsis): defined by Mark as 'the involuntary presence of former sins in the memory'. This state of 'prepossession' or prejudice results from repeated acts of sin which predispose a man to yield to particular temptations. In principle he retains his free choice and can reject demonic provocations; but in practice the force of habit makes it more and more difficult for him to resist.

(vi) *Passion* (q.v.). If a man does not fight strenuously against a prepossession, it will develop into an evil passion.

THEOLOGY (θεολογία – theologia): denotes in these texts far more than the learning about God and religious doctrine acquired through academic study. It signifies active and conscious participation in or perception of the realities of the divine world – in other words, the realization of spiritual knowledge (q.v.). To be a theologian in the full sense, therefore, presupposes the attainment of the state of stillness (q.v.) and dispassion (q.v.), itself the concomitant of pure and undistracted prayer, and so requires gifts bestowed on but extremely few persons.

THOUGHT (λογισμός – logismos; νόημα – noïma): (i) frequently signifies not thought in the ordinary sense, but thought provoked by the demons, and therefore often qualified in translation by the adjective 'evil' or 'demonic'; it can also signify divinely-inspired thought; (ii) a 'conceptual image', intermediate between fantasy (q.v.) and an abstract concept; this sense of noïma is frequent in the texts of St Maximos, where the rendering 'conceptual image' is normally adopted.

WATCHFULNESS (νῆψις – nipsis): literally, the opposite to a state of drunken stupor; hence spiritual sobriety, alertness, vigilance. It signifies an attitude of attentiveness (προσοχή – prosochi), whereby one keeps watch over one's inward thoughts and fantasies (q.v.), maintaining guard over the heart and intellect (φυλακὴ καρδίας/νοῦ – phylaki kardias/nou; τήρησις καρδίας/νοῦ – tirisis kardias/nou). In Hesychios, On Watchfulness and Holiness, §§ 1–6 (in our translation, vol. i, pp. 162–3), watchfulness is given a very broad definition, being used to indicate the whole range of the practice of the virtues. It is closely linked with purity of heart and stillness (q.v.). The Greek title of The Philokalia is 'The Philokalia of the Niptic Fathers', i.e. of the fathers who practised and inculcated the virtue of watchfulness. This shows how central is the role assigned by St Nikodimos to this state.

WRATH, wrathfulness: see Appetitive aspect of the soul.

INDEX

[Major entries are given in bold type]

PERSONS AND SOURCES

Agathon, Abba, of Egypt (4th cent.), 198, 199

Akindynos, Gregory (c. 1300–48), 287, 288, 291, 376, 378, 379, 380, 384, 385, 391, 392, 395, 396, 403, 405, 407, 408, 411, 412, 413, 415, 416

Ânân-Îshô (6th–7th cent.), 72n.

Andronikos II Palaiologos, Emperor (reigned 1282–1328), 287

Andronikos III Palaiologos, Emperor (reigned 1328–41), 287, 289

Antony the Great, St (251–356), 195–6

Apophthegmata: see Sayings of the Desert Fathers

Aristotle (384–322 B.C.), 350

Arsenios the Great, St (354—449), 99n., 197, 293n.

Arsenios, teacher of St Gregory of Sinai (13th cent.), 207, 209

Athanasios of Alexandria, the Great, St (c. 296–373), 196n., 399n., 421

Athanasios of Mount Auxentios (13th cent.), 341

Athanasios I, Patriarch of Constantinople (in office 1289–93, 1303–9), St, 341

Barlaam the Calabrian (c. 1290–1348), 287, 288, 290, 291, 376, 378, 379, 380, 384, 385, 388, 395, 400, 403, 404, 405, 408, 417

Barsanuphios of Gaza, St: *see* Varsanuphios of Gaza, St

Basil the Great, St (c. 330–79), 270, 319, 335–6, 377, 378, 379, 381, 385, 388, 391n., 396, 397, 403, 405, 413, 414–15

Cassian, St John (c. 360–435), 429

Chrysostom, St John (c. 347–407), 257, 294, 377, 380, 381, 391, 395, 396–7, 415

Constantine IX Monomachos, Emperor (reigned 1042–55), 76

Cyril of Alexandria, St (d. 444), 380, 392, 399–403, 405, 413

Cyril of Skythopolis (?525–?559), 198n.

Diadochos of Photiki, St (c. 400–c. 486), 202, 210n., 262, 270, 317–18, 423, 429, 432

Dionysios the Areopagite, St (c. 500), 77, 146n., 173n., 294, 336, 337, 376, 381n., 386–7, 388, 389–90, 394, 403, 406, 419

Ephrem the Syrian, St (c. 306–73), 260, 273

Eunomios (d. 394), 384–5, 405, 417

Evagrios the Solitary (of Pontos) (345/6–399), 77, 210n., 317n., 429

Gabriel (13th–14th cent.), 341

Gerontikon: see Sayings of the Desert Fathers

Gregoras, Nikiphoros (c. 1290–c. 1361), 287, 288

Gregory Akindynos: *see* Akindynos, Gregory

Gregory of Nyssa, St (c. 330–c. 395), 385, 405, 421

Gregory Palamas, St: *see* Palamas, St Gregory

Gregory of Sinai, St (c. 1265–1346), 207–11, 288

Gregory the Theologian (of Nazianzos), St (329–89), 13, 20, 38n., 242, 246, 369,

376n., 377, 378, 381n., 394, 396, 397, 404, 406–8, 414–15, 424

Gregory of Thessaloniki, St: *see* Palamas, St Gregory

Hesychios the Priest, St (?8th–?9th cent.), 72, 271, 437

Humbert of Silva Candida, Cardinal (d. 1061), 76

Ilias of Mount Auxentios (13th cent.), 341

Ilias the Presbyter (?late 11th–early 12th cent.), 267n.

Irene-Evlogia Choumnaina, Abbess (1291–c. 1355), 175, 176

Isaac the Syrian (of Nineveh), St (7th cent.), 77, 202, 266, 268, 270, 271, 318, 432

Isaiah the Solitary, St (?d. 489/91), 72, 201, 202, 264, 429, 433

Joachim 'the Vigilant' (14th cent.), 209

John Alexander, Tsar of Bulgaria (reigned 1331–71), 208

John Cassian, St: *see* Cassian, St John

John Chrysostom, St: *see* Chrysostom, St John

John of Damaskos, St (c. 675–c. 749), 217, 379, 383, 407–8, 413, 415, 422n., 435

John of Karpathos, St (?7th cent.), 203

John Klimakos, St: *see* Klimakos, St John

Kallistos I, Patriarch of Constantinople (in office 1350–3, 1355–63), 207, 209

Kiroularios, Michael: *see* Michael Kiroularios

Klimakos, St John (6th–7th cent.), 15n., 72, 73, 77, 196, 200, 264, 265, 266, 267, 268, 269, 271, 273, 277, 278, 279, 313, 335n., 336, 337, 431, 433, 435

Longinos 'the Confessor' (13th–14th cent.), 208–9, 257

Makarios of Corinth, St (1731–1805), 13, 64, 176, 208, 289

Makarios of Egypt, the Great, St (c. 300–c. 390), 99n., 320; *Makarian Homilies* (?late 4th cent.), 201–2, 334, 419, 421, 432

Mark the Monk (the Ascetic), St (?early 5th cent.), 13, 16–17, 72, 199–200, 259, 261, 269, 320, 435–6

Maximos the Confessor, St (580–662), 77, 251, 267, 271, 381, 384, 388, 397, 419, 421, 422, 427, 435, 437

Michael Kiroularios, Patriarch of Constantinople (in office 1043–58), 76

Michael VIII Palaiologos, Emperor (reigned 1259–82), 175, 192, 209

Neilos the Ascetic (of Ankyra), St (d. c. 430), 271, 317, 341n.

Neilos of Italy (13th cent.), 341

Nikiphoros Gregoras: *see* Gregoras, Nikiphoros

Nikiphoros the Monk (13th cent.), 64, 192–3, 204–6, 207, 209, 210, 341

Nikitas Stithatos (11th cent.), 11, 76–8, 173n., 271, 341n.

Nikodimos of the Holy Mountain, St (1749–1809), 13, 64, 176, 208, 289, 437

Niphon 'the Hesychast' (14th cent.), 209

Origen (c. 185–c. 254), 294

Palamas, St Gregory (1296–1359), 66, 175, 176, 192–3, 207, 208, 210, 287–92, 341n., 395n., 424

Palladius, Bishop of Helinopolis (c. 365–425), 72n.

Paradise of the Fathers, 72

Paul of Mount Latros, St (d. 955), 197–8

Philotheos of Sinai, St (?9th–10th cent.), 72, 271

Philotheos of Sinai (14th cent.), 209

Plato (c. 429–347 B.C.), 383, 428

Sabellius (3rd cent.), 403, 411, 412

Savvas, St (439–532), 198

Sayings of the Desert Fathers (Apophthegmata, Gerontikon), 72n., 73n., 99n., 197n., 199n., 293n.

Seliotis (13th–14th cent.), 341

Skliraina, mistress of Constantine IX (11th cent.), 76

Stithatos, Nikitas: *see* Nikitas Stithatos

Symeon Metaphrastis, St (10th cent.), 416n., 419n.

Symeon the New Theologian, St (949–1022), 11–15, 62, 64, 76–7, 192, 203, 210, 265, 271, 341

Symeon the Studite, St (the 'Pious' or 'Devout') (c. 917–986/7), 11–15, 77

Synesis, the nun (14th cent.), 295

Thalassios the Libyan, St (7th cent.), 261
Theodosios the Cenobiarch, St (d. 529), 196–7

Theoliptos of Philadelphia (c. 1250–1322), 175–6, 192, 209, 287, 341

Varsanuphios of Gaza, St (6th cent.), 59n., 72, 266, 270,

Xenia, the nun (14th cent.), 289

SUBJECTS

Abandonment by God, sense of, 92, 260; three reasons for, 91; withdrawal of God's grace, 111, 113, 136

Abbot, 35, 51, 53, 54, 55, 57, 58, 59. See Spiritual father

Accidents, not to be attributed to God, 406, 410

Adam, 83, 194, 296; before the fall, 189; Adam's rib, 189. See Fall

Aeon: see Age to come

Aether, enclosed by heavens, 348, 350

Afflictions, 54, 100. See Endurance, Suffering, Trials

Agapi, and eros, 432. See Love

Age to come, 110, 292, 377, **427**; beauty of, 419; foretaste in present life, 137–8, 171, 182, 316, 326, 328, 344, 418, 423; and the divine light, 415

Alleluia, 172, 269

Alms, to be given to everyone at all times, **49–50**; only with the blessing of spiritual father, 28; how to be accepted, 256

'Anagogical', as term of opprobrium, 165

Analogy, from creation to the Creator, 385

Angels, nine ranks, **172–3**; hierarchy of, 76, 146–7, 151–2; created beings, 357; bodiless, 358, 374; impassible, 323; possess intellect, logos, eros and spirit, 362–3, 366; possess free will, 358–9; termed 'secondary light', an emanation from the Primal Light, 376, 381; their circular movement, 376, 381; their delight in prayer, 237; have no vision of the divine essence, 416; the devil and demons can take the form of angels, 68, 244, 286; false visions of angels, 270, 283.

Contemplation of angels by men, 67, 248; angels as guardians, 375; they help and protect us, 44, 104; we derive our noetic aspect from, 142; angels superior to men, 357, 366, 381; they deserve our homage, 357, yet also serve us, 366; we are more in God's image than they are, 363, 366, 374, 375–6; but they are more in His likeness, 376, 377; in heaven we are equal to them, 222, 297, 300.

Prayer and contemplation assimilate us to the angels, 120, 130, 172–3; we dance with them, 381; we can live an angelic life on earth, 19, 81, 103, 118, 121, 125, 144, 147, 153, 197, 221, 317, 328, 344; angelic habit (of monks), 45. See Fall

Anger, 71, 89, 104, 113, 124, 142, **227–8**, 231, 329, 428; good use of, 89, 228; against demons, 73, 105, 236, 428; converted into joy, 214; righteous indignation or natural wrath, 236. See Incensive power

Animals: wild animals and man, 197, 213; demons resemble or take the form of animals, 224–5, 243–4; fall makes us similar to the animals, 213, 227–8, 243; animals are better than us, 238; their soul dies with their body, 359

Anointing of priests and kings, 250; Christ anoints our human nature with His Godhead, 309, 323, 396. See Oil

Antichrist, 219

Anxiety, freedom from 72, 315. See Detachment

Apatheia: see Dispassion

Apophatic approach, 176, 210, 394, 401, 404; God transcends all being, 248, 382–3;

He cannot be understood, 21, 140; nor can man, 140, 227; an ignorance that surpasses knowledge, 181. *See* Essence, Images, Thoughts

Appetitive aspect of soul: *see* Desire

Archetypes, celestial, 231, 246, 250, 430; God as Archetype, 142, 319, 362

Arrogance: see Pride

Ascension of Christ, 253, 298, 324

Ascetic life: *see* Practice of the commandments

Assent to temptations, 89, 223, 224, 254, 255–6, 308, 435–6

Assurance (*plirophoria*), 204, 237, 280. *See* Awareness

Athos, Holy Mountain of, 192, 193, 207, 209, 287–8, 289, 292, 341, 424–5

Attentiveness: *see* Watchfulness

Avarice, 82, 89, 90, 122–3, 124, 231

Awareness, conscious (direct experience of God), 13, 14, 17, 23, 29, 36, 39, 40, 42, 50, 72, 79, 81, 194, 206, 211, 231, 232–3, 247, 248, 253, 259, 276, 316, 317, 335, 419, 424, 432. *See* Assurance; Conscience; Spirit, the Holy

Awe: *see* Fear

Baptism, 40, 48, 164, 166, 168, 176, 177–8, 211, 237, 247–8, 253, 257, 258, 259, 265, 272, 276, 280, 289, 317, 338; baptism of Christ, 253; John's baptism of repentance, 54; royal priesthood of baptized, 250

Baths, to be avoided, 27. *See* Washing

Beauty, divine, 67, 103, 108, 147, 155, 221, 415; Christ as the divine beauty, 422; beauty of the age to come, 419; of creation, 78, 91, 98, 103, 163, 355, 385; original beauty of divine image in man, 83, 87, 364; natural beauty of soul, 96, 110, 132, 183, 319, 363; bodily beauty, 91–2; dangers of beauty, 310, 371

Bees, to be imitated, 180, 186, 233

Bible: *see* Scripture

Blasphemy, 94, 104, 249, 251

Body, as God's creation, 290; state before and after fall, 227–8; distinction between body and flesh, 431; unity of body and soul, 66, 67, 170, 227–8, 292, 356, 375, 423; energized by God, 227, 248, 358–9,

363, 374; divine image in man does not involve the body, 139–40, 357, 361, 374; body is less precious than soul, 46, 110, 114, 150; the body's temperament, 142, 254, 261, 435; composed of the four elements, 171; consists of teguments and cavities, 146; originally created without humours, 213, 227; will be without them after resurrection, 221; baneful fluidity, 96; defluxions from, 50–1, 96, 254–6; bodies vary greatly, 280.

Low estate of body, 105, 109, 118, 132, 134, 151; to be given enough only to keep it alive, 37; to be disciplined and mortified, 29, 30, 102; but such bodily discipline is of limited value, 131–2, 150, 154; bodily toil and afflictions, 46, 272–3; body to be mortified and spurned, 30, 301; to be hated, 326; an enemy, 108; sinful love of, 85, 86; passionate attachment to, 109; passions of body, 226; seduction of, 120; ugly pleasures of, 419; downward pull, 42, 150; hard to lead to virtue, 301; danger of bodily relaxation, 27; bodily torpor and exhaustion, 34, 55, 254, 255; bodily strength not equal to inner desire, 101.

Body not evil by nature, 290, 332–3; bodily beauty is in itself good, 91–2; body to be kept pure, 201–2; the bodiless intellect is to be enclosed within the body, 200, 331–7; union with God in the body, 44, 135; body to be used in prayer, 66; bodily gestures in prayer, 67, 70, 75, 128, 277; bodily technique with Jesus Prayer, 64–6, 72–3, 192–3, 205–6, 210, 264–5, 277, 290, 331–2, 337, 338–40; our inner state reflected in the body and influenced by it, 87, 88, 95, 338, 423; intellect transmits grace to body, 318; body transformed, 339; sanctified and rendered immortal by soul, 36, 363; shares soul's joy, 424; shares with soul in blessings of Age to come, 423; loved by soul, 363; rendered spiritual, 150, 221, 431; shares in fragrance of Spirit, 149; to be delivered from corruption, 164; glory of the body at Christ's transfiguration, 415, 422; God's dwelling-place, 332, 339. *See* Flesh; Person, the human; Resurrection; Senses; Soul

Breathing, control of, during prayer, 65, 72–3, 192–3, 205–6, 210, 264–5, 277, 285, 290, 331–2, 337

Bride, bridegroom: see Nuptial symbolism

Bulgaria, 208

Burial of Christ, 253

Cain, 375; curse of, 261

Carnal mode of life, 107–8

Cataphatic approach, 401, 404. See Apophatic approach

Categories, the ten, 409

Cell, need to remain in, 51, 53, 57, 73, 181, 307, 310–11; prayer in, 72, 183; time wasted in, 180

Cenobitic life, 14, 43, 68, 98, 99–100, 209, 279; relations within the community, 37, 51–5, 57, 58, 59–61. See Monastic life, Solitary life

Chastity: see Purity, Virginity

Cherubim, 146, 152, 172, 257, 324, 416. See Angels

Children, how far subject to passions, 304, 310

Christ, meaning of the title, 396; two natures as God and man, 31, 42, 134, 135, 217, 218, 221, 234, 327; obedience to the Father, 33; glorified by the Father, 46; as Comforter, 314; death for our salvation, 49, 50, 298; priest of the heavenly tabernacle, 220; presence in Eucharist, 62; presence in the hungry and thirsty, 49–50; washes our feet, 134; birth within our soul, 145, 151, 154; imitation of Christ, 46, 55, 93, 113, 122, 154, 222, 236, 253. See Ascension, Burial, Cross, Incarnation, Logos, Resurrection, Second coming, Transfiguration

Christ Philanthropos Sotir, monastery of, 175

Christmas, 58

Church, as bride of Christ, 41

Clothing, 55, 70, 307–8

Commandments: see Practice of the commandments

Communion, holy: see Holy communion

Communion with temptations, 201, 436

Community: see Cenobitic life

Compassion, 37, 82, 87, 109, 141, 143, 165, 166, 173. See Love

Compline, 53

Compunction, 39, 52, 53, 55, 61, 95, 96, 109, 112, 117, 118, 119, 120, 124, 126, 127, 128, 129, 134, 151, 152, 155, 157, 164, 166, 180, 181, 183, 308, 313, 314, 343, 373, 428; light of, 102, 136; distinguished from tears, 77, 97; from repentance, 97. See Grief, Tears

Confession of thoughts and sins, 32, 35, 40, 45, 53–4, 57–8, 186, 234, 327; to be done daily, 52, 276; can be made to one not a priest, 11, 12; how to hear confessions, 55–6, 58–9. See Spiritual father

Conscience and consciousness: listen to conscience, 13, 17, 19; cross-examination of, 117; how it accuses and torments us, 25, 97, 236, 314; pure and at peace, 54, 70, 72, 164, 315, 326; endemic spiritual consciousness, 97; intellect as father of consciousness, 116; consciousness as image of Son, 218; of Holy Spirit, 140–1, 142

Conscious awareness: see Awareness, conscious

Constantinople, Councils of (1341, 1347, 1351), 288, 415n.

Contemplation, 428–9; eight forms 248; of all things in the One, 31; contemplative vision of the creation, 245–7, 248, 251; Creator contemplated through created things, 385; intellect as organ of contemplation, 432; contemplation attained by the perfect, 73–4; gained through repentance, 204; through practice of the commandments, 36, 195, 279; through dispassion, 28–9; through stillness, 254; through the grace of the Spirit, 42; leads to vision of God, 263; as a banquet, 171; as the tree in Eden, 369; contemplation and theology, 83, 152. See Creation, Inner essences, Light, Mystical theology, Prayer, Teaching

Continence, grace of, 255

Contrition, 33, 78, 89, 92, 114, 117, 129, 180, 182, 205, 239, 260, 261, 262, 274, 276, 282, 313

Counsel: see Insight

Coupling with a temptation, 89, 254, 308, 436

Courage, 82, 153–4, 214, 229, 230, 231, 236, 272

Covetousness, 330

Cowardice, 34, 230

Creation: God as creator, 408–9; need for a first cause, 346; creation as an act of God's will, not of His nature, 393, 410, 413; as a free gift, 390; instantaneous, 354; God creates through His divine energies, 391–3; He creates out of non-being, 142, 153, 323, 354, 375; but eternally foreknows the inner essences of all things, 142; presence of the Logos in creation, 250; creation exists in God, 393; has an origin and a consummation, 346; goodness and beauty of, 48, 78, 91, 98, 103, 385; not originally subject to corruption, 214; forms an ordered cosmos, 355–6; to be apprehended as a unity, 245; laws of, 227; structure and arrangement of, 347–56; symbolized by the number two, 227; creative powers of man, 375; his misuse of created things, 244; but he can reconcile creation to God and transfigure it, 144, 214; creation to be transformed into higher state, 346–7. See Contemplation, Inner essences, Matter, Nature

Crete, 207

Cross, Christ's and our own, 33, 46, 55, 90–1, 122, 154, 203, 253, 324, 325; sacrifice of cross renewed in Eucharist, 135; sign of the cross, 105, 325

Cyprus, 207

Darkness, the divine, 77, 79, 90, 121, 150, 155, 220

David, King, 19

Death, 171, 258; not created by God, 367, 370; lacks substantial reality, 365; a result of the fall, 366–8, 370–2; many forms of, 371; two kinds of, 42–3; death of soul and death of body, 295–8, 299, 363, 366–7, 370–2; mindfulness of death, 25, 29, 89, 134, 267, 269; fear of, 37; voluntary death for Christ's sake, 22, 25, 35, 36, 44, 46, 91, 109; for others, 118; life-generating death of Christ or the Spirit, 112–13, 118, 126, 131, 164, 253, 325; death of dispassion, 142; pain experienced at moment of death, 138; feeling of confidence at death, 187, 290; our state at death determines future reward, 88, 161, 274; the second

death (eternal punishment), 296. See Martyrs

Decad, 173

Deer, why they eat snakes, 130

Defluxions, from body, 50–1, 96, 254–6

Deification (theosis), 56, 82, 135, 148, 189, 221, 222, 265, 292; deifying grace, 390, 419–21; gods by grace and adoption, 34, 38, 48, 130, 134, 139, 148, 153, 258, 381; but not gods by nature, 420; deification effected through participation in the divine energies, 291, 378, 389–90, 396–7; supranatural, 220; miraculous, 420; changeless, 213; varying degrees, 220; we are created for deification, 392

Dejection and despondency, 33, 34, 92, 94, 102, 104, 223, 231, 258, 299, 314

Delusion, 68, 210, 240, 244, 248–51, 259, 261, 262, 266, 268, 269, 278, 281–4, 336, 431, 434

Demons, 242–4; once celestial intelligences, 243; noetic and fleshless, 105; attacks of, 56, 61, 68, 74, 104–5, 127–8, 202, 203, 249–50, 255–6, 270–1, 282–3, 428, 429, 430, 434, 435; demons linked with passions, 34, 133, 134, 151, 169, 214, 224–5, 228, 244, 263, 280; three leading demons, 242–3; demonic possession, 249; demons as huntsmen, 111; adopt bodily form, 105; adopt form of animals, 224–5, 243–4; produce vicious materiality in us, 145; help us to predict future, 55, 249, 250; attacks increase as we mount higher, 130; anger to be used against, 73, 105, 236, 428; driven away by Jesus Prayer, 74, 105, 264, 269, 277; humans can be worse than demons, 21, 238–9. See Delusion, Devil, Discrimination, Exorcism, Temptation

Desert: fullness of virtue and contemplation possible without withdrawal into, 12, 14, 19, 20, 43, 77, 97–8, 197; desert of inner renunciation, 98–9. See Flight from world, Solitary life, Stillness

Desire: appetitive power, one of the three aspects of the soul, 82, 147, 165, 171, 428; before and after fall, 227–8; partakes in divine blessings 135; desire for God, 149, 339, 373; good use of desire, in accordance with nature, 83, 228, 333; bad use of, contrary to nature, 96; passions of, 226; sinful desire, 113, 223, 237, 242, 254, 262; healing of, 304, 310. See Unchastity

Despair: see Dejection

Detachment, 35, 72, 80, 107, 146, 177. See Renunciation

Devil, 323, 364–5; a murderer, 329; as our enemy, 48; his dominion on earth usurped, 375; transforms himself into angel of light, 68, 286. See Demons

Dialectic, dangers of, 335; dialectical nature of theology, 434. See Learning

Discernment, discretion: see Discrimination

Discrimination (diakrisis), 81, 82, 84, 86, 102, 132, 153, 208, 231, 240, 244, 271, 429, 431; discernment of spirits, 168, 169, 270, 283–4, 286, 429; discernment in matters of dogma, 222.

Dispassion (apatheia): in God, 139; in humans, 30, 35–6, 47, 68, 84, 85, 87, 88, 89–90, 93, 101, 104, 117, 118, 119, 121, 136, 137, 151, 154, 156, 162, 164, 194, 203, 228, 237, 250, 254, 255, 317, **429**; two kinds, **103**, 111, 112; life-quickening deadness of, 142; not a deathlike condition but a positive state, 423; attained through practice of the commandments (praktikē), 103, 134; brings inner freedom, 79, 103; brings peace, 159; linked with love, 108, 109, 129, 429; leads to contemplation, 28–9, 79, 90, 103; as the promised land, 221

Distraction, 178, 186, 235; in psalmody, 127–8, 182. See Thoughts

Dormition, of the Mother of God, 58

Dreams, 123–5

Drunkenness: see Intoxication

Dyad, 143–4. See Numbers

Eclipses, 354

Ecstasy and rapture, 120, 149, 155, 210, **222**, 227, 237, 240, 253, 279, 317, **429–30**, 432

Eden, 78, 119, 213. See Fall, Paradise

El, as name of God, 172

Elements, the four, 347; five, including aether, 350

Elijah, theophany at Horeb, 285; position at prayer, 340

Endurance, patient, 25, 46, 54, 95, 151, 187, 204, 229, 233, 236, 253, 262, 272, 307, 312, 319, 338, 373. See Trials

Energy, defined as the dynamic and essential activity of a nature, 407, 413; how distinguished from nature (or essence) and from hypostasis, 407; there is no essence that does not have an energy, 411; the energy of the soul differs from its essence, 335; divine and uncreated energies of God, 259, 291, 377–8, 407–8, 422; rightly termed 'divinity', 393; eternal, 388, 422–3; distinction between God's essence and His energies, 291, **377–417**, the energies of God are both single and multiple, 377–8, 385, 386; their multiplicity does not destroy divine unity, 291–2, 384; the energies proceed from the essence, 397; and make known the essence, 411, 412; God cannot be known except through His energies, 360, 385; the energies are common to all three persons of the Trinity, 291, 379, 389–90, 398–9, 403, 411; the energies of the Spirit, 259, 377–8; divine energies not identical with the hypostasis of the Son, 389, 399; or of the Spirit, 291, 378, 380, 389; yet inseparable from the Spirit, 390.

The act of creating pertains to God's energies, not to His essence, 413; energies not to be regarded as created effects, 387, 412; divine energies as paradigms, exemplars or predeterminations, 387; as God's pre-eternal will and providence, 384; termed 'processions' by Dionysios, 386; creative power of, 380, 388–9, 391–2; permeate creation, 291, 390; indwelling, 152; humans can participate in, 291, 378, 380, 382, 396–7; signify God's grace, 390; effect deification, 291, 390; at Christ's transfiguration, 414–16. See Essence, Grace

Envy, 245, 253, 258, 308; of demons, 250

Epektasis: see Heaven

Eros (intense longing), 107, 222, 362–3, 429, 432; Holy Spirit as eros, 361. See Love

Eschatology: see Age to come, Judgment, Second coming

Essence, the divine: uncreated, 291; transcendent, 291, 393; absolutely unknowable, 385, 393–4, 413–14, 416; inaccessible and imparticipable, 291, 380, 382, 390–1, 394–7, 414; yet not distant from us, 390; never mentioned in plural, 377; distinct from divine energies, 291, **377–417**; distinct from the uncreated light, 376; term 'God' does not describe His essence, 385–6; God's will is other than His nature or essence, 410; generation and procession (but not creation) are acts pertaining to God's essence, 392, 413; no essence without energy, 411. *See* Apophatic approach, Energy

Eternity: *see* Age to come

Eucharist: *see* Holy communion, Liturgy

Eustratios, prayer of St, 59

Evil, not to be attributed to God, 146, 147–8; due to our free will, 48. *See* Creation, Devil, Sin

Exorcism, gift of, 168

Experience, how we learn from, 338, 341–2. *See* Awareness

Face, external appearance of, 87, 88, 95

Faith, 16, **18–19**, 20–21, **25**, 122, 162, 164, 204, 212, 228, 234, 237, 245, 251, 430; to be confirmed by actions, 19, 40, **240–1**, 251; deeply-rooted, 80, 86, **87**, 109, 168; salvation by faith alone, 217

Fall, of devil and his angels, 105, 224, 243, 323, 357, 358, 364, 366, 375; of mankind, 193, 194, 203, 212, 280, 296, 298, 338, 363, **365–72**, 376–7, 381, 430, 431, 433, 435; not total, 375; makes us similar to animals, 213, 227–8, 243; affects our sense of time, 427; fragments the memory, 223; involves world in corruption, 214

Family, attitude towards one's, 14, 25, **26**, 53, 54, 178, 179, 180, 301, 326–7

Fantasy: image-producing faculty, **430–1**. *See* Images, Imagination, Thoughts

Fasting, 19, 58, 89, 90, 109, 125, 127, 129, 215, 229, 267, 272, 310; not to be excessive, 102. *See* Food

Fear of God, 20, 39, 177; two forms of, 132–3; three forms of awe, 261; caused by love, 93; changed into longing, 120; replaced by joy, 138; awe and joy combined, 259–60; fear of punishment hereafter, 37–8, 93; this differs from divine awe, 260–1. *See* Hell, Punishment

Fervour: *see* Warmth

Fire, the divine, 84, 106, 134, 263, 277, 419; non-material, 285. *See* Light

First hour (prime), 234

Flesh, various senses, 431; means the human person as fallen, 163; signifies dissolute way of life, 88; purified, 20. *See* Body, Carnal mode of life, Fall

Flight from world, 22, 53, 177; in inward sense, 79, 98–9. *See* Desert

Fluids, the two natural, 96; body originally created without humours, 213, 227. *See* Defluxions

Food, 29, 59, 60, 70, 98, 119, 154, 185–6, 209, 233, 234, 255, **280–1**, 313, 370. *See* Fasting

Fool, need to become, 47

Foreknowledge of God, differs from His will, 392–3

Foresight: *see* Prophecy

Forgetfulness, 199–200, 215, 223, 242, 264

Forgiveness, 276, 312; through confession, 45, 327; and through monastic profession, 45. *See* Confession

Form, God as the author of all, 382

Free will, 16, 48, 116–17, 141, 178, 186, 213, 225, 230, 236, 282, 283, 299, 312, 358–9, 365, 366, 367, 368, 372, 382, 389, 435, 436; dispassion confers freedom, 79, 103; so does stillness, 146. *See* Will

Gentleness, 231

Geometry, 383

George, a young man, 13, 16

Giants, the three noetic, 199

Glory: *see* Light

Gluttony, 50, 88, 102, 231, 235, 255, 309. *See* Food

Gnosis: see Knowledge

God: meaning of word *Theos*, 385; the only Being that truly is, 354; incomprehensible, 140, 418; no qualities in God, 140; and also no accidents, 406; utterly transcendent, 343, 359–60; eternal, 427; incorporeal, 357, 364; infinite, 21, 170; Intellect, and beyond all intellect, 139–40, 147, 170, 359; impassible, 407; dispassionate, and beyond all dispassion, 139; acts but is not acted upon, 407, 414; entire simplicity, 360; as One, 143–4, 145; as Monad, Triad and Decad, 173; indivisibly divided, 384; unions in God prevail over the distinctions, 384; three realities in God, essence, energy, hypostases, 380; as first cause, 346; known from the creation, 355, 385; outside everything yet within everything, 140, 170, 174, 349, 393; everywhere and nowhere, 374; archetype of the soul, 142; His compassion imitated by us, 143. *See* Apophatic approach, Creation, Energy, Essence, Trinity

Gospels: *see* Scripture

Grace, 56, 214, 216, 232, 257, 258, 261–2, 381; uncreated, 289, 322, 377, 380, 419; not God's essence but His energy, 378, 380, 389, 390, 420; deifying, 389, 390, 396–7, 418–21; common to all three Persons of the Trinity, 408; grace and nature, 395; effects of grace not to be confused with natural effects, 68; self-evident effects, 286; varied forms, 285; nothing can be achieved without, 54, 62, 212, 217, 220, 229, 247, 248, 277; works in heart, 334; sometimes quickly received, 266–7; consciousness of, 79; present unconsciously, 248; terrifies demons, 104; providential withdrawal of, 111, 113, 136; grace of baptism, 177, 272, 317. *See* Deification

Gratitude, 21, 54, 315

Greeks, the wisdom of the pagan, 291n., 309, 347, 349–50, 356–8; the Greeks worship demons, 358. *See* Learning

Grief, 38, 53, 56, 96, 119, 126, 150, 236, 267, 272, 284, **312–15**, **319–22**, 343, 345, 373. *See* Compunction, Sorrow

Guarding of the heart or intellect: *see* Heart, Intellect, Watchfulness

Hair shirt, 19

Hardship and toil, need for, 272–4, 275, 310–11. *See* Endurance, Practice of the Commandments

Healing, gift of, 168

Heart, **334–5**, **431**; centre of the human person, 65, 72–3, 290, 334; 'innermost body within the body', 334; source of life for the body, 205; how related to the breathing, 205; heart's blood overheated, 261; source of thoughts, both good and evil, 71, 105–6, 309; two forms of energy in heart, 261–2; intellect located in the heart, 334–5, 421; intellect activated by the heart, 344; watches over the heart, 70, 269; watchfulness of heart, 75, 81, 196, 242; guarding of the heart, 65, 71–2, 74–5, 201, 204, 266, 437; to be kept free from distractive thoughts, 213; finding the place of the heart, descending into the heart, **70–3**, 193, 201, 202, **205–6**, 264, 275, 338; prayer of the heart, 70, 240, 257, 259, 263, 266, 267, 284, 431; God manifested in the heart, 214; the Spirit present there, 215, 334; sanctuary of the heart, 211, 213; inward heaven of heart, 203; stillness of heart, 71; the earth of the heart, 71, 273; purity of, 70, 72, 429; impurity of, 329; depths of heart agitated by passion, 74; shattering of, 119; suffering of, 269, 273, 278. *See* Person, the human

Heaven, 324; foretaste of, 219, 320; variety in, 220; unending progress in, 222. *See* Kingdom of heaven

Heavens, rotation of, 347–9, 355, 358; sun, moon and other heavenly bodies, 353–4

Hell, **218–19**, 273, 324, 372; meditation on, 89, 129, 314; birthpangs of, 120; anticipated in this life, 239, 320. *See* Judgment, last; Punishment

Hermit life: *see* Solitary life

Hesychast controversy, 207–8, 288, 290

Hesychasts, 35, 200, 209–10, 268, 278, 280, 282, 285, 336; daily and nightly programme, 233–4; prayer is their life, 238; enemies of hesychasm, 235, 340; day-dreamer instead of hesychast, 240, 283. *See* Stillness

Hesychia: *see* Stillness

Hierissos, 292, 425

Holy communion, 51, 54, 135, 166; frequent, 12; each Sunday, 326; always receive with tears, 12, 59. *See* Liturgy

Holy of Holies, 324. *See* Tabernacle

Holy Name, invocation of: *see* Jesus Prayer

Holy Spirit: *see* Spirit, Holy

Hope, 54, 234, 316

Hours, not recited by monks of Sketis, 266

Human nature: *see* Person, the human

Humility, 16, 39, 54, 88, 90, 91, 92, 97, 100,

101, 102, 103, 109, **113–19**, 130, 143, 152, 158, 164, 166, 210, 217, 229, 231, 233, 235, 236, **238–40**, 241, 244, 254, 256, 262, 268, 272, 284, 285, 303, 310–11, 313, 314, 315, 345

Hymns: *see* Psalmody

Ioconography, 430

Ignorance, 132, 144–5, 163, 199–200, 218, 223, 225, 230, 243, 251; an ignorance that surpasses spiritual knowledge, 181

Ikons, restoration of, 287; of Christ and the saints, 324–5; humans as living ikons of Christ, 397. *See* Image

Illness: *see* Sickness

Illusion: *see* Delusion

Image of God in man, 31, 34, 116, **139–43**, 146, 153, 221, 243, 325, 356, 357, 365, 366, 431; man as image of Christ, 87, 148, 244, 381, 397; of the Trinity, 140–1, 183, 184, 218, 220n., **362–4**, 374–5; image and likeness linked, 83, 177, 184; distinguished, 141, 142–3, 317–18, 363, 375–6; image refers to intellect or soul, not to body, 139–40, 143, 357, 361, 374, 423; makes man sovereign over creation, 142, 374–5; restoring to God His own image, 132

Images, conceptual (*noïmata*), 81, 437; to be laid aside in prayer, 176, 181, 188, 239, 259, 264, 270, 283, 284, 316–17, 337; may lead us into delusion, 249; image-free provocation, 435; divine images derived from God, 216. *See* Fantasy, Thoughts

Imagination, 226, 244, 271; role in process of temptation, 254, 283; imaginative faculty, how related to sensation and the intellect, 353–4

Incarnation, 48, 99, 217, 245, 248, 251, 253, 298, 314, 324, 325, 336, 340, 361, 372–3, 377, 379, 421; hypostatic union is unique, 380; refashions our nature, 134–5; anoints our human nature, 309, 323, 396. *See* Christ

Incensive power: one of the three aspects of the soul, 82, 147, 165–6, 171, 261, 428; the virile aspect of the soul, 105; good use of, in accordance with nature, 83, 333; used against demons, 105, 134; bad use of,

contrary to nature, 96, 242; passions of, 223, 226; healing of, 304. *See* Anger

Inner essences or principles (*logoi*) of created things, 233, 434; pre-exist in God, 387; the thoughts of God, 433; present in man and known to him, 142; contemplation of the *logoi* (*physiki theoria*), 76, 78, 89, 90, 92, 103, 104, 109, 116, 117, 120, 121, 125, 126, 129, 131, 133, 136, 145, 148, 149, 151, 152, 153, 154, 155, 156, 159, 162, 163, 174, 318, 429, 432, 433. *See* Creation

Insight, visionary (*diorasis*), 55–6, 318; cognitive insight (*epistimi*), 81, 245, 266

Intellect (*nous*), **432**; has its abode in the divine Intellect, 147; image of God in man to be associated especially with the intellect, 139–40, 143, 218, 357, 361, 423; characteristics of the intellect, 141; pre-eminent among our inner powers, 344, 357; endowed with natural sovereignty, 171; but should recognize its own infirmity, 358; ever-active and volatile, 276–7, 290, 337; one of the five inner senses, 81; four principal faculties of, 81–2; it is three yet one, 343–4; constituted by thought and intuition, 344; intellect, imagination and sense-perception, 353–4; intellect, consciousness and spirit, 218; intellect as father of consciousness, 116; intellection (*noïsis*), 81, 432; the intellect's direct and circular movements, 336, 338, 376; intellect to be distinguished from *dianoia* (mind or reason), 226, 271, 277, 317, 360–1, 375, 432.

Intellect to be enclosed within the body, **331–7**, transmits grace to body, 318; watches over body, soul and senses, 333, 338; governs appetite and sense-perception, 374–5; can grow cloddish, 108; passions of, 226; consubstantial with soul, 116, 141; pilot of soul, 102; illumines soul, 126; to be united with soul, 205; converts powers of soul, 316, 319; located by some in the head, by others in the heart, **334–5**, 421, 432; activated by the heart, 344.

Guarding of the intellect, 71, 72, 74, 193, 198, 199, 200, 204, 207, 270n., 337, 343–4, 437; to be separated from materiality, 317; to be withdrawn from sensory things, 68, 72; to become deaf and speechless, 316; to be kept free from images and forms, 188, 240, 283, 284, 316; returns into itself, 315, 316, 319; beholds itself, 336; recreated, 316; possesses creative power, 143; purity of, 79; inward search by the intellect, 65, 72; its watch over the heart and descent into it, 70–3, 193, 205–6, 264, 269, 275, 277, 338; its prayer within the heart, 259, 263; reunited through prayer, 188.

Intellect gives knowledge of divine mysteries, 81; always to be directed to God, 56; its nature is to meditate on divine things, 103, 143, 179; contemplative, 151; dispassionate and visionary, 104; beholds light of life, 80–1; illuminated by light, 239, 316–18; attains vision of God, 114, 216; celebrates mystical eucharist, 144; to be guided by the Spirit, 216–17; acts as mediator, bringing all things closer to God, 317; undergoes resurrection, like that of Lazarus, 136–7; transcends itself and sees God, 336; union with God transcending the intellect, 245; in future life, we become intellects, 222. See Images, conceptual; Person, the human

Intelligent aspect of the soul, 82–3, 134, 147, 170, 171, 173, 212, 223, 247; intelligence distinguished from the intellect, 116, 163, 226; constitutes dignity of the intellect, 141; passions of, 226, 243; healing of, 304

Intense longing: see Eros

Intention, inner, to be carefully watched, 271–2

Intimate communion, 432–3

Intoxication, spiritual, 78, 222, 232; of compunction, 117

Invocation of the Holy Name: see Jesus Prayer

Israel: signifies contemplation, 263

Jacob: signifies ascetic practice, 263

Jesus Christ: see Christ

Jesus Prayer, 176, 207, 208, 275, 284, 431, 433; single-phrased, 344; formula may be varied, but not too frequently, 264, 275–6; may be said aloud or silently, 276; accompanied by prostrations, 185; offered by the intellect, 189; frequent, 182; unceasing, 181, 183, 184, 189, 206, 259,

263, 264, 268, 270n., 276; without form, thoughts or images, 206, 259, 264, 270n., 277; destroys distractive thoughts, 73; drives out demons, 74, 105, 264, 269, 277; need for spiritual guidance, 65, 193, 205, 210, 259, 269; accompanied by physical technique, 64–6, 72–3, 192–3, 205–6, 210, 264–5, 277, 288, 290, 331–2, 337, 338–40; and baptism, 211, 259; and the Holy Spirit, 211, 259, 276

Joy, 118, 146, 149, 155, 164, 188, 231, 232, 259, 285, 312, 313, 315; two kinds of joy, 260; mindless and confused joy, 262; joy and reverence, 103; and awe, 259–60; trembling of joy, 261; uninterrupted, 177; joy in midst of poverty, 108; joy of monastic life, 178; after meditating on hell, 120; on finding place of heart, 73, 205; anticipates age to come, 137–8; intellect should rise above, 104. See Compunction, Tears

Judgment, the last, 21, 39, 210, 245, 258; by fire, 165–6, 218–20; both now and hereafter, 215; we are not to judge others, 36–7, 52, 56, 91, 92, 95. See Hell, Punishment, Sound judgment

Justice or righteousness (dikaiosyni), 82, 136–7, 152, 153–4, 229–30

Kabbalah, 173n

Kingdom of heaven, differs from kingdom of God, 171; granted through Christ's incarnation, 373; many stages and levels in it, 220; contemplation of, 248; and the divine light, 414–15; anticipated in this life, 219; the kingdom within us, 202, 205–6, 335, 373

Kings, anointing of, 250

Klazomenai, 207

Knowledge, spiritual or intuitive (gnosis), 76, 81, 254, 345, 434; threefold, 375; and the grace of the Spirit, 42; knowledge derived from sense-perception, not to be called spiritual, 354

Laity, anointed as kings and priests, 250; can be spiritual guides, 11; can receive vision of divine light, 14, 20

Laughter, spiritual, 313, 315. See Tears

Lavra, 197, 198

Law, not binding on those who receive gifts of the Spirit, 139, 170; the three laws, 170; natural law, 227

Laziness, 223, 319. *See* Listlessness

Learning, secular or worldly, 46–7, 94, 159, 160, 212, 216, 245, 331. *See* Dialectic, Greeks

Lent, 58

Letters, wise not to write, 197

Light, the divine and uncreated, 208, 287, 288, 415, 419; identical with God's uncreated grace, 390; to be regarded as God's energy, not His essence, 292, 376; the light of the Trinity, 317, 318; the light of the Holy Spirit, 38, 120, 318; angels are emanations of the divine light, 376, 381; Adam clothed in divine light before the fall, 377; revealed at Christ's transfiguration on Tabor, 414–17, 422; seen by Paul on road to Damaskos, 377; the vision of divine light, 12, 13, 14, 18, 19, 23, 29, 47, 62, 77, 84, 97, 107, 118, 119, 125, 132, 139, 146, 148, 153, 176, 181, 182, 210, 240, 259, 285–6, 289, 316–17, 319, 376–8; transformation into, 18, 20, 216; unifies the soul, 145; produces rapture, 149; to be identified with the kingdom of God, 414–15; eschatological, 292, 419; deprival of divine light, 212–13; vision of oneself as luminous, 73; the light of the intellect, 109, 239, 316–18; false visions of light, 68, 210; how to distinguish divine from demonic light, 61, 283, 286. *See* Energy, Fire, Transfiguration

Likeness: see Image of God in man

Listlessness and sloth, 34, 53, 57, 128, 185, 199–200, 231, 236–7, 242, 251, 254, 272, 273, 277

'Little souls', title given to supposed saints, 249

Liturgy: the eucharist, 51, 52, 55, 62–3, 211, 288, 289; liturgy of the angels, 172; mystical eucharist or inner liturgy of the heart, 117, 144, 148, 163, 211, 213, 220, 237. *See* Holy communion

Logoi: see Inner essences

Logos, Christ the divine, 140, 360–1, 375, 433; presence in creation, 250; self-offering, 148; offered up by us, 163; *logos* as a

human faculty, 360–1. *See* Christ, Incarnation, Inner essences (*logoi*)

Lord's day, to be kept holy, 326; anticipates age to come, 326

Lord's Prayer, 266

Love, 148, 149, 217, 241, 254, 318, 333, 338; for God, 80, 93, 101, 107, 108, 118, 120, 129, 164, 166, 181, 189, 282, 321, 323–4, 363, 364, 373, 432; love and stillness, 146, 234; for fellow humans, 36–7, 49–50, 93, 108, 118, 119, 164, 166, 168, 169, 364; do not feel special love for particular persons, 53; love for parents, 326–7; love is greater than prayer, 15, 58, 77, 128; love as fundamental to the virtues, 229; to be expressed in actions, 122; linked with dispassion, 108, 109, 129, 429; makes us similar to God, 141; deifying, 177. *See* Compassion, *Eros*

Lust, 89, 91, 104, 218, 219, 223, 225, 236–7, 249, 261, 262, 277, 309–10. *See* Desire, Unchastity

Lyons, Council of (1274), 175

Madness, 68, 249

Magoula, *skete* of, 207, 425

Mamas, monastery of St, 12, 13

Man: see Person, the human

Marriage, a great mystery, 321; lawful, 328; married people can attain contemplation, 14; purity possible for them, but difficult, 300; better not to marry, 300–2. *See* Nuptial symbolism

Martyrs, 101. *See* Death

Mary the Virgin, St: see Mother of God

Matins, 52n., 55, 234

Matter: God creates from non-being, not from pre-existent matter, 354; material world is good, 78; not to be misused, 326. *See* Creation

Memory, 251; fragmented state, 222–3. *See* Mindfulness of God

Mercy, converts anger into joy, 214

Messalians, 395–6, 420, 421

Microcosm, man as, 242

Midnight office, 59n

Mind: see Intellect, Reason, Thoughts

Mindfulness of God, 233, 267, 434; continuous, 56, 180–1, 203, 215, 223, 259, 323, 364

Miracles, gift of working, 168, 172

Missionary vocation of the contemplative: see Teaching

Monastic life, **177–9**; the 'second covenant', renewing baptism, 178; signifies inner rather than outer renunciation, 99, 337; one-pointed concentration of the monk, 293; monastic life and repentance, 178; and dispassion, 129; joyfulness of, 178; monastic habit, 39, 45, 178; the first grade of rasophore, 207; monks as prophets, 292, **418–19**; an eschatological vocation, 292, 328, 418; monks can hear confessions even if not ordained, 11; the monk is like a wheel, 129. See Cenobitic life, Solitary life

Moon, phases of, 353–4

Moses, provides best account of creation, 346

Mother of God, Mary, 18, 19, 301, 324, 328; soul as mother of the Logos, and mind as mother of the Spirit, 120

Mourning: see Grief

Murder, 329

Muslims, 289

Mystical theology, 90, 150, 155, 220. See Contemplation, Theology, Union with God

Name, invocation of the Holy: see Jesus Prayer

Natural contemplation: see Inner essences

Nature, different senses, 394; three levels, according to, contrary to, and above, 224; grace and nature, 395. See Creation

Navel, 65, 72, 288, 338, 340

Nazirites, 109, 160, 166

Noetic perception, noïsis: see Intellect

Novices, 53, 283, 295

Number, spiritual meaning of, 173n., 227, 378

Nuptial symbolism, **40–1**, 120, 136, 183, 232, 301, 302, 316, 321, 367

Oaths, 325–6

Obedience, 14, 23, 37, 55, 69, 70, 215, 236, 241, 251, 268, 282, 285, 306; of Christ, 33, 122. See Abbot, Spiritual father

Odour of sanctity, after death, 280

Oil, 78, 127, 134, 232, 419. See Anointing

Omphalopsychoi ('navel-physics'), 288, 340

Oracles, pagan, 358

Orthodoxy, how defined, 217, 251

Orthros: see Matins

Pain: see Suffering

Paloukiton, 12

Paradise, differs from kingdom of heaven, 171; twofold, both sensible and spiritual, **213–14**; the noetic paradise, 149, 150, 315; humans as the new paradise, 45; the Church as paradise, 166; paradise of the virtues, 313; of prayer, 190. See Eden, Fall

Paroria, 208, 209

Passion of Christ: see Cross

Passions, 88, 210, **223–7**, 428, 429, 433, 436; to be distinguished from sinful acts, 89, 223; the three principal passions, 82, 89, 231; six universal passions, 235; eight ruling passions, 231; five passions hostile to obedience, 241; aroused in five ways, 244; passions of body and soul, 226, 260, 338; linked to incensive power of soul, 223; carnal passions, 309; material passions, 243; the passible aspect of the soul, 142, 171, 311, 333, 343, 423, 428; passions naturally implanted in children, 304, 310; some passions are voluntary, some rooted in nature, 305; spring from the mind or intellect, 309–10; provoke distractive thoughts, 223; provoked by fantasies, 224; eating as cause of passions, 370; the raw material of the passions, 84; linked to the fallen self, 144; contrary to nature, 230; associated with demons, 34, 133, 134, 151, 169, 214, 224–5, 228, 244, 263, 280, 339.

The passions are to be resisted and curtailed, 73, 74, 75, 98; to be expelled, 316; to be mortified, 103; to be hated, 37; as malady, 233; a plague, 99; a prison house, 156; rebellious, 80; anarchic, 146; linked to pride, 91; involve misuse of things, 225; disperse powers of soul, 183; stench of passions, 219; frost of, 81; darkness of, 179; cloak of dark passions, 86; Red Sea of passions, 131; brute-like, 151; as wild beasts, 101, 119, 224–5; evil love of passions, 201.

Good use of passions, 433; mastery of,

83; stilled, 85; deliverance and purification from, 29, 53, 56, 61, 97, 117, 151, 157, 161, 162, 260, 343; becoming dead to the passions, 190; love for God, shown by absence of passions, 373; transformation of passion-imbued thoughts, 130; union with God as a passion, 155. *See* Dispassion, Temptation, Thoughts

Passover of the soul, 163

Patience: *see* Endurance, patient

Peace, threefold, 121; of thoughts, 315

Penance, 186, 255. *See* Repentance

Pentecost, the mystical, 126, 131

Person, the human: defined, 116; our own nature incomprehensible to us, 140, 227; our different faculties, 374–5; triad of intellect, *logos* and *eros*, 362; of intellect, intelligence and spirit, 183–4; of intellect, consciousness and spirit, 218; of soul, intellect and consciousness, 140–1; composed of clay or matter and the divine image, 141, 356; of material substratum and spiritual essence, 170; unity of body and soul, 66, 67, 170, 227–8, 290, 423; creative possibilities resulting from this, 375; microcosm, 242; no other being superior to, 365–6; excels whole world, 46; sovereign over creation, 142, 366, 374–5; creation exists for our sake, 242, 356; we are created incorruptible but not immutable, 213; human nature essentially good, 78; great but petty, 110; our fall involves creation in corruption, 214; but we also reconcile the creation to God, 144; inner conflict between fallen and spiritual self, 144; threefold knowledge, noetic, rational and sensory, 375; knowledge of inner essences, 142; two forms of human life, social and solitary, 152. *See* Angels, Body, Fall, Heart, Image, Intellect, Reason, Senses, Soul, Trinity

Philosopher, the true, 245–7

Philotheou, monastery of, 207

Physiki: *see* Inner essences

Pleasure, two forms, 96; bitter, 111; pain-inducing, 85; counteracted by pain, 102; sensual pleasure, 434; to be kept under intelligent control, 319; leads us astray, 369; love of, 89, 107; we should rise above pain and pleasure, 123. *See* Self-indulgence

Poor: *see* Alms, Poverty

Popularity: *see* Praise, love of

Possessions, 46, 53, 54, 59; total shedding of, 231, 311, 314–15; love of, **304–6**. *See* Poverty

Poverty, 14, 50, 98, 235, 267, 303, 306, 319, 320, 322; four types, 313; presence of Christ in the poor, 49–50; poverty of spirit, 71, 303, 306, **310–14**, 315. *See* Possessions, Renunciation

Practice of the commandments and virtues, ascetic practice (*praxis, praktiki*), 17, 20, 21, 25, 36, 40, 41, **42**, 44, 48, 76, 79, 80, 83, 85, 86, 92, 93, 98, 102, 110, 145, 148, 151, 152, 161–2, 169, 203, 232, 240–1, 257, 266–7, **272–4**, 280, 345, 428–9; limited value of, 131–2, 154, 162, 166, 198–9, 214–16; need to advance beyond, 136, 150; but some never do so, 280; limitless, 101; leads to dispassion, 103, 134; commandments form a single unity, 216; comprehensive and particular commandments, 50, 215, 311; observance of the commandments guards grace, 265; reveals the power of baptism, 253, 257, 259; but presupposes faith, 217; asceticism is war against the flesh, not against the body, 431; ascetic practice and contemplation, 245–6, 263, 279. *See* Virtues

Praise, love of, 82, 89, 90, 107–8, 246, 307–9

Prayer, definition of: **237–8**; highest of all activities, 282; dialogue with God, 181; two forms of, 263; three methods of, 65, 67–73; four rungs, 73–4; prayer in church (liturgical), 52, 55, 185, 266; prayer in cell, interrupted by visitors, 60–1, 128–9; prayer differs from psalmody, 73–4, 266, 268, 278–9; prayer for others, 48, 61; for enemies, 28; use of the body in prayer, 64–6, 67, 70, 72–3, 75, 128, 192–3, 205–6, 210, 264–5, 277; seated position when praying, 205, 264, 266, 274, 277, 278; prayer as an activity of the intellect, 129, 188, 263; noetic prayer, 237, 239; prayer of the heart, 70, 240, 257, 259, 263, 266, 267, 284, 431; intellect, intelligence and soul united in prayer, 183, 184; prayer free from image and form, 176, 181, 188 206, 210, 239, 259, 270; distractions in prayer, 182; demonic disturbances, 61;

continual prayer, 50, **128–9**, 149, 234, 240, 264, 266, 276; persevere even when physically exhausted, 55; effort needed, 344; the change from entreaty to thanksgiving, 315; prayer teaches us all things, 58; makes us angels, 120; unites us to God, 118, 343; signs of God's presence in prayer, 259–60; prayer of fire, 261; love is greater than prayer, 15, 58, 77, 128. *See* Breathing, control of; Contemplation; Intellect; Jesus Prayer; Mindfulness of God; Lord's Prayer; Vigils; Warmth of heart

Prepossession (*prolipsis*) or predisposition, 37, 315, 436

Pride, 30, 39, 56, 68, 88–9, 91, 92, 93, 109, 166, 226, 231, 235, 249, 250, 308. *See* Praise, love of

Priesthood: qualities required in a priest, **62**; respect for priests, 58; royal priesthood of the baptized, 250

Prodigal son, 322

Prophecy and foresight, 19, 55, 103, 125, 155, 160, 168, 169, 215, 249, 250, 254, 292, 318–19, 341, 358, 381; prophetic role of monasticism, 292, 418–19

Prostrations, 185, 186, 266, 267

Provocations, 308; demonic, 224–5, 372, 435–6; mental, 264. *See* Demons, Temptation

Psalmody, 50, **127–8**, 169–70, 182, 183, 185, 209, 215, 233, 234, **266–70**, **278–80**; recited standing up, 266, 269, 278; distinguished from prayer, 73–4, 266, 268, 278–9

Psalms: the six, 52; the twelve, 59

Psychic mode of life, 107–9, 216, 247

Publican, prayer of, 340

Punishments, 93, **218–20**, 236; foretaste of future, 218–19; eternal punishment, 37–8, 39, 120, 133, 137, 248, 296, 298. *See* Hell, Judgment

Purification and purity, 20, 39, 62, 72, 79, 107, 120, 145, 146, 148, 153, 212, 231, 244, 248, 258, 345, 429, 437; partial and total, 344–5; purgative stage, 150–1

Pythagorean theory of numbers, 173n.

Reading, 170, 184–5, 232, 233, 269; suitable reading for a hesychast, 271; insufficient by itself, without spiritual guidance, 279; carry out what you read, 216

Reason or mind (*dianoia*), 81, 430, 434; distinguished from the spiritual intelligence, 212; and from the intellect, 226, 271, 277, 317, 360–1, 375, 432

Rebuttal, 71, 434

Refectory: *see* Food

Relics, veneration of, 325

Remembrance of God: *see* Mindfulness of God

Renunciation: of world, 26, 77, 241; of possessions, 306, 313; inner renunciation, 98–9; and obedience to spiritual father, 110. *See* Detachment, Possessions, Will

Repentance, 39, 42, 54, 78, 83, 98, 133, 134, 151, 167, 178, 185, 204, 273, 281, 299, 311, 312, 329, 371, 372–3, 434; constant and unending, 40, 41; different from compunction, 97. *See* Compunction, Grief, Tears

Resurrection of Christ, 253, 298, 324, 326; our resurrection with Christ, 163, 164, 222; resurrection of our intellect, 136–7; of our soul, 240, 251, 253, 258, 297; resurrection of the body, 213, 221, 228, 248, 296, **297–8**, 300, 326, 363; final resurrection anticipated in present life, 137–8, 221

Revelation: God revealed to us today as much as to those in the past, 251

Riches: *see* Possessions, Poverty

Righteousness: *see* Justice

Sabbath: kept spiritually, 337. *See* Lord's day

Sacraments: *see* Baptism, Holy communion, Liturgy

Saints: real sanctity, 240; a return to our natural state, 78; saints living even now in our midst, 47; their relationship with others, 47–8; hard to recognize, 39; their union with God, 421; have one energy with Him, 397; to be honoured, 324–5; as teachers, 232; their testimony to be believed, 331; never contradict one another, 227; look on others as saints, 52, 53, 103, 119; see your spiritual father as a saint, 57; the suffering of the saints, 294, 325; those who attack the saints, 340; false saints, 39, 249; the saints in heaven, 221

Salvation, through faith alone, 217. *See* Deification

Satan: *see* Devil

Scripture, 50, 58, 60, 68, 127, 149, 152, 156-7, 179, 214, 246-7, 257, 274n., 284; understood by only a few, 36, 47, 48; not understood by the 'psychic', 109; differently understood according to our spiritual state, 133-4; double meaning, literal and spiritual, 136; everything to be interpreted spiritually, 165; not to be read only in literal, 'Judaic' manner, 251

Second coming of Christ, 248, 292, 324, 325, 415. *See* Judgment, Resurrection

Sefiroth, 173n.

Self-conceit: *see* Pride

Self-control (*enkrateia*), 59, 80, 82, 83, 88, 90, 102, 103, 117, 127, 149, 217, 231, 233, 235, 261, 262, 267, 272, 281, 285, 313, 319, 333; all-embracing, 109, 120, 125, 131; more difficult than total abstinence, 302

Self-esteem (*kenodoxia*), 50, 51, 52, 60, 69, 70, 90, 100, 101, 124, 231, 255, 272. *See* Pride

Self-examination, 51-2, 285, 315, 326, 338-9

Self-flattery, 306-7, 340. *See* Self-esteem

Self-indulgence (*philidonia*), 82, 89, 90, 102, 142, 178, 180, 218, 219, 225, 226, 249, 254, 309, 313, 367

Self-knowledge, 83, 88, 98, 109-10, 116-17, 201, 235, 358, 366

Self-love (*philavtia*), 80, 85, 86, 98, 108, 226, 235, 245

Self-reproach, 285, 314. *See* Repentance

Self-restraint (*sophrosyni*), 82, 152, 153-4, 229-30, 310

Self-will: *see* Will

Semen, 50-1, 96, 254-6

Senses, the five physical, 352-3; higher and lower, 80; outer and inner, 80-1; in relation to the noetic and passible aspects of soul, 141-2; work together with the powers of the soul, 233; subordinate to the intellect, 375; subjected to the virtues, 171; sense of touch, 84; guarding and control of senses, 68, 70, 94, 164, 179, 313, 333; the senses transcended, 81, 84, 90, 109, 119, 124, 146, 149-50, 155, 163, 189, 222; to be spurned, 188; to be deadened, 233; to be turned inwards and introverted to the soul, 98, 197; to be transformed, 103; servitude to the senses, 84, 85; this makes us alien to God and leads to sin, 223, 382; senses arouse distractive thoughts and expose us to demonic attacks, 75; dispassionate use of, 84; sense-world as an image of the invisible world, 246.

The spiritual senses (the soul's organs of perception), 29, 31, 43, 80-1, 84, 87, 92, 98, 103-4, 105, 107, 108, 125, 145, 154, 216, 233, 344, 424

Sensual pleasure: *see* Pleasure

Seraphim, 152, 172. *See* Angels

Seth, 371, 375

Seven, the number, symbolizes time, 227; symbolizes multiplicity, 378

Sexual instinct: *see* Desire

Sickness, 59; unjustified fear of, 86; benefit and harm of, 102; rules of fasting do not apply when a person is ill, 281; but prayer should not be abandoned, 190-1; visits to the sick, 58, 60

Silence, 85, 126, 155, 197, 233, 235, 239, 262, 268, 272, 285, 293; indescribable, 103; eloquent, 274. *See* Stillness

Simantron, 185n.

Sin, 214, 319-20; as 'missing the mark', 434; sinful acts distinguished from passions, 89, 223; passion-free recollection of sin, 112. *See* Passion, Temptation, Vice

Sinai, 166, 207, 209

Sketis, 266

Sleep, 50-1, 280-1, 313; sleeping on the ground, 89, 90, 98, 105; attacks of demons during sleep, 105, 249, 255; as the image of death, 219. *See* Dreams, Vigils

Sloth: *see* Listlessness

Sobriety (*nipsis*): *see* Watchfulness

Solitary life, 14, 43, 68, 98, 152, 170, 235, 256. *See* Desert, Hesychast, Stillness, Withdrawal

Sorrow, 434; when prompted by God, different from dejection, 94-5. *See* Dejection, Grief

Soul: three different types of soul, intelligent, sentient, vegetative, 347; soul of animals, 359; characteristics of human soul:

created spiritual, immortal, intellective, intelligent, 116, 227, 243, 359, 364; two aspects, noetic and passible, 141–2; passible aspect, 142, 171, 311, 333, 343, 423, 428; three powers or aspects, intelligent, incensive, appetitive, 28, 82, 102, 121, 134–5, 147, 170–1, 183, 223, 225, 226–7, 229, 242, 304, 428; single, but with many powers, 334, 344; five senses of, 81; three psychic activities, 81; four principal virtues of soul, 82; passions of, 226; effects of fall on, 243; unity with body, 66, 67, 170, 227–8, 292, 356, 375, 423; the soul is the actuality of the body, 347; it loves the body, 363; it energizes the body, 227, 248, 358–9, 363, 374; present everwhere in the body, 374; not located in navel, 340; more precious than the body, 46, 110, 114, 150; natural beauty of, 96, 110, 132, 183, 319; deiform, 46, 135, 141, 227, 344, 347, 352, 432; as image of God, 140; as noetic altar, 211; superior to the whole world, 356; supracelestial, 348; capable of knowing God, 356; mother of the Logos, 120; unified by the divine Monad, 144; restored to natural state through stillness, 146; 'little souls', 249. See Body; Person, the human; Psychic mode of life; Senses

Sound understanding (phronisis), 82, 136–7, 153, 159, 161, 229–30

Spirit, the Holy: place within the Trinity, 361–2; proceeds from the Father, 140, 323; from the Father alone, 328, 361–2; from the Father through the Son, 217; common to both Father and Son, and sent by both, 362; as the pre-eternal rejoicing of Father and Son, 362; as eros, 361–2; energies of, 259, 377–8; but the hypostasis of the Holy Spirit is not to be identified with the divine energies, 291, 378, 380, 389; relationship with Christ, 42, 140, 361–2, 391; as the cloud at Christ's transfiguration, 155; uncreated, 388; Spirit of truth, 374.

How the Holy Spirit differs from the human spirit, 361; the Holy Spirit and human consciousness, 140–1, 142; speaks in the heart, 215; law of the Spirit in the heart, 257; signs of the Spirit's presence, 259–60; manifested in different forms,

285; gifts of, 168–9, 395; seven gifts of, 132–3, 378–9; the Spirit of adoption, 327; indwelling presence, 39–40, 45, 84, 85, 86, 93, 114, 134, 146, 149, 154–5, 315; conscious experience of, 13, 14, 17, 36, 40, 42, 81; becoming partakers of, 164; illumination by, 20, 38, 43, 47, 63, 79, 103, 143, 152, 318; becoming pregnant with, 157, 214, 273; pledge of, 40–1, 80, 237; firstfruits or foretaste of, 164, 253, 265, 419; fruits of, 115; dew of, 97; oil of, 134; milk and honey of, 216; rain from, 78, 167; freedom of, 163; unifying power of, 220; temple of, 190; sighing of, 260; intercedes for us, 164, 260; blasphemy against, 322.

The Holy Spirit and baptism, 40, 164, 168, 258, 259, 265; rebirth in, 121; all the baptized receive the Spirit, 248; but He is consciously experienced only by those who fulfil the commandments, 247–8, 259; presence of the Spirit at the Liturgy, 62; and at ordination, 62–3; nothing possible without the grace of the Spirit, 45; no true teaching without His inspiration, 247; gives power to speak clearly, 106, 157; the Spirit and contemplation, 42; prayer as an activity of the Spirit, 259; the Spirit received through stillness, 126; marks of the spiritual life, 109

Spirit, the human, 218; how different from the Holy Spirit, 361

Spiritual father or guide, 16, 27–8, 30–3, 37, 40, 51, 69, 70, 98, 110, 122, 268, 327–8; his crucial importance, 13, 77, 205, 241, 274, 279, 283–5; his prayers, 18, 23, 35; as a mediator, 88; needed when saying the Jesus Prayer, 65, 193, 205, 210, 259, 269; to be regarded as God, 31, 33, 52, 53; as Christ, 28; as a saint, 57; yet obedience to him is not altogether unqualified, 14, 30–1; or at any rate not initially, 32; can be a lay person, 11; should be dispassionate, 30; how he should give counsel, 58–9, 61; his counsel bestows life, 143; dangers of desiring to be a spiritual guide, 100; many are not qualified to guide others, 283–4. See Abbot, Confession

Spiritual knowledge: see Knowledge

Spiritual senses: see Senses

Spiritual way of life, 107–8, 109

Stages of the spiritual life: *praktiki, physiki, gnosis* (the practice of the commandments, natural contemplation, spiritual knowledge), 76, 129–30, 148, 152; moral, natural and theological, 245–6; purgative, illuminative, mystical, 77, 145, 150–1, 258; carnal, psychic, spiritual, 77, 107–8; beginners, those in the middle, the perfect, 38, 89, 102, 107, 111, 133, 150, 215, 234, 237, 255, 258, 272; five rungs on the ladder of perfection, 241; many stages or levels in the other world, 220

Stars, 357

Stealing, 329

Steward, in monastery, 35, 59

Stillness (*hesychia*), 19, 43, 71, 125–6, 146, 149, 177, 204, 228, 233, 234–6, 237, 246, 280, 285, 334, 337, 340, 341, 434–5; how life of stillness differs from community life, 279; no stillness without obedience, 306; produced by dispassion, 103; confers knowledge of God, 109; signifies the shedding of thoughts, 270, 278; stillness and prayer, 238, 254, 266, 272; as ever-moving stability, 147. *See* Silence, Withdrawal

Studios, monastery of, 11, 12, 14, 76

Suffering, mortifies body, 30; to be willingly accepted, 37; leads to joy, 38. *See* Afflictions

Sufism, 65

Suicide, 68

Suspicion of fellow humans, 95, 187. *See* Judgment

Tabernacle of Moses, 220. *See* Holy of Holies

Tabor, the mountain of contemplation, 167. *See* Transfiguration

Teaching, 231–2, 245–7, 250; mysteries of contemplative life are to be shared with others, 13, 23, 77, 98, 109, 126, 132, 139, 143, 145, 147, 148, 152, 156–7, 167, 189. *See* Writing

Tears, one of the two natural fluids in our body, 96; two kinds, acrid and joyful, 97; tears of repentance, 39, 40, 51–2, 78, 84, 89, 90, 110, 111, 133, 151, 165, 201; of compunction, 34, 52, 55, 57, 61, 90, 112, 117, 119, 120, 124, 129, 155, 157, 167, 180; tears of repentance different from tears of compunction, 97; compunction and tears distinguished, 77, 97; tears of sorrow, 95; of contrition, 205; of anguish, 61; of spiritual grief, 313, 315; of awe, 260; of humility, 118, 119, 129; shed for the dead, 119; painful, 78; painless, 90; tears of sweetness and joy, 13, 18, 38, 78, 85, 97, 119, 120, 127, 261, 315; cleansing fire of tears, 110; purifying tears, 28, 38, 61, 79, 84, 85, 96, 110, 117, 126, 127, 148, 221, 269, 322; during prayer, 58, 68; like rain from heaven, 87; gentle flow, 102; shed uncontrollably, 114; unquenchable, 56; unceasing, 38; as medicine of soul, 99; bread of tears, 136; refine the heart, 109; not experienced by the 'psychic', 109; a gift from God, 14, 262; never receive communion without tears, 12, 59

Temperament of body, 261, 435

Temptation, stages of, 435–6; from demons, 105, 239; allowed by God for our benefit, 111, 285; but He also prevents us from succumbing, 282. *See* Assent, Communion, Coupling, Provocations, Trials

Ten Commandments, 290

Tetractys, 173n.

Thanksgiving: *see* Gratitude

Theology, as contemplation and vision of God, 12–13, 76, 83, 152, 155, 246, 254, 436–7; impossible without Holy Spirit, 167; dialectical or antinomic character, 403. *See* Contemplation, Mystical theology

Theosis: *see* Deification

Theotokos: *see* Mother of God

Thessaloniki, 287, 288, 289

Thoughts (*logismoi*), 437; four types, 224; roused by senses, 75; and by passions, 223, 225; provoke fantasies, 223, 224, 225; changeable, 224; we should avoid evil thoughts as well as evil actions, 29; scrutiny of, 70, 71, 81; to be repulsed, 74, 186, 277; destroyed by Jesus Prayer, 73; prayer free from thoughts, 206, 210, 270, 278, 343; the heart to be kept empty of thoughts, 213. *See* Confession, Images, Imagination, Memory, Self-examination, Temptation, Watchfulness

Time, nature of, in kingdom of heaven, 171;

and eternity, 427–8; symbolized by number seven, 227

Tithe, to be offered from ourselves, 163

Tongues, gift of, 168

Tonsure, 55

Transfiguration of Christ, 155, 167, 208, 253, 292, 377, **414–17**, **422**; anticipates second coming, 415; transfiguration of creation, 214, 346, 347. *See* Light

Trembling, 261. *See* Fear

Trials (*peirasmoi*), 95, 113, 168, 250, 283, 311–13, 319. *See* Endurance, Temptation

Trinity, the Holy, **140**, 173, 174, **217–18**, 233, 238, 248, 323, 354, **361–2**, **397–9**, 418; God is Trinity but not triple, 386; Trinity revealed at Christ's transfiguration, 155; the divine energies as Trinitarian, 291, 379, 389, 398–9, 403, 411; indwelling of the Trinity, 79, 107; the human person as an image of the Trinity, 140–1, 183, 184, 218, 220n., 343, **362–4**, 423; angels also are in Trinitarian image, but less so than humans, 362–3

Trisagion, 53, 172, 266, 269

Troparion, 269

Truth, only attained through participation, 216

Turks, 289

Two, the number, symbolizes creation, 227

Unchastity, 89, 101, **111–12**, 231, 281, **328–9**; in soul as well as body, 201. *See* Desire, Lust

Union with God, 139, 148, 343; our natural desire for, 107; by grace alone, 421; not merely relative and imitative, 420; with the divine energy, not the divine essence, 381; direct, 246; immaterial, 318; transcending the intellect, 245; brings union with all fellow humans, 153. *See* Energy, Light

Universals and particulars, 383

Vanity: *see* Self-esteem, Self-flattery

Veroia, 288

Vespers, 233

Vices, close to virtue, 214; as that which falls short of or exceeds virtue, 230. *See* Passions

Vigilance: *see* Watchfulness

Vigils, **59**, 89, 90, 109, 129, 229, **233–4**, 267, 272, 279, 313

Virgin, the Blessed: *see* Mother of God

Virginity, 153; recovered through tears of compunction, 120–1; better than marriage, 301–2, 328

Virtues, **228–31**; the four principal or cardinal virtues, 82, 110, 153, 171, 229–30; eight other virtues related to them, 230; eight natural and general virtues, 153; the practical, natural and supranatural virtues, 230; the five virtues of the hesychast, 233; comprehensive and particular virtues, 50, 229; the triad of faith, hope and love, 79; the virtues form a single unity, 39, 42, 229; how connected, 272; all are equal to each other, 229; at the midpoint between deficiency and excess, 230; close to the vices, 214; virtue implanted in us at our creation, 97, 110, 230; our natural appetite for, 223; the virtues bring us close to God and make us similar to Him, 142, 343, 382; resemble bones in human body, 216; spring from prayer, 279; and from love, 373; express aspiration for beauty, 228; each virtue is a gift, 307; never possessed perfectly in this life, 254; foretaste of the kingdom of heaven, 219. *See* Practice of the commandments

Vision of God, 13, 114, 155, 166, 203; false visions from demons, 249, 259, 270. *See* Contemplation, Light, Theology, Union with God

Vocations, variety of, 14, 43, 45; we all have one calling, 250

Vows, monastic, 57, 178

Warfare, inner, three causes of, 244

Warmth of heart, 210; in prayer, 259, 263, 269, 270, 277, 284; how distinguished from demonic warmth, 271; three kinds of fervour, 261

Washing, 55. *See* Baths

Watchfulness (*nipsis*) and attentiveness, 67, 69, 70, 71, 72, 74–5, 81, 103, 110, 125, 181, 183, 196, 199, **204–6**, 207, 233, 308, 315, 333, 334, 338, 340, 341, 437. *See* Attentiveness

Water, covers most of the earth's surface, 350–2

Wealth: *see* Possessions

Wheel, monk resembles, 129

Will: of God, 45; differs from His foreknowledge, 392–3; and from His nature, 410; Christ has two wills, 217, 218; our human will, to be cut off, 14, 23, 33, 37, 45, 53, 77, 109; the mundane will, 79, 82, 88. *See* Flesh, Free will

Winds, 349

Wine, 59, 234, 281

Wisdom: the divine personal Wisdom, 85, 90, 143, 153, 229, 238, 250, 360, 362; cup of Wisdom, 129; true and false wisdom, 47. *See* Learning

Withdrawal of God's grace: *see* Abandonment

Withdrawal from world: *see* Flight from world

Work, manual, 185, 186, 233, 266, 269; not on Sundays or great feasts, 326

World, signifies sensory things, 177. *See* Creation, Flight from world, Nature

World soul, denied, 347–9

Worship, in spirit and in truth, possible everywhere, 374

Wrath: *see* Anger

Writing, three motives for, 251–2; avoid writing letters, 197; writing disturbs one's tranquillity, 293–4. *See* Teaching

Yoga, 65